The book of Wisdom; the Greek text, the Latin Vulgate, and the Authorised English version;

W J. 1823-1895 Deane

Nabu Public Domain Reprints:

You are holding a reproduction of an original work published before 1923 that is in the public domain in the United States of America, and possibly other countries. You may freely copy and distribute this work as no entity (individual or corporate) has a copyright on the body of the work. This book may contain prior copyright references, and library stamps (as most of these works were scanned from library copies). These have been scanned and retained as part of the historical artifact.

This book may have occasional imperfections such as missing or blurred pages, poor pictures, errant marks, etc. that were either part of the original artifact, or were introduced by the scanning process. We believe this work is culturally important, and despite the imperfections, have elected to bring it back into print as part of our continuing commitment to the preservation of printed works worldwide. We appreciate your understanding of the imperfections in the preservation process, and hope you enjoy this valuable book.

ΣΟΦΙΑ ΣΑΛΩΜΩΝ

THE BOOK OF WISDOM

W. J. DEANE

London

HENRY FROWDE

OXFORD UNIVERSITY PRESS WAREHOUSE

7 PATERNOSTER ROW

THE BOOK OF WISDOM

THE GREEK TEXT, THE LATIN VULGATE

AND

THE AUTHORISED ENGLISH VERSION

*WITH AN INTRODUCTION, CRITICAL APPARATUS
AND A COMMENTARY*

BY

WILLIAM J. DEANE, M.A.

ORIEL COLLEGE, OXFORD, RECTOR OF ASHEN, ESSEX

Oxford

AT THE CLARENDON PRESS

1881

[All rights reserved]

JS1751
1881

22258

PREFACE.

WHEN I turned my attention many years ago to the Book of Wisdom, there was no Commentary in the English language that treated fully of this work, save that of Arnald. This was copious indeed, but cumbersome and often speculative and uncritical. I felt also the want of some better revision of the text than was offered by the editions of the Septuagint usually met with in England. Even Tischendorf, who had sung the praises of his Sinaitic Codex far and wide, had made scarcely any use of this MS in his own editions of the Septuagint, contenting himself with noting the variations of the Alexandrian and the Codex Ephraemi rescriptus. Taking the Vatican text as a basis therefore, I collated it with the Sinaitic and the other uncial MSS, and with the cursives given in Holmes and Parsons' work, with occasional reference to the Complutensian and Aldine editions. It was not till my own collation was just completed that I became acquainted with Fritzsche's Libri Apocryphi Veteris Testamenti, a work of the utmost value, though not quite free from mistakes in recording the readings both of the Vatican and Sinaitic MSS. These errors have been noted by E. Nestle in an appendix to the last (eighth) edition of Tischendorf. In confirming the text by reference to the Fathers, I have derived great assistance from Observationes Criticae in Libr. Sap. by F. H. Reusch, who has carefully noted the passages of the Book quoted by early writers. Walton's Polyglot has provided me with the Armenian, Syriac, and Arabic versions. For the sake of comparison I have printed the Latin Vulgate, and the so-called authorised English Version, in parallel columns with the Greek. The former is particularly interesting as containing many unusual words or forms, which are duly noted in the Commentary. In elucidating the text I have endeavoured to give the plain grammatical and historical meaning of each passage, illustrating it by reference to the writings of Philo, Josephus, the Alexandrian writers, and early Fathers; but I have been sparing of quotations from Christian authors, not from want of materials, but because I did not wish my work to assume an homiletical form, or to be burdened by reflections which an educated reader is able to make for himself.

PREFACE.

The importance of the Septuagint in the study of the New Testament cannot be overrated; and I trust it will be found that I have not often omitted to note passages and words in the Book of Wisdom which illustrate the writings of the later Covenant. Many statements and allusions in the Book are confirmed by traditions found in the Targums these have been gathered from the works of Dr. Ginsburg and Etheridge In preparing the Commentary great use has been made of the works of C. L. W Grimm and Gutberlet; the former is too well known and appreciated to need commendation; the latter is useful, and the writer's judgment can be trusted where it is uninfluenced by the desire to condone the mistakes and interpolations of the Latin Vulgate. The great Commentary of Cornelius a Lapide has of course been constantly consulted The Rev. Canon Churton kindly permitted me to inspect his MS. when my own notes were almost completed; and I have availed myself of his paraphrase in some few passages Dr. Bissell's work reached me only as my own pages were passing through the press, but it does not afford any new light on obscure passages, and seems to be chiefly a compilation from German sources

Viewing the Book of Wisdom as an important product of Jewish-Alexandrine thought, it seemed desirable to offer a brief sketch of the course taken by Greek philosophy in discussing the momentous questions with which it attempted to cope. An effort is made to define the position occupied by our Book in the Jewish-Alexandrian school, and some notion is given of the influence exercised by that phase of thought on the language, though not on the doctrine, of Christianity The later development of this school, which led to many fatal errors, is barely noticed, as being beyond the scope of this work, which aims only at affording a help to the student of the period immediately antecedent to Christianity

CONTENTS.

PROLEGOMENA.

I. 1. The Book of Wisdom: its claims on attention 2 Sketch of the progress of Greek Philosophy 3 The Jewish-Alexandrian Philosophy 4 Its influence on the Theology of the New Testament 1

II. Title Plan Contents . . 23

III. Language and Character 27

IV Place and date of Composition Author . . 30

V. History Authority Relation to the Canon of Scripture . . 35

VI. Text 39

VII Versions, Editions, and Commentaries . . . 41

THE GREEK TEXT AND CRITICAL APPARATUS WITH THE ANGLICAN VERSION AND LATIN VULGATE . . . 45

COMMENTARY 111

INDEXES 221

PROLEGOMENA.

I.

1. The Book of Wisdom. its claims on attention —2 Sketch of the progress of Greek Philosophy —3 The Jewish-Alexandrian Philosophy —4 Its influence on the Theology of the New Testament

1. THE Book of Wisdom has many claims on our attention and respect. Whatever views we may adopt as to its date and author (matters which will be discussed later), we may confidently assert, that, occupying that period between the writing of the Old and New Testaments, when the more formal utterances of the Holy Spirit for a season had ceased to be heard, and, as far as remaining records attest, God had for the time ceased to speak by the prophets, it possesses an absorbing interest for every student of the history of Christianity. In conjunction with other writings of the same period, this Book exhibits the mind and doctrine of the Jews, the progress of religious belief among them, and the preparation for Christianity which was gradually being effected by the development of the Mosaic creed and ritual. The gap between the two covenants is here bridged over. Herein is presented a view of the Hebrew religion, definite and consistent, which may well be regarded as a necessary link in the chain of connection between the earlier and later revelations. Nowhere else can be seen so eloquent and profound an enunciation of the faith of a Hebrew educated away from the isolating and confining influence of Palestine, one who had studied the philosophies of East and West, had learned much from those sources, yet acknowledged and exulted in the superiority of his own creed, and who, having tried other systems by that high standard, had found them to fail miserably. Nowhere else can be read so grand a statement of the doctrine of the immortality of the soul as the vindication of God's justice. The identification of the serpent who tempted Eve with Satan, the reference of the introduction of death into the world to the devil, the typical significance assigned to the history and ritual of the Pentateuch, the doctrine of man's freedom of will exerted in bringing upon himself the punishment of his sins, and the sure retribution that accompanies transgression,—in treating of all these subjects, the Book is unique among prechristian writings, and its neglect or omission cannot be compensated by any other existing work.

It is remarkable how greatly this Book has been disregarded in England. While the Fathers have quoted it largely and continually, while commentators in old time delighted in plumbing its depths and in finding Christian verities underlying every page, while in later days Germany has poured forth a copious stream of versions and comments, England has been till lately[1] content with the single work of R. Arnald, and has

---

[1] Lately the Rev J. H. Blunt has published The Annotated Bible, London, 1879, vol ii of which contains the Apocrypha, and the Rev W. R. Churton has prepared an edition of the Book of Wisdom for the Society for Promoting Christian Knowledge

left the Book unstudied and uncriticized. Familiar as some of its chapters are to all English churchmen from their forming some of the daily and festival lections in the Calendar, no student of Holy Scripture has seemed to think the Book of Wisdom worth serious labour, and it has been left for other nations to bestow upon this remarkable work that diligence which it deserves and will well repay.

2. Before entering upon an examination of the text of the Book of Wisdom, some preliminary inquiries are necessary for determining its place in the history of religious development and its connection with preceding and subsequent systems. If, as we shall show reason hereafter for asserting, the work was produced at Alexandria, and is a genuine offspring of the Jewish-Alexandrian school which took its rise in that celebrated centre of commerce and philosophy, a short space must be devoted to an investigation into the origin, tenets, and influence of that school. To trace at length its effects in producing gnosticism and other heresies in Christian times is beyond the scope of this outline, which aims only at recording its rise, and making a brief examination of the question, whether the Gospel owes any of its doctrines to this system.

If we make a distinction between Theology and Philosophy, we must say Theology has to do with faith, Philosophy with research. Philosophy claims to systematise the conceptions furnished by Theology and Science, and to provide a doctrine which shall explain the world and the destiny of man [1]. The basis of Theology is revelation; this principle Philosophy ignores, and casting away the help thus offered endeavours and claims to elucidate the phenomena of the universe by analysis and generalisation.

Let us see first what progress the purely heathen Greek Philosophy made towards solving the great problems of being, and next how it fared when combined with a belief in revelation.

The history of Greek Philosophy may be divided into three periods, the Pre-Socratic, the Socratic, and the Post-Socratic [2].

Involved in a polytheistic religion, the earliest Greek philosophers attempted in vain to explain the mysteries around them by the agencies of the deities in whom the poets had taught them to believe. Failing to construct any satisfactory theory out of these elements, Thales [3] and the Ionic school tried other expedients. At one time water, at another time fire, at another air, became in their view the cause of life and power, the substance, as it were, of which all phenomena were only the modes. The utmost development at which these Physicists arrived was to endow this primary element, be it air or other substance, with intelligence, making it in fact equivalent to a soul possessed of reason and consciousness. Anaximander (B.C. 610) held that 'The Infinite' ($\tau\grave{o}$ $\check{a}\pi\epsilon\iota\rho o\nu$) was the origin of all things. What he meant exactly by this term it is perhaps impossible to discover; but being a mathematician, and 'prone to regard abstractions as entities,' he was led to formulate a 'distinction between all Finite Things and the Infinite All [4].' But this 'Infinite All' was not developed into the idea of Infinite mind till the school of the Eleatics arose.

Meantime the interest of the history centres itself upon the mysterious and justly celebrated Pythagoras, the great founder of the Mathematicians. He was a lover of Wisdom for its own sake, not for the practical purposes to which it may be applied; hence it was perhaps that he adopted the study of numbers as best able to draw the mind away from the finite to the

---

[1] Lewes, Hist. of Philosophy, I. xviii. ed. 1867. In the following brief sketch of Greek Philosophy I have chiefly followed Mr. Lewes.

[2] Zeller, Die Philosophie der Griechen, i. 111 ff.

[3] Ὁ τῆς τοιαύτης ἀρχηγὸς φιλοσοφίας. Aristot. Met. A. c. 3. Thales is considered to have been born about B.C. 636. Ritter. Hist. of Ancient Phil. i. bk. III. chap. 3. pp. 195, ff. Eng. trans. Mosheim's trans. of Cudworth's Intell. Syst. i. pp. 35, 147.

[4] Lewes, Hist. of Philos. i. 15.

infinite, from the sensible to the incorporeal In them he saw the principles of things, the cause of the material existence of things[1]. All numbers resolve into one: all parts can be reduced to unity. All that we see around us are only copies of numbers, and numerical existence is the only invariable existence. And as this is the farthest point to which we can conduct our speculations, One is the infinite, the absolute, the ἀρχή which is the object of the philosophers' search. We must remember that with Pythagoras numbers were not, as with us, mere symbols, but real entities[2]; we can thus readily conceive the meaning of his little-known theory. The doctrine of the transmigration of souls attributed to him is based on the same principle. The soul is One and perfect Connecting itself with man it passes into imperfection; and according as one or other of its three elements, νοῦς, φρήν, θυμός, rule, so is the man's scale in creation, rational, intelligent, sensual, so are the bodies which it may successively inhabit; but these changes are merely phenomena of the monad, the one invariable essence.

Unsatisfied with the answer to the problem of existence given by others, Xenophanes (B. C. 616) fixing his gaze on the vast heavens determined that the One is God[3]. The position which he maintained is found in a couplet of his which has been preserved[4]:

Εἷς θεὸς ἔν τε θεοῖσι καὶ ἀνθρώποισι μέγιστος,
οὔτε δέμας θνητοῖσιν ὁμοίιος οὔτε νόημα

He may be considered the apostle of Monotheism, the teacher, amid the corruptions of the prevalent belief in multitudinous gods, of a faith in one perfect Being, though he could not tell who or what this being was, and looked upon all things as manifestations of this one self-existent, eternal God His Monotheism was in fact Pantheism But his speculations opened the way to scepticism, led men to think that nothing could be known as certain.

Parmenides[5] (B.C 536) followed in his train, affirming that the only truth is obtained through reason without the aid of the senses, and that nothing really exists but the One Being. These two distinct doctrines, the latter of which was but little in advance of his predecessors, compose his system This was supported by his pupil and friend Zeno of Elea (B C. 500), the inventor of Dialectics, who, indeed, added nothing new, but contributed a mass of arguments, sophisms, and illustrations, many of which are more ingenious than solid, but which are valuable and interesting as being the earliest instances of that formal logic which plays so important a part in all subsequent discussions.

The immediate precursors of Socrates and his school were the Sophists, but the intermediate tenets of some other philosophers, especially of Democritus and Heraclitus, the so-called laughing and weeping philosophers, demand a passing notice. The men themselves may be mythical, but there is a germ of truth in all myths, and the story of these two represents doubtless a real step in the progress of inquiry. Heraclitus (B C. 503) rejected the idea of reason being the sole criterion of truth, and held that the senses rightly educated are never deceived. Error springs from the imperfection of human reason, not from the falsity of the information or ideas derived from sensation Perfect knowledge dwells with the universal Intelligence, and the more a man admits this into his soul, the more secure is he from error. The principle of all things is Fire, ever changing, moving, living, and out of the strife of contraries producing harmony. Democritus too (B C. 460) upheld the truth of sensation, but sensation controlled by reflection (διάνοια)[6], and he was the first to answer the question of the *modus operandi* of the senses by the sup-

---

[1] Τοὺς ἀριθμοὺς εἶναι τῆς οὐσίας Aristot. Metaph. i 6. ap Lewes, i p 28; Grote, Plato, 1 pp 10, ff (ed 1865), Mosheim's Cudworth, 1 pp. 567, 570, notes.

[2] See the point argued against Ritter by Lewes, Hist of Phil 1 pp 30, ff

[3] Τὸ ἓν εἶναί φησι τὸν θεόν. Aristot. Metaph. 1 5; Mosheim's Cudworth, i. pp 580, ff

[4] Xenoph. Colophon Fragm. illustr. S Karsten.

[5] Mosheim's Cudworth, 1 pp 592, ff

[6] Lewes, 1 p 98

position, that all things threw off images of themselves which entered the soul through the organs of the body. The primary elements were atoms which were self-existent and possessed of inherent power of motion, from which the universe received its form and laws. The notion of a supreme Being to control these elements is foreign to his system, which is the merest materialism; destiny, to which he attributed the formation of things, being a term used to cloke ignorance. Differing somewhat from former philosophers, Anaxagoras, while holding that all knowledge of phenomena came from the senses, regarded this information as delusive because it did not penetrate to the substance of things, and needed reason to correct it; and as regards cosmology, he taught that creation and destruction were merely other names for aggregating or decomposing pre-existent atoms, the Arranger being Intelligence, νοῦς, the Force of the universe, not a moral or divine power, but an all-knowing unmixed and subtle principle [1]. This principle Empedocles conceived to be Love, which was opposed by Hate, who however operated only in the lower world, for the one supreme power, which he termed Love, was a sphere above the world, ever calm, rejoicing, and restful. These forces are in some sort identical with good and evil; and it is the struggle between these powers that causes individual things and beings to come into existence, Hate separating the elements which are combined by Love into one all-including sphere.

To this period of Greek Philosophy belong the Sophists.

The Sophists did not form a school or sect [2]. They taught the art of disputation, how best to use language so as to convince and persuade; but they were the natural successors of preceding speculators. Thought is sensation, said one [3], 'man is the measure of all things,' human knowledge is relative, truth is subjective; therefore a wise man will regard all truth as opinion, and study only how to make what he considers true or expedient acceptable to others. It is easy to see how such sentiments might be perverted to the overthrow of morality, and hence we can understand the reason why Plato and others regarded the Sophists with such repugnance; but there is little evidence to show that the teachers who had the name ever pushed their opinions to such dangerous consequences.

To contend against these unsatisfactory sceptics an opponent arose who in most respects was a perfect contrast to them. In his abnegation of self, in his contempt for riches and honours, in his denunciation of abuses, in his proud humility, Socrates (B.C. 469) contradicted their most cherished principles and assaulted their most esteemed practices. No flow of words could persuade him to act contrary to his sober convictions; no arguments, however speciously propounded, could confuse his sense of right and wrong; no spurious wisdom could withstand his subtle questioning. To make him the model of a sophist leader, as Aristophanes has done in his *Clouds*, is to confound his method with his principles. If his method was, in some sort, sophistical, his object was quite distinct from that of the Sophists; for while they gave up the pursuit of abstract truth as hopeless, he never ceased his quest for it, showing men how ignorant they were of real knowledge and aiding them in its acquisition. But he founded no school, never set himself up as a teacher, left no system of philosophy behind him. Physics he early surrendered as incapable of satisfactory solution; and he turned his attention to Ethics, and the right method of inquiry. In the latter subject he is properly judged to be the inventor of two important processes, Inductive reasoning and Abstract

---

[1] Lewes, i. pp. 78, 79, 83; Maurice, Ment. and Mor. Phil. pt. I. chap. vi. § 3.

[2] For the fairest view of the Sophists see Grote, Hist of Greece, viii. 463; Lewes, pp. 105, ff.; Maurice, Philosophy, pt. I. chap. vi. div. ii. § 1.

[3] Protagoras, Ritter, pp. 573, ff.; Mosheim's Cudworth, lib. II. cap. iii.

PROLEGOMENA.

definition[1], by the first of which 'he endeavoured to discover the permanent element which underlies the changing forms of appearances and the varieties of opinion; by the second he fixed the truth which he had thus gained.' It was a great step to force men to free the mind of half-realised conceptions and hazy notions, and to see clearly what a thing is and what it is not. And this is what the method of Socrates aimed at effecting. That it led to the common error of mistaking explanation of words for explanation of things is as true of the ages since Socrates as it was then[2]. In his ethical deliveries he seems to have been somewhat inconsistent, maintaining at one time that virtue is knowledge, vice ignorance, and at another that virtue cannot be taught, and yet again that it is a matter of practice and natural disposition[3]. But he always affirmed that man had within him a faculty that discerned right from wrong; he upheld the supremacy of conscience; he considered that happiness consisted in knowing the truth and acting in accordance with it. The immortality of the soul, a doctrine so beautifully propounded in his last discourses, rested, in his view, on the beneficence of Divine Providence[4]. In his own profoundly religious mind that a voice divine (δαιμόνιόν τι) should seem to utter warnings and advice, is what we might have antecedently expected[5].

The method of Socrates was followed in a greater or less degree by other philosophers who have been distinguished as founders of three Schools, the Cyrenaic terminating in Epicurism, the Cynic combining to form Stoicism, and the Megarian, which contributed an important element to the speculations which in later times found their home at Alexandria[6].

But the real successor of Socrates is Plato, his pupil, friend, and biographer. To give an accurate description of Plato's many-sided philosophy would be a difficult matter in any case; in this present necessarily brief sketch it is impossible. Only a few salient points can here be indicated—opinions rather than a system being enunciated. And even this is only partly feasible, as he so often changes his opinions, refutes at one time that which at another he had maintained, implies doubts where he had previously stated certainties, repudiates the process which he himself often has adopted, that we are seldom sure, when we produce the views set forth in one Dialogue, whether they have not been modified or denied in another. One thing however is well assured, and that is, that in his search for truth he was severely logical. Universal propositions, abstract terms, were the materials with which he worked, and to discover these was the aim of all his teaching. To attribute to these general notions, or ideas, a substantive existence, to consider them not merely conceptions of the mind, but entities, *noumena* of which all individual things were the *phenomena*[7], is simply an explanation of a difficulty for which he was indebted to his imaginative faculty. The soul, in his grand view, was always immortal, and before it became clogged with the body had seen Existence as it is, and had had glimpses, more or less perfect, of those ideas, those great realities, of which material things were the defective copy. Man's knowledge is a reminiscence of the verities seen in the disembodied state sensation awakens the recollection it is our business to encourage this memory, to strengthen it, to guide it by reason. So that the teacher's object is not so much to impart new information, as to recall previous impressions, dim and weak, but still not wholly effaced. This

---

[1] Τούς τ' ἐπακτικοὺς λόγους καὶ τὸ ὁρίζεσθαι καθόλου Arist. Metaph. xiii. 4, Dict. of Bible, Art Philosophy, by Mr. Brooke Foss Westcott.

[2] Lewes, i p 161.

[3] Compare Xen Mem I ii. 19; III ix 1; Arist Eth Nic VI xiii. 3, Top. III i. 4, Plato, Meno, xxxvi-xxxix pp 96, 97, Protagoras, xl p 361

[4] Xen Mem I. iv

[5] Theages, x. xi pp 128, 129, Grote, Plato, i pp 433, 434

[6] Maurice, chap vi § 3 Compare Ueberweg, Hist. of Phil § 35, Eng ed.

[7] Lewes, i p 241, Ritter, ii. pp 265, ff, Grote, Plato, iii p 520.

tendency to seek for the idea of everything led to the conception of the one Good, that is God; and though Plato never set himself to oppose the religious belief of his countrymen, it is plain that his speculations pointed to Monotheism. Following up the manifold ideas, he arrived at the supreme essence of all, the great Intelligence. By this power he supposed the world to have been created, arguing however at one time that God created only types of individual things from which other things of the same class proceeded [1], and at another that God fashioned Chaos after the model of these types which have an independent and eternal pre-existence [2]. But however made, the world was an animal, and like other animals possessed a soul [3], and God, who is all good, rejoiced to see the animated creature, τὸ πᾶν ζῷον [4], and wished it to be all good likewise. Evil however dwells in this phenomenal world, which, being only a copy of the ideal world, must necessarily be imperfect, and which also, being composed of matter which is unintelligent, must be evil, for intelligence alone is good [5]. At the same time man, being endowed with free will, has his lot in his own hands, and may choose the evil or the good [6]. And on this choice depends the future destiny of the soul, which will have to pass into various bodies, undergo various transmigrations, till it return to its best and purest existence [7].

A new epoch begins with Aristotle (B.C. 384), who was born about a century before the translation of the Hebrew Scriptures into Greek and the formation of the Alexandrian library [8]. From the calm stand-point of strict logic, this philosopher, uninfluenced by imagination, pronounced a judgment upon the speculations of his predecessors. Plato's doctrine of ideas he unhesitatingly condemned, holding that these abstractions had no existence separate from their phenomena, and that error arose not from the falsity of sensuous perceptions, but from wrong interpretation thereof [9]. So in his view the great object of study was to set forth the rules and conditions under which the mind considers and discourses [10], the formulas whereby it makes known its judgments. But we cannot dwell on his method and his dialectics. A few words must be said on his ethics and theology, and then we must pass on to the schools that followed, with which we are more concerned.

A less devoutly religious man than Plato, Aristotle seems scarcely to have believed in a personal God, though he uses language that may imply such belief. A first Cause is that which he seeks to find, and whose attributes he seeks to establish by logic. And having demonstrated, with more or less success, the unity of this First Principle, he, perhaps in deference to popular opinion, does not further pursue the investigation [11]. There is no recognition of the perfection of God as the ground-work of morals, as in the Platonic doctrine; 'the absolute good' is eliminated from his system. The τέλος of mankind is Happiness, and this consists in the proper use of the highest faculties. Our faculties or energies have each their special excellence and virtue; the acts of virtue are exercised by voluntary choice, and these separate acts make habits, and habits form character. Now the best habit of the highest part of man's nature, and that which makes his life most divine, is Contemplation. But to attain to this, there is need of restraint, discipline, and education, which forces can only be properly and effectually applied in the State.

Thus we have seen that the early philosophers specu-

---

[1] De Rep. X. i. ii. pp. 596, 597; and v. vi. pp. 29, 30; Grote, Plato, iii. p. 248.
[2] Timaeus, xviii. p. 51.
[3] Timaeus, vi. p. 30.
[4] Timaeus, x. p. 37.
[5] Lewes, i. p. 262; Ritter, ii. pp. 275, 276.
[6] De Rep. X. xv. p. 619.
[7] Timaeus, xiv. p. 42; Ritter, ii. p. 377.

[8] Lewes, i. pp. 271, 272.
[9] Aristot. De Anima, III. iii; Metaph. IV. v.
[10] Maurice, Ment. and Metaph. Phil. pt. I. chap. vi. p. 184, ed. 1834; Lewes, Aristotle, chap. vi. pp. 108, ff; Ueberweg, § 48.
[11] In Met. xii. p. 1074, Bekker, Aristotle conceives God to be eternal Thought, and that his thought is life and action. See Maurice, pt. I. chap vi. § 6; Mosheim's edition of Cudworth, i. pp. 639, ff.

lated about nature, that Socrates turned their investigations on man, that Plato, while not wholly neglecting Physics, made this study subordinate to that of Ethics. Aristotle systematized the method of inquiry, and applied it to Physics, Metaphysics, and Ethics, paving the way for that invasion of Scepticism, which, using his instruments, exposed the vanity of philosophy [1]

The Sceptics, who next come on the stage, took their stand on the uncertainty of all knowledge. What had seemed determined in one age had failed to satisfy another the truth of this philosopher had seemed the vainest error to that. What is the criterion of truth? Sensation? Reason? No You cannot trust them absolutely, you cannot prove that they distinguish correctly. There is no criterion of truth the mystery of existence cannot be penetrated; all we can do is to study *appearances*, to make a science of *phenomena*. Such a negative doctrine had little real influence; but in thus denying the certainty of all higher speculations it prepared the way for the coming Philosophy, which concerned itself with questions of practical morality

Of the Post-Socratic School the Epicureans occupy a foremost place. Their founder Epicurus (B.C. 342) looked upon Philosophy as the Art of Life, the instructress in the method of securing happiness; and as to happiness, that, he said, is Pleasure—Pleasure regulated by common sense and experience; not momentary gratification at the cost of future pain and trouble, but a life-long enjoyment Now this can only be secured by virtue, and to live happily means really to live in accordance with justice, prudence, and temperance. It is easy to see how such teaching might be perverted, as we know it was, to fostering sensuality on the one side and a hard indifference on the other. Its basis was an enlightened selfishness, free from all high motive; for there was no supreme Power to make men account for their actions, the gods, if there were gods, being too much wrapped up in their own happiness to interfere with the concerns of mortals [2].

In startling contrast to the softness of Epicurus, Zeno the Stoic (died B C 263) preached a stern, spiritual morality, a life of active virtue—a life in which man realises his true manhood. Virtue is, as Socrates taught, the knowledge of good· knowledge is gained by sensation, and fashioned and utilised by reason, which is the God of the world. This, call it what you will, Reason, Fate, God, is that which gives its form to matter and the law to morals. Man bears within himself his ruling power he should give free scope to this dominion, crush relentlessly every feeling that wars against it, rise superior to pain and suffering, and encourage that apathetic indifference which is the highest condition of humanity. If there was in this theory much that really tended to lower man's standard and to confuse his view of the object of life, it possessed at least one element which was of vital importance It put man face to face with his conscience, bared to his sight his responsibility, and taught him to aim at an object higher than mere pleasure [3]

The New Academy, which evolved itself from Platonic elements, was what in modern times would be called an agnostic system Beginning with distinctions between probable and improbable perceptions, and between assent simple, and assent reflective, it ended with denying the possibility of the existence of any satisfactory criterion of truth Reason and Conception depend on Sensation for their knowledge, and the Senses are defective and convey only subjective effects, not the real nature of things. So neither Reason, Conception, nor Sensation can be the desired criterion What remains? Nothing but Common Sense, or a system of Probabilities, or utter Scepticism.

Some influence in preparation for the coming religion was exerted by these philosophies either in the way of

---

[1] Lewes, 1. pp 334, 335.   [2] Lewes, 1. pp 342-348, Maurice, pt I chap. 6 div. iv. § 2, Ueberweg, § 59
[3] Lewes, 1 pp 349-360, Maurice, pp 241, 242, ed. 1854

contrast or by their positive tenets they were in some sort a Praeparatio Evangelica. If on the one hand they had originated and encouraged that scepticism which springs from pride of intellect and the scornful denial of everything beyond and above nature, on the other hand they had fostered the need of something to believe, something which should have authority over the spirit of man and on which he might rest and be at peace. They had spiritualized to some extent the popular mode of regarding religion, they had restored a certain unity in the conception of the Divine essence, and had given man hopes of redemption from the blind power of nature and an elevation to a secure and higher life[1], but here they stopped. They offered these as mere speculative opinions. The best of philosophies had yet to learn that humility which a better religion teaches, and till this was received and acquiesced in, men might argue and criticize and theorize, but they would never arrive at the truth.

So that we may still sorrowfully ask, What had been the result of ages of speculation and keenest controversy? Had the problems been solved which philosophy had so long and so confidently discussed? No, baffled and defeated philosophy had almost ceased to prosecute its researches, and was ready to doubt if any adequate reward awaited further investigations. Whence comes this universe of things? What is the science of life? Is there any rule for virtue? Is there any method of happiness? What and whence is the soul? What will its future be? Is God one or many? Is there a God at all? Reason had attempted to answer these questions and had failed to afford any certain reply. Another element was needed to give assurance to inquiring minds, and that element was faith[2].

3. It was at Alexandria that Philosophy first came in contact with Revelation. Of its after struggle with Christianity we are not now to speak. Our sketch is limited to the time immediately preceding the Christian era and to the period in which it may have influenced the writers of the New Testament. No place in all the world could be more appropriate than Alexandria for the comparison of the doctrines of various schools. The population of this great city was mixed from the first, and owing to its extensive commerce, its world-famed library, the liberality of its rulers, and the advantages of its situation, it attracted to its shores all that was great and famous, learned and ambitious, in the East and West alike. The civilization of both quarters of the world here met at a common centre, and from this point sent forth an influence that extended through all countries[3]. It was however only by slow degrees that the rigid and unbending Oriental deigned to examine the tenets of other peoples. And when this investigation took place, the Greek did not absorb the Eastern philosophy, nor the Eastern the Greek; but from the fusion of the two a new system arose, a combination of revealed truth and speculative opinion, which has received the name of Neo-Platonism, and of which Philo Judaeus was the most eminent supporter, if not the founder. If it was a new phase of opinion among the Jews thus to view with favour the guesses of heathen philosophers, if, based as their religion was on the sure word of Revelation, the endeavour to amalgamate it with alien speculations marks a certain change in sentiment; we must remember that this people had been from the earliest times of their history always ready to introduce foreign superstitions into their religion. They never indeed fell into idolatry after their return from captivity; but short of such apostacy, the contact with other races and the intercourse with people of different faith, had influenced and modified their opinions and prejudices[4]. The Hebrew dwellers in Alexandria had been for some time gradually severing themselves from connection with their brethren in Palestine. The

---

[1] Neander, Hist. of Christ. Relig. i p. 46 (Bohn's transl.)
[2] Lewes, i p. 374, Ueberweg, § 62
[3] Vacherot, Hist. Crit. de l'Ecole d'Alexandrie, vol. i p. 101; Neander, Hist. of Christ. Relig. i pp. 68, ff (Bohn's transl.).
[4] See Burton, Bampt. Lect. iii. pp. 70, ff (ed. 1829).

translation of the Scriptures into Greek raised the barrier of language between the two bodies[1], and the separation was further strengthened by the policy of the Palestinians who, after the persecution of Ptolemy Philopator (B.C. 217), threw in their lot with the fortunes of Syria. The erection of a temple at Leontopolis[2] by the Egyptian Jews (B.C. 161), laying them open to the charge of schism, widened the breach; and though these still paid a nominal respect to Jerusalem, its exclusive claims and isolating prejudices had lost their influence with them. And then the atmosphere in which they dwelt, the eclecticism which they saw around them[3], the lectures of various philosophers, the restless activity of scholars and teachers, the magnificent library, produced a powerful effect. The conservatism of the Oriental was not proof against the bold and energetic speculativeness of the Greek. The Hebrew became at first patient and then enamoured of Greek culture, he searched the best writings of the West with the view of discovering truths that squared with his own divine traditions, he examined the creeds of the heathen by the light of Revelation, and in Hellenic myths saw the remnants of a higher religion. The sacred books moulded and limited his faith, they did not restrain his thoughts, they did not prevent him from interpreting and developing their statements with a freedom which often approached rationalism[4]. As it was with Judaism that the first contact of Eastern and Western doctrine was concerned, so the medium, the connecting link between the two systems, was Platonism. The teachings of Aristotle and Zeno doubtless had some influence, but the assimilating principle was found in the tenets of Plato. The idealism, sublimity, richness of his philosophy struck a chord in the Hebrew breast that responded harmoniously, and from the union of these elements arose a strain which combined, more or less perfectly, the beauties of both. The writings of this period which have survived (of which the so-called 'Apocrypha' forms an important portion) are few in number, but they show unmistakable traces of Greek culture, and of the spirit of compromise which enlarged its own conceptions in order to embrace those of heathendom[5].

Even in the Septuagint itself traces of this influence appear. Expressions that might have been misunderstood and have conveyed wrong impressions to heathen minds have been softened or altered. Thus, Exod. xxiv. 9-11, where it is said that Moses and Aaron, Nadab and Abihu, and seventy elders, went up to the mountain, and they saw the God of Israel, 'And upon the nobles of the children of Israel He laid not His hand: also they saw God, and did eat and drink,' the Greek renders: καὶ εἶδον τὸν τόπον οὗ εἱστήκει ὁ Θεὸς τοῦ Ἰσραήλ. καὶ τῶν ἐπιλέκτων τοῦ Ἰσραὴλ οὐ διεφώνησεν οὐδὲ εἷς καὶ ὤφθησαν ἐν τῷ τόπῳ τοῦ Θεοῦ, καὶ ἔφαγον καὶ ἔπιον. Here there seems to have been a studied attempt to obviate the plain meaning of the text lest it should give occasion to anthropomorphic ideas of God[6]. In the Books of Maccabees it is studiously shown that the Lord interferes in the affairs of the world only through

---

[1] The Jews of Palestine observed annually a three days' fast in humiliation for the profanation offered to God's word by this version, the length of the fast being regulated by the duration of the plague of darkness in Egypt.

[2] See Dollinger, The Gentile and Jew, ii p. 396 (English transl.)

[3] Alexander the Great built temples to Egyptian divinities as well as to his own Grecian gods. Arr Exped. Alex iii 1. The worship of Serapis, whose temple was one of the wonders of Alexandria, was introduced from Pontus. See Gibbon Decl and Fall, chap. xxviii. and references there. S Aug De Civ xviii 5.

[4] Vacherot, i p 127, and 106, ff.

[5] Among these writings, besides those in the Greek Bible, may be mentioned the works of Aristobulus, who expounded the Pentateuch allegorically. Fragments of this production are to be found in Euseb Praep Ev. vii 13, ff; viii 9. ff; xiii. 12. See Dahne, Jüdisch-Alexandr Relig Philos ii pp 73, ff. Another document of this period is the collection called the Sibylline Books or Oracles. Dahne, pp 228, ff; Gfrörer, Philo, ii pp 71, ff and 121, ff. These are spoken of further on.

[6] Gfrorer, Philo, ii pp 9, ff. The Targums of Onkelos and Jonathan paraphrase the passage in much the same way as the Septuagint. See Etheridge, pp 400, 526. Other instances are given by Gfrorer. See too Ginsburg, The Kabbalah, p 6, note.

His ministers and agents. When (2 Macc. iii) Heliodorus came to the temple at Jerusalem to pillage its treasures, the Lord ἐπιφάνειαν μεγάλην ἐποίησεν; and though a little after it is said (ver 30) that 'the Almighty Lord appeared,' the expression is used in reference to an angelic manifestation[1].

Of philosophic connection is the expression applied to Almighty God, τῶν ὅλων, or ἁπάντων, ἀπροσδεὴς in 2 Macc. xiv. 35 and 3 Macc. ii 9; and not in accordance with the usage of the Old Testament, which speaks (1 Kings viii 27) of the heaven of heavens not containing God, but never employs this term derived from Greek philosophy[2] From the same source are derived the phrases about reason, the mind, etc, in the Fourth Book, e g ὁ ἱερὸς ἡγεμὼν νοῦς (ii 23), λογισμὸς αὐτοδέσποτος (i. 1); παθῶν τύραννος (xvi 1), ἡ τοῦ θείου λογισμοῦ παθοκράτεια (xiii 16), and the four cardinal virtues (i 18), which are also named in Wisd viii. 7[3]

Of the Greek learning displayed in the Book of Wisdom we have spoken further on, when noting its character and language; we may here give an instance or two of the writer's acquaintance with Western Philosophy. The term νοερὸν applied to the spirit of Wisdom (vii. 22) reflects the Stoic's definition of God as πνεῦμα νοερὸν[4], the enumeration of the four cardinal virtues (viii 7), Justice, Temperance, Prudence, Courage, is quite Platonic[5] That the world was created ἐξ ἀμόρφου ὕλης (xi 17) is an orthodox opinion couched in Platonic language; it is a philosophical expression for that 'earth without form and void' from which this our globe was evolved[6]. The pre-existence of souls was a theory common to many systems of philosophy as well as to Platonism, and the author, in saying (viii 19, 20) · 'I was a witty child and had a good soul, yea, rather, being good, I came into a body undefiled,' showed that he was well acquainted with this opinion of the schools, while his statement was grounded on the language of Scripture[7]

If we cast our eyes upon writings outside the sacred volume we shall find the same blending of Greek and Hebrew notions In spite of Valckenaer's Diatribe[8] there seems no good reason to doubt that Aristobulus, of whose works Eusebius and Clemens Alex have preserved considerable fragments, is that Jewish priest, 'king Ptolemaeus' master' (2 Macc i. 10), who is addressed by Judas Maccabaeus as the representative of the Jews in Alexandria. The Ptolemy, whose teacher or counsellor (διδάσκαλος) he was, was Ptolemy Philometor (A D 150), and the work, remains of which have reached us, was an allegorical exposition of the Pentateuch, after the form with which we are familiar in the writings of Philo and the Alexandrian Fathers, Origen and Clement. In this treatise, perhaps with the hope of winning the king over to the Jewish faith, he labours to prove that the Law and the Prophets were the source from which the Greek philosophers, and specially the Peripatetics, had derived their doctrines To this end he cites Orpheus, who, in one of his sacred legends (ἱεροὶ λόγοι), speaks of God as the Creator, Preserver, and Ruler of all things, accom-

---

[1] Gfrorer, ii p 55 But see Grimm, Comment in 2 Macc iii 30 Dahne, ii. pp 181, ff Compare 3 Macc. ii. 9
[2] Dahne, ii p 187, and i p 120, Grimm in 2 Macc xiv 35
[3] See more, ap Dahne, i p. 194. The Fourth Book of Maccabees is not printed in Tischendorf's edition of the Septuagint It will be found, in Field, Apel, and Fritzsche
[4] Plut Plac. Philos vi (p 535), Zeller, Phil d Griech iii p 72
[5] Plato, de Rep. iv. pp 444, ff, Ritter, Hist. of Philos ii p 407 (Eng transl)
[6] See note on ch xi. 17
[7] Compare Isai xlix 1, 5, lvii 16, Jer i 5, and notes on ch viii 19, 20
[8] Diatribe de Aristobulo, 1806 See Dahne, ii pp. 73, ff, Gfrorer, Philo, ii pp. 71, ff, Vacherot, i pp 140, ff, Art Aristobulus, in Smith's Dict. of Bible, by Professor Westcott, Matter, Hist de l'École d'Alex. iii pp 153, ff, Eusebius entitles Aristobulus' work, Βίβλους ἐξηγητικὰς τοῦ Μωσέως νόμου (Hist. Eccl vii 32), or, Τὴν τῶν ἱερῶν νόμων ἑρμηνείαν (Praep Ev vii 13) The quotations in Clem Alex (Strom. i. p. 304, v p. 595, i p 342, vi p 632) are all found in Euseb Praep Ev See Dähne, p 89 Eusebius' Fragments are found, vii. 13, 14, viii 6, 8, 10; ix 6, xiii 12, pp 663, ff See also Dollinger, The Gentile and Jew, ii p 397 (Eng transl).

modating what is said of Zeus to the Lord of the Hebrews. in his view the letter of Holy Scripture is not to be pressed. Moses' imagery is only figurative: the transactions on Mount Sinai are only emblematic statements of great truths. He unhesitatingly sacrifices the literal meaning of the sacred story, and explains and allegorises till nothing historical remains. In the same way he treats the Greek myths, making them symbolise revealed truths, and striving to find for them a divine origin and a place in the Biblical records.

The letter of Aristeas[1], giving the well-known account of the production of the Septuagint translation, seems to have been the work of an Alexandrian Jew living at this period, though the writer, the better to maintain his assumed character, professes himself to be of another nation In it he speaks of the Jews worshipping the same God as the Greeks adored under the name of Zeus, but is careful to guard against Pantheism by maintaining that God's power and influence are through and in all things[2], he explains away the peculiar laws concerning meats clean and unclean, as symbolising purity and separation; he shows that all vice and evil springs from man's nature, all good from God, using the terms ἀρετή, ἀδικία, ἐγκράτεια, δικαιοσύνη, in a truly philosophic manner These sayings are supposed to be answers of the seventy-two elders to questions of the king; but as the whole story is fictitious, the doctrines asserted may well be taken to represent the views prevalent among the Jews in Alexandria in the century before Christ.

The Sibylline Books[3], which have come down to us, seem, on the best evidence, to be the production of Alexandrian Jews, and contain signs of their place and time of birth. Thus in the Proëmium we read[4].

Εἷς Θεός, ὃς μόνος ἄρχει ὑπερμεγέθης, ἀγένητος,
παντοκράτωρ, ἀόρατος, ὁρῶν μόνος αὐτὸς ἅπαντα,
αὐτὸς δ' οὐ βλέπεται θνητῆς ὑπὸ σαρκὸς ἁπάσης,
τίς γὰρ σὰρξ δύναται τὸν ἐπουράνιον καὶ ἀληθῆ
ὀφθαλμοῖσιν ἰδεῖν Θεὸν ἄμβροτον, ὃς πόλον οἰκεῖ, . . .
αὐτὸν τὸν μόνον ὄντα σέβεσθ' ἡγήτορα κόσμου,
ὃς μόνος εἰς αἰῶνα, καὶ ἐξ αἰῶνος ἐτύχθη,
αὐτογενής, ἀγένητος, ἅπαντα κρατῶν διὰ παντὸς
πᾶσι βροτοῖσιν ἐνὼν τὸ κριτήριον ἐν φάει κοινῷ . . .
οὐρανοῦ ἡγεῖται, γαίης κρατεῖ, αὐτὸς ὑπάρχει.

Here the expressions about God are wholly in accord with the Alexandrian philosophy, and seem also to embody a protest against the idolatry of Egypt.

Thus we see the progress of the attempt to reconcile Hebrew doctrine with Greek philosophy, to accommodate the one to the other, to read revealed truths in time-honoured myths, and to obtain, from a profound investigation into the inner sense of the sacred volume, ground for believing that the chief dogmas taught by the wisest of philosophers were contained therein.

But all these attempts are not comparable to what was effected by Philo Judaeus, whose voluminous works afford the most complete examples of the doctrine of the Jewish-Alexandrian school[5] Himself a resident in Alexandria, and from his early youth a devoted student, he was admirably fitted to examine the tenets of the philosophers before him and to combine them, if such combination were loyally possible, with those which he had received from his fathers and which he had no intention of disparaging or repudiating[6] Studious

---

[1] Gallandi, Bibl. Patr ii 771 ; Gfrorer, Philo, ii. pp. 61, ff., Dahne, ii pp 205, ff ; Hody, De Bibl Text. Orig.

[2] Μόνος ὁ Θεός ἐστι, καὶ διὰ πάντων ἡ δύναμις τοῦ αὐτοῦ ἐστι. φανερὰ γίνεται [πάντα αὐτῷ], πεπληρωμένου παντὸς τόπου τῆς δυναστείας This seems to favour the theory of the Neo-platonists concerning the Anima Mundi

[3] See Dahne, ii. pp 228, ff.

[4] Ap Theophil Ad Autol ii 36; Gfrorer, Philo, ii p 123

[5] For Philo's doctrine, see Gfrörer, Philo, i., Dahne, i.; Vacherot, i pp 142-167, Ritter, Hist Phil iv pp 407, ff (Eng transl).

Of Philo's works the best edition is that by Mangey, 2 vols fol, 1742, but this does not contain the treatises discovered by Mai and Aucher That by Richter (Lips 1828-1830) comprises all that is attributed to Philo There is a translation of his works in Bohn's Ecclesiastical Library For Philo's influence on succeeding theology see Mosheim's notes on Cudworth's Intellectual System, translated by Harrison, 1845, Kingsley, Alex and Her Schools, p 79, ff , J. Bryant, The Sentiments of Philo. Cambr. 1797

[6] Vit Mos iii 23 (ii. p 163 M) οὐκ ἀγνοῶ ὡς πάντα εἰσὶ

rather than original, more fanciful than profound, he was incapable of forming a complete system of theology, and being led away by side issues and verbal niceties, he is often inconsistent with himself, fails to convey a distinct impression, because he has but vague notions or unrealised conceptions to offer. Of his piety and earnestness there can be no doubt, equally certain it is that, owing to his want of logical method and division, his expressions are indefinite, and to frame any regular doctrine from his works is a matter of extreme difficulty, if it be possible.

The predominant idea of Philo was to present the Jewish religion in such a form as to make it acceptable to the Greek intellect. How to reconcile Revelation and Philosophy—this was the task to which he applied all the powers of his mind and all the stores of his learning. His great resource was allegory. In his hands the facts of history lost their reality and became only the embodiment of abstract truths, and the simple monotheism of Scripture was adapted to the refinements of Greek science [1].

First, as to the knowledge of God. Philo maintains that this is unattainable by man. He may know what God is not, he may know of His existence (ὕπαρξις), he can know nothing of His proper existence (ἰδία ὕπαρξις) or essence [2]. What we do know of God is that He is superior to the Good, more simple than the One, more ancient than the Unit [3]; He is unchangeable [4], eternal [5], uncompounded [6], wanting nothing [7], the source of all life [8], exclusively free [9] and exclusively blessed [10]; He fills all things [11], He is ever working [12], His love, justice, and providence are over all His works [13].

Such being the nature of God, so ineffable and unapproachable, what communication can there be between the Creator and the creature? It is true that man ought to strive with all his powers to know God, but of himself he cannot attain to this knowledge. He cannot rise to God: God must reveal Himself to him [14]. Now there are two kinds of revelation which God uses in His communications with men. The first and most perfect is bestowed only on some favoured seers, who, elevated above the condition of finite consciousness, become, as it were, one with Him whom they contemplate [15]. For the majority of men there remains only that in-

---

χρησμοὶ ὅσα ἐν ταῖς ἱεραῖς βίβλοις ἀναγέγραπται, χρησθέντες δι' αὐτοῦ κ.τ.λ. His views on inspiration are collected by Gfrorer, i pp. 54, ff.

[1] On Philo's reference of all that was best in Greek Philosophy to Moses see Quod omnis prob 8 (ii. p. 454), De Jud 2. (ii p 245), Quis rer div haer 43 (i p 503), De conf ling 20 (i p 419), De Vit Mos ii 4 (ii p 137)

[2] De Praem et Poen 7 (ii p. 415).

[3] De Vit Cont 1 (ii p. 472) τὸ ὄν, ὃ καὶ ἀγαθοῦ κρεῖττόν ἐστι, καὶ ἑνὸς εἰλικρινέστερον, καὶ μονάδος ἀρχεγονώτερον, where we may observe, that, while exalting God above the conceptions of philosophers, Philo says nothing of His Personality, substituting τὸ ὄν for ὁ ὤν of Exod iii 14

[4] Quod Deus immut § 5. (i p 276) τί γὰρ ἂν ἀσέβημα μεῖζον γένοιτο τοῦ ὑπολαμβάνειν τὸ ἄτρεπτον τρέπεσθαι,

[5] De Caritate, 2 (ii p 386) γενητὸς γὰρ οὐδεὶς ἀληθείᾳ Θεός, ἀλλὰ δόξῃ μόνον, τὸ ἀναγκαιότατον ἀφῃρημένος, ἀϊδιότητα

[6] Leg Alleg ii 1 ὁ δὲ Θεὸς μόνος ἐστί, καὶ ἕν, οὐ σύγκριμα, φύσις ἁπλῆ . οὐδὲ ἐκ πολλῶν συνεστώς. ἀλλὰ ἀμιγὴς ἄλλῳ (i. p. 66)

[7] Quod det potiori insid 16 (i p 202) δεῖται γὰρ οὐδενὸς ὁ πλήρης Θεός So Quod Deus immut 12 (i. p. 281). ὁ δὲ Θεὸς ἅτε ἀγέννητος ὤν, καὶ τὰ ἄλλα ἀγαγὼν εἰς γένεσιν, οὐδενὸς ἐδεήθη τῶν τοῖς γεννήμασι προσόντων.

[8] De Profug 36 (i p 575) ἡ μὲν γὰρ ὕλη, νεκρόν· ὁ δὲ Θεὸς πλέον τι ἢ ζωή, πηγὴ τοῦ ζῆν, ὡς αὐτὸς εἶπεν, ἀέννοος.

[9] De Somn 38 (i p 692) καὶ γὰρ ὁ Θεὸς ἑκούσιον

[10] De Septenar 5 (ii. p 280) μόνος γὰρ εὐδαίμων καὶ μακάριος, πάντων μὲν ἀμέτοχος κακῶν, πλήρης δὲ ἀγαθῶν τελείων

[11] De Confus ling. 27. (i. p. 425) ὑπὸ δὲ τοῦ Θεοῦ πεπλήρωται τὰ πάντα, περιέχοντος, οὐ περιεχομένου, ᾧ πανταχοῦ τε καὶ οὐδαμοῦ συμβέβηκεν εἶναι μόνῳ

[12] Leg Alleg i 3 (i p 44) παύεται γὰρ οὐδέποτε ποιῶν ὁ Θεός, ἀλλ' ὥσπερ ἴδιον τὸ καίειν πυρός, καὶ χιόνος τὸ ψύχειν, οὕτω καὶ Θεοῦ τὸ ποιεῖν

[12] De Vict offer 3 (ii p 253): τὸν εὐεργέτην καὶ σωτῆρα Θεόν Fragm ii p 685 M βασιλεὺς ἥμερον καὶ νόμιμον ἀνῃρημένος ἡγεμονίαν, μετὰ δικαιοσύνης τὸν σύμπαντα οὐρανόν τε καὶ κόσμον βραβεύει Ib ἁπάντων μὲν τῶν λογισμοῦ μεμοιραμένων κήδεται, προμηθεῖται δὲ καὶ τῶν ὑπαιτίων ζώντων, ἅμα μὲν καιρὸν εἰς ἐπανόρθωσιν αὐτοῖς διδούς κ τ λ

[14] De Abrah. 17 (ii. p 13) διὸ λέγεται, οὐχ ὅτι ὁ σοφὸς εἶδε Θεόν, ἀλλ' ὅτι ὁ Θεὸς ὤφθη τῷ σοφῷ· καὶ γὰρ ἦν ἀδύνατον καταλαβεῖν τινα δι' αὐτοῦ τὸ πρὸς ἀλήθειαν ὄν, μὴ παραφήναντος ἐκείνου ἑαυτὸ καὶ παραδείξαντος.

[15] De Abrah 24. (ii p 19), De Poster Cain. 5 (i. p 229);

PROLEGOMENA

ferior apprehension of God derived through some mediate existence or existences. This mediator in the first place is the Word (λόγος), the interpreter of God's will, and the God to imperfect beings, as the Lord or true God is God only to wise and perfect men[1]. This Logos is described as the image and firstborn of God[2], the archangel and high priest of the world[3], not the complete representative of the Supreme Being, but His figure and shadow[4], the ideal type of human nature, as it were, a celestial Adam[5], and God's instrument in the creation of the world. But there is a want of uniformity in Philo's doctrine of the Logos, the description being sometimes of a personal, sometimes of an impersonal, being[6]. He seems to have grasped the idea of a personal mediator, and yet to have shunned to enunciate it on every occasion, as though it were too earthly a conception for his soaring philosophy; and he takes refuge in abstractions whenever, if his terms are precisely weighed, the concrete comes too prominently to the surface.

The Logos, in Philo's view, is not the direct organ of communication between the Supreme God and His creatures. This office is discharged by inferior ministers, angels, and incorporeal existences, who pass between heaven and earth, and move in the minds of those who are still imperfect[7]. But his doctrine of angels is full of inconsistencies, as he calls by this name all the forces of nature, as well as divine powers, and introduces them on all occasions, and under various conditions, to suit his allegorising explanations of Holy Writ.

With regard to Creation, the simple cosmogony of the Hebrews was much modified and altered to bring it into harmony with philosophic speculations. In one place Philo says that God, who begat all things, not only, like the sun, brought to light hidden things, but even created what before had no existence, being not only the architect of the world, but the founder[8]. At another time he speaks of the impossibility of anything being generated out of nothing[9], and assumes an unformed and lifeless mass of matter, brought into shape and order by the spirit of God[10]. But he does not consider creation as a single act, that took place once for all; rather, God never ceases from making, it is His property to be always creating[11]. Only, His act is limited to willing; the act of creation is carried out by

---

48 (1. p. 258); Quis rer divin haer 13 and 14 (1 p 482). See Art Philosophy by Professor Mansel in Kitto's Cyclopaed a.

[1] Leg. Alleg. iii 73 (1 p 128) οὗτος γὰρ [ὁ ἑρμηνεὺς λόγος] ἡμῶν τῶν ἀτελῶν ἂν εἴη Θεός, τῶν δὲ σοφῶν καὶ τελείων, ὁ πρῶτος

[2] De Confus. ling. 28 (1 p. 427) τῆς ἀϊδίου εἰκόνος αὐτοῦ, λόγου τοῦ ἱερωτάτου Θεοῦ γὰρ εἰκὼν λόγος ὁ πρεσβύτατος. Ib τὸν πρωτόγονον αὐτοῦ λόγον, τὸν ἄγγελον πρεσβύτατον, ὡς ἀρχάγγελον πολυώνυμον ὑπάρχοντα

[3] De Somn. 1 37 (1. p. 653): ἀρχιερεὺς, ὁ πρωτόγονος αὐτοῦ θεῖος λόγος

[4] Leg Aleg iii. 31. (1. p 106)· σκιὰ Θεοῦ ὁ λόγος αὐτοῦ ἐστιν, ᾧ καθάπερ ὀργάνῳ προσχρησάμενος ἐκοσμοποίει αὕτη δὲ ἡ σκιὰ καὶ τὸ ὡσανεὶ ἀπεικόνισμα ἑτέρων ἐστὶν ἀρχέτυπον. ὥσπερ γὰρ ὁ Θεὸς παράδειγμα τῆς εἰκόνος, ἣν σκιὰν νυνὶ κέκληκεν, οὕτως ἡ εἰκὼν ἄλλων γίνεται παράδειγμα

[5] To the question why it is said, 'in the image of God made He man' and not 'in His own image,' Philo answers. θνητὸν γὰρ οὐδὲν ἀπεικονισθῆναι πρὸς τὸν ἀνωτάτω καὶ πατέρα τῶν ὅλων ἐδύνατο, ἀλλὰ πρὸς τὸν δεύτερον Θεόν, ὅς ἐστιν ἐκείνου λόγος Fragm ii. p. 625 M.

[6] See the question argued in Gfrorer, Philo, 1 pp 176, ff.,

Dorner, Person of Christ, i. pp 27, ff. (Engl. transl), Jowett, Epp. of S Paul, 1

[7] De Somn 1 22, 23 (1 p. 643) ταῖς δὲ τῶν ἔτι ἀπολουομένων, μήπω δὲ κατὰ τὸ παντελὲς ἐκνιψαμένων τὴν ῥυπῶσιν καὶ κεκηλιδωμένην σώμασι βαρέσι ζωήν, ἄγγελοι, λόγοι θεῖοι [ἐμπεριπατοῦσι], φαιδρύνοντες αὐτὰς τοῖς καλοκἀγαθίας ὄμμασιν. See Vacherot, i. pp. 152, 153

[8] De Somn 1. 13 (1 p 632) ἄλλοι τε ὡς ἥλιος ἀνατείλας τὰ κεκρυμμένα τῶν σωμάτων ἐπιδείκνυται, οὕτω καὶ ὁ Θεὸς τὰ πάντα γεννήσας, οὐ μόνον εἰς τὸ ἐμφανὲς ἤγαγεν, ἀλλὰ καὶ ἃ πρότερον οὐκ ἦν, ἐποίησεν, οὐ δημιουργὸς μόνον ἀλλὰ καὶ κτίστης αὐτὸς ὤν

[9] De Incorr Mundi, 2 (11 p 488) ἐκ τοῦ γὰρ οὐδαμῇ ὄντος ἀμήχανόν ἐστι γενέσθαι τι

[10] De Plantat 1 (1 p 829), De Cherub. 35 (1 pp 161, 162); De Victim offer 13 (ii p 261) ἐξ ἐκείνης γὰρ [ὕλης] πάντ' ἐγέννησεν ὁ Θεός, οὐκ ἐφαπτόμενος αὐτός· οὐ γὰρ ἦν θέμις ἀπείρου καὶ πεφυρμένης ὕλης ψαύειν τὸν εὐδαίμονα καὶ μακάριον, ἀλλὰ ταῖς ἀσωμάτοις δυνάμεσιν, ὧν ἔτυμον ὄνομα αἱ ἰδέαι, κατεχρήσατο πρὸς τὸ γένος ἕκαστον τὴν ἁρμόττουσαν λαβεῖν μορφήν. Cf. De Mund. Opif 2

[11] Leg Alleg. i. 3 (1 p 44) quoted above, p. 12, note 12.

the Word. As the pattern on which the world was formed Philo conceived the Platonic notion of a spiritual world composed of ideas or spiritual forms; and the powers which operated in the sensible creation he likened to the rays that proceed from a central light, the nearer (including in this idea the Logos) being the brightest effulgence, and the more distant, fainter and more imperfect reflections That this is one germ of the later Gnostic doctrine of Emanations seems undoubted [1]. In pursuing his cosmology Philo now teaches that the world ($ὁ\ νοητὸς\ κόσμος$) is nothing else but the Reason ($λόγος$) of God the Creator[2]. Thus the $λόγος\ ἐνδιάθετος$, Thought, as embracing all ideas, becomes $λόγος\ προφορικός$, Thought realised, the living word, the power of Jehovah manifested, is the archetypal idea of things, 'the supreme unity of the primitive forms of the created world' 'Some persons affirm,' he says[3], 'that the incorporeal ideas are an empty name, void of all reality, thus removing the most necessary of all essences from the number of existing things, while it is in fact the archetypal model of all things which have the distinctive qualities of essence, which are form and measure' This twofold notion of the Word combined with the belief in the Supreme God foreshadows, not the Christian Trinity, the three Persons in one God, where the Divine Three are equal and consubstantial, but the three Principles of the later Alexandrian school as they are found in Plotinus[4] Tending to a similar result is the comment on the three mysterious visitants to Abraham in the plain of Mamre[5] 'The one in the centre is the Father of the Universe,' he says, 'Who is called in the Scriptures "I am that I am;" and the beings on each side are those most ancient powers and nearest to Him Who is, one of which is called the creative, the other the kingly, power And the creative power is God; for by this He made and arranged the universe; and the kingly power is the Lord, for it is meet that the Creator should rule and govern the creature[6].' But on this subject Philo is incoherent and inconsistent, and it is vain to attempt to construct a regular system from his bewildered speculations.

As to psychology, Philo, after Aristotle, distinguishes the three parts or characters of the soul, the rational, the vegetative, and the appetitive[7], sometimes dividing the rational part into $αἴσθησις$, $λόγος$, and $νοῦς$, at another into $λόγος$, $θύμος$, and $ἐπιθυμία$[8]. The soul is immaterial and pre-existent, dwelling in the upper air till it sojourns in a mortal body; and those souls only which are earthly in desires and have a love for mortal life are thus embodied, others of higher aims and nobler ambition never assume a corporeal nature, but soar upwards to the vision of the Almighty, being what men call angels or demons[9].

Such is a very brief account of the philosophical theology of Philo. The attempt to combine philosophy and faith, however skilfully executed, appears to have been in his hands a failure philosophy gained little by it, faith suffered great loss. The simple narrative of Genesis was not improved or explained by imagining a twofold Logos, as concerned in the creation, the one being the archetypal idea, the other the sensible world; and Plato's cosmogony, which recognised three

---

[1] De Mund Opif 4, 6, 7 (1 pp 4. 5), De Somn 1 19 (i. p 638). Dähne, 1 pp 240, ff, Burton, Bampt. Lect iv note 49

[2] De Mund Opif 6 (1 p 5) $εἰ\ δέ\ τις\ ἐθελήσειε\ γυμνοτέροις\ χρήσασθαι\ τοῖς\ ὀνόμασιν,\ οὐδὲν\ ἂν\ ἕτερον\ εἴποι\ τὸν\ νοητὸν\ εἶναι\ κόσμον,\ ἢ\ θεοῦ\ λόγον\ ἤδη\ κοσμοποιοῦντος$ See Gfrörer, 1 p 177, Lewes, 1 p 379, Vacherot, i pp. 158, 159.

[3] De Vict offer 13 (ii. p 261)

[4] For Plotinus see Vacherot, 1. pp 360, ff., and specially pp 431, ff

[5] De Abraham. 24. (ii p. 19).

[6] See another analogous fancy, De Cherub 9 (1 pp 143. 144).

[7] Aristot Ethic Nicom I xiii, Philo, De congr erud grat. 6 (1. p 523), Fragm. ii. p 668, Leg Alleg 1 22 (1. p. 57). See Gfrörer, 1 pp 382, ff ; Dähne, i pp 288, ff

[8] De congr. erud. grat. 18. (i. p. 533), De Victim. 6 (ii p. 243); De Concupisc 2 (ii p 350).

[9] De Somn. i. 22. (i. pp. 641, 642), Quaest. in Gen. iii. 10. (vii pp 14, 15, Richt).

independent existences, the Demiurge, Matter, and the Idea, was not corrected by a theory which left Matter as eternal as God, and merely assigned Scriptural appellations to heathen notions

4 It has been confidently asserted that Christianity owes its prominent doctrines to Philo and the Alexandrian School; some writers have even not scrupled to maintain that the religion of Christ is simply a product of the allegories of Philo and his imitators[1]. The chief point with most of the writers who make such assertions is S. John's doctrine of the Logos, which is said to have been derived entirely from Philo's writings. Now we must distinguish between a doctrine and the language in which it is expressed. A writer may employ terms previously in existence to denote an opinion very different from that which other teachers have used it to signify There are limits to language, especially to philosophic language, and without the invention of new words it would have been impossible for Christianity to avoid fixing a different sense to many of the words and phrases which it adopted This has been the case with the term Λόγος The Hebrew equivalent (*Memra*) had been employed in the Scriptures in a more or less personal sense : the angel of the Lord, the angel of the covenant, was identified in the popular expositions of the Sacred Books with the Memra[2] the Books of Ecclesiasticus and Wisdom had further developed the idea of the Personality of the Word: the term Logos had been heard in the speculations of heathen and Jew : it contained a mighty truth which had been obscured by a mass of error, what wonder if S John was directed to make use of this term in order to set forth the doctrine of our Lord's Person, and at the same time to correct the mistakes and heresies which had gathered around it? Familiar with the true dogma, knowing the false notions of the Alexandrian School, the apostle thus tacitly rebuked the error by assigning a correct idea to that term which had been the subject of so much disputation, and whose meaning had been so greatly distorted[3] 'In the beginning was the Logos, and the Logos was with God, and the Logos was God' The language is philosophic and Alexandrian, the notion is solely Christian; and that notion, to use the words of Canon Liddon[4], is this: 'The divine Logos is God reflected in His own eternal Thought ; in the Logos God is His own object. The infinite Thought, the reflection and counterpart of God, subsisting in God as a Being or Hypostasis, and having a tendency to self-communication,—such is the Logos The Logos is the Thought of God, not intermittent and precarious like human thought, but subsisting with the intensity of a personal form' And He is eternal, ἐν ἀρχῇ, and not merely παρὰ τῷ Θεῷ, but πρὸς τὸν Θεόν, a phrase which implies not only 'coexistence and immanence, but also perpetuated intercommunion.' And more, the Logos is 'not merely a divine Being, but He is in the absolute sense God,' Θεὸς ἦν ὁ Λόγος.

Philo did not say this. He has certain vague notions of a personal mediator, and at times seems to state the doctrine without reserve ; but he is not stable in this opinion He is always fluctuating and hesitating and modifying ; and is very far from holding in its full meaning S John's simple enunciation, 'The Word was God' There is a grave difference between one who is dimly feeling after a truth which he has not realised and could not define, and one who is finding language to denote a doctrine revealed to him and enshrined in his heart.

Judging from Philo's language alone in certain passages one would say, without hesitation, that he maintained the Divinity and Personality of the Word, and

---

[1] Grossman, Quaest Philon. p 3, and among others of the German school, Ernesti, Lücke, De Wette, Straus; Gratz, Geschichte, in 217 , Baur, Paul u Christenth , Schwegler, Nachap. Zeitalt

[2] See Etheridge, The Targums of Onkelos, etc on the Pentateuch, Introd pp 17, ff

[3] See Liddon, Bampton Lectures, v pp 338, ff (ed 1866).

[4] Bampt Lect p 341

attributed to Him that nature and those offices and qualities which are assigned to Him by the New Testament writers Further investigation would considerably modify and correct this view. It would be seen that the teaching of the Jew and the Christian was similar in form only, not in substance · that while using the same language they held very different ideas If Philo calls the Logos, the image of God[1], His first-begotten Son[2], the second deity Who is the Word of the Supreme deity[3], he speaks of Him also, as we have seen, in quite other terms, which are not consistent with the belief in His perfect divinity[4]. Thus in stating that the world was made according to the image of the Word, the archetypal model, the idea of ideas[5], he plainly cannot mean that this Word is of the same nature as Almighty God, otherwise he would be guilty of a materialistic conception, which would be entirely repugnant to his religious views; whereas, if the Word is merely an exemplar produced in the mind of the Supreme Being, this entirely evacuates the expression of all personal meaning and reduces it to an architectural design subsequently carried out[6]. Besides this, the best and inmost part of God is regarded as incommunicable, in the inmost divine sphere the Absolute does not admit of distinctions, but has only a circle of rays in which it is reflected, so that in this sense also, the Logos, the revelation of God, is not itself partaker of divinity[7]

Certainly, as we have before noticed, Philo has no fixed belief in His Personality, he cannot conceive the notion of His incarnation; and the glorious hopes and aspirations which surround the Messiah he completely ignores Of Christ's two natures he has no notion whatever. He speaks indeed of the mediatorial character of the Logos[8], but by this he means something very different from the Christian doctrine, as we shall see further on

It was doubtless under divine guidance that S Paul, S. John, and other writers of the New Testament employed, in enunciating the truths which they had to promulgate, terms and expressions already used and partially understood Here were already provided words which were capable of conveying the thought which they purposed to imprint on the mind of their hearers The same terminology with which the converts had been familiarised in the Septuagint, the Greek philosophical writings, and the sapiential Books, needed only to receive a new modification of meaning to qualify it for the higher office of containing the form of Christian theology. The Greek language had already been forced into the service of Jewish thought[9] · it was now translated into a still nobler sphere, and under inspired manipulation learned to connote Christian ideas and revealed mysteries

In Christian hands the term Logos was employed to express two definite ideas, that the Word was a Divine Person, and that He became incarnate in Jesus Christ[10]. Thus the vague conception of pre-Christian teachers, which never advanced beyond the idea of the Logos as the undefined manifestation of the invisible God,

---

[1] De Mund Opif 8 (i. p 6). See Bryant, The Sentim of Philo, p 17, ff, who maintains that Philo derived many of his views from S. Paul

[2] De Agric. 12 (1 p 308), De conf ling. 28 · τὸν πρωτόγονον αὐτοῦ λόγον ... ἀρχὴ καὶ ὄνομα Θεοῦ καὶ λόγος

[3] Fragm (ii p 625)

[4] De Leg Alleg iii 73 (1 p 128) quoted above, p. 13, note 1.

[5] Quaest et Sol (ii p 625) θνητὸν γὰρ οὐδὲν ἀπεικονισθῆναι πρὸς τὸν ἀνωτάτω καὶ πατέρα τῶν ὅλων ἐδύνατο, ἀλλὰ πρὸς τὸν δεύτερον Θεόν, ὅς ἐστιν ἐκείνου λόγος Ἔδει γὰρ τὸν λογικὸν ἐν ἀνθρώπου ψυχῇ τύπον ὑπὸ θείου λόγου χαραχθῆναι ἐπειδὴ ὁ πρὸ τοῦ λόγου Θεὸς κρείσσων ἐστὶν ἢ πᾶσα λογικὴ φύσις τῷ δὲ ὑπὲρ τὸν λόγον, ἐν τῇ βελτίστῃ καί τινι ἐξαιρέτῳ καθεστῶτι ἰδέᾳ, οὐδὲν θέμις ἦν γενητὸν ἐξομοιοῦσθαι Euseb. Praep Ev vii 13.

[6] Cudworth, Intell. Syst transl. by Harrison, ii pp 329, ff note.

[7] Dorner, Person of Christ, vol 1, note A (Clarke's transl) See also Introduction, pp 22, 23

[8] Quis rer div haer 42 (1 p 501) · ὁ δ' αὐτὸς ἱκέτης μέν ἐστι τοῦ θνητοῦ κηραίνοντος ἀεὶ πρὸς τὸ ἄφθαρτον, πρεσβευτὴς δὲ τοῦ ἡγεμόνος πρὸς τὸ ὑπήκοον

[9] Jowett, on Ep to Galat p 452.

[10] Bishop J B Lightfoot, on Ep to Coloss i 15.

received precise and exact signification; and it seems impossible to resist the conclusion that, although the Jewish and the Christian writers use the same language and have certain ideas in common, their doctrines are very far from being identical, and that S John may be regarded rather as one who is correcting and defining the vague notions of the Alexandrian school, than as one who is influenced by that philosophy and dependent upon its teaching.

To turn for a moment to another portion of the same subject, the interpretation of Scripture, and to compare the treatment to which Philo subjected the historical statements of Holy Writ with the method pursued, for instance, by the author of the Epistle to the Hebrews and S Paul can any two processes be more distinct? In one case you have always a straining after allegorical interpretation, far-fetched and fanciful, a verbose exposition of details without regard to consistency or truth; in the other you find the chief attention concentrated on principles involved with little special reference to words and terms. Philo deals with the facts of revelation and history as *media* for mystical, spiritual, and allegorical interpretation, and as in a great measure not real history, but parables of heavenly or moral truths. The Christian writer treats his facts as events that happened in the sphere of God's Providence, that were transacted on the stage of this world in the fulfilment of the Creator's will and carrying out His plans, leading on to the Incarnation of the Divine Son and His exaltation to the heaven of heavens. Let us take one instance where Philo and S Paul have treated the same subject, and compare the method employed on either side S. Paul, Gal iv. 22–31, has expounded the history of Hagar and Sarah allegorically. In doing this he first gives the facts, states them as true records of events that really happened, and then elicits from them a spiritual sense, shows what is their spiritual signification 'It is written,' he says, 'that Abraham had two sons, one by the bondwoman, the other by the freewoman, but he who was of the bondwoman was born after the flesh, but he of the freewoman was by the promise.' This is the history. Then follows the allegorical interpretation[1]. These women represent two different covenants, the first given from Mount Sinai, which brings forth children unto bondage, inasmuch as it is Hagar For Hagar represents Mount Sinai in Arabia, and answers to the earthly Jerusalem, which with all her children is still in bondage. But the other covenant, inasmuch as it is Sarah, bears free children and answers to the heavenly Jerusalem, which with all her children is free. Philo[2] takes many pages to allegorise the history, and he executes his purpose in a verbose, pointless, unauthorised way, as different as possible from the terseness, strictness, and directness of S Paul. Sarah, 'my princedom,' is the wisdom, justice, temperance, and all the other virtues which govern me, he says. She indeed is always bringing forth good reasonings, blameless counsels, and praiseworthy actions, but she does not bring them forth for me unless I first call in the aid of her handmaid which is the encyclical knowledge of logic and music obtained by previous instruction. For Hagar is the emblem of grammar, geometry, astronomy, rhetoric, music, and all other rational objects of study, which one must pass in order to arrive at virtue And these are, as it were, infantile food prepared for the soul, till it is ready for the virtues of the perfect man The handmaid is an Egyptian, that is, 'earthly,' because the man who delights in encyclical learning has need of all his external senses to profit by what he learns; and her name is Hagar, that is, 'emigration,' because virtue is the only native citizen of the universe, and all other kinds of instruction are strangers and foreigners. 'The same relation that a mistress has to her handmaiden, or a wife, who

---

[1] Ἅτινά ἐστιν ἀλληγορούμενα Not 'which things are an allegory,' but as Vulg 'Quae sunt per allegoriam dicta.' The narrative contains an inner meaning See Wordsw. in loc., Picon Tripl Expos.; Dr. J. B. Lightfoot, Ep. to Galat. pp. 189, ff

[2] De congr. erud. grat. 1–5. (i. pp. 519, ff.).

is a citizen, to a concubine, that same relation has virtue, i e Sarah, to education, i e. Hagar, so that very naturally, since the husband, by name Abraham, is one who has an admiration for contemplation and knowledge, virtue, i.e. Sarah, would be his wife, and Hagar, i e all kinds of encyclical accomplishments, would be his concubine. Whoever, therefore, has acquired wisdom from his teachers, would never reject Hagar. For the acquisition of all the preliminary branches of education is necessary[1].' This is really a favourable specimen of Philo's allegorising treatment of Holy Scripture, and it is obvious that the arbitrary, fanciful transference of plain facts to force a moral lesson which has no connection with the history, is an extreme contrast with the method of S Paul, where the history is the framework on which the allegory depends for its applicability, coherence, and usefulness. The fancy (for it is nothing more) that the apostle derived his method of treating Holy Scripture from the Alexandrian school is very far from the truth, and could hardly have been upheld by any one who had studied the two systems with common attention or a mind free from prejudice[2].

Take another doctrine which Philo is said to have taught the Christian Church In a certain passage[3] he calls the Son of God παράκλητος, and herein is seen the source where S John (1 Ep. 1 2) derived the term as applied to Christ. But what are the facts? 'It was necessary,' says Philo, 'that one ministering to the Father of the world should use as Advocate the Son most perfect in virtue both for the forgiveness of sins and the supply of the richest blessings' He is speaking of the dress of the high-priest, and explains the vestment as representing the world which was thus, as it were, brought into the temple whenever the priest entered to perform his sacred offices. And then he proceeds as above, thus showing that by the Son he means the world[4], and implies, as does likewise the author of the Book of Wisdom (xviii 24), that the very sacrificial garments themselves were regarded as a means of intercession What is there in this ceremonial figure to teach S John the doctrine of the Advocacy of Jesus Christ the righteous, the propitiation for man's sin? There is another passage in Philo[5] bearing on the same subject, where he says, that the Father has given to His archangel and most ancient Logos a preeminent gift to stand on the confines and separate the created from the Creator And this Logos is continually a suppliant to the immortal God in behalf of the mortal race, and is also the ambassador sent by the Ruler of all to the subject man There is a similarity here to the verse of S Paul (1 Tim ii 5) 'There is one God and one Mediator between God and man, the man Christ Jesus,' but the coincidence is not essential In Philo the Logos is a mean between the good and the evil, as the cloud between Israel and the Egyptians, neither being uncreated as God, nor created as man, but being like a hostage to both parties, a pledge to God that the whole race would not rebel entirely, and to man that God will never overlook the work of His hands That Christ partakes of both natures, and is the only Mediator between God and man, is quite beyond the Jew's idea, who has mingled the particle of truth which he possessed with the Aristotelian notion of the mean and the Pythagorean theory of contrasts

There is throughout all such occasional coincidences the fundamental distinction between the ideal Logos of the Jewish philosopher and the one Christ, God and

---

[1] Bohn's transl, ii p 162

[2] See The Apostle Paul and the Christian Church at Philippi By Rev J F Todd, London, 1864 Here will be found a painstaking endeavour to show the contrast between the teaching and method of Philo and S Paul Burton's Bampton Lectures, note 93, &c., Dorner, Person of Christ, i. 22-41 (Clarke's ed).

[3] De Vit Mos iii 14 (ii p 155) ἀναγκαῖον γὰρ ἦν τὸν ἱερώ- μενον τῷ τοῦ κόσμου πατρὶ παρακλήτῳ χρῆσθαι τελειοτάτῳ τὴν ἀρετὴν υἱῷ, πρός τε ἀμνηστείαν ἁμαρτημάτων καὶ χορηγίαν ἀφθονω- τάτων ἀγαθῶν

[4] Philo calls the Logos κόσμος αὐτός De Mund Opif 48. (i p 33)

[5] Quis rer. div. haer. 42. (ii. p. 501). See Jowett, Ep. to Galat p 482.

man, of the Christian. With a writer who saw in matter the source of all evil, the idea of the Incarnation was inconceivable, was indeed repugnant to his conception of God and God's relation with the world. That the term Logos was well understood is evident, e g. from the abrupt commencement of S. John's Gospel; but none of the philosophers or theologians who were familiar with the expression would have admitted the statement that 'The Logos became flesh.' Such an assertion was utterly irreconcilable with their principles. With Philo the Logos is rather 'Reason' than 'Word,' metaphysical rather than personal, speculative rather than moral With the Apostle the reverse is the case. The Personality of the Word, His historical manifestation, are the points brought out. And in the full Christian doctrine we trace the truth for which preceding revelations had prepared the way, that the Son of God is that Angel of the Covenant who guided the ancient patriarchs, that Word who executed the Father's will, that Wisdom which was with God and was over all His works

Besides Philo and his school there are other sources whence Christianity is said to have derived its tenets and practices. Not satisfied with the opinion that Christianity is the ordained religion for which Judaism prepared the way, being itself the proper development of the earlier form, critics have, with a perseverance that might be better employed, sought to trace Christ's doctrines to human opinions prevalent in the age preceding his own, and to state precisely whence they were borrowed or adopted.

Among the heralds of Christianity have been reckoned the Essenes[1], many of whose tenets and practices are said to have prepared the way for the reception of a purer and more definite faith. They were indeed the saintly livers among the Jews in all ages of their history. From the time of Moses to the captivity, from the return to the era of the Maccabees and thence onward to Christian days, there had always been holy men, led by the Spirit of God, who, whether living in communities or solitary, kept in many respects to the strictest traditions of their faith, and by purity, unworldliness, and the practice of many virtues anticipated no few of the Christian doctrines Doubtless there were many excesses in their religion they often showed as mere fanatics, often espoused philosophical tenets alien from and inconsistent with revelation, but as their name connects them with the Chasidim, the holy[2], so all their rules and tenets and practices were intended to produce holiness. Of the analogy between their precepts and many of Christ's commands or of the usages of the early Christians, it is easy to judge[3]. Thus, the Essenes commended the poor in spirit, peacemakers, the merciful, the pure in heart; they contemned the laying up riches; they had all things in common, called no man master, sold their possessions and divided them among the poor, they swore no oaths, but their communication was yea, yea, nay, nay. They believed that by prayer and fasting they could cast out devils; that a man should abstain from marriage for the sake of the kingdom of heaven; that by living a life of holiness and purity their bodies would become temples of the Holy Ghost and they would be able to prophesy (1 Cor. xiv 1, 39). That Christianity derived any of its doctrines and practices from the Essenes is an unproved assertion, but that finding their principles and customs prevailing, Christ and His Apostles recognised what was good and right in them, while rejecting their excesses,

---

[1] The accounts of the Essenes are found in Philo, Quod omn prob lib 12, 13 (ii pp 457–460); Fragm. ii pp 632, ff., Mang, Joseph Bell Jud ii. 8; Antiq xiii. 5; xv 10, xviii 1, Solinus, Polyhist. xxv 7, ff ; Porphyr περὶ ἀποχ τῶν ἐμψύχ, p. 381, ed. 1620, Epiphan. Adv. Haer i 10 p 28, ed 1682; i 19 p 39; κατὰ Ὀσσηνῶν; Pliny, Hist Nat v. 17. See Dr Ginsburg's Essay, The Essenes their History and Doctrines, London, 1864, Gfrörer, Philo, ii pp 299, ff, Dahne, i. pp 469, ff

[2] See Art. Chasidim, in Kitto's Bibl Cyclop. This derivation is the subject of much dispute. See Lightfoot's Essay

[3] The following comparison is based on Dr Ginsburg's most complete and interesting Essay, where the whole literature of the subject is fully treated, and Dr. J B. Lightfoot's Essay in his edition of S Paul's Ep. to Coloss.

is certainly possible [1]. And the very existence of this sect, if it was a sect, or of these saintly persons, was doubtless one of those providential preparations for the triumph of the Gospel which the Christian student has at all times loved to trace. But much more has been made of the importance of these religionists than is warranted by their history or the tenets which are attributed to them.

The fact is that the Essenes were an insignificant body, and played no prominent part in the national life of the Jews. There is no evidence that any intercourse existed between Essenism and Christianity, and to assume that Christ Himself, John the Baptist, and James the Lord's brother were members of this sect, as some authors do, is to read into history preconceived views, not to base theories on well-established facts. The coincidences of practice and teaching between the two are only so far connected as all high morality may be said to be derived from one source, or as the special points mentioned may be considered as the growth of the same country, climate, and circumstances. In many of their opinions and customs they directly contravened the Mosaic law, as for instance in their abstention from animal sacrifices [2], and no more marked opposition to Christianity could be found than in their persistent denial of the Resurrection of the body.

From what has been said we may gather these inferences. The Jewish-Alexandrian philosophy was not the origin of any of the doctrines of the New Testament; nor was the allegorical method of interpreting certain parts of the historical Scriptures derived from or identical with that employed by Philo and his school. The two allegations to the contrary are based on verbal similitudes, sometimes accidental, sometimes intentional, but with no affinity in thought. But using the language current at the time as the vehicle of Christian truth, the Apostles explained their meaning intelligibly, suggested the origin of the erroneous speculations then prevalent, and at the same time corrected these mistakes. For it was indeed incumbent on them to notice the prevailing theories which were to become the parents of future heresies in the Christian Church. It is beyond our design to trace the course of these declensions from the faith, but we may state briefly the effect of this Judaic-Alexandrian philosophy on one or two points of Christian dogma.

The Arian heresy may reasonably be referred to the Logos doctrine of the Alexandrian school. This error gathered into one view all that had hitherto tended to lower the divinity of the Second Person of the Divine Trinity. The Logos, regarded by Philo often as not personal, sometimes as personal, but not so *per se*; the denial of any duality of Divine Persons; the separation of the Logos from the divine sphere, His subordination to God, and His creation in time; these and such-like opinions were a preparation for the notion that the Son was a creature begotten not eternally and not consubstantial with the Father.

Again, the Sabellian doctrine which substituted three names or conceptions of God in place of three Persons, which regarded the Trinity as different modes of the existence of God, had its prefiguration in the dream of Philo concerning the threefold perfections of God. The trinity of Plato, as it is called, the discussions of philosophers respecting the three great principles of things, with which the schools of Alexandria had familiarised him, led to a theory, which, while it retained the great dogma of Monotheism, embraced the idea of a triad of operations or virtues in the divine nature [3]. Vague and indeterminate as was Philo's conception of this

---

[1] That S. John the Baptist belonged to this order is argued from his ascetic life, and from the fact that Christ announced him to be Elias, which would be equivalent to saying that he had arrived at the highest degree among the Essenes. See Dr. Ginsburg's Art. The Essenes, Ap. Kitto's Cyclop.; Grätz, Gesch. d. Jud. iii. p. 217. The same opinion has been held concerning James, the Lord's brother, and even Christ Himself. See the refutation in Lightfoot.

[2] This has been denied by Neander, Hist. of Christ. Relig. i. p. 67 (Bohn's transl.); but see Lightfoot, p. 134.

[3] Cudworth, Intell. Syst. ii. 333, note (transl. by Harrison); Philo, De Cherub. 9 (i. p. 143); De Abrah. 24 (ii. p. 19); De Mut. Nom. 4 (i. p. 582).

trinity, it was the germ of that error which used the term while it destroyed the Christian connotation.

And once more, that Judaizing Platonism, which with certain additions merged into Gnosticism, derived some of its chief elements from these Alexandrian theologasters, as Erasmus would have called them. This widely penetrating system, which formed the chief danger of early Christianity, was the natural offspring of Oriental mysticism. Gnosticism furnished no essentially new speculations; it gave a new emphasis to truths already held, it combined them in new relations, but it did not create or invent novel theories and produce an altogether fresh system. Of the elements that contributed to this philosophy Alexandrian Judaism was one of the most important. If we may trace some of its factors to oriental Pantheism or Parsism, we are constrained to acknowledge the supreme influence of the school of Alexandria, and to look upon this as the medium by which the tenets of the various religionisms which composed it were held together and consolidated. The distinction between the highest God and the Demiurgus, the derivation of evil from an evil principle called matter ($\ddot{v}\lambda\eta$), the doctrine of emanation, the representation of the visible world as an image of the world of light, the arbitrary allegorising of Scripture, and the notion of a secret doctrine which belonged only to the highest intellects, all these were the direct product of the Jewish-Alexandrian philosophy.

To this school also we may trace many of the opinions and much of the method of the early Christian Fathers. In defending and developing Christian doctrines they were necessarily brought face to face with Alexandrian teachers, and were constrained either to accept or oppose their statements. With the writings of Philo Justin Martyr was well acquainted, and he adopts many of the Jew's opinions and uses his language. In his idea of God he is much more in accordance with Philo than with the Catholic Creed, conceiving the Father, the Word, and the Spirit, not as three Persons of one divine substance, but as three Principles of differing rank[1]. After Philo's example also he endeavours to reconcile the cosmogony of Plato with that of Moses, and at another time he introduces thoughts concerning the soul from the Stoics and other Greek philosophers[2].

Of the deep influences of the Graeco-Jewish philosophy upon the Alexandrian Fathers every student is aware. 'Any one,' say Vacherot[3], 'who desires to understand Clement and Origen, must keep in mind the three sources from which they drew their thoughts, Gnosticism, Philoism, and Platonism.'

Clemens Alexandrinus regarded Greek Philosophy as a mere plagiarism from the Jewish Scriptures[4]. In his *Stromata* his chief object is to furnish materials for the construction of a Christian philosophy on the basis of faith in revealed religion; and in carrying out this design he shows how in various particulars the heathens were indebted to Hebrew sources for their wisdom, thus following up the investigation in which Philo had led the way. Nor does he confine himself simply to the truths which philosophy has to teach: from her he borrows his method of inquiry; he calls to his aid dialectics, geometry, arithmetic and other sciences, to contribute their support to his theological speculations. All, in his view, have their part in this supreme science, which is Knowledge, Gnosis[5], and the end and object of this is union with God through the Word.

In Origen we see the allegorising method of interpreting the Scriptures reduced, as we may say, to a system. This great teacher seems to revel in the obscurities and dark sayings of the divine oracles. He finds in them subjects worthy of his deepest thought. It was in his opinion an error fraught with much evil to adhere to the external, the carnal part of Scripture;

---

[1] Apol. Prim. p. 51, Vacherot, 1 p. 230.
[2] Apol. Prim. p. 78, Cum Tryph. Dial. p. 221.
[3] Ib. 1 p. 248.
[4] Strom. xi. 1.
[5] Strom. vi. 10, Vacherot, 1 p. 251.

in every portion we should seek hidden and mystic meanings which are the spirit of the Word of God and its veritable substance. The letter leads astray and brings little benefit[1]. Consistently with this theory he lays comparatively little stress on the historical facts connected with Christ's life, and seeks to rise to the contemplation of the essence of the Logos, as He is in Himself, using the life and character of the historical Jesus as a symbol of the agency of the Divine Logos, seeing in all Scripture the incarnation of the Word[2]. Like Philo, he explained the earthly events narrated in the Bible and the temporary enactments recorded there as symbolical veils of spiritual mysteries. The outer husk he deemed to be suitable food for the uninstructed multitude; the higher truths were to be reserved for those who had arrived at the most perfect condition. If there were any persons standing between these two states, for them the allegorical sense was suitable, as best conveying to their capacities moral instruction and edification. There are many other points in which both Origen and Clement exhibited remarkable affinity in doctrine to Philo. In their language concerning God and the Word and the Holy Spirit and the destiny of man they are in close accord with the Jewish writer. They also owed much to Greek Philosophy; in their cosmology, their psychology, their ethics they introduced the ideas of Stoics and Platonists; and although, in the case of Origen, these foreign elements were developed into formal heresy, yet they were on the whole serviceable to the cause of Christianity, and formed a part of that Providential arrangement which prepared the way for the acceptance and dissemination of the true faith[3].

These writers and their followers had the high merit of introducing Christianity in the only form in which it would be likely to find acceptance with cultivated and scientific intellects; and if they exhibited a tendency to merge practice in speculation, to make men think rather than act, still both of these elements are necessary for all education, and we must not decry the merits of those who taught the one if they failed sufficiently to supply the other. The *argumentum ad hominem* which they were thus enabled to use was eminently serviceable to them in conciliating opponents and in establishing the doctrines which they laboured to disseminate. They could show how philosophers had long been feeling after a Trinity in the Divine nature, how the Word of God had been an object of abundant speculation for many a day. The very terms with which their adversaries were familiar could convey the instruction which they desired to give; the very dogmas which heathen sages had announced were echoes of revealed truths; and those who had set these forth were guided by that Holy Spirit whom Christians adored.

Before concluding this brief and necessarily imperfect sketch there is one other result of the Jewish-Alexandrian teaching which we must mention. An earnest pagan, when he turned his attention to the conclusions attained by his most eminent philosophers, and saw how empty, unsatisfactory and barren of issue were their speculations, naturally longed for something better, some completer solutions of the questions by which his mind was agitated. And, looking around on the varying faiths of the nations, he endeavoured to calm his disquiet and quench his longing by elaborating an eclectic philosophy which should combine in one the best points of heathenism and Oriental religion. In this connection it was impossible to avoid following in the steps of Philo and his school. In attempting to breathe into the expiring heathendom a new breath of life, a method, which had already more or less successfully glorified and exalted ancient myths and philosophic theories by conceding to them a place in the shrine of revealed religion, was the very element needed to inspire new zeal in behalf of the old rites, and to form the basis of polemical and apologetic

---

[1] Orig. in Ep. ad Rom. lib. viii. 8. p. 633 Ben.
[2] See Neander, Hist. of Christ. Relig. ii. p. 257, ff. (Bohn's transl.)
[3] Vacherot, i. p. 294, ff.

discussion. Successful opposition to Christianity could only be offered by a spiritualizing of the polytheistic religion which would conceal its grossness and soften the contrast between the popular superstitions and the pure doctrines by which they were being undermined and supplanted. This antagonistic system is known as the later Neo-Platonism. Its struggles with Christianity and its utter defeat form an interesting episode in Church history which it is beyond our scope to describe.

If then we allow that there is token of immediate connection between the Jewish-Alexandrian philosophy and the early Fathers, and if we concede that the attempt to conciliate philosophy and religion led the way to that new phase of doctrine which was so bitterly hostile to Christianity, we have shown that we dissent heartily and altogether from the opinion that any prominent doctrines of Christianity are derived from any alien sources, and we can see no ground for such opinion but certain verbal similarities which are capable of another and more reasonable explanation.

II

Title.—Plan.—Contents.

THE Book which we are about to consider has generally gone by the name of The Wisdom of Solomon. It is so entitled in the earliest Manuscripts. Thus the Sinaitic Codex calls it Σοφια Σαλομωντος, the Vatican Σοφια Σαλωμων, and the Alexandrian Σοφια Σολομωντος: the early translations have usually given it the like appellation, the Syriac terming it 'The Book of the Great Wisdom of Solomon,' and the Arabic 'The Book of the Wisdom of Solomon, the son of David.' But by many of the Greek Fathers, and by Western writers since the time of SS. Jerome and Augustine, the name of Solomon has been dropped. Epiphanius and Athanasius cite it under the designation of Πανάρετος Σοφία, 'All-virtuous Wisdom,' a title also applied to Proverbs and Ecclesiasticus. Clement of Alexandria[1] and Origen[2] called it Ἡ θεία Σοφία. The Latin Vulgate prefixes the title 'Liber Sapientiae,' and Augustine[3] names it 'Liber Christianae Sapientiae,' and says it is improperly termed Solomon's. That it had no claim to be considered a production of the royal author whose name it bore was generally felt, though some few writers in uncritical times maintained the contrary. Jerome, in his preface to the Books of Solomon, says 'Fertur et Panaretos Jesu Filii Sirach liber, et alius *pseud-epigraphus*, qui Sapientia Salomonis inscribitur,' intending probably by this epithet to shew merely that in his judgment it was wrongly attributed to King Solomon. Elsewhere he refers to it as 'The Wisdom that is ascribed to Solomon, if any one thinks proper to receive the Book.' Augustine in his *Retractations*[4] remarks 'Salomonis duo hi libri a pluribus adpellantur propter quamdam, sicut existimo, eloquii similitudinem. Nam Salomonis non esse nihil dubitant quique doctiores.' That the

---

[1] Strom. iv. 16. p. 515.   [2] In Ep. ad Rom. vii. 14.
[3] Ep. 130; De Doctr. Christ. ii. 8, Specul. p. 1127, O. D , De Civitat. Dei, xvii. 20. 'Alii vero duo, quorum unus Sapientia, alter Ecclesiasticus dicitur, propter eloquii nonnullam similitudinem, ut Salomonis dicantur, obtinuit consuetudo; non autem esse ipsius, non dubitant doctiores, eos tamen in auctoritatem, maxime occidentalis, antiquitus recepit Ecclesia.'
[4] ii. 4. Cf. Spec. de lib. Sap.

author assumes the name of Solomon is of course apparent. Such a use of fiction has been common in all ages without any suspicion of fraud being attached to the writer. Plato and Cicero in their Dialogues introduce real characters as vehicles for supporting or opposing their own views. If it could be proved that any of the Psalms ascribed to David were written after his time, we might reasonably suppose that they had his name prefixed to them, as being composed in his spirit or in that form of sacred poetry employed by him. So all the Sapiential Books, though some of them were confessedly of much later date, were commonly attributed to Solomon, as being himself the ideal of the personification of Wisdom and the author *par excellence* of works on this subject. And when the writer introduces Solomon himself speaking, this is not done with any intention of leading his readers to believe that the work was a genuine production of the Son of David. Written, as we shall see, at a period many centuries removed from the palmy days of Israel, at a place far distant from Jerusalem, in a language and style unfamiliar to the Hebrew king, the Book could never have claimed for itself the authority of that royal name except by a fiction universally understood and allowed. An analogous use of fiction is found in the Books of Tobit and Judith, where under circumstances professedly historical, but which in many particulars do violence to history, moral and political truths are forcibly enunciated. There is this further reason for the use of the name of Solomon in the title of the Book, namely, that many of the sentiments and much of the language found therein are derived from the genuine works of the royal author, as will be seen in the Commentary.

The plan and contents of the Book have next to be considered. And first we must ask, What is meant by Wisdom (Σοφία) of which it treats? Dismissing from our minds later definitions of the term, and taking our stand on the Old Testament Scriptures, we see that it is used chiefly in two pregnant senses. First, it signifies that quality, so named, which is an attribute of the Godhead, or the thought of God which has its expression in the Logos, the Son; secondly, it denotes the habit of mind infused in angels and men by God Himself, and the rules and dictates of religion and practical godliness. In the latter sense it is equivalent to what is elsewhere called the knowledge of God, a term which includes the high contemplation of glorified saints and angels, as well as the religious culture and practice of devout men on earth. As to the Divine Wisdom, this originally resides in God. As Job says (xii. 13), 'with Him are Wisdom and strength;' 'God understandeth the ways thereof, and He knoweth its place' (xxviii. 23). And then more definitely in the Book of Proverbs it is said of Wisdom: 'The Lord possessed me in the beginning of His way, before his works of old. I was set up from everlasting, from the beginning or ever the earth was. I was by Him, as one brought up with Him, and I was daily His delight, rejoicing always before Him' (ch. viii). Though we do not here see Wisdom actually distinguished as a Person of the Godhead, yet it is shown as more than a mere abstraction or poetical personification; it is shown at least as uncreated and as coeternal with God. Thus much we may gather from the canonical Scriptures of the Old Testament[1]. In the Book of Ecclesiasticus a further advance is made. 'Wisdom comes from the Lord and is with Him for ever' (i. 1); She is indeed said to be

---

[1] See Liddon, Bampton Lectures, ii. pp. 89-95, ed. 1867. Christ 'is stated, according to His earthly nature, to be "the firstborn of every creature"; a passage which bears out the opinion of S. Athanasius [Orat. II Contr. Arian. 47], that the reference to the creation of Wisdom in the Book of Proverbs is designed, among other things, to set forth the Incarnation of our Lord, as the head and pattern of humanity. S. Athanasius, following the Septuagint [Κύριος ἔκτισέ με ἀρχὴν ὁδῶν αὐτοῦ εἰς ἔργα αὐτοῦ], and expressing the Hebrew with more exactness than is done in our translation, renders Prov. viii. 22, "The Lord created me a beginning of His ways," which is equivalent, he observes, to the assertion that the Father prepared me a body, and He created me for man, on behalf of their salvation.' Wilberforce, Incarnat. chap. ii. pp. 24, 25. ed. 1852. The Revised Bible translates, 'The Lord possessed [*or*, prepared, *marg.*] me in the beginning of His way.'

created, 'created before all things' (i. 4), but she is also said to be 'poured out upon all God's works' (ver. 9), 'and never to fail' (xxiv. 9), 'but to have her habitation in Jacob, and to take root in the inheritance of the Lord' (ib 8, and 12). And thus we are led on to the doctrine of the Logos, the expression of the thought of God, and the manifestation of Wisdom among mankind and in all creation In the Book of Wisdom this idea has become more definite and precise. The nature and sphere and operation of Wisdom are clearly stated She is the breath of the power of God and a pure influence flowing from the glory of the Almighty, the brightness of the everlasting light, the unspotted mirror of the power of God, and the image of His goodness Being One she can do all things, remaining immutable herself she maketh all things new, and in all ages entering into holy souls she maketh them friends of God and prophets. She is privy to the mysteries of God, sits by His throne, loves His works, was present when He formed the world, and gives to men all the virtues which they need in every station and condition of life'

As regards Wisdom in its human aspect we may say generally that, as used in the Sapiential Books, the term expresses the perfection of knowledge showing itself in action, whether in the case of king or peasant, statesman or artisan, philosopher or unlearned. Its contradictory is Folly (ἄνοια), which signifies all wilful ignorance, sinfulness and carelessness, every act and habit opposed to the love of God and the practice of holiness. Professor Huxley remarks in one of his essays: 'The only medicine for suffering, crime, and all the other woes of mankind, is Wisdom' And though his notion of wisdom is very different from that of him who is called 'Pseudo-Solomon,' and involves no principle of divine revelation, yet taken as it stands the statement contains a great truth The habit of making a right choice, of using aright the knowledge and powers given, is enforced alike by the Jewish teacher and the modern philosopher. That gift of God the Holy Spirit which is called Wisdom directs men to seek God as the end and object of their life and faculties, to give themselves up to His guiding hand, to know and to do His will The Jew was not a speculative philosopher; he did not employ his mind on abstruse theories concerning the mutual connection and interdependence of nature and spirit Abstract investigation had little charm for him All his views were based on revealed truths, it was from reflection on past revelations that his literature arose Thus with him Wisdom embraces what a Greek would call virtue, a habit of choosing the good and excellent way; but it comprises also the notion of a deep knowledge, an appropriation of the history of God's dealings with His people, and a thorough trust in the divine aid which is never refused to the prayer of the faithful.

In the Book before us Divine Wisdom is presented under two aspects sometimes as the Spirit, sometimes as the Word of God, different operations being attributed to each[2] As the Spirit of God, Wisdom fills the world, is the means by which the Divine omnipresence is effectuated and expressed, and inspires men to be prophets, as the Word of God, Wisdom made the world, and is the executor of God's commands both

---

[1] Wisd. vii, viii, ix ; Vacherot, i pp. 134. 135, Dahne, pp 154, ff , Gfrörer, Philo, 1 pp 243, ff , ii pp. 216, ff.

[2] Thus, chap 1. 4-6 'Into a malicious soul wisdom shall not enter, nor dwell in the body that is subject to sin. For the holy spirit of discipline will flee deceit, and remove from thoughts that are without understanding. Wisdom is a loving spirit.' 'For the Spirit of the Lord filleth the world ; and that which containeth all things hath knowledge of the voice,' ver 7 Compare also ix. 17 Here Wisdom is identified with the Holy Spirit In the following passages it assumes the character of the Word vii 22, 'Wisdom, which is the worker of all things, taught me,' xviii 15, 'Thine Almighty word leaped down from heaven out of Thy royal throne, as a fierce man of war . and brought Thine unfeigned commandment ;' ix 1, 2, 'O God of my fathers, Who hast made all things with Thy Word, and ordained man through Thy Wisdom' In Philo also the conception of Wisdom is not consistent or uniform Some passages expressly identify the Logos and Wisdom, elsewhere Wisdom is represented as the spouse of God, and again as the mother of the Logos.

in the reward and punishment of His creatures. By personifying Wisdom in the former view the author prepares the way in a most remarkable manner for the full doctrine of the Personality of the Holy Ghost, which was not plainly revealed till later times; and by his personification of the Word he adumbrates the true Christian doctrine expressed by S. John.

Human Wisdom is portrayed as that gift of God to men which is the guide and aim of all good conduct in life, and which leads to a happy immortality. This gift contains all virtues, moral, physical, and intellectual, holy living, manual dexterity, cultivated understanding. In developing this principle the author is in advance of many of the books of the Old Testament in regard to the Providence of God, the immortality of the soul, and the future judgment, thus lighting the way to the full knowledge of Christianity. Incidentally, or it may be formally, he refutes the pernicious doctrines of Epicureans and materialists; he shews the superiority of the Hebrew religion to heathen philosophy in its purity and strictness, in its faith in a future life, in its trust in Divine Providence, and tacitly confutes many of those arguments alleged by Pagans both then and afterwards against Hebraism. And, further, as in the inspiration of his genius, and fired by the majesty of his subject, a poet is often led to give utterance to thoughts which have a meaning and a fulness far beyond anything that he intended, so the author of the Book of Wisdom, if not directly inspired by God as were the writers of the earlier Scriptures, has exhibited a deep knowledge of divine things, and a forward reach into mysteries still unrevealed, which seem greater than have been elsewhere displayed beyond the limits of Scripture. Those magnificent encomiums of Wisdom wherein our Book abounds seem to illustrate and glorify Him Who is the Wisdom of God. Nothing can be more appropriate to Christ than the grand personification of this attribute of Deity. In such passages as the following the writer seems to have been guided beyond his own thought to indicate the operations and attributes of the second Person of the Holy Trinity. 'O God of my fathers, and Lord of mercy, Who hast made all things by Thy Word' (ix 1). 'For it was neither herb, nor mollifying plaister that restored them [the people bitten by fiery serpents] to health, but Thy Word, O Lord, which healeth all things.' 'That Thy children, O Lord, whom Thou lovest, might know that it is not the growing of fruits that nourisheth man; but that it is Thy Word which preserveth them that put their trust in Thee' (xvi 12, 26). 'While all things were in quiet silence, and night was in the midst of her swift course, Thine Almighty Word leaped down from heaven out of Thy royal throne, as a fierce man of war in the midst of a land of destruction, and brought Thine unfeigned commandment as a sharp sword' (xviii 14–16). As regards the second passage here quoted, our Lord Himself has explained the allegorical import of the 'serpent lifted up in the wilderness.' The last passage has for ages been applied by the Latin Church to the Incarnation, and is interwoven into her offices for Christmas and Epiphany. And once more, that language which the author puts into the mouth of the wicked persecuting the righteous is more true of the mockery heaped upon the Saviour as He hung upon the Cross[1]. 'He professeth to have the knowledge of God, and he calleth himself the child of God. He maketh his boast that God is his Father. Let us see if his words be true: and let us prove what shall happen in the end of him. For if the just man be the Son of God, He will help him, and deliver him from the hand of his enemies.'

The Book itself may be broadly divided into two parts, the first nine chapters treating of Wisdom under its more speculative aspect, exhorting men to strive after it, and describing its origin, and its moral and intellectual effects; the last ten chapters being confined to the historical view, showing how Wisdom has displayed its power in the lives of the Fathers and in its

---

[1] Wisd. ii 13, 16–18, S. Matt. xxvii 42, 43. The words in Ps. xxii 8, are not so full or so similar.

dealings with the Israelites in connection with Egypt Herein incidentally are answered many of the heathen cavils against Hebraism; and that problem which Job found impossible to explain, the difficulties which occur to any one who reflects upon the moral government of the world, is in a measure resolved, and the faithful believers are comforted with the assurance that although they suffer here and the wicked prosper, yet a day of retribution is at hand, and in another life all shall be adjusted and rectified,—a fact, the truth of which, as regards individuals, may be inferred from God's dealings with nations which have no future, but are rewarded and punished in this world.

III.

Language and Character.

The language and style of the Book are very remarkable Compared with the Septuagint version of the canonical Scriptures, it is seen at once to be no mere translation from the Hebrew, but an original work of high character and of marked peculiarity. S Jerome was quite justified in the opinion expressed in his Preface to the Books of Solomon: 'Secundus apud Hebraeos nusquam est, quin et ipse stylus Graecam eloquentiam redolet.' It is indeed written in the purest form of Alexandrian Greek, free from the Hebraisms and anomalies of the Septuagint, and full of passages which combine the richest vocabulary with genuine rhetorical eloquence. The originality of the work is seen in many particulars. We may remark the many unusual compound words and novel and combined expressions with which it abounds; such are, κακόμοχθος (xv 8); ὑπέρμαχος (xvi 17); ἀκηλίδωτος (iv. 9); ἀναποδισμός (ii 5); εἰδέχθεια (xvi. 3), γενεσιάρχης (xiii. 3); εὐδράνεια (xiii 19), νηπιοκτόνος (xi. 7); βραχυτελής (xv 9). Many expressions in this Book have become, as it were, household words among us, others exhibit a remarkable felicity which has given them a general currency Mediaeval illuminations on the walls of Churches or in devotional manuals show how deeply the heart of the religious had imbibed the notion that 'the souls of the righteous are in the hand of God' (iii 1). Materialistic and rude as such representations may seem to modern eyes, they preach a great truth which is clearly set forth in Wisdom. Many a man quotes or hears the words 'a hope full of immortality' (iii. 4) without knowing the source of this noble expression. 'They are Thine, O Lord, Thou Lover of souls,' δέσποτα φιλόψυχε (xi 26). Here is an old term with a new and beautiful sense affixed to it, the classical notion of 'loving life too well,' and hence of being cowardly, being elevated into an attribute of Almighty God Who hateth nothing that He hath made Modern science is fond of talking about Protoplasm and the Protoplast, little imagining that it is indebted to Wisdom for the word[1]: 'I myself am a mortal man .. the offspring of him that was first made of the earth,' γηγενοῦς ἀπόγονος πρωτοπλάστου (viii. 1, x. 1) That saying of our Lord, 'Whoso committeth sin is the servant of sin,' and still more that of S. Paul, 'We are debtors not to the flesh

---

[1] Forgetting this, Wilberforce writes (Doctr. of Incarnat chap. iii. p 49, ed. 1852). 'Wherein did the Protoplast, as Bishop Bull calls him, after S Irenaeus, differ from us all?' as though the latter were the originator of the expression in its application to Adam.

to live after the flesh,' had already been shadowed forth by our author where he speaks of Wisdom not dwelling in the body pawned, pledged, bound over to sin, κατάχρεῳ ἁμαρτίας[1]. Classical Greek knows a verb ῥέμβω, ῥέμβομαι, to roam, be restless or unsteady; it remained with the author of the Book of Wisdom (iv. 12) to use the noun ῥεμβασμός to express the wandering desire of man, the restlessness of unchecked concupiscence, the giddiness and moral vertigo caused by passion.

As we have already seen, the author shews many traces of acquaintance with Greek thought and philosophy, and many of his expressions are couched in the phraseology of Plato and the Stoics. The phrase applied to the material of which the world was formed, ὕλη ἄμορφος (xi. 17), is Platonic, so are the terms πρόνοια (xiv. 3), πνεῦμα νοερόν (vii. 22).

To Greek literature and customs are owed many allusions and terms. Thus the manna is called ambrosial food (xix. 21); revellers are crowned with garlands (ii. 8); victors in athletic games are rewarded with a wreath (iv. 2); men have their household gods and ships their tutelary divinities (xiii. 15; xiv. 1).

From these circumstances the treatise presents a closer analogy to profane writings than any other book contained in the Greek Bible, and its language is consequently richer and more varied.

There are other points to remark in the form and character of the work. It is modelled in some degree on the ancient Hebrew poetry. That rhythm of thought, and parallelism of members, which are the distinguishing form of Hebrew poetry, are also conspicuous features in Wisdom. This is more carefully managed in the first portion, the latter part of the book being more rhetorical in construction. But that the whole was written in what has been called 'verse rhythm' is obvious, and the Alexandrian MS. has transmitted it to us in this form, in which it will be found printed in the text. Epiphanius[2] too speaks of Wisdom as written stichometrically, and critics[3] have ascertained that it is divided in our present Greek MSS. into 1098 stiches, while Nicephorus found 1100 verses in his codices. Hence it is argued[4] that one or two of the Vulgate additions are probably grounded on ancient authority. Be this as it may, the writer of Wisdom, while employing the familiar parallelism to give force and emphasis to his periods, has also availed himself of some other appliances more or less foreign to Hebrew poetry. Sometimes he seems to have adopted almost the strophe and antistrophe of the Greek poets; at other times he has condescended to paronomasias, alliterations, and assonances for the sake of giving greater effect to his contrasts or prominence to his verbal expressions. Some of these forms of parallelism may be observed in the very beginning of the Book.

Ἀγαπήσατε δικαιοσύνην οἱ κρίνοντες τὴν γῆν,
φρονήσατε περὶ τοῦ Κυρίου ἐν ἀγαθότητι,
καὶ ἐν ἁπλότητι καρδίας ζητήσατε αὐτόν·
ὅτι εὑρίσκεται τοῖς μὴ πειράζουσιν αὐτόν,
ἐμφανίζεται δὲ τοῖς μὴ ἀπιστοῦσιν αὐτῷ.

Here are seen the verbal artifice in the words ἀγαπήσατε, ζητήσατε, φρονήσατε, ἀγαθότητι, ἁπλότητι, and the parallelism of thought in the various members of the sentence; μὴ ἀπιστοῦσι and μὴ πειράζουσι are parallel to ἐν ἁπλότητι and ἐν ἀγαθότητι, εὑρίσκεται answer to ζητήσατε, ἐμφανίζεται to φρονήσατε.

Take the noble passage descriptive of Wisdom, vii. 24 ff.:—

'More active than all action is Wisdom;
And she passes and goes through all things by reason of her purity.
For a vapour is she of the power of God,
And a pure effluence of the glory of the Almighty,

---

[1] S. John viii. 34; Wisd. i. 4; Rom. vi. 16, 20; viii. 12.
[2] Epiph. De Mens. et Pond. iv: αἱ γὰρ στιχήρεις δύο βίβλοι, ἥτε τοῦ Σολομῶντος, ἡ πανάρετος λεγομένη, καὶ ἡ τοῦ Ἰησοῦ τοῦ υἱοῦ Σιρὰχ κ.τ.λ.
[3] Credner, Geschichte des Kanon. pp. 108, 120; Thilo, Specimen exercit. crit. p. 34.
[4] See Grimm on ch. i. 15.

Therefore falleth unto her naught defiled,
For a reflection is she of Eternal Light;
And a mirror unspotted of the majesty of God,
And an image of His goodness.'

Or again, mark the delicate balancing of sentences in the language put into the mouth of the sensualist, (ch. ii):—

'Short is our life and full of pain,
And there is no healing for the death of man,
And none was ever known to have returned from the grave
For we were born at all adventure,
And hereafter shall be as though we never had been;
For smoke is the breath in our nostrils,
And thought is a spark at the beat of our heart,
And when this is quenched the body shall turn to ashes,
And the spirit shall be dispersed as empty air;
And our name shall be forgotten in time,
And no man shall remember our works:
And our life shall pass away as track of cloud,
And shall be scattered abroad as a mist
Chased away by the beams of the sun
And by his heat oppressed
For the passage of a shadow is our life,
And there is no return of our death,
For it is fast sealed, and no man cometh back.'

As an instance of another kind of parallelism exhibiting great ingenuity may be mentioned the famous Sorites in chap vi, whereby the writer proves that the desire of Wisdom leads to a kingdom[1].—

'The desire of Wisdom is the beginning of Wisdom,
And the truest beginning of Wisdom is the desire for instruction,
And the care for instruction is love,
And love is the keeping of her laws,
And attention to her laws is assurance of immortality,
And immortality maketh us to be near unto God,
Therefore the desire of Wisdom leadeth unto a kingdom.'

The first member of the argument is not expressed, but is virtually contained in the preceding verse, and the final premiss before the conclusion might be, 'To be near unto God is to reign.' The wording of some of the clauses is a little varied, otherwise the Sorites is complete, and the predicate of the last of the premisses is predicated of the subject of the first in accordance with the rules of Logic.

Instances of verbal refinement meet us in every page Thus, οἱ φυλάξαντες ὁσίως τὰ ὅσια ὁσιωθήσονται (vi. 11); αὖς—θροῦς (i. 10); παισὶν—ἐμπαιγμὸν—παιγνίοις (xii 25, 26), ἀργὰ—ἔργα (xiv. 5), are examples of artificial adornment which, though not so frequent in other Greek authors, are not without example in either of the Testaments[2]. But it must be confessed that the straining after such effects sometimes degenerates into turgidity, and seems to be below the dignity of the subject. But while the contrasts are occasionally forced and the treatment is unequal, the general tenour of the work is highly pleasing, rising often into grand eloquence and expressing the noblest thought in the choicest diction.

There is another connection in which the language of the Book is most interesting and valuable Its utility in the study of the New Testament is undoubted. Many phrases that are commonly found in the later Scriptures can be traced to, or are illustrated by their use in, the Book of Wisdom. These are mentioned in the Commentary as they occur, but a few may be noticed here When the author of the Epistle to the Hebrews would express the co-eternity and consubstantiality of the Son with the Father, he uses the remarkable term ἀπαύγασμα τῆς δόξης—a phrase which is not found in the Old Testament elsewhere but in Wisdom vii 26, where Wisdom is called ἀπαύγασμα φωτὸς ἀϊδίου The expression χάρις καὶ ἔλεος, familiar to us in the New Testament (e g 1 Tim. i. 2), is used more than once in our Book[3]; so σημεῖα καὶ τέρατα (S John iv 48) occurs viii 8, and x. 16 That mysterious

---

[1] See note on vi. 18.
[2] Cf 2 Cor i. 3, 4, where S. Paul accumulates παρακαλεῖν and its derivatives. For such verbal refinements in Wisdom see Grimm, Einleit, p 7 For examples of play on words in the New Testament see Phil. iii 2, 3, κατατομή, περιτομή· Gal. v. 11, 12, περιτομήν, ἀποκόψονται Rom. i. 29, 30, 31, πορνείᾳ, πονηρίᾳ; φθόνου, φόνου; ἀσυνέτους, ἀσυνθέτους. Comp. notes in Bishop Wordsworth's Greek Test., Matt. xxvi. 2. and 2 Thess iii 11, and Jowett, on Rom i 28
[3] Chap. iii 9, iv. 15

phrase, of which so much has been made in modern controversy, εἰς τὸν αἰῶνα (1 John ii. 17) is used (ch. v. 15) in speaking of the just man's life beyond the gate of death. More than once in the Revelation we meet with the words, ἄξιοι γάρ εἰσι [1]: these are illustrated by the text in Wisdom: 'God proved them and found them worthy of Himself,' ἀξίους ἑαυτοῦ. 'The day of visitation,' ἐν ἡμέρᾳ ἐπισκοπῆς, of 1 S. Peter (ii. 12) is explained by the similar phrase in Wisd. iii. 7, ἐν καιρῷ ἐπισκοπῆς. The New Testament expressions, ἔξοδος meaning 'death'; παιδεία 'suffering'; παράπτωμα 'transgression'; ἀμίαντος 'undefiled'; ἐπιτιμία 'punishment'; are all illustrated by their use in this Book.

IV.

Place and date of Composition.—Author.

BEFORE we attempt to investigate the authorship of the Book of Wisdom, it will be necessary to settle the place and approximate date of its composition. With regard to the former we can have no hesitation in assigning it to Alexandria. In no other locality could a Jew, as the author confessedly is, have written such a work. A Palestinian Hebrew, at the era when we shall shew reason to suppose it to have been composed, would scarcely have possessed so thorough a command of the Greek language as the author displays. Such a passage as that in chap. xiii. 3, which speaks of the beauty of material objects and calls Almighty God 'the first author of beauty,' is essentially different from purely Hebrew thought and points to a Hellenistic writer [2]. Josephus himself confesses [3] that his countrymen had no taste for the study of foreign tongues, and were especially averse from Greek culture and education. The intimate acquaintance with Greek thought and philosophy displayed in this Book is superior to anything found at Jerusalem. The dogmas of the Old Testament were never developed in the form herein exhibited till the Jewish system came in contact with western philosophy, and thence drew terms, modifications, and contrasts before unknown. Where could this close contact have occurred but at Alexandria? and who but an Alexandrian Jew could have clothed the results in the only language that could adequately express them? Alexandria in the time of the Ptolemies was filled with Jews. It is computed that they numbered nearly one third of the whole population. Living thus in the very centre of heathen culture they could not fail to be influenced by the spirit of the place, and to compare their own imperishable belief and their own divine revelation with the restless speculations and manifold traditions which were presented to their notice by the heathens among whom they dwelt. Here they saw that Epicurean indifference, that luxurious selfishness, that gross materialism, that virtual denial of Providence, which are so sternly and eloquently rebuked in the Book of Wisdom. Here they witnessed that bestial idolatry, and that debased revolt against the pure worship of God, which meet with such severe handling in this work. A man who had these things daily before his eyes, whose righteous soul was continually vexed with this opposition to all his cherished beliefs, would naturally thus deliver his

---

[1] Rev. iii. 4; xvi. 6; Wisd. iii. 5.   [2] Gfrörer, Philo und die Alexandr. Theosophie, ii. p. 212.   [3] Ant. xx. 12.

testimony, and brand the surrounding heathenism with the fire of his words. The modes of worship thus assailed, the local colouring of details, the political allusions, are distinctively Egyptian, point conclusively to an Alexandrian author, are too personally antagonistic, and shew too familiar an acquaintance with the whole subject, to be the word of one who, living at a distance, merely described past events and gave an unbiassed judgment upon them. They lead irresistibly to the conclusion that the writer composed his work amid the people and the scenes to which he continually refers. Some persons[1] have thought that the Book ends abruptly, and that the present is only a portion of a larger treatise which carried on the author's historical view of the operations of divine wisdom down to the latest times of the Jewish commonwealth. But if we consider that the author is writing in Egypt, and partly with the purpose of exposing the corruptions of its idol worship in contrast with the pure religion of the Israelites, it is seen at once that in bringing his comparison down to the time of the Exodus and the judgment executed on the gods of Egypt, he leaves his subject at the most appropriate conclusion, and that a survey of succeeding events, in which that country had no concern, would rather have diminished than increased the effect of the contrast.

As we can assume Alexandria to be the birthplace of our Book, so by internal evidence we can approach the date of its production. Disregarding the fictitious name of Solomon adopted merely for literary purposes, we have two facts which limit the period during which it must have been composed. First, it contains evident traces of the use of the Septuagint version of the Scriptures, and must therefore have been written subsequently to that translation. Thus in ch. ii. 12 the ungodly are made to use the words of Isa. iii 10.

δήσωμεν [ἐνεδρεύσωμεν Wisd] τὸν δίκαιον, ὅτι δύσχρηστος ἡμῖν ἐστι, where the Hebrew has something quite different, and in xv. 10 the author writes σποδὸς ἡ καρδία αὐτοῦ, which is a quotation from the Septuagint of Isai xliv 20 where the variation from the Hebrew is remarkable[2]. Now the Septuagint version was begun at least in the time of the earlier Ptolemies about B C 280, and was continued at various intervals. When it was concluded is quite uncertain, For our purpose it is enough to fix a date earlier than which Wisdom could not have been written, and this limit we may set at B C 200. The second limitation is derived from the fact that the Book contains no trace of distinctively Christian doctrine. The Incarnation, the Atonement, and the Resurrection of the body, find no place in its teaching. It is true that some commentators[3] have satisfied themselves that there are passages which could only have come from a Christian hand, but as these are allowed by them to be interpolations, (though there is no evidence of the fact and the passages themselves are in accordance with the rest of the work), we may leave this opinion out of our consideration.

But in addition to these *data*, there is another fact to be inferred from the treatise which defines the period during which it could have been composed. Its language in many places points to a time of oppression wholly inappropriate to the era of Solomon. Such statements as these: 'The souls of the righteous are in the hand of God, and there shall no torment touch them' (iii 1), 'Then shall the righteous man stand in great boldness before the face of such as have afflicted him' (v. 1); seem to be the utterances of one who was consoling himself and others under persecution and affliction. Hence the author inveighs against unrighteous rulers, and threatens them with heavy

---

[1] Eichhorn, Einleit. in d. Apokryph ; Grotius, Annot in libr. Apocryph.
[2] Other instances of reference to the Septuagint version are found in the following vi 7, xi. 4, xii 8, xvi. 22, xix 21.

[3] Noack, Der Ursprung des Christenthums, i p 222, ff ; Kirschbaum, Der Jüd Alex p. 52, Grotius, in Comm. ; Gratz, Gesch der Jud iii p. 495, Erasmus, De Ratione Concion in. (vol v. p 1049).

judgment (vi. 5, 9); speaks of present sufferings and chastisements (xii. 22, 23); and connects these things with the diatribe against idolatry and the deification of man (xiv. etc.).

Now under the earlier Ptolemies the Jews in Alexandria enjoyed the utmost peace and prosperity, had all the privileges of Macedonian citizens, were in high favour at court, and exercised their own peculiar worship without restraint[1]. Such too was their condition under the later kings down to the time of the Christian era. The only persecutions which they suffered took place in the reigns of Ptolemy Philopator (B.C. 221–204), and Ptolemy VII or Physcon (B.C. 170–117). The sufferings of the Jews under the latter are mentioned by Josephus[2]. They had their rise in the inhuman and sanguinary temper of the king, and extended not merely to the Hebrews, but to all the inhabitants, insomuch that the populace in general fled from the scene of blood, and the city was almost deserted. The only special persecution of the Jews in the period of which we are speaking was that which raged under Ptolemy Philopator. This monarch on his return from the defeat of Antiochus (B.C. 217) passed through Jerusalem, and being repulsed in an attempt to penetrate, against the High Priest's remonstrances, into the Most Holy Place of the Temple, conceived an implacable hatred for the Jews, and on his return to Egypt revenged himself for his humiliation by the most atrocious persecutions. It is thought that the highly coloured account in the third Book of Maccabees refers to this occurrence. But be that as it may, without any undue assumption, and leaving undecided the special tribulation to which the writer of Wisdom refers, we may safely date the production of the Book between B.C. 217 and B.C. 145, that is between the epoch marked by the religious oppression under Philopator, and that rendered memorable by the enormities of the bloated sensualist Physcon.

If we come now to consider the question of the author of the Book, we are at once launched into a controversy which, with our present information, knows no possible settlement. It is easy to find objections to all the writers to whom the work has been attributed: to fix on a more probable name is beyond our power. We can here only very briefly indicate the line which this fruitless inquiry has taken.

We have seen already that the name of Solomon was assumed by the author for literary purposes[3], but many in old time[4] and some in later years[5] have contended for the Solomonic authorship. However, the language, the style, the development of doctrine, the local colouring, the quotations from the Septuagint, entirely preclude the notion of the writer being David's son. And as to the work being a translation from the Hebrew, or (as the critic[6] who attributes it to Zerubbabel suggests,) the Chaldee, considerations have already

---

[1] Joseph. Ant. xii. 1; Contr. Ap. ii. 4.

[2] Contr. Ap. ii. 5. See also Athenaeus, iv. p. 184; vi. p. 252, ed. Casaub.; Justin. Hist. xxxviii. 8, 9.

[3] Thus Eusebius, quoting vi. 24, says: καὶ ταῦτα δέ πη ἐξ αὐτοῦ λέγεται τοῦ προσώπου (i.e. personifying Solomon); Praep. Evang. vii. 12. (xxi. p. 544, Migne).

[4] E.g. Clem. Alex. Strom. vi. 11 (p. 786, Pott.), quoting xiv. 2, 3, says: ἔπειτα δὲ οὐκ ἀνέγνωσαν τὸ πρὸς τοῦ Σολομῶντος εἰρημένον, S. Cypr. Exh. Mart. xii.; Orig. Hom. in Jer. viii. (xiii. p. 337, M.): φησὶν ἡ Σοφία ἡ ἐπιγεγραμμένη Σολομῶντος. So Holkot in his Commentary. Didymus attributes the book to Solomon, De Trin. ii. 6. (xxxix. p. 536, M.): ὡς Σολομῶν λέγει· φειδὴ δὲ πάντων, xi. 26; and De Spir. § 54, he refers to vii. 18, 20, as showing that Solomon knew 'violentias spirituum, rapidos ventorum flatus.' De Trin. i. 16. (xxxix. p. 337, M.): Σολομῶν γὰρ λέγει· ἀναλόγως τῶν κτισμάτων ὁ γεν. θεωρ., xiii. 5. Eusebius, Hist. Eccl. iv. 13, blames Clem. Alex. because in his Stromata he cites as Scripture 'some books which are impugned by many, ἀπὸ τῶν ἀντιλεγομένων γραφῶν, as the Book of Wisdom which is attributed to Solomon, the epistles of Barnabas and Clement,' etc. Hippol. Rom. Demonstr. adv. Jud. p. 67. (ed. Lagarde): πάλιν Σολομῶν περὶ Χριστοῦ καὶ Ἰουδαίων φησὶν ὅτι ὅτε στήσεται ὁ δίκαιος ... πάντα ὡς σκιά. Tertullian, De Praescript. 7, refers to a passage in Wisdom thus: 'Nostra institutio de porticu Salomonis est, qui et ipse tradiderat Dominum in simplicitate cordis esse quaerendum.' (i. 1).

[5] Schmidt, Das Buch der Weisheit; Azariah de Rossi, Meor Enajim, p. 281 b. ed. 1829.

[6] Faber, Ap. Grimm, Einleit., pp. 8, 18. See Huetius, Demonstr. Evangel. p. 250, ed. 1722.

been adduced which render this theory untenable. S Jerome, in his Preface to the Books of Solomon[1], asserts that some ancient writers consider the author to be Philo Judaeus; and many in later times have adopted this opinion, referring the persecutions of which the text gives intimations to the oppressive acts of the Romans, culminating in Caligula's attempt to erect his statue in the Temple at Jerusalem, which was the occasion of Philo's legation to the Emperor[2] But this idea fails to command assent on internal evidence, even if there were not many reasons already mentioned which render the date of that learned Jew inapplicable. Roman Catholics, who are bound by the decrees of the Council of Trent to believe in the inspiration of the Book of Wisdom, have a summary method of dismissing Philo's claim Living at the time of our Lord he must be regarded as one of the unbelieving Jews, and to suppose such a man inspired by the Holy Spirit would be sacrilegious. 'Quis enim credat,' asks Corn. a Lapide, 'hominem Judaeum, jam abrogato Judaismo, infidelem et perfidum, esse auctorem libri canonici et sacri[3]?' But without adopting this very formidable argument, there are such great differences in style, in doctrine, in treatment, that we cannot for a moment acquiesce in the theory which identifies Philo with the author of the Book of Wisdom. Leaving the question of style, which is a matter more to be felt by readers than discussed on paper, we will notice a few discrepancies which are found in these two writers In Wisdom[4] the serpent who tempted Eve is identified with the devil; but Philo ignores that evil power, and terms the serpent a symbol of pleasure, which speaks with seductive voice to men, and draws them away from temperance and obedience to law In the same way the latter interprets the Brazen Serpent as σωφροσύνη or καρτερία in Wisdom the matter is treated in its plain historical sense[5]. And in general the treatment of Scriptural narratives by the two authors presents a very marked contrast, Philo always straining after spiritual, anagogical, recondite interpretations, and losing the reality of the history in the fanciful lessons evolved from it, the author of Wisdom taking the facts as they stand and meditating religiously upon them, with no attempt to explain away their obvious meaning. It would be entirely alien to the method and treatment of the latter to introduce the Pythagorean doctrine of numbers in speaking of the six days of creation, as Philo does[6], or to resolve the four rivers of Paradise into the four cardinal virtues[7], or to explain the manna as God's word[8] Philo scarcely ever refers to the Psalms and Prophets; in Wisdom the allusions to these writings and especially to Isaiah are numerous and important In his desire to maintain the absolute perfection of God, and looking on matter as the source of evil, Philo conceives the Logos as the mediate cause of the world, assisted by other powers, angels and demons The Book of Wisdom enters into none of these abstruse speculations, and is satisfied with the avowal that God made all things by His word (ix. 1). Where, if he held the opinion, the author might naturally have introduced the doctrine of ideas[9], which forms so prominent a feature in Philo's philosophy, we find no trace of the same The Egyptian darkness is said in Wisdom (xvii. 14) to have 'come upon them out of the bottoms

---

[1] 'Nonnulli Scriptorum veterum hunc esse Judaei Philonis affirmant' This opinion has been maintained by Lyranus, Postill, Luther, in the introduction to his translation of the Book; Cosin, Hist of the Canon; and many others See an ingenious conjecture by Dr Tregelles in reference to a corrupt passage of the Muratorian Canon, where the Latin text reads, 'Sapientia ab amicis Salomonis scripta,' and which he imagines may have been in the original ὑπὸ Φίλωνος instead of ὑπὸ Φίλων, Journal of Philol, 1855, p 37

[2] Joseph Ant xviii. 8, 1; Philo, De Leg ad Caium
[3] In Sap libr xv 14
[4] Chap ii. 24, Philo, De Mund Opif 56 (1 p 38), De Agric 22 (1 p 315)
[5] Wisd xvi 5, 7, Philo, Leg Alleg ii 20, De Agric 22
[6] De Mundi Opif 3 (1 p 3)
[7] Philo, De Poster Caini 37 (1 p 250)
[8] Philo, Leg Alleg iii 60 (i p 121)
[9] E g. i 3, vii 22, vi.i. 19, ff, ix 15.

of inevitable hell;' whereas Philo[1] attributes it to an eclipse of the sun. The description of the origin of idolatry in Wisdom and in Philo's works could never have been written by the same author, as there are many points discrepant and contradictory[2].

Such differences might be greatly extended, but enough has been said to show that the opinion which makes Philo the author of the Book of Wisdom is untenable; if indeed more proofs of the same were wanting, they might be found in contrasting the ideas of the two authors as to divine Wisdom, which will be found to be irreconcileable.

The theory[3] which assigns the work to Aristobulus, the favourite of Ptolemy Philometor, fails to satisfy for these reasons: the little that is known of his writings is quite different in style and treatment from Wisdom, and at any rate is too insignificant, even if we grant its genuineness, to support the notion; secondly, in his time the Jews were in great prosperity, and not suffering from the persecutions to which we have seen allusions in our Book; and thirdly, being a courtier and a king's favourite minister, Aristobulus is not likely to have inveighed against kings and tyrants, and to have proffered unpalatable advice.

Despairing of finding a single author to whom to attribute the Book, some writers[4] have impugned its unity. That perverse criticism which is always straining after startling effects, and which is never satisfied except it evolve new theories, and on very insufficient grounds uproot long-established convictions, has seen in the structure of this Book evidence of the handiwork of two or more authors. Solomon and his translators, according to Houbigant, have shared the work between them. Four Jews of varying sentiments, and one of them belonging to Christian times, seem to Bretschneider to have composed the treatise. Nachtigal finds herein a collection of sentences, or a kind of Psalm in praise of Wisdom, which two sets of Rabbis sung antiphonally at three separate sittings of the sacred company. Eichhorn, if he is not quite clear as to the work being the production of two different writers, assures himself that it was composed in a most peculiar fashion, the second part (from chap. xi.) being the offspring of the author's younger days, before he had learned to free himself from the shackles of Jewish prejudices and had enlarged his mind by the study of Greek Philosophy, the first portion giving token of riper years and maturer knowledge. For these theories of a plurality of authors there is really no evidence of any weight[5]. Uncertain as all such subjective criticism must be, it is remarkably ill-placed on this occasion, as we have seen that the Book presents an unity of design and an identity of treatment which imply the work of a single author, and which indeed would be marvellous if it were the production of two or more writers composing at different periods and under different circumstances. A theory started by Noack[6], attributing the authorship to Apollos, has recently been maintained by Professor Plumptre, who in two articles in The Expositor[7] claims this apostle as the writer of Wisdom and of the Epistle to the Hebrews, the former being the production of the author while unconverted, the latter the fruit of his mature Christianity. The hypothesis is attractive, but it rests on no secure basis, there being nothing in its favour except that Apollos was an eloquent Jew of Alexandria and might have written the Book. The argument is supported chiefly by a certain coincidence of phraseology in the two writings; and it is certain that there are many

---

[1] Vita Moys. i. 21. (ii. p. 100): ἴσως μὲν καὶ ἡλίου γενομένης ἐκλείψεως τῶν ἐν ἔθει τελειοτέρας. Ginsburg, ap. Kitto's Cyclop., Art. Wisdom of Solomon.

[2] Comp. Wisd. xii. xiii. and Philo, De Monarch. i. 1–3. (ii. pp. 212–216).

[3] Lutterbeck, Die Neutest. Lehrbegr. i. 407, ff.

[4] Houbigant, Proleg. in Not. Crit. i. pp. ccxvi, ccxxi; Eichhorn, Einleit. in d. Apokr. p. 142, ff.; Bretschneider, De libr. Sap. parte priore; Nachtigal, Das Buch Weisheit.

[5] The refutation of these dreamings *seriatim* may be seen in Grimm, Einleit. See also Migne, Script. Sacr. Curs. Compl. Prolegom. in libr. Sap.; Dähne, ii. p. 154, ff.

[6] Der Ursprung des Christenth. i. p. 222.

[7] Vol. i. pp. 329, ff. and 409, ff.

words and expressions common to both. But this correspondence may prove nothing more than the fact that the Christian author was acquainted with the Alexandrian work, or that they both drew from some common source. To any unprejudiced mind the contrast between the two is most marked; the difference of style is too great to be reasonably attributed to different phases of the same intellect. There is nothing in Wisdom like the continuous interweaving of Old Testament Scriptures which is found in the Epistle, there is no exhibition in the Epistle of the acquaintance with pagan learning which is so prominent a feature of the earlier work. The resemblances in language may be paralleled from Philo, and might be equally well used to support his claim to the authorship of either. For those who hold the Pauline origin of the Epistle to the Hebrews, no other argument is needed to discredit this theory; for those who leave the question about the Epistle doubtful, it is enough to say that the date of Apollos does not coincide with what we have shown to be the probable date of our Book, that we know absolutely nothing of that apostle's writings, that the verbal similarities are capable of another explanation, and that the scope and objects of the two writings are wholly different.

The authorship of the Book of Wisdom is a problem which will never be solved, and we may be well content to let it rest. The name of the writer could add little to the importance of the work, and we may believe that he, like the author of *De imitatione Christi*, would pray: 'Da mihi omnibus mori quae in mundo sunt, et propter Te amare contemni, et nesciri in hoc saeculo.'

V.

History, authority, and relation to the Canon of Scripture.

WE must now speak of the history of the Book, of its recognition as inspired, and its relegation to those which are called the Apocryphal writings. It seems to be quoted by no pre-christian writer[1]. Neither Philo nor Josephus notice or refer to it. There is however, as we have already hinted[2], evidence to show that some of the authors of the New Testament were acquainted with, if they did not quote, its language. Allusions to its phraseology are frequent in S. Paul's Epistles. That noble passage in the fifth chapter of Wisdom seems to be the groundwork of the grand description of the Christian's armour in Ephesians (vi 13-17). 'He shall take to him his jealousy for complete armour,' λήψεται πανοπλίαν· 'Take unto you the whole armour of God,' ἀναλάβετε τὴν πανοπλίαν τοῦ Θεοῦ. 'He shall put on righteousness as a breastplate,' ἐνδύσεται θώρακα δικαιοσύνην: 'Having on the breastplate of righteousness,' ἐνδυσάμενοι τὸν θώρακα τῆς δικαιοσύνης. 'And true judgment instead of a helmet. He shall take holiness for an invincible shield' 'above all taking the shield of faith ... and take the helmet of salvation.' The passage too about the potter in Rom. ix. is an echo

---

[1] Vacherot (Hist. de l'École d'Alexandr. i p. 134) says that Wisdom is quoted by Aristobulus, but I have not been able to identify the passage. The author has probably misappropriated a citation from Clemens, which occurs in Eusebius, immediately contiguous to a passage from Aristobulus.

[2] Prolegom. § iii. A copious list of supposed citations or references is given in Grimm, Einleit. p. 36, note 2. See also an article by Bleek, in Theol. Stud. und Krit. 1853, pp. 339. ff.

of a similar sentiment in Wisd. xv. 'Hath not the potter power over the clay, of the same lump to make one vessel unto honour and another unto dishonour?' says St Paul 'The potter tempering soft earth,' we find in Wisdom, 'fashioneth every vessel with much labour for our service; yea, of the same clay he maketh both the vessels that serve for clean uses and likewise all such as serve to the contrary, but what is the use of either sort, the potter himself is the judge.' We have already spoken of the remarkable expression ἀπαύγασμα applied (Heb. 1. 3) to the divine Son, being the 'brightness of the Father's glory and the express image (χαρακτήρ) of His Person,' which is found nowhere else in Scripture but in the description of Wisdom (chap vii. 26), 'She is the brightness (ἀπαύγασμα) of the everlasting light, the unspotted mirror of the power of God, and the image of His goodness.' The similarity here is too close to be accidental. Desiring to indicate the consubstantiality and coequality of the Son with the Father, the writer was guided to use the language with which he was familiar in the Book of Wisdom, and which has now been formulated in the Nicene Creed, Θεὸς ἐκ Θεοῦ, φῶς ἐκ φωτός. It seems very probable[1] that St Paul in writing to the Romans has many references to Wisdom. Thus, when he is showing the wilful wickedness of the Gentiles in not understanding the invisible things of God from the things that are made, he had, it may be, in his mind the passage in Wisdom, 'Surely vain are all men by nature, who are ignorant of God, and could not out of the good things that are seen know Him that is[2].' S. Paul's words in verses 24–27 of the same chapter, when he describes the iniquities of the heathen, read like a commentary on Wisd xiv. 21. 'The worshipping of idols not to be named is the beginning, the cause and the end of all evil.' Rom. ii. 4, τοῦ πλούτου τῆς χρηστότητος αὐτοῦ καὶ τῆς ἀνοχῆς καὶ τῆς μακροθυμίας, is like Wisd. xv. 1, σὺ δὲ ὁ θεὸς ἡμῶν χρηστὸς καὶ ἀληθής, μακρόθυμος καὶ ἐν ἐλέει διοικῶν τὰ πάντα; Rom. xi. 32, ἵνα τοὺς πάντας ἐλεήσῃ, corresponds with Wisd. xi. 24, ἐλεεῖς πάντας, ὅτι πάντα δύνασαι, καὶ παρορᾷς ἁμαρτήματα ἀνθρώπων εἰς μετάνοιαν. The passage Rom ix. 22, 23 has many striking parallelisms with Wisd vii 22–24; and these coincidences of thought and expression might be largely multiplied[3], but enough has been said to show that there is great probability that some of the New Testament writers were well acquainted with our Book.

The first direct quotation with which we are acquainted (though in this case the writer himself does not name the author whose words he cites), is found in Clemens Rom Ep. I ad Cor xxvii. 5, where we read· τίς ἐρεῖ αὐτῷ τί ἐποίησας, ἢ τίς ἀντιστήσεται τῷ κράτει τῆς ἰσχύος αὐτοῦ; Now although the words τίς ἐρεῖ αὐτῷ τί ἐποίησας are found in Job xi. 12, the second question τίς ἀντιστήσεται occurs nowhere but Wisd. xi 22 and xii. 12, and Clement, quoting from memory, has mingled the two passages together[4]. That Irenaeus made use of the Book is testified by Eusebius (Hist v. 8), who tells us that he cited certain passages therefrom, viz: ὅρασις Θεοῦ περιποιητικὴ ἀφθαρσίας, which does not occur, and ἀφθαρσία δὲ ἐγγὺς εἶναι ποιεῖ Θεοῦ, which is found in Wisd vi 20[5]. He also adds (v 26) that he has seen another work of Irenaeus, βιβλίον τι διαλέξεων διαφόρων, in which are inserted quotations from the Epistle to the Hebrews and τῆς λεγομένης Σοφίας Σαλομῶντος. From the time of Clemens Alexandrinus it is cited continually by the Fathers, often under Solomon's name, and often as inspired. With Clemens Alexandrinus[6] it is usually

---

[1] See Bleek, *ubi supr* p. 340, ff

[2] Rom i 20 ἐματαιώθησαν ἐν τοῖς διαλογισμοῖς αὐτῶν Wisd xiii. 1. μάταιοι γὰρ πάντες ἄνθρωποι κ τ λ.

[3] Compare also 1 Cor vi 2 with Wisd iii 8; 2 Cor v 4 with Wisd. ix 15, S. John xvii. 3 with Wisd. xv. 1, 3; S. Matt. xiii. 43 with Wisd iii 7, Rev ii 10 with Wisd v. 16.

[4] Wisd xi 22 κράτει βραχίονός σου τίς ἀντιστήσεται, xii. 12· τίς γὰρ ἐρεῖ, τί ἐποίησας, ἢ τίς ἀντιστήσεται, τῷ κρίματί σου. Grimm. Einleit. p. 36.

[5] This passage is found in Irenaeus' work, Adv. Haer. iv. 38, 3.

[6] Strom iv. 16. p. 609 Pott; v p 699; vi. p. 795.

PROLEGOMENA.

called ἡ θεία σοφία, S. Athanasius calls it ἡ Σοφία, but cites it as Scripture[1]; thus too Eusebius[2], after transcribing the passage vii 22—viii 1, ends with the words ταῦτα μὲν ἡ Γραφή. S Cyprian[3] introduces Wisd v 1-9 with the words· 'Secundum Scripturae sanctae fidem' S. Augustine[4] too on some occasions classes it with Scripture. The high regard in which it was held may be inferred from the frequent use made of it by Origen, Didymus, Ephraem Syrus, Hippolytus Romanus, Chrysostom[5], and other Fathers, who appeal to it in proof of doctrine as to the rest of the Bible. For those writers who knew the Word of God only as presented to them in the Greek language, it was natural to accord to the Book of Wisdom this high position. If we may judge from the Manuscripts that have come down to us, it would be impossible for anyone, looking merely to the Septuagint version and its allied works, to distinguish any of the Books in the collection as of less authority than others. There is nothing whatever to mark off the canonical writings from what have been called the deutero-canonical. They are all presented as of equal standing and authority, and if we must make distinctions between them, and place some on a higher platform than others, this separation must be made on grounds which are not afforded by the arrangement of the various documents themselves. The place which the Book of Wisdom occupies in the MSS which contain it is not in all cases identical, but in none is it relegated to a position apart from the universally allowed canonical Books. In the Sinaitic and Alexandrian Codices it stands between the Song of Solomon and Ecclesiasticus, in the Vatican MS Job stands next before it, and it must be observed that Isaiah and the other prophets are arranged after these, the Sapiential Books holding an intermediate position between the Historical and the Prophetical. The copies of the Greek Scriptures in use among the Jews at the time of our Lord contained the Books thus arranged without any distinctive mark, and, as far as we know, neither Christ nor His Apostles, in citing the Septuagint (which they continually do)[6], ever gave any warning against what we call the Apocryphal writings, many of which formed an integral part of the volume.

That the Book of Wisdom was not included among the twenty-two volumes of the Hebrew canon is obvious[7]. Its language alone would render its admission impossible. The first public recognition of its claims is said to have been made by a canon of the Council of Carthage, A D 397, though the same canon had already appeared in a provincial Council at Hippo four years previously[8]. This verdict is not confirmed by the Apostolic Canons, which place Ecclesiasticus in a secondary rank, but omit all mention of Wisdom. Very few of the private catalogues of Scripture class our Book with the canonical writings. S Augustine[9] includes it in his list, but seems elsewhere to speak somewhat apologetically thus 'Liber Sapientiae, qui tanta numerositate annorum legi meruit in Ecclesia Christi:' it is also found in the catalogues of Innocentius[10],

---

[1] S. Athan Apol de Fuga, 19 (p 262 Ben)· ὡς εἶπεν ἡ Σοφία, quoting Wisd iii 5, 6; Contr Gent. ii. (p 9) he introduces Wisd xiv. 12-21 with ἡ Γραφὴ λέγουσα. But in the Fest Ep. 39, he excludes it from the Canon

[2] Praep Ev vii 12 (p 322 Ben) and xi. 14 (p 532)

[3] Ad Demetr p 224 (ed. Paris, 1726); so, quoting Wisd. iii 4-8, he calls it 'Scriptura divina,' Ep 81

[4] De Civit Dei, xi 10, 1, he quotes 'Spiritus sapientiae multiplex' (Wisd. vii 22), as being 'in Scriptura sacra' See also in Ps lvii 1

[5] Numerous quotations will be found in the Commentary. To have inserted half that I have collected would have indeed enriched my notes, but at the same time would have swelled their dimensions unreasonably

[6] See Grinfield, Nov Test ed Hellen

[7] Joseph Contr Ap i 8, Euseb Hist Eccl iv 26

[8] Cosin, Hist of Canon, § 82, Smith's Bible Dict , Art. Canon, Labb Conc iii p. 891, wherein are enumerated as canonical 'Salomonis libri quinque' Hefele, Hist. of Counc ii. p 400 (Clarke)

[9] De Doctr Christ ii 8 Compare De Praedest i 27 (x p 807)

[10] Ep ad Exsup ap Galland. viii. pp 56, ff.

Cassiodorus[1], and Isidorus[2]. But individual writers continued to deny its claims to canonicity, while they maintained its importance and utility in moral teaching. Thus S. Jerome[3], after naming the twenty-two Books of the Hebrew Canon, proceeds: 'Hic prologus, Scripturarum quasi galeatum principium, omnibus libris quos de Hebraeo vertimus in Latinum, convenire potest, ut scire valeamus, quidquid extra hos est, inter apocrypha esse ponendum. Igitur Sapientia, quae vulgo Salomonis inscribitur, et Jesu filii Sirach liber, et Judith, et Tobias, et Pastor[4], non sunt in Canone.' And of the two Sapiential Books he says[5]: 'Sic et haec duo volumina legat [Ecclesia] ad aedificationem plebis, non ad auctoritatem ecclesiasticorum dogmatum confirmandam.' Similar sentiments are to be found in various authors down to the time of the Council of Trent, which put an end to all differences of opinion among the members of the Roman Catholic Church by decreeing the canonicity of this Book[6]. This hasty and uncritical enactment ordered all the Books of which a list was given, including Wisdom, to be received 'pari pietatis affectu,' on pain of incurring anathema.

The early Greek Church was naturally influenced by the use of the Septuagint version in its reception of the Book of Wisdom. But later the Confession of Cyril Lucar[7] confirmed the Catalogue of the Council of Laodicea[8], held between A.D. 343 and 381, in which our Book is wanting[9]. The same verdict is given in the Confession of Metrophanes Critopulus, the friend of Lucar, who enumerates the twenty-two books of the Hebrew Canon, and then adds: τὰ λοιπὰ δὲ βιβλία, ἄπερ τινὲς βούλονται συγκαταλέγειν τῇ ἁγίᾳ γραφῇ οἷον ... Σοφίαν τοῦ Σολομῶντος ... ἀποβλήτους μὲν οὐχ ἡγούμεθα· πολλὰ γὰρ ἠθικά, πλεῖστον ἐπαίνου ἄξια, ἐμπεριέχεται τούταις. ὡς κανονικὰς δὲ καὶ αὐθεντικὰς οὐδέποτ' ἀπεδέξατο ἡ τοῦ Χριστοῦ ἐκκλησία ... Διὸ οὐδὲ τὰ δόγματα ἡμῶν πειρώμεθα ἐκ τούτων παραστῆσαι[10]. The Orthodox Confession, which was put forth with authority A.D. 1643, merely refers the Canon to the decision of Oecumenical synods, but does not name the volumes which compose it[11]. On the other hand, the Synod of Jerusalem, A.D. 1672, introduced Wisdom and the other deutero-canonical Books to a place in Holy Scripture, and, following the lead of the Patriarch Dositheus, inveighed strongly against the Confession of Cyril Lucar which was of no authority in the Oriental Church. Having endorsed the Laodicean Canon of Scripture, the Council says: καὶ πρὸς τούτοις ἅπερ ἀσυνέτως καὶ ἀμαθῶς εἴτ' αὖν ἐθελοκακούργως ἀπόκρυφα κατωνόμασε [ὁ Κύριλλος]· τὴν Σοφίαν δηλαδὴ τοῦ Σολομῶντος ... ἡμεῖς γὰρ μετὰ τῶν ἄλλων τῆς θείας γραφῆς γνησίων βιβλίων καὶ ταῦτα γνήσια τῆς γραφῆς μέρη κρίνομεν[12]. In the Longer Catechism of the Russian Church, which gives the Catalogue of the Old Testament according to the Hebrew Canon, the question is asked, Why are not the Books of Wisdom and Ecclesiasticus mentioned in this list? The answer is: Athanasius says, that they have been appointed by the Fathers to be read by proselytes who are preparing for admission into the Church, but they are excluded from the catalogue because they do not exist in the Hebrew[13]. The present view of the rest of the Greek Church is in accordance with the verdict of the Synod of Jerusalem.

From the time of the Reformation Protestant Churches have always, following the example of

---

[1] De Instit. Div. Litt. xiv.
[2] De Orig. vi. 1.
[3] Prol. Galeat. in libr. Reg. See Bleek, Theol. Stud. u. Krit. 1853. pp. 270, ff.
[4] The Shepherd of Hermas is meant. This is found at the end of the Codex Sinaiticus.
[5] Praef. in libr. Salom.; Orig. περὶ Ἀρχ. iv. 33, says: 'Qui utique liber non ab omnibus in auctoritate habetur' (p. 193 Ben.).
[6] Concil. Trid. Sess. iv.; Sarpi, p. 139, ff. (ed. 1655).
[7] Kimmel, Monum. Fid. Eccles. Orient. P. lxxxviii; Bleek, ubi supr. p. 277.
[8] Kimmel, ib. i. p. 42.
[9] Hefele, Hist. of Counc. ii. p. 323 (Clarke).
[10] Kimmel, ii. pp. 105, 106.
[11] Kimmel, i. p. 159, and Proleg. p. lv; Blackmore, Doctr. of Russ. Ch. pp. xvi, ff.
[12] Kimmel, ii. p. 467; Migne, Dict. des Conc.
[13] Blackmore, Doctr. of Russ. Church, pp. 38, 39.

Luther[1], separated the so-called Apocryphal Books from the rest of the Scripture. The verdict of the Anglican Church is found in her Sixth Article, at the same time, with an inconsistency occasioned doubtless by the general use of the Latin Vulgate, she continually in her authorised Homilies quotes Wisdom as Scripture. Thus in the Homily Of Obedience, pt 1.[2], she introduces a citation with the words, 'the infallible and undeceivable word of God,' and in another place, 'as the word of God testifieth[3].'

With regard to the position and authority of the Book of Wisdom we may sum up our opinion in the following terms. Written anterior to Christianity, it is entirely in accordance with the mind of the Spirit as expressed in the Canonical Scriptures: many coincidences of thought and expression, designed or undesigned, exist between it and the writings of the New Covenant: it exhibits views and doctrines in advance of those found in the Old Testament: it shows in a marked manner the effect of the union of Jewish and Greek ideas, and in many respects anticipates the dogmas and the language which Christianity introduced. And further, it has been commonly quoted as Scripture by some Fathers and Councils, and is considered in this light by the Eastern and Roman Churches. On the other hand, it is certain that Wisdom was never included in the Hebrew Canon, was distinctly repudiated by many early writers, is wanting in evidence of general reception, and is rejected by the Anglican and all reformed Churches as inspired. We therefore regard as probable and safe the *dictum* of the Sixth Article, at the same time acknowledging that the absence of sufficient proof of canonicity, and not any internal marks of error or inferiority, is the chief ground for assigning to this work a lower place than the other writings of the Old Testament. Whether we consider its high tone, its moral and religious teaching, its devotional spirit, its polished diction, and its perfect accordance with the word of God[4], or whether we regard it as supplementary to the Old Testament, as filling a gap in the intellectual and religious history of God's people, as bridging over a space which would otherwise be left unoccupied, it is worthy of all respect, and claims an honour and a reverence which, with perhaps the exception of Ecclesiasticus, no other book, exterior to those universally acknowledged as divine Scripture, can be said to possess.

VI.

The Text

The authorities for the Text of the Book of Wisdom are chiefly the following Uncial Manuscripts.

1. The Codex Sinaiticus (S), discovered by Tischendorf at the Monastery on Mount Sinai in 1844 and 1859, written, as he supposes, (though others have seen reason to doubt this opinion,) in the middle of the fourth century, now in the possession of the Emperor of Russia, and of which a facsimile edition was published in 1862.

---

[1] Luther, in his translation of 'The Apocrypha,' assigned an inferior position to these Books. See Credner, Gesch d Kan pp 291, ff
[2] P. 97 ed Oxf 1844.
[3] Peril of Idolatry, pt iii p 220, comp p 216 and pt i p 164.
[4] The charges of Platonism, heathenism, and false teaching, brought against the Book by various writers, are noticed in the Commentary on the various passages referred to.

It contains the whole of Wisdom, but has not been used by Tischendorf, except in a chapter or two, in his own latest edition of the Septuagint. Since his death an edition (the sixth) has been published (1880) containing a collation of S and V by E Nestle. The corrections in the MS are in my edition noted S¹ and S².

2. The Codex Alexandrinus (A), written about the middle of the fifth century, presented to King Charles I in 1628 by Cyril Lucar, Patriarch of Constantinople, and now preserved in the British Museum. It contains the whole of the Book of Wisdom. A facsimile edition was published by Baber, Lond. 1816-1828. The various readings of this MS are very accurately given by Tischendorf. It forms the foundation of the Society for Promoting Christian Knowledge edition of the Lxx, ed. Field, though the learned editor has in some instances admitted doubtful corrections of the text, even where the reading of the original was quite intelligible. As above, A¹ and A² denote corrections in the MS. by first or second hand. So in V below.

3 The Codex Vaticanus (V), the most valuable of all the MSS. for antiquity and accuracy, now in the Vatican Library, written about the middle of the fourth century. It contains the whole of our Book. It was published, but very incorrectly, by Cardinal Mai in 1857; and has now been re-edited with great care by Vercellone and Cozza (Romae, 1868-1874), the types used in the magnificent facsimile of the Sinaitic Codex being employed. Tischendorf's last edition of the Septuagint gives a fairly accurate reprint of this text.

4. The Codex Ephraem rescriptus (C). This is a MS of certain portions of the text over which a work of S. Ephraem had been written. The original has been restored by a chemical process. Its date is probably the middle of the fifth century, and it contains the following portions of Wisdom viii 5—xii. 10; xiv. 19—xvii. 18, xviii. 24—xix. 22. Its readings are noted by Tischendorf.

5 Codex Venetus Marcianus (Ven). This is a MS of the eighth or ninth century in the library of S Mark at Venice. It was collated for Holmes and Parsons' edition of the Lxx, and numbered by them (23) on the erroneous supposition that it was written in cursive characters. Its readings in the majority of instances support the Vatican.

The cursive MSS. which contain the Book of Wisdom collated by Holmes and Parsons are of later age and much inferior authority. They are numbered 55, 68, 106, 155, 157, 248, 253, 254, 261, 296. The best of these is 68. The Complutensian edition chiefly follows 248. Besides the above, a partial collation of some Paris MSS was published by I C Thilo in his Specimen exercitation. critic. in Sapient. Sal. Halis, 1825 These are numbered A, Aa, B, C, D, E, F, H, I; they are of little critical value.

The two first editions of the Lxx have a peculiar interest though founded on inferior MSS. They are the Complutensian Polyglot of Cardinal Ximenes, 1517, and the Aldine, 1518. The former seems to have been the text generally used by the translators of the English Version.

A valuable assistance to the criticism of our Book has been put forth by F. H. Reusch, Observationes Criticae in Librum Sapientiae. Friburgi in Brisgovia, 1861 In this little work (which he designed as a companion volume to his edition of the Greek and Latin texts), he not only gives a selection of various readings, but a copious account of the passages quoted by the Fathers and early writers, which are of manifest utility in the confirmation and correction of the text.

The best edition of the text is that by O. F. Fritzsche, Libri Apocryphi Veteris Testamenti Graece. Lipsiae, 1871. This text is an original one, formed from a careful review of all attainable sources, the various readings being accurately given with a fulness to be found in no other edition of these Books.

The edition by Apel (Libri Vet. Test. Apocryphi Graece Accurate recognitos breviq ue diversarum lectionum delectu instructos, ed. H. E. Apel. Lipsiae, 1838) is of little critical value.

The groundwork of the present edition is the Vatican MS. as edited by Vercellone and Cozza, from which I have departed in very few instances, which are duly noted. The stichometrical arrangement of the text is from the Alexandrian MS. The critical apparatus contains the variations of the uncial MSS those of the cursive, given by Holmes and Parsons, and partially reprinted by Fritzsche, as of less importance, I have not thought it necessary to exhibit in their entirety

The references to the Septuagint are to Tischendorf's last edition. This is mentioned as in some Books the chapters and verses are differently numbered The references to the Old Testament are chiefly to the Greek text In quoting from Philo I have added in brackets the volume and page of Mangey's edition. In the references to the Fathers, where any difficulty was likely to arise, I have generally given the volume and page of the Benedictine editions The editions of other writers used are mentioned as they occur

VII.

Versions, Editions, and Commentaries.

OF the Versions, the Latin contained in the Vulgate is the most important for antiquity and literalness. It is really the old Italic rendering of the second or third century, and was left untouched by S Jerome when he re-edited the rest of the Bible In his Preface to the Books of Solomon he says · 'In eo libro, qui a plerisque Sapientia Salomonis inscribitur . calamo temperavi, tantummodo canonicas Scripturas vobis emendare desiderans.' Although this version has been authorized by the Council of Trent, and declared to be the very Word of God, impartial criticism will detect in it many errors arising from misunderstanding of the original, and many obscurities of expression which only tend to 'darken knowledge' There are also some additions to the text which are plainly not sanctioned by the original. But, with due allowance for these defects, it probably represents the reading of MSS. earlier than any that have come down to us, and in this respect, at any rate, is of great critical value, while its language is interesting as presenting provincialisms and phrases which point to an African origin. These are noted in the commentary as they occur. In their elucidation much use has been made of a work by H. Ronsch, Itala und Vulgata Marburg, 1875 ·

Other versions are the Syriac and Arabic, given in Walton's Polyglot, and the Armenian The former (Peschito) has been republished by Lagarde (Libri Veteris Testamenti Apocryphi e recognitione P Ant de Lagarde. Lips., 1861) It is too free and paraphrastic to be of much critical use, but it often supplies a traditional rendering which is serviceable in the exegesis of the text Much the same account may be given of the Arabic, which however seems not to be older than the seventh century. The Armenian Version is of higher antiquity and of much greater accuracy. So close is it to the original that it is easy to see what reading the translator has followed. The variations are noted by Reusch in his Observ Crit. The Book of Wisdom in Armenian, Greek, and Latin was published by the Mechitarists in 1827. (Reusch).

COMMENTARIES.

The following is a fairly complete list of the chief Commentaries on the Book of Wisdom, wherein Germany, as usual, is very copious, and England, till quite lately, has contributed scarcely anything. In early times we have these:

Rabanus Maurus. Commentariorum in Libr. Sap. libri tres. Migne, Patrol. Lat. cix.

Walafrid Strabo: Glossa Ordinaria. Migne, 113, 114.

Anselm, Episc. Laudunensis. Glossa interlinearis. Basil., 1502, etc.

Matthaeus Cantacuzenus. Scholia in Libr. Sap. Migne, Patrol. Graec. clii. The fragments are given in Tom. c. pp. 395, 411, 418, 447, 489.

Bonaventura. Expositio in Libr. Sap. Opp. vol. i. Romae, 1588; Venetiis, 1574.

Hugo a Sancto Caro: Postillae, sive breves commentar. in univ. Bibl. Basil. 1487, 1504, Lugd. 1669.

Nicolas Lyranus: Postillae in univ. Bibl. Romae, 1471-1472.

Robert Holkot († 1340), an English Dominican: In Libr. Sap. Praelectiones ccxiii. pub. in 1481, 1511, 1586, 1689.

Since the Reformation, among Roman Catholics, the following are the chief Commentaries:

Dionysius Cartbusianus: In quisque Libr. Sapient. Salom., Paris, 1548.

P. Nannius. Sap. Salomonis una cum Scholiis, Petro Nannio interprete. Bas. 1552.

Corn. Jansen, Bishop of Ghent. Adnotationes in Libr. Sap. Sol. Duac. 1577, 1660. Paraphrasis in omnes Psalmos David, etc. ac in Sapientiam Notae. Antv. 1614. This Comm. is given in Migne's Script. Sacr. Curs. Compl. Tom xvii.

Hier. Osorius. Paraphrasis in Salomonis Sapientiam. Boulogn. 1577.

Joann. Lorinus: Commentar. in Sap. Lugd. 1607, 1624.

De Castro. Comm. in Sap. Sal. Lugd. 1613.

Corn. a Lapide. Commentar. in Libr. Sap. Antv. 1638. Often reprinted.

Job. Maldonatus. Comm. in Sap. Sal. Paris 1643.

Pet. Gorsius: Explicatio in Lib. Sapientiae. Par. 1655.

Joh. Menochius. Brevis Explicatio sensus literalis totius Scripturae. Ant. 1678.

De Sacy. La Sainte Bible. Par. 1692. (Vol. 14 contains a commentary on Wisdom.)

Augustin Calmet. Commentaire littéral. Par. 1724.

Jac. Tirinus. Comment. in S. Scripturam, in the Biblia Magna of De la Haye, where are also the notes of Estius, Sa, and others.

Duguet et d'Asfeld. Explication du livre de la Sagesse. Paris, 1755.

Weitenauer: Job, Psalm., Salom., Siracides explic. 1768.

F. W. Smets. Sapientia Vulg. edit. Vers. Belgica notis Grammat. etc. Antv. et Amst. 1749.

Du Hamel. Salomonis Libri tres ... item Liber Sap. et Ecclesiasticus. Par. 1703.

C. F. Houbigant. Notae criticae in univ. Vet. Test. libros, etc. Francof. 1777.

Fr. Boaretti: Il Libro della Sapienza recato... con analisi, annotazioni, etc. Venezia, 1792.

T. A. Dereser. Die Sprüchwörter. das Buch der Weisheit ... übersetzt und erklärt. Frankf. 1825.

J. A. Schmid. Das Buch der Weisheit übersetzt und erklärt. Wien, 1858, 1865.

C. Gutberlet: Das Buch der Weisheit übersetzt und erklärt. Münster, 1874. This forms part of the new edition of the Old Testament by Roman Catholic expositors, under the title: Die heiligen Schriften des alten Testamentes nach katholischen Prinzipien übersetzt und erklärt von einem Verein befreundeter Fachgenossen.

Anglican:
R. Arnald A critical commentary upon the Apocryphal Books, 1744-1752 It is usually printed with the Commentaries of Patrick, Lowth, and Whitby

J H. Blunt· The Annotated Bible, vol. ii. Apocrypha. London, 1879

The Wisdom of Solomon, edited for the Society for Promoting Christian Knowledge, by the Rev W R. Churton, B D. 1880

Protestant:
Critici Sacri Amst 1698-1732. Of this ed. vol v contains the notes on 'Libri Apocryphi.' Herein are comprised the Annotations of Grotius

Conr Pellicanus· In Libros quos vocant Apocryphos vel potius Ecclesiasticos .. commentarii Tiguri, 1572.

Nic Selneccerus· Lib Sap ad tyrannos, etc Lips 1568.

Vict. Strigel Sapientia Sirach. Sapientia Francof. et Lips. 1691.

J. G. Hasse: Salomos Weisheit, neu übersetzt mit Anmerkungen und Untersuchungen. Jena, 1785

Brochmannus: Comm in iv capp. Sapientiae Hafn. 1656.

Wilh Petersen· Petachia, od schriftmassige Erklarung der Weish Sal Budingen, 1727

Gottfr. Schuband Das Buch der Weish. Sal. Magdeb. 1733.

J A. Steinmetz: Das Buch der Weish. Magd. und Leipz 1747

J F. Kleuker Salom Denkwürdigkeiten, Als Anhang: Das Buch der Weish etc. Riga, 1785.

Jac Wallenius Salomos Vishet Greifswald, 1786 Annotationes philologico-criticae in Libr qui inscribitur Σοφία Σαλωμών Gryphisw. 1786

J. C. C. Nachtigal. Das Buch der Weish. Halle, 1799

K G Kelle Die heiligen Schriften in ihrer Urgestalt. 1 Band Salom Schriften. Freib 1815.

A L. C Heydenreich Uebersetzung und Erläuterung des Buches der Weish, in Tzschirner's Memorabilien

W. F. Engelbreth Librum Sap. Sal interpretandi specimina. Hafniae, 1816

J. Schulthess: Exegetisch. theolog. Forschungen. Zurich, 1820

J. P. Bauermeister: Comment in Sap Sal. Gotting 1828

C L W Grimm· Commentar über das Buch der Weish. Leipz 1837.

Fritzsche und Grimm. Kurzgefasstes exegetisches Handbuch zu den Apocryphen des Alt. Test Leipz. 1851-1860. vi Lieferung Das Buch der Weish erklart von C. L W Grimm

Edwin Cone Bissell, D D · The Apocrypha of the Old Testament, with Historical Introductions, a Revised Translation, and Notes, Critical and Explanatory. Edinburgh, 1880.

Though not a Commentary, here must be added, Clavis Librorum Veteris Testamenti Apocryphorum Philologica, Auctore Christ Abrah Wahl. Lipsiae, 1853.

THE GREEK TEXT AND CRITICAL APPARATUS,
WITH THE ANGLICAN VERSION AND THE LATIN VULGATE.

LIBER SAPIENTIAE.
CAPUT I.

1 Diligite justitiam, qui judicatis terram. Sentite de Domino in bonitate, et in simplicitate
2 cordis quaerite illum; quoniam invenitur ab his, qui non tentant illum, apparet autem eis qui fidem habent in illum.
3 Perversae enim cogitationes separant a Deo; probata autem
4 virtus corripit insipientes. Quoniam in malevolam animam non introibit sapientia, nec habitabit in corpore subdito peccatis.
5 Spiritus enim sanctus disciplinae effugiet fictum, et auferet se a cogitationibus quae sunt sine in-

ΣΟΦΙΑ ΣΑΛΩΜΩΝ.
ΚΕΦΑΛΑΙΟΝ Α'.

1 ἈΓΑΠΉΣΑΤΕ δικαιοσύνην οἱ κρίνοντες τὴν γῆν,
φρονήσατε περὶ τοῦ Κυρίου ἐν ἀγαθότητι,
καὶ ἐν ἁπλότητι καρδίας ζητήσατε αὐτόν·
2 ὅτι εὑρίσκεται τοῖς μὴ πειράζουσιν αὐτόν,
ἐμφανίζεται δὲ τοῖς μὴ ἀπιστοῦσιν αὐτῷ.
3 σκολιοὶ γὰρ λογισμοὶ χωρίζουσιν ἀπὸ Θεοῦ,
δοκιμαζομένη τε ἡ δύναμις ἐλέγχει τοὺς ἄφρονας.
4 ὅτι εἰς κακότεχνον ψυχὴν οὐκ εἰσελεύσεται σοφία,
οὐδὲ κατοικήσει ἐν σώματι κατάχρεῳ ἁμαρτίας.
5 ἅγιον γὰρ πνεῦμα παιδείας φεύξεται δόλον,
καὶ ἀπαναστήσεται ἀπὸ λογισμῶν ἀσυνέτων,

THE WISDOM OF SOLOMON.
CHAPTER I.

1 Love righteousness, ye that be judges of the earth: think of the Lord with a good (heart), and in simplicity of heart seek
2 him. For he will be found of them that tempt him not; and sheweth himself unto such as do
3 not distrust him. For froward thoughts separate from God: and his power, when it is tried,
4 [1] reproveth the unwise. For [Or, maketh manifest] into a malicious soul wisdom shall not enter; nor dwell in the body that is subject unto
5 sin. For the holy spirit of discipline will flee deceit, and remove from thoughts that are

---

Titulus: Σοφια Σαλωμων V. Σ. Σολομωντος A. Σ. Σαλομωντος S.   I. 2. μη απιστουσιν αυτω S. V.   μη πιστευουσιν α. A. τοις πιστευουσιν 261 et fors. Vulg. Syr.   3. τε V. A. δε S.   4. αμαρτιας Omnes Codd. αμαρτιαις Eus. in Ps. 159; Ath. ii. 42, 378. Vulg. Syr.   5. παιδειας V. S. Ven. Vulg. Syr. Ar. σοφιας A. Arm.   απαναστησεται, αποστησεται S⁷.

[margin notes:
¹ Or, is rebuked, or, sheweth itself.
² Or, lips.
³ Or, upholdeth.
⁴ Or, reproving.
⁵ Or, slandereth.]

without understanding, and ¹will not abide when unrighteousness 6 cometh in. For wisdom is a loving spirit; and will not acquit a blasphemer of his ²words: for God is witness of his reins, and a true beholder of his heart, and a hearer of his 7 tongue. For the Spirit of the Lord filleth the world: and that which ³containeth all things hath knowledge of the voice. 8 Therefore he that speaketh unrighteous things cannot be hid: neither shall vengeance, when it punisheth, pass by him. 9 For inquisition shall be made into the counsels of the ungodly: and the sound of his words shall come unto the Lord for the manifestation⁴ of 10 his wicked deeds. For the ear of jealousy heareth all things: and the noise of murmurings 11 is not hid. Therefore beware of murmuring, which is unprofitable; and refrain your tongue from backbiting: for there is no word so secret, that shall go for nought: and the mouth that belieth ⁵ slayeth the

καὶ ἐλεγχθήσεται ἐπελθούσης ἀδικίας.
6 φιλάνθρωπον γὰρ πνεῦμα σοφία, καὶ οὐκ ἀθῳώσει βλάσφημον ἀπὸ χειλέων αὐτοῦ, ὅτι τῶν νεφρῶν αὐτοῦ μάρτυς ὁ Θεός, καὶ τῆς καρδίας αὐτοῦ ἐπίσκοπος ἀληθής, καὶ τῆς γλώσσης ἀκουστής·
7 ὅτι πνεῦμα Κυρίου πεπλήρωκε τὴν οἰκουμένην, καὶ τὸ συνέχον τὰ πάντα γνῶσιν ἔχει φωνῆς.
8 διὰ τοῦτο φθεγγόμενος ἄδικα οὐδεὶς μὴ λάθῃ, οὐδὲ μὴ παροδεύσῃ αὐτὸν ἐλέγχουσα ἡ δίκη.
9 ἐν γὰρ διαβουλίοις ἀσεβοῦς ἐξέτασις ἔσται, λόγων δὲ αὐτοῦ ἀκοὴ πρὸς Κύριον ἥξει εἰς ἔλεγχον ἀνομημάτων αὐτοῦ·
10 ὅτι οὖς ζηλώσεως ἀκροᾶται τὰ πάντα, καὶ θροῦς γογγυσμῶν οὐκ ἀποκρύπτεται.
11 φυλάξασθε τοίνυν γογγυσμὸν ἀνωφελῆ, καὶ ἀπὸ καταλαλιᾶς φείσασθε γλώσσης· ὅτι φθέγμα λαθραῖον κενὸν οὐ πορεύσεται, στόμα δὲ καταψευδόμενον ἀναιρεῖ ψυχήν.

tellectu, et corripietur a superveniente iniquitate. 6 Benignus est enim spiritus sapientiae, et non liberabit maledicum a labiis suis, quoniam renum illius testis est Deus, et cordis illius scrutator est verus, et linguae ejus 7 auditor. Quoniam spiritus Domini replevit orbem terrarum; et hoc, quod continet omnia, 8 scientiam habet vocis. Propter hoc qui loquitur iniqua non potest latere, nec praeteriet il9 lum corripiens judicium. In cogitationibus enim impii interrogatio erit; sermonum autem illius auditio ad Deum veniet, ad correptionem iniqui10 tatum illius. Quoniam auris zeli audit omnia, et tumultus murmurationum non abscondel11 tur. Custodite ergo vos a murmuratione quae nihil prodest, et a detractione parcite linguae, quoniam sermo obscurus in vacuum non ibit, os autem quod mentitur occidit animam.

---

5. αδικιας Codd. ανομιας Compl. 248. 6. πνευμα σοφια S.V. σοφιας A. Ven. Vulg. Syr. Ar. Arm. Didym. 299. αθωωσει V. αθωωσει S. A. V¹. αληθης S. V. A. Ven. αληθινος 106. 261. της γλωσσης αυτου ακ. A. Ar. Arm. 7. πεπληρωκε S. V. επληρωσεν A. 8. ουδε μην V. ουδε μη S. A. Ven. ουδεις ου μη 106. 253. 261. παροδευσῃ S. V. al. παρελευσηται Compl. παροδευσι S². 9. αυτου ακοη V. A. al. ακ. αυτη S. ανομηματων S. V. al. ασεβηματων 248. 10. ους ζηλωσεως S¹. 11. κενον V. A. al. καινον S. ου πορευσεται om. S. add. cor.

12 Nolite zelare mortem in errore vitae vestrae, neque acquiratis perditionem in operibus
13 manuum vestrarum. Quoniam Deus mortem non fecit, nec laetatur in perditione vivorum.
14 Creavit enim, ut essent omnia; et sanabiles fecit nationes orbis terrarum; et non est in illis medicamentum exterminii, nec inferorum regnum in terra.
15 Justitia enim perpetua est, et
16 immortalis. Impii autem manibus et verbis accersierunt illam; et aestimantes illam amicam, defluxerunt, et sponsiones posuerunt ad illam; quoniam digni sunt qui sint ex parte illius.

CAPUT II.

1 Dixerunt enim cogitantes apud se non recte: Exiguum, et cum taedio est tempus vitae nostrae, et non est refrigerium in fine hominis, et non est qui agnitus sit reversus ab inferis.

12 Μὴ ζηλοῦτε θάνατον ἐν πλάνῃ ζωῆς ὑμῶν,
μηδὲ ἐπισπᾶσθε ὄλεθρον ἔργοις χειρῶν ὑμῶν·
13 ὅτι ὁ Θεὸς θάνατον οὐκ ἐποίησεν,
οὐδὲ τέρπεται ἐπ' ἀπωλείᾳ ζώντων.
14 ἔκτισε γὰρ εἰς τὸ εἶναι τὰ πάντα,
καὶ σωτήριοι αἱ γενέσεις τοῦ κόσμου,
καὶ οὐκ ἔστιν ἐν αὐταῖς φάρμακον ὀλέθρου,
οὔτε ᾅδου βασίλειον ἐπὶ γῆς.
15 δικαιοσύνη γὰρ ἀθάνατός ἐστιν·
16 ἀσεβεῖς δὲ ταῖς χερσὶ καὶ τοῖς λόγοις προσεκαλέσαντο αὐτόν,
φίλον ἡγησάμενοι αὐτὸν ἐτάκησαν,
καὶ συνθήκην ἔθεντο πρὸς αὐτόν,
ὅτι ἄξιοί εἰσι τῆς ἐκείνου μερίδος εἶναι.

ΚΕΦΑΛΑΙΟΝ Β'.

1 Εἶπον γὰρ ἐν ἑαυτοῖς λογισάμενοι οὐκ ὀρθῶς·
ὀλίγος ἐστὶ καὶ λυπηρὸς ὁ βίος ἡμῶν,
καὶ οὐκ ἔστιν ἴασις ἐν τελευτῇ ἀνθρώπου,
καὶ οὐκ ἐγνώσθη ὁ ἀναλύσας ἐξ ᾅδου.

12 soul. Seek not death in the error of your life: and pull not upon yourselves destruction with the works of your hands.
13 For God made not death: neither hath he pleasure in the
14 destruction of the living. For he created all things, that they might have their being: and the generations of the world were healthful; and there is no poison of destruction in them, nor the kingdom of death upon
15 the earth: (For righteousness is
16 immortal:) But ungodly men with their works and words called *it* to them: for when they thought to have it their friend, they consumed to nought, and made a covenant with it, because they are worthy to take part with it.

CHAPTER II.

1 For the *ungodly* said, reasoning with themselves, but not aright, Our life is short and tedious, and in the death of a man there is no remedy: neither was there any man known to have returned from the grave.

---

12. εργοις S. V.   εν εργοις A. Vulg.   13. επ' απωλεια S. V. al.   επ' αγγελια A.   εν απωλεια Ald. Orig. iii. 137.
14. ου γαρ εκτισεν εις γαρ εις το ειναι S¹.   ουτε αδου V. S.   ουδε α A. Compl.   επι γης V. S.   επι της γης A.   15. δικ. γαρ A. V. S. al.   δικ. δε 248. Compl.   16. λογοις S A. V.   λογισμοις 248.   II. 1. εν εαυτ. A. S. V. Ven. Ald. Compl.

THE BOOK OF WISDOM.

[1 Or, moist.]
[2 Or, oppressed.]
[3 Or, he.]
[4 Or, earnestly.]

2 For we are born at all adventure: and we shall be hereafter as though we had never been: for the breath in our nostrils is as smoke, and a little spark in the moving of our heart: 3 Which being extinguished, our body shall be turned into ashes, and our spirit shall vanish as the soft[1] air, And our name shall be forgotten in time, and no man shall have our works in remembrance, and our life shall pass away as the trace of a cloud, and shall be dispersed as a mist, that is driven away with the beams of the sun, and overcome[2] with the heat thereof. 5 For our time is a very shadow that passeth away; and after our end there is no returning: for it[3] is fast sealed, so that no man cometh again. 6 Come on therefore, let us enjoy the good things that are present: and let us speedily[4] use the creatures like as in youth. 7 Let us fill ourselves with costly wine

2 ὅτι αὐτοσχεδίως ἐγεννήθημεν,
καὶ μετὰ τοῦτο ἐσόμεθα ὡς οὐχ ὑπάρξαντες·
ὅτι καπνὸς ἡ πνοὴ ἐν ῥισὶν ἡμῶν,
καὶ ὁ λόγος σπινθὴρ ἐν κινήσει καρδίας ἡμῶν,
3 οὗ σβεσθέντος τέφρα ἀποβήσεται τὸ σῶμα,
καὶ τὸ πνεῦμα διαχυθήσεται ὡς χαῦνος ἀήρ.
4 καὶ τὸ ὄνομα ἡμῶν ἐπιλησθήσεται ἐν χρόνῳ,
καὶ οὐθεὶς μνημονεύσει τῶν ἔργων ἡμῶν·
καὶ παρελεύσεται ὁ βίος ἡμῶν ὡς ἴχνη νεφέλης,
καὶ ὡς ὁμίχλη διασκεδασθήσεται,
διωχθεῖσα ὑπὸ ἀκτίνων ἡλίου
καὶ ὑπὸ θερμότητος αὐτοῦ βαρυνθεῖσα.
5 σκιᾶς γὰρ πάροδος ὁ καιρὸς ἡμῶν,
καὶ οὐκ ἔστιν ἀναποδισμὸς τῆς τελευτῆς ἡμῶν,
ὅτι κατεσφραγίσθη, καὶ οὐδεὶς ἀναστρέφει.
6 δεῦτε οὖν καὶ ἀπολαύσωμεν τῶν ὄντων ἀγαθῶν,
καὶ χρησώμεθα τῇ κτίσει ὡς νεότητι σπουδαίως.
7 οἴνου πολυτελοῦς καὶ μύρων πλησθῶμεν,

2 Quia ex nihilo nati sumus, et post hoc erimus tanquam non fuerimus; quoniam fumus flatus est in naribus nostris, et sermo scintilla ad commovendum cor 3 nostrum; qua extincta, cinis erit corpus nostrum, et spiritus diffundetur tanquam mollis aër, et transibit vita nostra tanquam vestigium nubis, et sicut nebula dissolvetur, quae fugata est a radiis solis, et a calore illius 4 aggravata; et nomen nostrum oblivionem accipiet per tempus, et nemo memoriam habebit operum 5 nostrorum. Umbrae enim transitus est tempus nostrum, et non est reversio finis nostri; quoniam consignata est, et nemo 6 revertitur. Venite ergo, et fruamur bonis quae sunt, et utamur creatura tanquam in 7 juventute celeriter. Vino pretioso et unguentis nos implea-

---

2. ως ουχ Vulgo. ως μη 157. υπαρξαντες Vulgo. υπαρχοντες S¹. καπνος η πνοη η A. V. al. καπνος εν ρισιν η πνοη ημων S. η πνοη εν ρ. S¹. ο λογος Vulgo. ολιγος Compl. C. Par. 3. σβεσθεντος V. σβενσθεντος A. σβενθεντος S. διαχυθησεται V. S. διαχυθησεται A. διαλυθησεται 55. 248. 254. 4. μνημονευσει V. A. al. μνημονευει S. μνημονευσει S¹. παρελ. Vulgo. πορευσεται 106. 261. βαρυνθεισα Vulgo. μαρανθεισα 106. 5. καιρος A¹. S. V². Compl. Ald. Vulg. βιος V. Vulgo. αναπ. A. V. al. ανταποδισμος S. 6. ουν και. A. om. και. νεοτητι V. Ven. νεοτητος A. S. νεοτητει S². εν νεοτητι Compl. al. Athan. ad Matt. ii. 8.

mus; et non praetereat nos flos 8 temporis. Coronemus nos rosis, antequam marcescant; nullum pratum sit quod non pertranseat luxuria nostra. Nemo nostrum exsors sit luxuriae nostrae; ubique relinquamus signa laetitiae; quoniam haec est pars 10 nostra, et haec est sors. Opprimamus pauperem justum, et non parcamus viduae, nec veterani revereamur canos multi temporis. Sit autem fortitudo nostra lex justitiae; quod enim infirmum est inutile invenitur. Circumveniamus ergo justum, quoniam inutilis est nobis, et contrarius est operibus nostris, et improperat nobis peccata legis, et diffamat in nos peccata disciplinae nostrae. Promittit se scientiam Dei habere, et filium Dei se nominat. Factus est nobis in traductionem cogitationum nostrarum. Gravis est nobis etiam ad videndum,	καὶ μὴ παροδευσάτω ἡμᾶς ἄνθος ἔαρος. 8 στεψώμεθα ῥόδων κάλυξι πρὶν ἢ μαρανθῆναι· 9 μηδεὶς ἡμῶν ἄμοιρος ἔστω τῆς ἡμετέρας ἀγερωχίας, πανταχῇ καταλίπωμεν σύμβολα τῆς εὐφροσύνης, ὅτι αὕτη ἡ μερὶς ἡμῶν καὶ ὁ κλῆρος οὗτος. 10 καταδυναστεύσωμεν πένητα δίκαιον, μὴ φεισώμεθα χήρας, μηδὲ πρεσβύτου ἐντραπῶμεν πολιὰς πολυχρονίους. 11 ἔστω δὲ ἡμῶν ἡ ἰσχὺς νόμος τῆς δικαιοσύνης, τὸ γὰρ ἀσθενὲς ἄχρηστον ἐλέγχεται. 12 ἐνεδρεύσωμεν τὸν δίκαιον, ὅτι δύσχρηστος ἡμῖν ἐστι, καὶ ἐναντιοῦται τοῖς ἔργοις ἡμῶν, καὶ ὀνειδίζει ἡμῖν ἁμαρτήματα νόμου, καὶ ἐπιφημίζει ἡμῖν ἁμαρτήματα παιδείας ἡμῶν. 13 ἐπαγγέλλεται γνῶσιν ἔχειν Θεοῦ, καὶ παῖδα Κυρίου ἑαυτὸν ὀνομάζει. 14 ἐγένετο ἡμῖν εἰς ἔλεγχον ἐννοιῶν ἡμῶν. 15 βαρύς ἐστιν ἡμῖν καὶ βλεπόμενος,	and ointments: and let no flower of the spring pass by 8 us: Let us crown ourselves with rosebuds, before they be 9 withered: Let none of us go without his part of our [1] voluptuousness: let us leave tokens of our joyfulness in every place: for this is our portion, and our 10 lot is this. Let us oppress the poor righteous man, let us not spare the widow, nor reverence the ancient grey hairs of the 11 aged. Let our strength be the law of justice: for that which is feeble is found to be nothing 12 worth. Therefore let us lie in wait for the righteous; because he is not for our turn, and he is clean contrary to our doings: he upbraideth us with our offending the law, and objecteth to our infamy the trans- 13 gressions of our education. He professeth to have the knowledge of God: and he calleth himself the child of the Lord. 14 He was made to reprove our 15 thoughts. He is grievous unto us even to behold: for his life

[1] Or, jollity.

7. ἡμᾶς. με S. sed cor.¹ ημας   εαρος A. 55. 106. 157. 261. 296. Arm. Vulg.   αερος V. S. al.   9. εσται. εστι S.   καταλιπ. S. V.   καταλειτωμεν A.   ουτος S. V.   ημων A.   10. πρεσβυτου V. S.   πρεσβυτερου A.   πολυχρονιους S. A. V.   πολυχρονιου Ven.   12. ενεδρ. δε V.   om. δε A. S. (S¹ addit.)   τα αμαρτ. νομ. S.   παραπτωματα 248.   παιδειας V.   παιδιας S. A.

is not like other men's, his ways are of another fashion. We are esteemed of him as counterfeits[1]: he abstaineth from our ways as from filthiness: he pronounceth the end of the just to be blessed, and maketh his boast that God is his father. 17 Let us see if his words be true: and let us prove what shall happen in the end of him. 18 For if the just man be the son of God, he will help him, and deliver him from the hand of his enemies. 19 Let us examine him with despitefulness and torture, that we may know his meekness, and prove his patience. 20 Let us condemn him with a shameful death: for by his own saying he shall be respected. 21 Such things they did imagine, and were deceived: for their own wickedness hath blinded them. 22 As for the mysteries of God, they knew them not: neither hoped they for the wages of righteousness, nor discerned[2] a reward for blameless souls. 23 For God created man to

[1] Or, *false coin*.

[2] Gr. *preferred, or, esteemed the reward*.

ὅτι ἀνόμοιος τοῖς ἄλλοις ὁ βίος αὐτοῦ,
καὶ ἐξηλλαγμέναι αἱ τρίβοι αὐτοῦ.
16 εἰς κίβδηλον ἐλογίσθημεν αὐτῷ,
καὶ ἀπέχεται τῶν ὁδῶν ἡμῶν ὡς ἀπὸ ἀκαθαρσιῶν·
μακαρίζει ἔσχατα δικαίων,
καὶ ἀλαζονεύεται πάτερα Θεόν.
17 ἴδωμεν εἰ οἱ λόγοι αὐτοῦ ἀληθεῖς,
καὶ πειράσωμεν τὰ ἐν ἐκβάσει αὐτοῦ.
18 εἰ γάρ ἐστιν ὁ δίκαιος υἱὸς Θεοῦ, ἀντιλήψεται αὐτοῦ
καὶ ῥύσεται αὐτὸν ἐκ χειρὸς ἀνθεστηκότων.
19 ὕβρει καὶ βασάνῳ ἐτάσωμεν αὐτόν,
ἵνα γνῶμεν τὴν ἐπιείκειαν αὐτοῦ
καὶ δοκιμάσωμεν τὴν ἀνεξικακίαν αὐτοῦ.
20 θανάτῳ ἀσχήμονι καταδικάσωμεν αὐτόν·
ἔσται γὰρ αὐτοῦ ἐπισκοπὴ ἐκ λόγων αὐτοῦ.
21 Ταῦτα ἐλογίσαντο, καὶ ἐπλανήθησαν·
ἀπετύφλωσε γὰρ αὐτοὺς ἡ κακία αὐτῶν·
22 καὶ οὐκ ἔγνωσαν μυστήρια Θεοῦ,
οὐδὲ μισθὸν ἤλπισαν ὁσιότητος,
οὐδὲ ἔκριναν γέρας ψυχῶν ἀμώμων.
23 ὅτι ὁ Θεὸς ἔκτισε τὸν ἄνθρωπον ἐπ᾽ ἀφθαρσίᾳ,

quoniam dissimilis est aliis vita illius, et immutatae sunt viae 16 ejus. Tanquam nugaces aestimati sumus ab illo; et abstinet se a viis nostris tanquam ab immunditiis, et praefert novissima justorum, et gloriatur patrem se habere Deum. 17 Videamus ergo si sermones illius veri sint, et tentemus quae ventura sunt illi, et sciemus quae erunt 18 novissima illius. Si enim est verus filius Dei, suscipiet illum, et liberabit eum de manibus 19 contrariorum. Contumelia et tormento interrogemus eum, ut sciamus reverentiam ejus, et probemus patientiam illius. 20 Morte turpissima condemnemus eum; erit enim ei respectus ex sermonibus illius.

21 Haec cogitaverunt, et erraverunt; excaecavit enim illos malitia eorum. 22 Et nescierunt sacramenta Dei, neque mercedem speraverunt justitiae, nec judicaverunt honorem animarum 23 sanctarum. Quoniam Deus crea-

---

16. ελογισθημεν V. A. S². εγενηθημεν S.   οδων S. A. V. εργων Ven. εσχατα. εργα των δ. 155.   17. και ειδωμεν S¹.
18. αντιληψεται V. al. αντιλημψεται S. A.   19. δοκιμ. A. S. δικασωμεν V. Vercell. 68. Ald.   21. ελογισαντο V. A.
ελογισθησαν S. (ελογισαντο S².) addunt 55. 106. 261. al. οι αφρονες. απετυφλ. A. V. ετυφλωσεν S. Orig. ii. 712.   22. εκρειναν V.
ψυχων. ψυχαν S.

vit hominem inexterminabilem, et ad imaginem similitudinis
24 suae fecit illum. Invidia autem diaboli mors introivit in orbem
25 terrarum; imitantur autem illum qui sunt ex parte illius.

CAPUT III.

1 Justorum autem animae in manu Dei sunt, et non tanget
2 illos tormentum mortis. Visi sunt oculis insipientium mori, et aestimata est afflictio exitus
3 illorum; et quod a nobis est iter, exterminium; illi autem
4 sunt in pace. Et si coram hominibus tormenta passi sunt, spes illorum immortalitate plena
5 est. In paucis vexati, in multis bene disponentur, quoniam Deus tentavit eos, et invenit illos
6 dignos se. Tanquam aurum in fornace probavit illos, et quasi holocausti hostiam accepit illos, et in tempore erit respectus
7 illorum. Fulgebunt justi, et tanquam scintillae in arundi-

καὶ εἰκόνα τῆς ἰδίας ἰδιότητος ἐποίησεν αὐτόν·
24 φθόνῳ δὲ διαβόλου θάνατος εἰσῆλθεν εἰς τὸν κόσμον, πειράζουσι δὲ αὐτὸν οἱ τῆς ἐκείνου μερίδος ὄντες.

ΚΕΦΑΛΑΙΟΝ Γ´.

1 Δικαίων δὲ ψυχαὶ ἐν χειρὶ Θεοῦ, καὶ οὐ μὴ ἅψηται αὐτῶν βάσανος.
2 ἔδοξαν ἐν ὀφθαλμοῖς ἀφρόνων τεθνάναι, καὶ ἐλογίσθη κάκωσις ἡ ἔξοδος αὐτῶν,
3 καὶ ἡ ἀφ᾽ ἡμῶν πορεία σύντριμμα· οἱ δέ εἰσιν ἐν εἰρήνῃ.
4 καὶ γὰρ ἐν ὄψει ἀνθρώπων ἐὰν κολασθῶσιν, ἡ ἐλπὶς αὐτῶν ἀθανασίας πλήρης·
5 καὶ ὀλίγα παιδευθέντες μεγάλα εὐεργετηθήσονται, ὅτι ὁ Θεὸς ἐπείρασεν αὐτούς, καὶ εὗρεν αὐτοὺς ἀξίους ἑαυτοῦ.
6 ὡς χρυσὸν ἐν χωνευτηρίῳ ἐδοκίμασεν αὐτούς, καὶ ὡς ὁλοκάρπωμα θυσίας προσεδέξατο αὐτούς.
7 καὶ ἐν καιρῷ ἐπισκοπῆς αὐτῶν ἀναλάμψουσιν, καὶ ὡς σπινθῆρες ἐν καλάμῃ διαδραμοῦνται.

he immortal, and made him to be an image of his own eternity.
24 Nevertheless through envy of the devil came death into the world: and they that do hold of his side do find it.

CHAPTER III.

1 But the souls of the righteous are in the hand of God, and there shall no torment touch
2 them. In the sight of the unwise they seemed to die: and their departure is taken for
3 misery, And their going from us to be utter destruction: but
4 they are in peace. For though they be punished in the sight of men, yet is their hope full
5 of immortality. And having been a little chastised, they shall be greatly rewarded[1]: for God [1] Or, benefited. proved them, and found them
6 worthy[2] for himself. As gold [2] Or, meet. in the furnace hath he tried them, and received them as a
7 burnt offering. And in the time of their visitation they shall shine, and run to and fro like sparks among the stubble.

---

23. ιδιοτητος V. A. S. Ven. Ald. Compl. αιδιοτητος Field. 248. 253. E. F. G. H. Par. Ath. i. 41. Method. 788. Niceph. ii. 200. Epiph. 543. 557. ομοιοτητος 106. 261. Aa. B. Par. Vulg. Syr. III. 2. εδοξαν γαρ S². αφρονων. ανθρωπων Ven. 3. η αφη ημων V. Vercell. 6. ολοκάρπωμα. ολοκαντωμα Ven.

THE BOOK OF WISDOM.

¹ Or, and such as be faithful shall remain with him in love.

² Or, light, or, unchaste.

³ Gr. the chosen.

8 They shall judge the nations, and have dominion over the people, and their Lord shall 9 reign for ever. They that put their trust in him shall understand the truth: and[1] such as be faithful in love shall abide with him: for grace and mercy is to his saints, and he hath 10 care for his elect. But the ungodly shall be punished according to their own imaginations, which have neglected the righteous, and forsaken the Lord. 11 For whoso despiseth wisdom and nurture, he is miserable, and their hope is vain, their labours unfruitful, and their 12 works unprofitable: Their wives are foolish[2], and their children 13 wicked: Their offspring is cursed. Wherefore blessed is the barren that is undefiled, which hath not known the sinful bed: she shall have fruit in 14 the visitation of souls. And *blessed* is the eunuch, which with his hands hath wrought no iniquity, nor imagined wicked things against God: for unto him shall be given the[3] special gift of faith, and an inheritance

8 κρινοῦσιν ἔθνη καὶ κρατήσουσι λαῶν,
καὶ βασιλεύσει αὐτῶν Κύριος εἰς τοὺς αἰῶνας.
9 οἱ πεποιθότες ἐπ' αὐτῷ συνήσουσιν ἀλήθειαν,
καὶ οἱ πιστοὶ ἐν ἀγάπῃ προσμενοῦσιν αὐτῷ,
ὅτι χάρις καὶ ἔλεος ἐν τοῖς ὁσίοις αὐτοῦ
καὶ ἐπισκοπὴ ἐν τοῖς ἐκλεκτοῖς αὐτοῦ.
10 Οἱ δὲ ἀσεβεῖς καθ' ἃ ἐλογίσαντο ἕξουσιν ἐπιτιμίαν,
οἱ ἀμελήσαντες τοῦ δικαίου καὶ τοῦ Κυρίου ἀποστάντες.
11 σοφίαν γὰρ καὶ παιδείαν ὁ ἐξουθενῶν ταλαίπωρος,
καὶ κενὴ ἡ ἐλπὶς αὐτῶν, καὶ οἱ κόποι ἀνόνητοι,
καὶ ἄχρηστα τὰ ἔργα αὐτῶν.
12 αἱ γυναῖκες αὐτῶν ἄφρονες, καὶ πονηρὰ τὰ τέκνα αὐτῶν·
13 ἐπικατάρατος ἡ γένεσις αὐτῶν. ὅτι μακαρία στεῖρα ἡ ἀμίαντος,
ἥτις οὐκ ἔγνω κοίτην ἐν παραπτώματι,
ἕξει καρπὸν ἐν ἐπισκοπῇ ψυχῶν·
14 καὶ εὐνοῦχος, ὁ μὴ ἐργασάμενος ἐν χειρὶ ἀνόμημα,
μηδὲ ἐνθυμηθεὶς κατὰ τοῦ Κυρίου πονηρά·
δοθήσεται γὰρ αὐτῷ τῆς πίστεως χάρις ἐκλεκτή

8 neto discurrent. Judicabunt nationes, et dominabuntur populis, et regnabit Dominus illo- 9 rum in perpetuum. Qui confidunt in illo intelligent veritatem, et fideles in dilectione acquiescent illi; quoniam donum et pax est electis ejus. 10 Impii autem secundum quae cogitaverunt correptionem habebunt, qui neglexerunt justum, 11 et a Domino recesserunt. Sapientiam enim et disciplinam qui abjicit, infelix est; et vacua est spes illorum, et labores sine fructu, et inutilia 12 opera eorum. Mulieres eorum insensatae sunt, et nequissimi 13 filii eorum. Maledicta creatura eorum, quoniam felix est sterilis et incoinquinata, quae nescivit thorum in delicto; habebit fructum in respectione 14 animarum sanctarum. Et spado, qui non operatus est per manus suas iniquitatem, nec cogitavit adversus Deum nequissima;

---

9. ἐπ' αὐτῷ. επι Κυριου Ven. χαρις και ελεος τοις εκλεκτοις αυτου V. Vulg. al. χαρ. και ελ. εν τοις εκλ. αυτου και επιτκοπη εν τοις οσιοις αυτου Λ. Ven. ελεος τ. οσιοις αυτ. και επισκοπη εν τ. εκλ. αυτου S. εν τ. οσιοις Ald. Compl. Ita Syr. Arm. Ar.
10. καθα ed. rom. ἐπιτιμίαν, ατιμιαν 248.   11. σοφιαν δε S. γαρ S². παιδειαν V. παιδιαν A. S. κοποι αυτων ανονητοι S.
12. αι γυν. A. V. και αι S.   13. γεννησεις S. η ante αμαρτ. om. S. ψυχων αυτων Λ.   14. ὁ μή. ο om. S. εν χειρι S. V. A. εν χερσιν Ven.

dabitur enim illi fidei donum electum, et sors in templo Dei
15 acceptissima. Bonorum enim laborum gloriosus est fructus, et quae non concidat radix sa-
16 pientiae. Filii autem adulterorum in inconsummatione erunt, et ab iniquo thoro semen
17 exterminabitur. Et si quidem longae vitae erunt, in nihilum computabuntur, et sine honore erit novissima senectus illorum.
18 Et si celerius defuncti fuerint, non habebunt spem, nec in die
19 agnitionis allocutionem. Nationis enim iniquae dirae sunt consummationes.

CAPUT IV.

1 O quam pulchra est casta generatio cum claritate! immortalis est enim memoria illius, quoniam et apud Deum nota est et apud homines.
2 Cum praesens est, imitantur illam, et desiderant eam cum se eduxerit; et in perpetuum coronata triumphat incoinquinatorum certaminum praemium
3 vincens. Multigena autem impiorum multitudo non erit utilis,

καὶ κλῆρος ἐν ναῷ Κυρίου θυμηρέστερος.
15 ἀγαθῶν γὰρ πόνων καρπὸς εὐκλεής,
καὶ ἀδιάπτωτος ἡ ῥίζα τῆς φρονήσεως.
16 τέκνα δὲ μοιχῶν ἀτέλεστα ἔσται, καὶ ἐκ παρανόμου κοίτης σπέρμα ἀφανισθήσεται.
17 ἐάν τε γὰρ μακρόβιοι γένωνται, εἰς οὐδὲν λογισθήσονται,
καὶ ἄτιμον ἐπ' ἐσχάτων τὸ γῆρας αὐτῶν.
18 ἐάν τε ὀξέως τελευτήσωσιν, οὐχ ἕξουσιν ἐλπίδα,
οὐδὲ ἐν ἡμέρᾳ διαγνώσεως παραμύθιον.
19 γενεᾶς γὰρ ἀδίκου χαλεπὰ τὰ τέλη.

ΚΕΦΑΛΑΙΟΝ Δ'.

1 Κρείσσων ἀτεκνία μετὰ ἀρετῆς· ἀθανασία γάρ ἐστιν ἐν μνήμῃ αὐτῆς,
ὅτι καὶ παρὰ Θεῷ γινώσκεται καὶ παρὰ ἀνθρώποις.
2 παροῦσάν τε μιμοῦνται αὐτήν, καὶ ποθοῦσιν ἀπελθοῦσαν·
καὶ ἐν τῷ αἰῶνι στεφανηφοροῦσα πομπεύει,
τὸν τῶν ἀμιάντων ἄθλων ἀγῶνα νικήσασα.
3 πολύγονον δὲ ἀσεβῶν πλῆθος οὐ χρησιμεύσει,

in[1] the temple of the Lord more acceptable to his mind.
15 For glorious is the fruit of good labours: and the root of wis-
16 dom shall never fall away. As for the children of adulterers, they shall not come[2] to their perfection, and the seed of an unrighteous bed shall be rooted
17 out. For though they live long, yet shall they be nothing regarded: and their last age shall
18 be without honour. Or, if they die quickly, they have no hope, neither comfort in the day of
19 trial[3]. For horrible is the end of the unrighteous generation.

[1] Or, among the people.

[2] Or, be partakers of holy things.

[3] Or, hearing.

CHAPTER IV.

1 Better it is to have no children, and to have virtue: for the memorial thereof is immortal: because it is known[4] with God, and with men.
2 When it is present, men take example at it; and when it is gone, they desire it: it weareth a crown, and triumpheth for ever, having gotten the victory, striving for undefiled rewards. But the multiplying

[4] Or, approved.

---

14. θυμηδέστερος Ven. 253. 15. ὁ καρπὸς V¹. 17. εἰς οὐδὲν Compl. 55. 106. 254. 261. 18. S. ita: (εαν τε γὰρ οξεως τελευτησουσιν) εις ουδεν λογισθησονται (και ατιμον επ' εσχατον το γηρας αυτων) εαν τε γὰρ οξεως τελευτησουσιν ουχ εξουσιν ελπιδα. ουχ εχουσιν V. 19. χαλεπὰ πονηρα 106. 261. IV. 1. Κρεισσων γαρ S. γαρ om. S¹. 2. μιμουνται S. V. Ven. Vulg. Syr. Ar. Arm. τιμωσιν A. Method. 676. πομπεύει. MS. A: τοπεμπει. ‡ αποπεμπει Tisch.

brood of the ungodly shall not thrive, nor take deep rooting from bastard slips, nor lay any 4 fast foundation. For though they flourish in branches for a time; yet standing not fast, they shall be shaken with the wind, and through the force of winds they shall be rooted 5 out. The imperfect branches shall be broken off, their fruit unprofitable, not ripe to eat, 6 yea, meet for nothing. For children begotten of unlawful beds[1] are witnesses of wickedness against their parents in 7 their trial. But though the righteous be prevented with death, yet shall he be in rest. 8 For honourable age is not that which standeth in length of time, nor that is measured by 9 number of years. But wisdom is the grey hair unto men, and an unspotted life is old age. 10 He pleased God, and was beloved of him: so that living among sinners he was trans- 11 lated. Yea, speedily was he taken away, lest that wickedness should alter his understanding, or deceit beguile his

[1] Gr. *dequ.*

καὶ ἐκ νόθων μοσχευμάτων οὐ
δώσει ῥίζαν εἰς βάθος,
οὐδὲ ἀσφαλῆ βάσιν ἑδράσει.
4 κἂν γὰρ ἐν κλάδοις πρὸς καιρὸν
ἀναθάλῃ,
ἐπισφαλῶς βεβηκότα ὑπὸ ἀνέμου σαλευθήσεται,
καὶ ὑπὸ βίας ἀνέμων ἐκριζωθήσεται·
5 περικλασθήσονται κλῶνες ἀτέλεστοι,
καὶ ὁ καρπὸς αὐτῶν ἄχρηστος,
ἄωρος εἰς βρῶσιν, καὶ εἰς οὐθὲν
ἐπιτήδειος.
6 ἐκ γὰρ ἀνόμων ὕπνων τέκνα
γεννώμενα
μάρτυρές εἰσι πονηρίας κατὰ
γονέων ἐν ἐξετασμῷ αὐτῶν.
7 Δίκαιος δὲ ἐὰν φθάσῃ
τελευτῆσαι, ἐν ἀναπαύσει
ἔσται.
8 γῆρας γὰρ τίμιον οὐ τὸ πολυχρόνιον,
οὐδὲ ἀριθμῷ ἐτῶν μεμέτρηται·
9 πολιὰ δέ ἐστι φρόνησις ἀνθρώποις,
καὶ ἡλικία γήρως βίος ἀκηλίδωτος.
10 εὐάρεστος Θεῷ γενόμενος ἠγαπήθη,
καὶ ζῶν μεταξὺ ἁμαρτωλῶν
μετετέθη·
11 ἡρπάγη, μὴ ἡ κακία ἀλλάξῃ
σύνεσιν αὐτοῦ,
ἢ δόλος ἀπατήσῃ ψυχὴν αὐτοῦ.

et spuria vitulamina non dabunt radices altas, nec stabile 4 firmamentum collocabunt. Et si in ramis in tempore germinaverint, infirmiter positi, a vento commovebuntur, et a nimietate ventorum eradicabuntur. 5 Confringentur enim rami inconsummati; et fructus illorum inutiles et acerbi ad manducandum, et ad nihilum apti. 6 Ex iniquis enim somnis filii qui nascuntur testes sunt nequitiae adversus parentes in interrogatione sua.

7 Justus autem si morte praeoccupatus fuerit, in refrigerio 8 erit. Senectus enim venerabilis est non diuturna, neque annorum numero computata; cani 9 autem sunt sensus hominis, et aetas senectutis vita immaculata. 10 Placens Deo factus est dilectus, et vivens inter peccatores trans- 11 latus est. Raptus est, ne malitia mutaret intellectum ejus, aut ne fictio deciperet animam

---

3. μοχευματων S. μοσχ. S². 4. κἂν γάρ. και γαρ S¹. καν S². βεβηκότα. βεβιωκοτα S. βεβηκοτα S¹. 5. αυτων κλωνες S. 106. 253. 261. αυτ. S. corr. improb. ατελεστοι V. S. ατελεστατοι A. 9. ἀνθρώποις. εν ανθρ. S². 10. τῳ θεῷ S. V. om. τῳ A. Ven. V¹. γενομ. θ. Ven. 11. μη η κακια S. Compl. μη κακ. V. A. πριν η κακ. Ven. Theod. iv. 1227. αυτου post συνεσιν om. S. add. S². ἀπατήσῃ. απατησει S.

12 illius. Fascinatio enim nugacitatis obscurat bona, et inconstantia concupiscentiae transvertit sensum sine malitia.
13 Consummatus in brevi explevit
14 tempora multa; placita enim erat Deo anima illius; propter hoc properavit educere illum de medio iniquitatum. Populi autem videntes et non intelligentes, nec ponentes in prae-
15 cordiis talia, quoniam gratia Dei, et misericordia est in sanctos ejus, et respectus in electos
16 illius. Condemnat autem justus mortuus vivos impios, et juventus celerius consummata
17 longam vitam injusti. Videbunt enim finem sapientis, et non intelligent quid cogitaverit de illo Deus, et quare munierit
18 illum Dominus. Videbunt, et contemnent eum; illos autem Dominus irridebit; et erunt post haec decidentes sine honore, et in contumelia inter
19 mortuos in perpetuum; quoniam disrumpet illos inflatos

12 (βασκανία γὰρ φαυλότητος ἀμαυροῖ τὰ καλά,
 καὶ ῥεμβασμὸς ἐπιθυμίας μεταλλεύει νοῦν ἄκακον.)
13 τελειωθεὶς ἐν ὀλίγῳ ἐπλήρωσε χρόνους μακρούς.
14 ἀρεστὴ γὰρ ἦν Κυρίῳ ἡ ψυχὴ αὐτοῦ·
 διὰ τοῦτο ἔσπευσεν ἐκ μέσου πονηρίας.
15 οἱ δὲ λαοὶ ἰδόντες καὶ μὴ νοήσαντες,
 μηδὲ θέντες ἐπὶ διανοίᾳ τὸ τοιοῦτο,
 ὅτι χάρις καὶ ἔλεος ἐν τοῖς ἐκλεκτοῖς αὐτοῦ,
 καὶ ἐπισκοπὴ ἐν τοῖς ὁσίοις αὐτοῦ.
16 κατακρινεῖ δὲ δίκαιος καμὼν τοὺς ζῶντας ἀσεβεῖς,
 καὶ νεότης τελεσθεῖσα ταχέως πολυετὲς γῆρας ἀδίκου.
17 ὄψονται γὰρ τελευτὴν σοφοῦ,
 καὶ οὐ νοήσουσι τί ἐβουλεύσατο περὶ αὐτοῦ,
 καὶ εἰς τί ἠσφαλίσατο αὐτὸν ὁ Κύριος.
18 ὄψονται καὶ ἐξουθενήσουσιν,
 αὐτοὺς δὲ ὁ Κύριος ἐκγελάσεται·
 καὶ ἔσονται μετὰ τοῦτο εἰς πτῶμα ἄτιμον,
 καὶ εἰς ὕβριν ἐν νεκροῖς δι᾿ αἰῶνος.
19 ὅτι ῥήξει αὐτοὺς ἀφώνους πρηνεῖς,

12 soul. For the bewitching of naughtiness doth obscure things that are honest; and the wandering of concupiscence doth undermine[1] the simple mind. [1] Gr. *pervert*
13 He, being made perfect[2] in a [2] Or, *satisfied, or, ruined* short time, fulfilled a long time:
14 For his soul pleased the Lord: therefore hasted he *to take him away* from among the wicked.
15 This the people saw, and understood it not, neither laid they up this in their minds, That his grace and mercy is with his saints, and that he hath respect
16 unto his chosen. Thus the righteous that is dead shall condemn the ungodly which are living; and youth that is soon perfected the many years and
17 old age of the unrighteous. For they shall see the end of the wise, and shall not understand what God in his counsel hath decreed of him, and to what end the Lord hath set him in safety.
18 They shall see him, and despise him; but God shall laugh them to scorn: and they shall hereafter be a vile carcase, and a reproach among the dead for
19 evermore. For he shall rend them, and cast them down head-

---

14. εν κυριῳ S. εν impr. S². ην εν 106. leguntur in A. Vulg. Compl. Ald. Syr. Ar. Arm. νεοτης V. S. Compl. νεοτητος A. Ald. αυτον Ven. οψονται αυτον και S¹. οψ. γαρ και S². 15. λαοι. αλλοι A cor. 155. 296. εν bis om. S. εκλεκτ. et οσιοις inv. ord. 16. καμων V. S. Ven. θανων A. V². Compl. Ald. θανατῳ 106. 261. B. Par. 17. ησφαλισατο. ησφαλισας. αυτον. εαυτον 106. 248. Compl. 18. εξουθεν. δι᾿ αιωνος S. V. om. δι᾿ A.

[1 Or, to the casting up of the account.]

long, that they shall be speechless; and he shall shake them from the foundation; and they shall be utterly laid waste, and be in sorrow; and their memorial shall perish. And when[1] they cast up the accounts of their sins, they shall come with fear: and their own iniquities shall convince them to their face.

CHAPTER V.

1 Then shall the righteous man stand in great boldness before the face of such as have afflicted him, and made no account of 2 his labours. When they see it, they shall be troubled with terrible fear, and shall be amazed at the strangeness of his salvation, so far beyond all that they 3 looked for. And they repenting and groaning for anguish of spirit shall say within themselves, This was he, whom we had sometimes in derision, and 4 a proverb[2] of reproach: We fools accounted his life madness, and his end to be without ho-5 nour: How is he numbered

[2 Or, parable.]

καὶ σαλεύσει αὐτοὺς ἐκ θεμελίων,
καὶ ἕως ἐσχάτου χερσωθήσονται, καὶ ἔσονται ἐν ὀδύνῃ,
καὶ ἡ μνήμη αὐτῶν ἀπολεῖται.
20 ἐλεύσονται ἐν συλλογισμῷ ἁμαρτημάτων αὐτῶν δειλοί,
καὶ ἐλέγξει αὐτοὺς ἐξεναντίας τὰ ἀνομήματα αὐτῶν.

ΚΕΦΑΛΑΙΟΝ Ε΄.

1 Τότε στήσεται ἐν παρρησίᾳ πολλῇ ὁ δίκαιος
κατὰ πρόσωπον τῶν θλιψάντων αὐτὸν
καὶ τῶν ἀθετούντων τοὺς πόνους αὐτοῦ.
2 ἰδόντες ταραχθήσονται φόβῳ δεινῷ,
καὶ ἐκστήσονται ἐπὶ τῷ παραδόξῳ τῆς σωτηρίας.
3 ἐροῦσιν ἐν ἑαυτοῖς μετανοοῦντες,
καὶ διὰ στενοχωρίαν πνεύματος στενάζοντες· καὶ ἐροῦσιν·
οὗτος ἦν ὃν ἔσχομέν ποτε εἰς γέλωτα
καὶ εἰς παραβολὴν ὀνειδισμοῦ.
4 οἱ ἄφρονες τὸν βίον αὐτοῦ ἐλογισάμεθα μανίαν,
καὶ τὴν τελευτὴν αὐτοῦ ἄτιμον.
5 πῶς κατελογίσθη ἐν υἱοῖς Θεοῦ,

sine voce, et commovebit illos a fundamentis, et usque ad supremum desolabuntur; et erunt gementes, et memoria il-20 lorum peribit. Venient in cogitatione peccatorum suorum timidi, et traducent illos ex adverso iniquitates ipsorum.

CAPUT V.

1 Tunc stabunt justi in magna constantia adversus eos qui se angustiaverunt, et qui abstu-2 lerunt labores eorum. Videntes turbabuntur timore horribili, et mirabuntur in subitatione in-3 speratae salutis; dicentes intra se, poenitentiam agentes, et prae angustia spiritus gementes: Hi sunt quos habuimus aliquando in derisum, et in simi-4 litudinem improperii. Nos insensati vitam illorum aestimabamus insaniam, et finem illorum 5 sine honore; ecce quomodo

---

19. σαλευσει S. V. A. σαλευθησει Ven. ἐσχάτου. εσχατων A. 20. δηλοι S². τὰ ἀνομήματα. τα νοηματα 155. V. 1. ὁ δικαιος εν παρρ. πολ. Ven. θλιψαντων S.V. θλιψοντων A. πόνους. λογους 55. 254. 2. σωτηριας αυτου S. 55. 253. 254. 3. ερουσιν S. V. και ερουσιν A. Compl. ερουσιν γαρ Ven. al. εαυτοις S. εν εαυτ. V. A. Ven. 55 Compl. Ald. Vulg. Ephr. στεναζοντες V. Vulg. στεναζουσιν και ερουσιν S. Ven. στεναζονται και ερουσιν A. Compl. Ald. 4. οι αφρονες cum anteced. conj. A. S. ημεις οι αφρ. Von. 253. ατιμαν S. ατιμον S².

THE BOOK OF WISDOM.

computati sunt inter filios Dei, et inter sanctos sors illorum est. 6 Ergo erravimus a via veritatis, et justitiae lumen non luxit nobis, et sol intelligentiae non 7 est ortus nobis. Lassati sumus in via iniquitatis et perditionis, et ambulavimus vias difficiles, viam autem Domini ignoravi- 8 mus. Quid nobis profuit superbia? aut divitiarum jactantia 9 quid contulit nobis? Transierunt omnia illa tanquam umbra, et tanquam nuntius percurrens, 10 et tanquam navis, quae pertransit fluctuantem aquam, cujus, cum praeterierit, non est vestigium invenire, neque semitam 11 carinae illius in fluctibus; aut tanquam avis quae transvolat in aëre, cujus nullum invenitur argumentum itineris, sed tantum sonitus alarum verberans levem ventum, et scindens per vim itineris aërem; commotis alis

καὶ ἐν ἁγίοις ὁ κλῆρος αὐτοῦ ἐστιν·
6 ἄρα ἐπλανήθημεν ἀπὸ ὁδοῦ ἀληθείας,
καὶ τὸ τῆς δικαιοσύνης φῶς οὐκ ἔλαμψεν ἡμῖν,
καὶ ὁ ἥλιος οὐκ ἀνέτειλεν ἡμῖν.
7 ἀνομίας ἐνεπλήσθημεν τρίβοις καὶ ἀπωλείας,
καὶ διωδεύσαμεν ἐρήμους ἀβάτους,
τὴν δὲ ὁδὸν Κυρίου οὐκ ἔγνωμεν.
8 τί ὠφέλησεν ἡμᾶς ἡ ὑπερηφανία;
καὶ τί πλοῦτος μετὰ ἀλαζονείας συμβέβληται ἡμῖν;
9 παρῆλθεν ἐκεῖνα πάντα ὡς σκιά
καὶ ὡς ἀγγελία παρατρέχουσα·
10 ὡς ναῦς διερχομένη κυμαινόμενον ὕδωρ,
ἧς διαβάσης οὐκ ἔστιν ἴχνος εὑρεῖν,
οὐδὲ ἀτραπὸν τρόπιος αὐτῆς ἐν κύμασιν·
11 ἢ ὡς ὀρνέου διαπτάντος ἀέρα οὐθὲν εὑρίσκεται τεκμήριον πορείας,
πληγῇ δὲ ταρσῶν μαστιζόμενον πνεῦμα κοῦφον
καὶ σχιζόμενον βίᾳ ῥοίζου κινουμένων πτερύγων διωδεύθη,

among the children of God, and his lot is among the saints! 6 Therefore have we erred from the way of truth, and the light of righteousness hath not shined unto us, and the sun of right- 7 eousness rose not upon us. We wearied ourselves[1] in the way of wickedness and destruction: yea, we have gone through deserts, where there lay no way: but as for the way of the Lord, 8 we have not known it. What hath pride profited us? or what good hath riches with *our* vaunt- 9 ing brought us? All those things are passed away like a shadow, and as a post that 10 hasted by; And as a ship that passeth over the waves of the water, which when it is gone by, the trace thereof cannot be found, neither the pathway of 11 the keel in the waves; Or as when a bird hath flown[2] through [2 Or, *flieth.*] the air, there is no token of her way to be found, but the light air being beaten with the stroke of her wings, and parted with the violent noise and motion

[1 Or, *filled ourselves*; or, *surfeited.*]

---

6. ελαμψεν V. A. επελαμψεν S. Ven. Ephr.   ημιν και V. S.   εν ημιν και A.   ηλιος της δικαιοσυνης Ven. Compl. Arm.
7. διωδευσαμεν S. V. ωδευσαμεν A.   εγνωμεν V. A. επεγνωμεν S.   8. υπερηφανια ημων Ven. 253.   και τι V. S.   η τι A. Vulg.   αλαζονιας A. S.   συνβεβληται S.   10. η ως S².   τροπιος V.   τροπιας S.   τροπεως S². A.   τριβον V¹.
11. διπταντος V. Ephr. διαπταντος A. S. V². Compl. Ald.   πορειας.   πονηριας S.   ποριας S².   μαστιζ. ταρσων V¹.   εν αυτῳ. αυτου S. Ephr.   εν αυτῳ S².

THE BOOK OF WISDOM.

of them, is passed through, and therein afterwards no sign where 12 she went is to be found; Or like as when an arrow is shot at a mark, it parteth the air, which immediately cometh together again, so that a man cannot know where it went through: 13 Even so we in like manner, as soon as we were born, began to draw to our end, and had no sign of virtue to shew; but were consumed in our own 14 wickedness. For the hope of the ungodly is like dust[1] that is blown away with the wind; like a thin froth that is driven away with the storm; like as the smoke[2] which is dispersed here and there with a tempest, and passeth away as the remembrance of a guest that tarrieth but a day. But the righteous live for evermore; their reward also is with the Lord, and the care of them is with 16 the most High. Therefore shall they receive a glorious kingdom[3], and a beautiful crown from the Lord's hand: for with his right hand shall he cover them, and with his arm shall 17 he protect them. He shall take to him his jealousy for complete

[1] Gr. thistledown.

[2] Or, chaff.

[3] Or, palace; unless the word be taken improperly, as 2 Mac. 2. 17.

καὶ μετὰ τοῦτο οὐχ εὑρέθη σημεῖον ἐπιβάσεως ἐν αὐτῷ·
12 ἢ ὡς βέλους βληθέντος ἐπὶ σκοπὸν
τμηθεὶς ὁ ἀὴρ εὐθέως εἰς ἑαυτὸν ἀνελύθη,
ὡς ἀγνοῆσαι τὴν δίοδον αὐτοῦ·
13 οὕτως καὶ ἡμεῖς γεννηθέντες ἐξελίπομεν·
καὶ ἀρετῆς μὲν σημεῖον οὐδὲν ἔσχομεν δεῖξαι,
ἐν δὲ τῇ κακίᾳ ἡμῶν κατεδαπανήθημεν.
14 ὅτι ἐλπὶς ἀσεβοῦς ὡς φερόμενος χνοῦς ὑπὸ ἀνέμου,
καὶ ὡς πάχνη ὑπὸ λαίλαπος διωχθεῖσα λεπτή,
καὶ ὡς καπνὸς ὑπὸ ἀνέμου διεχύθη,
καὶ ὡς μνεία καταλύτου μονοημέρου παρώδευσε.
15 Δίκαιοι δὲ εἰς τὸν αἰῶνα ζῶσι,
καὶ ἐν Κυρίῳ ὁ μισθὸς αὐτῶν,
καὶ ἡ φροντὶς αὐτῶν παρὰ Ὑψίστῳ.
16 διὰ τοῦτο λήψονται τὸ βασίλειον τῆς εὐπρεπείας
καὶ τὸ διάδημα τοῦ κάλλους ἐκ χειρὸς Κυρίου·
ὅτι τῇ δεξιᾷ σκεπάσει αὐτούς,
καὶ τῷ βραχίονι ὑπερασπιεῖ αὐτῶν.
17 λήψεται πανοπλίαν τὸν ζῆλον αὐτοῦ,

transvolavit, et post hoc nullum signum invenitur itineris illius; 12 aut tanquam sagitta emissa in locum destinatum, divisus aër continuo in se reclusus est, ut 13 ignoretur transitus illius; sic et nos nati continuo desivimus esse; et virtutis quidem nullum signum valuimus ostendere, in malignitate autem nostra 14 consumti sumus. Talia dixerunt in inferno hi, qui peccaverunt; 15 [14] quoniam spes impii tanquam lanugo est, quae a vento tollitur; et tanquam spuma gracilis, quae a procella dispergitur; et tanquam fumus, qui a vento diffusus est; et tanquam memoria hospitis unius diei praetereuntis.
16 [15] Justi autem in perpetuum vivent, et apud Dominum est merces eorum, et cogitatio illo17 rum apud Altissimum. [16] Ideo accipient regnum decoris, et diadema speciei de manu Domini; quoniam dextera sua teget eos, et brachio sancto suo 18 defendet illos. [17] Accipiet ar-

---

12. ανελυσεν Ven. την οδον S. διοδον S². Apcl. al. χνους S. A. V. Ven. Compl. Ald. Vulg. διελυθη 248. Compl. ως μνειαν S. η ως μνεια S². διωδευσεν S. 15. φροντις. φροντησις 248. Compl. τη δ. αυτου 106. Compl. υπερασπισει αυτου S. imp. S². 13. γενηθεντες V. εξελιπομεν S. V. εξελειπομεν A. Compl. 14. χους παχνη V. A. S. αχνη 157. F. G. Par. Vulg. Syr. αραχνη Ven. διεχυθη. η και ως μνεια 248 Compl. μονοημερου. μονημερου S. παρωδευσε V. A. 16. λημφονται S. A. Ita vv. 17. 19 λημψεται. δεξια κυριου S. 17. το ζηλος S. imp. S².

THE BOOK OF WISDOM.

maturam zelus illius, et armabit creaturam ad ultionem inimi-
19 corum. [18] Induet pro thorace justitiam, et accipiet pro galea
20 judicium certum: [19] sumet scutum inexpugnabile, aequitatem;
21 [20] acuet autem duram iram in lanceam, et pugnabit cum illo orbis terrarum contra insen-
22 satos. [21] Ibunt directe emissiones fulgurum, et tanquam a bene curvato arcu nubium exterminabuntur, et ad certum locum
23 insilient. [22] Et a petrosa ira plenae mittentur grandines; excandescet in illos aqua maris, et flumina concurrent duriter.
24 [23] Contra illos stabit spiritus virtutis, et tanquam turbo venti dividet illos; et ad eremum perducet omnem terram iniqnitas illorum, et malignitas evertet sedes potentium.

καὶ ὁπλοποιήσει τὴν κτίσιν εἰς ἄμυναν ἐχθρῶν·
18 ἐνδύσεται θώρακα δικαιοσύνην, καὶ περιθήσεται κόρυθα κρίσιν ἀνυπόκριτον·
19 λήψεται ἀσπίδα ἀκαταμάχητον ὁσιότητα,
20 ὀξυνεῖ δὲ ἀπότομον ὀργὴν εἰς ῥομφαίαν,
συνεκπολεμήσει δὲ αὐτῷ ὁ κόσμος ἐπὶ τοὺς παράφρονας.
21 πορεύσονται εὔστοχοι βολίδες ἀστραπῶν,
καὶ ὡς ἀπὸ εὐκύκλου τόξου τῶν νεφῶν ἐπὶ σκοπὸν ἁλοῦνται·
22 καὶ ἐκ πετροβόλου θυμοῦ πλήρεις ῥιφήσονται χάλαζαι·
ἀγανακτήσει κατ' αὐτῶν ὕδωρ θαλάσσης,
ποταμοὶ δὲ συγκλύσουσιν ἀποτόμως·
23 ἀντιστήσεται αὐτοῖς πνεῦμα δυνάμεως,
καὶ ὡς λαῖλαψ ἐκλικμήσει αὐτούς·
καὶ ἐρημώσει πᾶσαν τὴν γῆν ἀνομία,
καὶ ἡ κακοπραγία περιτρέψει θρόνους δυναστῶν.

armour, and make the creature his weapon for the revenge of
18 his enemies. He shall put on righteousness as a breastplate, and true judgment instead of
19 an helmet. He shall take holiness[1] for an invincible shield.[1]
20 His severe wrath shall he sharpen for a sword, and the world shall fight with him against the un-
21 wise. Then shall the right aiming thunderbolts go abroad; and from the clouds, as from a well drawn bow, shall they fly
22 to the mark. And hailstones full of wrath shall be cast as out of a stone bow, and the water of the sea shall rage against them, and the floods
23 shall cruelly drown them. Yea, a mighty wind shall stand up against them, and like a storm shall blow them away: thus iniquity shall lay waste the whole earth, and ill dealing shall overthrow the thrones of the mighty.

CAPUT VI.

1 Melior est sapientia quam vires, et vir prudens quam fortis.
2 [1] Audite ergo, reges, et intelligite; discite, judices finium ter-

ΚΕΦΑΛΑΙΟΝ ϛ'.

1 Ἀκούσατε οὖν, βασιλεῖς, καὶ σύνετε,
μάθετε, δικασταὶ περάτων γῆς·

CHAPTER VI.

1 Hear therefore, O ye kings, and understand; learn, ye that be judges of the ends of the earth.

---

17. ὁπλοποιήσει. ὁδοποιήσει S. imp. S¹. δε ante αυτ. om. A. al. 21. ευστροφοι 253. ποτ. τε S. συγκλυσουσιν S. V. συγκλυσουσιν Α. 18. δικαιοσυνης S. Ven. al. νεφων. νεφελων S. συγκλεισουσιν 106. 157. 261. και περιθησεται δε Ven. 22. και εκ. και om. S. 20. συνπολεμησει S. πληρης S. ποταμοι δε. 23. εκλιμμησει A. λικμησει 296.
VI. 1. βασιλευς S. βασιλεις S².

2 Give ear, ye that rule the people, and glory in the multitude of
3 nations. For power is given you of the Lord, and sovereignty from the Highest, who shall try your works, and search
4 out your counsels. Because, being ministers of his kingdom, ye have not judged aright, nor kept the law, nor walked after
5 the counsel of God; Horribly and speedily shall he come upon you: for a sharp judgment shall be to them that be in high
6 places. For mercy will soon pardon the meanest: but mighty men shall be mightily tormented.
7 For he which is Lord over all shall fear no man's person, neither shall he stand in awe of any man's greatness: for he hath made the small and great,
8 and careth for all alike. But a sore trial shall come upon the
9 mighty. Unto you therefore, O kings, do I speak, that ye may learn wisdom, and not fall away.

2 ἐνωτίσασθε, οἱ κρατοῦντες πλήθους,
καὶ γεγαυρωμένοι ἐπὶ ὄχλοις ἐθνῶν·
3 ὅτι ἐδόθη παρὰ τοῦ Κυρίου ἡ κράτησις ὑμῖν,
καὶ ἡ δυναστεία παρὰ Ὑψίστου,
ὃς ἐξετάσει ὑμῶν τὰ ἔργα,
καὶ τὰς βουλὰς διερευνήσει.
4 ὅτι ὑπηρέται ὄντες τῆς αὐτοῦ βασιλείας οὐκ ἐκρίνατε ὀρθῶς,
οὐδὲ ἐφυλάξατε νόμον,
οὐδὲ κατὰ τὴν βουλὴν τοῦ Θεοῦ ἐπορεύθητε.
5 φρικτῶς καὶ ταχέως ἐπιστήσεται ὑμῖν,
ὅτι κρίσις ἀπότομος ἐν τοῖς ὑπερέχουσιν γίνεται.
6 ὁ γὰρ ἐλάχιστος συγγνωστός ἐστιν ἐλέους,
δυνατοὶ δὲ δυνατῶς ἐτασθήσονται.
7 οὐ γὰρ ὑποστελεῖται πρόσωπον ὁ πάντων Δεσπότης,
οὐδὲ ἐντραπήσεται μέγεθος·
ὅτι μικρὸν καὶ μέγαν αὐτὸς ἐποίησεν,
ὁμοίως τε προνοεῖ περὶ πάντων·
8 τοῖς δὲ κραταιοῖς ἰσχυρὰ ἐφίσταται ἔρευνα.
9 πρὸς ὑμᾶς οὖν, ὦ τύραννοι, οἱ λόγοι μου,
ἵνα μάθητε σοφίαν καὶ μὴ παραπέσητε.

3 rae. [2] Praebete aures vos, qui continetis multitudines, et placetis vobis in turbis nationum:
4 [3] quoniam data est a Domino potestas vobis, et virtus ab Altissimo, qui interrogabit opera vestra, et cogitationes scruta-
5 bitur; [4] quoniam cum essetis ministri regni illius, non recte judicastis, nec custodistis legem justitiae, neque secundum volun-
6 tatem Dei ambulastis. [5] Horrende et cito apparebit vobis; quoniam judicium durissimum
7 his qui praesunt fiet. [6] Exiguo enim conceditur misericordia; potentes autem potenter
8 tormenta patientur. [7] Non enim subtrahet personam cujusquam Deus, nec verebitur magnitudinem cujusquam, quoniam pusillum et magnum ipse fecit, et aequaliter cura est illi
9 de omnibus. [8] Fortioribus autem fortior instat cruciatio.
10 [9] Ad vos ergo, reges, sunt hi sermones mei, ut discatis sapien-

---

2. επι οχλους S.   3. του om. A. al. Compl.   υμιν A. V. S. Ven.   υμων 106. 155.   ημων 261.   του υψιστ. Ven. 253.
4. διερευνησει A.   εξεραυνησει S.   εξερευνησει S².   διεραυνησει V.   5. επιστησεται υμιν ολεθρος Ven. al.   6. συγγνωστος V.
συγνωστος A. S².   ευγνωστος S.   εστιν om. 55. 254. 296.   ελεου A.   7. μέγαν.   μεγα 106. 155. 296.   προνοει A. V. Ven.
προνοειται S. Compl. al.   8. επισταται V.   εραυνα V.   ερευνα V².

THE BOOK OF WISDOM.

11 tiam, et non excidatis. [10] Qui enim custodierint justa juste, justificabuntur; et qui didi-
12 cerint ista, invenient quid respondeant. [11] Concupiscite ergo sermones meos, diligite illos, et habebitis disciplinam.
13 [12] Clara est, et quae nunquam marcescit, sapientia; et facile videtur ab his qui diligunt eam, et invenitur ab his qui quae-
14 runt illam. [13] Praeoccupat qui se concupiscunt, ut illis se prior
15 ostendat. [14] Qui de luce vigilaverit ad illam non laborabit; assidentem enim illam foribus
16 suis inveniet. [15] Cogitare ergo de illa sensus est consummatus; et qui vigilaverit propter illam
17 cito securus erit. [16] Quoniam dignos se ipsa circuit quaerens, et in viis ostendit se illis hilariter, et in omni providentia occurrit
18 illis. [17] Initium enim illius verissima est disciplinae con-
19 cupiscentia. [18] Cura ergo disciplinae, dilectio est; et dilectio custodia legum illius est; custoditio autem legum consummatio

10 οἱ γὰρ φυλάξαντες ὁσίως τὰ ὅσια ὁσιωθήσονται,
καὶ οἱ διδαχθέντες αὐτὰ εὑρήσουσιν ἀπολογίαν.
11 ἐπιθυμήσατε οὖν τῶν λόγων μου,
ποθήσατε καὶ παιδευθήσεσθε.
12 Λαμπρὰ καὶ ἀμάραντός ἐστιν ἡ σοφία,
καὶ εὐχερῶς θεωρεῖται ὑπὸ τῶν ἀγαπώντων αὐτήν,
καὶ εὑρίσκεται ὑπὸ τῶν ζητούντων αὐτήν·
13 φθάνει τοὺς ἐπιθυμοῦντας προγνωσθῆναι.
14 ὁ ὀρθρίσας ἐπ' αὐτὴν οὐ κοπιάσει,
πάρεδρον γὰρ εὑρήσει τῶν πυλῶν αὐτοῦ.
15 τὸ γὰρ ἐνθυμηθῆναι περὶ αὐτῆς φρονήσεως τελειότης,
καὶ ὁ ἀγρυπνήσας δι' αὐτὴν ταχέως ἀμέριμνος ἔσται·
16 ὅτι τοὺς ἀξίους αὐτῆς αὕτη περιέρχεται ζητοῦσα,
καὶ ἐν ταῖς τρίβοις φαντάζεται αὐτοῖς εὐμενῶς,
καὶ ἐν πάσῃ ἐπινοίᾳ ἀπαντᾷ αὐτοῖς.
17 ἀρχὴ γὰρ αὐτῆς ἡ ἀληθεστάτη παιδείας ἐπιθυμία,
18 φροντὶς δὲ παιδείας ἀγάπη,
ἀγάπη δὲ τήρησις νόμων αὐτῆς,
προσοχὴ δὲ νόμων βεβαίωσις ἀφθαρσίας,

10 For they that keep holiness holily shall be judged holy[1]: [1 Or, justifie]
and they that have learned such things shall find what to
11 answer[2]. Wherefore set your [2 Or, a defe] affection upon my words; desire them, and ye shall be in-
12 structed. Wisdom is glorious, and never fadeth away: yea, she is easily seen of them that love her, and found of such as
13 seek her. She preventeth them that desire her, in making herself first known unto them.
14 Whoso seeketh her early shall have no great travail: for he shall find her sitting at his
15 doors. To think therefore upon her is perfection of wisdom: and whoso watcheth for her shall quickly be without care.
16 For she goeth about seeking such as are worthy of her, sheweth herself favourably unto them in the ways, and meeteth
17 them in every thought. For the very true beginning of her is the desire of discipline[3]; and [3 Or, nurtur]
the care of discipline is love;
18 And love is the keeping of her laws; and the giving heed unto her laws is the assurance of in-

---

10. φυλαξοντες V. τα οσια οσιως S. 106. 261. 12. λαμπρα γαρ Ven. 253. 13. επιθυμ. αυτην S. 155. 261. αυτης 106. προ του γνωσθηναι 106. 261. 14. επ' αυτην S. V. προς αυτ. A. al. Compl. πυλων. πλουταν S. imp. S⁷. 15. περι αυτης ενθ. S. 16. αυτη om. S. 253. φαντ. αυτους Ven. al. απαντα S. A. Ven. al. Compl. υπαντα V. Clem. Al. 18. παιδ. αγάπη. παιδ. επιθυμια αγαπη S. αφθαρσια S. imp. S⁷.

19 corruption; And incorruption maketh us near unto God:
20 Therefore the desire of wisdom
21 bringeth to a kingdom. If your delight be then in thrones and sceptres, O ye kings of the people, honour wisdom, that ye
22 may reign for evermore. As for wisdom, what she is, and how she came up, I will tell you, and will not hide mysteries from you: but will seek her out from the beginning of her nativity, and bring the knowledge of her into light, and will not
23 pass over the truth. Neither will I go with consuming envy; for such a man shall have no
24 fellowship with wisdom. But the multitude of the wise is the welfare of the world: and a wise king is the upholding of
25 the people. Receive therefore instruction through my words, and it shall do you good.

19 ἀφθαρσία δὲ ἐγγὺς εἶναι ποιεῖ Θεοῦ·
20 ἐπιθυμία ἄρα σοφίας ἀνάγει ἐπὶ βασιλείαν.
21 εἰ οὖν ἥδεσθε ἐπὶ θρόνοις καὶ σκήπτροις, τύραννοι λαῶν, τιμήσατε σοφίαν, ἵνα εἰς τὸν αἰῶνα βασιλεύσητε.
22 Τί δέ ἐστι σοφία καὶ πῶς ἐγένετο, ἀπαγγελῶ,
καὶ οὐκ ἀποκρύψω ὑμῖν μυστήρια,
ἀλλ' ἀπ' ἀρχῆς γενέσεως ἐξιχνιάσω,
καὶ θήσω εἰς τὸ ἐμφανὲς τὴν γνῶσιν αὐτῆς,
καὶ οὐ μὴ παροδεύσω τὴν ἀλήθειαν·
23 οὔτε μὴν φθόνῳ τετηκότι συνοδεύσω,
ὅτι οὗτος οὐ κοινωνήσει σοφίᾳ.
24 πλῆθος δὲ σοφῶν σωτηρία κόσμου,
καὶ βασιλεὺς φρόνιμος εὐστάθεια δήμου.
25 ὥστε παιδεύεσθε τοῖς ῥήμασί μου, καὶ ὠφεληθήσεσθε.

20 incorruptionis est; [19] incorruptio autem facit esse proximum Deo. [20] Concupiscentia itaque sapientiae deducit ad regnum perpetuum. [21] Si ergo delectamini sedibus et sceptris, o reges populi, diligite sapientiam, ut in perpetuum regnetis.
23 Diligite lumen sapientiae, omnes
24 qui praeestis populis. [22] Quid est autem sapientia, et quemadmodum facta sit referam, et non abscondam a vobis sacramenta Dei; sed ab initio nativitatis investigabo, et ponam in lucem scientiam illius, et non
25 praeteribo veritatem. [23] Neque cum invidia tabescente iter habebo, quoniam talis homo non erit
26 particeps sapientiae. [24] Multitudo autem sapientium sanitas est orbis terrarum; et rex sapiens stabilimentum populi est.
27 [25] Ergo accipite disciplinam per sermones meos, et proderit vobis.

CHAPTER VII.

1 I myself also am a mortal man, like to all, and the offspring of him that was first made of the

ΚΕΦΑΛΑΙΟΝ Ζ´.

1 Εἰμὶ μὲν κἀγὼ θνητὸς ἄνθρωπος, ἴσος ἅπασιν,
καὶ γηγενοῦς ἀπόγονος πρωτοπλάστου.

CAPUT VII.

1 Sum quidem et ego mortalis homo, similis omnibus, et ex genere terreni illius qui prior factus est; et in ventre matris

---

20. επιθυμια γαρ ασοφιας A. επιθυμια γ' αρα σοφιας Field. επιθυμιας γαρ αναιρει επι βασ. S. επιθυμια γαρ σοφιας αναγει S². γαρ 106. 155. al.   21. ω τυραννοι Ven. al.   22. τις δε S. imp. cor.   εγενετο εν ανθρωποις 248.   23. ουτε μη D. Par. ουδε μη B. Par. 106. 261.   κοινωνησει V. S.   κοινωνει A. Ven. 55. 157.   VII. 1. ανθρωπος om. S. V².   απογονον S. απογονος S².

2 figuratus sum caro, decem mensium tempore coagulatus sum in sanguine, ex semine hominis, et delectamento somni conve-
3 niente. Et ego natus accepi communem aërem, et in similiter factam decidi terram, et primam vocem similem omnibus
4 emisi plorans. In involumentis nutritus sum, et curis magnis.
5 Nemo enim ex regibus aliud
6 habuit nativitatis initium. Unus ergo introitus est omnibus ad
7 vitam, et similis exitus. Propter hoc optavi, et datus est mihi sensus; et invocavi, et venit
8 in me spiritus sapientiae; et praeposui illam regnis et sedibus, et divitias nihil esse duxi
9 in comparatione illius; nec comparavi illi lapidem pretiosum, quoniam omne aurum in comparatione illius arena est exigua, et tanquam lutum aestimabitur argentum in conspectu
10 illius. Super salutem et speciem dilexi illam, et proposui

2 καὶ ἐν κοιλίᾳ μητρὸς ἐγλύφην σὰρξ δεκαμηνιαίῳ χρόνῳ,
παγεὶς ἐν αἵματι ἐκ σπέρματος ἀνδρὸς καὶ ἡδονῆς ὕπνῳ συνελθούσης.
3 καὶ ἐγὼ δὲ γενόμενος ἔσπασα τὸν κοινὸν ἀέρα,
καὶ ἐπὶ τὴν ὁμοιοπαθῆ κατέπεσον γῆν,
πρώτην φωνὴν τὴν ὁμοίαν πᾶσιν ἴσα κλαίων.
4 ἐν σπαργάνοις ἀνετράφην καὶ ἐν φροντίσιν.
5 οὐδεὶς γὰρ βασιλεὺς ἑτέραν ἔσχε γενέσεως ἀρχήν·
6 μία δὲ πάντων εἴσοδος εἰς τὸν βίον, ἔξοδός τε ἴση.
7 Διὰ τοῦτο ηὐξάμην, καὶ φρόνησις ἐδόθη μοι·
ἐπεκαλεσάμην, καὶ ἦλθέ μοι πνεῦμα σοφίας.
8 προέκρινα αὐτὴν σκήπτρων καὶ θρόνων,
καὶ πλοῦτον οὐδὲν ἡγησάμην ἐν συγκρίσει αὐτῆς·
9 οὐδὲ ὡμοίωσα αὐτῇ λίθον ἀτίμητον,
ὅτι ὁ πᾶς χρυσὸς ἐν ὄψει αὐτῆς ψάμμος ὀλίγη,
καὶ ὡς πηλὸς λογισθήσεται ἄργυρος ἐναντίον αὐτῆς.
10 ὑπὲρ ὑγίειαν καὶ εὐμορφίαν ἠγάπησα αὐτήν,
καὶ προειλόμην αὐτὴν ἀντὶ φωτὸς ἔχειν,

2 earth, And in my mother's womb was fashioned to be flesh in the time of ten months, being compacted in blood, of the seed of man, and the pleasure that
3 came with sleep. And when I was born, I drew in the common air, and fell upon the earth, which is of like nature, and the first voice which I uttered was
4 crying, as all others do. I was nursed in swaddling clothes,
5 and that with cares. For there is no king that had any other
6 beginning of birth. For all men have one entrance into life,
7 and the like going out. Wherefore I prayed, and understanding was given me: I called *upon God*, and the spirit of
8 wisdom came to me. I preferred her before sceptres and thrones, and esteemed riches nothing in comparison of her.
9 Neither compared I unto her any precious stone[1], because [1] Gr. *stone of inestimable price*.
all gold in respect of her is as a little sand, and silver shall be counted as clay before her.
10 I loved her above health and beauty, and chose to have her

---

2. υπνω V. A. υπνου S. Ven. Field. ομοιαν απασι κλαιων S. om. ισα. Ita F. Par. 3. κοινον ημιν αερα Compl. 248. κατεπεσα S. Compl. 248. ισα V. A. al. ηκα Compl. φρ. V. 4. ανετραφην V. S. ανεστραφην A. 157. και φροντ. A. S. και εν 5. βασιλευς V. S. βασιλεων A. 6. βιον V. A. κοσμον S. ειση S. 7. ευξαμην V. 9. αυτη V. S. al. αυτην A. ως ψαμμος Ven. S². 10. υγιαν S. προειλομην V. S. προειλαμην A. Ven. Compl.

	instead of light: for the light that cometh from her never 11 goeth out. All good things together came to me with her, and innumerable riches in her 12 hands. And I rejoiced in *them* all, because wisdom goeth before them: and I knew not that she was the mother of ¹ Gr. *without guile.* 13 them. I learned diligently¹ and do communicate her libe-² Gr. *without envy.* rally²: I do not hide her riches. 14 For she is a treasure unto men that never faileth: which they that use become the friends of ³ Or, *enter friendship with God.* God³, being commended for the gifts that come from learning. ⁴ Or, *God grant.* 15 God hath granted⁴ me to speak as I would, and to conceive as is meet for the things that ⁵ Or, *are to be spoken of.* are given me⁵: because it is he that leadeth unto wisdom, 16 and directeth the wise. For in his hand are both we and our words; all wisdom also, and knowledge of workmanship. 17 For he hath given me certain knowledge of the things that are, namely, to know how the world was made, and the opera-	ὅτι ἀκοίμητον τὸ ἐκ ταύτης φέγγος. 11 ἦλθε δέ μοι τὰ ἀγαθὰ ὁμοῦ πάντα μετ' αὐτῆς, καὶ ἀναρίθμητος πλοῦτος ἐν χερσὶν αὐτῆς. 12 εὐφράνθην δὲ ἐπὶ πᾶσιν, ὅτι αὐτῶν ἡγεῖται σοφία, ἠγνόουν δὲ αὐτὴν γενέτιν εἶναι τούτων. 13 ἀδόλως τε ἔμαθον, ἀφθόνως τε μεταδίδωμι, τὸν πλοῦτον αὐτῆς οὐκ ἀποκρύπτομαι. 14 ἀνεκλιπὴς γὰρ θησαυρός ἐστιν ἀνθρώποις, ὃν οἱ χρησάμενοι πρὸς Θεὸν ἐστείλαντο φιλίαν, διὰ τὰς ἐκ παιδείας δωρεὰς συσταθέντες. 15 Ἐμοὶ δὲ δῴη ὁ Θεὸς εἰπεῖν κατὰ γνώμην, καὶ ἐνθυμηθῆναι ἀξίως τῶν δεδομένων· ὅτι αὐτὸς καὶ τῆς σοφίας ὁδηγός ἐστι καὶ τῶν σοφῶν διορθωτής. 16 ἐν γὰρ χειρὶ αὐτοῦ καὶ ἡμεῖς καὶ οἱ λόγοι ἡμῶν, πᾶσά τε φρόνησις καὶ ἐργατειῶν ἐπιστήμη. 17 αὐτὸς γάρ μοι ἔδωκε τῶν ὄντων γνῶσιν ἀψευδῆ, εἰδέναι σύστασιν κόσμου καὶ ἐνέργειαν στοιχείων,	pro luce habere illam, quoniam inextinguibile est lumen illius. 11 Venerunt autem mihi omnia bona pariter cum illa, et innumerabilis honestas per manus 12 illius; et laetatus sum in omnibus, quoniam antecedebat me ista sapientia, et ignorabam quoniam horum omnium mater 13 est. Quam sine fictione didici, et sine invidia communico, et honestatem illius non abscondo. 14 Infinitus enim thesaurus est hominibus; quo qui usi sunt, participes facti sunt amicitiae Dei, propter disciplinae dona 15 commendati. Mihi autem dedit Deus dicere ex sententia, et praesumere digna horum quae mihi dantur, quoniam ipse sapientiae dux est, et sapientium 16 emendator. In manu enim illius, et nos, et sermones nostri, et omnis sapientia, et operum 17 scientia, et disciplina. Ipse enim dedit mihi horum quae sunt scientiam veram, ut sciam dispositionem orbis terrarum,

11. εν χερσιν V. A. Ven. εν χειρι S. εν ταις χερσιν V¹. 12. ευφρανθην V. S. ηυφρανθην A. επι παντων V. al. επι πασιν A. S. Compl. ηγνοαν S¹. γενετιν A. γενετην 261 B. Par. γενεσιν V. S. Ven. 14. εστιν θησαυρος S. ον V. A. S. φ Ven. 253. H. Par. χρησαμενοι V. S. Ven. κτησαμενοι A. S². vol. scrib. vid. Ita al. συσταθεντες Vulgo. ου σταθεντες 106. 261. 15. δῴη. δεδωκεν Compl. Ald. Arab. Vulg. των δεδομενων V. 68. al. τ. διδομενων 253. Compl. Vulg.τ. λεγομενων A. S, Ven. al. Syr. Arab. Arm. 16. εργατιων S.

18 et virtutes elementorum, initium, et consummationem, et medietatem temporum, vicissitudinum permutationes, et commutationes
19 temporum, anni cursus, et stel-
20 larum dispositiones, naturas animalium, et iras bestiarum, vim ventorum, et cogitationes hominum, differentias virgulto-
21 rum, et virtutes radicum. Et quaecunque sunt absconsa et improvisa didici; [22] omnium enim artifex docuit me sapientia.

22 Est enim in illa spiritus intelligentiae, sanctus, unicus, multiplex, subtilis, disertus, mobilis, incoinquinatus, certus, suavis, amans bonum, acutus, quem nihil
23 vetat, benefaciens, humanus, benignus, stabilis, certus, securus, omnem habens virtutem, omnia prospiciens, et qui capiat omnes spiritus, intelligibilis,
24 mundus, subtilis. Omnibus enim mobilibus mobilior est sapientia; attingit autem ubique
25 propter suam munditiam.. Vapor est enim virtutis Dei, et emanatio quaedam est claritatis

18 ἀρχὴν καὶ τέλος καὶ μεσότητα χρόνων,
τροπῶν ἀλλαγὰς καὶ μεταβολὰς καιρῶν,
19 ἐνιαυτῶν κύκλους καὶ ἄστρων θέσεις,
20 φύσεις ζώων καὶ θυμοὺς θηρίων, πνευμάτων βίας καὶ διαλογισμοὺς ἀνθρώπων,
διαφορὰς φυτῶν καὶ δυνάμεις ῥιζῶν·
21 ὅσα τέ ἐστι κρυπτὰ καὶ ἐμφανῆ ἔγνων.
22 ἡ γὰρ πάντων τεχνῖτις ἐδίδαξέ με σοφία.
Ἔστι γὰρ ἐν αὐτῇ πνεῦμα νοερόν, ἅγιον,
μονογενές, πολυμερές, λεπτόν, εὐκίνητον, τρανόν, ἀμόλυντον, σαφές, ἀπήμαντον, φιλάγαθον, ὀξύ,
23 ἀκώλυτον, εὐεργετικόν, φιλάνθρωπον,
βέβαιον, ἀσφαλές, ἀμέριμνον, παντοδύναμον, πανεπίσκοπον,
καὶ διὰ πάντων χωροῦν πνευμάτων
νοερῶν καθαρῶν λεπτοτάτων.
24 πάσης γὰρ κινήσεως κινητικώτερον σοφία,
διήκει δὲ καὶ χωρεῖ διὰ πάντων διὰ τὴν καθαρότητα.
25 ἀτμὶς γάρ ἐστι τῆς τοῦ Θεοῦ δυνάμεως,
καὶ ἀπόρροια τῆς τοῦ παντοκράτορος δόξης εἰλικρινής·

18 tion of the elements: The beginning, ending, and midst of the times: the alterations of the turning *of the sun*, and the
19 change of seasons: The circuits of years, and the positions of
20 stars: The natures of living creatures, and the furies of wild beasts: the violence of winds, and the reasonings of men: the diversities of plants, and the
21 virtues of roots: And all such things as are either secret or
22 manifest, them I know. For wisdom, which is the worker of all things, taught me: for in her is an understanding spirit, holy, one only[1], manifold, subtil, lively, clear, undefiled, plain, not subject to hurt, loving the thing that is good, quick, which cannot be letted, ready to do
23 good, Kind to man, stedfast, sure, free from care, having all power, overseeing all things, and going through all understanding, pure, and most subtil,
24 spirits. For wisdom is more moving than any motion: she passeth and goeth through all things by reason of her pureness.
25 For she is the breath[2] of the power of God, and a pure influence[3] flowing from the glory

[1] Gr. *only begotten*.
[2] Or. *vapour*.
[3] Or. *stream*.

18. καιρων om. 106. 261.   19. ενιαυτων V. Ven. al. Syr. Arm.   ενιαυτου A. S. al. Compl. Vulg. Arab.   κυκλου S.   αστρων S. θεσεις.   συνθεσεις 55.   δρομους 248.   20. θυμους.   νομους και θηριων S.   22. εστιν V.   εν αυτη V. S. Ven. al. Vulg. Syr. Arab. Arm.   αυτη A. 55. 106. al. Euseb. Praep. vii. 12.   ευεργετον S.   23. παντεπισκοπον A. S², al.   νοερον 261. καθαρον 106.   καθαρωτατον 261.   λεπτοτατον 106. 261. Cf. Vulg.   24. καθαριοτητα S. Ven. 261. Ald.   ι autem eras. S¹. 25. απορροια S. (imp. S².)   ειλικρινης V. S.   ιλικρινειας A.

of the Almighty: therefore can no defiled thing fall into her. 26 For she is the brightness of the everlasting light, the unspotted mirror of the power of God, and the image of his goodness. 27 And being but one, she can do all things: and remaining in herself, she maketh[1] all things new: and in all ages entering into holy souls, she maketh them friends of God, and prophets. 28 For God loveth none but him that dwelleth with wisdom. 29 For she is more beautiful than the sun, and above all the order of stars: being compared with the light, 30 she is found before it. For after this cometh night: but vice shall not prevail against wisdom.

[1] Or, createth.

CHAPTER VIII.

1 *Wisdom* reacheth from one end to another mightily: and sweetly[2] doth she order all things. 2 I loved her, and sought her out from my youth, I desired to make *her* my spouse[3], and I was a lover of her beauty.

[2] Or, profitably.

[3] Or, to marry her to myself.

διὰ τοῦτο οὐδὲν μεμιαμμένον εἰς αὐτὴν παρεμπίπτει. 26 ἀπαύγασμα γάρ ἐστι φωτὸς ἀϊδίου, καὶ ἔσοπτρον ἀκηλίδωτον τῆς τοῦ Θεοῦ ἐνεργείας, καὶ εἰκὼν τῆς ἀγαθότητος αὐτοῦ. 27 μία δὲ οὖσα πάντα δύναται, καὶ μένουσα ἐν αὑτῇ τὰ πάντα καινίζει, καὶ κατὰ γενεὰς εἰς ψυχὰς ὁσίας μεταβαίνουσα φίλους Θεοῦ καὶ προφήτας κατασκευάζει. 28 οὐθὲν γὰρ ἀγαπᾷ ὁ Θεὸς εἰ μὴ τὸν σοφίᾳ συνοικοῦντα. 29 ἔστι γὰρ αὕτη εὐπρεπεστέρα ἡλίου, καὶ ὑπὲρ πᾶσαν ἄστρων θέσιν, φωτὶ συγκρινομένη εὑρίσκεται προτέρα· 30 τοῦτο μὲν γὰρ διαδέχεται νύξ, σοφίας δὲ οὐκ ἀντισχύει κακία.

ΚΕΦΑΛΑΙΟΝ Η'.

1 Διατείνει δὲ ἀπὸ πέρατος εἰς πέρας εὐρώστως, καὶ διοικεῖ τὰ πάντα χρηστῶς. 2 Ταύτην ἐφίλησα καὶ ἐξεζήτησα ἐκ νεότητός μου, καὶ ἐζήτησα νύμφην ἀγαγέσθαι ἐμαυτῷ, καὶ ἐραστὴς ἐγενόμην τοῦ κάλλους αὐτῆς.

---

omnipotentis Dei sincera; et ideo nihil inquinatum in eam 26 incurrit; candor est enim lucis aeternae, et speculum sine macula Dei majestatis, et imago 27 bonitatis illius. Et cum sit una, omnia potest; et in se permanens omnia innovat, et per nationes in animas sanctas se transfert, amicos Dei et prophetas 28 constituit. Neminem enim diligit Deus, nisi eum qui cum 29 sapientia inhabitat. Est enim haec speciosior sole, et super omnem dispositionem stellarum; luci comparata invenitur 30 prior. Illi enim succedit nox, sapientiam autem non vincit malitia.

CAPUT VIII.

1 Attingit ergo a fine usque ad finem fortiter, et disponit omnia suaviter.

2 Hanc amavi, et exquisivi a juventute mea, et quaesivi sponsam mihi eam assumere, et amator factus sum formae

---

25. μεμιασμενον 248 Compl.   27. εν αυτη V. S.   εν εαυτη A. Ven. al. Compl.   τὰ πάντα. τα om. A.   28. ουδεν γαρ ο θεος αγαπα A. al.   29. αστερων A.   προτέρα. λαμπροτερα 106. 261. B. Par.   30. σοφιας V. σοφια S. (imp. cor.). σοφιαν A. 55. 254.   ουκ αντισχυει V. ου κατισχυει S. A. al. ου κατισχυσει 248. Compl.   VIII. 1. εις περας V. Ven. al. επι περας S. A². διοικειται A. Ven. τα om. Ven.

3 illius. Generositatem illius glorificat, contubernium habens Dei; sed et omnium Dominus
4 dilexit illam; doctrix enim est disciplinae Dei, et electrix operum illius. Et si divitiae
5 appetuntur in vita, quid sapientia locupletius quae operatur omnia?
6 Si autem sensus operatur, quis horum quae sunt magis quam
7 illa est artifex? Et si justitiam quis diligit, labores hujus magnas habent virtutes: sobrietatem enim, et prudentiam docet, et justitiam, et virtutem, quibus utilius nihil est in vita homi-
8 nibus. Et si multitudinem scientiae desiderat quis, scit praeterita, et de futuris aestimat, scit versutias sermonum, et dissolutiones argumentorum; signa et monstra scit antequam fiant, et eventus temporum et saecu-
9 lorum. Proposui ergo hanc adducere mihi ad convivendum, sciens quoniam mecum commu-

3 εὐγένειαν δοξάζει συμβίωσιν Θεοῦ ἔχουσα,
καὶ ὁ πάντων Δεσπότης ἠγάπησεν αὐτήν.
4 μύστις γάρ ἐστι τῆς τοῦ Θεοῦ ἐπιστήμης,
καὶ αἱρετὶς τῶν ἔργων αὐτοῦ.
5 εἰ δὲ πλοῦτός ἐστιν ἐπιθυμητὸν κτῆμα ἐν βίῳ,
τί σοφίας πλουσιώτερον τῆς τὰ πάντα ἐργαζομένης;
6 εἰ δὲ φρόνησις ἐργάζεται,
τίς αὐτῆς τῶν ὄντων μᾶλλόν ἐστι τεχνίτης;
7 καὶ εἰ δικαιοσύνην ἀγαπᾷ τις,
οἱ πόνοι ταύτης εἰσὶν ἀρεταί·
σωφροσύνην γὰρ καὶ φρόνησιν ἐκδιδάσκει,
δικαιοσύνην καὶ ἀνδρείαν,
ὧν χρησιμώτερον οὐδέν ἐστιν ἐν βίῳ ἀνθρώποις.
8 εἰ δὲ καὶ πολυπειρίαν ποθεῖ τις,
οἶδε τὰ ἀρχαῖα καὶ τὰ μέλλοντα εἰκάζει,
ἐπίσταται στροφὰς λόγων καὶ λύσεις αἰνιγμάτων,
σημεῖα καὶ τέρατα προγινώσκει,
καὶ ἐκβάσεις καιρῶν καὶ χρόνων.
9 ἔκρινα τοίνυν ταύτην ἀγαγέσθαι πρὸς συμβίωσιν,
εἰδὼς ὅτι ἔσται μοι σύμβουλος ἀγαθῶν,

3 In that she is conversant with God, she magnifieth her nobility: yea, the Lord of all things himself loved her.
4 For she is privy[1] to the mysteries of the knowledge of God, and a lover[2] of his works.
5 If riches be a possession to be desired in this life; what is richer than wisdom, that worketh all things?
6 And if prudence work; who of all that are is a more cunning
7 workman than she? And if a man love righteousness, her labours are virtues: for she teacheth temperance and prudence, justice and fortitude: which are such things, as men can have nothing more profit-
8 able in their life. If a man desire much experience, she knoweth things of old, and conjectureth *aright* what is to come: she knoweth the subtilties of speeches, and can expound dark sentences: she foreseeth signs and wonders, and the events
9 of seasons and times. Therefore I purposed to take her to me to live with me, knowing that she would[3] be a counsellor of

[1] Or, *teacher*.
[2] Or, *chooser*.
[3] Gr. *will*.

---

4. αιρετις A. V. ερετις S. αιρετης Par. I. V. A. Ven. τιμιωτερον S. περιεργαζομενης S. ευρετις Par. A. 55. 106. ευρετης Par. C. D. H. 261. 5. πλουσιωτερον
6. εργαζεται τι 55. 253. 254. τεχνιτης V. A. al. τεχνιτις S. 106.
7. σωφροσυνην τε και Ven. ανδριαν A. S. C. 8. πολυπειραν A. εικαζειν V. C. 55. al. Arm. εικαζει A. S³. Ven. Vulg. Compl.
9. αγαγεσθαι om. C. αγ. εμαυτῳ 106. 248. Compl.

K 2

good things, and a comfort in
10 cares and grief. For her sake I shall have estimation among the multitude, and honour with the elders, though
11 I be young. I shall be found of a quick conceit in judgment, and shall be admired in the
12 sight of great men. When I hold my tongue, they shall bide my leisure, and when I speak, they shall give good ear unto me: if I talk much, they shall lay their hands upon their mouth.
13 Moreover by the means of her I shall obtain immortality, and leave behind me an everlasting memorial to them that come
14 after me. I shall set[1] the people in order, and the nations
15 shall be subject unto me. Horrible tyrants shall be afraid, when they do but hear of me; I shall be found[2] good among the multitude, and valiant in
16 war. After I am come into mine house[3], I will repose myself with her: for her conversation hath no bitterness; and to live with her hath no sorrow,
17 but mirth and joy. Now when I considered these things in myself, and pondered them in my heart, how that to be allied unto wisdom is immortality;
18 And great pleasure it is to have

[1] Or, govern.
[2] Or, appear.
[3] Or, Being entered into mine house.

καὶ παραίνεσις φροντίδων καὶ λύπης.
10 ἕξω δι' αὐτὴν δόξαν ἐν ὄχλοις, καὶ τιμὴν παρὰ πρεσβυτέροις ὁ νέος.
11 ὀξὺς εὑρεθήσομαι ἐν κρίσει, καὶ ἐν ὄψει δυναστῶν θαυμασθήσομαι.
12 σιγῶντά με περιμενοῦσι, καὶ φθεγγομένῳ προσέξουσι, καὶ λαλοῦντος ἐπὶ πλεῖον χεῖρα ἐπιθήσουσιν ἐπὶ στόμα αὐτῶν.
13 ἕξω δι' αὐτὴν ἀθανασίαν, καὶ μνήμην αἰώνιον τοῖς μετ' ἐμὲ ἀπολείψω.
14 διοικήσω λαούς, καὶ ἔθνη ὑποταγήσεταί μοι.
15 φοβηθήσονταί με ἀκούσαντες τύραννοι φρικτοί,
ἐν πλήθει φανοῦμαι ἀγαθὸς καὶ ἐν πολέμῳ ἀνδρεῖος.
16 εἰσελθὼν εἰς τὸν οἶκόν μου προσαναπαύσομαι αὐτῇ·
οὐ γὰρ ἔχει πικρίαν ἡ συναναστροφὴ αὐτῆς,
οὐδὲ ὀδύνην ἡ συμβίωσις αὐτῆς, ἀλλὰ εὐφροσύνην καὶ χαράν.
17 Ταῦτα λογισάμενος ἐν ἐμαυτῷ,
καὶ φροντίσας ἐν καρδίᾳ μου, ὅτι ἀθανασία ἐστὶν ἐν συγγενείᾳ σοφίας,
18 καὶ ἐν φιλίᾳ αὐτῆς τέρψις ἀγαθή,

nicabit de bonis, et erit allocutio
10 cogitationis et taedii mei. Habebo propter hanc claritatem ad turbas, et honorem apud
11 seniores juvenis; et acutus inveniar in judicio, et in conspectu potentium admirabilis ero, et facies principum mirabuntur
12 me; tacentem me sustinebunt, et loquentem me respicient, et sermocinante me plura, manus
13 ori suo imponent. Praeterea habebo per hanc immortalitatem, et memoriam aeternam his qui post me futuri sunt relin-
14 quam. Disponam populos, et nationes mihi erunt subditae.
15 Timebunt me audientes reges horrendi; in multitudine videbor bonus, et in bello fortis.
16 Intrans in domum meam, conquiescam cum illa; non enim habet amaritudinem conversatio illius, nec taedium convictus illius, sed laetitiam et gaudium.
17 Haec cogitans apud me, et commemorans in corde meo, quoniam immortalitas est in cog-
18 natione sapientiae, et in amicitia

10. εν οχλῳ C. 12. χειρα V. A. χειρα δε C. χειρας S. 55. 157. 253. επιθ. χειρα Ven. το στομα S. 13. Post αθανασ. add. C. και τιμην παρα (cetera non liquent). απολειψω. καταλειψω C. 14. υποταγησεται A. V. S. al. υποταγησονται S³. 106. 148. 261. Compl. 15. φανησομαι C. 16. ουδε ... αυτης om. 106. 261. η συμβ. αυτης om. 254. 17. αθανασια εστιν A. S. V². C. Ven. al. εστιν αθαν. V. al. εν ευγενεια 248. εν om. S. suppl. S³. 18. τερψις. τρεψις C.

illius delectatio bona, et in operibus manuum illius honestas sine defectione, et in certamine loquelae illius sapientia, et praeclaritas in communicatione sermonum ipsius, circuibam quaerens, ut mihi illam assumerem.

19 Puer autem eram ingeniosus, et sortitus sum animam bonam.

20 Et cum essem magis bonus, veni ad corpus incoinquinatum.

21 Et ut scivi quoniam aliter non possem esse continens, nisi Deus det; et hoc ipsum erat sapientiae, scire cujus esset hoc donum; adii Dominum, et deprecatus sum illum, et dixi ex totis praecordiis meis :

CAPUT IX.

1 Deus patrum meorum, et Domine misericordiae, qui fecisti
2 omnia verbo tuo, et sapientia tua constituisti hominem, ut dominaretur creaturae quae a

καὶ ἐν πόνοις χειρῶν αὐτῆς πλοῦτος ἀνεκλιπής,
καὶ ἐν συγγυμνασίᾳ ὁμιλίας αὐτῆς φρόνησις,
καὶ εὔκλεια ἐν κοινωνίᾳ λόγων αὐτῆς,
περιῄειν ζητῶν ὅπως λάβω αὐτὴν εἰς ἐμαυτόν.

19 παῖς δὲ ἤμην εὐφυὴς, ψυχῆς τε ἔλαχον ἀγαθῆς·

20 μᾶλλον δὲ ἀγαθὸς ὢν ἦλθον εἰς σῶμα ἀμίαντον.

21 Γνοὺς δὲ ὅτι οὐκ ἄλλως ἔσομαι ἐγκρατής, ἐὰν μὴ ὁ Θεὸς δῷ,
(καὶ τοῦτο δ' ἦν φρονήσεως τὸ εἰδέναι τίνος ἡ χάρις,)
ἐνέτυχον τῷ Κυρίῳ, καὶ ἐδεήθην αὐτοῦ,
καὶ εἶπον ἐξ ὅλης τῆς καρδίας μου·

ΚΕΦΑΛΛΑΙΟΝ Θ'.

1 Θεὲ πατέρων καὶ Κύριε τοῦ ἐλέους,
ὁ ποιήσας τὰ πάντα ἐν λόγῳ σου,

2 καὶ τῇ σοφίᾳ σου κατασκευάσας ἄνθρωπον,
ἵνα δεσπόζῃ τῶν ὑπὸ σοῦ γενομένων κτισμάτων,

her friendship; and in the works of her hands are infinite riches; and in the exercise of conference with her, prudence; and in talking with her, a good report[1]; I went about seeking [1 Or, *fame*] how to take her to me[2]. For [2 Or, *marry her*]

19 I was a witty child, and had
20 a good spirit. Yea rather, being good, I came into a body un-
21 defiled. Nevertheless, when I perceived that I could not otherwise obtain her, except God gave her me; and that was a point of wisdom also to know whose gift she was; I prayed [3 Or, *went*] unto the Lord, and besought him, and with my whole heart I said,

CHAPTER IX.

1 O God of my fathers, and Lord of mercy, who hast made all
2 things with thy word, And ordained man through thy wisdom, that he should have dominion over the creatures which

3 thou hast made, And order the world according to equity and righteousness, and execute judgment with an upright
4 heart: Give me wisdom, that sitteth by thy throne; and reject me not from among thy
5 children: For I thy servant and son of thine handmaid am a feeble person, and of a short time, and too young for the understanding of judgment and
6 laws. For though a man be never so perfect among the children of men, yet if thy wisdom be not with him, he shall be nothing regarded.
7 Thou hast chosen me to be a king of thy people, and a judge of thy sons and daughters:
8 Thou hast commanded me to build a temple upon thy holy mount, and an altar in the city wherein thou dwellest, a resemblance of the holy tabernacle, which thou hast prepared from the beginning.
9 And wisdom was with thee: which knoweth thy works, and was present when thou madest the world, and knew what was acceptable in thy sight, and right in thy commandments.
10 O send her out of thy holy

3 καὶ διέπῃ τὸν κόσμον ἐν ὁσιότητι καὶ δικαιοσύνῃ,
καὶ ἐν εὐθύτητι ψυχῆς κρίσιν κρίνῃ·
4 δός μοι τὴν τῶν σῶν θρόνων πάρεδρον σοφίαν,
καὶ μή με ἀποδοκιμάσῃς ἐκ παίδων σου.
5 ὅτι ἐγὼ δοῦλος σὸς καὶ υἱὸς τῆς παιδίσκης σου,
ἄνθρωπος ἀσθενὴς καὶ ὀλιγοχρόνιος
καὶ ἐλάσσων ἐν συνέσει κρίσεως καὶ νόμων.
6 κἂν γάρ τις ᾖ τέλειος ἐν υἱοῖς ἀνθρώπων,
τῆς ἀπὸ σοῦ σοφίας ἀπούσης εἰς οὐδὲν λογισθήσεται.
7 σύ με προείλω βασιλέα λαοῦ σου
καὶ δικαστὴν υἱῶν σου καὶ θυγατέρων.
8 εἶπας οἰκοδομῆσαι ναὸν ἐν ὄρει ἁγίῳ σου,
καὶ ἐν πόλει κατασκηνώσεώς σου θυσιαστήριον,
μίμημα σκηνῆς ἁγίας ἣν προητοίμασας ἀπ' ἀρχῆς.
9 καὶ μετὰ σοῦ ἡ σοφία ἡ εἰδυῖα τὰ ἔργα σου,
καὶ παροῦσα ὅτε ἐποίεις τὸν κόσμον,
καὶ ἐπισταμένη τί ἀρεστὸν ἐν ὀφθαλμοῖς σου
καὶ τί εὐθὲς ἐν ἐντολαῖς σου.
10 ἐξαπόστειλον αὐτὴν ἐξ ἁγίων οὐρανῶν,

3 te facta est; ut disponat orbem terrarum in aequitate et justitia, et in directione cordis
4 judicium judicet; da mihi sedium tuarum assistricem sapientiam, et noli me reprobare
5 a pueris tuis; quoniam servus tuus sum ego, et filius ancillae tuae, homo infirmus, et exigui temporis, et minor ad intellec-
6 tum judicii et legum. Nam et si quis erit consummatus inter filios hominum, si ab illo abfuerit sapientia tua, in nihi-
7 lum computabitur. Tu elegisti me regem populo tuo, et judicem filiorum tuorum, et filia-
8 rum; et dixisti me aedificare templum in monte sancto tuo, et in civitate habitationis tuae altare, similitudinem tabernaculi sancti tui, quod praeparasti ab
9 initio; et tecum sapientia tua quae novit opera tua, quae et affuit tunc cum orbem terrarum faceres, et sciebat quid esset placitum oculis tuis, et quid directum in praeceptis tuis.
10 Mitte illam de caelis sanctis

6. εαν γαρ 55. 157. η τις C. εις om. S. C. ουθεν A. C. λογισθησονται S. -σεται S². 7. προειλω V. A. προειλου S. Ven. al. Compl. προσειλου C. 8. οικοδομησω C. κατασκηνεσεως A. 9. εποιει C. εν οφθ. σου. ενωπιον 248. 10. αγιων σου 157. Vulg.

tuis, et a sede magnitudinis tuae, ut mecum sit et mecum laboret, ut sciam quid acceptum sit 11 apud te; scit enim illa omnia, et intelligit, et deducet me in operibus meis sobrie, et cus- 12 todiet me in sua potentia. Et erunt accepta opera mea, et disponam populum tuum juste, et ero dignus sedium patris mei. 13 Quis enim hominum poterit scire consilium Dei? aut quis poterit cogitare quid velit Deus? 14 Cogitationes enim mortalium timidae, et incertae providentiae 15 nostrae. Corpus enim, quod corrumpitur, aggravat animam, et terrena inhabitatio deprimit 16 sensum multa cogitantem. Et difficile aestimamus quae in terra sunt, et quae in prospectu sunt invenimus cum labore. Quae autem in caelis sunt quis 17 investigabit? Sensum autem tuum quis sciet, nisi tu dederis

καὶ ἀπὸ θρόνου δόξης σου πεμψον αὐτήν,
ἵνα συμπαροῦσά μοι κοπιάσῃ,
καὶ γνῶ τί εὐάρεστόν ἐστι παρὰ σοί.
11 οἶδε γὰρ ἐκείνη πάντα καὶ συνιεῖ,
καὶ ὁδηγήσει με ἐν ταῖς πράξεσί μου σωφρόνως,
καὶ φυλάξει με ἐν τῇ δόξῃ αὐτῆς.
12 καὶ ἔσται προσδεκτὰ τὰ ἔργα μου,
καὶ διακρινῶ τὸν λαόν σου δικαίως,
καὶ ἔσομαι ἄξιος θρόνων πατρός μου.
13 τίς γὰρ ἄνθρωπος γνώσεται βουλὴν Θεοῦ;
ἢ τίς ἐνθυμηθήσεται τί θέλει ὁ Κύριος;
14 λογισμοὶ γὰρ θνητῶν δειλοί, καὶ ἐπισφαλεῖς αἱ ἐπίνοιαι ἡμῶν.
15 φθαρτὸν γὰρ σῶμα βαρύνει ψυχήν,
καὶ βρίθει τὸ γεῶδες σκῆνος νοῦν πολυφρόντιδα.
16 καὶ μόλις εἰκάζομεν τὰ ἐπὶ γῆς,
καὶ τὰ ἐν χερσὶν εὑρίσκομεν μετὰ πόνου,
τὰ δὲ ἐν οὐρανοῖς τίς ἐξιχνίασεν;
17 βουλὴν δέ σου τίς ἔγνω, εἰ μὴ σὺ ἔδωκας σοφίαν

heavens, and from the throne of thy glory, that being present she may labour with me, that I may know what is pleasing 11 unto thee. For she knoweth and understandeth all things, and she shall lead me soberly in my doings, and preserve me 12 in her power[1]. So shall my works be acceptable, and then shall I judge thy people righteously, and be worthy to sit in 13 my father's seat. For what man is he that can know the counsel of God? or who can think what the will of the Lord 14 is? For the thoughts of mortal men are miserable[2], and our 15 devices are but uncertain. For the corruptible body presseth down the soul, and the earthy tabernacle weigheth down the mind that museth upon many 16 things. And hardly do we guess aright at things that are upon earth, and with labour do we find the things that are before us[3]: but the things that are in heaven who hath searched 17 out? And thy counsel who hath known, except thou give

[1] Or, by her power, or, glory.
[2] Or, fearful.
[3] Gr. at hand.

---

10. συνπαρουσα S. συνπαρουσαν μοι κοπιασει C.   11. τα παντα 55. 106. al.   εν ταις. εν om. C.   εαυτης S. αυτης S². 12. δικαιως V. A. S. al. σωφρονως C. θρονου S.   13. ανθρωπων 248. Compl.   ὁ κυριος. θεος Ald. Compl. Vulg.   15. σκηνος. σωμα 106. 261.   16. μολις V. μογις A. S. C. al.   χερσιν V. A. ποσιν S. Ven.   εξιχνιασει 106. 261. Vulg.   17. συ εδωκας. συνεδωκας C.

wisdom, and send thy Holy
18 Spirit from above? For so the
ways of them which lived on
the earth were reformed, and
men were taught the things
that are pleasing unto thee, and
were saved through wisdom.

CHAPTER X.

1 She preserved the first formed
father of the world, that was
created alone, and brought him
2 out of his fall, And gave him
3 power to rule all things. But
when the unrighteous went
away from her in his anger,
he perished also in the fury
wherewith he murdered his
4 brother. For whose cause the
earth being drowned with the
flood, wisdom again preserved
it, and directed the course of
the righteous in a piece of
5 wood of small value. Moreover, the nations in their
wicked conspiracy being confounded, she found out the
righteous, and preserved him
blameless unto God, and kept
him strong against[1] his tender
compassion towards his son.
6 When the ungodly perished,
she delivered the righteous

καὶ ἔπεμψας τὸ ἅγιόν σου
πνεῦμα ἀπὸ ὑψίστων;
18 καὶ οὕτως διωρθώθησαν αἱ τρίβοι τῶν ἐπὶ γῆς,
καὶ τὰ ἀρεστά σου ἐδιδάχθησαν
ἄνθρωποι,
καὶ τῇ σοφίᾳ ἐσώθησαν.

ΚΕΦΑΛΑΙΟΝ Ι'.

1 Αὕτη πρωτόπλαστον πατέρα
κόσμου μόνον κτισθέντα διεφύλαξεν,
καὶ ἐξείλατο αὐτὸν ἐκ παραπτώματος ἰδίου,
2 ἔδωκέ τε αὐτῷ ἰσχὺν κρατῆσαι
πάντων.
3 ἀποστὰς δὲ ἀπ' αὐτῆς ἄδικος
ἐν ὀργῇ αὐτοῦ,
ἀδελφοκτόνοις συναπώλετο θυ-
μοῖς·
4 δι' ὃν κατακλυζομένην γῆν πάλιν
ἔσωσεν σοφία,
δι' εὐτελοῦς ξύλου τὸν δίκαιον
κυβερνήσασα.
5 αὕτη καὶ ἐν ὁμονοίᾳ πονηρίας
ἐθνῶν συγχυθέντων ἔγνω
τὸν δίκαιον,
καὶ ἐτήρησεν αὐτὸν ἄμεμπτον
Θεῷ,
καὶ ἐπὶ τέκνου σπλάγχνοις
ἰσχυρὸν ἐφύλαξεν.
6 αὕτη δίκαιον ἐξαπολλυμένων
ἀσεβῶν ἐρρύσατο

sapientiam, et miseris spiritum
sanctum tuum de altissimis;
18 et sic correctae sint semitae
eorum qui sunt in terris, et
quae tibi placent didicerint ho-
19 mines? Nam per sapientiam
sanati sunt quicunque placuerunt
tibi Domine a principio.

CAPUT X.

1 Haec illum qui primus formatus est a Deo pater orbis
terrarum, cum solus esset crea-
2 tus, custodivit; et eduxit illum
a delicto suo, [2] et dedit illi vir-
3 tutem continendi omnia. Ab
hac ut recessit injustus in ira
sua, per iram homicidii fraterni
4 deperiit. Propter quem cum
aqua deleret terram, sanavit
iterum sapientia, per contemptibile lignum justum gubernans.
5 Haec et in consensu nequitiae
cum se nationes contulissent,
scivit justum, et conservavit
sine querela Deo, et in filii
misericordia fortem custodivit.
6 Haec justum a pereuntibus
impiis liberavit fugientem, de-

---

17. απο υψηλων S. αφ υψους C.   18. διορθωθησαν S. C.   των εθνων επι της γης C.   αριστα C. αρεστα σοι 248. Compl.
τη σοφ. σου S. 106. 296.   X. 1. εξειλατο. εξετεινεν 68. Ald.   2. εδωκε δε C.   απαντων V. παντων S. A. C. al.
απο παντων S².   4. δι ον V. A. S². Ven. Vulg. διο S. C.   διεσωσε V. εσωσεν S. A. C. Ven. al. Compl. Ald.   δι' ευτ.
δι' om. C.   5. συγχυθ. S.   εγνω S. A. C. Ven. Compl. Vulg. al.   ευρε V. 68.   τω θεω C. Compl.   τεκνοις 106. 261.
σπλαγχνον 106.   6. ερυσατο C. ita vs. 9, 13, 15.

| [−X, 12.] | THE BOOK OF WISDOM. | 73 |

scendente igne in Pentapolim;
7 quibus in testimonium nequitiae fumigabunda constat deserta terra, et incerto tempore fructus habentes arbores, et incredibilis animae memoria stans
8 figmentum salis. Sapientiam enim praetereuntes, non tantum in hoc lapsi sunt ut ignorarent bona, sed et insipientiae suae reliquerunt hominibus memoriam, ut in his quae peccave-
9 runt nec latere potuissent. Sapientia autem hos qui se observant a doloribus liberavit.
10 Haec profugum irae fratris justum deduxit per vias rectas, et ostendit illi regnum Dei, et dedit illi scientiam sanctorum, honestavit illum in laboribus,
11 et complevit labores illius. In fraude circumvenientium illum affuit illi, et honestum fecit
12 illum. Custodivit illum ab inimicis, et a seductoribus tutavit illum, et certamen forte dedit

φυγόντα πῦρ καταβάσιον Πενταπόλεως·
7 ἧς ἔτι μαρτύριον τῆς πονηρίας καπνιζομένη καθέστηκε χέρσος,
καὶ ἀτελέσιν ὥραις καρποφοροῦντα φυτά,
καὶ ἀπιστούσης ψυχῆς μνημεῖον ἑστηκυῖα στήλη ἁλός.
8 σοφίαν γὰρ παροδεύσαντες οὐ μόνον ἐβλάβησαν τοῦ μὴ γνῶναι τὰ καλά,
ἀλλὰ καὶ τῆς ἀφροσύνης ἀπέλιπον τῷ βίῳ μνημόσυνον,
ἵνα ἐν οἷς ἐσφάλησαν μηδὲ λαθεῖν δυνηθῶσι.
9 σοφία δὲ τοὺς θεραπεύσαντας αὐτὴν ἐκ πόνων ἐρρύσατο.
10 αὕτη φυγάδα ὀργῆς ἀδελφοῦ δίκαιον ὡδήγησεν ἐν τρίβοις εὐθείαις,
ἔδειξεν αὐτῷ βασιλείαν Θεοῦ, καὶ ἔδωκεν αὐτῷ γνῶσιν ἁγίων, εὐπόρησεν αὐτὸν ἐν μόχθοις, καὶ ἐπλήθυνε τοὺς πόνους αὐτοῦ.
11 ἐν πλεονεξίᾳ κατισχυόντων αὐτὸν παρέστη,
καὶ ἐπλούτισεν αὐτόν·
12 διεφύλαξεν αὐτὸν ἀπὸ ἐχθρῶν, καὶ ἀπὸ ἐνεδρευόντων ἠσφαλίσατο,
καὶ ἀγῶνα ἰσχυρὸν ἐβράβευσεν αὐτῷ,

man, who fled from the fire which fell down upon the five
7 cities[1]. Of whose wickedness even to this day the waste land that smoketh is a testimony, and plants bearing fruit that never come to ripeness: and a standing pillar of salt *is* a monument of an unbelieving
8 soul. For regarding not wisdom, they gat not only this hurt, that they knew not the things which were good; but also left behind them to the world a memorial of their foolishness: so that in the things wherein they offended they could not so much as be
9 hid. But wisdom delivered from pain those that attended
10 upon her. When the righteous fled from his brother's wrath, she guided him in right paths, shewed him the kingdom of God, and gave him knowledge of holy things, made him rich in his travels, and multiplied
11 *the fruit* of his labours. In the covetousness of such as oppressed him she stood by him,
12 and made him rich. She defended him from his enemies, and kept him safe from those that lay in wait, and in a sore conflict she gave him the vic-

[1] Gr. *Pentapolis.*

---

6. φεύγοντα S. φυγ. S¹. καταβ. πυρ S. A. C. Ven. Compl. ης εστιν Ven. η εστι μαρτ. C. και απιστ. 106. 261. Vulg. Syr. Arab.
8. παροδ. ανθρωποι 55. 254. της εαυταν αφρ. 157. 248. Compl. απελειπον A.
9. θεραπευσαντας V. Ven. 68. 254. θεραπευοντας S. A. C. al. 10. αυτη και φυγ. C. ανθρωπων C. πονους. κοπους S. A. Ven.
11. επλουτισεν αυτ. εν μοχθοις C. εβραβ. αυτον 161.

7. οἷς ἐπί vulgo legitur. ητ ετι S. A. V. al. Compl. Ald. μνημεῖον. μνημοσυνον 106. 241. σημειον 248. εστηκυιη S. μνημην S. μνημοσυνον S¹. εφ οις Ven. εν τριβ. εν om. Ven. αγιου Ven. 253.
12. διεφυλ. και εφυλαξεν S. Ven. 248.

L

tory; that he might know that
godliness is stronger than all.
13 When the righteous was sold,
she forsook him not, but delivered him from sin: she went
down with him into the pit,
14 And left him not in bonds,
till she brought him the sceptre
of the kingdom, and power
against those that oppressed
him[1]: as for them that had accused him, she shewed them to
be liars, and gave him per-
15 petual glory. She delivered
the righteous[2] people and blameless seed from the nation that
16 oppressed them. She entered
into the soul of the servant of
the Lord, and withstood dreadful kings in wonders and signs;
17 Rendered to the righteous
a reward of their labours,
guided them in a marvellous
way, and was unto them for
a cover by day, and a light[3]
of stars in the night season;
18 Brought them through the Red

[1] Or, the power of them that ruled over him.
[2] Or, holy.
[3] Or, flame.

ἵνα γνῷ ὅτι παντὸς δυνατωτέρα
ἐστὶν εὐσέβεια.
13 αὕτη πραθέντα δίκαιον οὐκ
ἐγκατέλιπεν,
ἀλλὰ ἐξ ἁμαρτίας ἐρρύσατο
αὐτόν.
συγκατέβη αὐτῷ εἰς λάκκον,
14 καὶ ἐν δεσμοῖς οὐκ ἀφῆκεν
αὐτὸν,
ἕως ἤνεγκεν αὐτῷ σκῆπτρα
βασιλείας
καὶ ἐξουσίαν τυραννούντων αὐ-
τοῦ·
ψευδεῖς τε ἔδειξε τοὺς μωμησαμένους αὐτὸν,
καὶ ἔδωκεν αὐτῷ δόξαν αἰώνιον.
15 αὕτη λαὸν ὅσιον καὶ σπέρμα
ἄμεμπτον ἐρρύσατο ἐξ ἔθ-
νους θλιβόντων.
16 εἰσῆλθεν εἰς ψυχὴν θεράποντος
Κυρίου,
καὶ ἀντέστη βασιλεῦσι φο-
βεροῖς ἐν τέρασι καὶ ση-
μείοις.
17 ἀπέδωκεν ὁσίοις μισθὸν κόπων
αὐτῶν,
ὡδήγησεν αὐτοὺς ἐν ὁδῷ θαυ-
μαστῇ,
καὶ ἐγένετο αὐτοῖς εἰς σκέπην
ἡμέρας
καὶ εἰς φλόγα ἄστρων τὴν
νύκτα.
18 διεβίβασεν αὐτοὺς θάλασσαν
ἐρυθρὰν,

illi ut vinceret, et sciret quoniam omnium potentior est
13 sapientia. Haec venditum justum non dereliquit, sed a peccatoribus liberavit eum; des-
cenditque cum illo in foveam,
14 et in vinculis non dereliquit
illum, donec afferret illi scep-
trum regni, et potentiam adversus eos qui eum deprimebant;
et mendaces ostendit qui ma-
culaverunt illum, et dedit illi
15 claritatem aeternam. Haec
populum justum et semen sine
querela liberavit a nationibus
16 quae illum deprimebant. In-
travit in animam servi Dei, et
stetit contra reges horrendos in
17 portentis et signis. Et reddi-
dit justis mercedem laborum
suorum, et deduxit illos in via
mirabili, et fuit illis in velamento dei, et in luce stellarum
18 per noctem; transtulit illos per

12. παντως S. παντων S². η ευσεβεια A. al. Compl. 13. εγκατελειπεν A. 248. Compl. ερυσατο S. C. 14. συν-
κατεβη S. βασιλεων 261. τυραννων. αυτον Ven. O. al. S². 16. αντεστη. ανεστη βασιλευς S. 'Sed post v. 19, ubi hic vs., ut
scriba ipse punctis indicavit, errore repetitus est, recte legitur αντεστη βασιλευσιν.' Fritzsche. ισχυροις κ. φοβ. 106. 261. 17.
μισθον οσιοις A. al. μισθον οσιον 106. 261. οσιοις μισθον οσιοτητος 248. Compl. κοπων αυτου S. C. αυτων S². φλογας S. αο-
τεραν A. C. S². 18. εις θαλασσ. S. C.

mare Rubrum, et transvexit
illos per aquam nimiam. Inimicos autem illorum demersit in
mare, et ab altitudine inferorum
eduxit illos. [20] Ideo justi
tulerunt spolia impiorum, et
decantaverunt, Domine, nomen
sanctum tuum, et victricem manum tuam laudaverunt pariter;
quoniam sapientia aperuit os
mutorum, et linguas infantium
fecit disertas.

CAPUT XI.

1 Direxit opera eorum in mani-
2 bus prophetae sancti. Iter fecerunt per deserta, quae non
habitabantur, et in locis de-
3 sertis fixerunt casas. Steterunt
contra hostes, et de inimicis se
4 vindicaverunt. Sitierunt, et
invocaverunt te; et data est
illis aqua de petra altissima, et
requies sitis de lapide duro.
5 Per quae enim poenas passi
sunt inimici illorum a defectione
potus sui, et in eis cum abundarent filii Israel laetati sunt,
6 per haec, cum illis deessent, bene

καὶ διήγαγεν αὐτοὺς δι' ὕδατος
πολλοῦ.
19 τοὺς δὲ ἐχθροὺς αὐτῶν κατέκ-
λυσε,
καὶ ἐκ βάθους ἀβύσσου ἀνέβρασεν αὐτούς.
20 διὰ τοῦτο δίκαιοι ἐσκύλευσαν
ἀσεβεῖς,
καὶ ὕμνησαν, Κύριε, τὸ ὄνομα
τὸ ἅγιόν σου,
τήν τε ὑπέρμαχόν σου χεῖρα
ᾔνεσαν ὁμοθυμαδόν.
21 ὅτι ἡ σοφία ἤνοιξε στόμα
κωφῶν,
καὶ γλώσσας νηπίων ἔθηκε
τρανάς.

ΚΕΦΑΛΑΙΟΝ ΙΑ΄.

1 Εὐώδωσε τὰ ἔργα αὐτῶν ἐν
χειρὶ προφήτου ἁγίου.
2 διώδευσαν ἔρημον ἀοίκητον,
καὶ ἐν ἀβάτοις ἔπηξαν σκηνάς.
3 ἀντέστησαν πολεμίοις, καὶ ἐχθροὺς ἠμύναντο.
4 ἐδίψησαν καὶ ἐπεκαλέσαντό σε,
καὶ ἐδόθη αὐτοῖς ἐκ πέτρας
ἀκροτόμου ὕδωρ,
καὶ ἴαμα δίψης ἐκ λίθου σκλη-
ροῦ.
5 Δι' ὧν γὰρ ἐκολάσθησαν οἱ
ἐχθροὶ αὐτῶν,
διὰ τούτων αὐτοὶ ἀποροῦντες
εὐεργετήθησαν.

sea, and led them through much
19 water: But she drowned their
enemies, and cast them up out
of the bottom of the deep.
20 Therefore the righteous spoiled
the ungodly, and praised thy
holy name, O Lord, and mag-
nified with one accord thine
hand, that fought for them.
21 For wisdom opened the mouth
of the dumb, and made the
tongues of them that cannot
speak eloquent.

CHAPTER XI.

1 She prospered their works in
the hand of the holy prophet.
2 They went through the wilderness that was not inhabited,
and pitched tents in places where
3 there lay no way. They stood
against their enemies, and were
avenged of their adversaries.
4 When they were thirsty, they
called upon thee, and water
was given them out of the flinty
rock, and their thirst was
quenched out of the hard stone.
5 For by what things their enemies were punished, by the
same they in their need were

---

18. δια υδατ. S. 19. εχθρους αυτου C. κατεκλυσαν Λ. κατεπαυσεν S. βάθ. ἀβυσσ. θαμβους sine αβυσσ. S. ἀνέβρασεν.
διεβιβασεν C. εισηλθεν (v. 16) usque ad σημιοις repetivit S¹. et uncis inclusit. 20. την δε C. χειραν C. S. 21. ηνοιξεν S.
XI. 1. Ευοδωσεν A. S. C. V¹. αυτου A. eorum Vulg. προφητων αγιων A. 3. εχθρ. ημυναντο S. A. C. Ven. V². al. ημυν.
εχθ. V. 5. γαρ om. 106. 261.

6 benefited. For instead of a fountain of a perpetual running river troubled with
7 foul blood, For a manifest reproof of that commandment, whereby the infants were slain, thou gavest unto them abundance of water by a means which
8 they hoped not for: Declaring by that thirst then how thou hadst punished their adver-
9 saries. For when they were tried, albeit but in mercy chastised, they knew how the ungodly were judged in wrath and tormented, thirsting in another
10 manner than the just. For these thou didst admonish and try, as a father: but the other, as a severe king, thou didst
11 condemn and punish. Whether they were absent or present,
12 they were vexed alike. For a double grief came upon them, and a groaning for the remem-
13 brance of things past. For when they heard by their own punishments the other to be benefited, they had some feel-
14 ing[1] of the Lord. For whom they rejected with scorn, when he was long before thrown out at the casting forth *of the infants*, him in the end, when they saw what came to pass,

[1] Or, *perceived*.

6 ἀντὶ μὲν πηγῆς ἀενάου ποταμοῦ αἵματι λυθρώδει ταραχθέντος,
7 εἰς ἔλεγχον νηπιοκτόνου διατάγματος,
ἔδωκας αὐτοῖς δαψιλὲς ὕδωρ ἀνελπίστως·
8 δείξας διὰ τοῦ τότε δίψους πῶς τοὺς ὑπεναντίους ἐκόλασας.
9 ὅτε γὰρ ἐπειράσθησαν, καίπερ ἐν ἐλέει παιδευόμενοι,
ἔγνωσαν πῶς ἐν ὀργῇ κρινόμενοι ἀσεβεῖς ἐβασανίζοντο.
10 τούτους μὲν γὰρ ὡς πατὴρ νουθετῶν ἐδοκίμασας,
ἐκείνους δὲ ὡς ἀπότομος βασιλεὺς καταδικάζων ἐξήτασας.
11 καὶ ἀπόντες δὲ καὶ παρόντες ὁμοίως ἐτρύχοντο.
12 διπλῆ γὰρ αὐτοὺς ἔλαβε λύπη, καὶ στεναγμὸς μνήμων τῶν παρελθόντων.
13 ὅτε γὰρ ἤκουσαν διὰ τῶν ἰδίων κολάσεων εὐεργετουμένους αὐτούς,
ᾔσθοντο τοῦ Κυρίου.
14 ὃν γὰρ ἐν ἐκθέσει πάλαι ῥιφέντα ἀπεῖπον χλευάζοντες,
ἐπὶ τέλει τῶν ἐκβάσεων ἐθαύμασαν,
οὐχ ὅμοια δικαίοις διψήσαντες.

7 cum illis actum est. [6] Nam pro fonte quidem sempiterni fluminis, humanum sanguinem
8 dedisti injustis. [7] Qui cum minuerentur in traductione infantium occiserum, dedisti illis abundantem aquam insperate,
9 [8] ostendens per sitim, quae tunc fuit, quemadmodum tuos exaltares, et adversarios illos necares.
10 [9] Cum enim tentati sunt, et quidem cum misericordia disciplinam accipientes, scierunt quemadmodum cum ira judicati impii
11 tormenta paterentur; [10] hos quidem tanquam pater monens probasti; illos autem tanquam durus rex interrogans condem-
12 nasti. [11] Absentes enim et praesentes similiter torquebantur.
13 [12] Duplex enim illos acceperat taedium, et gemitus cum memoria
14 praeteritorum. [13] Cum enim audirent per sua tormenta bene secum agi, commemorati sunt Dominum, admirantes in finem
15 exitus. [14] Quem enim in expositione prava projectum deriserunt, in finem eventus mirati sunt, non similiter justis si-

---

6. ων αντι μεν Ven. αεναου A. S. V. αεννάου V². al. ταραχθέντοι S. A. A. F. G. Par. ταραχθέντες V. al. λυθρω διαταραχθέντες Ven. 7. ελεγχον. επαινον 106. 261. δαψιλες om. 106. 261. δαψειλες S. 8. κολασας S. εκολασας S. cor. εκαλεσας C. 9. εν οργη A. V. μετ' οργης S. C. Ven. 106. 253. 261. Vulg. 12. μνημων των παρελθοντων V. C. 68. 253. Arm. μνημη των παρελθοντων 296. B. Par. μνημων των παρελθοντων A. S. Ven. al. Compl. παρεληλιθοτων 55. 254. A. Par. 13. ευεργετουμενους V. 68. al. ευεργετημενους S. A. C. 55. τοῦ κυρίου. σου κυριε Ven. 253. S². 14. τον γαρ V. S. ον γαρ A. al. Compl. εχθεσει S. A. εχθεσι C. παλιν Ven. παλαι impv. S². ριφεντα παλαι ανθρωπον απειποντες εχλευαζον C. απειπαν S². εθαυμαζον A. τοις δικαιοις S. διψησαντες. ψηφισαντες 106. 261.

16 tientes. [15] Pro cogitationibus autem insensatis iniquitatis illorum, quod quidam errantes colebant mutos serpentes, et bestias supervacuas, immisisti illis multitudinem mutorum animalium in
17 vindictam: [16] ut scirent, quia per quae peccat quis, per haec et
18 torquetur. [17] Non enim impossibilis erat omnipotens manus tua, quae creavit orbem terrarum ex materia invisa, immittere illis multitudinem ursorum, aut
19 audaces leones, [18] aut novi generis ira plenas ignotas bestias, aut vaporem ignium spirantes, aut fumi odorem proferentes, aut horrendas ab oculis scintillas
20 emittentes; [19] quarum non solum laesura poterat illos exterminare, sed et aspectus per timorem
21 occidere. [20] Sed et sine his uno spiritu poterant occidi, persecutionem passi ab ipsis factis suis, et dispersi per spiritum virtutis tuae; sed omnia in mensura, et numero, et pon-

15 ἀντὶ δὲ λογισμῶν ἀσυνέτων ἀδικίας αὐτῶν,
ἐν οἷς πλανηθέντες ἐθρήσκευον ἄλογα ἑρπετὰ καὶ κνώδαλα εὐτελῆ,
ἐπαπέστειλας αὐτοῖς πλῆθος ἀλόγων ζώων εἰς ἐκδίκησιν,
16 ἵνα γνῶσιν, ὅτι δι' ὧν τις ἁμαρτάνει, διὰ τούτων καὶ κολάζεται.
17 οὐ γὰρ ἠπόρει ἡ παντοδύναμός σου χεὶρ
καὶ κτίσασα τὸν κόσμον ἐξ ἀμόρφου ὕλης
ἐπιπέμψαι αὐτοῖς πλῆθος ἄρκων, ἢ θρασεῖς λέοντας,
18 ἢ νεοκτίστους θυμοῦ πλήρεις θῆρας ἀγνώστους,
ἤτοι πυρπνόον φυσῶντας ἆσθμα,
ἢ βρόμον λικμωμένους καπνοῦ,
ἢ δεινοὺς ἀπ' ὀμμάτων σπινθῆρας ἀστράπτοντας,
19 ὧν οὐ μόνον ἡ βλάβη ἠδύνατο συνεκτρίψαι αὐτοὺς,
ἀλλὰ καὶ ἡ ὄψις ἐκφοβήσασα διολέσαι.
20 καὶ χωρὶς δὲ τούτων ἑνὶ πνεύματι πεσεῖν ἐδύναντο
ὑπὸ τῆς δίκης διωχθέντες
καὶ λικμηθέντες ὑπὸ πνεύματος δυνάμεώς σου·
ἀλλὰ πάντα μέτρῳ καὶ ἀριθμῷ καὶ σταθμῷ διέταξας.

15 they admired. But for the foolish devices of their wickedness, wherewith being deceived they worshipped serpents void of reason, and vile beasts, thou didst send a multitude of unreasonable beasts upon them for
16 vengeance; That they might know, that wherewithal a man sinneth, by the same also shall
17 he be punished. For thy Almighty hand, that made the world of matter without form, wanted not means to send among them a multitude of bears,
18 or fierce lions, Or unknown wild beasts, full of rage, newly created, breathing out either a fiery vapour, or filthy scents of scattered smoke, or shooting horrible sparkles out of their
19 eyes: Whereof not only the harm might dispatch them at once, but also the terrible sight
20 utterly destroy them. Yea, and without these might they have fallen down with one blast, being persecuted of vengeance, and scattered abroad through the breath of thy power: but thou hast ordered all things in measure and number and weight.

15. εθησκευον S. εθρησκ. S. cor. κλωδαλα A. (?). επαποστειλαι 106. 261. 16. και κολαζεται S. Ven. 253. Athan. 17. και κτισασα. η και κτ. Ven. S². η κτ. 106. 261. η πληθος A. 296. 18. νεοκτιστους V. Ven. S. Arm. νεοκτιστον A. C. al. Compl. θυμοις πληρης S. θρασυγγωστους S. θηρας αγνωστους S². πυρπνεον S. 296. πυρφρορον 106. πυρφροραν 261. ασθματα 261. βρομους V. 68 157. 248. βρομον A. C. S. Ven. al. Compl. Vulg. Arm. βραμων 106. 261. λικμωμενους V. A. S. λικμωμενου 248. Compl. πινθηρας S. σπινθ. S². 19. ηδυνατο. εδυν. S. A. συνεκτριψαι V. S. Ven. al. εκτριψαι A. C. S². al. εκτρεψαι 106. 261. 20. εν ενι πν. C. 253. δικης om. S. add. cor. σου om. C. και σταθμω om. C. 261.

21 For thou canst shew thy great strength at all times when thou wilt; and who may withstand
22 the power of thine arm? For the whole world before thee is as a little grain[1] of the balance, yea, as a drop of the morning dew that falleth down upon the
23 earth. But thou hast mercy upon all; for thou canst do all things, and winkest at the sins of men, because they should
24 amend. For thou lovest all the things that are, and abhorrest nothing which thou hast made: for never wouldest thou have made any thing, if thou hadst
25 hated it. And how could any thing have endured, if it had not been thy will? or been preserved, if not called by
26 thee? But thou sparest all: for they are thine, O Lord, thou lover of souls.

[1] Or, little weight.

21 τὸ γὰρ μεγάλως ἰσχύειν σοὶ πάρεστιν πάντοτε,
καὶ κράτει βραχίονός σου τίς ἀντιστήσεται;
22 ὅτι ὡς ῥοπὴ ἐκ πλαστίγγων ὅλος ὁ κόσμος ἐναντίον σου,
καὶ ὡς ῥανὶς δρόσου ὀρθρινὴ κατελθοῦσα ἐπὶ γῆν.
23 ἐλεεῖς δὲ πάντας, ὅτι πάντα δύνασαι,
καὶ παρορᾷς ἁμαρτήματα ἀνθρώπων εἰς μετάνοιαν.
24 ἀγαπᾷς γὰρ τὰ ὄντα πάντα,
καὶ οὐδὲν βδελύσσῃ ὧν ἐποίησας,
οὐδὲ γὰρ ἂν μισῶν τι κατεσκεύασας.
25 πῶς δὲ ἔμεινεν ἄν τι εἰ μὴ σὺ ἠθέλησας;
ἢ τὸ μὴ κληθὲν ὑπὸ σοῦ διετηρήθη;
26 φείδῃ δὲ πάντων, ὅτι σά ἐστι, Δέσποτα φιλόψυχε.

22 dere disposuisti. [21] Multum enim valere, tibi soli supererat semper; et virtuti brachii
23 tui quis resistet? [22] Quoniam tanquam momentum staterae, sic est ante te orbis terrarum, et tanquam gutta roris antelucani quae descendit in terram.
24 [23] Sed misereris omnium, quia omnia potes, et dissimulas peccata hominum propter poeniten-
25 tiam. [24] Diligis enim omnia quae sunt, et nihil odisti eorum quae fecisti; nec enim odiens aliquid constituisti, aut fecisti.
26 [25] Quomodo autem posset aliquid permanere, nisi tu voluisses? aut quod a te vocatum non
27 esset conservaretur? [26] Parcis autem omnibus, quoniam tua sunt, Domine, qui amas animas.

CHAPTER XII.

1 For thine incorruptible Spirit
2 is in all things. Therefore chastenest thou them by little and little that offend, and warnest them by putting them in remembrance wherein they

ΚΕΦΑΛΑΙΟΝ ΙΒ΄.

1 Τὸ γὰρ ἄφθαρτόν σου Πνεῦμά ἐστιν ἐν πᾶσι.
2 Διὸ τοὺς παραπίπτοντας κατ᾽ ὀλίγον ἐλέγχεις,
καὶ ἐν οἷς ἁμαρτάνουσιν ὑπομιμνήσκων νουθετεῖς,

CAPUT XII.

1 O quam bonus et suavis est, Domine, Spiritus tuus in omnibus!
2 Ideoque eos qui exerrant partibus corripis, et de quibus peccant admones et alloqueris,

---

21. σοι παρεστιν A. C. S. V². Ven. al. παρεστι σοι V. al. σου τις ουθεις C. 22. πλαστιγαν S. κατεναντιον C. ορθινη C. ορθρινης 55. 264. Vulg. επι γην V. S. A. επι την γην 157. 248. 296. Compl. επι γης C. S². 106. 261. 24. και ουδενα A. 25. πως γαρ C. εμεινεν V. A. Ven. al. διεμεινεν S. C. al. τις C. κληθηναι C. πως αν διετηρηθη Ven. 55. 253. 254. 26. σα εστι V. S. Ven. al. Vulg. Ar. Arm. σα εστι παντα A. C. 55. al. Orig. Syr. XII. 2. αμαρτανωσιν 248. Compl.

ut relicta malitia, credant in te,
3 Domine. Illos enim antiquos inhabitatores terrae sanctae tuae,
4 quos exhorruisti, quoniam odibilia opera tibi faciebant per medicamina et sacrificia injusta,
5 et filiorum suorum necatores sine misericordia, et comestores viscerum hominum, et devoratores sanguinis [6] a medio sacra-
6 mento tuo, et auctores parentes animarum inauxiliatarum, perdere voluisti per manus parentum nostrorum, ut dignam per-
7 ciperent peregrinationem puerorum Dei, quae tibi omnium
8 charior est terra. Sed et his tanquam hominibus pepercisti, et misisti antecessores exercitus tui vespas, ut illos paulatim exterminarent.
9 Non quia impotens eras in bello subjicere impios justis, aut bestiis saevis, aut verbo duro simul extermi-
10 nare; sed partibus judicans dabas locum poenitentiae, non

ἵνα ἀπαλλαγέντες τῆς κακίας πιστεύσωσιν ἐπὶ σέ, Κύριε.
3 καὶ γὰρ τοὺς παλαιοὺς οἰκήτορας τῆς ἁγίας σου γῆς μισήσας,
4 ἐπὶ τῷ ἔχθιστα πράσσειν ἔργα φαρμακειῶν καὶ τελετὰς ἀνοσίους,
5 τέκνων τε φονέας ἀνελεήμονας, καὶ σπλαγχνοφάγων ἀνθρωπίνων σαρκῶν θοῖναν
6 καὶ αἵματος, ἐκ μέσου μύστας θιάσου,
καὶ αὐθέντας γονεῖς ψυχῶν ἀβοηθήτων,
ἐβουλήθης ἀπολέσαι διὰ χειρῶν πατέρων ἡμῶν,
7 ἵνα ἀξίαν ἀποικίαν δέξηται Θεοῦ παίδων ἡ παρὰ σοὶ πασῶν τιμιωτάτη γῆ.
8 ἀλλὰ καὶ τούτων ὡς ἀνθρώπων ἐφείσω,
ἀπέστειλάς τε προδρόμους τοῦ στρατοπέδου σου σφῆκας,
ἵνα αὐτοὺς καταβραχὺ ἐξολεθρεύσωσιν·
9 οὐκ ἀδυνατῶν ἐν παρατάξει ἀσεβεῖς δικαίοις ὑποχειρίους δοῦναι,
ἢ θηρίοις δεινοῖς, ἢ λόγῳ ἀποτόμῳ ὑφ᾽ ἓν ἐκτρῖψαι·
10 κρίνων δὲ καταβραχὺ ἐδίδους τόπον μετανοίας,

have offended, that leaving their wickedness they may believe on
3 thee, O Lord. For it was thy will to destroy by the hands of our fathers both those old[1] inhabitants of thy holy land,

[1] Or, ancient

4 Whom thou hatedst for doing most odious works of witchcrafts[2], and wicked sacrifices;

[2] Or, sorceries

5 And also those merciless murderers of children, and devourers of man's flesh, and the feasts of
6 blood, With their priests out of the midst of their idolatrous crew, and the parents, that killed with their own hands
7 souls destitute of help: That the land, which thou esteemedst above all other, might receive a worthy colony[3] of God's

[3] Or, inhabitance

8 children. Nevertheless even those thou sparedst as men, and didst send wasps, forerunners of thine host, to destroy them by little and little.
9 Not that thou wast unable to bring the ungodly under the hand of the righteous in battle, or to destroy them at once with cruel beasts, or with one rough
10 word: But executing thy judgments upon them by little and little, thou gavest them place of repentance, not being igno-

---

2. πιστευσωσιν om. S. add. S. cor. πιστευσωμεν A. αυτου επι σε S. αυτου S². impr. 3. παλαι S. 106. 4. φαρμακιων S. φαρμακιας C. ανοσιων C. 5. σπλαγχνοφαγοις Compl. σαρκος C. θοιναν 55. 254. και ανθρωπινων σαρκων, και θοιναν, και αιματος Compl. εκ μεσου μυσταθεια[s] σου V. μυσου μυσταθειασου V. a Sec. Man. εκ μεσου μυσταθιασου S. 55. 106. al. εμμεσου C. μυσταθειασου A. S². μυστας θειας σου Compl. εκ μυσου μυστας τε θειας σου Ald. 6. αυθέντας. λυθεντας C. εαν βουληθης S. εβουληθης S². δια χειρος 55. 106. al. 7. ινα αξ. κατα αξιαν S. ινα αξ. S. cor. και θεου 106. 261. παιδων 55. 254. η παρα σοι S. om. η. η παρα σοι. παντων S². 8. τους στρατοπεδους V. S. εξολεθρευσωσιν A. C. V. 9. διδοναι S. 10. κεινων γαρ S. κρεινων δε S².

rant that they were a naughty generation, and that their malice was bred in them, and that their cogitation would never be 11 changed. For it was a cursed seed from the beginning; neither didst thou for fear of any man give them pardon for those things wherein they sinned. 12 For who shall say, What hast thou done? or who shall withstand thy judgment? or who shall accuse thee for the nations that perish, whom thou hast made? or who shall come to stand against thee[1], to be revenged[2] for the unrighteous 13 men? For neither is there any God but thou that careth for all, to whom thou mightest shew that thy judgment is not un-14 right. Neither shall king or tyrant be able to set his face against thee for any whom thou 15 hast punished. Forsomuch then as thou art righteous thyself, thou orderest all things righteously: thinking it not agreeable with thy power to condemn him that hath not deserved to be 16 punished. For thy power is the beginning of righteousness, and because thou art the Lord of all, it maketh thee to be

[1] Or, *in thy presence*.
[2] Or, *a revenger*.

οὐκ ἀγνοῶν, ὅτι πονηρὰ ἡ γένεσις αὐτῶν
καὶ ἔμφυτος ἡ κακία αὐτῶν,
καὶ ὅτι οὐ μὴ ἀλλαγῇ ὁ λογισμὸς αὐτῶν εἰς τὸν αἰῶνα·
11 σπέρμα γὰρ ἦν κατηραμένον ἀπ' ἀρχῆς·
οὐδὲ εὐλαβούμενός τινα, ἐφ' οἷς ἡμάρτανον ἄδειαν ἐδίδους.
12 τίς γὰρ ἐρεῖ, τί ἐποίησας;
ἢ τίς ἀντιστήσεται τῷ κρίματί σου;
τίς δὲ ἐγκαλέσει σοι κατὰ ἐθνῶν ἀπολωλότων, ἃ σὺ ἐποίησας;
ἢ τίς εἰς κατάστασίν σοι ἐλεύσεται ἔκδικος κατὰ ἀδίκων ἀνθρώπων;
13 οὔτε γὰρ Θεός ἐστι πλὴν σοῦ, ᾧ μέλει περὶ πάντων,
ἵνα δείξῃς, ὅτι οὐκ ἀδίκως ἔκρινας·
14 οὔτε βασιλεὺς ἢ τύραννος ἀντοφθαλμῆσαι δυνήσεταί σοι περὶ ὧν ἐκόλασας.
15 δίκαιος δὲ ὢν δικαίως τὰ πάντα διέπεις,
αὐτὸν τὸν μὴ ὀφείλοντα κολασθῆναι καταδικάσαι
ἀλλότριον ἡγούμενος τῆς σῆς δυνάμεως.
16 ἡ γὰρ ἰσχύς σου δικαιοσύνης ἀρχή,
καὶ τὸ πάντων σε δεσπόζειν πάντων φείδεσθαί ποιεῖ.

ignorans quoniam nequam est natio eorum, et naturalis malitia ipsorum, et quoniam non poterat mutari cogitatio illorum in per-11 petuum. Semen enim erat maledictum ab initio; nec timens aliquem, veniam dabas peccatis 12 illorum. Quis enim dicet tibi: Quid fecisti? aut quis stabit contra judicium tuum? aut quis in conspectu tuo veniet vindex iniquorum hominum? aut quis tibi imputabit, si perierint na-13 tiones quas tu fecisti? Non enim est alius Deus quam tu, cui cura est de omnibus, ut ostendas quoniam non injuste ju-14 dicas judicium. Neque rex neque tyrannus in conspectu tuo inquirent de his quos per-15 didisti. Cum ergo sis justus, juste omnia disponis; ipsum quoque qui non debet puniri condemnare exterum aestimas 16 a tua virtute. Virtus enim tua justitiae initium est, et ob hoc quod omnium Dominus es,

---

10. οτι ante ου om. S. addit S. cor.   11. κεκατηραμενον S.   12. ελευσεται σοι S. Ven.   13. διξης S. et S¹. διξη S².
14. ουτε γαρ 106. 261.   δυνησονται 106. 261.   εκλασας. απωλεσας Reusch. Vulg (?). εκολασας S. A. V. Ven. Compl. Ald. al. Arm. Ar.   15. τα παντα δικαιως S.   ηγουμενον S. ηγουμενος S².   16. φειδ. σε ποιει A. S². al. Compl.

17 omnibus te parcere facis. Virtutem enim ostendis tu, qui non crederis esse in virtute consummatus, et horum qui te nesciunt
18 audaciam traducis. Tu autem dominator virtutis, cum tranquillitate judicas, et cum magna reverentia disponis nos; subest enim tibi, cum volueris, posse.
19 Docuisti autem populum tuum per talia opera, quoniam oportet justum esse et humanum, et bonae spei fecisti filios tuos, quoniam judicans das locum in
20 peccatis poenitentiae. Si enim inimicos servorum tuorum, et debitos morti, cum tanta cruciasti attentione, dans tempus et locum per quae possent mu-
21 tari a malitia; cum quanta diligentia judicasti filios tuos, quorum parentibus juramenta et conventiones dedisti bonarum
22 promissionum! Cum ergo das nobis disciplinam, inimicos nostros multipliciter flagellas, ut

17 ἰσχὺν γὰρ ἐνδείκνυσαι ἀπιστούμενος ἐπὶ δυνάμεως τελειότητι,
καὶ ἐν τοῖς εἰδόσι τὸ θράσος ἐξελέγχεις.
18 σὺ δὲ δεσπόζων ἰσχύος ἐν ἐπιεικείᾳ κρίνεις,
καὶ μετὰ πολλῆς φειδοῦς διοικεῖς ἡμᾶς·
πάρεστι γάρ σοι ὅταν θέλῃς τὸ δύνασθαι.
19 ἐδίδαξας δέ σου τὸν λαὸν διὰ τῶν τοιούτων ἔργων,
ὅτι δεῖ τὸν δίκαιον εἶναι φιλάνθρωπον
καὶ εὐέλπιδας ἐποίησας τοὺς υἱούς σου,
ὅτι δίδως ἐπὶ ἁμαρτήμασι μετάνοιαν.
20 εἰ γὰρ ἐχθροὺς παίδων σου καὶ ὀφειλομένους θανάτῳ
μετὰ τοσαύτης ἐτιμώρησας προσοχῆς καὶ διέσεως,
δοὺς χρόνους καὶ τόπον δι' ὧν ἀπαλλαγῶσι τῆς κακίας·
21 μετὰ πόσης ἀκριβείας ἔκρινας τοὺς υἱούς σου,
ὧν τοῖς πατράσιν ὅρκους καὶ συνθήκας ἔδωκας ἀγαθῶν ὑποσχέσεων;
22 ἡμᾶς οὖν παιδεύων, τοὺς ἐχθροὺς ἡμῶν ἐν μυριότητι μαστιγοῖς,

17 gracious unto all. For when men will not believe that thou art of a full[1] power, thou shewest thy strength, and among them that know it thou makest
18 their boldness manifest. But thou, mastering thy power, judgest with equity, and orderest us with great favour: for thou mayest use power when thou
19 wilt. But by such works hast thou taught thy people that the just man should be merciful, and hast made thy children to be of a good hope that thou givest
20 repentance for sins. For if thou didst punish the enemies of thy children, and the condemned to death, with such deliberation, giving them time and place, whereby they might be delivered from their malice:
21 With how great circumspection didst thou judge thine own sons, unto whose fathers thou hast sworn, and made covenants of
22 good promises? Therefore, whereas thou dost chasten us, thou scourgest our enemies a thousand times more, to the intent that, when we judge, we

---

17. ισχυν (cor. ισχυς) γαρ ενδεικνυσο S. ενδεικνυσαι S². ο απιστ. 55. 106. 254. οτι απιστ. A. εν τοις ουκ ειδοσι A. Vulg. Arm. σε ειδοσιν S. ειδοσι σου 55. 254. θαρσος 248. Compl. σου το κρατος S². εξελεγχεται S. εξελεγχεις S². 18. δε om. Ven. al. 19. οτι τον om. S. add. S². διδοις V. A. 68. Ald. διδως edd. 20. ετιμωρησαι V. S. Ven. al. ετιμωρησαι A. 55. 106. al. Compl. και δεησεως vulgo lect. om. A. al. Compl. Vulg. και διεσεως S. και διεσωσας 296. C. D. H. Par. Arm. δους αυτοις Ven. χρονον και τοπον A. 55. 106. al. Vulg. Syr. χρονον και τροπον 248. Compl. τοπον και χρονον Ven. 21. μετα ποσης. και μετα πασης S². κρινεις Ven. υποσχης S. υποσχεθων S². 22. εν μυριοτησι 106. 261.

M

should carefully think of thy goodness, and when we ourselves are judged, we should 23 look for mercy. Wherefore, whereas men have lived dissolutely and unrighteously, thou hast tormented them with their 24 own abominations[1]. For they went astray very far in the ways of error, and held them for gods, which even among the beasts of their enemies were despised, being deceived, as children of no understanding. 25 Therefore unto them, as to children without the use of reason, thou didst send a judg- 26 ment to mock them. But they that would not be reformed by that correction, wherein he dallied with them, shall feel a 27 judgment worthy of God. For, look, for what things they grudged, when they were punished, that is, for them whom they thought to be gods; [now] being punished in them, when they saw it, they acknowledged him to be the true God, whom before they denied to know; and therefore came extreme damnation upon them.

[1] Or, *abominable idols*.

CHAPTER XIII.

1 Surely vain are all men by nature, who are ignorant of God,

ἵνα σου τὴν ἀγαθότητα μεριμνῶμεν κρίνοντες,
κρινόμενοι δὲ προσδοκῶμεν ἔλεος.
23 ὅθεν καὶ τοὺς ἐν ἀφροσύνῃ ζωῆς βιώσαντας ἀδίκους
διὰ τῶν ἰδίων ἐβασάνισας βδελυγμάτων.
24 καὶ γὰρ τῶν πλάνης ὁδῶν μακρότερον ἐπλανήθησαν,
θεοὺς ὑπολαμβάνοντες τὰ καὶ ἐν ζώοις τῶν ἐχθρῶν ἄτιμα,
νηπίων δίκην ἀφρόνων ψευσθέντες.
25 διὰ τοῦτο ὡς παισὶν ἀλογίστοις τὴν κρίσιν εἰς ἐμπαιγμὸν ἔπεμψας·
26 οἱ δὲ παιγνίοις ἐπιτιμήσεως μὴ νουθετηθέντες
ἀξίαν Θεοῦ κρίσιν πειράσουσιν.
27 ἐφ' οἷς γὰρ αὐτοὶ πάσχοντες ἠγανάκτουν,
ἐπὶ τούτοις οὓς ἐδόκουν θεοὺς, ἐν αὐτοῖς κολαζόμενοι,
ἰδόντες ὃν πάλαι ἠρνοῦντο εἰδέναι, Θεὸν ἐπέγνωσαν ἀληθῆ.
διὸ καὶ τὸ τέρμα τῆς καταδίκης ἐπ' αὐτοὺς ἐπῆλθεν.

ΚΕΦΑΛΑΙΟΝ ΙΓ΄.

1 Μάταιοι μὲν γὰρ πάντες ἄνθρωποι φύσει, οἷς παρῆν Θεοῦ ἀγνωσία,

bonitatem tuam cogitemus judicantes, et cum de nobis judicatur, speremus misericordiam 23 tuam. Unde et illis, qui in vita sua insensate et injuste vixerunt, per haec quae coluerunt dedisti summa tormenta. 24 Etenim in erroris via diutius erraverunt, deos aestimantes haec quae in animalibus sunt supervacua, infantium insensa- 25 torum more viventes. Propter hoc tanquam pueris insensatis judicium in derisum dedisti. 26 Qui autem ludibriis et increpationibus non sunt correcti, dignum Dei judicium experti 27 sunt. In quibus enim patientes indignabantur, per haec quos putabant deos, in ipsis cum exterminarentur videntes, illum, quem olim negabant se nosse, verum Deum agnoverunt; propter quod et finis condemnationis eorum venit super illos.

CAPUT XIII.

1 Vani autem sunt omnes homines, in quibus non subest scientia Dei; et de his quae

---

22. ελεον Ven.   23. αφροσυναις S. Compl.   ζωης om. Ven.   αδικους S. V. 55. 68. Ar.   αδικως A. S³. Ven. al. Vulg. Syr. Arm.
25. εμπαιγμον. ενπεγμον S.   26. πεγνιοις S.   κρισιν θεου S.   27. ους. ουν S. οις (248. 261) εδοκουν θεοις (261) κολαζομενοι εν αυτοις 106.   ιδοντες δε S.   ειδεναι om. S. 157.   επ' αυτους. επ' αυτον S. επ αυταν S².   ηλθεν Ven.
XIII. 1. ματαιοι γαρ παντες φυσι ανθρ. S.

videntur bona, non potuerunt intelligere cum qui est, neque operibus attendentes agnoverunt 2 quis esset artifex; sed aut ignem, aut spiritum, aut citatum aërem, aut gyrum stellarum, aut nimiam aquam, aut solem et lunam, rectores orbis terrarum 3 deos putaverunt. Quorum si specie delectati, deos putaverunt, sciant quanto his Dominator eorum speciosior est; speciei enim generator haec 4 omnia constituit. Aut si virtutem et opera eorum mirati sunt, intelligant ab illis quoniam qui haec fecit, fortior est 5 illis; a magnitudine enim speciei et creaturae cognoscibiliter poterit creator horum videri. 6 Sed tamen adhuc in his minor est querela; et hi enim fortasse errant, Deum quaerentes, 7 et volentes invenire. Etenim cum in operibus illius conver-

καὶ ἐκ τῶν ὁρωμένων ἀγαθῶν οὐκ ἴσχυσαν εἰδέναι τὸν ὄντα,
οὔτε τοῖς ἔργοις προσχόντες ἐπέγνωσαν τὸν τεχνίτην·
2 ἀλλ' ἢ πῦρ, ἢ πνεῦμα, ἢ ταχινὸν ἀέρα,
ἢ κύκλον ἄστρων, ἢ βίαιον ὕδωρ,
ἢ φωστῆρας οὐρανοῦ πρυτάνεις κόσμου θεοὺς ἐνόμισαν.
3 ὧν εἰ μὲν τῇ καλλονῇ τερπόμενοι ταῦτα θεοὺς ὑπελάμβανον,
γνώτωσαν πόσῳ τούτων ὁ Δεσπότης ἐστὶ βελτίων·
ὁ γὰρ τοῦ κάλλους γενεσιάρχης ἔκτισεν αὐτά·
4 εἰ δὲ δύναμιν καὶ ἐνέργειαν ἐκπλαγέντες,
νοησάτωσαν ἀπ' αὐτῶν πόσῳ ὁ κατασκευάσας αὐτὰ δυνατώτερός ἐστιν.
5 ἐκ γὰρ μεγέθους καὶ καλλονῆς κτισμάτων
ἀναλόγως ὁ γενεσιουργὸς αὐτῶν θεωρεῖται.
6 ἀλλ' ὅμως ἐπὶ τούτοις ἐστὶ μέμψις ὀλίγη,
καὶ γὰρ αὐτοὶ τάχα πλανῶνται Θεὸν ζητοῦντες καὶ θέλοντες εὑρεῖν.
7 ἐν γὰρ τοῖς ἔργοις αὐτοῦ ἀναστρεφόμενοι διερευνῶσι,

and could not out of the good things that are seen know him that is: neither by considering the works did they acknowledge 2 the workmaster; But deemed either fire, or wind, or the swift air, or the circle of the stars, or the violent water, or the lights of heaven, to be the gods 3 which govern the world. With whose beauty if they being delighted took them to be gods; let them know how much better the Lord of them is: for the first author of beauty hath 4 created them. But if they were astonished at their power and virtue, let them understand by them, how much mightier he is 5 that made them. For by the greatness and beauty of the creatures proportionably the 6 maker of them is seen. But yet for this they are the less to be blamed: for they peradventure err, seeking God, and de- 7 sirous to find him. For being conversant in his works they

---

1. εκ τωνδε Ven. ενεκα των 106. ουδε S. οτε Ven. προσχοντες V. 55. 68. 253. προσεχοντες A. S. Ven. al. Compl. εγνωσαν S. 2. η και πνευμα 248. αστερων S². 3. θεους V. 55. 68. Vulg. ταυτα θεους A. Ven. al Compl. Syr. Arm. Ar. ταυθ sine θεους S. του S². θεους υπελαμβανον ειναι 253. υπελ. θ. ειναι Ven. βελτειον S². βελτειων S². κάλλους. κοσμον S². 4. δε om. S. εις δε S². την δυν. 106. δυναμει και ενεργεια V. Ven. 68. Compl. Ald. δυναμιν κ. ενεργειαν S. A. V. Mai. και εκπλ. S. και S. cor. impr. ποσῳ μαλλον 55. 254. 5. καλλονης και κτισμ. S. Ven. al. Compl. Ald. Vulg. και καλλονης S². 55. 248. al. Compl. μεγεθους καλλονης κτισματων V. A. 68. 157. Syr. 6. επί. ετι A. μεμψις εστιν A. 157. al. Compl. 7. διεραυνωσιν S. V. διερευνωσι S².

84 THE BOOK OF WISDOM [XIII 8–

[1 Or, *track*.]

search[1] him diligently, and believe their sight because the things are beautiful that are
8 seen. Howbeit neither are they
9 to be pardoned. For if they were able to know so much, that they could aim at the world, how did they not sooner find out the Lord thereof?
10 But miserable are they, and in dead things is their hope, who called them gods, which are the works of men's hands, gold and silver, to shew art in, and resemblances of beasts, or a stone good for nothing, the work of
11 an ancient hand. Now a carpenter[2] that felleth timber, after he hath sawn down a tree meet for the purpose, and taken off all the bark skilfully round about, and hath wrought it handsomely, and made a vessel thereof fit for the service of
12 man's life, And after spending the refuse[3] of his work to dress his meat, hath filled himself,
13 And taking the very refuse among those which served to no use, being a crooked piece of wood, and full of knots, hath carved it diligently, when he had nothing else to do, and

[2 Or, *timber-wright*.]
[3 Or, *chips*.]

καὶ πείθονται τῇ ὄψει, ὅτι καλὰ τὰ βλεπόμενα.
8 πάλιν δὲ οὐδ' αὐτοὶ συγγνωστοί.
9 εἰ γὰρ τοσοῦτον ἴσχυσαν εἰδέναι,
ἵνα δύνωνται στοχάσασθαι τὸν αἰῶνα,
τὸν τούτων Δεσπότην πῶς τάχιον οὐχ εὗρον;
10 Ταλαίπωροι δὲ καὶ ἐν νεκροῖς αἱ ἐλπίδες αὐτῶν,
οἵτινες ἐκάλεσαν θεοὺς ἔργα χειρῶν ἀνθρώπων,
χρυσὸν καὶ ἄργυρον τέχνης ἐμμελέτημα καὶ ἀπεικάσματα ζώων,
ἢ λίθον ἄχρηστον χειρὸς ἔργον ἀρχαίας.
11 εἰ δὲ καί τις ὑλοτόμος τέκτων εὐκίνητον φυτὸν ἐκπρίσας,
περιέξυσεν εὐμαθῶς πάντα τὸν φλοιὸν αὐτοῦ,
καὶ τεχνησάμενος εὐπρεπῶς κατεσκεύασε χρήσιμον σκεῦος εἰς ὑπηρεσίαν ζωῆς,
12 τὰ δὲ ἀποβλήματα τῆς ἐργασίας
εἰς ἑτοιμασίαν τροφῆς ἀναλώσας ἐνεπλήσθη,
13 τὸ δὲ ἐξ αὐτῶν ἀπόβλημα εἰς οὐθὲν εὔχρηστον,
ξύλον σκολιὸν καὶ ὄζοις συμπεφυκός,
λαβὼν ἔγλυψεν ἐν ἐπιμελείᾳ ἀργίας αὐτοῦ,

sentur inquirunt, et persuasum habent quoniam bona sunt quae
8 videntur. Iterum autem nec
9 his debet ignosci. Si enim tantum potuerunt scire, ut possent aestimare saeculum, quomodo hujus Dominum non facilius invenerunt?
10 Infelices autem sunt, et inter mortuos spes illorum est, qui appellaverunt deos opera manuum hominum, aurum et argentum, artis inventionem, et similitudines animalium, aut lapidem inutilem opus manus anti-
11 quae. Aut si quis artifex faber de sylva lignum rectum secuerit, et hujus docte eradat omnem corticem, et arte sua usus, diligenter fabricet vas utile in con-
12 versationem vitae; reliquiis autem ejus operis ad praepara-
13 tionem escae abutatur, et reliquum horum quod ad nullos usus facit, lignum curvum et vorticibus plenum, sculpat diligenter per vacuitatem suam, et

---

8 συγγνωστοι S συγνωστοι A   9 τουτου δεσπ. 106 261   10 εμμελητηματα S³ 106 253 ευμελητηματα Ven
11 ευκινητον εκκινηται Ald περιεξεσεν Ven. 248. Compl ευτρεπως S   12 αποβληματα V το δε αποβλητον Ven.
υπολιμματα A υπολειμματα 55 296 al αποβλητα 106 261 ετοιμασιαν υπηρεσιαν A αναλωσεως S ενεπλησεν Ven
13. συμπεφυκως S. συμπεφυκος S². εμπεφυκος 157 εν επιμελεια V al. εν abest ab A. S αργιας V S. Ven. al Vulg. εργασιας
S². A Codd Par plerique Syr Ar Arm

per scientiam suae artis figuret illud, et assimilet illud imagini 14 hominis, aut alicui ex animalibus illud comparet, perliniens rubrica, et rubicundum faciens fuco colorem illius, et omnem maculam quae in illo est per- 15 liniens; et faciat ei dignam habitationem, et in pariete ponens illud, et confirmans ferro, 16 ne forte cadat, prospiciens illi, sciens quoniam non potest adjuvare se; imago enim est, et 17 opus est illi adjutorium. Et de substantia sua, et de filiis suis, et de nuptiis votum faciens inquirit. Non erubescit loqui cum illo, qui sine anima est; 18 et pro sanitate quidem infirmum deprecatur, et pro vita rogat mortuum, et in adjutorium 19 inutilem invocat; et pro itinere petit ab eo, qui ambulare non potest; [19] et de acquirendo, et de operando, et de omnium rerum

καὶ ἐμπειρίᾳ ἀνέσεως ἐτύπωσεν αὐτό,
ἀπείκασεν αὐτὸ εἰκόνι ἀνθρώπου,
14 ἢ ζώῳ τινὶ εὐτελεῖ ὡμοίωσεν αὐτό,
καταχρίσας μίλτῳ, καὶ φύκει ἐρυθήνας χρόαν αὐτοῦ,
καὶ πᾶσαν κηλῖδα τὴν ἐν αὐτῷ καταχρίσας,
15 καὶ ποιήσας αὐτῷ αὐτοῦ ἄξιον οἴκημα,
ἐν τοίχῳ ἔθηκεν αὐτὸ ἀσφαλισάμενος σιδήρῳ.
16 ἵνα μὲν οὖν μὴ καταπέσῃ προενόησεν αὐτοῦ,
εἰδὼς ὅτι ἀδυνατεῖ ἑαυτῷ βοηθῆσαι·
καὶ γάρ ἐστιν εἰκών, καὶ χρείαν ἔχει βοηθείας.
17 περὶ δὲ κτημάτων καὶ γάμων αὐτοῦ καὶ τέκνων προσευχόμενος
οὐκ αἰσχύνεται τῷ ἀψύχῳ προσλαλῶν·
18 καὶ περὶ μὲν ὑγιείας τὸ ἀσθενὲς ἐπικαλεῖται,
περὶ δὲ ζωῆς τὸ νεκρὸν ἀξιοῖ,
περὶ δὲ ἐπικουρίας τὸ ἀπειρότατον ἱκετεύει,
περὶ δὲ ὁδοιπορίας τὸ μηδὲ βάσει χρῆσθαι δυνάμενον,
19 περὶ δὲ πορισμοῦ καὶ ἐργασίας καὶ χειρῶν ἐπιτυχίας

formed it by the skill of his understanding, and fashioned it 14 to the image of a man; Or made it like some vile beast, laying it over with vermilion, and with paint colouring it red, and covering every spot therein; 15 And when he had made a convenient room for it, set it in a wall, and made it fast with iron: 16 For he provided for it that it might not fall, knowing that it was unable to help itself; for it is an image, and hath need of 17 help: Then maketh he prayer for his goods, for his wife and children, and is not ashamed to speak to that which hath no life. 18 For health he calleth upon that which is weak: for life prayeth to that which is dead: for aid humbly beseecheth that which hath least means to help[1]: and for a good journey he asketh of that which cannot set a foot 19 forward: And for gaining and getting, and for good success of his hands, asketh ability to

[1] Gr. it hath no experience at all.

---

13. και εν εμπειρια Ven. συνεσεως V², S². ανεσεως A. S. V¹. Ven. al. Ald. απεικασεν τε A. 14. αφωμοιωσεν S. 296. μιλτω. γη μιλτω S². Ven. 253. ερυθηνας 248. Compl. ερυθημα S. ερυθηνας S². V. ερυθηνος A. χροας S. V². χροαν S². χροιαν 106. 261. καταχρησας γη Ven. γη add. S². 15. αυτου om. S. Ven. 261. 16. εαυτῷ. αυτω S. 106. 17. γαμου Ven. αυτου om. Ven. 106. al. τεκνων αυτου Ven. 253. ευχομενος S. Ven. λαλων Ven. 18. υγιας S. υγειας 106. 261. το νεκρον S. A. V. 157. 248. Compl. επικουριας. εμπειριας S. επικουριας S². το απειροτατον S. A. al. Compl. ικετευει om. S. add. S². ποριας S. οδοιποριας S². χρησασθαι 55. 253. al. 19. και περι δε S. δε S. cor. impr. και χειρων. και om. S.

CHAPTER XIV.

1 Again, one preparing himself to sail, and about to pass through the raging waves, calleth upon a piece of wood more rotten than the vessel[2] that carrieth 2 him. For verily desire of gain devised that[2], and the workman 3 built it by his skill. But thy providence, O Father, governeth it; for thou hast made a way in the sea, and a safe path in 4 the waves; Shewing that thou canst save from all danger: yea, though a man went to sea 5 without art. Nevertheless thou wouldest not that the works of thy wisdom should be idle, and therefore do men commit their lives to a small piece of wood, and passing the rough sea in 6 a weak vessel are saved. For in the old time also, when the proud giants perished, the hope of the world governed by thy

[1] Or, ship.
[2] Or, vessel, or, ship.

ΚΕΦΑΛΑΙΟΝ ΙΔ΄.

1 Πλοῦν τις πάλιν στελλόμενος
καὶ ἄγρια μέλλων διοδεύειν κύματα,
τοῦ φέροντος αὐτὸν πλοίου σαθρότερον ξύλον ἐπιβοᾶται.
2 ἐκεῖνο μὲν γὰρ ὄρεξις πορισμῶν ἐπενόησε,
τεχνίτης δὲ σοφίᾳ κατεσκεύασεν.
3 ἡ δὲ σὴ, Πάτερ, διακυβερνᾷ πρόνοια,
ὅτι ἔδωκας καὶ ἐν θαλάσσῃ ὁδὸν
καὶ ἐν κύμασι τρίβον ἀσφαλῆ,
4 δεικνὺς ὅτι δύνασαι ἐκ παντὸς σώζειν,
ἵνα κἂν ἄνευ τέχνης τις ἐπιβῇ.
5 θέλεις δὲ μὴ ἀργὰ εἶναι τὰ τῆς σοφίας σου ἔργα·
διὰ τοῦτο καὶ ἐλαχίστῳ ξύλῳ πιστεύουσιν ἄνθρωποι ψυχὰς,
καὶ διελθόντες κλύδωνα σχεδίᾳ διεσώθησαν.
6 καὶ ἀρχῆς γὰρ ἀπολλυμένων ὑπερηφάνων γιγάντων,
ἡ ἐλπὶς τοῦ κόσμου ἐπὶ σχεδίας καταφυγοῦσα

CAPUT XIV.

1 Iterum alius navigare cogitans, et per feros fluctus iter facere incipiens, ligno portante se, 2 fragilius lignum invocat. Illud enim cupiditas acquirendi excogitavit, et artifex sapientia 3 fabricavit sua. Tua autem, Pater, providentia gubernat; quoniam dedisti et in mari viam, et inter fluctus semitam 4 firmissimam, ostendens quoniam potens es ex omnibus salvare, etiam si sine arte aliquis adeat 5 mare. Sed ut non essent vacua sapientiae tuae opera, propter hoc etiam et exiguo ligno credunt homines animas suas, et transeuntes mare per ratem li- 6 berati sunt. Sed et ab initio cum perirent superbi gigantes, spes orbis terrarum ad ratem

---

19. το αδρανες S. εὐδρ. αἰτεῖται. αδρανιαν επικαλειται S. αιτειται S². XIV. 1. διοδευειν μελλων Ven. πλοιου V. S. Ven. al. ξυλου A. 157. Ar. Vulg. επιβοα Ven. 253. 2. επενθησε Ven. τεχνιτις δε σοφια A. S. V. al. Compl. τεχνιτηι edd. Ven. Vulg. Syr. Ar. Arm 3. διακυβερναται 106. 261. 4. εκ παντος δυνασαι S. εκ παντων A. Vulg. ινα om. Ven. 253. S². καν V. S Ven. al. και A. 55. 106. al. 5. της σης σοφιας 253. σου om. S. Ven. 253. εν ελαχ. Ven. 106. 157. κλυδωνας Ven. 55. 254. 6. και om. Ven. 106. 261.

confugiens, remisit saeculo semen nativitatis, quae manu tua erat 7 gubernata. Benedictum est enim lignum, per quod fit jus- 8 titia. Per manus autem quod fit idolum, maledictum est et ipsum, et qui fecit illud; quia ille quidem operatus est, illud autem cum esset fragile, deus 9 cognominatus est. Similiter autem odio sunt Deo impius et 10 impietas ejus. Etenim quod factum est cum illo qui fecit 11 tormenta patietur. Propter hoc et in idolis nationum non erit respectus, quoniam creaturae Dei in odium factae sunt, et in tentationem animabus hominum, et in muscipulam pedibus in- 12 sipientium. Initium enim fornicationis est exquisitio idolorum; et adinventio illorum cor- 13 ruptio vitae est; neque enim erant ab initio, neque erunt in 14 perpetuum. Supervacuitas enim hominum haec advenit in orbem terrarum; et ideo brevis illorum finis est inventus. 15 Acerbo enim luctu dolens pater cito sibi rapti filii fecit imaginem; et illum, qui tunc quasi

ἀπέλιπεν αἰῶνι σπέρμα γενέσεως τῇ σῇ κυβερνηθεῖσα χειρί.
7 εὐλόγηται γὰρ ξύλον δι' οὗ γίνεται δικαιοσύνη.
8 τὸ χειροποίητον δὲ ἐπικατάρατον αὐτὸ, καὶ ὁ ποιήσας αὐτὸ,
ὅτι ὁ μὲν εἰργάζετο, τὸ δὲ φθαρτὸν θεὸς ὠνομάσθη.
9 ἐν ἴσῳ γὰρ μισητὰ Θεῷ καὶ ὁ ἀσεβῶν καὶ ἡ ἀσέβεια αὐτοῦ·
10 καὶ γὰρ τὸ πραχθὲν σὺν τῷ δράσαντι κολασθήσεται.
11 διὰ τοῦτο καὶ ἐν εἰδώλοις ἐθνῶν ἐπισκοπὴ ἔσται,
ὅτι ἐν κτίσματι Θεοῦ εἰς βδέλυγμα ἐγενήθησαν
καὶ εἰς σκάνδαλα ψυχαῖς ἀνθρώπων
καὶ εἰς παγίδα ποσὶν ἀφρόνων.
12 Ἀρχὴ γὰρ πορνείας ἐπίνοια εἰδώλων,
εὕρεσις δὲ αὐτῶν φθορὰ ζωῆς.
13 οὔτε γὰρ ἦν ἀπ' ἀρχῆς, οὔτε εἰς τὸν αἰῶνα ἔσται.
14 κενοδοξίᾳ γὰρ ἀνθρώπων εἰσῆλθεν εἰς τὸν κόσμον,
καὶ διὰ τοῦτο σύντομον αὐτῶν τέλος ἐπενοήθη.
15 ἀώρῳ γὰρ πένθει τρυχόμενος πατὴρ
τοῦ ταχέως ἀφαιρεθέντος τέκνου εἰκόνα ποιήσας,

hand escaped in a weak vessel, and left to all ages a seed of 7 generation. For blessed is the wood whereby righteousness 8 cometh. But that which is made with hands is cursed, as well it, as he that made it: he, because he made it; and it, because, being corrupt- 9 ible, it was called god. For the ungodly and his ungodliness are both alike hateful unto God. 10 For that which is made shall be punished together with him 11 that made it. Therefore even upon[1] the idols of the Gentiles shall there be a visitation: because in the creature of God they are become an abomination, and stumblingblocks[2] to the souls of men, and a snare[3] to 12 the feet of the unwise. For the devising of idols was the beginning of *spiritual* fornication, and the invention of them the 13 corruption of life. For neither were they from the beginning, neither shall they be for ever. 14 For by the vainglory of men they entered into the world, and therefore shall they come 15 shortly to an end. For a father afflicted with untimely mourning, when he hath made an image of his child soon taken away, now honoured him as a

[1] Or, *to*, or, *by*.
[2] Gr. *scandals*.
[3] Or, *trap*.

6. απελιπεν V. υπελιπεν S. απελειπεν A. κατελειπεν 296. κατελιπεν 261. τω αιωνι S. V. τῳ impr. V². 7. ευλογειται 248. ευλογημενον 106. 261. εν δικαιοσ. S. εν S. cor. impr. 8. το δε χειρ. S. 157. 248. Compl. οτι ο μεν V. A. al. και ο μεν S. ειργαζετο V. ηργαζετο A. S. 253. ειργασατο 55. 254. 11. καὶ ἐν. και om. S. εν om. 106. 261. 296. κτισμασιν Ven. σκανδαλον 261. ποσ. ανθρωπων αφρ. 106. 261. 12. γαρ om. 261. Compl. ευρεσεις V¹. αυτων S. 13. ἔσται. μενει 157. 14. κενοδ. γάρ. κεν. δε Von. S². ανθρ. θανατος εισηλθεν S. θανατος S. cor. impr. εις κοσμον V. 68. εις τον κ. A. S. Ven. al. Compl. αυτων το τελος A. 55. 157. al. Compl. το τελος αυτων 106. 296. το om. V. S. Ven. 68. 253. Athan.

god, which was then a dead man, and delivered to those that were under him ceremonies and
16 sacrifices. Thus in process of time[1] an ungodly custom grown strong was kept as a law, and graven images were worshipped by the commandments of kings[2].
17 Whom men could not honour in presence[3], because they dwelt far off, they took the counterfeit of his visage from far, and made an express image of a king whom they honoured, to the end that by this their forwardness they might flatter him that was absent, as if he were pre-
18 sent. Also the singular diligence of the artificer did help to set forward the ignorant
19 to more superstition. For he, peradventure willing to please one in authority, forced all his skill to make the resemblance
20 of the best fashion[4]. And so the multitude, allured by the grace of the work, took him now for a god, which a little before was but honoured as a
21 man. And this was an occasion to deceive the world: for

[1] Gr. *in time.*
[2] Or, *tyrant.*
[3] Or, *in sight.*
[4] Gr. *to the better.*

τὸν τότε νεκρὸν ἄνθρωπον νῦν ὡς θεὸν ἐτίμησε,
καὶ παρέδωκε τοῖς ὑποχειρίοις μυστήρια καὶ τελετάς.
16 εἶτα ἐν χρόνῳ κρατυνθὲν τὸ ἀσεβὲς ἔθος ὡς νόμος ἐφυλάχθη,
καὶ τυράννων ἐπιταγαῖς ἐθρησκεύετο τὰ γλυπτά·
17 οὓς ἐν ὄψει μὴ δυνάμενοι τιμᾶν ἄνθρωποι διὰ τὸ μακρὰν οἰκεῖν,
τὴν πόρρωθεν ὄψιν ἀνατυπωσάμενοι,
ἐμφανῆ εἰκόνα τοῦ τιμωμένου βασιλέως ἐποίησαν,
ἵνα τὸν ἀπόντα ὡς παρόντα κολακεύωσι διὰ τῆς σπουδῆς.
18 εἰς ἐπίτασιν δὲ θρησκείας καὶ τοὺς ἀγνοοῦντας
ἡ τοῦ τεχνίτου προετρέψατο φιλοτιμία.
19 ὁ μὲν γὰρ τάχα τῷ κρατοῦντι βουλόμενος ἀρέσαι
ἐξεβιάσατο τῇ τέχνῃ τὴν ὁμοιότητα ἐπὶ τὸ κάλλιον·
20 τὸ δὲ πλῆθος ἐφελκόμενον διὰ τὸ εὔχαρι τῆς ἐργασίας
τὸν πρὸ ὀλίγου τιμηθέντα ἄνθρωπον νῦν σέβασμα ἐλογίσαντο.
21 καὶ τοῦτο ἐγένετο τῷ βίῳ εἰς ἔνεδρον,

homo mortuus fuerat, nunc tanquam deum colere coepit, et constituit inter servos suos sacra et sacrificia. Deinde interveniente tempore, convalescente iniqua consuetudine, hic error tanquam lex custoditus est, et tyrannorum imperio colebantur
17 figmenta. Et hos quos in palam homines honorare non poterant propter hoc quod longe essent, e longinquo figura eorum allata, evidentem imaginem regis quem honorare volebant fecerunt, ut illum qui aberat tanquam praesentem colerent
18 sua sollicitudine. Provexit autem ad horum culturam et hos qui ignorabant artificis eximia
19 diligentia. Ille enim, volens placere illi qui se assumpsit, elaboravit arte sua ut similitudinem in melius figuraret.
20 Multitudo autem hominum abducta per speciem operis, eum, qui ante tempus tanquam homo honoratus fuerat, nunc deum
21 aestimaverunt. Et haec fuit vitae humanae deceptio, quo-

---

15. τον τοτε V. S. Ven. al. τ. ποτε A. 296. 16. κρατηθεν 106. Ald. Compl. εθνος S. (ν erasum) νομον S. νομος S¹. ἐφυλάχθη. ωνομασθη 106. 261. εθρησκευοντο 106. 261. 17. τυπω ανατυπωσαμενοι Ven. 253. τυπωσαμενοι 254. τετιμημενον 157. Athan. των απ. ως παρ. V. A. al. ως παρ. των απ. S. Ven. al. κολακευωσι V. S. Ven. al. κολακευσωσιν A. 55. 106. al. της σπουδης S. V. Ven. al. Ath. της om. A. 55. 106. al. 18. μετα τουτο η του 253. 19. τῳ κρατ. V. Mai. τῳ om. S. A. C. V. Vercell 253. al. Ald. τῃ om. 253. 20. ἐφελκομενον. ἐξερχομενον 106. 261. ευχαρι V. S. al. ευχαρις A. C. εις σεβασμα 55. 254. σεβασμιον 261. 21. εις ενεδρα S. ενεδρον S².

niam aut affectui aut regibus deservientes homines, incommunicabile nomen lapidibus et
21 lignis imposuerunt. Et non suffecerat errasse eos circa Dei scientiam; sed et in magno viventes inscientiae bello, tot et tam magna mala pacem appel-
23 lant. Aut enim filios suos sacrificantes, aut obscura sacrificia facientes, aut insaniae plenas
24 vigilias habentes, neque vitam, neque nuptias mundas jam custodiunt; sed alius alium per invidiam occidit aut adulterans
25 contristat; et omnia commista sunt, sanguis, homicidium, furtum et fictio, corruptio et infidelitas, turbatio et perjurium,
26 tumultus bonorum, Dei immemoratio, animarum inquinatio, nativitatis immutatio, nuptiarum inconstantia, inordinatio moe-
27 chiae et impudicitiae. Infandorum enim idolorum cultura omnis mali causa est, et initium, et finis.
28 Aut enim dum laetantur, insaniunt, aut certe vaticinantur

ὅτι ἢ συμφορᾷ ἢ τυραννίδι δουλεύσαντες ἄνθρωποι
τὸ ἀκοινώνητον ὄνομα λίθοις καὶ ξύλοις περιέθεσαν.
22 εἶτ᾽ οὐκ ἤρκεσε τὸ πλανᾶσθαι περὶ τὴν τοῦ Θεοῦ γνῶσιν,
ἀλλὰ καὶ ἐν μεγάλῳ ζῶντες ἀγνοίας πολέμῳ
τὰ τοσαῦτα κακὰ εἰρήνην προσαγορεύουσιν.
23 ἢ γὰρ τεκνοφόνους τελετὰς, ἢ κρύφια μυστήρια,
ἢ ἐμμανεῖς ἐξάλλων θεσμῶν κώμους ἄγοντες,
24 οὔτε βίους οὔτε γάμους καθαροὺς ἔτι φυλάσσουσιν,
ἕτερος δ᾽ ἕτερον ἢ λοχῶν ἀναιρεῖ, ἢ νοθεύων ὀδυνᾷ.
25 πάντα δ᾽ ἐπιμὶξ ἔχει αἷμα καὶ φόνος, κλοπὴ καὶ δόλος,
φθορά, ἀπιστία, τάραχος, ἐπιορκία,
26 θόρυβος ἀγαθῶν, χάριτος ἀμνηστία,
ψυχῶν μιασμός, γενέσεως ἐναλλαγή,
γάμων ἀταξία, μοιχεία καὶ ἀσέλγεια.
27 ἢ γὰρ τῶν ἀνωνύμων εἰδώλων θρησκεία
παντὸς ἀρχὴ κακοῦ καὶ αἰτία καὶ πέρας ἐστίν.
28 ἢ γὰρ εὐφραινόμενοι μεμήνασιν, ἢ προφητεύουσι ψευδῆ,

men, serving either calamity or tyranny, did ascribe unto stones and stocks the incommunicable
22 name[1]. Moreover this was not enough for them, that they erred in the knowledge of God; but whereas they lived in the great war of ignorance, those so great
23 plagues called they peace. For whilst they slew their children in sacrifices, or used secret ceremonies, or made revellings of
24 strange rites; They kept neither lives nor marriages any longer undefiled: but either one slew another traitorously, or grieved
25 him by adultery. So that there reigned in all men without exception[2] blood, manslaughter, theft, and dissimulation, corruption, unfaithfulness, tumults,
26 perjury, Disquieting of good men, forgetfulness of good turns, defiling of souls, changing of kind[3], disorder in marriages, adultery, and shameless un-
27 cleanness. For the worshipping of idols not to be named[4] is the beginning, the cause, and the
28 end, of all evil. For either they are mad when they be merry,

[1] Or, of God.
[2] Or, confused'y.
[3] Or, sex.
[4] Gr. nameless.

---

21. περιεθεσαν V. A. S.   περιθηκαν S². C. 106. 157. 248. Compl.   22. ηρκεσε τo V.   ηρκεσεν πλανασθαι S.   ηρκεσεν αυτοις A. a sec. man. 106. 261.   ηρκεσθησαν Ven.   μεγαλῳ V. Ven.   εν μεγαλω A. C. 157. al. Compl. S².   μεγαλας S.   24. ετι καθαρους 148. Compl   λοχευων S³.   25. παντας Ven. 253.   παντα S. A. V. C. 55. al. Compl. Vulg. Syr. Ar. Arm.   επιμιξιν S. 296.   επιμξιαν S².   εχει om. 248. S².   απιστειας C.   ταραχη Ven. 254.   ταραχοι S. A. V. C. 55. al. Compl. Ald.   εφιορκια C.
26. αμνησια S. V. 68. al.   αμνηστια A. C. S³. Ven. al. Compl.   μοιχειαι και ασελγειαι 296.   27. θρησκια A.

or prophesy lies, or live unjustly, or else lightly forswear themselves. 29 For insomuch as their trust is in idols, which have no life; though they swear falsely, yet they look not to be hurt. 30 Howbeit for both causes shall they be justly punished: both because they thought not well of God, giving heed[1] unto idols, and also unjustly swore in deceit, 31 despising holiness. For it is not the power of them by whom they sware: but it is the just vengeance of sinners, that punisheth always the offence of the ungodly.

[1] Or, *devoted*.

CHAPTER XV.

1 But thou, O God, art gracious and true, longsuffering, and in 2 mercy ordering all things. For if we sin, we are thine, knowing thy power: but we will not sin, knowing that we are counted 3 thine. For to know thee is perfect righteousness: yea, to know thy power is the root of

ἢ ζῶσιν ἀδίκως, ἢ ἐπιορκοῦσι ταχέως.
29 ἀψύχοις γὰρ πεποιθότες εἰδώλοις,
κακῶς ὀμόσαντες ἀδικηθῆναι οὐ προσδέχονται.
30 ἀμφότερα δὲ αὐτοὺς μετελεύσεται τὰ δίκαια,
ὅτι κακῶς ἐφρόνησαν περὶ Θεοῦ προσσχόντες εἰδώλοις,
καὶ ἀδίκως ὤμοσαν ἐν δόλῳ καταφρονήσαντες ὁσιότητος.
31 οὐ γὰρ ἡ τῶν ὀμνυμένων δύναμις,
ἀλλ' ἡ τῶν ἁμαρτανόντων δίκη ἐπεξέρχεται ἀεὶ τὴν τῶν ἀδίκων παράβασιν.

ΚΕΦΑΛΑΙΟΝ ΙΕ΄.

1 Σὺ δὲ ὁ Θεὸς ἡμῶν χρηστὸς καὶ ἀληθής,
μακρόθυμος καὶ ἐν ἐλέει διοικῶν τὰ πάντα.
2 καὶ γὰρ ἐὰν ἁμάρτωμεν, σοί ἐσμεν, εἰδότες σου τὸ κράτος·
οὐχ ἁμαρτησόμεθα δέ, εἰδότες ὅτι σοὶ λελογίσμεθα.
3 τὸ γὰρ ἐπίστασθαί σε ὁλόκληρος δικαιοσύνη,
καὶ εἰδέναι σου τὸ κράτος ῥίζα ἀθανασίας.

falsa, aut vivunt injuste, aut 29 pejerant cito. Dum enim confidunt in idolis quae sine anima sunt, male jurantes noceri se 30 non sperant. Utraque ergo illis evenient digne, quoniam male senserunt de Deo, attendentes idolis, et juraverunt injuste, in dolo contemnentes jus- 31 titiam. Non enim juratorum virtus, sed peccantium poena perambulat semper injustorum praevaricationem.

CAPUT XV.

1 Tu autem, Deus noster, suavis et verus es, patiens, et in miseri- 2 cordia disponens omnia. Etenim si peccaverimus, tui sumus, scientes magnitudinem tuam; et si non peccaverimus, scimus quoniam apud te sumus com- 3 putati. Nosse enim te, consummata justitia est; et scire justitiam, et virtutem tuam ra-

28. εφιορκουσιν A. 30. αμφοτ. δε αυτου C. τα δικια S. τα δικαια S². V. τα αδικα A. *a pr. man.* οτι και κακ. S. προσχοντες V. 68. al. προσεχοντες S. A C. Ven. al. Compl. 31. η *post* γαρ *om.* S. *add.* S. cor. ομνυομενων V². al. ομνυμενων A. S. V¹. 55. 106. al. Ald. XV. 1. αληθης και επιεικης 253. εν ελεει V². εν *om.* S. A. V¹. C. al. ελεημων S². 2. αν 253. αμαρτανωμεν S. 106. 261. αμαρτωμεν V. A. S². al. σου εσμεν 106. 296. κρατος. κριμα S. κρατος S². δε *om.* V¹. σου λελογ. 106. 261. 3. το ειδεναι Ven. 253. 296. S². το κρατος σου V. Mai. σου τ. κρ. S. A. V. Vercell. Ven. al. Compl.

₄ dix est immortalitatis. Non enim in errorem induxit nos hominum malae artis excogitatio, nec umbra picturae labor sine fructu, effigies sculpta per ₅ varios colores, cujus aspectus insensato dat concupiscentiam, et diligit mortuae imaginis effigiem sine anima. ₆ Malorum amatores digni sunt qui spem habeant in talibus, et qui faciunt illos, et qui diligunt, et qui co- ₇ lunt. Sed et figulus mollem terram premens laboriose fingit ad usus nostros unumquodque vas, et de eodem luto fingit quae munda sunt in usum vasa, et similiter quae his sunt contraria; horum autem vasorum quis sit usus, judex est figulus. ₈ Et cum labore vano deum fingit de eodem luto, ille qui paulo ante de terra factus fuerat, et post pusillum reducit se unde acceptus est, repetitus animae ₉ debitum quam habebat. Sed cura est illi, non quia labora-

₄ οὔτε γὰρ ἐπλάνησεν ἡμᾶς ἀνθρώπων κακότεχνος ἐπίνοια, οὐδὲ σκιαγράφων πόνος ἄκαρπος, εἶδος σπιλωθὲν χρώμασι διηλλαγμένοις· ₅ ὧν ὄψις ἄφρονι εἰς ὄρεξιν ἔρχεται, ποθεῖ τε νεκρᾶς εἰκόνος εἶδος ἄπνουν. ₆ κακῶν ἐρασταὶ ἄξιοί τε τοιούτων ἐλπίδων, καὶ οἱ δρῶντες καὶ οἱ ποθοῦντες καὶ οἱ σεβόμενοι. ₇ καὶ γὰρ κεραμεὺς ἁπαλὴν γῆν θλίβων ἐπίμοχθον, πλάσσει πρὸς ὑπηρεσίαν ἡμῶν ἓν ἕκαστον, ἀλλ' ἐκ τοῦ αὐτοῦ πηλοῦ ἀνεπλάσατο τά τε τῶν καθαρῶν ἔργων δοῦλα σκεύη, τά τε ἐναντία, πάνθ' ὁμοίως· τούτων δὲ ἑκατέρου τίς ἑκάστου ἐστὶν ἡ χρῆσις, κριτὴς ὁ πηλουργός. ₈ καὶ κακόμοχθος θεὸν μάταιον ἐκ τοῦ αὐτοῦ πλάσσει πηλοῦ, ὃς πρὸ μικροῦ ἐκ γῆς γεννηθεὶς μετ' ὀλίγον πορεύεται ἐξ ἧς ἐλήφθη, τὸ τῆς ψυχῆς ἀπαιτηθεὶς χρέος. ₉ ἀλλ' ἔστιν αὐτῷ φροντὶς οὐχ ὅτι μέλλει κάμνειν,

₄ immortality. For neither did the mischievous invention of men deceive us, nor an image spotted with divers colours, the ₅ painter's fruitless labour; The sight whereof enticeth fools to lust after it[1], and so they desire the form of a dead image, that ₆ hath no breath. Both they that make them, they that desire them, and they that worship them, are lovers of evil things, and are worthy to have such ₇ things to trust upon. For the potter, tempering soft earth, fashioneth every vessel with much labour for our service: yea, of the same clay he maketh both the vessels that serve for clean uses, and likewise also all such as serve to the contrary: but what is the use of either sort, the potter himself is the judge. ₈ And employing his labours lewdly, he maketh a vain god of the same clay, even he which a little before was made of earth himself, and within a little while after returneth to the same, out of the which he was taken, when his life which was lent him shall be ₉ demanded. Notwithstanding his care is, not that he shall

[1] Or, *turneth reproach the fool*

---

4. ουδε γαρ 106. 261. ουτε σκ. 157. 248. Ald. al. σκιογραφ. S³. 296. Ald. σπινωθεν S. Ven. σπιλαθεν S³. et caet. διηλλαγμενοι S. διηλλαγμενοις S². et caet. 5. ων η S². 55. 254. αφρονι S. A. (?) 55. 106. al. Vulg. αφροσιν V. C. Ven. S². al. ορεξιν S. A. C. Ven. Compl. al. Vulg. Syr. Arm. Ar. ορειδος V. ποθει τε. ποθειται C. Ven. αγνουν A. 7. εκθλιβων 157. εν om. V. Ven. add. S. A. C. al. Compl. εκαστος Ven. ταυτα A. S. C. om. τα τε εναντια πανθ ομ. εκατερου V. A. εκατερουν C. εκατερων 253. ετερον S. 106. ετερου S². Ven. Ald. η χρ. S. om. η. 8. α κακομ. 157. πλασσει εκ του αυτου A. γενηθεις C. V. πορευεται 55. 157. al. Compl. ελημφθη A. S. C.

THE BOOK OF WISDOM.

[marginal notes: ¹ Or, be sick, or, die. ² Gr. life. ³ Or, So.]

have much labour¹, nor that his life is short: but striveth to excel goldsmiths and silversmiths, and endeavoureth to do like the workers in brass, and counteth it his glory to make 10 counterfeit things. His heart is ashes, his hope is more vile than earth, and his life of less 11 value than clay: Forasmuch as he knew not his Maker, and him that inspired into him an active soul, and breathed in a 12 living spirit. But they counted our life a pastime, and our time² here a market for gain: for, say they, we must be getting every way, though it be by evil means. 13 For³ this man, that of earthly matter maketh brittle vessels and graven images, knoweth himself 14 to offend above all others. And all the enemies of thy people, that hold them in subjection, are most foolish, and are more

οὐδ' ὅτι βραχυτελῆ βίον ἔχει,
ἀλλ' ἀντερείδεται μὲν χρυσουργοῖς καὶ ἀργυροχόοις,
χαλκοπλάστας τε μιμεῖται,
καὶ δόξαν ἡγεῖται ὅτι κίβδηλα πλάσσει.
10 σποδὸς ἡ καρδία αὐτοῦ,
καὶ γῆς εὐτελεστέρα ἡ ἐλπὶς αὐτοῦ,
πηλοῦ τε ἀτιμότερος ὁ βίος αὐτοῦ·
11 ὅτι ἠγνόησε τὸν πλάσαντα αὐτόν,
καὶ τὸν ἐμπνεύσαντα αὐτῷ ψυχὴν ἐνεργοῦσαν,
καὶ ἐμφυσήσαντα πνεῦμα ζωτικόν·
12 ἀλλ' ἐλογίσατο παίγνιον εἶναι τὴν ζωὴν ἡμῶν
καὶ τὸν βίον πανηγυρισμὸν ἐπικερδῆ·
δεῖν γάρ φησιν ὅθεν δὴ κἂν ἐκ κακοῦ πορίζειν.
13 οὗτος γὰρ παρὰ πάντας οἶδεν ὅτι ἁμαρτάνει,
ὕλης γεώδους εὔθραυστα σκεύη καὶ γλυπτὰ δημιουργῶν.
14 πάντες δ' ἀφρονέστατοι καὶ τάλανες ὑπὲρ ψυχὴν νηπίου,
οἱ ἐχθροὶ τοῦ λαοῦ σου καταδυναστεύσαντες αὐτόν·

turus est, nec quoniam brevis illi vita est, sed concertatur aurificibus et argentariis; sed et aerarios imitatur, et gloriam praefert, quoniam res supervacuas fingit. 10 Cinis est enim cor ejus, et terra supervacua spes illius, et luto vilior vita ejus; 11 quoniam ignoravit qui se finxit, et qui inspiravit illi animam quae operatur, et qui insufflavit ei 12 spiritum vitalem. Sed et aestimaverunt lusum esse vitam nostram, et conversationem vitae compositam ad lucrum, et oportere undecunque etiam ex malo 13 acquirere. Hic enim scit se super omnes delinquere, qui ex terrae materia fragilia vasa et 14 sculptilia fingit. Omnes enim insipientes, et infelices supra modum animae superbi, sunt inimici populi tui, et impe-

---

9. χρυσουργοῖς. αργυρουργοις Ven. πλάσσει. πρασσει C. 157.   10. καρδ. αυτων 157. 248. ευτερα S. ευτελεστερα S⁴. ελπ. αυτων 157. 248. Compl.   11. ηγνοει 261. πλασαντα S. V. Ven. al. Vulg. Syr. Arm. ποιησαντα A. C. 55. al. Ar. εις ψυχην C. 55. al. ενφυσησαντα S. αυτω πνευμα Ven. S². C¹. 106 261.   12. αλλα A. ελογισαντο V. S. A. C. Ven. Vulg. Syr. Arm. Ar. ελογισατο V¹. S². 106. al. φησιν V. Ven. S. al. Ar. φασιν A. C. 157. al. Compl. Arm. οθεν δη om. S. δη και εκ A. 55. al. δη εκ C. κακων 106. 248. 261.   13. αυτος 261. 296. γαρ om. Ven. ευθραστα S. A. C. Ven. 157. ευθραυστα V. 55. al.   14. παντες δε S. V. Ven. al. Vulg. Syr Arm. Ar. παντων δε A. C. 154. 296. παντως 253. αφρονεστατοι V. Ven. A. al. Vulg. Syr. Arm. Ar. αφρονεστεροι S. C. 106. al. ψυχην νηπιου V. Ven. S. al. ψυχας νηπιων A. C. 248. 296. Compl. ψυχας om. 55. 254. οι καταδ. V. Ven. 105. al. S².   αυτων S³.

15 rantes illi; quoniam omnia idola nationum deos aestimaverunt, quibus neque oculorum usus est ad videndum, neque nares ad percipiendum spiritum, neque aures ad audiendum, neque digiti manuum ad tractandum, sed et pedes eorum pigri ad ambu-
16 landum. Homo enim fecit illos; et qui spiritum mutuatus est, is finxit illos. Nemo enim sibi similem homo poterit deum
17 fingere. Cum enim sit mortalis, mortuum fingit manibus iniquis. Melior enim est ipse his quos colit, quia ipse quidem vixit, cum esset mortalis, illi
18 autem nunquam. Sed et animalia miserrima colunt; insensata enim comparata his, illis
19 sunt deteriora. Sed nec aspectu aliquis ex his animalibus bona potest conspicere; effugerunt autem Dei laudem et benedictionem ejus.

15 ὅτι καὶ πάντα τὰ εἴδωλα τῶν ἐθνῶν ἐλογίσαντο θεούς,
οἷς οὔτε ὀμμάτων χρῆσις εἰς ὅρασιν,
οὔτε ῥῖνες εἰς συνολκὴν ἀέρος,
οὔτε ὦτα ἀκούειν,
οὔτε δάκτυλοι χειρῶν εἰς ψηλάφησιν,
καὶ οἱ πόδες αὐτῶν ἀργοὶ πρὸς ἐπίβασιν.
16 ἄνθρωπος γὰρ ἐποίησεν αὐτούς,
καὶ τὸ πνεῦμα δεδανεισμένος ἔπλασεν αὐτούς.
οὐδεὶς γὰρ αὑτῷ ὅμοιον ἄνθρωπος ἰσχύει πλάσαι θεόν·
17 θνητὸς δὲ ὢν νεκρὸν ἐργάζεται χερσὶν ἀνόμοις·
κρείττων γάρ ἐστι τῶν σεβασμάτων,
ἀνθ' ὧν αὐτὸς μὲν ἔζησεν, ἐκεῖνα δὲ οὐδέποτε.
18 καὶ τὰ ζῷα δὲ τὰ ἔχθιστα σέβονται·
ἀνοίᾳ γὰρ συγκρινόμενα τῶν ἄλλων ἐστὶ χείρονα.
19 οὐδ' ὅσον ἐπιποθῆσαι ὡς ἐν ζώων ὄψει καλὰ τυγχάνει,
ἐκπέφευγε δὲ καὶ τὸν τοῦ Θεοῦ ἔπαινον καὶ τὴν εὐλογίαν αὐτοῦ.

15 miserable than very babes. For they counted all the idols of the heathen to be gods: which neither have the use of eyes to see, nor noses to draw breath[1], nor ears to hear, nor fingers of hands to handle; and as for their feet,
16 they are slow to go. For man made them, and he that borrowed his own spirit fashioned them: but no man can make a
17 god like unto himself. For being mortal, he worketh a dead thing with wicked hands: for he himself is better than the things which he worshippeth: whereas he lived *once*, but they never.
18 Yea, they worshipped those beasts also that are most hateful: for being compared together, some are worse than others.
19 Neither are they beautiful, so much as to be desired in respect of beasts: but they went without the praise of God and his blessing.

---

15. ὅτι καὶ πάντα. και om. A. C. al. Compl. Vulg. τα ειδωλα A. S. C. V. Ven. al. τα om. V². al. οις ουδε 55. 157. 254. χρησεις S. 261. εἰς ὅρασιν. εις om. C. ρεινες S. 16. δεδανεισμενος V. δεδανισμενος A. V¹. C. S². δεδανισμενον S. αὐτῷ. εαυτω Ven. αὐτῷ ὅμοιον ἄνθρωπος. αυτων ομοι. ανθρωπος (ανθρωπῳ 55. 254. ανθρωποις 253. ανθρωπαν 246.) 248. Compl. al. ανθρωποις ομοιον ανθρωπων 106. 261. ανθρωπων ομοιον ισχυει A². ανθρωπων πλασαι θεον ομοιον ισχυει S. αυτων ομοιον ανθρωπος ισχυει πλασαι θεον S². 17. κρισσον A. C. κρισσον S. κρεισσον 261. κρειττων V. σεβηματων A. αυτον αν V. caet. ανθ' αν S. αν om. 157. 253. αυτος μεν γαρ 157. 18. εκθιστα S. ανοια ed. Sixt. et Mai. Ald. Compl.

CHAPTER XVI.

1 Therefore by the like were they punished worthily, and by the multitude of beasts tormented. 2 Instead of which punishment, dealing graciously with thine own people, thou preparedst for them meat of a strange taste, even quails to stir up their appetite; 3 To the end that they, desiring food, might for the ugly sight of the beasts sent among them loathe even that, which they must needs desire: but these, suffering penury for a short space, might be made partakers of a strange taste. 4 For it was requisite, that upon them exercising tyranny should come penury, which they could not avoid: but to these it should only be shewed how their enemies were tormented. 5 For when the horrible fierceness of beasts came upon these[1], and they perished with the stings of crooked serpents, thy wrath

[1] Or, thy people.

ΚΕΦΑΛΛΑΙΟΝ ΙΣ´.

1 Διὰ τοῦτο δι᾽ ὁμοίων ἐκολάσθησαν ἀξίως,
καὶ διὰ πλήθους κνωδάλων ἐβασανίσθησαν.
2 ἀνθ᾽ ἧς κολάσεως εὐεργετήσας τὸν λαόν σου,
εἰς ἐπιθυμίαν ὀρέξεως ξένην γεῦσιν,
τροφὴν ἡτοίμασας ὀρτυγομήτραν,
3 ἵνα ἐκεῖνοι μὲν ἐπιθυμοῦντες τροφὴν,
διὰ τὴν εἰδέχθειαν τῶν ἐπαπεσταλμένων
καὶ τὴν ἀναγκαίαν ὄρεξιν ἀποστρέφωνται,
οὗτοι δὲ ἐπ᾽ ὀλίγον ἐνδεεῖς γενόμενοι
καὶ ξένης μετάσχωσι γεύσεως.
4 ἔδει γὰρ ἐκείνοις μὲν ἀπαραίτητον ἔνδειαν ἐπελθεῖν τυραννοῦσι,
τούτοις δὲ μόνον δειχθῆναι πῶς οἱ ἐχθροὶ αὐτῶν ἐβασανίζοντο.
5 καὶ γὰρ ὅτε αὐτοῖς δεινὸς ἐπῆλθε θηρίων θυμὸς,
δήγμασί τε σκολιῶν διεφθείροντο ὄφεων,
οὐ μέχρι τέλους ἔμεινεν ἡ ὀργή σου·

CAPUT XVI.

1 Propter haec et per his similia passi sunt digne tormenta, et per multitudinem bestiarum exterminati sunt. 2 Pro quibus tormentis bene disposuisti populum tuum, quibus dedisti concupiscentiam delectamenti sui novum saporem, escam parans 3 eis ortygometram; ut illi quidem concupiscentes escam propter ea quae illis ostensa et missa sunt, etiam a necessaria concupiscentia averterentur. Hi autem in brevi inopes facti novam gustaverunt escam. 4 Oportebat enim illis sine excusatione quidem supervenire interitum exercentibus tyrannidem; his autem tantum ostendere quemadmodum inimici eorum exterminabantur. 5 Etenim cum illis supervenit saeva bestiarum ira, morsibus perversorum colubro-

XVI. 2. ευηργετησεν S. ευηργετησαν S². ευηργετησας 253. οις εις Α. 55. 248 Vulg. γευσεως S. γευσειν S¹. τροφητ 106. Ald. 3. τροφητ S. Ven. al. ειδεχθειαν C. 55. Field. Ap. Fr. Mai. Reusch. Tisch. διχθεισαν S. διχθησαν Ven. δειχθεισαν Α. V. 68. al. Compl. Ald. Vulg. Ar. Arm. δειχθεισαν των επαπ. Vercell. επεσταλμενων 55. απεσταλμενων 157. επαποστρεφονται C. αυτοι δε V. Ven. ουτοι δε S. A. C. al. Compl. επ' ολιγω 248. Compl. μετ' ολιγον 106. γινομενοι 106. 261. 4. μεν om. V¹. 5. εφθειροντο S. διεφθειροντο S².

6 rum exterminabantur. Sed non in perpetuum ira tua permansit, [6] sed ad correptionem in brevi turbati sunt, signum habentes salutis ad commemorationem 7 mandati legis tuae. Qui enim conversus est, non per hoc quod videbat sanabatur, sed per te 8 omnium salvatorem; in hoc autem ostendisti inimicis nostris, quia tu es qui liberas ab omni 9 malo. Illos enim locustarum et muscarum occiderunt morsus, et non est inventa sanitas animae illorum, quia digni erant ab hujuscemodi exterminari. 10 Filios autem tuos nec draconum venenatorum vicerunt dentes; misericordia enim tua adveniens 11 sanabat illos. In memoria enim sermonum tuorum examinabantur, et velociter salvabantur, ne in altam incidentes oblivionem, non possent tuo uti adjutorio. 12 Etenim neque herba, neque malagma sanavit eos, sed tuus, Domine, sermo, qui sanat omnia.

6 εἰς νουθεσίαν δὲ πρὸς ὀλίγον ἐταράχθησαν,
σύμβολον ἔχοντες σωτηρίας,
εἰς ἀνάμνησιν ἐντολῆς νόμου σου.
7 ὁ γὰρ ἐπιστραφεὶς οὐ διὰ τὸ θεωρούμενον ἐσώζετο,
ἀλλὰ διὰ σὲ τὸν πάντων σωτῆρα.
8 καὶ ἐν τούτῳ δὲ ἔπεισας τοὺς ἐχθροὺς ἡμῶν,
ὅτι σὺ εἶ ὁ ῥυόμενος ἐκ παντὸς κακοῦ.
9 οὓς μὲν γὰρ ἀκρίδων καὶ μυιῶν ἀπέκτεινε δήγματα,
καὶ οὐχ εὑρέθη ἴαμα τῇ ψυχῇ αὐτῶν,
ὅτι ἄξιοι ἦσαν ὑπὸ τοιούτων κολασθῆναι·
10 τοὺς δὲ υἱούς σου οὐδὲ ἰοβόλων δρακόντων ἐνίκησαν ὀδόντες,
τὸ ἔλεος γάρ σου ἀντιπαρῆλθε καὶ ἰάσατο αὐτούς.
11 εἰς γὰρ ὑπόμνησιν τῶν λογίων σου ἐνεκεντρίζοντο,
καὶ ὀξέως διεσώζοντο, ἵνα μὴ εἰς βαθεῖαν ἐμπεσόντες λήθην
ἀπερίσπαστοι γένωνται τῆς σῆς εὐεργεσίας.
12 καὶ γὰρ οὔτε βοτάνη οὔτε μάλαγμα ἐθεράπευσεν αὐτούς,
ἀλλὰ ὁ σός, Κύριε, λόγος ὁ πάντα ἰώμενος.

6 endured not for ever: But they were troubled for a small season, that they might be admonished, having a sign of salvation, to put them in remembrance of the commandment of 7 thy law. For he that turned himself toward it was not saved by the thing that he saw, but by thee, that art the Saviour 8 of all. And in this thou madest thine enemies confess, that it is thou who deliverest from all 9 evil: For them the bitings of grasshoppers and flies killed, neither was there found any remedy for their life: for they were worthy to be punished by 10 such. But thy sons not the very teeth of venomous dragons overcame: for thy mercy was *ever* by them, and healed them. 11 For they were pricked[1], that [1 Gr. *stung*.] they should remember thy words: and were quickly saved, that not falling into deep forgetfulness, they might be continually mindful of[2] thy good- [2 Or, *never drawn from*.] 12 ness. For it was neither herb, nor mollifying plaister, that restored them to health: but thy word, O Lord, which healeth

---

6. εταραχθη S¹. εταραχθησαν S². συμβουλον S. A. Ven. Ald. συμβολον V. Fr. Field. νομον A.* 248. 296. σου om. S. 106. Ald.   8. εχθρ. σου S. ε. ημων S².   9. γαρ om. S¹. add. S².   μυων 106. 157. Ald.   απεκτειναν 157.   δηματα S. δηγματα S². δηγματι 261. Ald.   τοιουτων. τουτων S.   τοιουτων S¹.   10. τους δε δουλους Ven.   δρακ. ιοβολων Ven.   σου γαρ S.   κυριε add. 106. 261.   αντιπαρηγεν Ven. 253.   ιατο S. Ven. 253.   11. λογων σου 106. 261.   ενκεντριζοντο A. C. (?)   οξεως. ενθεως Ven. ινα μη εις βαθ. om S. add. S. cor.   απερισπατοι Ven. 253.   12. ο λογοσ ο S.   παντας A. 55. al.   ιωμενος. δυναμενος S².

13 all things. For thou hast power of life and death: thou leadest to the gates of hell, and bringest
14 up again. A man indeed killeth through his malice: and the spirit, when it is gone forth, returneth not; neither the soul
15 received up cometh again. But it is not possible to escape thine
16 hand. For the ungodly, that denied to know thee, were scourged by the strength of thine arm: with strange rains, hails, and showers, were they persecuted, that they could not avoid, and through fire were
17 they consumed. For, which is most to be wondered at, the fire had more force in the water, that quencheth all things: for the world fighteth for the right-
18 eous. For sometime the flame was mitigated, that it might not burn up the beasts that were sent against the ungodly; but themselves might see and perceive that they were persecuted with the judgment of God.
19 And at another time it burneth even in the midst of water above

13 σὺ γὰρ ζωῆς καὶ θανάτου ἐξουσίαν ἔχεις,
καὶ κατάγεις εἰς πύλας ᾅδου καὶ ἀνάγεις.
14 ἄνθρωπος δὲ ἀποκτέννει μὲν τῇ κακίᾳ αὐτοῦ,
ἐξελθὸν δὲ πνεῦμα οὐκ ἀναστρέφει,
οὐδὲ ἀναλύει ψυχὴν παραληφθεῖσαν.
15 τὴν δὲ σὴν χεῖρα φυγεῖν ἀδύνατόν ἐστιν.
16 ἀρνούμενοι γάρ σε εἰδέναι ἀσεβεῖς
ἐν ἰσχύϊ βραχίονός σου ἐμαστιγώθησαν,
ξένοις ὑετοῖς καὶ χαλάζαις καὶ ὄμβροις διωκόμενοι ἀπαραιτήτοις
καὶ πυρὶ καταναλισκόμενοι.
17 τὸ γὰρ παραδοξότατον, ἐν τῷ πάντα σβεννύντι ὕδατι πλεῖον ἐνήργει τὸ πῦρ·
ὑπέρμαχος γὰρ ὁ κόσμος ἐστὶ δικαίων.
18 ποτὲ μὲν γὰρ ἡμεροῦτο φλόξ,
ἵνα μὴ καταφλέξῃ τὰ ἐπ' ἀσεβεῖς ἀπεσταλμένα ζῷα,
ἀλλ' αὐτοὶ βλέποντες ἴδωσιν ὅτι Θεοῦ κρίσει ἐλαύνονται·
19 ποτὲ δὲ καὶ μεταξὺ ὕδατος ὑπὲρ τὴν πυρὸς δύναμιν φλέγει,

13 Tu es enim, Domine, qui vitae et mortis habes potestatem, et deducis ad portas mortis, et re-
14 ducis. Homo autem occidit quidem per malitiam, et cum exierit spiritus, non revertetur, nec revocabit animam quae re-
15 cepta est; sed tuam manum
16 effugere impossibile est. Negantes enim te nosse impii, per fortitudinem brachii tui flagellati sunt; novis aquis, et grandinibus, et pluviis persecutionem passi, et per ignem consumti.
17 Quod enim mirabile erat, in aqua, quae omnia extinguit, plus ignis valebat; vindex est
18 enim orbis justorum. Quodam enim tempore mansuetabatur ignis, ne comburerentur quae ad impios missa erant animalia, sed ut ipsi videntes scirent quoniam Dei judicio patiuntur per-
19 secutionem. Et quodam tempore in aqua supra virtutem ignis

---

13. και ζωης και 106. 261. εχεις κυριε 106. 261. αδου πυλας Ven. πυλας om. 106. 261.   14. ανθρωπος μεν S.   μεν γαρ 106. 261. αποκτενι τη κακια S. αποκτενη Ven. αποκτενει 106. al. Ald. αποκτεινει Compl. εαυτου Ven. το ante πνευμα add. S². παραλημφθεισαν A. S. C.   15. εκφυγειν 157.   16. και ante ομβρ. om. 106. 261. απαρετητος A. απαραιτητας 157. 248. Compl.   17. τα παντα S. σβεννυοντι 106. 261. πλεον S. εστιν ο κοσμ. S. 106. 296. δικαιοις A.   18. ειμερουτο V¹. S. ημερουτο S². επαπεσταλμενα Ven. αποσταλεντα 157. αποστελλομενα 106. ζωα om. S. add. S². αλλα βλεποντες S. αλλ' ινα S². οι βλεποντες Ven. κρισει θεου C. 248. Compl. ελαυνωνται Λ.   19. την του πυρος 106. 261.

exardescebat undique, ut iniquae terrae nationem extermi-
20 naret. Pro quibus angelorum esca nutrivisti populum tuum, et paratum panem de caelo praestitisti illis sine labore, omne delectamentum in se habentem, et omnis saporis suavi-
21 tatem. Substantia enim tua dulcedinem tuam quam in filios habes ostendebat, et deserviens uniuscujusque voluntati, ad quod quisque volebat convertebatur.
22 Nix autem et glacies sustinebant vim ignis, et non tabescebant, ut scirent quoniam fructus inimicorum exterminabat ignis ardens in grandine et pluvia
23 coruscans. Hic autem iterum ut nutrirentur justi, etiam suae
24 virtutis oblitus est. Creatura enim tibi Factori deserviens, exardescit in tormentum adversus injustos, et lenior fit ad benefaciendum pro his qui in te

ἵνα ἀδίκου γῆς γεννήματα καταφθείρῃ.
20 ἀνθ' ὧν ἀγγέλων τροφὴν ἐψώμισας τὸν λαόν σου,
καὶ ἕτοιμον ἄρτον αὐτοῖς ἀπ' οὐρανοῦ παρέσχες ἀκοπιάτως,
πᾶσαν ἡδονὴν ἰσχύοντα καὶ πρὸς πᾶσαν ἁρμόνιον γεῦσιν.
21 ἡ μὲν γὰρ ὑπόστασίς σου τὴν σὴν γλυκύτητα πρὸς τέκνα ἐνεφάνισε,
τῇ δὲ τοῦ προσφερομένου ἐπιθυμίᾳ ὑπηρετῶν,
πρὸς ὅ τις ἐβούλετο μετεκιρνᾶτο.
22 χιὼν δὲ καὶ κρύσταλλος ὑπέμεινε πῦρ καὶ οὐκ ἐτήκετο,
ἵνα γνῶσιν ὅτι τοὺς τῶν ἐχθρῶν καρποὺς κατέφθειρε πῦρ φλεγόμενον,
ἐν τῇ χαλάζῃ καὶ ἐν τοῖς ὑετοῖς διαστράπτον,
23 τοῦτο δὲ πάλιν, ἵνα τραφῶσι δίκαιοι,
καὶ τῆς ἰδίας ἐπιλελῆσθαι δυνάμεως.
24 ἡ γὰρ κτίσις σοι τῷ ποιήσαντι ὑπηρετοῦσα
ἐπιτείνεται εἰς κόλασιν κατὰ τῶν ἀδίκων,
καὶ ἀνίεται εἰς εὐεργεσίαν ὑπὲρ τῶν εἰς σὲ πεποιθότων.

the power of fire, that it might destroy the fruits of an unjust
20 land. Instead whereof thou feddest thine own people with angels' food, and didst send them from heaven bread prepared without their labour, able to content every man's delight, and agreeing to every taste.
21 For thy sustenance[1] declared thy sweetness unto thy children, and serving to the appetite of the eater, tempered itself[2] to
22 every man's liking. But snow and ice endured the fire, and melted not, that they might know that fire burning in the hail, and sparkling in the rain, did destroy the fruits of the
23 enemies. But this again did even forget his own strength, that the righteous might be
24 nourished. For the creature that serveth thee, who art the Maker, increaseth his strength against the unrighteous for their punishment, and abateth his strength for the benefit of such as put their trust in thee.

[1] Or, manna
[2] Or, was tempered

---

19. γενηματα C V. διαφθειρη V. 68. al. καταφθειρη A. S. Ven. 55. al. καταφθαρει C. καταφθαρη 254. 20. αρτον απ' ουρανου παρεσχες αυτοις A. S. C. (?) 55. 106. al. A. B. E. H. Par. αρτον εξ Ven. παρέσχες. επεμψας V. 248. Compl. ακοπιατως V. S. C. Ven. ακοπιαστως A. 106. al. προς πασαν ηδ. 248. Compl. ισχυουσαν Ven. 106. προς αυτε πασ. αρμ. om. 106. 261. και ante προς om. 155. αρμονιαν S. 21. σου om. C. 55. αυτου 248. προς τεκ. γλυ. S. Ven. 51. al. ενεφανιζεν S. A. ενεφανισεν Ven. 155. προς τ. ενεφ. γλ. A. 155. al. Compl. επιθ. επιποθων και υπηρ. 155. μετεκριματο S¹. 22. υπεμεινε A. γνωμεν S¹. Pro εχθρων εθνων A. φλεγον S. Ven. 155. al. εν τοις. ξενοις S¹. 23. δε παλιν A. C. 106. al. δε om. S. παλιν δ' V. Ven. al. επιλελησθαι V. Ven. 68. 261. επιλελησται A. S. C. 55. al. Compl. 24. ποιησαντι τα παντα 248. Compl. ποιησαντι αυτον C. εις σε V. Ven. 68. 296. επι σοι A. S. C. 55. al. Compl. επι σε 155. 284. 261.

[1 Or, things.]

25 Therefore even then was it altered into all fashions[1], and was obedient to thy grace, that nourisheth all things, according to the desire of them that had

[2 Or, of them that prayed.]

26 need[2]: That thy children, O Lord, whom thou lovest, might know, that it is not the growing of fruits that nourisheth man: but that it is thy word, which preserveth them that put their

27 trust in thee. For that which was not destroyed of the fire, being warmed with a little sun-

28 beam, soon melted away: That it might be known, that we must prevent the sun to give thee thanks, and at the day-

29 spring pray unto thee. For the hope of the unthankful shall melt away as the winter's hoar frost, and shall run away as unprofitable water.

CHAPTER XVII.

[3 Or, souls that will not be reformed.]

1 For great are thy judgments, and cannot be expressed: therefore unnurtured souls[3] have

---

25 διὰ τοῦτο καὶ τότε εἰς πάντα μεταλλευομένη
τῇ παντοτρόφῳ σου δωρεᾷ ὑπηρέτει
πρὸς τὴν τῶν δεομένων θέλησιν,
26 ἵνα μάθωσιν οἱ υἱοί σου, οὓς ἠγάπησας, Κύριε,
ὅτι οὐχ αἱ γενέσεις τῶν καρπῶν τρέφουσιν ἄνθρωπον,
ἀλλὰ τὸ ῥῆμά σου τοὺς σοὶ πιστεύοντας διατηρεῖ.
27 τὸ γὰρ ὑπὸ πυρὸς μὴ φθειρόμενον
ἁπλῶς ὑπὸ βραχείας ἀκτῖνος ἡλίου θερμαινόμενον ἐτήκετο,
28 ὅπως γνωστὸν ᾖ ὅτι δεῖ φθάνειν τὸν ἥλιον ἐπ' εὐχαριστίαν σου,
καὶ πρὸς ἀνατολὴν φωτὸς ἐντυγχάνειν σοι.
29 ἀχαρίστου γὰρ ἐλπὶς ὡς χειμέριος πάχνη τακήσεται,
καὶ ῥυήσεται ὡς ὕδωρ ἄχρηστον.

ΚΕΦΑΛΑΙΟΝ ΙΖ'.

1 Μεγάλαι γάρ σου αἱ κρίσεις καὶ δυσδιήγητοι·
διὰ τοῦτο ἀπαίδευτοι ψυχαὶ ἐπλανήθησαν.

---

25 confidunt. Propter hoc et tunc in omnia transfigurata omnium nutrici gratiae tuae deserviebat, ad voluntatem eorum qui a te

26 desiderabant; ut scirent filii tui quos dilexisti, Domine, quoniam non nativitatis fructus pascunt homines, sed sermo tuus hos qui in te crediderint

27 conservat. Quod enim ab igne non poterat exterminari, statim ab exiguo radio solis calefactum

28 tabescebat; ut notum omnibus esset quoniam oportet praevenire solem ad benedictionem tuam, et ad ortum lucis te

29 adorare. Ingrati enim spes tanquam hibernalis glacies tabescet, et disperiet tanquam aqua supervacua.

CAPUT XVII.

1 Magna sunt enim judicia tua, Domine, et inenarrabilia verba tua: propter hoc indisciplinatae

---

25. εις παντα om. S. γενεσεις των ανθρωπων A. διαφθειρομενον S. ανατολης του φωτος S³. αι κρισις S. μεταλλευομενη η γη 253. γη 106. δωραια S. δεαμενων σου Ven. 55. S². Vulg. Syr. εκτρεφουσιν 157. τον ανθρωπον Ven. 106. 261. S². πιστευσαντας Ven. 253. Vulg. 28. γνωστον ην V. διαφθαυιν S. δει φθαυειν S². φθαννειν A. C. ευχαριστια 106. 261. 26. μαθωσιν C. 27. μη om. S. προ 29. αχαριστον 155. ωσπερ 106. 261. χιμερινη S. χιμερινη A. χιμεριος S². V. XVII. 1.

THE BOOK OF WISDOM.

2 animae erraverunt. Dum enim persuasum habent iniqui posse dominari nationi sanctae, vinculis tenebrarum et longae noctis compediti, inclusi sub tectis, fugitivi perpetuae providentiae
3 jacuerunt. Et dum putant se latere in obscuris peccatis, tenebroso oblivionis velamento dispersi sunt, paventes horrende, et cum admiratione nimia per-
4 turbati. Neque enim quae continebat illos spelunca sine timore custodiebat, quoniam sonitus descendens perturbabat illos, et personae tristes illis apparentes pavorem illis praestabant.
5 Et ignis quidem nulla vis poterat illis lumen praebere, nec siderum limpidae flammae illuminare poterant illam noctem horren-
6 dam. Apparebat autem illis subitaneus ignis, timore plenus; et timore perculsi illius quae non videbatur faciei aestimabant deteriora esse quae videbantur;
7 et magicae artis appositi erant

2 ὑπειληφότες γὰρ καταδυναστεύειν ἔθνος ἅγιον ἄνομοι,
δέσμιοι σκότους καὶ μακρᾶς πεδῆται νυκτὸς,
κατακλεισθέντες ὀρόφοις, φυγάδες τῆς αἰωνίου προνοίας ἔκειντο.
3 λανθάνειν γὰρ νομίζοντες ἐπὶ κρυφαίοις ἁμαρτήμασιν,
ἀφεγγεῖ λήθης παρακαλύμματι ἐσκορπίσθησαν,
θαμβούμενοι δεινῶς καὶ ἰνδάλμασιν ἐκταρασσόμενοι.
4 οὐδὲ γὰρ ὁ κατέχων αὐτοὺς μυχὸς ἀφόβους διεφύλασσεν,
ἦχοι δὲ καταράσσοντες αὐτοὺς περιεκόμπουν,
καὶ φάσματα ἀμειδήτοις κατηφῆ προσώποις ἐνεφανίζετο.
5 καὶ πυρὸς μὲν οὐδεμία βία κατίσχυε φωτίζειν,
οὔτε ἄστρων ἔκλαμπροι φλόγες καταυγάζειν ὑπέμενον τὴν στυγνὴν ἐκείνην νύκτα.
6 διεφαίνετο δ' αὐτοῖς μόνον αὐτομάτη πυρὰ φόβου πλήρης,
ἐκδειματούμενοι δὲ τῆς μὴ θεωρουμένης ἐκείνης ὄψεως,
ἡγοῦντο χείρω τὰ βλεπόμενα.
7 μαγικῆς δὲ ἐμπαίγματα κατέκειτο τέχνης,

2 erred. For when unrighteous men thought to oppress the holy nation; they being shut up in their houses[1], the prisoners of darkness, and fettered with the bonds of a long night, lay [there] exiled[2] from the eternal
3 providence. For while they supposed to lie hid in their secret sins, they were scattered under[3] a dark veil of forgetfulness, being horribly astonished, and troubled with [strange] ap-
4 paritions[4]. For neither might the corner that held them keep them from fear: but noises [as of waters] falling down sounded about them, and sad visions appeared unto them with heavy
5 countenances. No power of the fire might give them light: neither could the bright flames of the stars endure to lighten
6 that horrible night. Only there appeared unto them a fire kindled of itself, very dreadful: for being much terrified, they thought the things which they saw to be worse than the sight
7 they saw not. As for the illusions of art magick, they were

[1] Or, under their roofs.
[2] Or, fugitives.
[3] Or, in.
[4] Or, sights.

2. επειληφοτες C. ανομον δεσμοις S. ανομοι δεσμοι S². 3. κρυφιοις Ven. ληθη C. εσκορπισθησαν V. Ven. 68. al. Compl. Vulg. Syr. Ar. Arm. διεσκορπισθησαν S. εσκοτισθησαν A. C. 55. al. B. C. H. Par. εν ινδαλμασιν ταρασσομενα 106. 261. 4. μοιχος S. μυχος S. cor. μυθος A. αφοβως V. S. 68. 296. αφοβους A. C. Ven. 55. al. Compl. διεφυλαττεν A. C. δεκ^αταρασσοντες (sic) V. (A. C. Ven. al.) δ' εκταρασσοντες V¹. 55. 253. 254. ταρασσοντες S. 106. 261. κατηφη S. κατηφη S². κατηφεσι Ven. 5. φωτειν C. (†) αστρων. πυρων 155. A. Par. πυρογενεις add. S². καταγαυζειν S. καταυγαζειν S². 6. μονοις 157. πληρης S. εκδειμ. δε V. al. τε S. A. Ven. al. μεν C. της. τις Ven. μη om. A. 106. 261. τοις θεωρουμενοις εκεινοις 261. τα μη βλεπομενα 106. 261. 7. εμπεγματα S. κατεκιντο A. κατεκειντο 157. 254. 296. 248.

100 THE BOOK OF WISDOM. [XVII. 8–

put down, and their vaunting in wisdom was reproved with dis-8 grace. For they, that promised to drive away terrors and troubles from a sick soul, were sick themselves of fear, worthy to 9 be laughed at. For though no terrible thing did fear them; yet being scared with beasts that passed by, and hissing of 10 serpents, They died for fear, denying that they saw[1] the air, which could of no side be 11 avoided. For wickedness, condemned by her own witness, is very timorous, and being pressed with conscience, always fore-12 casteth grievous things. For fear is nothing else but a betraying of the succours which 13 reason offereth. And the expectation from within, being less, counteth the ignorance more than the cause which 14 bringeth the torment. But they sleeping the same sleep that night, which was indeed intolerable[2], and which came upon them out of the bottoms 15 of inevitable hell, Were partly vexed with monstrous apparitions, and partly fainted, their

[1] Or, refusing to look upon.

[2] Or, wherein they could do nothing.

καὶ τῆς ἐπὶ φρονήσει ἀλαζονείας ἔλεγχος ἐφύβριστος.
8 οἱ γὰρ ὑπισχνούμενοι δείματα καὶ ταραχὰς ἀπελαύνειν ψυχῆς νοσούσης,
οὗτοι καταγέλαστον εὐλάβειαν ἐνόσουν.
9 καὶ γὰρ εἰ μηδὲν αὐτοὺς ταραχῶδες ἐφόβει,
κνωδάλων παρόδοις καὶ ἑρπετῶν συρισμοῖς ἐκσεσοβημένοι,
10 διώλλυντο ἔντρομοι
καὶ τὸν μηδαμόθεν φευκτὸν ἀέρα προσιδεῖν ἀρνούμενοι.
11 δειλὸν γὰρ ἰδίως πονηρία μαρτυρεῖ καταδικαζομένη,
ἀεὶ δὲ προσείληφε τὰ χαλεπὰ συνεχομένη τῇ συνειδήσει.
12 οὐθὲν γάρ ἐστι φόβος εἰ μὴ προδοσία τῶν ἀπὸ λογισμοῦ βοηθημάτων·
13 ἔνδοθεν δὲ οὖσα ἥττων ἡ προσδοκία
πλείονα λογίζεται τὴν ἄγνοιαν τῆς παρεχούσης τὴν βάσανον αἰτίας.
14 οἱ δὲ τὴν ἀδύνατον ὄντως νύκτα
καὶ ἐξ ἀδυνάτου ᾅδου μυχῶν ἐπελθοῦσαν
τὸν αὐτὸν ὕπνον κοιμώμενοι,
15 τὰ μὲν τέρασιν ἠλαύνοντο φαντασμάτων,

derisus, et sapientiae gloriae 8 correptio cum contumelia. Illi enim qui promittebant timores et perturbationes expellere se ab anima languente, hi cum derisu pleni timore languebant. 9 Nam etsi nihil illos ex monstris perturbabat, transitu animalium et serpentium sibillatione commoti, [10] tremebundi peribant, et aërem, quem nulla ratione quis effugere posset, negantes se 10 videre. [11] Cum sit enim timida nequitia, dat testimonium condemnationis; semper enim praesumit saeva, perturbata consci-11 entia. [12] Nihil enim est timor nisi proditio cogitationis anxili-12 orum. [13] Et dum ab intus minor est expectatio, majorem computat inscientiam ejus causae, de qua tormentum praestat. 13 [14] Illi autem qui impotentem vere noctem, et ab infimis, et ab altissimis inferis supervenientem, eundem somnum dormientes, 14 [15] aliquando monstrorum exagitabantur timore, aliquando

---

7. επιφερομενης φρονησει αλαζονια S. φρον. αλαζονιας S². A. C. V¹. 8. διματα S. διγματα C. διμα φοβους τα τε και Ven. ταραχάτ. καταρχας S. ταραχας S². ευλοβιαν S. ευλαβιαν S². 9. μηθεν Ven. τερατωδες Ven. S². συριγμοις V. S². al. συριμοις S. A. C. Compl. εκσεσοβημενοι V. C. S. Ven. al. εκσεσοβισμενοι 155. εκπεφοβημενοι A. 106. εκπεφοβουμενων 261. 10. εν τρομῳ C. και το μηδ. S. και τον S². αφευκτον S. a eras. pr. man. προσιδιν S. 11. ινων Ven. γαρ om. C. ιδιῳ Compl. S². μαρτυρει V. Ven. al. Vulg. Syr. Ar. Arm. μαρτυρι A. S. 55. Compl. al. μαρτυρια C. προσειληφεν S. προσιληφεν S². 12. ουθεν V. al. ουδεν A¹. S. C. ουδε A². 106. 253. προδοσία. προδοκια S. 13. αναλογιζεται αγνοιαν S. Ven. 253. 14. αδυνάτου ᾅδου. αδυνατων 106. 261. 15. ηλαυνετο S. ηλαυνοντο S².

[—XVII. 20.] THE BOOK OF WISDOM. 101

animae deficiebant traductione; subitaneus enim illis et insperatus
15 timor supervenerat. [16] Deinde si quisquam ex illis decidisset, custodiebatur in carcere sine fer-
16 ro reclusus. [17] Si enim rusticus quis erat, aut pastor, aut agri laborum operarius praeoccupatus esset, ineffugibilem sustinebat
17 necessitatem. Una enim catena tenebrarum omnes erant colligati. [18] Sive spiritus sibilans, aut inter spissos arborum ramos avium sonus suavis, aut vis aquae
18 decurrentis nimium, [19] aut sonus validus praecipitatarum petrarum, aut ludentium animalium cursus invisus, aut mugientium valida bestiarum vox, aut resonans de altissimis montibus echo, deficientes faciebant
19 illos prae timore. [20] Omnis enim orbis terrarum limpido illuminabatur lumine, et non impeditis operibus continebatur.

τὰ δὲ τῆς ψυχῆς παρελύοντο προδοσίᾳ·
αἰφνίδιος γὰρ αὐτοῖς καὶ ἀπροσδόκητος φόβος ἐπεχύθη.
16 εἶθ' οὕτως, ὃς δήποτ' οὖν ἦν, ἐκεῖ καταπίπτων
ἐφρουρεῖτο εἰς τὴν ἀσίδηρον εἱρκτὴν κατακλεισθείς.
17 εἴτε γὰρ γεωργὸς ἦν τις, ἢ ποιμήν,
ἢ τῶν κατ' ἐρημίαν ἐργάτης μόχθων,
προληφθεὶς τὴν δυσάλυκτον ἔμενεν ἀνάγκην·
μιᾷ γὰρ ἁλύσει σκότους πάντες ἐδέθησαν.
18 εἴτε πνεῦμα συρίζον,
ἢ περὶ ἀμφιλαφεῖς κλάδους ὀρνέων ἦχος εὐμελής,
ἢ ῥυθμὸς ὕδατος πορευομένου βίᾳ,
19 ἢ κτύπος ἀπηνὴς καταρριπτομένων πετρῶν,
ἢ σκιρτώντων ζώων δρόμος ἀθεώρητος,
ἢ ὠρυομένων ἀπηνεστάτων θηρίων φωνὴ,
ἢ ἀντανακλωμένη ἐκ κοιλότητος ὀρέων ἠχώ,
παρέλυσεν αὐτοὺς ἐκφοβοῦντα.
20 ὅλος γὰρ ὁ κόσμος λαμπρῷ κατελάμπετο φωτί,
καὶ ἀνεμποδίστοις συνείχετο ἔργοις·

heart failing them: for a sudden fear, and not looked for, came
16 upon them. So then whosoever there fell down was straitly kept, shut up in a prison with-
17 out iron bars. For whether he were husbandman, or shepherd, or a labourer in the field[1], he was overtaken, and endured that necessity, which could not be avoided: for they were all bound with one chain of darkness.
18 Whether it were a whistling wind, or a melodious noise of birds among the spreading branches, or a pleasing fall of
19 water running violently, Or a terrible[2] sound of stones cast[2] down, or a running that could not be seen of skipping beasts, or a roaring voice of most savage wild beasts, or a rebounding echo from the hollow mountains; these things made
20 them to swoon for fear. For the whole world shined with clear light, and none were hin-

15. εφνιδιος S. επεχιθη S. Ven. al. επηλθεν V. al. επελιθη 261. 17. γεωργος τις ην S 157. 296. η ante ποιμην om. S. add S¹. κατ' ερημιας S. προλημφθεις S. A. C. δυσαληκτον S. A. δυσαλυτον 106. εμεινεν Ven. al. εδεηθησαν Ven. 18. διασυριζον S, δια eras. pr. man. περι αμφις κλαδους S. αμφιλαφις S¹. η ορνεων A. εμμελης 254. εμμελεις 155. 19. καταρριπτομενων S. A. V. θηριων απην S. απηνεστατος A. κοιλοτατον Tisch. Reusch 157. 251. Arm. κοιλοτητος V. S. A. Ven. al. plur. Compl. Ald. πορελυεν A. 55. 148 Compl. παρελυσεν V. S. εκφοβουσα S². 155. 20. φωτει S². κατελαμπρυνετο 155.

21 dered in their labour: Over them only was spread an heavy night, an image of that darkness which should afterward receive them: but yet were they unto themselves more grievous than the darkness.

CHAPTER XVIII.

1 Nevertheless thy saints had a very great light, whose voice they hearing, and not seeing their shape, because they also had not suffered the same things, 2 they counted them happy. But for that they did not hurt them *now*, of whom they had been wronged before, they thanked them, and besought them pardon for that they had been enemies. 3 Instead whereof thou gavest them a burning pillar of fire, both to be a guide of the unknown journey, and an harmless sun to entertain them ho-4 nourably. For they were worthy to be deprived of light, and imprisoned in darkness, who had kept thy sons shut up, by whom the uncorrupt[1] light of the law was to be given unto

[1] Or, incorruptible.

21 μόνοις δὲ ἐκείνοις ἐπετέτατο βαρεῖα νύξ,
εἰκὼν τοῦ μέλλοντος αὐτοὺς διαδέχεσθαι σκότους,
ἑαυτοῖς δὲ ἦσαν βαρύτεροι σκότους.

ΚΕΦΑΛΑΙΟΝ ΙΗ΄.

1 Τοῖς δὲ ὁσίοις σου μέγιστον ἦν φῶς,
ὧν φωνὴν μὲν ἀκούοντες, μορφὴν δὲ οὐχ ὁρῶντες,
ὅ τι μὲν οὖν κἀκεῖνοι ἐπεπόνθεισαν, ἐμακάριζον,
2 ὅτι δὲ οὐ βλάπτουσι προηδικημένοι, εὐχαριστοῦσι,
καὶ τοῦ διενεχθῆναι χάριν ἐδέοντο.
3 ἀνθ' ὧν πυριφλεγῆ στύλον,
ὁδηγὸν μὲν ἀγνώστου ὁδοιπορίας,
ἥλιον δὲ ἀβλαβῆ φιλοτίμου ξενιτείας παρέσχες.
4 ἄξιοι μὲν γὰρ ἐκεῖνοι στερηθῆναι φωτὸς καὶ φυλακισθῆναι ἐν σκότει,
οἱ κατακλείστους φυλάξαντες τοὺς υἱούς σου,
δι' ὧν ἤμελλε τὸ ἄφθαρτον νόμου φῶς τῷ αἰῶνι δίδοσθαι.

20 [21] Solis autem illis superposita erat gravis nox, imago tenebrarum, quae superventura illis erat. Ipsi ergo sibi erant graviores tenebris.

CAPUT XVIII.

1 Sanctis autem tuis maxima erat lux, et horum quidem vocem audiebant, sed figuram non videbant. Et quia non et ipsi eadem passi erant, magnifica-2 bant te; et qui ante laesi erant, quia non laedebantur, gratias agebant; et ut esset differentia 3 donum petebant. Propter quod iguis ardentem columnam ducem habuerunt ignotae viae, et solem sine laesura boni hos-4 pitii praestitisti. Digni quidem illi carere luce, et pati carcerem tenebrarum, qui inclusos custodiebant filios tuos per quos incipiebat incorruptum legis

---

21. επετατο A. V. 68. 106. Ald. επεκειτο S. επετετακτο 254. εδεδοτο Ven. αυτούς. αυτου S. αυτους S². XVIII. 1. ην φωνην S². μεν om. V¹. ορωντες ετρυχοντο 106. 261. ουν V. S. al. Syr. Ar. Arm. Ald. ου A. 254. Compl. Vulg. γαρ Ven. 2. βλαστουσιν S. βλεπουσιν S². ευχαριστουσι V. S. 68. ηυχαριστουν A. Ven. caet. ιδέοντο. ιδεχοντο Ven. οδαντων S. ιδοντο S². 3. οδηγον. ολιγον S. οδηγον S². φιλοτιμαι παρεσχε (sic) S. φιλοτιμου ξενιτιας παρεσχες S². ξενητιας A. παρεσχου Ven. παρεσχεν 155. παρεσχον 248. 4. εκεινου A. εν σκοτει V. 68. 106. 157. εν om. A. Ven. 55. al. σκοτους S. σκοτει S². φυλασσοντες S. εμελλεν S. φως. φωτοι S. φως S².

[—XVIII. 10.] THE BOOK OF WISDOM. 103

<table>
<tr><td>

5 lumen saeculo dari. Cum cogitarent justorum occidere infantes et, uno exposito filio et liberato, in traductionem illorum, multitudinem filiorum abstulisti, et pariter illos perdi-
6 disti in aqua valida. Illa enim nox ante cognita est a patribus nostris, ut vere scientes quibus juramentis crediderunt animae-
7 quiores essent. Suscepta est autem a populo tuo sanitas quidem justorum, injustorum
8 autem exterminatio. Sicut enim laesisti adversarios, sic et nos
9 provocans magnificasti. Absconse enim sacrificabant justi pueri bonorum, et justitiae legem in concordia disposuerunt, similiter et bona et mala recepturos justos, patrum jam
10 decantantes laudes. Resonabat autem inconveniens inimicorum vox, et flebilis audiebatur planc-

</td><td>

5 Βουλευσαμένους δ' αὐτοὺς τὰ τῶν ὁσίων ἀποκτεῖναι νήπια,
καὶ ἑνὸς ἐκτεθέντος τέκνου καὶ σωθέντος εἰς ἔλεγχον,
τὸ αὐτῶν ἀφείλω πλῆθος τέκνων,
καὶ ὁμοθυμαδὸν ἀπώλεσας ἐν ὕδατι σφοδρῷ.
6 ἐκείνη ἡ νὺξ προεγνώσθη πατράσιν ἡμῶν,
ἵνα ἀσφαλῶς εἰδότες οἷς ἐπίστευσαν ὅρκοις ἐπευθυμήσωσι.
7 προσεδέχθη δὲ ὑπὸ λαοῦ σου σωτηρία μὲν δικαίων, ἐχθρῶν δὲ ἀπώλεια.
8 ὡς γὰρ ἐτιμωρήσω τοὺς ὑπεναντίους,
τούτῳ ἡμᾶς προσκαλεσάμενος ἐδόξασας.
9 κρυφῇ γὰρ ἐθυσίαζον ὅσιοι παῖδες ἀγαθῶν,
καὶ τὸν τῆς θειότητος νόμον ἐν ὁμονοίᾳ διέθεντο,
τῶν αὐτῶν ὁμοίως καὶ ἀγαθῶν καὶ κινδύνων μεταλήψεσθαι,
τοὺς ἁγίους πατέρων ἤδη προαναμέλποντες αἴνους.
10 ἀντήχει δ' ἀσύμφωνος ἐχθρῶν βοή,
καὶ οἰκτρὰ διεφέρετο φωνὴ θρηνουμένων παίδων.

</td><td>

5 the world. And when they had determined to slay the babes of the saints, one child being cast forth, and saved, to reprove them, thou tookest away the multitude of their children, and destroyedst them altogether
6 in a mighty water. Of that night were our fathers certified afore, that assuredly knowing unto what oaths they had given credence, they might afterwards
7 be of good cheer. So of thy people was accepted both the salvation of the righteous, and
8 destruction of the enemies. For wherewith thou didst punish our adversaries, by the same thou didst glorify us, whom
9 thou hadst called. For the righteous children of good men did sacrifice secretly, and with one consent made a holy law[1], [1 Or, a covenant of God, or, league.]
that the saints should be like partakers of the same good and evil, the fathers now singing out
10 the songs of praise. But on the other side there sounded an ill according cry of the enemies, and a lamentable noise was carried abroad for children

</td></tr>
</table>

5. δ' om. S. 106. 253. Ald.   δ' αυτους om. 157.   οσιων σου 261.   αποκτινειν S.   αποκτιναι S².   εις εκδικησιν 253.   των αυτων A. των αυτων 55. al. Compl.   το om. 106. al. impr. S. cor.   αφιλου A.   αφειλου 55. 106. al. Compl.   αφιλες Ven.   Post τεκνων S.: τους δε εχθρους του λαου ομοθυμαδον απωλεσας.   S. cor. sicut V.   6. τοις πατρασιν 106. al.   επιθυμησωσιν S. 106. 248. al. ευχαριστησωσιν Ven.   7. δε om. S. V¹. 106. 261. Ald.   προσδεχθη A.   8. ω γαρ V. a sec. m. Ven. al. Arm.   ως γαρ S. A. V. a pr. m. Compl. Ald. Vulg. Ar.   9. οσιοι om. A.   θειοτητος V. A. Ven. al.   οσιοτητος S. 106. al. Vulg. Syr. Arm.   και αγαθων.   και impr. S².   μεταλημψεσθαι S. A.   προαναμελποντων V. S. 68. 261. Ar.   προαναμελποντες A. S². 55. 106. al. Compl. Vulg.   προαναμελποντος Ven.   αναμελποντες S².   10. η βοη S.   η cras. S. cor.   διεφ. φωνη A. S. Ven. 55. al. Compl. Vulg. Ar. Arm.   φωνη om. V. 68. al.   διεφερετο A.

11 that were bewailed. The master and the servant were punished after one manner; and like as the king, so suffered the common 12 person. So they all together had innumerable dead with one kind of death; neither were the living sufficient to bury them: for in one moment the noblest offspring of them was 13 destroyed. For whereas they would not believe any thing by reason of the enchantments; upon the destruction of the firstborn, they acknowledged this people to be the sons of 14 God. For while all things were in quiet silence, and that night was in the midst of her swift 15 course, Thine Almighty word leaped down from heaven out of thy royal throne, as a fierce man of war into the midst of a land 16 of destruction, And brought thine unfeigned commandment as a sharp sword, and standing up filled all things with death; and it touched the heaven, but 17 it stood upon the earth. Then suddenly visions[1] of horrible dreams troubled them sore, and

[1] Or, *imaginations*.

11 ὁμοίᾳ δὲ δίκῃ δοῦλος ἅμα δεσπότῃ κολασθείς,
καὶ δημότης βασιλεῖ τὰ αὐτὰ πάσχων.
12 ὁμοθυμαδὸν δὲ πάντες ἐν ἑνὶ ὀνόματι θανάτου
νεκροὺς εἶχον ἀναριθμήτους·
οὐδὲ γὰρ πρὸς τὸ θάψαι οἱ ζῶντες ἦσαν ἱκανοί,
ἐπεὶ πρὸς μίαν ῥοπὴν ἡ ἐντιμοτέρα γένεσις αὐτῶν διέφθαρτο.
13 πάντα γὰρ ἀπιστοῦντες διὰ τὰς φαρμακίας,
ἐπὶ τῷ τῶν πρωτοτόκων ὀλέθρῳ ὡμολόγησαν Θεοῦ υἱὸν λαὸν εἶναι.
14 ἡσύχου γὰρ σιγῆς περιεχούσης τὰ πάντα,
καὶ νυκτὸς ἐν ἰδίῳ τάχει μεσαζούσης,
15 ὁ παντοδύναμός σου λόγος ἀπ' οὐρανῶν ἐκ θρόνων βασιλείων,
ἀπότομος πολεμιστὴς εἰς μέσον τῆς ὀλεθρίας ἥλατο γῆς,
16 ξίφος ὀξὺ τὴν ἀνυπόκριτον ἐπιταγήν σου φέρων,
καὶ στὰς ἐπλήρωσε τὰ πάντα θανάτου·
καὶ οὐρανοῦ μὲν ἥπτετο, βεβήκει δ' ἐπὶ γῆς.
17 τότε παραχρῆμα φαντασίαι μὲν ὀνείρων δεινῶν ἐξετάραξαν αὐτούς,

11 tus ploratorum infantium. Simili autem poena servus cum domino afflictus est, et popularis 12 homo regi similia passus. Similiter ergo omnes, uno nomine mortis, mortuos habebant innumerabiles. Nec enim ad sepeliendum vivi sufficiebant, quoniam uno momento, quae erat praeclarior natio illorum exter- 13 minata est. De omnibus enim non credentes, propter veneficia; tunc vero primum eum fuit exterminium primogenitorum, spoponderunt populum Dei esse. 14 Cum enim quietum silentium contineret omnia, et nox in suo cursu medium iter haberet, 15 omnipotens sermo tuus de caelo a regalibus sedibus, durus debellator in mediam exterminii 16 terram prosilivit, gladius acutus insimulatum imperium tuum portans, et stans replevit omnia morte, et usque ad caelum at- 17 tingebat stans in terra. Tunc continuo visus somniorum malorum turbaverunt illos, et ti-

11. βασιλεια S. βασιλει S². 12. δε om. S. add. S². γαρ om. 106. 261. ροπήν. ωραν 106. 261. η om. S 106. 261. add. S². διεφθαρη V. al. Ap. διεφθαρτο S. A. 55. al. pl. 13. λαον θεου Ven. 14. εν om. 106. 248. 261. μεσουσης 106. 261. μεσαζουσης τα παντα V¹. 16. επιταγην V. S. al. υποταγην A. al. εβεβηκει 106. επι om. S. Ven. add. S². 17. δεινως V. Ven. al. δεινων A. S. 55. al. Compl. Vulg. Syr. Ar. Arm. εταραξαν 155. 254.

mores supervenerunt insperati.
18 Et alius alibi projectus semivivus, propter quam moriebatur causam demonstrabat mortis.
19 Visiones enim quae illos turbaverunt haec praemonebant, ne inscii quare mala patiebantur
20 perirent. Tetigit autem tunc et justos tentatio mortis, et commotio in eremo facta est multitudinis; sed non diu permansit ira tua.
21 Properans enim homo sine querela deprecari pro populis, proferens servitutis suae scutum, orationem et per incensum deprecationem allegans, restitit irae, et finem imposuit necessitati, ostendens quoniam tuus est famulus.
22 Vicit autem turbas, non in virtute corporis, nec armaturae potentia; sed verbo illum qui se vexabat subjecit, juramenta parentum, et testamentum commemorans.
23 Cum enim jam acervatim cecidissent super alterutrum mortui, interstitit, et amputavit impetum, et divisit illam quae ad vivos ducebat

φόβοι δὲ ἐπέστησαν ἀδόκητοι·
18 καὶ ἄλλος ἀλλαχῇ ῥιφεὶς ἡμίθνητος,
 δι' ἣν ἔθνησκεν αἰτίαν ἐνεφάνιζεν.
19 οἱ γὰρ ὄνειροι θορυβήσαντες αὐτοὺς τοῦτο προεμήνυσαν,
 ἵνα μὴ ἀγνοοῦντες δι' ὃ κακῶς πάσχουσιν ἀπόλωνται.
20 ἥψατο δὲ καὶ δικαίων πεῖρα θανάτου,
 καὶ θραῦσις ἐν ἐρήμῳ ἐγένετο πλήθους·
 ἀλλ' οὐκ ἐπὶ πολὺ ἔμεινεν ἡ ὀργή.
21 σπεύσας γὰρ ἀνὴρ ἄμεμπτος προεμάχησε·
 τὸ τῆς ἰδίας λειτουργίας ὅπλον,
 προσευχὴν καὶ θυμιάματος ἐξιλασμὸν κομίσας,
 ἀντέστη τῷ θυμῷ, καὶ πέρας ἐπέθηκε τῇ συμφορᾷ,
 δεικνὺς ὅτι σός ἐστι θεράπων.
22 ἐνίκησε δὲ τὸν ὄχλον
 οὐκ ἰσχύϊ τοῦ σώματος, οὐχ ὅπλων ἐνεργείᾳ,
 ἀλλὰ λόγῳ τὸν κολάζοντα ὑπέταξεν,
 ὅρκους πατέρων καὶ διαθήκας ὑπομνήσας.
23 σωρηδὸν γὰρ ἤδη πεπτωκότων ἐπ' ἀλλήλων νεκρῶν,
 μεταξὺ στὰς ἀνέκοψε τὴν ὀργήν,
 καὶ διέσχισε τὴν πρὸς τοὺς ζῶντας ὁδόν.

and terrors came upon them un-
18 looked for. And one thrown here, and another there, half dead, shewed the cause of his
19 death. For the dreams that troubled them did foreshew this, lest they should perish, and not know why they were
20 afflicted. Yea, the tasting of death touched the righteous also, and there was a destruction of the multitude in the wilderness: but the wrath en-
21 dured not long. For then the blameless man made haste, and stood forth to defend them; and bringing the shield of his proper ministry, even prayer, and the propitiation of incense, set himself against the wrath, and so brought the calamity to an end, declaring that he was
22 thy servant. So he overcame the destroyer, not with strength of body, nor force of arms, but with a word subdued he him that punished, alleging the oaths and covenants made with the
23 fathers. For when the dead were now fallen down by heaps one upon another, standing between, he stayed the wrath, and parted [1] the way to the living. [1] Or, *cut off.*

---

17. και φοβοι δε 155. επεπεσον 157. απροσδοκητοι 157. 18. ριφθις A. εθνησκεν V. Ven. S². al. ενεφανιζεν V. S. Ven. al. ενεφανιζον A. 55. 157. al. 19. τουτο om. S. προεμηνυσαν V. S. προσεμηνυσαν A. 20. δε ποτε 248. Compl. ποτε πειρα Ven. 253. τοτε πειρα S. ποτε π. S². εγενετο εν ερημω Ven. οργη σου S. Ven. 55. al. Vulg. σου eras. S². 21. οπλον λαβων 253. προσευχης Ven. S¹. τω om. S. add. S². 22. οχλον Mss. fere omn. ολοθρευοντα 157. 248. Compl. ημιθανης 157. 296. εθνησκον A. S. 55. al. 23. διεσχισε. διεκοψεν S².

THE BOOK OF WISDOM.

24 For in the long garment was the whole world, and in the four rows of the stones was the glory of the fathers graven, and thy Majesty upon the dia-
25 dem of his head. Unto these the destroyer gave place, and was afraid of them: for it was enough that they only tasted of the wrath.

CHAPTER XIX.

1 As for the ungodly, wrath came upon them without mercy unto the end: for he knew before
2 what they would do; How that having given them leave to depart, and sent them hastily away, they would repent and pursue
3 them. For whilst they were yet mourning and making lamentation at the graves of the dead, they added another foolish device, and pursued them as fugitives, whom they had in-
4 treated to be gone[1]. For the destiny, whereof they were worthy, drew them unto this end, and made them forget the things that had already happened, that

[1] Or, cast out by intreaty.

24 ἐπὶ γὰρ ποδήρους ἐνδύματος ἦν ὅλος ὁ κόσμος,
καὶ πατέρων δόξαι ἐπὶ τετραστίχου λίθου γλυφῆς,
καὶ μεγαλωσύνη σου ἐπὶ διαδήματος κεφαλῆς αὐτοῦ.
25 τούτοις εἶξεν ὁ ὀλοθρεύων, ταῦτα δὲ ἐφοβήθη·
ἦν γὰρ μόνη ἡ πεῖρα τῆς ὀργῆς ἱκανή.

ΚΕΦΑΛΑΙΟΝ ΙΘ΄.

1 Τοῖς δὲ ἀσεβέσι μέχρι τέλους ἀνελεήμων θυμὸς ἐπέστη·
προῄδει γὰρ αὐτῶν καὶ τὰ μέλλοντα,
2 ὅτι αὐτοὶ ἐπιστρέψαντες τοῦ ἀπεῖναι,
καὶ μετὰ σπουδῆς προπέμψαντες αὐτούς,
διώξουσι μεταμεληθέντες.
3 ἔτι γὰρ ἐν χερσὶν ἔχοντες τὰ πένθη,
καὶ προσοδυρόμενοι τάφοις νεκρῶν,
ἕτερον ἐπεσπάσαντο λογισμὸν ἀνοίας,
καὶ οὓς ἱκετεύοντες ἐξέβαλον, τούτους ὡς φυγάδας ἐδίωκον.
4 εἷλκε γὰρ αὐτοὺς ἡ ἀξία ἐπὶ τοῦτο τὸ πέρας ἀνάγκη,
καὶ τῶν συμβεβηκότων ἀμνηστίαν ἐνέβαλεν,

24 viam. In veste enim poderis quam habebat totus erat orbis terrarum; et parentum magnalia in quatuor ordinibus lapidum erant sculpta, et magnificentia tua in diademate capitis illius
25 sculpta erat. His autem cessit qui exterminabat, et haec extimuit; erat enim sola tentatio irae sufficiens.

CAPUT XIX.

1 Impiis autem usque in novissimum sine misericordia ira supervenit; praesciebat enim et
2 futura illorum; quoniam cum ipsi permisissent ut se educerent, et cum magna sollicitudine praemisissent illos, consequebantur illos poenitentia acti.
3 Adhuc enim inter manus habentes luctum, et deplorantes ad monumenta mortuorum, aliam sibi assumserunt cogitationem inscientiae, et quos rogantes projecerant, hos tanquam fugitivos
4 persequebantur. Ducebat enim illos ad hunc finem digna necessitas; et horum quae acciderant commemorationem amit-

---

24. λιθου V. S. 68. al.   λιθαν A. C. Ven. 55. al. Compl.   λιθων 155.   γλυφη S.   γλυφης S².   η ante μεγαλ. add. S².
25. ολεθρευων A. C.   δε om. Ven. 253. S².   εφοβηθησαν V. S. 68. al. Syr. Ar.   εφοβηθη A. Ven. S¹. 55. al. Compl. Vulg.   μονον Ven.   οργης σου S.   XIX. 2. επιστρεψαντες. V. S¹. C. Ven. al.   επιτρεψαντες A. S². 55. al. Compl. Vulg.   απιεναι 106. al. Compl.
3. οτι γαρ Ven.   ανοιας om. S. add. S².   4. το om. S. V. Ven. al. Ald.   εβαλεν C.   ενεβαλλεν Ven.

tebant, ut quae deerant tormentis, repleret punitio, et populus quidem tuus mirabiliter transiret, illi autem novam mortem invenirent. Omnis enim creatura ad suum genus ab initio refigurabatur, deserviens tuis praeceptis, ut pueri tui custodirentur illaesi. Nam nubes castra eorum obumbrabat; et ex aqua quae ante erat, terra arida apparuit, et in mari Rubro via sine impedimento, et campus germinans de profundo nimio; per quem omnis natio transivit quae tegebatur tua manu, videntes tua mirabilia et monstra. Tanquam enim equi depaverunt escam, et tanquam agni exultaverunt, magnificantes te, Domine, qui liberasti illos. Memores enim erant adhuc eorum, quae in incolatu illorum facta fuerant, quemadmodum pro natione animalium eduxit terra muscas, et pro piscibus eructavit fluvius multitudinem ra-

ἵνα τὴν λείπουσαν ταῖς βασάνοις προσαναπληρώσωσι κόλασιν,
5 καὶ ὁ μὲν λαός σου παράδοξον ὁδοιπορίαν περάσῃ,
ἐκεῖνοι δὲ ξένον εὕρωσι θάνατον.
6 ὅλη γὰρ ἡ κτίσις ἐν ἰδίῳ γένει πάλιν ἄνωθεν διετυποῦτο,
ὑπηρετοῦσα ταῖς ἰδίαις ἐπιταγαῖς,
ἵνα οἱ σοὶ παῖδες φυλαχθῶσιν ἀβλαβεῖς.
7 ἡ τὴν παρεμβολὴν σκιάζουσα νεφέλη,
ἐκ δὲ προϋφεστῶτος ὕδατος ξηρᾶς ἀνάδυσις γῆς ἐθεωρήθη,
ἐξ ἐρυθρᾶς θαλάσσης ὁδὸς ἀνεμπόδιστος,
καὶ χλοηφόρον πεδίον ἐκ κλύδωνος βιαίου,
8 δι' οὗ πᾶν ἔθνος διῆλθον οἱ τῇ σῇ σκεπαζόμενοι χειρί,
θεωρήσαντες θαυμαστὰ τέρατα.
9 ὡς γὰρ ἵπποι ἐνεμήθησαν,
καὶ ὡς ἀμνοὶ διεσκίρτησαν,
αἰνοῦντές σε, Κύριε, τὸν ῥυόμενον αὐτούς.
10 ἐμέμνηντο γὰρ ἔτι τῶν ἐν τῇ παροικίᾳ αὐτῶν,
πῶς ἀντὶ μὲν γενέσεως ζώων ἐξήγαγεν ἡ γῆ σκνῖπα,
ἀντὶ δὲ ἐνύδρων ἐξηρεύξατο ὁ ποταμὸς πλῆθος βατράχων.

they might fulfil the punishment which was wanting to their torments: And that thy people might pass a wonderful way: but they might find a strange death. For the whole creature in his proper kind was fashioned again anew, serving the peculiar commandments that were given unto them, that thy children might be kept without hurt: *As namely*, a cloud shadowing the camp; and where water stood before, dry land appeared; and out of the Red sea a way without impediment; and out of the violent stream a green field: Wherethrough all the people went that were defended with thy hand, seeing thy marvellous strange wonders. For they went at large like horses, and leaped like lambs, praising thee, O Lord, who hadst delivered them. For they were yet mindful of the things that were done while they sojourned in the strange land, how the ground brought forth flies[1] instead of cattle, and how the river cast up a multitude of

[1] Or, *lice*.

---

4. λιπουσαν S. προσαναπληρωσωσι A. C. 155. προσαναπληρωσωσι V. Ven. al. προσαναπληρωσουσιν S. 5. πειρασῃ S. V¹. 6. Post γενει add. S². ταχι († ταχει vel ταξει). ανετυπουτο 55. 248. 254. Compl. Vulg. ιδιαις V. C. Ven. al. Ar. σαις A. S. 106. al. Vulg. Syr. Arm. υποταγαις 106. 261. αβλαβοι 261. 7. τη την π. σκιαζουσῃ A. εκ δε του Ven. εκ γαρ S¹. αναδοσις 261. εθεωρειτο S. εθεωρειτο A. εθεωρηθη V. S². al. και εξ ερυθρ. 248. S². Compl. Vulg. παιδιον S. 8. πανεθνι V¹. Ven. S². al. πανεθνει (*sic*) V². παν εθνος A. S. C. 55. al. Compl. Ald. Vulg. Syr. Ar. τερατα. πραγματα 106. 9. διενεμηθησαν 106. 261. ρυομενον V. S. Ven. al. ρυσαμενον A. C. 55. al. Ald. Vulg. Arm. 10. μεν om. C. γενεσεως. χερσαιαν 155. A. Par. ἡ γῆ. η om. C. σκνιπα V. C. 68. al. Arm. σκνιφας A. Ven. 106. 261. Ald. Vulg. S². σκνιφα S. 55. 157. al. ενυδραν V. S. al. ανυδραν A. βατραχους S. πληθος suppl. in marg. βατραχων S².

P 2

11 frogs instead of fishes. But afterwards they saw a new generation of fowls, when, being led with their appetite, they asked
12 delicate meats. For quails came up unto them from the sea for
13 their contentment[1]. And punishments came upon the sinners not without former signs by the force of thunders: for they suffered justly according to their own wickedness, insomuch as they used a more hard and hateful behaviour toward strangers.
14 For the *Sodomites* did not receive those, whom they knew not when they came: but these brought friends into bondage, that had well deserved of them.
15 And not only so, but peradventure some respect shall be had of those, because they used
16 strangers not friendly: But these very grievously afflicted them, whom they had received with feastings, and were already made partakers of the same
17 laws with them. Therefore even with blindness were these stricken, as those were at the doors of the righteous man: when, being compassed about with horrible great darkness,

[1] Or, *comfort*.

11 ἐφ' ὑστέρῳ δὲ εἶδον καὶ νέαν γένεσιν ὀρνέων,
ὅτε ἐπιθυμίᾳ προαχθέντες ᾐτήσαντο ἐδέσματα τρυφῆς.
12 εἰς γὰρ παραμυθίαν ἀνέβη αὐτοῖς ἀπὸ θαλάσσης ὀρτυγομήτρα.
13 Καὶ αἱ τιμωρίαι τοῖς ἁμαρτωλοῖς ἐπῆλθον
οὐκ ἄνευ τῶν προγεγονότων τεκμηρίων τῇ βίᾳ τῶν κεραυνῶν·
δικαίως γὰρ ἔπασχον ταῖς ἰδίαις αὐτῶν πονηρίαις·
καὶ γὰρ χαλεπωτέραν μισοξενίαν ἐπετήδευσαν·
14 οἱ μὲν γὰρ τοὺς ἀγνοοῦντας οὐκ ἐδέχοντο παρόντας,
οὗτοι δὲ εὐεργέτας ξένους ἐδουλοῦντο.
15 καὶ οὐ μόνον, ἀλλ' ἥτις ἐπισκοπὴ ἔσται αὐτῶν,
ἐπεὶ ἀπεχθῶς προσεδέχοντο τοὺς ἀλλοτρίους·
16 οἱ δὲ μετὰ ἑορτασμάτων εἰσδεξάμενοι
τοὺς ἤδη τῶν αὐτῶν μετεσχηκότας δικαίων δεινοῖς ἐκάκωσαν πόνοις.
17 ἐπλήγησαν δὲ καὶ ἀορασίᾳ,
ὥσπερ ἐκεῖνοι ἐπὶ ταῖς τοῦ δικαίου θύραις,
ὅτε ἀχανεῖ περιβληθέντες σκότει

11 narum. Novissime autem viderunt novam creaturam avium, cum adducti concupiscentia postulaverunt escas epulationis. In
12 allocutione enim desiderii ascendit illis de mari ortygometra; [13] et vexationes peccatoribus supervenerunt, non sine illis quae ante facta erant argumentis per vim fulminum; juste enim patiebantur secundum suas nequitias. Etenim detestabiliorem
13 inhospitalitatem instituerunt: [14] alii quidem ignotos non recipiebant advenas, alii autem bonos hospites in servitutem redigebant. [15] Et non solum haec,
14 sed et alius quidam respectus illorum erat, quoniam inviti recipiebant extraneos. [16] Qui autem cum laetitia receperunt hos
15 qui eisdem usi erant justitiis, saevissimis afflixerunt doloribus.
16 [17] Percussi sunt autem caecitate, sicut illi in foribus justi, cum subitaneis cooperti essent

---

11. ιδον A. C. γενεσιν νεαν A. al. Compl. οτι Reusch. Tisch. 68. οτε V. S. A. C. Ven. al. 12. παραμυθιον Ven. 106. 261. εκ θαλασσης ανεβη αυτοις S. εκ θαλ. 248. Compl. 13. αι om. 106. 261. ανευ. ανισοι 106. 261. γεγονοταν V. Ven. al. προγεγονοταν A. S. C. al. Compl. Vulg. Syr. Ar. Arm. τεκμηριον om. 106. 261. των κεραυνων S. των er. S. cor. πονηριαις αυτων S. γαρ om. S. 261. 14. παροντας. ως παριοντας 106. 261. αυτοι δε C. 16. μεθ' εορτασμων Ven. 253. ηδη μετεσχηκοτας των δικαιων S. 17. οι επι ταις Ven. σκοται Ven.

THE BOOK OF WISDOM.

tenebris, unusquisque transitum ostii sui quaerebat. [18] In se enim elementa dum convertuntur, sicut in organo qualitatis sonus immutatur, et omnia suum sonum custodiunt; unde aestimari ex ipso visu certo potest. [19] Agrestia enim in aquatica convertebantur; et quaecunque erant natantia in terram transibant. [20] Ignis in aqua valebat supra suam virtutem, et aqua extinguentis naturae obliviscebatur. [21] Flammae e contrario corruptibilium animalium non vexaverunt carnes coambulantium, nec dissolvebant illam, quae facile dissolvebatur sicut glacies, bonam escam. [22] In omnibus enim magnificasti populum tuum, Domine, et honorasti, et non despexisti, in omni tempo e et in omni loco assistens eis.

ἕκαστος τῶν αὐτοῦ θυρῶν τὴν δίοδον ἐζήτει.
18 δι' ἑαυτῶν γὰρ τὰ στοιχεῖα μεθαρμοζόμενα,
ὥσπερ ἐν ψαλτηρίῳ φθόγγοι τοῦ ῥυθμοῦ τὸ ὄνομα διαλλάσσουσι,
πάντοτε μένοντα ἤχῳ,
ὅπερ ἐστὶν εἰκάσαι ἐκ τῆς τῶν γεγονότων ὄψεως ἀκριβῶς.
19 χερσαῖα γὰρ εἰς ἔνυδρα μετεβάλλετο,
καὶ νηκτὰ μετέβαινεν ἐπὶ γῆς·
20 πῦρ ἴσχυεν ἐν ὕδατι τῆς ἰδίας δυνάμεως,
καὶ ὕδωρ τῆς σβεστικῆς φύσεως ἐπελανθάνετο·
21 φλόγες ἀνάπαλιν εὐφθάρτων ζώων οὐκ ἐμάραναν σάρκας ἐμπεριπατούντων,
οὐδὲ τηκτὸν κρυσταλλοειδὲς εὔτηκτον γένος ἀμβροσίας τροφῆς.
22 κατὰ πάντα γὰρ, Κύριε, ἐμεγάλυνας τὸν λαόν σου καὶ ἐδόξασας,
καὶ οὐχ ὑπερεῖδες, ἐν παντὶ καιρῷ καὶ τόπῳ παριστάμενος.

every one sought the passage of his own doors. For the elements were changed in themselves[1] by a kind of harmony, like as in a psaltery notes change the name of a tune, and yet are always sounds; which may well be perceived by the sight of the things that have been done. For earthly things were turned into watery, and the things, that before swam in the water, now went upon the ground. The fire had power in the water, forgetting his own virtue: and the water forgat his own quenching nature. On the other side, the flames wasted not the flesh of the corruptible livingthings, though they walked therein: neither melted they the icy kind of heavenly meat, that was of nature apt to melt. For in all things, O Lord, thou didst magnify thy people, and glorify them, neither didst thou lightly regard them: but didst assist them in every time and place.

[1] Gr. by themselves.

---

17. των αυτου V. S. Ven. al. των εαυτου A. C. al. Compl. την οδον 106. 261. παντοτε. παντα Ven. S². εν ηχω Ven. 157. 254. S². 19. χερσεα S. ενεδρα S. ενυδρα S². επι γην Ven. εις γην S. 155. 253. επι γης S². 20. ισχυσεν V. Ven. al. ισχυεν S. A. C. al. ιδιας δυναμεως. post δυν. addunt. A. C. al. Compl. επιλελησμενον. σβεστικης δυναμεως V. 68. al. Syr. σβ. φυσεως S. A. C. Ven. al. Compl. Ald. Vulg. Ar. Arm. 21. εμπεριπατουντων S. ευτηκτον κρυστ. V¹. 68. κρυσταλλοειδες ευτηκτον S. A. C. V². Ven. al. Compl. Ald. τρυφης S. τροφης S². 22. κυριε om. Ven. εμνημονευσας του λαου σου 253. και ουχ. και om. C. τοπραι S. περισταμενος C. Subscriptio: Σοφια Σαλομωνος A. Σοφ. Σαλομωνος V. Σοφ. Σαλομωντος S. Σ. Σαλομωντος C.

COMMENTARY.

CHAPTER I.

CHAPTERS I–IX. WISDOM SPECULATIVELY REGARDED: ITS SPIRITUAL, INTELLECTUAL, AND MORAL ASPECT.

CHAPTERS I–V COMMENDATION OF WISDOM AS GUIDE TO HAPPINESS AND IMMORTALITY

I 1–5. *Exhortation to the pursuit of Wisdom, in which pursuit the condition is purity in thought,* 6–11 *and in word.*

1. Δικαιοσύνην, 'righteousness,' not merely justice between man and man, but moral uprightness, which is equivalent to Wisdom in its full theoretical and practical meaning. Comp 2 Sam. xxiii 2, 3.

Οἱ κρίνοντες τὴν γῆν, i e kings and princes (cp. vi. 1, 4, ix. 7); for, as Grimm quotes, κρίνειν τὸ ἄρχειν ἔλεγον οἱ παλαιοί, Artemid. ii. 12, p. 56, ed. Ald. In Ecclus. x. 1, 2, the words κριτὴς and ἡγεμὼν are interchanged as synonymous, and Solomon's prayer, 1 Kings iii 9, is that he may judge (κρίνειν) the people righteously. Comp Exod. ii 14, 1 Sam. viii 20; Ep Jer. 14 (13 Tisch.) In the Oriental point of view judgment appertains to the office of ruler.

Φρονήσατε περὶ τ K. ἐν ἀγαθότητι A Lap 'Sentite et sapite de Deo, quod ipse sit probissimus, honestissimus, sanctissimus, justissimus.' But this spoils the parallelism with ἁπλότητι, which belongs to the verb ζητήσατε. Ἐν ἀγαθότητι is = ἀγαθῶς, 'think of the Lord with sincerity.' See on ἀγαθωσύνη, the word in N. T., Trench, Syn. of N. T., Ser. II. § xiii.

Ἐν ἁπλότητι καρδίας, 'in singleness of heart,' with pure intention, a Hebraistic expression, 1 Chron. xxix. 17, Eph. vi. 5. The opposite vice is duplicity Comp. S Matt. vi 22. In Acts ii. 46 we find ἐν ἀφελότητι καρδίας. With this verse comp Ps. ii. 10 ff

Ζητήσατε. The expression ζητεῖν τὸν Κύριον is common, e.g Deut. iv 29, Isai lv 6, Hebr xi 6, Philo, De Mon. 5 (ii p 217, Mang): οὐδὲν ἄμεινον τοῦ ζητεῖν τὸν ἀληθῆ Θεόν. The first verse contains the subject of the whole Book, to recommend righteousness, which is Wisdom, to all men, and specially to princes and governors

2 The parallelism is to be remarked· εὑρίσκεται answers to ζητήσατε, ἐμφανίζεται to φρονήσατε, μὴ πειράζουσι and μὴ ἀπιστοῦσι to ἐν ἁπλότητι καρδίας and ἐν ἀγαθότητι Gutb Comp. 2 Chron xv. 2, and Proleg. p. 28.

Πειράζουσιν, 'tempt' God by doubting His power, justice, and love, and by trusting in themselves S. Matt. iv 7 Comp. Deut vi 16; Acts v 9, 1 Cor x. 9

A reads τοῖς μὴ πιστεύουσιν for τοῖς μὴ ἀπιστοῦσιν, in which case ἐμφανίζεται would imply, 'showeth Himself in hostile fashion' But the reading of the text has highest authority. The Vulg. seems to have read τοῖς πιστεύουσιν, 'eis qui fidem habent in illum,' unless the translators expressed the phrase μὴ ἀπιστεῖν by 'fidem habere;' Reusch. Origen, Exc in Ps xiii. (vol xvii p. 108, Migne) quotes τοῖς μὴ ἀπιστοῦσιν αὐτῷ, also Schol in Luc i 14 (xvii. p 317, Migne), and so S Jer. iv 649, vi. 853 Didym. in Ps. ix. 11 (xxxix p. 1193, Migne). παρίσταται ὁ τρόπος ὡς δεῖ ζητεῖν τὸν Θεὸν, ἐκ τῶν ἐν τῇ Σοφίᾳ οὕτως ἐχόντων φρονήσατε κ.τ.λ. τοῖς μὴ ἀπιστοῦσιν αὐτῷ. Ἀπιστεῖν occurs x 7; xii 17; xviii 13 Comp. S Mark xvi 16

Ἐμφανίζεται, 'manifests himself,' as S. John xiv. 21, 22. 'Apparet his qui non sunt ei increduli.' Hieron. in Isai lv (iv. p. 649).

3. Σκολιοί, 'perverse,' opp. to 'simple;' Deut. xxxii 5, Acts ii 40; Phil ii. 15 Such thoughts separate from God as leading to sin.

Δοκιμαζομένη τε, κ τ λ, 'His (God's) power when tried,' tried by men's unbelief Tu in 'potentia Dei tentata et lacessita impiorum diffidentia et infidelitate.' Ps. xciv. 9 Sept. Comp ch. ii. 17 19, 2 Cor. xiii 5, Hebr iii. 9, where δοκιμάζ. is found in connection with πειράζειν. The many similar expressions in Wisd. and Hebr have often been noticed See Prolegom. pp 29, 34.

Ἐλέγχει, 'convicts,' convinces the fools of folly by punishing their unbelief.

Τοὺς ἄφρονας 'Fool,' in the Sapiential Books, means a godless, impious man, a sinner. Folly is the opposite of Wisdom; it is the work of the devil, as wisdom is the effect of the grace of God Prov ii 6 and xxiv 9. 'The Lord giveth wisdom; but the thought of foolishness is sin.' Comp Prov. x 21: 'Fools die for want of wisdom' The wicked woman is the personification of folly (ix 13 ff), and the dead are in her house and her guests in the depths of hell. Thus ἀφροσύνη, Judg xx 6 (Al. Codex), plainly means gross wickedness, and ἄφρων, 2 Sam xiii. 13, is an evil man And thus throughout the Book of Proverbs. Comp. Prov i 22, xiii 19, 20, xix. 1, Eccles. vii 25, 26. So S Paul, Rom i 30, uses ἀσύνετος, of moral degradation. Comp. Ps. xiii. 1 ff, 2 Macc. iv. 6; xv 33

4 Ὅτι gives the reason why perverse thoughts separate from God, and shows in what the punishment of fools consists. S. Bas. Mag. Hom in Prov 4 (xxxi. 393, Migne): καθαίρει πρότερον διὰ τοῦ θείου φόβου τὰς ψυχὰς τῶν μελλόντων τῇ σοφίᾳ προσομιλεῖν.

Κακότεχνος, 'using evil arts,' 'artful,' xv. 4; Hom. Il. xv 14 κακότεχνος δόλος.

Σοφία, here first mentioned, includes the knowledge of things divine and human, and the practice of godliness, and is identical with the 'holy Spirit of discipline,' verse 5 As personified by Solomon and our author (Prov i. 20; Wisd. vii. 27, and elsewhere) it becomes applicable sometimes to the Son of God and sometimes to the Holy Spirit As defined by the Stoics Σοφία is ἐπιστήμη θείων καὶ ἀνθρωπίνων καὶ τῶν τούτων αἰτιῶν So Cicer De Offic ii. 2, § 5; Philo, Congr erud grat 14 (i p 530) Σοφία, φρόνησις, and σύνεσις are in Aristot (Eth Nic. vi 6, 7) the three intellectual virtues (διανοητικαὶ ἀρεταί) See Dr. J. B. Lightfoot on Ep. to Col. i. 9.

Κατάχρεῳ ἁμαρτίας, a happy expression, not found elsewhere in Scripture It means, 'pledged, pawned to sin.' A Lap 'peccato obnoxio [corpore], oppignorato, et velut acre peccati obaerato et obstricto' Comp S. John viii 34, Rom vii 14 Some Fathers read ἁμαρτίαις; but Didym. De Trin ii 20 (xxxix 740, Migne) has ἁμαρτίας. So Orig. Contr. Cels iii. 60. Pseudo-Ath. De Pass. Dom. 4 (ii p. 82 Ben.): ἅγιον γὰρ Πνεῦμα παιδείας ἀσυνέτων, καὶ οὐ κατοικήσει ἐν σώματι κατάχρεῳ ἁμαρτίαις Comp S James iii 15 'Soul and body,' in O'd Testament use, make up the whole man. 2 Macc vii. 37. Christianity added a new element, spirit, 1 Thess v 23 Some have deduced from this passage that the author saw in the body the source of all moral evil; but the words do not speak of the original creation, and we are taught elsewhere that holiness is necessary for the knowledge of the Lord. Ps. cxi 10; Jer. iv. 14; and comp Wisd. i 14; viii. 20.

5 Ἅγιον Πνεῦμα, without the article, as a Proper Name. So S. Matt. i. 18, 20, S. John xx. 22; Acts ii. 4. The expression τὸ Πνεῦμα τὸ ἅγιον occurs in Isai

lxiii. 11; τὸ Πνεῦμα τὸ ἅγιον αὐτοῦ, Ib v 10   So Wisd. ix 17· τὸ ἅγιόν σου Πνεῦμα. Ps l 13 τὸ Πνεῦμα τὸ ἅγιόν σου. Thus the way was prepared for the later use. At this time the Jews had scarcely realised the distinct Personality of the Holy Ghost, though there are intimations of the truth in the Old Testament, as in the Psalm just quoted, and Gen i 2· 'The Spirit of God moved upon the face of the waters,' where, while the Targum of Onkelos translates 'a wind from before the Lord blew upon the face of the waters,' the Targum of Jonathan paraphrases: 'the Spirit of mercies from before the Lord breathed upon the face of the waters' Etheridge, The Targums, etc., vol 1. pp 33, 157 Comp. Isai. xlviii. 16· 'The Lord God and His Spirit hath sent me' See on ver 6.

Παιδείας (σοφίας, the reading of A, was probably introduced from ver 6) belongs to πνεῦμα, not to δόλον, as some take it 'The Holy Spirit of (= which teaches) discipline, instruction, education.' 'Sanctus enim quum sit spiritus ad morum humanorum conformationem spectans,' Wahl Clav. in voc   Comp Isai xi 2. Didym De Trin ii 3 (xxxix. 468, Migne)· πνεῦμα παιδείας, τοῦτ' ἔστι, σοφίας 'Η γὰρ Σοφία λέγει, πνεῦμα παιδείας φεύξεται δόλον

Δόλον. Vulg 'fictum'= fictionem, which occurs iv. 11; xiv 25. It is not found elsewhere in Vulg.

'Ελεγχθήσεται, 'corripietur,' Vulg ; 'will not abide,' Eng ; 'will be scared away, hasten away in shame,' Gutb, Grimm. Literally, 'will be reproved' by men's sins. Gen. vi. 3· 'my spirit shall not remain (οὐ μὴ καταμείνῃ) in men' So the people are said, Isai lxiii. 10, to 'have vexed' (παρώξυναν) the Holy Spirit. Comp. Eph. iv. 30

6 Γάρ. The connection seems to be this: Evil in a man's heart drives Wisdom away from him; for Wisdom knows man too well and loves him too dearly not to punish the blasphemer by withdrawing her presence from him and leaving him to vengeance. Cp vii 23 Didym. De Trin. ii. 26. (xxxix 752, Migne) introduces this passage vers 6, 7, thus 'Η Σοφία θεολογοῦσα τὸ θεῖκον Πνεῦμα, καὶ ἀπ' αὐτοῦ ἀπειλοῦσα τοῖς βλασφημοῦσιν αὐτό, λέγει· φιλάνθρωπον γὰρ πνεῦμα σοφίας, καὶ οὐκ ἀθῴώσει, κ.τ λ

Σοφία. The reading σοφίας was probably derived from the previous verse, where A gives ἅγ. πνεῦμα σοφίας.

'Αθῴώσει, 'will let go unpunished,' 'absolve.' The verb does not occur in classical Greek   Comp. Ecclus xi. 10 ; xvi 11

Βλάσφημον, 'a blasphemer of God' This word and those akin to it are in Scriptural use restricted commonly to this one sense, as in modern languages.

Χειλέων = ῥημάτων   Isai. xxix 13.

Τῶν νεφρῶν αὐτ   There is an inverted climax here . God is a witness of a man's reins (his inmost feelings), much more of his heart (his thoughts unexpressed), still more of his tongue (his spoken words) 1 Chr xxviii 9 , Hebr. iv. 12 , Rev ii 23

'Επίσκοπος, applied to God, Job xx. 29 ; 1 Pet. ii. 25. Clem. Rom. Ep ad Cor. lix. 3 · τὸν παντὸς πνεύματος κτίστην καὶ ἐπίσκοπον

7 'Οτι, the proof that God knows all things and that no one can escape Him.   Prov. xv 3 ; Ps vii. 9

Πνεῦμα Κ. without the article, as vers. 5, 6 , Judg iii 10.

Πεπλήρωκε, 'hath filled and doth fill,'= completam tenet rerum universitatem. Otto in Act. Mart. Just. 3. The reading of A, ἐπλήρωσεν, is not supported by the Fathers who quote the passage See below Comp Jer xxiii 24   Grimm compares Philo, Leg. Alleg iii 2 · 'God has filled (πεπλήρωκεν) everything and has penetrated everything, and has left no one of all His works empty or deserted.' So De Conf. Ling. 27. S. Cyr. Al De Recta Fide ad Pulcher · αὐτὸς ὁ Σωτὴρ πέμπειν ἔφασκε πρὸς ἡμᾶς τὸν Παράκλητον, καίτοι πληροῦντος τὰ πάντα τοῦ ἁγίου Πνεύματος· Πνεῦμα γὰρ κυρίου, φησὶ, πεπλήρωκε τὴν οἰκουμένην, p. 137 Aub.

Τὸ συνέχον, Vulg 'Hoc quod continet,' not referring the words grammatically to ' Spiritus Domini,' just preceding, with which they are plainly connected 'That which containeth all things' (Eng), i.e. holds all together, keeps from falling asunder. So Xen Mem.

iv. 3 13: ὁ τὸν ὅλον κόσμον συντάττων τε καὶ συνέχων. Philo, Vit. Mos ii 31 'The Creator of the universe, the Father of the world, Who holds together (συνέχων) earth and heaven' There is nothing in the text about the 'anima mundi' of Plato. The writer speaks merely of the Omniscience and Omnipresence of God, even as the Psalmist, Ps. cxxxix, and Zech iv 10 Comp Eph. i. 23. The use of συνέχω is parallel with S Paul's phrase, Col i 17· τὰ πάντα ἐν αὐτῷ συνέστηκε. S. Aug. says that there is no necessity to refer this passage to the spirit that is supposed by some to animate the world, 'invisibilem scilicet creaturam cuncta visibilia universali quadam conspiratione vegetantem atque continentem Sed,' he proceeds, 'neque hic video quid impediat intelligere Spiritum Sanctum, cum ipse Deus dicat apud Prophetam, "Caelum et terram ego impleo." Non enim sine Suo Spiritu Sancto implet Deus caelum et terram' De div. quaest ad Simpl ii 25, (vi. 108 Ben) Compare S. Bas Magn. Adv Eunom v. (p 321 Ben.)· καθάπερ γὰρ ἡλίου βολαὶ φωτίσασθαι νέφος καὶ λάμπειν ποιοῦσι, χρυσοειδῆ ὄψιν ποιοῦσαι οὕτω καὶ Πνεῦμα ἅγιον, ἐπελθὸν εἰς ἀνθρώπου σῶμα, ἔδωκε μὲν ζωήν, ἔδωκε δὲ ἀθανασίαν, ἔδωκεν ἁγιασμόν, ἤγειρε δὲ κείμενον τὸ δὲ κινηθὲν κίνησιν ἀΐδιον ὑπὸ Πνεύματος ἁγίου ζῶον ἅγιον ἐγένετο Ἔσχε δὲ ἀξίαν ἄνθρωπος, Πνεύματος εἰσοικισθέντος, προφήτου, ἀποστόλου, ἀγγέλου Θεοῦ, ὢν πρὸ τούτου γῆ καὶ σποδός. Arn and others mention a reading ὁ συνέχων; but this is found in no uncial MS, nor in Holmes and Parsons' revision. Clem Al Strom i 5 (p. 332 Pott.) quotes the verse as given in the text On the Soul of the world S. Cyril Al. has the following passage: οἱ δὲ τῶν Ἑλλήνων λογάδες ἀντὶ τοῦ ἁγίου Πνεύματος τρίτον εἰσκομίζουσι ψυχήν, ὑφ' ἧς καὶ ἅπαν ψυχοῦται ζῶον, ἐνιείσης αὐτοῖς τὴν ζωήν, καὶ τὰς τοῦ ἁγίου Πνεύματος δυνάμεις τε καὶ ἐνεργείας προσνενεμήκασιν αὐτῇ... Ἄραρε δὲ ὅτι καὶ ἑτέρα φύσις, παρὰ πάντα ἐστὶ τὰ δι' αὐτοῦ κινούμενα, τὸ θεῖόν τε καὶ ζωοποιόν, καὶ ἅγιον Πνεῦμα. Καὶ γὰρ ἐστιν ἀγεννήτου Θεοῦ Πνεῦμα, ἴδιον αὐτοῦ καὶ ἐξ αὐτοῦ προϊόν, ἐνυπόστατόν τε καὶ ζῶν, καὶ ἀεὶ ὄν, ὅτι τοῦ Ὄντος ἐστί, καὶ αὐτὸ τὰ πάντα πληροῖ, καὶ τῶν ὅλων ἐστὶ περιεκτικόν, ἐπεί τοι καὶ ὁμοούσιον τῷ πληροῦντι τὰ πάντα, καὶ ἀμερίστως ὄντι πανταχοῦ. πάντα γὰρ αὐτοῦ μεστά Contr. Jul. viii p 275 (Aub) See note on xii 1

8 Οὐδεὶς μὴ is used on the analogy of οὐ μὴ with conjunctive.

Οὐδὲ μὴ παροδεύσῃ I have edited from S. A Ven The reading of V. οὐδὲ μὴν occasions a difficulty with the verb in the subj., no such use being found for certain elsewhere The MSS vary between μὴν and μὴ in other places, e g ch vi. 23 Job xxvii 6, xxviii 13

Παροδεύσῃ Vulg 'praeteriet,' a verb inflected on the analogy of ambire, as Ecclus. xi. 20; xxxix. 37, though we find 'praeteribo,' Wisd vi. 24 and 'transibit,' ii. 3 Comp Deut xxii 1; Jer v 22, and see on ch xvi. 27.

Ἐλέγχουσα, 'justice when it punisheth,' Heb xii 5, Rev iii 19 Comp Philo, In Flacc. 18 (II. p 538) τὴν ἔφορον τῶν ἀνθρωπείων δίκην.

Ἡ δίκη. Justice personified, as Acts xxviii. 4; 2 Macc viii. 11; 4 Macc iv 13, 21

9 Διαβουλίοις Διαβαύλιον, a late word, used by Polyb. iii 20 1, etc Comp. Ps. ix. 23 Sept, Hos. iv 9

Λόγων ἀκοή = λόγαι ἀκουσθέντες, as in Thuc i. 73, where see Poppo Ἀκοή is used objectively for 'the thing heard,' 1 Kings ii. 28, S. Matt iv 24, xiv. 1. So 'auditio,' as in Cic Pro Planc xxiii : 'fictae auditiones' S Aug reads 'sermonum autem illius auditio a Domino veniet,' instead of 'ad Deum veniet.' De Mendac I xvi 31

Εἰς ἔλεγχον, 'ad correptionem.' Vulg 'For the reproving of his wicked deeds' Eng Marg, as v. 8, ἐλέγχουσα, 'when it punisheth.' 'Correptio' in the sense of 'reproof' is late Latin. It occurs continually in the Vulg e g ch. iii 10; xvii 7, Ecclus viii 6, xvi. 13

10 Οὓς ζηλώσεως = the jealous ear Comp οἰκονόμος ἀδικίας, κριτὴς ἀδικίας, S Luke xvi 8, xviii 6. S. John xvii 12 S James i 25, v 15 There is a play of words in οὓς and θροῦς.

Οὐκ ἀποκρύπτεται. 'Non abscondetur.' Vulg Rather, 'absconditur'

11 Ἀνωφελῆ. The commentators consider this to be a litotes for 'very hurtful.' Comp. S. Jude 16.

Καταλαλιᾶς, 'detractione' Vulg 'Backbiting.' Eng. Rather, as the connection shows, calumny against God, blasphemy, is meant. The word καταλαλιά, not found in classical writers, is used in N. T., 2 Cor. xii 20, 1 Pet. ii 1. Clem. Rom Ep ad Cor 30· φεύγοντες καταλαλιάς. 'Detractio' in the sense of 'slander,' 'detraction' is also unclassical. Comp Ecclus xlii. 11.

Πορεύσεται, 'shall come from the lips;' it can scarcely mean 'pass away.'

Καταψευδόμενον, lying against God, speaking falsely of things pertaining to Him, His ways and attributes.

'Αναιρεῖ ψυχὴν, 'slayeth the soul' The writer evidently refers not to physical, but to eternal death The doctrine of future rewards and punishments, only darkly adumbrated in the O T, is greatly developed in the Book of Wisdom, and men's actions are always regarded as influencing the life beyond the grave Comp. iii. 1, 4, 5, 18, 19 S. Aug Serm. cvii. 10, Ben. ' Occides me? Melius tu occides carnem meam, quam ego per linguam falsam animam meam. Quid facturus es mihi? Occisurus es carnem exit anima libera, in fine saeculi et ipsam quam contempsit carnem receptura Quid ergo mihi facturus es? Si autem falsum testimonium dixero pro te, de lingua mea occido me et non in carne occido me: Os enim quod mentitur occidit animam' See also De Mendac. 31 ff (vi p 437 Ben)

12–16. *A third condition of the pursuit of Wisdom is holiness in action. Sin is the cause of death, which men, being possessed of free will, may choose or reject.*

12 Ζηλοῦτε with acc. 'strive after,' as 1 Cor xii 31, or 'court,' as Gal iv. 17 Vulg . 'Nolite zelare mortem.' Zelo is a verb formed from the Greek and common in the Latin Fathers, but unknown previously Thus S Aug Conf 1 7 'vidi ego et expertus sum zelantem parvum.' Tert. Carm. Adv. Marc iv. 36. Words of similar formation used in Vulg are these: thesaurizare, Matt vi. 19, 20, sabbatizare, Lev xxv 2, anathematizare, Mark xiv. 71, evangelizare, Luke ii 10, scandalizare, Matt xvii. 26; catechizare, Gal vi. 6, agonizare, Ecclus iv 33.

'Εν πλάνῃ, i e by leading a life that strays from the path of virtue. There is no allusion to suicide, as some have thought See Blunt *in loc.*

'Επισπᾶσθε ὄλεθρον, a stronger expression than ζηλοῦτε θάνατον, 'draw not upon yourselves destruction' Both expressions imply that men using their free will amiss constrain God to punish them Death spiritual as well as temporal is meant. This distinction is found in Philo, Leg. All. 1. 33 (I. p 65, M.). διττός ἐστι θάνατος, ὁ μὲν ἀνθρώπου, ὁ δὲ ψυχῆς ἴδιος. 'Ο μὲν οὖν ἀνθρώπου χωρισμός ἐστι ψυχῆς ἀπὸ σώματος, ὁ δὲ ψυχῆς θάνατος ἀρετῆς μὲν φθορά ἐστι, κακίας δὲ ἀνάληψις. Παρ' ὃ καί φησιν οὐκ ἀποθανεῖν αὐτὸ μόνον, ἀλλὰ θανάτῳ ἀποθανεῖν, δηλῶν οὐ τὸν κοινὸν, ἀλλὰ τὸν ἴδιον καὶ κατ' ἐξοχὴν θάνατον, ὅς ἐστι ψυχῆς ἐντυμβευομένης πάθεσι καὶ κακίαις ἁπάσαις. We may remark here Philo's method of explaining direct statements of Scripture in a moral or spiritual sense in such a way as to eliminate their historical character

13 It is men who bring death upon themselves, for God designed not that man should die physically or eternally. If Adam had not sinned, that separation of soul and body which we call death would not have taken place, and the second death was prepared not for man, but for 'the devil and his angels,' S Matt. xxv. 41 Comp Prov viii. 36; Ezek. xviii 32; Hos. xiii. 9, 2 Esdr viii 59 Thus Const. Apost vii 1 φυσικὴ μέν ἐστιν ἡ τῆς ζωῆς ὁδός, ἐπείσακτος δὲ ἡ τοῦ θανάτου, οὐ τοῦ κατὰ γνώμην Θεοῦ ὑπαρξάντος, ἀλλὰ τοῦ ἐξ ἐπιβουλῆς τοῦ ἀλλοτρίου.

Τέρπεται ἐπ' ἀπωλ ζώντων Comp Ezek l. c and xxxiii. 11; 2 Pet iii. 9. ζώντων is probably neuter. S. Aug explains the apparent anomaly between this statement and the fact that it is by God's judgment that the sinner dies. 'Convenit judicio ejus ut moriatur peccator; nec tamen operi ejus convenit mors. Ejus quippe justum est judicium ut peccato suo quisque pereat, cum peccatum Deus non faciat; sicut mortem non fecit, et tamen quem morte dignum censet, occidit.' Contr. Jul. Op. imperf. iv 32 (x 1150 B.). A good comment on the passage is found in the sermon of

Florus, prefixed to Hincmar's Dissert. ii de Praedest. (lxxv p. 58, Migne) 'Non ergo omnipotens Deus ulli hominum causa mortis vel perditionis existit, sed ipsam mortem et perditionem manibus et verbis ipsi impii accersunt, dum nequiter operando, et nequius aliis persuadendo, et sibi et illis damnationem adducunt; dum viam iniquitatis et perditionis amantes, a recto itinere deflectuntur, et ad perpetuam damnationem, tanquam datis inter se dextris, pari consensu nequitiae, quasi ex voto et sponsione festinant, foederati mortis, et vitae aeternae inimici, ipsi secundum duritiam suam et cor impenitens, thesaurizant sibi iram in die irae'

14. Εἰς τὸ εἶναι, 'that they might *be*,' carry out the laws of their proper existence This would include the growth and decay of plants and brutes, and the immortality of man. Comp. Gen. i. 28, 31; Rom viii 20, 21; Rev iv. 11. Cp. S Cyr. Al De rect. Fid. ad Pulch p 152

Σωτήριοι, sc εἰσί, 'saving, not hurtful' but tending to preserve life, 'salutares'

Γενέσεις τ κόσμ. 'the creatures,' created things of the world (xvi 26, xix. 11), as commonly in Philo, e g. De Leg. Alleg. ii. 21, (I p 81). The Vulg. gives 'nationes' in the sense of 'races' or 'species,' which the word sometimes bears in classical Latin. Plin. xxii. 24 50 · 'Nationesque et indicationem in apium ac deinde florum natura diximus.'

Φάρμακον ὀλέθρου, 'medicamentum exterminii.' Vulg. Ὀλέθρου is added because φάρμακον is used in a bad or good sense. Comp. Ecclus. vi. 16 φίλος πιστὸς φάρμακον ζωῆς A Lap. thinks that the author means to assert that though noxious animals and plants were created at first, yet that they had no power to injure man before he fell. But the wording, 'there is in them no poison of destruction,' points rather to the nature of things generally, and implies that there is no destructive agency in nature, this clause being parallel to the one immediately preceding The Vulg. word 'exterminium' occurs iii 3; xviii. 13, 15, and in ecclesiastical Latin. So Tertull. Adv Jud. viii · 'exterminii civitatis Jerusalem.' S. Aug. Conf. ii. 4.

Ἅιδου βασίλειον. 'Nor is the kingdom of death upon the earth.' Βασίλειον and plur. βασίλεια mean in classical Greek 'a royal palace.' So S Luke vii. 25. But it seems here to be = βασιλεία, and in ch v 16, and 1 Kings xiv 8 (Cod. Alex). Calmet however and some others retain the usual meaning of 'court' or 'palace' 'Le roi des enfers n'avoit pas son palais sur la terre' Hades is personified as king of death, Hos. xiii 14; Isai. v. 14, Rom. v. 14, Rev. vi. 8; xx 14. Some commentators (see Burton, Bampt. Lect note 30) find Platonism in vers. 13–15, but the author says no more than is warranted by Old Testament Scriptures, and he explains how death was introduced, ii. 24.

15 This verse is placed in a parenthesis in the English Version, but this is unnecessary. 'Righteousness' (as in ver 1 = Wisdom) leads to immortality. The Vulg has 'justitia enim perpetua est et immortalis,' where the Greek has nothing to represent 'perpetua.' The Sixt. ed. adds: 'injustitia autem mortis acquisitio est,' which is received by Fritzsche and Grimm This is probably a gloss added by one who wished to complete the parallelism and to give αὐτὸν in ver. 16 something to refer to It has no authority from any Greek MS, and is found in very few Latin MSS of weight. For the sentiment comp Prov. iii 18 : ξύλον ζωῆς ἐστι (ἡ σοφία) πᾶσι τοῖς ἀντεχομένοις αὐτῆς

16. This verse repeats the thought of ver 12 with an emphatic irony. There is a fine climax here; men's frantic love for their own destruction is exhibited in a terrible picture. First, they call death to them like an honoured guest with inviting gestures (χερσὶν) and words, they are, as it were, love-sick and faint (ἐτάκησαν) with desire of death, and then to keep it always with them they make with it a covenant of truth and love. Gutb. See quotation from Hincmar in note on ver 12

'Called *it* to them.' Eng. 'It' is wrongly italicised as it represents αὐτὸν, i. e θάνατον, which is understood from ἀθάνατος, ver. 15 Vulg : 'accersierunt,' from accersio = arcesso, with the change of one s into r, both verbs being causatives from accedo. Comp Acts x 5, 32, Vulg So we find linio for lino, Ezek. xiii 15

'Ετάκησαν, 'they were consumed, they pined away for love' Vulg 'defluxerunt' Eng : 'They consumed to nought.' But if they perished, how could they be said to make a covenant with death? Arnald, seeing this difficulty, wishes to transpose the clauses; but this is unnecessary if we take ἐτάκ. as above. The 'making a covenant with death' is from Isai xxviii 15, 18, (comp Ecclus. xiv. 12.) There is a close connection between this book and the Greek version of Isaiah

'Εκείνου μερίδος, as in ii 25, where see note If ἐκείνου refers to a different object from αὐτὸν, it is best to refer it to ᾅδου, v 14 Cp. 2 Macc i. 26

Additional note on v. 13. Our author's teaching on the subject of death and judgment has been thus epitomised by Grimm and others. (i) God is not the author of death, but gave their being to all things, and willed man to be immortal, ii. 23 (ii) The envy of Satan brought death into the world, ii. 24. (iii.) But through virtue and wisdom men obtain immortality, i 15, ii 22; vi. 18, viii. 17, xv. 3, and a blessed life with God in heaven, iii 1 ff, iv 2, 7, 16 ff ; v 2 15; vi. 19 Only the ungodly meet with the punishment of θάνατος, i 12, 16; ii 24; they have no hope, iii. 11, 18, v. 14; xv 6, 10, darkness will cover them, xvii. 21; their souls shall perish, in that they will be in torment, and deprived of the comfort of God's presence, i 11, iv 19, but they will have knowledge of the blessedness of the righteous and be conscious of what they have lost when it is too late, v 1 ff The author assumes that judgment follows immediately upon death, and that sinners are not annihilated, but suffer the second death (Rev. ii. 11 ; xxi 8), i e positively, pain and consciousness of guilt, negatively, the loss of blessedness There is no trace in the Book of the doctrine of the resurrection of the body. The souls of the righteous are in heaven, the souls of the evil in hell, the body perishes like all other material substances, and there is no return for it.

CHAPTER II

II. 1-20 *The reasoning of the materialist or sensualist.* 1-5 *His view of life*

This is one of the finest passages in the Book, full of a kind of evil grandeur rhythmically expressed.' Comp. 1 Cor xv. 32 'Let us eat and drink, for tomorrow we die.' Isai xxii 13; lvi 12. Hor Sat. II. vi 93 ff

1. Εἶπον γὰρ, sc. οἱ ἀσεβεῖς, i 16. This is the reason why 'they are worthy to take part with death:' their own thoughts and words prove it.

'Εν ἑαυτοῖς (for which reading there is most authority: thus Vulg.: 'cogitantes apud se,') must be taken with λογισάμ. 'reasoning one with another' = ἀλλήλοις, as v. 3 1 Macc x 71.

Λυπηρός, Vulg . 'cum taedio.' Eng. 'tedious,' used in the sense of 'painful,' like Jacob's words · 'Few and evil have the days of the years of my life been.' Gen. xlvii. 9 Comp. Job xiv. 1 ; Eccles. ii. 23.

'Εν τελ. ἀνθρ, 'in the death of man,' when death comes, 'there is no remedy,' ἴασις, Vulg. · 'refrigerium,' MS Corb 2 'sanatio' Schleusner conjectures that the Vulg translator read ἴανσις from ἰαίνομαι, but the word is unknown. 'Refrigerium' is found iv 7; Isai xxviii. 12, Acts iii. 20, and in the Latin Fathers, e g Tertull. Apol 39 med.; Fug 12 p. 194 Idol 13: 'Lazarus apud inferos in sinu Abrahae refrigerium consecutus' Pseudo-Ambr. Serm. 19 (p 515 B).

'Αναλύσας, 'reversus,' Vulg. : 'having returned,' as 1 Esdr. iii 3. Tob. ii. 9 ἀνέλυσα θάψας, 'I returned home after burying.' So S. Luke xii. 36. Comp. the

Latin solvo, to loose from moorings, hence, to depart. Ὁ ἀναλύσας may also be taken as = a redeemer, saviour, liberator. But comp. ch. xvi. 14; Eccles. viii. 8.

2 Αὐτοσχεδίως, usually αὐτοσχεδόν, off-hand, at haphazard. Vulg.: 'ex nihilo,' which misrepresents the meaning. Eng.: 'at all adventure.' Comp. Lev. xxvi. 21, marg. Thus Shakspeare, Com. of Errors, ii 2.

'I'll say as they say, and persèver so,
And in this wish at all adventures go'

Grimm quotes Lactant Instt II i 2 · 'Homines .. ne se, ut quidam philosophi faciunt, tantopere despiciant, neve se infirmos et supervacuos et frustra omnino natos putent, quae opinio plerosque ad vitia compellit.' Comp Cicero, Tusc i. 49. 'Non temere nec fortuito sati et creati sumus,' et caet

Μετὰ τοῦτο, 'afterwards,' when this life is over

Οὐχ is closely joined with ὑπάρξ, so the correction μή is unnecessary. Obad 16 · καὶ ἔσονται καθὼς οὐχ ὑπάρχοντες.

Ὁ λόγος. Eng.. 'a little spark.' The Eng version here, as usually, follows the Compl which reads ὀλίγος σπινθήρ. Vulg. 'sermo scintilla ad commovendum cor nostrum.' Guth understands by 'sermo' λόγος ἐνδιάθετος = thought. The meaning is, our thought is a spark which arises at the beating of the heart. This is like the notion of our modern materialists, who see in the movements of the mind only certain molecular, chemical, or electrical, changes and nothing beyond. Ancient philosophers have similar speculations. Thus Heraclitus deemed that Fire was the ἀρχή, the principle, the moving power of all things; and if we may believe Cicero (Tusc Disp i. 9), Zeno considered that the 'animus' itself was fire. (See Wolf's note, l. c. § 19.) 'Aliis,' says Cicero, 'cor ipsum animus videtur, ex quo excordes, vecordes, concordesque vocantur.' See Prolegom § I 2. Isidor Pelus. Ep iv. 146, refers to this passage · οἱ γὰρ ἀσεβεῖς σπινθῆρα νομίσαντες εἶναι τὴν ψυχὴν, οὗ ἀποσβεσθέντος, ὡς ἔφασαν, τέφρα ἀποβήσεται τὸ σῶμα, μόνον τεθνάναι νομίζοντες, μὴ κρίνεσθαι δέ.

3 Τέφρα ἀποβ. as if the life were a spark of fire which gradually consumed the body and left only ashes.

The notion in Eccles iii. 20 and Ecclus. xvii. 1 is different.

Χαῦνος ἀήρ. Vulg · 'mollis,' whence Eng 'soft' Rather, 'empty, unsubstantial' With the general sentiment contained in vers. 1–3 we may compare Lucret De Rer. Nat iii. 233 ff and 456, 457.

4. The Vulg. transfers the first clause of this verse to the end. Similar transpositions occur iv. 19; xii. 12 Reusch

'Our name shall be forgotten' Comp. Eccles. ii 16 and ix 5. Ἐπιλησθήσεται, passive, as Ecclus. iii. 14. xxxii 9 · τὸ μνημόσυνον αὐτῆς οὐκ ἐπιλησθήσεται. So S. Luke xii. 6.

Μνημονεύσει Found with acc S Matt. xvi 9, Rev. xviii 5. On the desire to live in the memory of posterity see Ecclus xxxvii. 26; xliv. 7 ff.

Βαρυνθεῖσα, 'aggravata,' Vulg., 'overcome,' Eng Arn conjectures μαρανθεῖσα, which indeed is found in one cursive MS. Retaining the word βαρυνθεῖσα, we must take Bauermeister's comment as satisfactory: 'nebula vi caloris pressa redit in aquam atque decidit,' the science of those days being rather phenomenal than accurate.

5 Σκιᾶς The comparison of man's life to a shadow is frequent in O T Comp. Job xiv 2, 1 Chr xxix. 15, Ps. cii 11; cix. 23, cxliv. 4, Eccl. vi. 12; viii 13.

Καιρός, 'tempus nostrum.' Vulg.. 'non est reversio finis nostri' 'There is no return of our end,' i e 'no death a second time.' 'It is appointed unto men once to die,' Heb ix 27. The Eng version makes tautology · 'after our end is no returning .. no man cometh again'

Κατεσφραγίσθη, sc. ἀναποδισμός, 'Return is sealed up, closed,' as if in a sealed tomb. The ancients sealed what we shut or lock up. Job xiv 17; Dan. vi. 17; S Matt xxvii 66; Rev xx 3

'No man cometh again.' Comp Job vii. 9; 2 Sam xii 23, Ecclus. xxxviii 21. The doctrine of the resurrection of the body is not found in this Book. The prevalent idea is that, though the soul lived for ever, it would never return to earth.

6–9 *First result of the materialist's view of life: sensual gratifications are to be pursued with eagerness.*

With this paragraph comp. 1 Cor xv. 32; Isai. xxii. 13; Horat. Sat. II. vi. 93 ff.

6. Τῶν ὄντων ἀγαθῶν, 'present, actual good things,' in opposition to imaginary blessings, as virtue, wisdom, or future, as happiness in another state. The author seems to have in mind Isai xxii 13. Cp. S Luke xii. 19.

Ὡς νεότητι. The MSS. vary between νεότητι and νεότητος Vulg · 'tanquam in juventute' Syr · 'in juventute nostra.' Arab. 'quamdiu durat tempus juventutis.' Νεότητι may be dat. of time, or as κτίσει, dependent on χρησώμεθα. Perhaps the clause is best translated · 'Let us use the creature eagerly as in youth,' with the energy which youth is wont to exert.

Τῇ κτίσει, 'the creature,' i e. created things, as often in N. T. Rom. viii 19, 20; Heb iv 13. Some cursive MSS. read κτήσει, the two words being often confounded

7. Πλησθῶμεν is applied by *zeugma* to μύρων as well as οἴνου to which it properly belongs. Amos, vi. 6, speaks of the luxury of those οἱ πίνοντες τὸν διυλισμένον οἶνον, καὶ τὰ πρῶτα μύρα χριόμενοι. Comp. Ps xxiii. 5, S Luke vii 46.

Ἄνθος ἔαρος 'Flower of spring' 'Non praetereat nos flos temporis,' Vulg probably reading ἔαρος, as it translates 'the early rain,' S James v 7, by 'temporaneum,' and the 'early fig,' Isai xxviii 4, by the same word. Gutb. The reading ἀέρος probably was originally a mere oversight in copying Arn suggests that the meaning may be, 'Let no fragrant breath of air arising from the wine or ointments pass by or escape us.' This is more ingenious than solid Mr Churton paraphrases 'the flower that scents the air.'

8. Στεψώμεθα The crowning with flowers is a notion derived from the Greeks See Judith xv. 13 for something similar.

'Nullum pratum sit quod non pertranseat luxuria nostra,' Vulg; this addition is possibly correct It is true that nothing to correspond with this clause is found in any existing Greek MS, but a clause parallel to the first half of the verse is required, if we regard the careful balancing of periods exhibited in the rest of the paragraph. There are too, it seems (see Prolegom p. 28), two more stiches in the Latin version than in the present Greek text, which ought to consist of 1100 verses, but contains only 1098, hence it is thought that some have fallen out of the Greek Further, in a glossary attached to the Codex Coislinianus 394 collated by Thilo, the word λειμὼν is mentioned as occurring in this Book Now it is found nowhere in the existing text, and the only natural conjecture is that the original of the Vulg. addition commenced with the words μηδεὶς λειμὼν, and that these were accidentally omitted owing to the *itacismus* in ver 9, μηδεὶς ἡμῶν. The Rheims version translates. 'Let no meadow escape our riot'

9 Ἀγερωχίας This word in classical Greek means insolence, haughtiness Here, 'unrestrained voluptuousness,' insolentia in luxurie vitaeque mollitie conspicua, Wahl Clav Comp 2 Macc ix 7, 3 Macc ii. 3. It is derived from ἀ intensive, γέρας, and ἔχω.

Ὅτι αὕτη To enjoy life while it lasts we have nothing else to do, nothing more to expect Grimm

10–20 *Second result of the materialist's view oppression of the weak and the righteous*

10 Καταδυναστ 'Let us tyrannize over, oppress,' Ezek xviii 12, Acts x 38, S James ii. 6 Comp. the advice of Κακία to Hercules in the story of Prodicus, Xenoph. Mem. II i. 25 οἷς ἂν οἱ ἄλλοι ἐργάζωνται, τούτοις σὺ χρήσῃ, οὐδενὸς ἀπεχόμενος ὅθεν ἂν δυνατὸν ᾖ τι κερδᾶναι παντοχόθεν γὰρ ὠφελεῖσθαι τοῖς ἐμοὶ ξυνοῦσιν ἐξουσίαν ἔγωγε παρέχω

Ἐντραπῶμεν, 'reverence,' as S Matt. xxi 37.

11. 'Let might be right.' Juven Sat vi. 223.

'Hoc volo, sic jubeo, sit pro ratione voluntas'

For 'lex justitiae,' Vulg, some MSS read 'lex injustitiae'

Ἐλέγχεται, 'proves itself'

12 Ἐνεδρεύσ. κ τ λ. This passage seems to be a citation from Isai iii 10 according to the Sept : δήσωμεν τὸν δίκαιον, ὅτι δύσχρηστος ἡμῖν ἐστι, where the Hebrew gives something quite different. 'Say ye to the righteous that it shall be well with him.' It is quoted by many of the Fathers as referring to Christ. Comp.

S. Barnab. Ep. vi. 7; Just. Dial. xvii; Euseb. Ecl. Proph. iv. 2 (Praep. Ev. xiii. 13)· ἄρωμεν ἀφ' ἡμῶν τὸν δίκαιον. And so Clem. Alex. Strom. v. 14 (p. 714 Pott.): ἄρωμεν ἀφ' ἡμῶν τὸν δίκαιον· ὅτι δύσχρηστος ἡμῖν ἐστιν. He then partly quotes Plato, De Rep. ii. 5 (p. 361 Steph.). ὅσῳ διακείμενος ὁ δίκαιος μαστιγώσεται, στρεβλώσεται, δεδήσεται, ἐκκαυθήσεται τὼ ὀφθαλμὼ, τελευτῶν πάντα κακὰ παθὼν ἀνασχινδυλευθήσεται· καὶ γνώσεται, ὅτι οὐκ εἶναι δίκαιον, ἀλλὰ δοκεῖν δεῖ ἐθέλειν. Hippol. Rom. Demonstr. Adv. Jud. pp. 66, 67, (ed. Lagarde). φέρω δὴ ἐς μέσον καὶ τὴν προφητείαν Σολομὼν, τὴν λέγουσαν περὶ Χριστοῦ, τὰ πρὸς Ἰουδαίους σαφῶς καὶ ἀριδήλως διαγγέλλουσαν, οὐ μόνον τὰ κατὰ τὸν παρόντα καιρὸν, ἀλλὰ τὰ κατὰ τὸν μέλλοντα αἰῶνα αὐτοῖς συμβαίνειν διὰ τὴν αὐθάδειαν καὶ τόλμαν, ἢν ἐποίησαν ἀρχηγῷ τῆς ζωῆς. λέγει· γὰρ ὁ προφήτης, αὐ διελογίσαντο οἱ ἀσεβεῖς, περὶ Χριστοῦ εἰπόντες, ἀρθῶς ἐνεδρεύσωμεν . ἔσχατα δικαίων καὶ πάλιν ἄκουσον, ὦ Ἰουδαῖε. οὐδεὶς ἐκ τῶν δικαίων ἢ προφητῶν ἐκάλεσεν ἑαυτὸν υἱὸν Θεοῦ. λέγει οὖν αὖθις ὡς ἐκ προσώπου Ἰουδαίων ὁ Σολομὼν περὶ τούτου τοῦ δικαίου, ὅς ἐστιν ὁ Χριστὸς, ὅτι ἐγένετο ἡμῖν εἰς ἔλεγχον . ἐκ λόγων αὐτοῦ So S. Cypr. Testim. lib. ii. 14 These words are used in Hegesippus' account of the martyrdom of S. James the Just. Ap. Routh, Rel. Sacr. vol. i. p. 195, quoted from Euseb. Hist. ii. 23.

Δύσχρηστος, Vulg.: 'inutilis.' Eng.: 'not for our turn,' i.e. not for our convenience, not to our purpose. Thus Shakspeare: 'My daughter Catharine is not for your turn,' Taming of the Shrew, ii. 1. So Christ ἠτιμάσθη καὶ οὐκ ἐλογίσθη, Isai. liii. 3.

Ὀνειδίζει ἡ ἁμαρτ. νόμου 'Casts in our teeth offences against the law.' Νόμος without the article means 'The Mosaic law' (see Winer, Gr. § 19). Hence the sensualists in this chapter must be regarded as renegade Jews, who with Greek culture had adopted Greek vices. See Gutberl. Einleit §§ 3, 4; Neander, Hist. of Chr. Rel. i. p. 70 (Bohn). Thus Philo, Vit. Mos. i. 6 (II. p. 85) νόμους παραβαίνουσι καθ' οὓς ἐγεννήθησαν καὶ ἐτράφησαν, ἤδη δὲ πάτρια, οἷς μέμψις οὐδεμία πρόσεστι δικαία, κινοῦσιν ἐκδεδιῃτημένοι, καὶ διὰ τὴν τῶν παρόντων ἀποδοχὴν, οὐδενὸς ἔτι τῶν ἀρχαίων μνήμην λαμβάνουσιν. Comp. De Conf. Ling. 2 (I. p. 405). See note on iv. 15.

Vulg.: 'improperat nobis,' 'casts as a reproach.' So Rom. xv. 3· 'improperia improperantium.' This is a rare post-Aug. word formed from 'in,' 'probrum.' It is found in some MSS. of Plautus, Rud. III. iv. 28; but others read 'opprobas.' See on v. 3. Comp. Ecclus viii· 6, S. Matt. xxvii. 44, Vulg.

Ἐπιφημίζει ἡμῖν, Vulg · 'diffamat in nos.' Eng.: 'objecteth to our infamy.' Or simply, 'utters, asserts against us.'

Ἁμαρτ. παιδείας ἡμῶν 'Offences against our religious training.' There is continual confusion in MSS between παιδία and παιδεία.

13 Ἐπαγγέλ. 'professes.' 1 Tim. ii. 10; vi. 21. So Christ claimed 'to know' God. Matt. xi. 27, John vi. 46. In the text the knowledge of God means the knowledge of His will and requirements, what He rewards and what He punishes.

Παῖδα Κυρίου This expression seems here to mean 'child of the Lord,' as it is said ver. 16, 'he maketh his boast that God is his father,' and ver. 18, 'if the just man be the Son of God,' though in the latter passage the term is Θεοῦ υἱὸς not παῖς. But the two expressions are used interchangeably in this Book, comp. ix. 4, 7; xii. 19, 20. Our Saviour is called τὸν παῖδα αὐτοῦ (Θεοῦ) Ἰησοῦν, Acts iii. 13, where the word probably means 'servant,' παῖς not being used to express the eternal generation of the Son. It is applied in this sense to Christ, Is. xlii. 1, while, xlviii. 20, δοῦλος is used in the same connection. So xlix. 3: δοῦλός μου εἶ σύ, Ἰσραήλ, and ver. 6: μέγα σοί ἐστι τοῦ κληθῆναί σε παῖδά μου. Of Christ it is said, S. Matt. xxvii. 43 εἶπε γὰρ Ὅτι Θεοῦ εἰμι υἱός. S. John xix. 7. The Syriac of the text is translated 'He says, I am the Son of God.'

In all this passage the Fathers have generally seen a prophecy of the Passion of Christ, and there are some wonderful coincidences of thought and language between it and the Gospel. Comp. here S. Matt. xxvii. 43, S. John xix. 7. But the similarity may be owing partly to the O. T. quotations embodied in the text, partly to the recurrence of each typical form of reproach in the Passion of Christ. See Is. Williams,

The Passion, p. 226, (ed 1870) Comp the quotations in note on ver 12. S Aug. De Civit. xvii 20 'Quorum [librorum] in uno, qui appellatur Sapientia Salomonis, passio Christi apertissime prophetatur Impii quippe interfectores ejus commemorantur dicentes. "Circumveniamus justum,"' etc. Comp. also Cont Faust. xii. in Ps. xlviii. Enarr., Serm 1. 11 ; Ep. cxl. 20.

14. Ἐγένετο : he tended to expose our views to public reproach, by forcing comparisons with his own So Vulg : 'factus est nobis in traductionem cogitationum nostrarum.' Comp. S. John iii. 20; vii. 7. Mr. Churton paraphrases 'the effect of his words is to rebuke our inward thoughts and purposes.'

'Traductio,' blame, reproof. See on ch iv 20, and comp. xi. 7, xviii. 5, Vulg.

15. Καὶ βλεπόμενος, 'even when merely seen,' *i e.* the mere sight of him is annoying. Prov. xxi. 15 ὅσιος ἀκάθαρτος παρὰ κακούργοις. Comp. 1 Kings xxi. 20 ; Isai. liii. 3 , S. Matt. viii. 34 ; S. John xv. 19.

Τοῖς ἄλλοις = τῷ (βίῳ) τῶν ἄλλων, like Homer's κόμαι Χαρίτεσσιν ὁμοῖαι, Il. xvii. 51. So ch. vii. 3. φωνὴν ὁμοίαν πᾶσιν, where see note

Ἐξηλλαγμέναι, 'immutatae,' Vulg. 'strange, unusual;' Aristot. Poet. xxi. 20 : ἅπαν ὄνομά ἐστιν ἢ κύριον ... ἢ ἐξηλλαγμένον.

Τρίβοι, as ὁδὸς ver. 16 and in N. T., 'path of life,' religious views. Comp. Acts xix. 9; xxiv 14.

16. Εἰς κίβδηλον. 'We were reckoned by him as dross, impure.' The Eng translation 'counterfeits' (which indeed is the usual meaning of the word) conveys a wrong impression, as the persons mentioned would probably not take the trouble to assume the mask of religion. The parallel member ὡς ἀπὸ ἀκαθαρσιῶν supports this view. The Vulg. 'tanquam nugaces' seems weak, though Gloss. Philox. gives : 'nugas σαπρός.' The word 'nugax' does not occur again in the Vulg. It is found in S. Ambr. Ep. 58, when he is quoting 2 Sam. vi. 22 : 'ero nugax ante oculos tuos,' where Vulg gives 'humilis' (p 1099 Ben).

Μακαρίζει, 'praefert,' Vulg , rather, 'calls blessed the end of the just.' Ἔσχατα, 'the death,' as Ecclus. i. 13 ; vii. 36 ; li. 14. Comp Numb. xxiii. 10 (Heb); Rev. xiv. 13 In Job xlii. 12 τὰ ἔσχατα means the latter part of life.

Ἀλαζονεύεται, 'maketh his boast,' a fine expression Comp. ver. 13. This is the complaint made against Christ, John v. 18.

17. 'If his words be true,' viz. that he is a child of God. Comp. Ps. xxii. 7, 8, Matt. xxvii. 41 ff.

Τὰ ἐν ἐκβάσει αὐτοῦ, 'quae in exitu ejus eventura sunt,' Grimm; *i e* whether his end is blessed, ver 16. The sensualist himself thinks of no life beyond this 'end.' The Vulg. adds : 'et sciemus quae erunt novissima illius.' Gutberlet deems this to be merely an expansion of the idea contained in the Greek, but it is more probably another version of the same which has crept into the text. It is not found in S Cypr Test. Adv. Jud. ii. 14, where this passage is cited; but it occurs in S. Aug. De Civ. Dei, xvii. 20 Ἔκβασις in the sense of 'end' or 'issue' is of late Greek. Polybius has περὶ τὴν ἔκβασιν τὴν ἐκ τοῦ Φιλίππου πολέμου, Hist. iii. 7. 2. Comp. Wisd. viii. 8 ; xi. 14 ; Heb. xiii 7.

18. Some see in this verse an interpolation by a Christian hand, owing to its marvellous similarity to the taunts levelled at the Saviour, S Matt xxvii 43. But see on ver 13, and comp. Ps xxii. 8, 9. So Euseb Hist. Eccles v 1, tells of the treatment of martyrs by their persecutors who derided them in similar terms. ποῦ ὁ Θεὸς αὐτῶν, καὶ τί αὐτοὺς ὤνησεν ἡ θρησκεία, ἣν καὶ πρὸ τῆς ἑαυτῶν εἵλοντο ψυχῆς; ... νῦν ἴδωμεν εἰ ἀναστήσονται, καὶ εἰ δύναται βοηθῆσαι αὐταῖς ὁ Θεὸς αὐτῶν, καὶ ἐξελίσθαι ἐκ τῶν χειρῶν ἡμῶν.

Ὁ δίκαιος, Vulg. 'Si enim est verus filius Dei,' where 'verus' is the translation of ὁ δίκαιος.

19 Ἐτάσωμεν, 'let us test.' Acts xxii. 24. See on vi 7. Comp Jer. xi. 19.

Ἐπιείκειαν, 'meekness, goodness,' opp. to ὕβρει, as ἀνεξικακίαν is to βασάνῳ Acts xxiv. 4. Vulg.. 'reverentiam ejus,' as Heb v 7: 'exauditus pro sua reverentia' Gutb See on xii. 18.

Ἀνεξικακίαν, 'patience, forbearance.' 2 Tim. ii 24 : ἀνεξίκακον. Comp. Is liii. 7

20 Καταδικάσωμεν, as Jas. v. 6. κατεδικάσατε, ἐφονεύσατε τὸν δίκαιον. Grimm

Ἐπισκοπὴ is used in a good or bad sense Comp iii. 7, and xiv. 11. Here it means 'regard, respect,' (xix 14), with an ironical turn, 'God is sure to regard him.' Comp Gen xxxvii 20, Jer xi. 19, xviii. 18.

Ἐκ λόγων α. 'ex sermonibus illius.' Vulg. 'according to his words,' as he boasts, vers. 16, 18. The Greek will hardly bear Mr. Churton's paraphrase 'there shall be an inquiry into the truth of his words'

21-24 *Such views spring from wilful ignorance of the purpose of God who created man to be immortal, but death came into the world with sin by reason of the devil's envy*

21. Ἐλογίσ. καὶ ἐπὶ, like ver. 1: εἶπον ἑαυτοῖς λογισάμενοι οὐκ ὀρθῶς. This is one of the passages supposed (by Graetz and others) to have been introduced by a Christian copyist. The supposition is quite gratuitous, and unsupported by any evidence.

Ἀπετύφλωσε, Aristot. Eth Nic VI v 6 ἔστι γὰρ ἡ κακία φθαρτικὴ ἀρχῆς. S. Athan. Hist. Arian. 71 (i. p. 386 Ben)· ἐτύφλωσε γοῦν αὐτῶν ἐν τούτοις τὴν διάνοιαν ἡ κακία S Ephr.'s translator (de Humil '94) reads ἀπετύφλωσεν. Comp Eph. iv 18

22 Μυστήρια Θ 'Sacramenta Dei,' Vulg See on vi. 22 'The secret counsel of God' with regard to the trials of the just, and the reward that awaits them in the future life. Comp. iv. 17. For a similar use of the word in the N. T. see Rom. xvi. 25, Col. i. 26; Eph i 9.

Οὐδὲ ἔκρ. γέρας, sc εἶναι, 'nor judged that there is a reward.'

Ἀμώμων Rev. xiv. 5.

23. Ἐπ' ἀφθαρσίᾳ, 'with a view to incorruption,' 'to be immortal' (comp. vi. 18, 19, 4 Macc. ix 22, 23, 1 Cor. xv. 50, 53, 54), referring to the eternal life beyond the grave, as θάνατος in the next verse denotes rather the second death than physical death. Gutb

'Hominem inexterminabilem,' Vulg. This adjective is very uncommon. It is mentioned as occurring in Claud Mamert. De Stat. Anim. ii. 3 See note on x 4.

Ἰδιότητος, 'proprietatis.' 'His own peculiar nature, being;' 'q d Homo est imago Divinae naturae, quae Deo est propria, vel, Homo est imago divinarum proprietatum, attributorum et dotum, quae Deo sunt propria,' A. Lap. Comp Gen. i. 26, 27, ii 7, v. 1; Ecclus. xvii. 3, 1 Cor. xi. 7 Col iii 10 κατ' εἰκόνα τοῦ κτίσαντος αὐτόν See 2 Pet. i 4, which, however, refers to the Incarnation of Christ, and the Christian's sacramental incorporation with Him The reading ἰδιότητος has the greatest weight of authority The Eng translators read ἀϊδιότητος, which has some patristic, but little MS. authority. Thus S. Method. De Resur xi. (xviii p 280, Migne). ἔκτισε τὸν ἄνθρωπον ὁ Θεὸς ἐπ' ἀφθαρσίᾳ, καὶ εἰκόνα τῆς ἰδίας ἀϊδιότητος ἐποίησεν αὐτόν. οὐκ ἄρα ἀπόλλυται τὸ σῶμα· ὁ γὰρ ἄνθρωπος ἐκ ψυχῆς καὶ σώματος. And Athanas Cont. Apoll. 1 7 (i p 927, Ben): ὅτι ἔκτισεν ὁ Θεὸς τὸν ἄνθρωπον ἐπ' ἀφθαρσίᾳ, καὶ εἰκόνα τῆς ἰδίας ἀϊδιότητος ἐποίησεν αὐτόν ... κόσμον; and ib. (p. 934): ἐπ' ἀφθαρσίᾳ καὶ εἰκόνι τῆς ἰδίας ἀϊδιότητος, ἐποίησεν αὐτὸν φύσιν ἀναμάρτητον, καὶ θέλησιν αὐτεξούσιον φθόνῳ .. κόσμον, εὐραμένου τῆς παραβάσεως τὴν ἐπίνοιαν. The Vulg and Syr. read ὁμοιότητος, which seems to have reached the text from the gloss of some scribe who wished to make the wording conform to Gen i. 26. ποιήσωμεν ἄνθρωπον κατ' εἰκόνα ἡμετέραν καὶ καθ' ὁμοίωσιν. Clem. Alex. Strom. vi. 12, reads ἰδιότητος. Thus οὐκ ἔγνωσαν μυστήρια Θεοῦ· ὅτι ὁ Θεὸς ἔκτισε τὸν ἄνθρωπον ἐπ' ἀφθαρσίᾳ, καὶ εἰκόνα τῆς ἰδίας ἰδιότητος ἐποίησεν αὐτόν. P. 788, Pott Epiphan ap. Hieron i. 251. 'imaginem suae proprietatis dedit ei'

24. 'Through envy of the devil came death into the world' The serpent is here identified with the Devil and Satan, a very remarkable development of O T. teaching, anticipating the Christian revelation of the existence and personality of the great evil spirit. See Rev. xii. 9; xx. 2; S. John viii. 44. Philo allegorizes the whole story of the fall, making the serpent the symbol of pleasure, De Mund Opif. 56 (I. p. 38). Orig. in Joan. tom. xx. 22 (i. p. 343 Ben):

αὔτω φθόνῳ θάνατος εἰσῆλθεν εἰς τὸν κόσμον, ἀεὶ ἐν οἷς ἐὰν εὔρῃ ζῶσιν ἀνθρωποκτονοῦντος (Διαβόλου), ἕως ἂν πάντων τῶν ἐχθρῶν ὑποτεθέντων τοῖς ποσὶ τοῦ υἱοῦ τοῦ Θεοῦ, ἔσχατος ἐχθρὸς αὐτοῦ θάνατος καταργηθῇ So ib. t. xxii (p. 407). That the serpent who seduced our first parents is the same as Satan is stated in the Kabbalah and Talmud See Ginsburg, The Kabbalah, p 29

Διαβόλου, without the article, as 1 Chr xxi 1; Acts xiii 10; 1 Pet v 8 The word διάβολος means, 'one who sets at variance,' then 'a slanderer,' and it is used throughout the Sept. as the translation of the Hebrew Satan. For the O. T. idea of the Devil's envy, see Job i. 9–11, etc., and Isai. xiv. 13. Josephus, Ant. I. i. 4, speaks thus of the serpent's envy ὁ ὄφις συνδιαιτώμενος τῷ δὲ Ἀδάμῳ καὶ τῇ γυναικὶ φθονερῶς εἶχεν ἐφ᾽ οἷς αὐτοὺς εὐδαιμονήσειν ᾤετο πεπεισμένους τοῖς τοῦ Θεοῦ παραγγέλμασι S. Bernard makes the following suggestion as to the cause of this envy 'Potuit contingere (si tamen incredibile non putetur), plenum sapientia et perfectum decore, homines praescire potuisse futuros, etiam et profecturos in pari gloria. Sed si praescivit, in Dei verbo absque dubio vidit, et in livore suo invidit, et molitus est habere subjectos, socios dedignatus. Infirmiores sunt, inquit, inferioresque natura. non decet esse concives, nec aequales in gloria.' In Cant. Sermo xvii (p 2758 A)

Θάνατος εἰσῆλθεν εἰς τ κόσμον. Comp Rom v 12 θάνατος is the death of the soul See on ver 23 κόσμον is not the universe, but the world of men, as 2 John 7 The devil is called 'him that hath the power of death,' Hebr ii 14

Πειράζουσι δὲ αὐτόν. Vulg 'imitantur autem illum,' i. e diabolum Eng. 'do find it,' i e. death. Rather, 'they who are his (ἐκείνου, the devil's) portion, who have given themselves over unto him, tempt, court it,' (αὐτὸν, death) Comp. Rom. vi 23 · 'The wages of sin is death' See also the ending of chap i with which this is parallel

Τῆς ἐκείνου μερ. Comp. 1 John iii 12 Κάϊν ἐκ τοῦ πονηροῦ ἦν

CHAPTER III.

III.–V. *Contrast between the godly and the evil.*
III. 1–9. *How the godly are rewarded for their sufferings.*

1 Ἐν χειρὶ Θεοῦ 'Hoc est, habitant in adjutorio altissimi, et in protectione Dei caeli commorantur' S. Aug. Enarr in Ps lxxxvii. 5. The souls of departed saints are under God's special protection For χειρὶ Θ. comp. Deut. xxxiii 3, and Isai li. 16, and see 1 Pet. iv. 19. The words Δικαίων ... Θεοῦ are found in Const Apost l. vi cap 30. Pseudo-Clem. Rom. Ep. II ad Cor. xvii 7 οἱ δὲ δίκαιοι εὐπραγήσαντες καὶ ὑπομείναντες τὰς βασάνους καὶ μισήσαντες τὰς ἡδυπαθείας τῆς ψυχῆς, ὅταν θεάσωνται τοὺς ἀστοχήσαντας καὶ ἀρνησαμένους διὰ τῶν λόγων ἢ διὰ τῶν ἔργων τὸν Ἰησοῦν, ὅπως κολάζονται δειναῖς βασάνοις πυρὶ ἀσβέστῳ, ἔσονται δόξαν διδόντες τῷ Θεῷ αὐτῶν λέγοντες, ὅτι ἔσται ἐλπὶς τῷ δεδουλευκότι Θεῷ ἐξ ὅλης καρδίας. Clem Alex Strom iv 11 quotes δικαίων ... βάσανος. He then adduces, apparently from memory, Plat Apol. Socr 18 : ἐμὲ μὲν γὰρ Ἄνυτός τε καὶ Μέλιτος ἀποκτείνειεν μέντ᾽ ἂν, βλάψειε δ᾽ ἂν οὐδ᾽ ὁπωστιοῦν· οὐ γὰρ οἶμαι θεμιτὸν εἶναι τὸ ἄμεινον πρὸς τοῦ χείρονος βλάπτεσθαι. Comp. S. Luke xxiii. 46; Rev. xx. 4

Βάσανος Vulg.: 'tormentum mortis.' Some MSS. give 'tormentum malitiae,' and S Aug. Serm. cccvi. 1, notes that 'malitia' here means 'poena.' The meaning is 'torment after death,' as S. Luke xvi. 23, 28

2 Ἔδοξαν .. τεθνάναι. 'They seemed to be dead.' The author of the Ep. ad Diognet. x. 7 speaks of good men despising τοῦ δοκοῦντος ἐνθάδε θανάτου.

Ἐν ὀφθαλμοῖς = in the judgment, as ix. 9; Ecclus. viii 16; x 20

Ἔξοδος, 'departure' = death, as vii 6 Ecclus xxxviii 23; S. Luke ix 31; 2 Pet. i. 15.

3. Πορεία, as S Luke xxii. 22: ὁ υἱὸς τοῦ ἀνθρώπου πορεύεται. So to Abraham God said, Gen. xv. 15· σὺ δὲ ἀπελεύσῃ πρὸς τοὺς πατέρας σου ἐν εἰρήνῃ.

Σύντριμμα, 'breaking to pieces,' 'destruction.' Vulg. 'exterminium' Comp. Ps ii 9; Jer. xix 11, Isai. xxii. 4, lix 7; Ecclus. xl. 9; Rom. iii. 16 Like some modern philosophers who consider death equivalent to annihilation.

Ἐν εἰρήνῃ This is somewhat in advance of O. T. doctrine, which seems to have been content with the notion of rest in the grave, though there is an intimation of something more in Isai. lvii 2. Comp Job iii. 17, 18 Grimm appositely quotes Philo, Quod det. pot invid 15 (I p 200) ὁ μὲν δὴ σοφὸς τεθνηκέναι δοκῶν τὸν φθαρτὸν βίον ζῇ τὸν ἄφθαρτον.

4. Ἐὰν κολασθῶσιν, 'if they shall have been punished' as men think. The writer may refer to those who perished in the time of Antiochus Epiphanes, 1 Macc i 57 ff

'Yet is their hope full of immortality,' a beautiful expression, which has become, as has been said, a household word He here gives the reason why the righteous endure with patience all the ills of this life; they have full assurance of immortality. Heb. vi. 19; 1 Pet. i. 3. 2 Macc. vii. 9· Σὺ μέν, ἀλάστωρ, ἐκ τοῦ παρόντος ἡμᾶς ζῆν ἀπολύεις, ὁ δὲ τοῦ κόσμου βασιλεὺς ἀποθανόντας ἡμᾶς ὑπὲρ τῶν αὐτοῦ νόμων εἰς αἰώνιον ἀναβίωσιν ζωῆς ἡμᾶς ἀναστήσει See also ib. ver. 14. Comp. 2 Cor v. 1. Clem. Alex. Strom. iv. 15, quotes vers. 2–8

5-6. These verses give the reason why God lets the righteous suffer in this life Trouble educates, proves, purifies them, gives them opportunities of self-sacrifice. This is high teaching, to which the life and death of Christ put the crown. Gutb

5 Ὀλίγα παιδευθ. 'In paucis vexati,' Vulg. 'Having been lightly chastised.' ὀλίγα being opposed to μεγάλα cannot be = ὀλίγον, 'for a little time,' but must refer to the littleness of earthly afflictions compared with the greatness of future reward Comp Rom viii. 18; 2 Cor iv 17; 1 Pet 1 6, 7 The sufferings of the saints are termed παιδεία in Heb. xii 11; and 'whom the Lord loveth He chasteneth,' παιδεύει, Heb xii. 6, Rev. iii. 19. To complain, as some do, of the author as confining God's merciful providence to the Jews, while representing Him as hostile to all others, is not warranted by the general tone of his utterances. God hateth nothing that He hath made (xi 24), and chastises even His elect to win them to what is good.

Μεγάλα εὐεργετηθήσονται, 'in multis bene disponentur,' Vulg., reading as Grimm. suggests, εὐθετηθήσονται, which, however is found in no MS

Ἐπείρασεν, 'put them to the proof.' Heb. xi 37 Gen. xxii. 1· ὁ θεὸς ἐπείρασε τὸν Ἀβραάμ. Ex xv 25

Ἀξίους ἑαυτοῦ, 'worthy of (communion with) Himself.' S. Matt. x. 37, 38. Clem. Alex. Strom. iv. 15: ἐπείρασεν αὐτούς· τουτέστιν, εἰς δοκίμιον καὶ δυσωπίαν τοῦ πειράζοντος εἴασεν αὐτοὺς πειρασθῆναι· καὶ εὗρεν αὐτοὺς ἀξίους ἑαυτοῦ, υἱοὺς κληθῆναι, δηλονότι Cf 1 Thess. ii. 12, Rev. iii 4; xvi 6.

6. Χωνευτήριον. 'Smelting furnace' The word is peculiar to Sept and ecclesiastical writers. 1 Kings viii 51; Zech xi 13.

Ἐδοκίμασεν. 'He tested them.' Prov. xvii. 3; Ecclus. ii 5, 1 Pet. i. 7 Comp. Isai xlviii 10.

Θυσίας, an epexegetical genitive, 'a perfect sacrificial offering' Comp. Ecclus xlv 14: θυσίαι αὐτοῦ ὁλοκαρπωθήσονται The word ὁλοκάρπωμα loses its sense of 'an offering of fruits,' and is used for any 'burnt-offering.' Lev. i. 14; xvi. 24. S. Paul speaks triumphantly of his own death as a drink-offering, 2 Tim. iv 6: ἐγὼ γὰρ ἤδη σπένδομαι. Comp Phil ii. 17 S. Basil the Great thus speaks about temptation, Hom de Divit. in Luc xii 18 (p. 43 Ben.): Διπλοῦν τὸ εἶδος τῶν πειρασμῶν· Ἤ γὰρ αἱ θλίψεις βασανίζουσι τὰς καρδίας, ὥσπερ χρυσὸν ἐν καμίνῳ, διὰ τῆς ὑπομονῆς τὸ δοκίμιον αὐτῶν ἀπελέγχουσαι· ἤ καὶ πολλάκις οὗταί αἱ εὐθηνίαι τοῦ βίου ἀντὶ πειρατηρίου γίνονται τοῖς πολλοῖς

7. Ἐπισκοπῆς 'The time of their visitation,' i.e. of their recompence in the other world, as ver. 13. Comp. Jer. vi. 15: ἐν καιρῷ ἐπισκοπῆς αὐτῶν ἀπολοῦνται. 1 Pet. ii. 12 As the whole passage evidently refers to the life beyond the grave, it is a mistake to understand 'the time of visitation' as alluding to this world. The Vulg. connects this with the former verse, making two distinct statements. 'Et in tempore erit respectus eorum. Fulgebunt justi et . . .' 'In time there shall be respect had to them,' Douai. Reusch thinks that the original Latin ran: 'Et in tempore respectus illorum fulgebunt;' and then, from mistaking 'respectus' for nom. instead of gen., 'erit' was added, and 'fulgebunt' joined to the next sentence. Gutberlet, on the other hand, who always defends the renderings of the Vulgate, asserts that the change was made intentionally in order to bring out distinctly the two thoughts contained in the original clause, viz. that the just should be recompensed, and that they should shine.

Ἀναλάμψουσιν, according to the idea in Dan. xii. 3: 'They shall shine (ἐκλάμψουσι) as the brightness of the firmament, and . . . as the stars for ever and ever;' and in S. Matt. xiii. 43. 4 Esdr. vii. 55: 'super stellas fulgebunt facies eorum.' In Eclog. ex Script. Proph. xli. appended to the works of Clem. Alex. (p. 1000, Pott) we have: ὁ δίκαιος ὡς σπινθὴρ διὰ καλάμης ἐκλάμπει καὶ κρινεῖ ἔθνη.

Διαδραμοῦνται. Explica καὶ ἔσονται ὡς σπινθῆρες ἐν καλάμῃ διαδραμοῦσαι Wahl The passage refers to the exceeding swiftness and brightness of the disembodied spirit. S. Thomas Aquinas refers to this passage to prove the agility of the glorified body, but there is no trace of the doctrine of the resurrection of the body in this book. In Symb. Apost Expos xxxviii. Blunt thinks the idea to be, that the martyrdom of the saints would raise a flame in the 'stubble' of heathendom, by which it would be consumed. But this thought is alien from the whole tenour of the passage. Churton, referring the scene to this life,

paraphrases: 'when the fire of God's wrath shall consume the ungodly as stubble, they shall be as the sparks which fly upward (Job v 7), or like the torch of fire in the sheaf of corn (Zech. xii 16), witnesses to the justice of God, and to the guilt of His enemies.' Cp Mal. iv. 1.

8 'They shall judge nations, and have dominion over peoples.' So in Dan. vii 22 it is said: 'Judgment was given to the saints of the Most High; and the time came that the saints possessed the kingdom.' And in the N T. the saints are to be assessors with Christ at the final judgment. Matt xix 28, 1 Cor. vi. 2, Rev. xx 4 Comp Ecclus iv 15.

Αὐτῶν. 'Regnabit Dominus illorum.' Vulg Αὐτῶν is best governed by βασιλεύσει, 'The Lord shall be their King,' He whose service is perfect freedom For 'Deo servire regnare est.' Gutb. In the Vulg version 'illorum' is probably governed by 'regnavit,' as 1 Macc. xii. 39. 'et cum cogitasset Tryphon regnare Asiae.' This construction is also found in classical authors, e.g Hor. Carm. III. xxx. 12. There is no trace in this passage of a personal Messiah.

Εἰς τοὺς αἰῶνας 'In perpetuum' Vulg See on iv 2.

9. Οἱ πεποιθότες, 'they who have trusted and still do trust in Him,' the same as οἱ πιστοί

Ἀλήθειαν, 'shall understand truth,' shall possess the knowledge of divine things. S John vii. 17.

Ἐν ἀγάπῃ is best taken, as Eng marg., with προσμενοῦσιν, 'His faithful shall abide with Him in love.' S. John xv 9, Acts xi 23

Χάρις καὶ ἔλεος, as 1 Tim. i. 2. The clause occurs again iv. 15, and there is much variety in MSS respecting the wording and arrangement. The Vulg and Vat. omit καὶ ἐπισκοπὴ ἐν τοῖς ὁσίοις αὐτοῦ· but the authority of the Sinaitic, Alexandrian, and Venetian MSS, and all the versions except the Latin, seems to be conclusive of its genuineness. See on iv. 15

Ἐπισκοπὴ, 'care, regard.'

Ἐκλεκτοῖς. Comp Esth. viii 40 (xvi. 21); Tob. viii 15; S Matt. xxiv 22

10–IV 6. *Contrast of the good and evil, specially in their families.*

10 Καθ' ἃ ἐλογίσ 'Secundum quae cogitaverunt.' Vulg. The allusion is to their language in chap. ii.

'Ἐπιτιμίαν,' 'correptionem,' 'punishment.' In classical Greek ἐπιτίμιον is used for 'penalty,' ἐπιτίμησις, (xii. 26) for 'punishment,' never ἐπιτιμία, which means 'citizenship.' It is used once for 'punishment' in the N. T., 2 Cor ii 6. For the punishment of 'fools' in the moral sense see Prov i 29–31.

Τοῦ δικαίου, probably neuter = 'justice.' 'Justitiam violarunt.' A Lap. So S Aug Spec, quoting this passage, 'Qui neglexerunt justitiam.' That this is right the parallelism with σοφίαν ἐξουθενῶν seems to show. We have τὸ δίκαιον used 2 Macc iv 34; x. 12.

11 Αὐτῶν, referring to the collective term ὁ ἐξουθενῶν.

12 According to the Hebrew notion barrenness was the greatest misfortune to a woman, and a numerous progeny the greatest blessing. See Gen. xxx. 23; Isai. iv. 1, S Luke i. 25. The author takes another view. Comp. Ecclus xvi. 1, 2.

"Ἄφρονες, 'insensatae' Vulg. 'Light, or unchaste.' Eng marg. Folly being = wickedness in the Sapiential Books (see on i. 3), ἄφρονες here means 'evil, godless.' The Vulg. word 'insensatus' is not classical. It is found often in the Vulg. Thus, Wisd v. 4, 21; xi. 16, xii. 24; xv. 5; Gal iii. 1. And it frequently occurs in ecclesiastical writers, e g S Iren Haer ii 30 8 (p. 163, Ben). 'Deus qui omnia fecit solus omnipotens . . . et sensibilia et insensata.' Hieron in Gal c iii. p. 416 · 'post peccatum comparatus est peccatoribus insensatis.' S. Aug De Gen ad lit. iii c. 12. 19. In Ps. xlviii. Enarr Serm. ii. fin. (iv. p. 443, Ben.) Tertull De praescr. Haer. 27 See note on xvii. 1.

'Their children wicked.' As Ezek. xvi. 44; Ecclus xvi 1, 2; xli 5; 2 Esdr ix. 17.

13 Ἐπικατάρατος, 'doubly accursed,' xiv. 8; Gal iii 10, 13. In Tobit xiii 12 it is opposed to εὐλογημένος.

Γένεσις, 'offspring,' as xviii 12. Vulg = 'creatura,' in the same sense.

Ὅτι, which Arn regards as pleonastical, gives a further illustration of the author's position, that the happiness of the ungodly is false and baseless. It was promised by the Mosaic law that the righteous should be blessed with children, and that the wicked should be childless (Comp Ps cxxvii. 3; Ex. xxiii 26; Deut. vii. 14; Lev xx 20, 21; Hos. ix. 14.) But the unfruitful wife, being chaste and pure, is happier now than the evil mother of children, and shall be highly blessed hereafter. The same is true of the eunuch to whom by the Law (Deut. xxiii 1) some imperfection attached. This passage is supposed by Graetz to be an interpolation by a Christian writer who desired to teach high ascetic doctrine. But it really teaches no special view of celibacy, but merely shows that to be childless is better than to have ungodly children, and that a blessing awaits the continent.

Στεῖρα 'A barren wife.' Some think the author is referring to mixed marriages, as in Ezra ix, x, others see a reference to the celibacy practised by the Therapeutae, and thus described by Philo, De Vita Contempl. § 8 (II. p 482). Συνεστιῶνται καὶ γυναῖκες, ὧν πλεῖσται γηραιαὶ παρθένοι τυγχάνουσι τὴν ἁγνείαν, οὐκ ἀνάγκῃ, καθάπερ ἔνιαι τῶν παρ' Ἕλλησιν ἱερειῶν, διαφυλάξασαι μᾶλλον ἢ καθ' ἑκούσιον γνώμην, διὰ δὲ ζῆλον καὶ πόθον σοφίας, ᾗ συμβιοῦν σπουδάζουσι, τῶν περὶ σῶμα ἡδονῶν ἠλόγησαν, οὐ θνητῶν ἐκγόνων, ἀλλ' ἀθανάτων ὀρεχθεῖσαι, ἃ μόνη τίκτειν ἀφ' ἑαυτῆς οἷά τε ἐστὶν ἡ θεοφιλὴς ψυχή, σπείραντος εἰς αὐτὴν ἀκτῖνας νοητὰς τοῦ πατρός, αἷς δυνήσεται θεωρεῖν τὰ σοφίας δόγματα. The passage in the text seems to be intended to console the childless.

Ἡ ἀμίαντος, 'incoinquinata,' Vulg. A late Latin word found four times in this Book (iv. 2; vii 22; viii. 20), and nowhere else in Vulg. Comp. Heb. vii 24, xiii 4.

Ἥτις, 'such an one as,' defining more exactly ἡ ἀμίαντος.

Κοίτην ἐν παραπτ. 'concubitum cum peccato conjunctum.' Wahl. Comp. ver. 16. παρανόμου κοίτης, and iv. 6. Num. xxxi. 18: ἥτις οὐκ ἔγνω κοίτην ἄρσενος. For παράπτωμα comp x 1.

Καρπὸν, recompence better than the fruit of the womb (Ps cxxvii 3)

'Επισκοπῇ ψυχ. See on ver. 7 Vulg · 'In respectione animarum sanctarum' MS. Egert. and others omit 'sanctarum' Possibly the translators read ἁγίων instead of αὐτῶν, which A gives. S. Jer in Isai 56, (col. 410 a,) has 'in visitatione animarum.' 'Respectio' is a late word, occurring nowhere else in Vulg See on vi 18. The 'visitation of souls' is the judgment, when all anomalies shall be righted.

14. Καὶ εὐνοῦχος, sc μακάριός ἐστι. Εὐνοῦχος doubtless in the first two senses mentioned by our Lord, Matt. xix. 12. See Is. lvi. 4, 5. Vulg. · 'spado'= σπάδων. So Ecclus xxx. 21.

'Εργασ... ἐνθυμ.=in deed or thought,—parall. with ἡ ἀμίαντος

Τῆς πίστ. χάρις ἐκλ. 'The special gift of faith' Eng But the words must refer to the future life, as 'the visitation of souls,' ver. 13, and the 'inheritance' (κλῆρος) below. So Arn translates, 'some special gift or reward shall be given him for his faithfulness;' and the Syr · 'Dabitur ei pro ipsius gratia et fidelitate haereditas desiderii' Holkot and Lorinus refer the words to the 'aureola virginum' Gutb. takes them as denoting the eternal reward in store for the continent. So we may best render, 'a choice reward of his faithfulness.' χάρις and μισθὸς are interchanged, Matt v 46, Luke vi 32

Κλῆρος. In Isai lvi. 4, 5: 'a place and a name,' which they may have lost upon earth by having no children Comp Numb xxvii 4.

'Εν ναῷ Κ, 'in heaven,' as Ps. x. 4, Bar. ii 16, Rev. vii. 15. 'He shall have a place in the eternal temple,' with special reference to his exclusion from the Jewish sanctuary. Deut. xxiii. 1 For 'in the temple,' the Eng marg gives 'among the people,' reading ἐν λαῷ, for which there is no authority. This clause shows that in the opinion of the writer heaven is to be the dwelling-place of righteous souls. Comp. Tob iii. 6.

Θυμηρέστερος, 'more acceptable than aught else.' Vulg. 'acceptissima.' This passage is quoted by Clem. Alex. Strom vi 14 (p. 797, Pott)

15. Γὰρ, proof of the blessedness of the two classes mentioned above. 'For the reward (as ver 13) of good works is glorious.'

Τῆς φρονήσεως, gen. epexeget. 'The root (from which such fruit springs) which is wisdom' Ecclus i 6 No dry tree is the childless righteous man, but a fruitful tree that falleth not away (ἀδιάπτωτος). See Ps cxii 6, 7

16 The writer carries on the thought in ver 13, 'their offspring is cursed,' taking adultery as a typical characteristic of the ungodly.

'Ατέλεστα ἔσται, 'shall not come to perfection.' 'Neque in hac vita ad gloriam, neque in altera ad felicitatem perveniunt' Bauerm ap. Wahl Comp. iv. 4, 5 S Method Conv dec. Virg iii. (xviii. p 52, Migne): τέκνα μοιχῶν ἀτελεσφόρητα The Vulg word 'inconsummatio' is found nowhere else in that version ('inconsummatus,' iv. 5), but occurs in Tertull Adv. Val. x. 'inconsummatio generationis' The marg. rendering of Eng., 'be partakers of holy things,' regards the other meaning of ἀτελ, 'uninitiated,' and the restriction in Deut xxiii 2 'a bastard shall not enter into the congregation of the Lord.' But this sense seems less suitable in the present connection.

'Εκ παραν. κοίτ. σπέρμα. See on ver. 13.

'Αφανισθήσεται, 'shall come to nothing.' So David's child by Bathsheba died 2 Sam. xii 14.

17. Μακρόβ γένωνται, sc. τὰ τέκνα Constructio ad sensum

'Επ' ἐσχάτων 'At last,' as Prov xxv 8 Vulg.: 'novissima senectus,' whence Eng, 'their last age' See iv 8

18. 'Οξέως, 'quickly,' i. e. early. Vulg: 'celerius.' Comp xvi 11, Ecclus xlii. 4

'Ελπίδα They shall have no hope of acceptance with God

Διαγνώσεως, 'trial,' Eng. or, 'decision,' when the

cause is decided, for which the regular law term is διαγιγνώσκω Comp Acts xxv 21. Vulg · 'agnitionis,' which seems to be a mistranslation, unless it be equivalent to the revelation of the secrets of all hearts.' Rom. ii 16. Comp. Mal iii. 18

Παραμύθιον. Phil. ii 1. Vulg.: 'allocutionem,' which is a late word for 'comfort,' found in this sense in Catull. Carm. xxxviii. 5: 'Qua solatus es allocutione.' Senec Cons ad Helv c. 1. 'Quid quod novis verbis, nec ex vulgari et quotidiana sumtis allocutione, opus erat homini ad consolandos suos, ex ipso rogo caput allevanti . ' See on viii. 9.

19. Γενεᾶς γάρ. S Matt xvi. 4. This sums up the preceding statements, which are enforced in the following chapter, iv 1–6. See Ps. lxxiii 17–20; Phil iii 19 Vulg: 'nationis,' = breed, stock The whole paragraph is an amplification of the truth that God visits the sins of parents upon children. Deut. v. 9; Ex. xxxiv. 7, 2 Kings xxiv. 3, 4. See a different view Ezek xviii 19, 20

CHAPTER IV

1. The Vulg here (as in xii. 1) introduces an exclamation not warranted by the original: 'O quam pulchra est casta generatio cum claritate.' 'Casta' seems to be the translation of μετ' ἀρετῆς, but it does not appear whence the words 'cum claritate' were derived, unless from a double translation of μετ' ἀρετῆς Brev Moz 208 has 'Melior enim est generatio cum claritate' Pseudo-Cypr p. 866, Migne: 'Melius est sine filiis cum claritate.'

Ἀτεκνία refers to the cases of στεῖρα and εὐνοῦχος mentioned in chap. iii Blunt thinks that the author is referring to mixed marriages But see on iii. 13

Ἀρετῆς, 'moral excellence.' Gutb. would confine the sense here to chastity, but it may well be taken generally. In ver. 2 the sense is more limited Comp. Ecclus xvi 3. On the view of marriage entertained by the Therapeutae (which sect some suppose our author to have favoured) see Philo, De Vit. Cont. 8. Comp. notes iii. 13 and x. 9

Ἐν μνήμῃ αὐτῆς, 'the remembrance of it,' i e. of ἀτεκνία μετ' ἀρετῆς Vulg : 'immortalis est memoria illius' See on viii 13.

Γινώσκεται, 'is known, marked, recognised.' Comp Nah. i 7, S. Matt. vii 23, 2 Tim ii 19 S Method. Conv dec Virg iii (xviii. p. 44, Migne). ἐν τῇ πανα- ρέτῳ Σοφίᾳ, γυμνῶς ἤδη τοὺς ἀκροατὰς εἰς ἐγκράτειαν ἐφελκόμενον καὶ σωφροσύνην τὸ Πνεῦμα τὸ ἅγιον, τοιαῦτα μελῳδεῖ· κρεῖσσον ἀτεκνία μετ' ἀρετῆς, κεκραγὸς ... παραινῶν τε τιμῶσιν αὐτήν . . νικήσασα.

2 The writer seems here to have in view the virtue of chastity A Lap. . 'Castitas adeo speciosa est, ut, cum se praesentem in castis exhibet, multos trahat ad sui amorem et imitationem, cum vero absens est sui acuat desiderium.' Horat. Carm. III. xxiv. 31 sqq.

Ἐν τῷ αἰῶνι. 'In perpetuum.' Vulg 'For ever.' Eng. Better, 'in the life to come, the eternal future.' The word αἰών is derived from the same root as ἀεί, aevum, aeternus, Sanskrit êvas, Goth. aivs, Germ. ewig, Eng. ever This same root ΑΙϜ is probably seen in εἶμι, ire; and the original idea expressed by it is 'going, motion onwards.' Hence αἰών denotes extended time, and takes its limitation or modification from the connection in which it appears. No one could apply αἰώνιος in the same sense to material things as mountains (Hab iii 6), and to Almighty God (Bar. iv. 8) The αἰών of God is everlasting, the αἰών of a mountain is limited Applied to man, αἰών is his age, his period, applied to the world it denotes one of the successive cycles in the onward march of the universe. As the duration of each αἰών is practically unknown, the word has come to be used of prolonged indefinite existence, and hence for that which is perpetual and endless 1 Tim. vi. 19. See notes on xiii. 9; xviii 4.

Στεφανηφοροῦσα Crowns of rejoicing (ch. ii. 8, Lam v 16; Ecclus. i 11) were used among the Jews at festivals, etc., but the idea of a crown of victory was imported later from Greece. Thus 4 Macc xvii 15 θεοσέβεια ἐνίκα, τοὺς ἑαυτῆς ἀθλητὰς στεφανοῦσα. Comp. 4 Esdr ii 43; 1 Cor ix 25; Rev ii 10

Τὸν τ ἀμιάντ 'Having conquered in the struggle of (consisting in) undefiled contests.' Ἀγῶνα νικᾶν, like Ὀλύμπια νικᾶν, 'to conquer in the games.' Comp 2 Tim. iv 7. Ἄθλων from ἆθλος Κληρονομία ἀμίαντος occurs 1 Pet i 4 The Vulgate renders: 'incoinquinatorum certaminum praemium vincens,' where Reusch thinks that 'proelium' ought to be read Philo, Congr. Erud. Grat. 29 (I p. 543) τὸν ἀγῶνα τοῦ βίου διήθλησαν ἀδιάφορον καὶ ἀήττητον φυλάξαντες

3–6. The idea started in iii. 16 ('children of adulterers shall not come to perfection') is here enforced

3. Χρησιμεύσει, 'shall be useful.' A late Greek word. Ecclus xiii 4, Diod Sic. i 81.

Ἐκ νόθων μοσχευμάτων, sc. γιγνόμενον πλῆθας, 'being from bastard slips, i e. whereas this brood springs from illegitimate sources' Vulg · 'spuria vitulamina,' a rendering censured by S. Aug. Doctr. Christ. ii. 12: 'Quoniam μόσχος Graece vitulus dicitur, μοσχεύματα quidam non intellexerunt esse *plantationes*, et *vitulamina* interpretati sunt' Gutb thinks it possible that the translator used 'vitulamina' in the sense of 'suckers,' on the analogy of μόσχος, which means primarily 'a young shoot,' or else that the word may be connected with 'vitis,' as Ducange gives: 'vitulamen, planta illa infructuosa, quae nascitur a radice vitis.' The word is used by S. Ambrose, Ep. xxvii: 'Quid Theclam, quid Agnen, quid Pelagiam loquar, quae tanquam nobilia vitulamina pullulantes ad mortem quasi ad immortalitatem festinaverunt?' (p. 1006, Ben.)

Οὐδὲ .. ἑδράσει, 'nor lay a secure foundation.' Cf. Col. ii. 7.

4. Πρὸς καιρὸν ἀναθάλῃ, sc. μοσχεύματα. We see from the word βεβηκότα that the subject can no longer be πλῆθος. 'For even if they flourish in branches for a time.' Πρὸς καιρὸν, as 1 Cor vii 5, in the sense of the adj πρόσκαιρος, lasting only a short time. Matt. xiii 21.

Ἐπισφαλῶς βεβηκότα, 'standing not fast,' Eng. 'Infirmiter posita,' Vulg, where we may note the late form of the adverb for 'infirme.' See on xiii. 5. Βεβηκὼς in the sense of 'standing' is found in the phrase ἀσφαλέως βεβηκὼς, 'standing steady' Archil 52. So εὖ βεβηκὼς, Soph El. 979; Herod vii. 164 Others translate the word here, 'ascendentia,' 'succrescentia,' 'as they have grown insecurely.' The meaning, however, is much the same whichever way it is taken. Comp. Ps. xcii 7; S. Matt. vii 27. The Sin. MS. reads βεβιωκότα, which is probably an alteration

Ὑπὸ βίας, 'a nimietate,' Vulg. 'Nimietas' is a post-classical word found in late authors, and does not occur again in Vulg. Thus. Colum. vi 24 · 'Naturalia congruunt desideria, quoniam nimietate verni pabuli pecudes exhilaratae lasciviunt.' Pallad vii 7: 'Sanguinis nimietatem prohibet' Comp. Hieron Ep lxii. 1 · Tert. Adv Hermog xlii; Eutrop Brev x 9 See note on vii. 5.

5. Κλῶνες, 'branches,'=children Comp Rom xi 17

Ἀτέλεστοι, 'immature.' Vulg. . 'inconsummati,' a very uncommon word, which occurs in Ammian. xxi. 10; xxxi. 14

Καρπὸς αὐτῶν, the works of the unrighteous. S. Matt vii. 16, 20.

Ἄχρηστος, sc. ἐστι Profitless for the master's service Comp Ps. xxxvii. 35, 36; S. Matt. iii. 10.

6. Γὰρ introduces an illustration of the temporal and eternal misery of the children of the ungodly who follow their parents' example. See Ecclus. xxiii. 25, 26; xli 6, 7

Ὕπνων, 'concubitus,' an euphemism, as vii. 2; Hom Od xi 245.

Ἐν ἐξετασμῷ αὐτῶν, 'in their trial,' i. e. the judgment of parents and children

Ἕξει = ἡμέρα διαγνώσεως, iii 18 S Method Conv. dec. Virg vi (xviii p 57, Migne) gives ἐν ἕξει πιθανῶν λόγων

7–20. *Contrast of the good and evil as regards length of life*

7–15. These verses occur in the Mozarab Missal, p 20, ed. Leslie (lxxxv p. 144, Migne).

7. Ἐὰν φθάσῃ τελευτῆσαι, 'Si morte praeoccupatus fuerit' Vulg 'If he die prematurely' Comp. Isa lvii. 1; Wisd xvi 28, S. Matt. xvii. 25. φθάνειν with inf. instead of part. as in Eurip Med. 1169. So in ch. vi. 13 · φθάνει προγνωσθῆναι

Ἀναπαύσει, 'rest, peace,' iii 3. Vulg. 'refrigerium,' which in the Ital is the translation of ἀνάψυξις, οἱ ἀνάψυχή; Ps. lxv. 12; Acts iii. 20. But no such reading is found here See on ii. 1. The Syr. adds 'Sive in longitudine dierum moriatur, in honore invenietur.' No extant Gr. MS authorizes this interpolation, which indeed is inconsistent with the following verse S. Ephr quotes from ver 7 to ver. 17, i. pp 241, 242.

8. Comp Philo. De Abr. § 46 (II. p 39) ὁ ἀληθείᾳ πρεσβύτερος, οὐκ ἐν μήκει χρόνου, ἀλλ' ἐν ἐπαινετῷ βίῳ θεωρεῖται. So, speaking of the Therapeutae, he says, De Vita Contempl § 8 (II p 481)· πρεσβυτέρους οὐ τοὺς πολυετεῖς καὶ παλαιοὺς νομίζουσιν, ἀλλ' ἔτι κομιδῇ νέους παῖδας, ἐὰν ὀψὲ τῆς προαιρέσεως ἐρασθῶσιν, ἀλλὰ τοὺς ἐκ πρώτης ἡλικίας ἐνηβήσαντας καὶ ἐνακμάσαντας τῷ θεωρητικῷ μέρει φιλοσοφίας, ὃ δὴ κάλλιστον καὶ θειότατόν ἐστι.

9. Φρόνησις and βίος ἀκηλ. are the subjects. 'Judgment, sound sense, is gray hair' 'Cani sunt sensus hominis' Vulg, q d 'Cani capilli, puta canities hominis aestimatur et censetur esse non coma cana, sed ipse sensus et prudentia' A Lap Comp Cic De Senect. xviii 62: 'Non cani, non rugae repente auctoritatem arripere possunt, sed honeste acta superior aetas fructus capit auctoritatis extremos.' Pseudo-Bas. in Isai. iii. (p. 451, Ben.)· πλεῖον γὰρ τῷ ὄντι εἰς πρεσβυτέρου σύστασιν τῆς ἐν θριξὶ λευκότητος, τὸ ἐν φρονήσει πρεσβυτικόν Thus S Ambrose, Ep. xvi: 'Ipsa est vere senectus illa venerabilis, quae non canis, sed meritis albescit; ea est enim reverenda canities, quae est canities animae, in canis cogitationibus et operibus effulgens' (P 865, Ben)

Ἡλικία γήρως, 'the age of greyness,' hoary age. 'Mature old age' Arn

Ἀκηλίδωτος. 'Immaculata' Vulg 'Immaculatus' is a post-classical word, found in Vulg Ps xvii. 24, 1 Pet. i 19, Lucan Phars ii 736.

10 The author cites Enoch as an example that the removal of the righteous is a mark of God's love. That Enoch is meant seems to be proved by the comparison with Gen v 24. εὐηρέστησεν Ἐνὼχ τῷ Θεῷ, καὶ οὐχ ηὑρίσκετο, διότι μετέθηκεν αὐτὸν ὁ Θεός. So Ecclus. xliv. 16 Ἐνὼχ εὐηρέστησε Κυρίῳ, καὶ μετετέθη. See also Ecclus xlix 14, Heb. xi 5 Clem. Rom 1 ad Cor ix. 3. λάβωμεν Ἐνὼχ, ὃς ἐν ὑπακοῇ δίκαιος εὑρεθεὶς μετετέθη, καὶ οὐχ εὑρέθη αὐτοῦ θάνατος Comp the promise to Josiah, 2 Kings xxii. 20.

Θεῷ The τῷ before Θεῷ has been expunged in V It is added by the translator of S. Ephr 1 p 241, ed. Assem

Γενόμενος, 'having become (proved himself by life and conduct) well pleasing to God' Prov xiv. 18

Μετετέθη, 'he was translated,' taken to the unseen world without dying, being thus rewarded as the first example of eminent piety. In Ecclus xliv. 16, Vulg. renders the word, 'translatus est in paradisum' Μετετέθη is applied to Enoch, Heb. xi 5, and he is said εὐηρεστηκέναι τῷ Θεῷ

11. Ἡρπάγη. The 1st aor. is usual in Attic. 'Raptus est.' Vulg. Ἁρπάζω is used of the miraculous disappearance of Philip, Acts viii. 39, and of the rapture of S Paul, 2 Cor. xii 2. Comp. 1 Th iv. 17. For the sentiment comp Isai. lvii. 1. Thus Hom. Od. xv. 250, of the early death of Cleitus·

ἀλλ' ἦ τοι Κλεῖτον χρυσόθρονος ἥρπασεν Ἠὼς
κάλλεος εἵνεκα οἷο, ἵν' ἀθανάτοισι μετείη.

Σύνεσιν, 'understanding' of divine things, 'insight' into truth.

Δόλος. 'Fictio.' Vulg See on xiv. 25. It means

the crafts and wiles which the wicked use to pervert the good. God knows not only the absolute future, but also the conditional future; and foreseeing that under certain circumstances a good man would fall away, He removes him before the occasion arises. S Augustine's view is different: 'Dictum est secundum pericula vitae hujus, non secundum praescientiam Dei, qui hoc praescivit quod futurum erat, non quod futurum non erat id est, quod ei mortem immaturam fuerat largiturus ut tentationum subtraheretur incerto, non quod peccaturus est, qui mansurus in tentatione non esset' De Praedest 26 (x p 807, Ben) In another place he argues from this passage that God does not punish men for sins foreseen, but not actually committed. 'Quod si qui baptizatus hinc raptus est apostata erat futurus, si viveret; nullumne illi beneficium putabimus esse collatum, quod "raptus est ne malitia mutaret intellectum ejus;" et propter Dei praescientiam, non sicut fidele membrum Christi, sed sicut apostatam judicandum esse censebimus?' De Anima, i. § 15 (x. 345, Ben.).

Ἀπατήσῃ, Gen. iii. 13 · ὁ ὄφις ἠπάτησέ με. James i. 26 : ἀπατῶν καρδίαν αὐτοῦ

12 Βασκανία φαυλότητος. 'The fascination, witchery, of wickedness' Gal iii. 1 : τίς ὑμᾶς ἐβάσκανεν, Βασκαίνω is the Latin 'fascino,' and is often applied in Sept. to the effect of the eye, e.g. Deut xxviii 54; Ecclus. xiv. 8. 'Fascinatio nugacitatis.' Vulg. 'For 'fascinatio' see note on vi. 18 'Nugacitas' is a late word, which A. Lap. explains as 'malitia nugax, h. e. nugis suis illiciens' It is found nowhere else in Vulg, but occurs S Aug. Ep 67 'Omnis ab eo deleta est nugacitas' And De Music 6 See note on vii 5.

Ῥεμβασμός, an uncommon word, formed from ῥεμβάζω = ῥέμβομαι, 'to reel, to be giddy or unsteady' 'Ῥεμβ. ἐπιθυμ, 'the giddiness, intoxication of (caused by) passion' The Eng. 'Wandering of concupiscence,' misses the point, as does the Vulg., 'inconstantia concupiscentiae.' Prov. vii 12 · χρόνον γάρ τινα ἔξω ῥέμβεται (ἡ πόρνη). See Prolegom. p 28. 'Ῥέμβομαι is used in the Sibylline verses of persons who stray away from the true God after other objects of worship. Thus

βροτοὶ παύσασθε μάταιοι
ῥεμβόμενοι σκοτίῃ, καὶ ἀφεγγεῖ νυκτὶ μελαίνῃ

Theoph ad Autol. ii 36 See Gfrorer, Philo, ii pp 122, 123 Jer Taylor 'Sensual pleasure is a great abuse in the spirit of a man, being a kind of fascination or witchcraft, blinding the understanding, and enslaving the will. . . A longing after sensual pleasures is a dissolution of the spirit of a man, and makes it loose, soft, and wandering; unapt for noble, wise, or spiritual employments, because the principles upon which pleasure is chosen and pursued are sottish, weak, and unlearned, such as prefer the body before the soul, the appetite before reason, sense before the spirit, the pleasures of a short abode before the pleasures of eternity.' Holy Living, chap ii § 1.

Μεταλλεύει. This verb in class Greek means 'to mine,' or 'to get by mining,' and later 'to explore' A Lap., trying to adhere to the usual signification, takes it to mean here, 'mines out, digs out, all prudence, innocence,' etc. But this will not suit xvi 25, where it recurs. The Vulg. renders, 'transvertit,' as if = μεταλλοιοῖ. Eng : 'doth undermine.' Grimm thinks that the author uses it here and l c.= μεταλλάσσειν, 'to change, transform,' deriving it by a false etymology from ἄλλος. And this seems most probable, especially as Suidas explains. μεταλλεύειν, μεταφέρειν It is not, however, found in this sense anywhere but in Wisdom. The Greek translator of S Ephr ad init. Prov. (i. p. 67, Assem.) gives · ὁ χαλιναγωγῶν ὀφθαλμοὺς ἑαυτοῦ κουφότερος ἔσται· ὁ δὲ ῥεμβαζόμενος ἐπιθήσει ἑαυτῷ βάρος ῥεμβασμὸς γάρ, φησίν, ἐπιθυμίας μεταλλεύει νοῦν ἄκακον. This last clause is rendered by the Lat. translator. 'Distractio concupiscentiae puram ac simplicem [mentem] immutat.' As an instance of an erroneous use of a Greek word by an Hellenistic writer, Grimm quotes κεφαλαιοῦν, used by S Mark xii. 4, to mean, 'to wound in the head,' a signification found nowhere else See Kuinoel, in loc See note ch. v. 14.

13 Τελειωθ ἐν ὀλίγῳ 'Having been perfected in a

short time,' not as τέκνον μοιχῶν ἀτέλεστον (iii. 16), nor as κλῶν ἀτέλεστος (iv 5), but after he had reached his term Gutb His education for eternal life was early completed For τελειωθείς (which is a word used in the Grecian mysteries) comp. Ecclus vii 32, xxxiv. 10, Phil iii 12; Heb. v 9, x. 14. The author here returns to the subject of Enoch, ver. 12 being parenthetical. For ἐν ὀλίγῳ, Orig., Enarr in Job xxii. 16, reads ἐπ' ὀλίγῳ, but in Prov iii. p. 10, Ben, ἐν ὀλίγῳ.

'Fulfilled a long time' Advanced in holiness as much as if he had lived a long life S Ambr. De Obit. Theodor. 'Perfecta est aetas ubi perfecta est virtus' Enoch's age of 365 years was short as compared with that of the other antediluvians. Hooker applies the passage to Edward VI: 'The son and successor of which famous king (Henry VIII.) as we know was Edward the saint; in whom (for so by the event we may gather) it pleased God righteous and just to let England see what a blessing sin and iniquity would not suffer it to enjoy. Howbeit that which the wise man hath said concerning Enoch (whose days were though many in respect of ours, yet scarce as three to nine in comparison of theirs with whom he lived) the same to that admirable child most worthily may be applied, "Though he departed this world soon, yet fulfilled he much time"' Eccl. Pol IV. xiv. 7.

14. Ἀρεστὴ γάρ... πονηρίας shows how God regarded him as τελειωθείς.

Ἔσπευσεν, sc. Κύριος, 'sped him, took him hastily away' Vulg · 'properavit educere illum,' whenceEng 'hasted He to take him away.' Thus S Cypr · 'Per Salomonem docet Spiritus Sanctus eos qui Deo placeant maturius istinc eximi et citius liberari, ne dum in isto mundo diutius immorantur, mundi contactibus polluantur.' De Mortal. p. 235 Ben Ἔσπευσεν may be taken intransitively here, making ψυχή the subject, 'it hasted'

15 Οἱ δὲ λαοί, not 'the people,' (Eng) but 'the peoples.' The plur. is used of heathen nations; here it includes the renegade Jews, who are chiefly intended by the term 'ungodly' in this Book. Comp ii 12 and note. The words οἱ δὲ λαοί have no verb in the sentence. Some commentators take the participles ἰδόντ. and νοήσ. as equivalent to finite verbs by an Hebraistic use; Gutb makes ὄψονται, ver 17, the principal verb, putting ver. 16 in a parenthesis. The truth is, there is an anacoluthon occasioned by the introduction of the paragraph ver. 16, the author resuming his sentence ver. 17, with a change of construction : 'Because the heathen perceived this (viz. the early death of the righteous), and did not understand nor lay to heart that grace and mercy, etc .. for they shall see ...' ὄψονται repeating ἰδόντες, and νοήσουσι, νοήσαντες The object of νοήσ. and θέντες is τὸ τοιοῦτο, explained by ὅτι χάρις κ.τ.λ.

Θέντες ἐπὶ διανοίᾳ. Comp S Luke ix 44 θέσθε εἰς τὰ ὦτα. Acts xix. 21. Hom Od. xviii. 158 τῇ δ' ἄρ' ἐπὶ φρεσὶ θῆκε With this verse and ver. 17 comp Isai. lvii. 1.

Χάρις κ ἔλεος, 'Grace (help and favour) and mercy,' sc ἐστί See on iii. 9, where this clause also occurs. The arrangement of the words varies here as there in MSS

Ἐκλεκτοῖς αὐτοῦ, 'God's chosen people.' Tob viii. 15; 1 Chr xvi. 13; 2 Macc. i 25; Rom. viii 33

Ἐπισκοπή See on ii. 20, and iii. 9 The idea is that the righteous are the object of God's favour and mercy on earth, and after death shall receive their full fruition.

16. Κατακρινεῖ, 'condemnat,' Vulg. in the present. The righteous man dying early virtually condemns the wicked, because that in his short life he became perfected in righteousness (νεότης τελεσθεῖσα), while they, though they lived long, were still ἀτέλεστοι. Comp. S Matt. xii. 41, 42.

Καμών = θανών, which, doubtless originally a gloss, has found its way into the text in some MSS. S. Ephraem has θανών, and omits ταχέως at the end of the verse, I p. 241 ed Assem. Καμών with the meaning of 'dead' is found frequently in classical Gieek (e. g. Hom. Il. iii 278, Aesch. Suppl 231), but in Sept. only here and, as some think, ch. xv. 9, where see note.

17. Ὄψονται γάρ. Γάρ is epexegetical, reintroducing and confirming the statement in ver. 15. This verse is cited by Clem Al Strom vi 14 (p 795, Pott.).

Σοφοῦ = the righteous, vers. 7, 16.

Ἐβουλεύσατο, 'decreed,' vers 8 ff.

Εἰς τί, as S. Matt. xiv. 31.

Ἠσφαλίσατο, 'set him in safety,' (Eng) by removing him from the wicked world S. Eph. has περὶ αὐτῶν, instead of αὐτοῦ, I. p. 241.

18. Ἐκγελάσεται, Ps ii. 4; lviii 9. This and the foll. verses (to ver 20) point out the fate of the ungodly in this world.

Μετὰ τοῦτο, 'hereafter,' after all this contempt of the righteous

Εἰς πτῶμα ἄτιμον, 'a vile carcase' (Eng.), without the rites of sepulture, as Isai xiv. 19, Grimm But it seems unnatural to speak of all the wicked as being 'a carcase,' and the connection with what follows is better observed by taking πτῶμα in the sense of 'a fall,' as Ecclus. xxxiv. 6. So Vulg. 'decidentes sine honore' A Lap. 'Erunt in ruinam, casum, lapsum inhonoratum.' Arn 'shall fall shamefully' To the same effect the Syr. and Arab. versions. The metaphor of a tall tree, that bears no fruit, being rooted up (comp ver 3 ff) is intended, but is not absolutely maintained Thus the expressions εἰς ὕβριν ἐν νεκροῖς, ἀφώνους πρηνεῖς, and ἐν ὀδύνῃ, can only be used of persons

Δι' αἰῶνος, 'for ever' Deut v 29

19. Ῥήξει, sc ὁ Κύριος This is the punishment of their pride Comp. Ps. xxxvii. 35, 36 'He shall rend them so that they fall headlong speechless.' Thus their great swelling words shall be requited. We may compare the account of the death of king Antiochus, 1 Macc vi. 8-16, and of Herod, Acts xii 20-23 Ῥήγνυμι sometimes is used = ῥάσσω, 'to knock down, to fell,' of combatants, as Artem. 1 60 Wahl The reference in Liddell and Scott to Demosth. 1259 10 is erroneous, as the reading there is ῥάξαντες. Schäfer's remark is pithy. 'Passovio, cum in Lex. Gr. eundem citaret s. v. ῥήγνυμι, humani quid accidit.'

Πρηνεῖς, 'disrumpet illos inflatos,' Vulg What was the reading of the Latin translator is hard to conjecture. Even Gutberlet can make nothing of it. Some suggest πρηθείς or πρηστούς from πρήθω; but no such words exist, or πρήσεις, 'inflationes,' which gives no sense 'Pronos' or 'in faciem lapsos' gives the correct meaning 'Disrumpet illos sine voce pronos,' Pagnin 'Speechless,' as the wedding guest in Matt. xxii 12.

Ἐκ θεμελίων. The metaphor here is of a building overthrown.

Ἕως ἐσχάτου χερσ., 'they shall be left utterly desolate.'

Ἔσονται ἐν ὀδύνῃ. This is appropriate to the ungodly personally, the metaphor of trees being dropped So in the foll words. There is intended a contrast to the condition of the righteous who are 'in rest,' iii 1; iv. 7.

20 This verse refers rather to the future state of the ungodly, which is further developed in the next chapter.

Ἐλεύσονται. 'They shall come fearing in the reckoning up of their sins;' i.e fear shall seize them as they count over their sins, whether at death or after death

Ἐλέγξει, 'traducent' Vulg: 'shall censure, put to shame.' So xii 17. 'audaciam traducis.' S. Matt. i 19, Col ii. 15 Hence we see the origin of the common meaning of the Eng. word 'traduce,' French 'traduire' Comp 'traductio,' ii 14.

Ἐξεναντίας, 'ex adverso,' Vulg. 'To their face.' Eng. rather, 'appearing against them' Comp Judg ix. 17; Mark xv. 39 Ps xlix. 21. ἐλέγξω σε καὶ παραστήσω κατὰ πρόσωπόν σου. Here is a very remarkable anticipation of the effect of conscience in the punishment of the judgment day. Jer. ii 19; Rom ii. 15. Thus S. Aug Serm. lx 10, Ben.. 'Considerando conscientias suas, considerando omnia vulnera animae suae, auderent dicere, Injuste damnamur? De quibus ante in Sapientia dictum est: Traducent eos ex adverso iniquitates eorum. Sine dubio videbunt se juste damnari pro sceleribus et criminibus suis.'

CHAPTER .

V. CONTRAST OF THE GODLY AND THE WICKED AFTER DEATH

1–14. *The wicked under remorse of conscience.*

1. Τότε, i e in the day of account alluded to in the last verse of ch iv S Augustine refers this to the Day of Judgment. Ep. clxxxv. 41, Contr. Gaudent. 1. 51; Serm lviii 7, Ben

Στήσεται, as S Luke xxi 36

Παρρησίᾳ πολλῇ, 'much confidence,' as 1 John ii. 28, iv. 17. Comp Prov. xiii 5, Sept. The ungodly 'come fearing' to the judgment (ch iv 20) and in στενοχωρίᾳ πνεύματος (ver. 3)

Κατὰ πρόσωπον, 'before the face, in the sight of' Part of the punishment of the ungodly shall be the sight of the happiness of the blessed, as in S. Luke xiii. 28. See on verse 2.

Θλιψάντων The aor., as Gutb observes, expresses the past acts of the ungodly, the pres ἀθετούντων their habitual principle. The Vulg translates θλιψάντ. by 'qui se angustiaverunt.' 'Angustio' is = post-Aug 'angusto,' and is found often in Vulg, e. g. Ecclus. iv. 3, 2 Cor iv 8; Heb. xi. 37. The pronoun 'se' is the translation of αὐτόν, pronouns being used very loosely in that version.

Ἀθετούντων τ. πόνους αὐτ., 'despise his labours,' viz for eternal life. See vers. 3, 4, and comp. ii 17; iii. 2, 3. The Vulg. gives a very different meaning to the words 'qui abstulerunt labores eorum,' understanding them of oppressors who robbed the righteous of the labours of their hands. So S Cypr p 309, Ben : 'diripuerunt labores eorum' But this seems to strain the received signification of ἀθετεῖν, which is common in both Testaments Πόνους might mean 'sufferings,' but taking into consideration the passages named above, I think 'labours' is the best rendering

2 Ἰδόντες, at the sight of the confidence of the righteous. The author represents the righteous and the wicked as standing together before the judgment seat and witnessing each others' destiny. Our Lord introduces the same idea in the parable of the rich man and Lazarus. S Luke xvi. 23. S Ephr (1 241) has ἰδόντες αὐτόν

Ἐκστήσονται ἐπὶ τῷ π, 'shall be astonished at' Ex xviii. 9, S. Luke ii. 47.

Τῷ παραδόξῳ τῆς σωτηρίας The S MS and one or two Cursives add αὐτοῦ. The weight of evidence is against it; and if it is omitted we must consider that the author makes the ungodly wonder not so much at the 'salvation' of the righteous, as at 'the unexpected allotment of happiness,' the strange interchange of fates between those who thought themselves alone happy, and him whom they deemed wretched and contemptible. Now he is comforted and they are tormented. Luke xvi 23, 25. The Eng gives a long paraphrase: 'the strangeness of his salvation, so far beyond all that they looked for' The Vulg has 'in subitatione insperatae salutis.' This word 'subitatio' occurs nowhere else in the Vulg., whence it found its way into the writings of some of the Latin Fathers It seems to have been derived from the vernacular use of Africa, where this ancient version was made S. Cypr uses the verb 'subitare' (Ep. 57), and the subst, ad Demetrian. c 21. An unusual word of similar formation is 'sibilatio,' xvii 9 So 'salvatio,' Is. xxxvii. 32.

3 Here begins the fine description of the vain remorse of the ungodly, the gnawing of the worm that never dies, vers. 3–13 Comp Pseudo-Clem Rom Ep. ii ad Cor xvii 5; S Barn. Ep vii. 9.

Ἐν ἑαυτοῖς, 'within themselves,' or better, as ii. 1 'one with another,' this passage being the counterpart to the former, ii. 1–20, Grimm.

Μετανοοῦντες. Vulg.: 'poenitentiam agentes,' and

Eng· 'repenting,' if taken in the usual theological sense, give an erroneous idea. The time of repentance is past 'Changing their opinion, learning the truth too late,' is rather the meaning. In Judas' case the word used is μεταμεληθείς, S. Matt. xxvii 3 S Athanasius applies the passage to the judgment of Christ, Serm. Mag de Fide, 28 (ii p 15, Montf): ὅνπερ ἐν τῇ κρίσει ὁρῶντες κρίνοντα ζῶντας καὶ νεκρούς . μεταμελόμενοι, φυλὴ κατὰ φυλῆς, ἐροῦσιν Οὗτος ἦν ὃν ἐσχομέν ποτε εἰς γέλωτα, λέγοντες αὐτῷ, Ἄλλους ἔσωσας, ἑαυτὸν οὐ δύνασαι σῶσαι.

Διὰ στενοχωρίαν πνεύματ 'Prae angustia spiritus,' Vulg So Ecclus. x. 26: ἐν καιρῷ στενοχωρίας Comp. 4 Macc. ix. 11, Rom. ii. 9, viii. 35, 2 Cor. vi. 4. See also Ps. lxv. 14

Καὶ ἐροῦσιν, 'yea, they shall say.' All the best MSS., except V., add these words here Clem. Alex Strom vi. 14 (p. 795, Pott) ἐπί τε τῆς δόξης ἐροῦσιν αὐτοῦ Οὗτος ἦν ὃν ἐσχομέν ποτε εἰς ... ὀνειδισμοῦ, οἱ ἄφρονες.

Παραβολὴν ὀνειδισμοῦ, 'in similitudinem improperii,' Vulg Rather, 'as a proverb of reproach,' as 2 Chr. vii 20; Tob. iii. 4 Comp Jer. xxiv. 9. Παραβολή in the sense of 'proverb' occurs S. Luke iv. 23; vi 39 'Improperium' occurs continually in the Vulg, e.g. Rom. xv. 3, Heb. xi. 26. The term 'improperia,' the reproaches, is applied to an anthem used in some Churches on Good Friday See on ii. 12

4. Μανίαν So our blessed Lord and S. Paul were taunted, John x 20, Acts xxvi 24. Compare 4 Macc x. 13 Merc. Tris ad Aesculap. xv 43 : οἱ ἐν γνώσει ὄντες οὔτε τοῖς πολλοῖς ἀρέσκουσι, οὔτε οἱ πολλοὶ αὐτοῖς· μεμηνέναι δὲ δοκοῦσι, καὶ γέλωτα ὀφλισκάνουσι, quoted by Hooker, Eccl. Pol Pref. iii. 14.

Ἐλογισάμεθα, with double acc. as xiv 20; Rom. vi 11; Grimm. There is a play of words with κατελογίσθη in the next verse, lost in the Vulg and Eng. versions

5. Ἐν υἱοῖς Θεοῦ some take 'among the angels,' comparing Job i. 6, ii. 1, etc, but it is probably equivalent to ἁγίοις (Hos. i 10) and refers to ch. ii 13, 18. Comp. xviii 13, 1 John iii 2 Arn. 'The very same scoffers, who rallied the just man upon his glorious title of "Son of God," at length confess the truth of what he said.'

Κλῆρος, alluding to iii. 14. Col. i 12 Comp Dan. xii. 13 'Thou shalt rest and stand in thy lot (ἀναστήσῃ εἰς τὸν κλῆρόν σου) at the end of the days.' Translate : 'and how is his lot among the saints !' the force of πῶς being carried on

6 Ἆρα as a particle of inference never stands first in Attic Greek, but is thus placed in Hellenistic, e g. S. Luke xi. 48; Gal. ii. 21, iii 29, v. 11; Heb iv. 9.

'The way of truth,' i.e the right path of life. Comp S James v 19, 2 Pet ii 2.

'The light of righteousness,' the manifestation of, that which shows, what is the only true object of life, viz virtue and godliness.

Ὁ ἥλιος. This belongs to τ. δικαιοσ. as much as φῶς does, and hence one MS. (Ven.) inserts τῆς δικαιοσύνης here again, and is followed by the Arm. version, Vulg, Compl, and Eng, but the words are evidently an interpolation. The phrase ἥλιος δικαιοσύνης occurs Mal. iv 2. Sin is that which blinds the light, S. John iii 19, 20; 2 Cor. iv. 4 S Aug.· 'Illis non est ortus Christus, a quibus non est agnitus Christus. Sol ille justitiae, sine nube, sine nocte, ipse non oritur malis, non oritur impiis, non oritur infidelibus.' Serm ccxcii. 4.

7. Ἐνεπλήσθημεν, 'lassati sumus,' Vulg So Eng: 'we wearied ourselves' Rather 'we were surfeited with the ways of sin.' Comp. xiii. 12, Ecclus xxxiv. 3. Arn suggests ἐνεπλάγχθημεν; others propose ἐνεπλέχθημεν or ἐνεπλανήθημεν, but there is no necessity for any change. The received text seems to be a mixture of two phrases, ἀνομίας ἐνεπλήσθημεν and ἐνεπορεύθημεν τρίβοις ἀπωλείας, 'improbitate oppleti et tramite ad perniciem ducente ingressi sumus' Wahl. Καὶ ἀπωλ. a climax, 'yea, of destruction.'

Ἐρήμους ἀβάτους, 'pathless deserts.' Vulg.. 'vias difficiles,' perhaps making ἀβάτους (sc. ὁδοὺς) a substantive. Reusch supposes that 'vias' was originally a clerical error for 'eremias,' which reading is noted by Luc Brug Comp Job xii 24. Ps cvi. 40. ἐπλάνησεν αὐτοὺς ἐν ἀβάτῳ καὶ οὐχ ὁδῷ.

Ὁδὸν Κυρίου, so Ps xxv 4: 'Shew me Thy ways (τὰς ὁδούς σου), O Lord.'

8 Καὶ τί. 'Aut,' Vulg. Whence Eng.: 'or.'

Πλοῦτος μετὰ ἀλαζονείας, 'divitiarum jactantia,' Vulg. 'Riches accompanied with arrogant ostentation.' Eng: 'What good hath riches with our vaunting brought us?' 'Hath,' not 'have,' 'riches' being singular = richesse. So Rev. xviii 17 'great riches is come to nought.' Shakesp Othello, III. 3.

'Riches, fineless, is as poor as winter
To him that ever fears he shall be poor.'

Elsewhere the word is plural, as Wisd viii 18; Ecclus xiii. 24.

Συμβέβληται, 'quid contulit nobis?' Vulg 'Contributed to us,' as Acts xviii. 27.

9. Ἐκεῖνα πάντα, 'earthly pleasures, goods,' etc

Σκιά. See on ii 5.

Ὡς ἀγγελία παρατρέχουσα, 'tanquam nuntius percurrens,' Vulg. 'As a post that hasted by,' Eng. So Gutb and others taking ἀγγ as = ἄγγελος, 'a courier,' comparing Job ix 25, 26, which is very similar to the passage here. But such an use of ἀγγελία is probably unprecedented, and it seems preferable to take it in the sense of 'rumour, report.' Thus Arn. and Grimm. There is a various reading in Hes. Theog 781: ἀγγελίη πωλεῖται, where ἀγγ. may mean 'messenger.' But probably ἀγγελίης is genuine. Polyb. has παρῆν ἀγγελίη, Hist iii 61. 8

10. Ὡς ναῦς, sc παρῆλθε.

Ἴχνος ... ἀτραπόν, acc governed by οὐκ ἔστιν εὑρεῖν, 'it is not possible to find' Comp. xix. 18: ἐστὶν εἰκάσαι. Vulg. 'non est invenire,' as Ecclus. xiv. 17.

Τρόπος. A. and the corrector of S read the Attic form τροπέως The var lect πυρείας (Ven. Compl al) is derived from the following verse There may be a paronomasia in ἀτραπὸν τρόπιος Τρόπις is ἅπ. λεγ. in the Greek Bible

11 Ἦ ὡς. This commences a new paragraph and set of similes, which are concluded by οὕτως καὶ ἡμεῖς, ver. 13 Comp Prov xxx. 19.

Διαπτάντος. The form διϊπτάντος given by V. does not occur, and is contrary to analogy There is a late present διΐπταμαι, but the aor is διέπτην, διαπτάς.

Ταρσὸς, 'the flat of the wing,' hence, 'the wing.'

Βίᾳ ῥοίζου κιν πτερ, 'parted with the violent noise and motion of them,' Eng This seems to be a somewhat feeble paraphrase 'Scindens (sc. avis) per vim itineris acrem,' Vulg This is better, though the translator has mistaken the construction of the sentence. Ῥοῖζος means here not 'the sound' but 'the rush,' 'the impulse,' κινουμ πτερ 'as the wings move.' Comp 2 Macc. ix. 7, where ῥοίζῳ is rightly rendered, 'impetu euntem.' The adv. ῥοιζηδόν occurs 2 Pet. iii 10.

The aorists διωδεύθη, εὑρέθη, ἀνελύθη (ver. 12), mark the rapidity of the actions spoken of.

12 Εἰς ἑαυτὸν ἀνελύθη, 'in se reclusus est,' Vulg, perhaps reading ἀνεκλείθη. 'Cometh together again,' Eng, which is like a translation of Grotius' conjecture ἀνελήλυθε. Various explanations are given of ἀνελύθη, but it seems most simple to take it in the sense of 'returns,' as in 1. 'Aër sagitta divisus in se rediens in pristinum statum restituitur.' Wahl Ven. reads ἀνέλυσεν, which would have the same meaning 'Is at once resolved into itself again.' Bissell.

Ὡς ἀγνοῆσαι, sc. τινά, 'so that one knows not' ὡς = ὥστε with infin Comp 4 Macc. xiv. 1. ὡς μὴ μόνον τῶν ἀλγηδόνων περιφρονῆσαι αὐτούς. Acts xx. 24.

13 Οὕτως καί Here begins the apodosis to vers 11, 12.

Γεννηθέντες, 'having been born,' not 'as soon as we were born'

Ἐξελίπομεν. 'Continuo desivimus esse,' Vulg. 'Died,' as Gen xxv 8. Luke xvi 9 ὅταν ἐκλίπητε (acc. to the common reading); Tobit xiv. 11 We were born, we died this takes the point of comparison of swiftness and transitoriness The following words 'we had no sign of virtue to show,' embrace the point of leaving no trace behind The Eng: 'began to draw to our end,' is probably from the Compl reading ἐξελείπομεν.

Κατεδαπανήθημεν, 'we were consumed, cut off, in the midst of our wickedness,' and thus 'had no sign of virtue to show' Comp. Ps lviii 14 Here end the words of remorse supposed to be spoken by the wicked.

The Vulgate, to make this plainer, inserts a paragraph which has no equivalent in the Greek: 'Talia dixerunt in inferno hi qui peccaverunt.' It may have been suggested by our Lord's parable of Dives and Lazarus, Luke xvi. 23, 24 S. Cypr · 'Erit tunc sine fructu poenitentiae dolor poenae, inanis ploratio, et inefficax deprecatio. In aeternam poenam sero credent qui in vitam aeternam credere noluerunt. Securitati igitur et vitae, dum licet, providete.' Ad Demetr. (p 224).

14. Ὅτι This gives the ground for putting the above words in the mouth of the ungodly

Ἐλπίς, that on which the ungodly rest their hope, e. g riches, pleasure, etc, Prov x 28.

Χνοῦς, 'dust, down' Vulg : 'lanugo.' The other reading is χοῦς (Mark vi. 11). It seems more likely that χνοῦς was altered to χοῦς, than vice versa. Comp Ps. i. 4; xvii. 43, Isai xvii 13 S. Ephr i 242, reads χοῦς In Job xxi. 18 the ungodly are compared to ἄχυρα and κονιορτός.

Πάχνη ('hoar frost') is the reading of the best MSS., but it is not very satisfactory, ἄχνη ('foam') being much more suitable. The Vulg gives 'spuma,' to the same effect the Arab. and Arm. versions, and some inferior MSS It is possible that the author himself confused the meaning of the words. S. Ephr. has πάχνη See note on ch iv 12

Καπνός, Eng. Marg translates 'chaff,' why, it is difficult to say. Comp. Ps. lxvii. 3. 'Which is dispersed,' Eng, where 'which' is not in the Greek, and ought to be printed in italics But the use of italics in this Book is very capricious

Καταλύτου μου, 'the guest (at an inn) for a day.'

Διεχύθη . παρώδευσε The construction is slightly changed. See on ver. 11.

15, 16. *The recompense of the righteous in the life to come*

15. Εἰς τὸν αἰῶνα ζῶσι, 'live for evermore.' Ecclus xli. 13 Grimm compares 1 John ii. 17: 'He that doeth the will of God abideth for ever,' μένει εἰς τὸν αἰῶνα. Ζῆν is used of a blessed life, the life of grace and glory. S. John vi. 57, 1 John iv. 9.

Ἐν Κυρίῳ, sc. ἐστί. 'In the Lord is their reward,' in communion with Him, in possessing Him, as Gen. xv 1 'I am thy shield and thy exceeding great reward.' Ps. xvi 5 Or, 'Their recompense is in the Lord's keeping,' which the parallel clause seems rather to favour Comp Rev. xxii 12.

Φροντὶς αὐτῶν. 'Care for them.' Comp 1 Pet. v. 7.

16. Διὰ τοῦτο. Because God cares for them.

Τῆς εὐπρεπείας . τοῦ κάλλους, genitive of quality = the glorious kingdom, the beautiful diadem.

Βασίλειον, 'kingdom' (as 1 14; 2 Macc ii. 17), as is shown by διάδημα. S Matt. xxv. 34

Διάδημα τ καλ. This is an advance on the O. T revelation of the future reward of the righteous, and may be compared with S. Paul's words: 'Henceforth there is laid up for me a crown of righteousness,' etc 2 Tim. iv. 8, 1 Pet. v. 4, Rev. ii. 10. But comp Is xxviii 5; xxxv 10, lxii. 3, and see 2 Esdr ii 43–46.

16–23. *God protects the righteous, and fights against the wicked in this life.*

Σκεπάσει. Comp. xix. 8, Ps. xc 1.

Βραχίονι 'Brachio sancto suo.' Vulg. The addition 'sancto' has little MS authority in the Latin, and none in the Greek Deut xxxiii 27

Ὑπερασπιεῖ, 'will hold His shield over them.' So the Psalmist calls God his 'buckler' (ὑπερασπιστής), Ps. xvii 3 Comp. Ps. v. 12; xc. 4

17. Almighty God is here introduced as an earthly warrior arming himself for the battle. Such descriptions of God as 'a man of war' (Ex xv 3) are not unusual in Scripture. Is. lix 17 : ἐνεδύσατο δικαιοσύνην ὡς θώρακα, καὶ περιέθετο περικεφαλαίαν σωτηρίου ἐπὶ τῆς κεφαλῆς, καὶ περιεβάλετο ἱμάτιον ἐκδικήσεως, καὶ τὸ περιβόλαιον αὐτοῦ (ζήλου, Field) Comp also Ezek xxxviii 18–23, Ps xvii. 13, 14. It seems probable that S. Paul had this passage in his mind when he wrote Eph. vi. 11–17. Comp. 1 Thess v. 8. The panoplia consisted of the greaves, breastplate, sword, shield, helmet, and spear If 'thunderbolts' stand for spear, all those parts are mentioned except greaves. See Hom. Il iii. 328 ff.

T

Τὸν ζῆλον S reads the later form τὰ ζῆλος, which may be nominative, as the Vulg 'zelus' Zech. i 14: ἐζήλωκα τὴν Ἱερουσαλὴμ καὶ τὴν Σίων ζῆλον μέγαν

Ὁπλοποιήσει τ. κτίσιν. 'He shall use creation as His weapon' The verb is not found elsewhere, though ὁπλοποιὸς and ὁπλοποιία occur. Comp. the song of Deborah, Judg. v. 20: 'They fought from heaven, the stars in their courses fought against Sisera' The same thought is found in Ecclus xxxix 25-31. See on ver 20 Cod Sin. gives ὁδοποιήσει, 'shall make the creature His way' This is a fine expression, but is probably a mere clerical error It is corrected in the MS. by an early hand.

Εἰς ἄμυναν. 'Ad ultionem inimicorum' Vulg, whence Eng.: 'For the revenge of His enemies.' Better, 'For the repulse of His enemies,' i e 'defending the righteous from them' Philo, Vit Mos 1 17 (II. p. 96)· τὰ γὰρ στοιχεῖα τοῦ παντός, γῆ, καὶ ὕδωρ, καὶ ἀήρ, καὶ πῦρ ἐπιτίθενται δικαιώσαντος Θεοῦ, οἷς ἀπετελέσθη ὁ κόσμος, τὴν ἀσεβῶν χώραν φθαρῆναι So Pseudo-Bas.· ἐπὶ τῶν πληγῶν τῶν Αἰγυπτιακῶν, πανταχόθεν αὐτοῖς ὁ πόλεμος, ἀπὸ ἀέρος, ἀπὸ γῆς, ἀπὸ ὕδατος In Isai. 181 (p 511, Ben).

18 Δικαιοσύνην, 'justice' He will proceed according to the eternal rules of justice, and deliver a plain and impartial sentence (κρίσιν ἀνυπόκριτον). 'True judgment instead of a helmet,' Eng. (omitting περιθήσεται) is from the Vulg: 'Pro galea certum judicium.' Translate: 'Shall put on as helmet judgment without disguise.' Comp xviii 16· ἀνυπόκριτος ἐπιταγή Rom. xii 9; Jas iii. 17 Vers 18-21 are quoted accurately by Orig., Sel. in Psalm. xxxiv. 2 (ii. p. 650)

19. Ὁσιότητα, 'holiness,' which repels the slanders and reproaches of the impious when they presume to question the motive of God in punishing them. Vulg. 'aequitatem,' whence Eng Marg 'equity.' But this quality has been implied above Ὅσιος, as applied to God, occurs Deut. xxxii 4; Rev. xv. 4, xvi. 5 Ὁσιότης means 'piety towards God' in the N T., S Luke i 75, Eph iv. 24.

20 Ἀπότομον, 'severe, stern' 'Duram,' Vulg. Grimm compares the use of 'abscisus,' e g. Val. Max.

II. vii. 14 'Aspero et absciso castigationis genere militaris disciplina aget.' So 'abscissa sententia,' 'abscissior justitia,' VI. iii. 10; VI v 4. Comp. Rom xi 22, 2 Cor xiii 10.

Εἰς ῥομφαίαν, 'shall sharpen into a sword' 'In lanceam,' Vulg., in which sense the word seems not to occur. Comp Rev ii 16 'I will fight against thee with the sword of My mouth,' ἐν τῇ ῥομφαίᾳ τοῦ στόματός μου Is. xlix. 2.

Συνεκπολεμήσει, 'shall with Him fight it out,' 'fight to the end, against the unwise'

Ὁ κόσμος This still further illustrates how God employs created things (ver 17) to do His will against the unrighteous Of this the plagues of Egypt are the great example. Comp xi. 15-20, xvi. 24, 25; xix 6. See note on ver. 17

Τοὺς παράφρονας = τοὺς ἄφρονας, 1 3 On this passage S Greg M, Hom in Evang 35 (1613, Ben), comments thus 'Qui in cunctis deliquimus, in cuncta ferimur... Omnia namque quae ad usum vitae accepimus, ad usum convertimus culpae, sed cuncta, quae ad usum pravitatis infleximus, ad usum nobis vertuntur ultionis Tranquillitatem quippe humanae pacis ad usum vertimus humanae securitatis, peregrinationem terrae pro habitatione dileximus patriae, salutem corporum redegimus in usum vitiorum, ubertatis abundantiam non ad necessitatem carnis, sed ad perversitatem intorsimus voluptatis, ipsa serena blandimenta aëris ad amorem nobis servire coëgimus terrenae delectationis Jure ergo restat, ut simul nos omnia feriant, quae simul omnia vitiis nostris male subacta serviebant, ut quot prius in mundo incolumes habuimus gaudia, tot de ipso postmodum cogamur sentire tormenta.'

21 Εὔστοχοι βολίδες ἀστραπῶν. 'Well-aimed lightning flashes.' Ἀστρ is a gen of apposition, 'missiles which are flashes' So τῶν νεφῶν. Vulg reads 'directe;' this seems to be an error for 'directae,' which some MSS give 'And from the clouds, as from a well-drawn bow, shall they fly to the mark.' Eng 'Tanquam a bene curvato arcu nubium exterminabuntur et ad certum locum insilient.' Vulg This is

right in that it attributes τ νεφῶν to τόξου, but the addition of 'exterminabuntur' is unwarranted. It must mean 'shall be driven beyond limits.' Translate· 'As from a well-curved (=tight-stretched) bow of clouds (i e which the clouds compose) shall leap to the mark.' Comp. Ps. vii. 13. 'He ordaineth His arrows against the persecutors' 2 Sam. xxii 15, 2 Esdr xvi. 13. Grimm notes that ἅλλεσθαι is used of the flight of an arrow, Hom Il iv 125. The 'bow in the clouds' (Gen ix 13), which is a sign of mercy, is turned away from the earth; this, the engine of wrath, is aimed at earth.

22. Ἐκ πετροβόλου θυμοῦ πλήρεις ῥιφ. χάλ. These words may be taken in various ways. Πετροβόλου may be an adj, in which case it agrees with θυμ., 'From his wrath that hurls stones.' Vulg 'a petrosa ira.' Or πετροβ may be a subst. meaning 'an engine for throwing stones,' a 'balista' Eng 'a stone bow,' i.e. a bow for hurling stones, as Shakesp. Twelfth Night, ii 5· 'Oh, for a stone-bow to hit him in the eye.' Θυμοῦ may be governed by πλήρεις, or be in app. with πετροβ, 'stone-bow which is His wrath,' in which case πλήρεις must mean 'solid, massy' It seems most natural to take the sentence as Eng, though Grimm and Guth translate: 'from the sling of His anger.' Comp Josh x. 11; Rev viii 7.

Χάλαζαι, as in the plagues of Egypt (Ex ix. 23-25), which seem here to be adumbrated.

Ἀγανακτήσει, 'shall show its wrath.' Vulg.· 'excandescet,' which makes a strange confusion of metaphors This word occurs nowhere else in Vulg

Συγκλύσουσιν, 'shall wash over them,' as the sea overwhelmed the Egyptians, Ex. xiv. 27 The act. voice of this verb is not found in classical Greek, but is used in the Sept., e g. Cant viii 7 ποταμοὶ οὐ συγκλύσουσιν αὐτήν Is xliii 2 Κατακλύζω is found in N. T, 2 Pet iii. 6, and in Wisd. x. 4, 19. Vulg. translates 'concurrent'

Ἀποτόμως, 'inexorably' There is a paronomasia in ποταμοὶ .. ἀποτόμως.' Vulg. 'duriter.' See on xiii. 5.

23 Πνεῦμα δυνάμεως 'Spiritus virtutis,' Vulg. 'A mighty wind,' Eng This might stand were it not for the following clause But to say 'a wind shall blow them away like a storm' is inadmissible. We might take Θεὸς as the subject of ἐκλικμήσει, but this would be harsh. It is best with Gr. and Guth. to take πν. δυν. as 'the breath of God's power.' See xi. 20, where the same expression, coupled with λικμηθέντες, occurs Comp. Is. xi 4; 2 Thess ii. 8.

Ἐκλικμήσει, 'shall winnow.' Judith ii 27. Comp. Is xli. 16; S Matt xxi 44

Καὶ ἐρήμ 'And so,' consecutive.

Δυναστῶν. This brings the author back to his original address to rulers and judges, which is carried on in the following chapter.

CHAPTER VI.

CHAPTERS VI–IX COMMENDATION OF WISDOM AS THE GUIDE OF LIFE.

vi 1–11 *Rulers are enjoined to learn wisdom, which is always to be found by those who seek it*

1 The Vulg begins this chapter with an interpolation which has no authority. It seems to have been introduced as a heading, and is compiled from Eccles ix. 16, 18, and Prov. xvi. 32, 'Melior est sapientia quam vires, et vir prudens quam fortis.'

Ἀκούσατε. The writer speaks with authority in

the person of King Solomon Hence λόγοι μου, ver 11, etc. This section begins like Ps. ii. 10. Comp. ch 1 1

'Ακούειν and συνιέναι are used together, Isai. vi. 9 · ἀκοῇ ἀκούσετε καὶ οὐ μὴ συνῆτε. S Matt. xiii 14.

Περάτων γῆς Ps. ii. 8, xxi. 28; S. Matt. xii. 42. Thus Hom. Od. iv. 563

ἀλλά σ' ἐς 'Ηλύσιον πεδίον καὶ πείρατα γαίης
ἀθάνατοι πέμψουσιν

2 'Ενωτίσασθε, 'give ear.' This is a word of later Greek found in Byzantine writers Comp. Gen. iv. 23; Ecclus. xxx. 27 (Tisch); Acts ii. 14, where see Kuinoel.

Πλήθους Vulg. 'multitudines' Or, as some MSS · 'multitudinem' Comp xiv. 20 Not 'the people,' as Eng., but 'a multitude,' a host of subjects.

Γεγαυρωμένοι, 'priding yourselves,' in a middle sense. Usually with dat. 3 Macc. iii. 11, vi. 5, with ἐπί, Xen. Hiero, ii. 15. The expression, 'ends of the earth,' ver. 1, and 'multitudes of nations' here, point to some great world power. Grimm suggests that Rome is referred to.

3. ̔́Οτι introduces that to which rulers have to listen

Παρὰ τ. Κυρίου. Prov. viii. 15 'By Me kings reign.' Comp. 1 Chr. xxix. 11, 12; Rom xiii. 1. Gutb. notes that Christian kings are said to reign 'Gratia Dei.' Clem. Ep. I. ad Cor lxi. 1 · σύ, Δέσποτα, ἔδωκας τὴν ἐξουσίαν τῆς βασιλείας αὐτοῖς

Κράτησις, an unclassical word, and ἅπ λεγ. in Sept It occurs in Jos contr Ap. i 26, p. 461 : ὥστε τὴν τῶν προειρημένων κράτησιν χειρίστην φαίνεσθαι τοῖς τότε τὰ τούτων ἀσεβήματα θεωμένοις.

4. ̔́Οτι, 'because,' the ground of God's judgment of them

Τῆς αὐτ. βασ. For 'His kingdom ruleth over all' Ps ciii 19

Νόμον, that law of right and wrong, to which even heathens are subject. Rom. i. 19 ff. The Vulg. has 'legem justitiae,' which is well as an explanation, but is not found in the Greek.

5 'Επιστήσεται, sc ὁ Θεός Ven. unnecessarily introduces ὄλεθρος as the subject of the verb 'Εφίσταμαι is used in a hostile sense with a dative, 'to stand up against, to˙ surprise.' S. Luke xxi. 34, Acts xvii 5, 1 Th. v. 3.

'Εν τοῖς ὑπερέχουσιν Vulg. 'his' (or 'in his,' as some MSS give) 'qui praesunt' 'Those in authority' Gen xli. 40; Rom xiii 1; 1 Pet. ii 13

Γίνεται. 'Fiet' Vulg 'Shall be' Eng. Better 'is,' 'cometh to pass,' the general ground of what precedes.

6. Συγγνωστός ἐστιν ἐλέους 'The mean man is to be pardoned for pity's sake.' 'Ελέους is a gen. of cause, whereas usually the gen after συγγνωστ denotes the object to which the pardon extends The Vulg. has 'exiguo conceditur misericordia.' Grimm quotes Philostr. Soph 1 8, 3 συγγνωστὸς φιλατιμίας Maxim Tyr. iv. 3 · ψυχὴ συγγνωστὸς τῆς ἀγνοίας. Comp. Prov. vi 30 'Men do not despise a thief if he steal to satisfy his soul when he is hungry.'

'Ετασθήσονται, 'shall be punished' 'Tormenta patientur.' Vulg Whence Eng : 'shall be tormented' 'Ετάζω in classical Greek means 'to test,' but it is used as ἐξετάζω in Sept for 'to chastise', e. g Gen. xiii 17 : ἤτασεν ὁ Θεὸς τὸν Φαραὼ ἐτασμοῖς μεγάλοις. Examples of what seem light faults in 'mighty men,' being heavily punished, are seen in the case of Moses (Numb xx 12), David (2 Sam xxiv 12), Hezekiah (2 Kings xx 17, 18). Comp. S. Luke xii. 47, 48. In the commentary on Isaiah which passes under the name of Basil the Great, this passage is applied as a warning not only to the rich and powerful in material resources, but thus · καὶ εἴ τις ἑτέρου τὴν διάνοιαν ἐντρεχέστερος, μὴ ἀποχρῆται τῇ ἰσχύϊ τῆς φύσεως πρὸς τὴν τῶν θείων ἔρευναν καὶ τούτῳ οὐαί, ὅταν ἀπαιτῆται κατὰ τὴν ἀναλογίαν τῶν δεδομένων τὸ ἔργον (p 420, Ben)

7 Οὐ γὰρ ὑποστελεῖται πρόσωπ. 'The lord of all (Ecclus. xxxiii. 1, Tisch.) shall cower before no man's person.' Matt. xxii. 16, Eph. vi. 9. Comp. Deut. i. 17:

οὐ μὴ ὑποστείλῃ πρόσωπον ἀνθρώπου. Job xxxiv 19. In the sense of 'shrink from,' 'draw back,' the verb is found in Job xiii. 8; Hab. ii 4; Acts xx. 27, Heb x 38 The Vulg has, 'Non subtrahet personam cujusquam Deus,' 'scilicet,' adds a Lap, 'judicio suo et vindictae,' which is not at all the meaning of the Greek. Clem. Al. Strom vi. 6 (p 766, Pott.) gives· οὐ γὰρ ὑποστέλλεται προσωπον...ὁμοίως τε προνοεῖ πάντων.

Ὁμοίως, 'alike,' in so far as none are excluded from His care. Comp xii 13; Ps cxlv. 9; S. Matt. v. 45.

Προνοεῖν is generally constructed with the gen. without a preposition, as xiii. 16, 2 Macc. xiv. 9, 1 Tim v 8.

8. Ἰσχυρὰ ἔρευνα, 'severe scrutiny,' i e for the misuse of power Vulg, 'cruciatio,' a word unknown to classical Latin, and ἅπ λεγ in Vulg S. Aug, Tract. in Joan, has 'usque ad immanem cruciationem.' See note on ver. 18

9. Τύραννοι, 'kings,'=βασιλεῖς, ver. 1. Comp. Prov. viii. 15, 16; Hab. i 10.

Οἱ λόγοι μου, sc γίνονται. Solomon is introduced speaking.

Παραπέσητε, 'excidatis.' Vulg. 'Fall away' Eng 'Swerve from right,' 'sin,' xii. 2; Heb. vi. 6. Comp. παράπτωμα, iii. 13; Matt. vi. 15; Gal. vi. 1. Παραπίπτειν, in the sense of 'to err, to make a mistake,' is classical, e. g. Xen. Hist Gr i. 6 4. διαθροούντων ἐν ταῖς πόλεσιν ὅτι Λακεδαιμόνιοι μέγιστα παραπίπτοιεν ἐν τῷ διαλλάττειν τοὺς ναυάρχους

10 Τὰ ὅσια = the commandments of God. Clem. Al. Strom. vi. 11 (p. 786, Pott.) has οἱ γὰρ φυλάσσοντες instead of φυλάξαντες.

Ὁσίως, 'piously,' with pious intention, without which outward obedience is of little worth.

Ὁσιωθήσονται Vulg 'Qui custodierint justa juste justificabuntur.' Lit 'shall be made holy.' Comp. 2 Sam xxii. 26. Thus 1 John iii 7: 'He that doeth righteousness is righteous' 'Justifico' is a post-classical word, common in the Vulg, e.g. Ecclus vii 5, Rom. iii. 4, etc. For the language comp. Pseudo-Clem. Epist. de Gest S Pet xviii · οὐδὲ γὰρ καλὸν τὸ καλὸν ὅταν μὴ καλῶς γίνηται Greg Naz. Orat 33 (p. 531): τὸ καλὸν οὐ καλόν, ὅταν μὴ καλῶς γίνηται.

Οἱ διδαχθέντες αὐτά, sc. τὰ ὅσια, 'they who have learned them' Obedience precedes perfect knowledge. S. John vii 17.

Εὑρήσουσιν ἀπολογίαν, 'shall find what to answer.' Eng Vulg i e shall be able to endure the scrutiny into their actions, ver. 8.

11 Παιδευθήσεσθε, 'ye shall be taught,' shall learn true wisdom, which is the daily practice of virtue.

12–16. *Wisdom is easily found.*

12. Ἀμάραντος, 'unfading,' used by S. Peter (I. i. 4) of the heavenly inheritance It seems here to refer to the unfailing beauty of wisdom rather than to its imperishable nature. See Clem. Al. Strom. vi 15 (p 800, Pott)

Εὐχερῶς θεωρ. 'She is easily seen and recognised,' because she is λαμπρά, 'bright and beauteous.' See Is. Williams, The Resurrection, Pt. I. § ii. extr. p. 158. Comp Prov. viii 17 · 'I love them that love Me. and those that seek Me early shall find Me;' Ecclus. xxvii. 8; S. Matt. xi. 19.

13. Προγνωσθῆναι with φθάνει, as iv. 7. 'Praevenit illos qui appetunt ipsam. ut praenoscatur.' Schl. Comp. Prov. i. 20, 21, viii. 3, 34, etc. Ps. lviii. 11: ὁ Θεός μου τὸ ἔλεος αὐτοῦ προφθάσει με. S. Bern. De dilig. Deo, vii. (I p 1347) · 'Sed enim in hoc est mirum, quod nemo Te quaerere valet, nisi qui prius invenerit Vis igitur inveniri ut quaeratis, quaeri ut inveniaris. Potes quidem quaeri et inveniri, non tamen praeveniri.'

14. Ὁ ὀρθρίσας, 'he who rises early after her.' Prov. viii. 17. Ὀρθρίζω is a late word = ὀρθρεύω. See 1 Macc iv 52; Ecclus iv. 12 (πρὸς αὐτήν); Luke xxi 38. Clem. Al. Strom vi. 15 (p 800, Pott.) reads ὁ ὀρθρίσας ἐπ' αὐτήν.

Πάρεδρον..πυλῶν. Like a counsellor of a king as he sits at the gate to administer justice. 2 Sam. xix. 8, Jer. xxxix. 3.

15. Τὸ γὰρ ἐνθυμ. Wisdom is close at hand to those

who seek her, *for* to ponder deeply on her is the perfection of prudence, *i e* is wisdom. 'Sensus est consummatus,' Vulg, which Gutb. takes in the same meaning.

Φρονήσ. τελειότ. seems to be a synonym for wisdom. φρόνησις usually means practical wisdom, wisdom in the conduct of life. This may be seen in the parable of the unjust steward, Luke xvi. 8 · ἐπῄνεσεν ὁ κύριος τὸν οἰκονόμον τῆς ἀδικίας, ὅτι φρονίμως ἐποίησεν· ὅτι οἱ υἱοὶ τοῦ αἰῶνος τούτου φρονιμώτεροι ὑπὲρ τοὺς υἱοὺς τοῦ φωτὸς εἰς τὴν γενεὰν τὴν ἑαυτῶν εἰσι

'Ἀγρυπνήσας. Prov. viii 34. μακάριος... ἄνθρωπος ὅς τὰς ἐμὰς ὁδοὺς φυλάξει, ἀγρυπνῶν ἐπ' ἐμαῖς θύραις καθ' ἡμέραν 'He that watcheth for her sake.' Eph vi 18. εἰς αὐτὸ τοῦτο ἀγρυπνοῦντες, like the Latin, 'invigilare rei.' Virg Georg iv 158: 'Namque aliae victu invigilant.'

'Ἀμέριμνος, vii 23.

16. Ὅτι, a still further confirmation of ver. 14.

Περιέρχεται ζητοῦσα, viii. 18 περιῄειν ζητῶν. Comp. 1 Pet. v 8 Mr Churton paraphrases: 'She circumvents those whom she seeks,' but the notion of deluding people even to their good is foreign to the passage.

Ταῖς τρίβοις, 'ways, roads,' as Prov viii 2. In outer life. Comp also Prov i 20 ff Thus S. Aug: 'Quoquo enim te verteris, vestigiis quibusdam, quae operibus suis impressit, loquitur tibi, et te in exteriora relabentem, ipsis exteriorum formis intro revocat.' De Lib. Arbitr ii § 41.

Ἐν πάσῃ ἐπινοίᾳ, 'in every thought,' in their inner life Vulg. 'in omni providentia;' referring ἐπινοίᾳ to wisdom, 'with all care and foresight,' but this seems to injure the parallelism with τρίβοις, which refers to the seekers after wisdom.

'Ἀπαντᾷ. This reading has most authority V. has ὑπαντᾷ

17-21. *Wisdom leads to a kingdom*

17. Here begins the famous sorites, the conclusion of which is, 'The desire of wisdom leadeth to a kingdom,' ver. 20. As this should consist of the first subject and last predicate of the premisses, the first premiss is not formally expressed. It should run: The desire of Wisdom is the beginning of Wisdom; and then, through the rest of the series, the predicate of one premiss is the subject of the next. See Prolegom p. 29. It is quoted by Clem Alex. Strom vi. 15 (p 800, Pott).

Γὰρ introduces the argument to prove that Wisdom is worth man's thought and pains, 'for... it leads to eternal happiness'

Αὐτῆς, sc σοφίας.

'Ἀρχὴ, 'beginning, foundation.' Ps cxi 10, Prov. i. 7. 'Ἀρχὴ σοφίας φόβος Κυρίου

Ἡ ἀληθεστάτη is taken by Vulg. with ἐπιθυμία. S. Aug however quotes, 'initium enim illius verissimum,' De Mor Eccl i § 32 (p 699, D.) This is perhaps best. 'the truest, most real, and solid foundation of Wisdom is the desire of instruction, or training.' The Sin. Codex seems to have intended to substitute ἀγάπη for ἐπιθυμία. Clem. Al Strom. vi. 15 (p. 800, Pott.) reads. ἀρχὴ γὰρ αὐτῆς ἀληθεστάτη παιδείας ἐπιθυμία, τουτέστιν τῆς γνώσεως.

18. Φροντὶς, changed for ἐπιθυμία in the former premiss This is quoted by Clem Al Paedag ii 1 (p 167, Pott.)

'Ἀγάπη, i.e. of Wisdom.

Τήρησις νόμ αὐτ. The Decalogue speaks of 'them, that love Me and keep my commandments,' Ex. xx. 6, and Christ's word is, 'If ye love Me, keep my commandments' S John xiv. 15. Comp. Rom xiii 10 Grimm observes that the plural νόμοι = ἐντολαὶ occurs in N. T. only Heb. x. 16 in a citation, but frequently in O. T., e.g Jer. xxxviii 33; Ezek v. 6; 2 Macc. iv. 17.

Προσοχὴ = τήρησις. Obedience to the commands works assurance of immortality. So our Blessed Lord says 'If thou wilt enter into life, keep the commandments,' Matt. xix 17 Προσοχή Vulg. 'custoditio,' ἅπ. λεγ. Unusual words in Vulg. of like formation are these. 'cruciatio,' ver 9; 'exquisitio,' xiv. 12, 'exterminatio,' xviii 7; 'fascinatio,' iv. 12; 'increpatio,' xii. 26; 'respectio,' iii. 13, 'sibilatio,' xvii 9, 'subitatio,' v. 2; 'tribulatio,' Matt xiii. 21; 'salvatio,' Is. xxxvii. 32, 'sanctificatio,' Am. vii. 9, 'contritio,'

Rom. iii. 16; 'abominatio,' Ex viii. 26; 'compunctio,' Rom. xi. 8, 'corrogatio,' Ecclus. xxxii. 3; 'justificatio,' Luke i. 6; 'regeneratio,' Tit. iii. 5; with many others.

'Ἀφθαρσίας, 'blessed immortality,' as ii 23. 4 Macc. xvii. 12: τὸ νῖκος ἀφθαρσία ἐν ζωῇ πολυχρονίῳ. So 2 Tim. i. 10. Vulg.: 'incorruptionis,' a post-classical word. Comp. Rom. ii 7; 1 Cor xv 53, Vulg.

19 'Immortality maketh us near unto God,' even in His heavenly kingdom; whence it follows, ver. 20, that 'the desire of Wisdom leads to a kingdom.' This verse is quoted by S. Iren. Contr. Haer iv. 38 3 (ap. Migne), who gives the following sorites (ib p 285, Ben). ἔδει τὸν ἄνθρωπον πρῶτον γενέσθαι, καὶ γενόμενον αὐξῆσαι, καὶ αὐξήσαντα ἀνδρωθῆναι, καὶ ἀνδρωθέντα πληθυνθῆναι, καὶ πληθυνθέντα ἐνισχῦσαι, καὶ ἐνισχύσαντα δοξασθῆναι, καὶ δοξασθέντα ἰδεῖν τὸν ἑαυτοῦ Δεσπότην Θεὸς γὰρ ὁ μέλλων ὁρᾶσθαι ὅρασις δὲ Θεοῦ περιποιητικὴ ἀφθαρσίας· [ἀφθαρσία δὲ ἐγγὺς εἶναι ποιεῖ Θεοῦ, Migne]. Clem. Alexandr (Strom. vi 15, p. 801, Pott) sums up the argument thus· διδάσκει γὰρ, οἶμαι, ὡς ἀληθινὴ παιδεία ἐπιθυμία τις ἐστὶ γνώσεως· ἄσκησις δὲ παιδείας συνίσταται ἀγάπην γνώσεως· καὶ ἡ μὲν ἀγάπη τήρησις τῶν εἰς γνῶσιν ἀναγουσῶν ἐντολῶν· ἡ τήρησις δὲ αὐτῶν βεβαίωσις τῶν ἐντολῶν, δι' ἣν ἡ ἀφθαρσία ἐπισυμβαίνει· ἀφθαρσία δὲ ἐγγὺς εἶναι ποιεῖ Θεοῦ

20. The MSS vary here, but the reading in the text seems plainly to be correct.

'Ἐπὶ βασιλ., 'ad regnum perpetuum,' Vulg. S. Aug De Mor Eccl 1 32 (T i p 699 D) omits 'perpetuum.' So S. Paul says: 'They who receive abundance of grace and of the gift of righteousness shall reign in life by Jesus Christ.' Rom v. 17 Comp. Philo, Quod Deus imm 30 (I. p. 294). κατέφθειρε πᾶσα σὰρξ τὴν τοῦ αἰωνίου καὶ ἀφθάρτου τελείαν ὁδὸν τὴν πρὸς Θεὸν ἄγουσαν. Ταύτην ἴσθι σοφίαν. Διὰ γὰρ ταύτης ὁ νοῦς ποδηγετούμενος, εὐθείας καὶ λεωφόρου ὑπαρχούσης, ἄχρι τῶν τερμάτων ἀφικνεῖται τὰ δὲ τέρματα τῆς ὁδοῦ γνῶσίς ἐστι καὶ ἐπιστήμη Θεοῦ.

21 Ἥδεσθε ἐπὶ θρόνοις. This verb is found with ἐπὶ and the dat in Xen Mem. IV. v 9, Cyr. VIII iv 12. For the sentiment comp. Prov viii 15, 16.

Βασιλεύσητε. Prov. ix 6 ἀπολείπετε ἀφροσύνην, ἵνα εἰς τὸν αἰῶνα βασιλεύσητε Rev. xxii. 5. The Vulg. adds to this verse a second translation which has crept into the text of the MSS: 'Diligite lumen sapientiae, omnes qui praeestis populis.'

22-25. *Nature of Wisdom.*

22. Τί ἐστι σοφία, The author nowhere gives a definition of Wisdom, but presents to us her properties and her effects on men's lives.'

Πῶς ἐγένετο 'How she came into being' Comp. Prov. viii. 23 ff; Job xxviii 20 ff Some understand ἐμοὶ with ἐγέν, 'how she came unto me,' with a reference to the next chapter, but this seems an unnecessary restriction. The expression however may mean, 'how she began her work in man' So Mr Churton takes it, remarking that in herself she is immortal. Perhaps Dr. Bissell's rendering, 'how she arose,' is safest.

Μυστήρια Vulg 'sacramenta Dei,' as ii 22; Dan. ii 30; Eph. i. 9, and often. The author differs from the heathen, who made a profound secret of their mysteries, and professes his willingness to divulge all that he knows about Wisdom.

'Ἀπ' ἀρχῆς γενέσεως 'From the beginning of her nativity,' referring to πῶς ἐγένετο. This, which is the Eng. rendering, would require the addition of αὐτῆς. It is better with Arn., Grimm, and others to understand, 'from the beginning of creation' Prov. viii. 22, 23 Vulg 'ab initio nativitatis' 'Nativitas' is a post-classical word found in Ulpian and Tertull. and frequently in Vulg, whence it made its way into English. See on vii. 5

Ἐξιχνιάζω = classical ἐξιχνεύω Comp ix 16; Ecclus. i 3; xviii. 4, 6.

Παροδεύσω, 'pass by, neglect, despise,' as x. 8. The Vulg gives 'praeteribo,' which is used in the same sense.

23 Φθόνῳ τετηκότι. So Ovid 'Livor edax,' Am. i. 15 1; Pers. Sat iii 37:

'Virtutem videant, intabescantque relicta'

Συνοδεύσω, a play of words If this be subj we must read οὔτε μή. Retaining οὔτε μὴν, we must take συνοδ as fut. See on i 8 The meaning is I will disclose all I know without envy or grudging. Comp. vii. 13; Acts xx. 20, 27 Philo, De Vict Offer 12 (II p. 260): τί γάρ, εἰ καλὰ ταῦτ' ἐστίν, ὦ μύσται, καὶ συμφέροντα, συγκλεισάμενοι ἑαυτοὺς ἐν σκότῳ βαθεῖ, τρεῖς ἢ τέτταρας μόνους ὠφελεῖτε, παρὸν ἅπαντας ἀνθρώπους ἐν ἀγορᾷ μέσῃ τὰ τῆς ὠφελείας προθέντας, ἵνα πᾶσιν ἀδεῶς ἐξῇ βελτίονος καὶ εὐτυχεστέρου κοινωνῆσαι βίου, φθόνος γὰρ ἀρετῆς διῴκισται.

Οὗτος, i e either φθόνος, or as Vulg 'talis homo,' ὁ τῷ φθόνῳ συνοδεύων

Κοινωνεῖν with dat. 'to go shares with,' 'have dealing with.' Plat. Rep 1. p. 343 D. . ὅπου ἂν ὁ τοιοῦτος τῷ τοιούτῳ κοινωνήσῃ.

24. 'I will do my best to increase the roll of wise men, for the more numerous they are, the better it is for the world' Comp. Philo, De Sacr Ab. et Cain § 37 (I p. 187) πᾶς σοφὸς λύτρον ἐστὶ τοῦ φαύλου . καθάπερ ἰατρὸς τοῦ νοσοῦντος ἀντιτεταγμένος ταῖς ἀρρωστήμασι κ.τ.λ.

Εὐστάθεια, 'the upholding,' Eng., 'stabilimentum,' Vulg The word is generally applied to 'good health,' which is the meaning here Comp 2 Macc xiv. 6, 3 Macc. iii 26, Addit ad Esth. iii 18 (Tisch) Comp. Clem. Rom Ep. I. ad Cor. lxi 1 . οἷς δός, Κύριε, ὑγίειαν, εἰρήνην, ὁμόνοιαν, εὐστάθειαν, εἰς τὸ διέπειν αὐτοὺς τὴν ὑπὸ σοῦ δεδομένην αὐτοῖς ἡγεμονίαν ἀπροσκόπως See Eccles. ix. 13-18 In confirmation of vers. 24, 25 one may recall that dictum πολυθρύλλητον of Plato, De Rep. v p 473: ἐὰν μὴ ἢ οἱ φιλόσοφοι βασιλεύσωσιν ἐν ταῖς πόλεσιν, ἢ οἱ βασιλεῖς τε νῦν λεγόμενοι καὶ δυνάσται φιλοσοφήσωσι γνησίως τε καὶ ἱκανῶς, καὶ τοῦτο εἰς ταὐτὸν ξυμπέσῃ, δύναμίς τε πολιτικὴ καὶ φιλοσοφία, τῶν δὲ νῦν πορευομένων χωρὶς ἐφ' ἑκάτερον αἱ πολλαὶ φύσεις ἐξ ἀνάγκης ἀποκλεισθῶσιν, οὐκ ἔστι κακῶν παῦλα ταῖς πόλεσι, δοκῶ δὲ οὐδὲ τῷ ἀνθρωπίνῳ γένει.

25 Ὥστε, 'and so,' 'therefore,' as 1 Cor. iv. 5, 1 Pet iv. 19 Soph. El. 1172
θνητὸς δ' Ὀρέστης ὥστε μὴ λίαν στένε.

CHAPTER VII.

1-10 *Solomon, realising his mortality, prayed for Wisdom, which he valued above every earthly good.*

1. Εἰμὶ μὲν κἀγώ, 'I too as others.' The author speaks in the character of Solomon, at the same time humbling himself as knowing that wisdom is given only to the meek. The μέν has no answering δέ. See Jelf, Gr Gram § 766 Perhaps ver. 7 is meant to be the corresponding member, the δέ being omitted owing to the long paragraph, vers 1-6, preceding So Grimm Comp Acts x. 26; xiv 15.

Γηγενοῦς. Gen ii 7 ἔπλασεν ὁ Θεὸς τὸν ἄνθρωπον χοῦν ἀπὸ τῆς γῆς. Comp. Ecclus. xvii. 1, 1 Cor xv. 47. So Philo calls man γηγενής, De Mund Op. 47 (I. p 32), and Plato, De Legg v. 1 (p 727 E.) οὐδὲν γηγενὲς Ὀλυμπίων ἐντιμότερον

Πρωτόπλαστος, only here and x. 1 From its use in this Book the word came to be employed commonly as the designation of our first parent. (See Prolegom p. 27) Thus Clem. Alex. Strom iii 17: κἂν ἀπὸ τῶν ἀλόγων ξύλων τὴν ἐπιτήδευσιν τῆς συμβουλίας ὁ ὄφις εἰληφώς, καὶ παραπείσας τῇ κοινωνίᾳ τῆς Εὔας συγκαταθέσθαι τὸν Ἀδάμ, λέγῃ, ὡς ἂν μὴ φύσει ταύτῃ κεχρημένων τῶν πρωτοπλάστων, ὥς ἀξιοῦσί τινες S Athan. cont Apoll 1 15· ἢ πάντως κατὰ τὴν τῆς σαρκὸς ἐπίδειξιν, καὶ κατὰ τὴν μορφὴν τοῦ δούλου, τουτέστι τοῦ πρωτοπλάστου Ἀδάμ, ἣν ἔλαβεν ὁ ἐν μορφῇ Θεοῦ ὑπάρχων Θεός. S. Iren. Haer. iii. 21. 10. 'Et quemadmodum protoplastus ille Adam de rudi terra, et de adhuc virgine, ("nondum enim pluerat Deus, et homo non erat operatus terram,") habuit substantiam, et plasmatus est manu Dei, i e. verbo Dei, ("omnia enim per Ipsum facta sunt,") et sumpsit Dominus limum a terra et plasmavit hominem ..' And so Christian poets, with a painful disregard of quantities S Avitus, Poem ii. 35·

'His protoplastorum sensuum primordia sacra
Continuere bonis, donec certamine primo
Vinceret oppressos fallacem culpa per hostem'

Ovientius, Commonit. ii. 108:

'Per pomum, Protoplaste, cadis; cruce, Christe, mederis;
Illic mortiferam draco pestifer detulit escam'

2 Ἐγλύφην σάρξ, 'I was formed flesh.' Comp. xiii. 13. Prop. 'was carved,' 'cut out;' used of 'engraving,' Ecclus xxxviii. 27. The ἐγώ (with which παγείς agrees) implies the whole man. Another question arises about the derivation of the soul, viii 19, where see notes

Δεκαμηνιαίῳ χ 4 Macc. xvi. 7, Plut. Num. 12. The period of gestation is from 273 to 280 days = 40 weeks, or 10 lunar months at 4 weeks to the month. Speaking of the reasons which induced Romulus to make the year ten months long, Ovid says, Fast. i. 33·

'Quod satis est utero matris dum prodeat infans,
Hoc anno statuit temporis esse satis.'

Comp. Virg. Ecl. iv. 61. In 2 Macc vii 27 however the period is stated at 'nine months.'

Παγείς, as Job x 10 ἔπηξας (ἐτύρωσας, V) δέ με ἴσα τυρῷ, Al. MS. The author follows the common opinion of his age, and as Calmet properly asks. 'Quis jubet sacros auctores ex physicorum principiis loqui?'

Καὶ ἡδονῆς dep. on ἐκ, not gen. abs. as Gutb. takes it.

Ὕπνος, euphemistic, as iv 6

3 Ἔσπασα, 'I drew in,' 'sucked in,' expressive of the breathing of a new-born child.

Ὁμοιοπαθῆ. 'Similiter factam,' Vulg. 'Which is of like nature,' Eng In this sense the word occurs Acts xiv 15 Plat Timae xvi. p 45 C· ὁμοιοπαθὲς δὴ δι' ὁμοιότητα πᾶν γενόμενον. Arab: 'dolores meos reddentem' Grimm and Gutb. translate: 'the earth which endures the same from all her children,' = 'aeque omnibus calcatum,' or, 'upon whom all her children fall in helpless infancy.'

Κατέπεσον expresses the helplessness of the new-born infant. Comp. Hom Il xix 110·

ὅς κεν ἐπ' ἤματι τῷδε πέσῃ μετὰ ποσσὶ γυναικός.

Φωνὴν, acc. cogn. after κλαίων.

Ὁμοίαν πᾶσιν, a shortened expression for ὁμ. τῇ πάντων φωνῇ Comp ii. 15. Rev xiii 11. κέρατα ὅμοια ἀρνίῳ

Ἶσα, adv = ἐν ἴσῳ, xiv 9, 'aequaliter,' 'perinde ac' Job x. 10, quoted in note on ver 2. The Vulg. has 'emisi,' Eng. 'I uttered,' reading apparently, as Compl, ἧκα, which is found in no existing MS The Sin. Cod omits ἴσα, which indeed is hardly necessary to the sense. 'I cried when I was born,' says an old proverb, and 'every day tells me why' We may compare Lucret. v. 223 ff

'Tum porro puer, ut saevis projectus ab undis
Navita, nudus humi jacet, infans, indigus omni
Vitali auxilio, quom primum in luminis oras
Nixibus ex alvo matris Natura profudit,
Vagituque locum lugubri complet, ut aequum est,
Quoi tantum in vita restet transire malorum'

4 Ἐν φροντίσιν, 'curis magnis,' Vulg. Comp. S. Luke ii. 7.

5 Γενέσεως ἀρχὴν, vi 24. Gutb takes γενέσεως as a genit explicativus elucidating ἀρχήν The expression means simply 'beginning of existence.' Vulg 'nativitatis initium.' 'Nativitas' (vi. 24, xvi 26, q v. Ps. cvi. 37), a late word, may be compared with other words of like formation used in Vulg, e.g. 'nimietas,' iv 4; 'nugacitas,' iv 12; 'praeclaritas,' viii. 18, 'possibilitas,' Neh v 8; 'longiturnitas,' Bar. iii. 14; 'otiositas,' Ecclus. xxxiii 29

6 Theodoret. Orat. ix De Provid. (p. 577)· ἀέρα μέσον ἐξέχεε (ὁ Θεὸς) κοινόν τινα καὶ τοῦτον πλοῦτον πᾶσιν ὁμοίως προτεθεικώς. οὔτε γὰρ σπῶσιν αὐτὸν πλέον τῶν πενήτων οἱ πλούσιοι, ἀλλὰ τὴν ἴσην μοῖραν κἀνταῦθα ἡ πενία λαμβάνει .. βλέπε δὲ καὶ τὰ τικτόμενα ὁμοίως γυμνὰ προσιόντα· οὐ γὰρ τὸ τοῦ πλουσίου βρέφος ἀλουργίδα περιβέβληται, τὸ δὲ τοῦ πένητος ῥάκια περίκειται, ἀλλὰ ἄμφω γυμνὰ προέρχεται, τοῦ δημιουργοῦ κηρύσσοντος τὴν ἰσότητα ὁμοίως σπᾷ τὸν ἀέρα, ὁμοίως ἕλκει τὴν θηλήν· οὐχ ἑτέρῳ γάλακτι τὸ τοῦ πένητος τρέφεται, ἕτερον δὲ τῷ τοῦ πλουσίου προσφέρεται,

ἀλλ' ἴσης καὶ τοῦτο κἀκεῖνο καὶ τῆς αὐτῆς ἀπολαύει τροφῆς Οὐ μόνον δὲ τὴν εἰς τὸν βίον εἴσοδον μίαν, ἀλλὰ καὶ τὴν ἔξοδον ἴσην ἔχομεν εἰς γὰρ ἡμᾶς ὑποδέχεται θάνατος

Ἔξοδος. See on iii. 2, and comp. Job i. 21, xxi 23-26, Eccl iii 19, 20. Horat. Carm. I iv 13

'Pallida mors aequo pulsat pede pauperum tabernas
Regumque turres'

7 Διὰ τοῦτο Because by nature he was no wiser than others, and yet as king had more constant need for the exercise of wisdom

Ηὐξάμην. 1 Kings iii 5-12, Wisd viii 21
Φρόνησις, parallel but not identical with πνεῦμα σοφίας, meaning good sense, understanding 1 Kings iv. 29. See on vi 15.

Πν. σοφίας, not the Holy Spirit, but the principle of wisdom, as Eph. i 17 Comp Deut. xxxiv 9: πνεύματος συνέσεως 'If any of you lack wisdom,' says S James i 5, 'let him ask of God. and it shall be given him.'

Ἐπεκαλεσάμην, 'I called upon, invoked God.' So Acts vii. 59: ἐλιθοβόλουν τὸν Στέφανον, ἐπικαλούμενον καὶ λέγοντα κ τ λ, where however one must supply τὸν Κύριον Ἰησοῦν from the following prayer The verb usually is joined with Θεὸν or Κύριον, as Judith vi 21 So Herod. ii 39· ἐπικαλέσαντες τὸν θεόν

8. Ἐν συγκρίσει, 'in comparison.' So συγκρίνω, ver. 29, xv 18, 1 Cor. ii 13, 2 Cor. x 12. This is a late use of the word, found, e g, in Plut. Vit Flamin 21 extr; Aeli Var Hist. iii. 16 Comp S. Matt xiii 44.

9 Comp Job xxviii 12 ff., Prov iii. 14 ff.; viii. 10, 11, 19. Ἀτίμητον, 'priceless,' 'beyond value,' as 3 Mac. iii. 23: τὴν ἀτίμητον πολιτείαν. Sophocles, Lex sub voc refers for this use of the word to Greg. Naz. iii. 1232 A; and Greg Nyss 1092 D (Migne) See also Eustathius, 781. 19. Schleusner, s v 'eodem sensu Graecis φίλος ἀτίμητος dicitur Etiam adjectivum ἄτιμον per πολύτιμον explicatur a Schol Aeschyl Agam 421' Vulg 'lapidem pretiosum.' The Compl ed. reads τίμιον.

Ὁ πᾶς χρυσός, 'all the gold in the world,' sc. ἐστι.
Ἐν ὄψει, 'in comparatione,' Vulg. So possibly xv 19, where see note. Here comp. the parallel expression ἐναντίον αὐτῆς, 'adversus illam,' and xi 22. S Method. Conv. dec. Virg xi (xviii p 205, Migne) quotes from memory πᾶς γὰρ πλοῦτος ἐνώπιον αὐτῆς, καὶ χρυσὸς ὡς ψάμμος ὀλίγη.

10. Ἀντὶ φωτός, 'pro luce,' Vulg. 'Instead of light,' Eng, Gutb, Grimm. The interpretation of the Vulg is preferred by Arn, who paraphrases · 'I determined to have her for a light or guide.' But the context favours the other explanation · 'I had rather lose light itself than wisdom, because,' as he continues, 'the light of day wanes and perishes, but the light of wisdom never fails' Comp Ps cxix 105

Ἀκοίμητον, 'never goes to rest,' as the poets feign the sun sinks to sleep. 'Inextinguibile,' Vulg Matt. iii 12, Mark ix. 42, 44 See on x 4. Clem Alex Paed. ii 10 seems to allude to this passage when he says, λογισμοὺς ἀνδρῶν ἀγαθῶν οὓς ἀκοιμήτους λύχνους ὠνόμασεν ἡ γραφή. P. 230, Pott.

11-21 *With her came all earthly blessings, friendship with God, and scientific knowledge*

11. 1 Kings iii. 13 'I have also given thee that which thou hast not asked, both riches and honour.' Comp Prov iii 16, viii. 17-35; Ecclus. li 28; S Matt vi 33

Ἀναρίθμητος πλοῦτος. 'Innumerabilis honestas.' Vulg Sc ἦν or ἦλθε. The Vulg. often renders πλοῦτος and πλούσιος by 'honestas,' and 'honestus.' Comp ver 13, viii 18, Ecclus xi. 14, 23, xiii. 2. This is a use unknown to classical Latin The lexicons refer to a remark of Asconius in Cic. Verr. II i. 47 'An vetuste bonos pro magnis, honestos pro divitibus posuit ?' This sense is found in the Fathers, e.g. S. Aug. Contr Adim xix. (viii. 142 D), translating Wisdom vii 8. 'Et honestatem nihil esse duxi ad comparationem ipsius' So S Ambr. De Parad 3, renders Heb. xi 26: 'majorem honestatem aestimavit' (p. 175, Ben.).

12. Ἐπὶ πᾶσιν. The MSS vary between πάντων and πᾶσιν, but the dat. is the more usual construction Comp. Ps. cxxi. 1, Ecclus xvi. 1, 2; Rev. xviii. 20, acc. to the best MSS

Ἡγεῖται. 'Heads them,' brings them with her, the term being parallel with γενέτιν εἶναι τούτων ' I rejoiced in them all because they had their value from being the accompaniments of Wisdom' The Vulg gives· 'quoniam antecedebat me ista sapientia.' Quasi dux deducens me ad omnia bona jam dicta. A. Lap. Comp 2 Chr. i 12.

Ἡγνόουν. I knew not when I prayed. I had no lower motive.

Γενέτις = γενέτειρα, is found nowhere else, but is formed after the usual manner, as δεσπότις, τεχνῖτις, etc. The Vulg. and Arm. give 'mater.' There is good MS authority for γένεσιν, but the uncommon word is more probably genuine Apel, Field, and Tisch. read γενέτιν See the praise of Wisdom, Prov iii. 13–20

13 Ἀδόλως, with pure intentions, without any secret reservation, not hoping to gain any selfish or earthly benefit 'Quam sine fictione didici' Vulg. For 'fictio' see on xiv. 25. The Eng. 'diligently' is very weak, the margin is better, 'without guile' Comp vi 23 Observe the neat balancing of words, ἀδόλως ἀφθόνως. Euseb. in Psalm. xxxiii 8 (p 132, Ben)· ἀδόλως ἔλαβον, ἀφθόνως μεταδίδομαι Just. Mart Apol 1. 6: παντὶ βουλομένῳ μαθεῖν, ὡς ἐδιδάχθημεν, ἀφθόνως παραδιδόντες.

Τὸν πλοῦτον, 'honestatem,' Vulg See on ver. 11 1 Pet. iv. 10· 'As every man hath received the gift, even so minister the same one to another, as good stewards of the manifold grace of God.' Comp. Ecclus. xx. 30, S. Matt x. 8.

14. Ἀνεκλιπής = ἀνέκλειπτος. See on viii 18

Ὃν οἱ χρησ. This reading has the highest authority The unusual construction of χράομαι with acc. has led to the change into ᾧ in the one case, and κτησάμενοι in the other. There is a similar variation in the MSS in 1 Cor. vii 31 οἱ χρώμενοι τὸν κόσμον (Tisch), where some read τῷ κόσμῳ, and Acts xxvii 17 In 2 Macc iv 19 all MSS give the acc· ἃς ἠξίωσαν οἱ παρακομίσαντες μὴ χρῆσθαι πρὸς θυσίαν But the author may have intended ἅς to be governed by παρακομίσαντες. Bp. Wordsworth, in his note on 1 Cor. vii. 31, says that the acc. after χρᾶσθαι is not found in Sept, which is true, if we confine the name Septuagint to the canonical portion of the Old Testament The Vulg. of our passage is 'quo qui usi sunt.'

Πρὸς Θεὸν ἐστείλαντο φιλίαν. 'Participes facti sunt amicitiae Dei.' Vulg 'Prepare for themselves friendship with God.' So Abraham for his faith was called 'the friend of God' S James ii 23, Is xli 8. Comp. S John xv 14. The use of the grace of wisdom makes men beloved by God Comp. ver 27. Philo, De Sobr. 11 (I p 401): φίλον γὰρ τὸ σοφὸν Θεῷ μᾶλλον ἢ δοῦλον παρ' ὃ καὶ σαφῶς ἐπὶ Ἀβραὰμ φάσκει, Μὴ ἐπικαλύψω ἐγὼ ἀπὸ Ἀβραὰμ τοῦ φίλου μου, (Gen. xviii. 17).

Συσταθ. 'Being recommended to God.' 1 Macc. xii 43, Rom iii 5, v 8, 2 Cor. iv 2. 'The gifts that come from discipline' are the fruits of the due use of Wisdom, the good works which a holy man will do, energizing from the grace given to him

15. Δῴη is undoubtedly correct. The Vulg 'dedit' probably arose from the reading 'det,' which is found in MSS. Sang. and Corb., noted by Sabatier. The Eng 'hath granted' is in accordance with the Compl. and Ald. editions, which give δέδωκε without any existing MS authority.

Κατὰ γνώμην, 'according to my opinion or wishes,' 'ex sententia' 1 Cor. vii 40 It is a prayer for eloquence, the power of expressing his thoughts.

Ἐνθυμηθῆναι, the Vulg. translates by 'praesumere,' 'to conceive thoughts,' a meaning scarcely recognized by the lexicons, though it occurs in the sense of 'imagining,' 'picturing beforehand,' in Virg. Aen xi 18·

'Arma parate animis et spe praesumite bellum.'

Δεδομένων, 'in a way worthy of the gifts bestowed upon me' The reading λεγομένων has high authority, and is received by Fr. The Eng 'that are given me' may be the rendering of the Compl. διδομένων The Marg rendering, 'are to be spoken of,' is meant for a translation of τ. λεγομένων. Vulg. 'digna horum quae mihi dantur' 'Dignus' with gen. occurs also ix 12 Plaut. Trin V ii. 29· 'non ego sum salutis dignus,' where however some read 'salute.' In a letter of Balbus to Cicero (Ad Attic viii. 15) we have: 'cogitationem dignissimam tuae virtutis' It is found with dat. 2 Macc vi 24. 'Non enim aetati nostrae dignum est.'

Αὐτὸς, emphatic, as ver 17 'He and no other' is both the guide (ὁδηγὸς) of Wisdom, leading her whither He wills, and the director of those who possess her (διορθωτὴς τῶν σοφῶν) For διορθ cp Plut. Sol. 16.

16. Ἡμεῖς Comp. Acts xvii 28 ἐν αὐτῷ ζῶμεν καὶ κινούμεθα καὶ ἐσμέν

Λόγοι. Comp. Exod. iv. 11.

Φρόνησις, practical good sense for the conduct of affairs, vi 15.

Ἐργατειῶν, 'handicrafts' Comp Exod xxxi 3, where God is said to have inspired Bezaleel: καὶ ἐνέπλησα αὐτὸν πνεῦμα θεῖον σοφίας καὶ συνέσεως καὶ ἐπιστήμης ἐν παντὶ ἔργῳ. The Vulg. gives a double translation of ἐπιστήμη, 'operum scientia et disciplina.' Some of Sabatier's MSS read 'operum scientiae disciplina' This verse is quoted by Clem. Al. Strom. vi. 11 (p 786, Potter) ἐν χειρὶ αὐτοῦ, τουτέστι, τῇ δυνάμει καὶ σοφίᾳ.

17. Εἰδέναι, κτλ, explains τ ὄντων γνῶσιν. Wisdom is an 'universitas literarum' See 1 Kings iv. 29 ff, Exod. xxxi 3. Ἡ σοφία, says Philo, de Ebriet. 22 (I. p 370), τέχνη τεχνῶν οὖσα δοκεῖ μὲν ταῖς διαφόροις ὕλαις ἐναλλάττεσθαι, τὸ δὲ αὐτῆς ἀληθὲς εἶδος ἄτρεπτον ἐμφαίνει ταῖς ὀξυδορκοῦσι.

Σύστασιν, 'constitution,' 'construction,' used by Plato in this connection, Tim vii. p 32 C· τῶν δὲ δὴ τεττάρων ἐν ὅλον ἕκαστον εἴληφεν ἡ τοῦ κόσμου ξύστασις ἐκ γὰρ πυρὸς παντὸς ὕδατός τε καὶ ἀέρος καὶ γῆς ξυνέστησεν αὐτὸν ὁ ξυνιστάς. Comp. Clem. Rom. Ep. I. Ad Cor. lx 1: σὺ τὴν ἀέναον τοῦ κόσμου σύστασιν διὰ τῶν ἐνεργουμένων ἐφανεροποίησας Philo, De Vit Cont. 8 (II p 481): ὅπερ ἐστὶν ἀρχὴ τῆς τῶν ὅλων γενέσεως καὶ συστάσεως In this passage of Wisdom the author claims the knowledge of natural philosophy S Athan, Or. c. Gent. 44, applies the word σύστασις to Christ, thus: αὐτὸς ἐπὶ πάντων ἡγεμών τε καὶ βασιλεὺς καὶ σύστασις γενόμενος τῶν πάντων

Ἐνέργειαν στοιχείων, 'the operation of the elements.' 2 Pet. iii. 10, 12. Comp Philo, De Incorr Mundi, § 21 (II p. 508): τεττάρων ὄντων στοιχείων, ἐξ ὧν ὁ κόσμος συνέστηκε, γῆς, ὕδατος, ἀέρος, πυρός

18, 19 Ἀρχὴν..θέσεις These terms would include chronology and astronomy.

18 'Beginning, ending, and midst of times,' a poetical circumlocution for the difference and variety of the periods concerned in astronomical chronology, Grimm, Gutb

Μεσότητα Vulg 'medietatem,' a word which Cicero (De Univ. vii.) scarcely acknowledges, occurs often in the Vulg, e. g. Ex. xxvi. 12, 2 Chr ix. 6.

Τροπῶν ἀλλαγὰς, sc ἡλίου, as Deut xxxiii. 14. 'The solstices.' So Hom Od xv 404. ὅθι τροπαὶ ἠελίοιο. Τροπῶν is from τροπή. The reading τρόπων, from τρόπος, which was given by Mai, is opposed to the context

Μεταβολὰς καιρῶν, not only 'changes of seasons,' but all changes produced by the position of the sun, as day and night, heat and cold, etc

19. Ἐνιαυτῶν κύκλους, 'the cycles of years,' the lunar and solar cycles, the intercalary method, the sacred and civil reckonings, etc.

Ἄστρων θέσεις, ver 29, 'positions of stars' at various times of the year. With this passage Grimm compares Cic. De Nat Deor ii 61. 'Hominum ratio non in caelum usque penetravit? Soli enim ex animantibus nos astrorum ortus, obitus, cursusque cognovimus: ab hominum genere finitus est dies, mensis, annus: defectiones solis et lunae cognitae, praedictaeque in omne posterum tempus, quae, quantae, quando futurae sint'

20 Φύσεις. θηρίων. This would comprise zoology.

Φυσ ζώων. 'Natures of animals' This includes the more general department; θυμοὺς θηρίων, 'the rage of wild beasts,' the special. This latter phrase occurs xvi 5. Comp Deut xxxii. 33· θυμὸς δρακόντων.. θυμὸς ἀσπίδων. Solomon, we are told, 1 Kings iv 33, 'spake of trees, from the cedar tree in Lebanon, even unto the hyssop that springeth out of the wall: he spake also of beasts, and of fowl, and of creeping things, and of fishes.' The Book of Proverbs teems with allusions to the life and habits of animals, e g i. 17, vi. 6-8, xxvi 2, 11; xxx 15, 19, 25-31

Πνευμάτων βίας, 'vim ventorum,' Vulg. This translation seems plainly erroneous, though the phrase does occur in this sense in Philo, De Mund. Opif. 19 (I. p. 13): *νηνεμίας καὶ βίας πνευμάτων*. Our author uses *βίας ἀνέμων*, iv 4. The enumeration of the objects of Wisdom is given in pairs connected together in thought. Πνευμ βίας is joined to *διαλογισμοὺς ἀνθρώπων* both refer to rational beings, and therefore can have nothing to do with winds The meaning doubtless is, 'the powers of spirits.' The opinion of Solomon's supremacy over the spirit-world was widely spread Thus Joseph. Ant viii 2 : *παρέσχε δ' αὐτῷ μαθεῖν ὁ Θεὸς καὶ τὴν κατὰ τῶν δαιμόνων τέχνην εἰς ὠφέλειαν καὶ θεραπείαν τοῖς ἀνθρώποις Ἐπῳδάς τε συνταξάμενος αἷς παρηγορεῖται τὰ νοσήματα, καὶ τρόπους ἐξορκώσεων κατέλειπεν, οἷς ἐνδούμενα τὰ δαιμόνια ὡς μηκέτ' ἐπανελθεῖν ἐκδιώκουσι. Καὶ αὕτη μέχρι νῦν παρ' ἡμῖν ἡ θεραπεία πλεῖστον ἰσχύει*. See Fabric, Cod. Pseud V T. vol. 1. cap. cxciv.

Διαλογισμοὺς ἀνθρ Not 'the thoughts of men,' which none but God can know, but 'reasonings,' the ways in which men reason and argue,=psychology This would also include insight into character

Διαφορὰς φυτῶν, 'differences of plants,'=botany.

Δυνάμεις ῥιζῶν, 'virtues of roots,'=pharmacy. Clem Alex quoting this passage, Strom II 2 (p 430, Pott.), remarks : *ἐν τούτοις ἅπασι τὴν φυσικὴν ἐμπεριείληφε θεωρίαν τὴν κατὰ τὸν αἰσθητὸν κόσμον ἁπάντων τῶν γεγονότων· ἑξῆς δὲ καὶ περὶ τῶν νοητῶν αἰνίττεται, δι' ὧν ἐπάγει· ὅσα τέ ἐστι κ τ λ*. On the proper use of medicines see Ecclus. xxxviii 1-15.

21. Κρυπτά Vulg. ' 'absconsa,'=abscondita. See on xviii. 9.

'All such things as are secret or manifest' include all the objects of Wisdom before mentioned. For *ἐμφανῆ* the Vulg gives 'improvisa,' reading, it may be, *ἀφανῆ*, which is found in no MS, but is quoted by Euseb Praep. Evang xi. 7. So S. Ambr de Abrah. ii 7 (p 383, Ben.).

Ἔγνων. 'Them I know,' Eng. Rather : 'I knew,' 'didici,' Vulg

22. Τεχνῖτις.. σοφία, so xiv. 2, according to some MSS God (ver 15), who used Wisdom to frame the worlds, taught him Hence he can call Wisdom his teacher, because it was through her mediately that he arrived at his knowledge. See Prov iii 19 and viii. 22-31, which tells how Wisdom was with God when He created the universe. This personifying of Wisdom is a prophecy of its use as a title of the Son of God Comp. a similar personification Ecclus xxiv. S. Aug says, De Trin. iv. 20 ' Cum pronunciatur in Scriptura aut enarratur aliquid de sapientia sive dicente ipsa sive cum de illa dicitur, Filius nobis potissimum insinuatur.'

22-viii. 1. *Properties of Wisdom; her nature and effects*

In this very fine description of Wisdom her attributes are stated to be twenty-one, in which some have seen a cabalistic use of numbers, taking that number as the product of the sacred 3 and 7, 3 being the symbol of what is divine, 7 of completion and rest. The number of epithets varies in some of the versions, but this seems to have arisen from the double translations of some words, as in the Vulg. *φιλάνθρωπος* is rendered by 'humanus,' 'benignus' For an accumulation of epithets similar to those in this passage Grimm quotes (from Nitzsch) Clem. Alex. Protr. vi 72, who gives a long catalogue of attributes to *τ' ἀγαθόν*.

Ἔστι γὰρ ἐν αὐτῇ. The reading *αὐτῇ*, found in A. and Euseb. Praep Ev vii 12, and xi 14, favours the patristic identification of Wisdom with the Holy Spirit ; a notion which is somewhat in advance of the author's theology, though half implied in ix. 17. The ideas of divine and human wisdom are not always clearly distinguished, and run up into each other. S. Method. Conv dec. Virg. vii (xviii p 121, Migne) has *τὸ τῆς σοφίας νοερὸν πνεῦμα καὶ ἅγιον καὶ μονογενές*.

Γὰρ gives the reason for the first clause of ver. 22, especially proving that Wisdom is *πάντων τεχνῖτις*. Many of the epithets in this famous passage are applicable to our Blessed Lord Comp. Heb iv. 12. S. Aug. : 'Neque enim multae, sed una sapientia est, in qua sunt immensi quidam atque infiniti thesauri rerum intelligibilium, in quibus sunt omnes invisibiles atque incommutabiles rationes rerum, etiam visibilium et mutabilium, quae per ipsam factae sunt.' De Civ XI. x 3

Νοερόν, 'intelligent,' 'intellectual.' S Greg Naz Carm lib. i § 11 83 (11 p. 303, Ben.) calls angels νόες

ἤδη μὲν καθαροὶ καὶ ἀείζωοι θεράποντες·
οὐρανὸν εὐρὺν ἔχουσιν, ἁγνοὶ νόες, ἄγγελοι ἐσθλοί.

So again, ἐπεὶ νόες εἰσιν ἐλαφροί, and ἁπλοῖ τε νοεροί τε Ib This passage has been accused of Platonism See Burton, Bampt. Lect. III. note 30. The Stoics called the Supreme Being τὸ περιέχον τὰ ὅλα νοερὸν (Cudworth, Syst. Intell. iv. 25, p 655, ed Mosh), and πνεῦμα νοερὸν καὶ πυρῶδες, Plut Plac Philos. c. vi The author uses philosophical terms to express orthodox doctrine. He nowhere oversteps the limits of Scriptural belief. We may note that Philo, De Concup 10 (II. p 356), divides the soul into νοερα, λογική, and αἰσθητική

Μονογενές, 'unicus,' Vulg 'Single in nature,' 'alone of its kind,' in opposition to πολυμερές (Heb i 1), which means 'manifold' in its attributes and operations 1 Cor xii. 11 'All these worketh that one and the self-same spirit, dividing to every man severally as He will' This epithet, as applied to the Son of God, occurs John i. 14, 18, etc. Clem. Rom Ep. I. ad Cor. xxv. uses it of the Phoenix: τοῦτο μονογενὲς ὑπάρχον For the use of μονογενής in Plato (expressing the universe figuratively) see Bunsen, God in Hist vol ii note O, Append. p 317, Eng ed

Λεπτόν, 'subtle,' 'immaterial,' beyond the ken of the natural man. 1 Cor ii 14

Εὐκίνητον (ver. 24), 'active,' 'energetic,' ever in motion.

Τρανόν, 'disertus,' Vulg, which also places this epithet before 'mobilis' (εὐκίν.) The usual word is τρανής, 'piercing.' Τρανὸς in connection with γλῶσσα is found x 21, and Is xxxv. 6, where it means 'eloquent' Here probably the signification is 'penetrating,' 'keen' So Philo, De Mund. Opif. 21 (I p 15)

Ἀμόλυντον, like the sunbeam, 'unpolluted' by its contact with earthly objects. Epict iv. 11. 8

Σαφές, 'certus,' Vulg 'Sure,' 'unerring' Euseb. Praep Ev. vii. 12 and xi. 14 omits from σαφές to ἀμέριμνον inclusive.

Ἀπήμαντον, 'suavis,' Vulg Taking it in the active sense, 'unharming,' which seems a little weak. 'Unharmed' is better, as Gutb expresses it, 'which works in everything, but is affected and influenced by none'

Φιλάγαθον 2 Tim. iii. 3; Tit. i 8; Polyb vi. 53. 9.

Ὀξύ, 'acute,' keen and sagacious.

Ἀκώλυτον, 'which cannot be letted,' Eng 'irresistible.'

Εὐεργετικόν. 'Beneficent' even to the unthankful. Luke vi 35

23. Φιλάνθρωπον the Vulg translates by two words, 'humanus,' 'benignus.'

Βέβαιον, ἀσφαλές, 'stedfast and secure' in all its operations.

Ἀμέριμνον, a litotes for αὐτάρκες, = 'self-sufficing' Gutb.

Παντοδύναμον, a new word, xi 17; xviii. 15, 'having all power' Method. p 373 A (Migne)

Πανεπίσκοπον, 'all-surveying,' overlooking all the operations of mind and nature.

Διὰ πάντων χωροῦν πνευμάτων, 'permeating, penetrating all spirits,' the intelligent, as men (νοερῶν), the pure, as angels (καθαρῶν), yea, the most subtle of all (λεπτοτάτων). The Vulg. gives · 'qui capit omnes spiritus, intelligibilis, mundus, subtilis,' reading νοερόν, καθαρόν, λεπτότατον, which is found only in one or two inferior cursive MSS For 'intelligibilis' (Ecclus. iii. 32, Vulg) see on x 4.

24–26. See Prolegomena, pp 28 f.

24 Γάρ She penetrates all spirits, for she exerts the greatest activity.

Κινήσεως, 'motion,' 'action.' 'Mobilibus,' Vulg. Reusch proposes 'motibus,' which S. Aug. indeed once reads, iii. 304.

Διήκει δὲ καὶ χωρεῖ The Vulg renders 'attingit autem ubique' Arn compares Tertullian's phrase, 'Permeator universitatis spiritus' (Apol c. 21), which, however, he attributes to Seneca. Hooker, Eccl Pol. V. lvi 5 'All things are partakers of God, they are His offspring, His influence is in them, and the personal Wisdom of God is for that very cause said to excel in nimbleness or agility, to pierce into all intellectual, pure and subtile spirits, to go through all, and to reach unto everything. Otherwise, how should the same Wisdom be that which supporteth, beareth up (Heb. i. 3), and sustaineth all?' Clem Al Strom v. 14 (p. 699, Pott.) quotes διήκει . . καθαρότητα Grimm notes that the verbs διήκειν and χωρεῖν are used by Stoical writers in connection with the spirituality and immateriality of the Anima mundi Thus he quotes Plutarch, Plac Phil 1 8 17 · οἱ Στωικοὶ θεὸν ἀποφαίνονται . . . πνεῦμα μὲν διῆκον δι' ὅλου τοῦ κόσμου, τὰς δὲ προσηγορίας μεταλαμβάνον διὰ τὰς τῆς ὕλης, δι' ἧς κεχώρηκε, παραλλάξεις. Athenag. Suppl. vi. (pp. 32, 34, ed Otto) οἱ ἀπὸ τῆς στοᾶς δι' ὕλης . . φασι τὸ πνεῦμα χωρεῖν τοῦ θεοῦ . . . διήκει δὲ δι' ὅλου τοῦ κόσμου

25 Γάρ The proof of the purity and immateriality of Wisdom.

Ἀτμὶς, (parallel with ἀπόρροια,) 'breath,' Eng Ecclus xxiv. 3 · 'I came out of the mouth of the Most High, and covered the earth as a cloud.' Usually 'vapour' It serves to show the Divine nature of Wisdom. S Ath an , quoting Dionysius, applies this passage to Christ, De Sent. Dion. 15 (I. p. 254) ἀναλόγως πάλιν ὁ Χριστὸς ἀτμὶς λέγεται· Ἀτμὶς γάρ, φησίν, ἐστι τῆς τοῦ Θεοῦ δυνάμεως

Ἀπόρροια, 'effluence,' 'emanatio quaedam,' Vulg (perhaps reading τις for τῆς) These and the following expressions prepare the way for the recognition of the Λόγος, the Son of God. There is no Platonism here The passage is quoted by Orig Cont Cels iii 72 (I p 494), who reads εἰλικρινής, and may be compared with Ecclus. i 1 , Prov. ii. 6.

Μεμιαμμένον. The usual form is μεμιασμένος, but μεμιαμμ. is found Tob. ii. 9, and in Dio Cass. 51, 52.

Orig. Fragm in Prov. (xiii p. 20, Migne), quoting memoriter, reads, οὐδὲν γὰρ εἰς αὐτὴν σκοτεινὸν ἐμπίπτει. Comp. S James iii 15

Παρεμπίπτει, lit. 'steals in unnoticed'

26. Ἀπαύγασμα, 'reflection,' or 'radiance.' The latter probably is the meaning here, 'light emitted,' 'splendour,' like φῶς ἐκ φωτὸς of the Nicene Creed. The word does not occur again in O. T S Paul, Heb i 3, speaking of Christ (it may be with this passage in his memory), calls Him ἀπαύγασμα τῆς δόξης καὶ χαρακτὴρ τῆς ὑποστάσεως αὐτοῦ See also 2 Cor. iii. 18 Philo uses the word De Mund. Op. 51 (I p 35). πᾶς ἄνθρωπος κατὰ μὲν τὴν διάνοιαν ᾠκείωται θείῳ λόγῳ, τῆς μακαρίας φύσεως ἐκμαγεῖον ἢ ἀπόσπασμα ἢ ἀπαύγασμα γεγονώς And De Concup 11, referring to the 'breath (πνεῦμα) breathed into man,' he calls it τῆς μακαρίας καὶ τρισμακαρίας φύσεως ἀπαύγασμα (II p 356) The meaning of ἀπαύγ. may be doubtful in these passages, but in the following it must be taken in the sense of 'reflection.' He is commenting on Ex. xv. 17 'Thou . . . shalt plant them . . . in the Sanctuary which Thy hands have established.' τὸ δὲ ἁγίασμα, οἷον ἁγίων ἀπαύγασμα, μίμημα ἀρχετύπου, De Plantat. § 12 (I. p. 337) S Aug (De Trinit. iv 20) uses the passage to show the consubstantiality of the Father and the Son, and indeed takes generally what is said of Wisdom to be spoken of the Son. Thus Serm. cxviii. 2. Ben. 'De sapientia Patris, quod est Filius, dictum est, Candor est enim lucis aeternae. Quaeris Filium sine Patre? Da mihi lucem sine candore. Si aliquando non erat Filius, Pater lux obscura erat Quomodo enim non obscura lux erat, si candorem non habebat? Ergo semper Pater, semper Filius Si semper Pater, semper Filius.' And this is usual among the Fathers. See Arn. and A Lap. in l. Our author probably means (primarily) that Wisdom is a divine attribute, communicated in some sort to man, and seen in creation

Ἀκηλίδωτον This word occurs in Philo, De Cherub 28 (I p 156), De Nobil 6 (II p. 443)

Ἐνεργείας, 'majestatis,' Vulg. Gutb Rather, 'operation,' 'action.' Eph. iii. 7.

Εἰκών, so Christ is called εἰκὼν τοῦ Θεοῦ, 2 Cor iv. 4. Euseb in Psalm lxxii 1 (p. 426, Ben.) gives τῆς τοῦ Πατρὸς ἐνεργείας. Orig in Matt Tom xv § 10 (III. p. 665) καὶ ὁ Σωτὴρ δέ, ὥς ἐστιν εἰκὼν τοῦ Θεοῦ ἀοράτου, οὕτως καὶ τῆς ἀγαθότητος αὐτοῦ εἰκών. So in Joann. Tom. vi § 37 (IV p. 156), and Tom xiii § 25 (IV. p 236). Cont Cels vi. 62 πᾶς ἀνήρ, οὗ Χριστός ἐστι κεφαλή, εἰκὼν καὶ δόξα Θεοῦ ὑπάρχει. For εἰκών implying not likeness only, but also representation and manifestation, see Dr. J. B Lightfoot, on Ep to Coloss i. 15. It is frequently used by Philo, e.g. De Conf. Ling. 20 (I. p. 419) τὴν εἰκόνα αὐτοῦ, τὸν ἱερώτατον λόγον. De Profug. 19 (I p 561), De Somn. I 41 (I p. 656).

27. Μία δὲ οὖσα. 'Though she is one,' with reference to the epithets ver 22, μονογενές, πολυμερές. 1 Cor. xii 11 πάντα ταῦτα ἐνεργεῖ τὸ ἓν καὶ τὸ αὐτὸ Πνεῦμα.

Μένουσα ἐν αὑτῇ. Remaining the same, without change.

Καινίζει. She is the author of all changes and spiritual renovations. Ps. civ. 30: 'Thou sendest forth Thy Spirit, they are created, and Thou renewest (ἀνακαινιεῖς) the face of the earth.' Comp Ps cii 26, 27; Heb vi 6; Rev. xxi 5. Grimm compares Aristot Phys viii 5 διὸ καὶ Ἀναξαγόρας ὀρθῶς λέγει, τὸν νοῦν ἀπαθῆ φάσκων καὶ ἀμιγῆ εἶναι, ἐπειδήπερ κινήσεως ἀρχὴν αὐτὸν ποιεῖ εἶναι· οὕτω γὰρ ἂν μόνως κινοίη ἀκίνητος ὢν καὶ κρατοίη ἀμιγὴς ὤν. S Aug, De Fid. et Symb cap iii, refers the words to the Word· 'Manet enim illud Verbum incommutabiliter: nam de ipso dictum est, cum de Sapientia diceretur, in se ipsa manens innovat omnia.'

Κατὰ γενεάς, 'per nationes,' Vulg. 'Quaque hominum aetate,' Wahl. 'Through (all) generations,' as Esth. ix 27.

Μεταβαίνουσα, passing from one to another.

Φίλους Θεοῦ. As Abraham. Comp ver. 14; 2 Chron xx. 7; Is xli. 8; Jas. ii 23. So Philo says πᾶς σοφὸς Θεοῦ φίλος Fragm ii p. 652. Comp Clem. Rom Ep ad Cor. I. x. 1. and xvii 2. Hooker, Eccl. Pol. I. v. 3, writes thus. 'With Plato what one thing more usual, than to excite men unto love of wisdom, by showing how much wise men are thereby exalted above men; how knowledge doth raise them up into heaven; how it maketh them, though not gods, yet as gods, high, admirable, and divine?'

Προφήτας. Προφήτης means 'an interpreter of God's will,' not necessarily 'one who foretells the future,' just as the Eng. word 'prophesying' is used of prediction and of preaching or interpreting. Abraham is called 'a Prophet,' Gen. xx 7, Tob iv. 12 Comp Rom. xii. 6; 1 Cor xiv 3. Nothing can be determined from this passage concerning the continuance or cessation of prophecy after the return from captivity. But see 1 Macc. iv 46, ix 27, xiv. 41 Josephus mentions various instances of prophecy in later Jewish history. Thus, Bell. Jud. I iii 5, he relates how one Judas foretold the murder of Antigonus, and (III. viii. 3 and 9) how he himself was inspired to predict certain events. He also says that the Essenes aspired to this gift, and that their predictions generally were verified by the event, Bell. Jud II viii 12 See Prolegom. p 19

Canon Liddon, after quoting some of the remarkable terms applied to Wisdom in this Book, observes (Bampton Lectures, ii. pp 94, 95, ed 1867)· 'Her [Wisdom's] sphere is not merely Palestine, but the world, not this or that age, but the history of humanity. All that is good and true in human thought is due to her· "in all ages ... prophets." Is there not here, in an Alexandrian dress, a precious and vital truth sufficiently familiar to believing Christians? Do we not already seem to catch the accents of those weighty formulae by which Apostles will presently define the pre-existent Glory of their Majestic Lord? Yet are we not steadily continuing, with no very considerable measure of expansion, in that very line of sacred thought to which the patient servant of God in the desert, and the wisest of kings in Jerusalem, have already and so authoritatively, introduced us?'

28 Οὐθέν. MSS often vary between οὐθέν and οὐδέν Vulg. gives 'neminem.'

Συνοικοῦντα, 'making a home with,' 'being wedded to.' Used commonly with φόβῳ, ἄχθει, etc.

29, 30 The arrangement of the words in these verses is very forcible.

29. Γάρ gives the reason why God loves those who are wedded to Wisdom, ver 28. It is because of the beauty and purity which she imparts to them

Θέσιν, 'order,' 'harmonious arrangement.'

30 Τοῦτο, sc φῶς Light yields its place to darkness

Ἀντισχύει, 'withstands,' 'prevails against' Diod xvii 88 (var. lect.), Dion Cass xlviii. 11, 2 Vice is never conqueror as long as a man is governed by practical Wisdom. When the wise are led astray, as Solomon was, they cease to be wise. S Bern (Serm xiv De Sept Donis) joins this verse to the next chapter (vol i. p 2343, ed Mab) 'Sapientia vincit malitiam, dum Satanam conterit Dei virtus, et Dei sapientia Christus. Attingit ergo a fine usque ad finem fortiter, in caelo quidem dejiciendo superbum, in mundo superando malignum, in inferno spoliando avarum'

CHAPTER VIII.

1. This verse is best joined to the preceding chapter, δέ carrying on the same subject, and not = 'ergo,' as the Vulg. gives it The Eng version omits the particle altogether See on vii. 30

Διατείνει, 'she reacheth,' 'extendeth herself.' This verb is used intransitively by late authors, e g. Polyb. and Diod. Thus Polyb Hist. V lxxxvi: οὕτως . . διέτεινε πρὸς Γάζαν Diod. Sic. xii 70 In Attic the intr sense is expressed by the middle voice of this verb

Ἀπὸ πέρατος εἰς πέρας 'From one end of the universe to the other.' Cp. Rom. x. 18, Philo, Vit. Mos 1. 19 (II. p 98). This passage is often quoted and explained by the Fathers, e g S Bern. I p. 2343, A, B, p. 1680, C; pp 1387, 1388 (ed Mab); Orig in Matt tom. xvi. (III. p. 712, Ben) οὗ (Jesu Christi) τὸ μέγεθος φαίνεται διατείνοντας ἀπὸ πέρατος γῆς εἰς τὸ πέρας αὐτῆς εὐρώστως, καὶ διοικοῦντος τὰς Ἐκκλησίας χρηστῶς The Antiphon in the old English Church, sung Dec 16, and still marked in the P. B. Calendar as 'O Sapientia,' is taken from this verse: 'O Sapientia, quae ex ore Altissimi prodiisti, attingens a fine usque ad finem fortiter, suaviterque disponens omnia, veni ad docendum nos viam prudentiae.' Boethius, who is said not to have quoted Scripture in his De Consol. Phil, has in this work the following words, which look like a recollection of this passage 'Est igitur, inquit, summum bonum, quod regit cunctos fortiter, suaviterque disponit,' iii 12

Εὐρώστως... χρηστῶς 'Fortiter suaviter,' Vulg 'Mightily . . sweetly,' Eng Energy and mildness ('fortiter in re,' 'suaviter in modo') are requisites of good government 'In most decent and comely sort,' says Hooker, Eccl. Pol I ii 3

2–20 *Properties of Wisdom under the representation of a Bride. how she sways all life, gives ability to govern, and largely blesses him who loves her.*

2. The author returns to his quest for Wisdom, vii. 7 ff.

Ἐξεζήτησα . ἐζήτησα. 'Exquisivi . . quaesivi,' Vulg.

Ἐκ νεότητος Ecclus vi 18: τέκνον, ἐκ νεότητός σου ἐπίλεξαι παιδείαν, καὶ ἕως πολιῶν εὑρήσεις σοφίαν

Ἀγαγέσθαι, 'to take home,' with ἐμαυτῷ, as 3 Macc 1. 12: προφερόμενος ἑαυτόν. For ἄγομαι, 'to take a wife,' comp Hom Od. vi. 159 xiv 211: ἠγαγόμην δὲ γυναῖκα. Τὸν φιλόσοφον, says Plato, De Rep vi p. 475, σοφίας φήσομεν ἐπιθυμητὴν εἶναι οὐ τῆς μέν, τῆς δ' οὔ, ἀλλὰ πάσης. S. Dionys. Areop. (i. e. the author writing under his name), quoting part of this verse, speaks of our Book as a preparation for, or an entrance into, Holy Scripture: ἐν ταῖς προεισαγωγαῖς τῶν λογίων εὑρήσεις τινὰ λέγοντα κ τ λ De Div Nom iv. 12

3. Εὐγένειαν. 'Generositatem illius glorificat,' Vulg. 'She glorifies *his* noble birth,' i.e. the lover's. Eng. 'She magnifieth *her* nobility.' One cannot be quite sure that the Vulg. did not mean 'illius' to be = 'suam,' as it uses pronouns with some irregularity, e.g. S. Luke i. 51. 'Dispersit superbos mente cordis sui,' where the use of the reflexive pronoun has misled S. Augustine, who refers 'sui,' which really represents αὐτῶν, to 'Deus.' S. Hil. in Ps. cxxvii (p. 427, C) renders 'Honestatem glorificat convictum Dei habens.' But it seems most natural to take εὐγέν. as belonging to Wisdom herself, as Calmet says: 'Elle fait voir la gloire de son origine, en ce qu'elle est étroitement unie à Dieu.' In connection with vers. 5-8 the meaning is: 'If a man wants noble birth in a bride, who is nobler born than Wisdom?' S. Aug. 'An vero generositas solet significare aliud quam parentes? Contubernium vero nonne cum ipso patre aequalitatem clamat atque asserit?' De Mor. Eccl. 28.

Συμβίωσιν Θ. ἔχουσα. Comp. ver. 9, 16. 'Dwelling with God, as a wife with her husband.' See Prov. viii. 22. Thus Philo, De Ebriet. § 8 (I. p. 361) τὸν γοῦν τόδε τὸ πᾶν ἐργασάμενον δημιουργὸν ὁμοῦ καὶ πατέρα εἶναι τοῦ γεγονότος εὐθὺς ἐν δίκῃ φήσομεν μητέρα δὲ τὴν τοῦ πεποιηκότος ἐπιστήμην, ᾗ συνὼν ὁ Θεός, οὐχ ὡς ἄνθρωπος, ἔσπειρε γένεσιν. For συμβ. comp. Ecclus. xxxi. 26, Polyb. v. 81. 2, Cic. ad Att. xiii. 23. Συμβιωτής occurs Bel and Drag. 2.

4. Γάρ. We know that God loves her because she is privy to His mysteries.

Μύστις, fem. of μύστης = μυσταγωγὸς, 'one who initiates into mysteries,' 'a teacher,' as Eng. Marg. Here, 'a teacher of God's knowledge,' which He imparts to her. Vulg., 'doctrix.' This word is found nowhere else in the Vulg. or in class. authors, but occurs in S. Aug. De Mor. Eccl. xvi, and in Serv. in Virg. Aen. xii. 159. Μύστις means sometimes 'one initiated,' and is by some so taken in this passage.

Αἱρετίς. Vulg. 'electrix,' ἅπ. λεγ. 'Lover,' Eng., is certainly wrong. The marg. rendering, 'chooser,' is correct. God shares His works with Wisdom, who chooses what His works shall be. Unusual words of similar formation to 'doctrix' and 'electrix' in Vulg. are these: 'assistrix,' ix. 4, 'apostatrix,' Ezek. ii. 3, 'auguratrix,' Isai. lvii. 3; 'provocatrix,' Zeph. iii. 1, 'criminatrix,' Tit. ii. 3, 'aversatrix,' Jer. iii. 6, 'exasperatrix,' Ezek. ii. 8.

5. Τῆς τὰ πάντα ἐργαζομένης. 'The creator and preserver of all things.' S. Aug. De Mor. Eccl. i. 698 A. 'Quodsi honestas est possessio quae concupiscitur in vita, quid sapientia est honestius, quae omnia operatur?' Comp. Prov. viii. 18: 'Riches and honour are with me, yea, durable riches and righteousness,' and 2 Chron. i. 12.

6. 'If practical intelligence is wanted in a bride, where can it be found better than in Wisdom?' Comp. Prov. xxxi. 10 ff.

Τίς αὐτῆς τῶν ὄντων μ. ε. τεχν., 'Quis horum quae sunt.. artifex?' Vulg. The Eng., 'Who of all that are?' is opposed to the collocation of the words and to the parallel τὰ πάντα, ver. 5. Translate 'Who more than she is the artificer of all things that are?'

Τεχνίτης. This has been altered into τεχνῖτις as vii. 22; but it is not uncommon to find the masc. substantive as predicate to the feminine. So xiv. 2, in some MSS.

7. Δικαιοσύνην in its fullest sense, including all virtues, and among the four cardinal virtues δικαιοσύνην in a more restricted signification = 'justice.' Clem. Al., Strom. vi. 11 (p. 788, Pott.), has σωφροσύνη καὶ φρόνησις ἐκδιδάσκει δικαιοσύνην καὶ ἀνδρείαν κ.τ.λ.

Οἱ πόνοι ταύτης. 'Her (Wisdom's) labours among men are virtues.' Vulg.: 'Labores hujus magnas habent virtutes,' which waters down the forcible expression of the Greek. Πόνοι may well mean 'the produce of labour,' as x. 10, where see note.

Σωφροσύνην. Here are named the four cardinal virtues of Greek Ethics, σωφροσύνη, φρόνησις, δικαιοσύνη, and ἀνδρεία. In 4 Macc. v. 22, 23 the four virtues are σωφροσύνη, ἀνδρεία, δικαιοσύνη, and εὐσέβεια; but i. 18 we read τῆς δὲ σοφίας ἰδέαι καθεστᾶσι φρόνησις καὶ δικαιοσύνη καὶ ἀνδρεία καὶ σωφροσύνη. With the latter enumeration agrees Philo, Quod Omn. Prob. § 10 (II.

875), and Leg. Alleg. i. 19 (I 56), where he speaks of the four rivers of Eden: διὰ τούτων βούλεται τὰς κατὰ μέρος ἀρετὰς ὑπογράφειν. Εἰσὶ δὲ τὸν ἀριθμὸν τέσσαρες, φρόνησις, σωφροσύνη, ἀνδρία, δικαιοσύνη. This is derived from the Platonic school. Cicero, De Fin. v. 23 § 67 'Proprium suum cujusque munus est, ut Fortitudo in laboribus periculisque cernatur; Temperantia in praetermittendis voluptatibus, Prudentia in delectu bonorum et malorum; Justitia in suo cuique tribuendo.' Comp. De Off. i. 5. See Tit. ii 11, 12, and for the Christian virtues, Faith, Hope, and Charity, 1 Cor. xiii.

Ἐκδιδάσκει, 'she teacheth thoroughly,' 'edocet' 4 Macc. v 22: σωφροσύνην γὰρ ἡμᾶς ἐκδιδάσκει

Ὧν χρησιμώτερον Past. Herm. Mand. viii. 9: τούτων ἀγαθώτερον οὐδέν ἐστιν ἐν τῇ ζωῇ τῶν ἀνθρώπων Ecclus. xxv. 11; xl. 27.

8 Πολυπειρίαν, 'wide experience.' Ecclus xxv. 6. But as experience cannot be concerned with the future (τὰ μέλλοντα), the word is probably used in a secondary sense = 'great knowledge.' So Vulg. 'multitudinem sapientiae,' in which signification Wahl quotes Ael. Var. Hist. iv. 19. This verse is partially quoted by Clem. Al., Strom. vi. 8. (p. 755, Pott), who has εἰκάζει.

Εἰκάζει seems more correct than εἰκάζειν, for 'to conjecture things of old' is absurd as said by an unscientific Jew. What is meant is, that Wisdom, in her perfection of knowledge, knows the past and conjectures the future. In the 'locus classicus' about Calchas, Hom. Il. i. 70, it is said:

ὃς ᾔδη τά τ' ἐόντα, τά τ' ἐσσόμενα, πρό τ' ἐόντα.

Στροφὰς λόγ 'Subtilties of words' 'Breviter, sententiose et acute dicta,' Wahl. Applied to proverbs, Prov. i. 3. Comp. Ecclus. xxxix. 2, 3 'He will keep the sayings of the renowned men, and where subtle parables are (ἐν στροφαῖς παραβολῶν), he will be there also. He will seek out the secrets of grave sentences (παροιμιῶν), and be conversant in dark parables (ἐν αἰνίγμασι παραβολῶν).'

Αἰνιγμάτων 'Argumentorum,' Vulg. Forsit. 'aenigmatum,' Reusch. The word is used of the 'hard questions' of the Queen of Sheba, 1 Kings x. 1 Comp. Numb. xii. 8, 1 Cor. xiii 12 For instances of aenigmas see Ezek. xvii. 3 ff., and Judg xiv 12, 14, and 1 Esdr. iii. and iv.

Σημεῖα καὶ τέρατα, x 16 This expression has been imported into the N T., e.g. S John iv. 48; Acts ii. 19 Comp Jer xxxix. 20 Σημεῖον is a 'sign' or 'credential' of a mission from God, not necessarily supernatural τέρας is a 'portent' or 'prodigy' transcending experience. See Trench, Syn of N T. pt. ii

Προγινώσκει, 'foreseeth,' Eng. Rather, 'understandeth beforehand,' 'interprets their meaning'

Καιρῶν, definite part of time, χρόνων, indefinite, translated in Vulg. 'saeculorum.' Comp. Acts i 7, 1 Thess. v. 1; Dan. ii 21. The two words are clearly distinguished in Dem (?) Contr Naeer. p. 1357, 2 ἦν δὲ ὁ χρόνος οὗτος ᾧ Ἀστεῖος μὲν ἦν ἄρχων Ἀθήνησιν, ὁ καιρὸς δὲ ἐν ᾧ ἐπολεμεῖθ᾽ ὑμεῖς πρὸς Λακεδαιμονίους τὸν ὕστερον πόλεμον Schaf. in loc 'χρόνος simpliciter tempus καιρὸς tale tempus, cujus sit momentum in causa de qua agitur.'

9 Ἀγαγέσθαι, see on ver. 2. Πρὸς συμβίωσ. ver. 3.

Σύμβουλ. ἀγαθῶν, 'giving counsel by which I might obtain all good things.' 'Mecum communicabit de bonis,' Vulg.

Παραίνεσις, usually taken as = παραμυθία, 'comfort,' of which sense it is difficult to find another example, though the Vulg. 'allocutio,' which is used to signify 'an address for the sake of consolation,' shows how the above sense is obtained. So 'alloqui' and 'alloquium' are used. See Orell in Hor Epod xiii. 18, and note on ch. iii. 18 In S John xi. 31 instead of the usual reading, 'consolabantur eam,' MS Corb. gives 'adloquebantur eam'

Φροντίδων. 'Cogitationis,' Vulg. 'Cogitatio,' in the sense of 'anxiety,' 'care,' is uncommon In this signification 'cogitatus' occurs Ecclus. xxxi 1, 2

10-16 These verses are in thought dependent on εἰδὼς ὅτι, ver. 9, and express Solomon's hopes and expectations when he was seeking after Wisdom

10. Δι' αὐτήν 'On account of her,' as the final cause. So ver. 13, where Eng. wrongly changes the translation.

Ὁ νέος. Solomon says, 1 Kings iii. 7 'I am but a little child.' Comp. ch. ix. 5. Ecclus. xlvii. 14.

11. Ἐν κρίσει. This refers doubtless to Solomon's famous judgment, 1 Kings iii. 16–28, where it is said that 'all Israel feared the king, for they saw that the wisdom of God was in him, to do judgment.' The Vulg. adds at the end of the verse. 'et facies principum mirabuntur me;' a clause which has arisen from a double translation of the Greek. 'Of a quick conceit,' Eng. 'Conceit' is conception, thought, understanding. Comp. Shakesp., The Merchant of Venice, I. i.

'With purpose to be dressed in an opinion
Of wisdom, gravity, profound conceit'

12. Περιμενοῦσι, 'sustinebunt.' 'Sustinere,' in the sense of 'to wait,' occurs often in Vulg., e.g. Ps. xxiv. 3, Ecclus. i. 29, xxxvi. 18.

Προσέξουσιν, sc. τὸν νοῦν, 'give heed.' Comp. xiii. 1, xiv. 30; Acts viii. 6; 1 Tim. i. 4.

Λαλοῦντος ἐπὶ πλεῖον 'When I discourse at greater length.' Suppl. μου. So 2 Macc. xii. 36: τῶν δὲ περὶ τὸν Ἔσδριν ἐπὶ πλεῖον μαχομένων.

Χεῖρα. An expression implying keeping the utmost silence, as in Job xxi. 5; xxix. 9, etc., Ecclus. v. 12.

13. 'Praeterea,' Vulg. 'Moreover,' Eng. There is nothing to answer to this in the Greek.

Ἀθανασίαν (parall. with μνήμ. αἰών.), 'immortal fame.' Comp. iv. 1. The word has a higher meaning ver. 17 and xv. 3. The MS. Ephr. (C) here adds a clause commencing καὶ τιμὴν παρά, the rest being illegible. It is found nowhere else.

Μνήμ. αἰών. Ps. cxi. 6: εἰς μνημόσυνον αἰώνιον ἔσται δίκαιος.

14. Λαούς, 'my own people.' Ἔθνη, 'foreign nations.' Solomon is represented speaking as an ideal king. Grimm. So ver. 15. Comp. 1 Kings iv. 21, 24.

15. Με, with φοβηθ.

Ἀκούσαντες, 'when they hear of me.'

Ἐν πλήθει, 'my own people,' contrasted with ἐν πολέμῳ. 'Good and gentle to my subjects, and brave in war.' Comp. Hom. Il. iii. 179:

ἀμφότερον, βασιλεύς τ' ἀγαθὸς, κρατερός τ' αἰχμητής.

Πλῆθος used absolutely, as 1 Esdr. viii. 88. κλαυθμὸς γὰρ ἦν μέγας ἐν τῷ πλήθει. Dr. Bissel, following Bunsen (Bibelwerk), translates 'in counsel,' or 'the popular assembly.' But this is an idea quite foreign to our author's notions.

*16. Εἰσελθών, 'returning to private life, I shall rest at her side, as by a beloved wife.'

For προσαναπ. comp. Polyb. iv. 73. 3, Jos. Ant. xx. 2. 1.

Συναναστροφή. 3 Macc. ii. 31, 33, Diod. Sic. iii. 18.

Εὐφροσύνην κ. χαράν. 1 Macc. v. 54. Ps. l. 10 ἀκουτιεῖς με ἀγαλλίασιν καὶ εὐφροσύνην. Joel i. 16, Isai. xxii. 13, li. 3, S. Luke i. 14. Aristot. Eth. Nic. x. 7. ἡδίστη τῶν κατ' ἀρετὴν ἐνεργειῶν ἡ κατὰ τὴν σοφίαν ὁμολογουμένως ἐστίν. δοκεῖ γοῦν ἡ φιλοσοφία θαυμαστὰς ἡδονὰς ἔχειν καθαριότητι καὶ τῷ βεβαίῳ.

17. Ταῦτα, the considerations mentioned in vers. 3–16.

Ἀθανασία, v. 13.

Ἐν συγγενείᾳ, 'in affinity with Wisdom,' speaking still of Wisdom as a bride who imparts of her possessions to her husband. Comp. Eccles. vii. 12 περισσεία γνώσεως τῆς σοφίας ζωοποιήσει τὸν παρ' αὐτῆς.

18. Ἐν φιλίᾳ, 'married love,' parallel with συγγεν., ver. 17.

Τέρψις ἀγαθή, 'pure delight.' Ecclus. xiv. 14. ἐπιθυμίας ἀγαθῆς. The Eng. 'great pleasure,' is feeble.

'In the works of her hands are infinite riches.' Comp. the description of a good wife, Prov. xxxi. 10–31; and Eccles vii. 11, 12.

Πλοῦτος. Vulg., 'honestas.' See on vii. 11.

Ἀνεκλιπής, 'that fadeth not away,' as vii. 14. S. Luke xii. 33 θησαυρὸν ἀνέκλειπτον.

Ἐν συγγυμν. ὁμιλίας αὐτ. 'In the practice of intercourse with her.' S. Paul exhorts Timothy γύμναζε σεαυτὸν πρὸς εὐσέβειαν, 1 Tim. iv. 7, 8.

Εὔκλεια Vulg., 'praeclaritas,' ἅπ λεγ See on vii 5 'Fame, in the participation of her words'

19 After describing the qualities of the bride, the author mentions what the suitor has to offer on his part.

Ἤμην, as in S. John xvi 4, etc

Εὐφυής, 'of good natural parts,' referring to body and disposition, and explained by what follows, ψυχῆς τε ἔλαχον and ἦλθον εἰς σῶμα ἀμίαντον Gutb The passage has been interpreted of the pre-existence and Incarnation of Christ. Thus S. Aug., De Gen ad Lit. lib. x. cap. 18, of which chapter the heading in the Bened ed is 'De anima Christi, an possit in ipsum convenire illud, "Puer autem ingeniosus eram?" etc' He says here 'Neque enim negligendi sunt, seu errent, seu verum sapiant, qui hoc specialiter et singulariter de anima illa dictum putant mediatoris Dei et hominum hominis Christi Jesu.'

Ἔλαχον, 'I obtained,' a word which, as it might convey a wrong impression, as if the soul was a fortuitous addition, the writer corrects by μᾶλλον δέ, ver. 20 So that the whole passage may be thus paraphrased 'I was by nature endowed with good qualities of body and soul, or rather, it was because my soul was good and pure that a corresponding body was given it, and thus the εὐφυΐα was brought about' The author thus maintains that men are not 'born at all adventure' (ii 2), but come into the world by God's appointment See Church Quart Rev Apr. 1874, art. 'The Book of Wisdom' Compare Isai lvii. 16 πνεῦμα γὰρ παρ' ἐμοῦ ἐξελεύσεται, καὶ πνοὴν πᾶσαν ἐγὼ ἐποίησα. Jer. xxxviii (xlv Sept) 16. That the soul comes from God is maintained by Solomon, Eccles ii 21; xii 7 Cp. Zech xii. 1 These passages seem to favour the doctrine of Creationism, i e that souls are not derived by propagation from parents (which is Traducianism), but are created by God, and infused into the child before birth. S. Aug., commenting on this passage, says 'Magis enim videtur adtestari opinioni, qua non ex una propagari, sed desuper animae venire creduntur ad corpora' De Gen ad Lit lib x.

cap vii § 12. And again, interpreting S. John i 9, he says 'Fortasse hoc dictum est ad discernendum spiritalem illuminationem ab ista corporali quae sive per caeli luminaria, sive quibusque ignibus illuminat oculos carnis, ut hominem interiorem dixerit venientem in hunc mundum, quia exterior corporeus est, sicut hic mundus; tanquam diceret, Illuminat omnem hominem venientem in corpus, secundum illud quod scriptum est "Sortitus sum . incoinquinatum"' De Peccat Merit i. 25 § 38

Ψυχῆς ἀγαθῆς 'Dicendum animam bonam hoc loco intelligi non bonitate morali,' aut gratiae justificantis, sed bonitate naturali, quae est quaedam ad multas virtutes morales, in quibusdam hominibus, dispositio, ex qua dicuntur esse bona indole, et bonas habere propensiones' Estius, in l.

20 Μᾶλλον δέ the Vulg takes with ἀγαθός, 'magis bonus' (cp. 'magis versutus,' Plaut. Asin. I. i 105), which is plainly wrong It is a common form of correcting a previous statement, and here it modifies ἔλαχον, ver 19 See above. Agreeably with this view, Mr. Churton paraphrases thus 'If I should not rather say that I myself am the immortal soul, the offspring of God, the Father of spirits from whom that soul derived its goodness and generous nature, and came into a body that was free from blemish, and fitted to be its servant and instrument.' From this passage it is inferred that the author believed in the pre-existence of souls, an idea supposed to be foreign to the purely Hebrew thought, and introduced from Plato and Pythagoras Josephus, however (Bell. Jud. II viii. 11, 14), mentions that the Pharisees believed that the souls of good men passed into other bodies, and that the Essenes held that souls pre-existed, and were drawn into bodies by a natural yearning (ἴυγγί τινι) The doctrine is found in the Talmud, e g Chagiga, 12 b, and in the Kabbalah According to this all souls pre-exist in the World of Emanations, and are without exception destined to inhabit human bodies, and pursue their course upon earth for a certain number of years Hence we are told that 'when the Holy One wished

to create the world, the universe was before Him in idea. He then formed all the souls which were destined for the whole human race All were minutely before Him in the same form which they were to assume in the human body' Ginsburg, The Kabbalah, pp 31, 32 Philo has many passages on this subject. Thus De Somn 22 (I. pp 641, 642)· οὗτος δέ (ὁ ἀὴρ) ἐστι ψυχῶν ἀσωμάτων οἶκος . τούτων τῶν ψυχῶν αἱ μὲν κατίασιν ἐνδεθησόμεναι σώμασι θνητοῖς, ὅσαι προσγειόταται καὶ φιλοσώματοι αἱ δὲ ἀνέρχονται, διακριθεῖσαι πάλιν κατὰ τοὺς ὑπὸ φύσεως ὁρισθέντας ὁρισμοὺς καὶ χρόνους. See also De Mundo, 3 (II p 604), and De Gigant. 2, 3 (I pp 263, 264) Traces of this opinion are said to be found in Deut xxix 14, 15; Job xxxviii 19-21, Sept., and in S John ix. 2, where the Apostles ask Christ whether the blind man or his parents had sinned that he was born with this infirmity But this passage is capable of another interpretation. The author's opinion certainly is not identical with the Neo-Platonic, for by speaking of σῶμα ἀμίαντον he plainly does not consider all matter necessarily evil Nor is it the same as Philo's, who deems that souls are confined in bodies as punishment for sins committed in their disembodied state ; while here the soul is good, and on that account is sent into a pure body. The doctrine of the pre-existence of souls has been condemned in Christian times as heretical (e g in the Second Council of Constantinople), and those who hold the inspiration of the Book of Wisdom are necessarily obliged to refuse to see it in this passage But the plain meaning of the words points to some such opinion, which indeed may be held in an orthodox manner, as that in God's foreknowledge and purpose all souls pre-exist (see quotations on ver 19), and that they descend from Him Isai xlix 1, 5, Jer i 5. Tertull, de Anim Artic 11, says ' Consequens est, ut ex Dei flatu animam professi, initium ei deputemus. Hoc Plato excludit, innatam et infectam animam volens· et natam autem docemus et factam, ex initii constitutione.' The author says nothing of what is called the transmigration of souls, nor that God made some souls good and others evil.

Ἦλθον The personality in ἦλθον and ἤμην, ver 19, is rather confused, as we use the term 'I' sometimes of body and soul regarded as an unity, sometimes of soul alone

Ἀμίαντον There is no question here of original sin The author seems to hold that there is a kind of harmony between soul and body, and that the purity of the former necessitates a pure corporeal receptacle. That the outward form does in some measure express the inward character we all allow. The passage has been interpreted of the Incarnation of Christ, to which it readily accommodates itself. See on ver. 19.

21. *Wisdom is the gift of God in answer to prayer.*

Ἐγκρατής Vulg · 'Et ut sciri quoniam aliter non possem esse continens.' S. Aug quotes the passage as referring to the grace of continency. De S. Virgin § 43 (tom iv. 362 g); Confess vi 11, Serm. clx 7 But there is no question of chastity here, and the word 'continens' may mean 'possessed of,' 'participant of,' as Ecclus xv. 1 : 'continens justitiae,' ἐγκρατὴς τοῦ νόμου Certainly the Eng is right : 'that I could not otherwise obtain her,' i e Wisdom. Ἐγκρατής occurs in the same sense Ecclus vi 27 : ἐγκρατὴς γενόμενος μὴ ἀφῆς αὐτήν (σοφίαν)

Καὶ τοῦτο χάρις A parenthesis 'And this was a part of good sense,' viz to know whose gift Wisdom is Comp S James i. 5, 17.

Ἐνέτυχον, 'I addressed,' 'approached in prayer.' Comp xvi 28, 3 Macc vi. 37, Rom xi 2; Hebr. vii 25

Ἐξ ὅλης τῆς καρδίας μου This expression occurs Deut. vi. 5, Josh. xxii. 5, and elsewhere, *e.g.* S. Mark xii 30

CHAPTER IX.

1–18 *Solomon's Prayer for Wisdom.*

1 For Solomon's Prayer see 1 Kings iii. 6 ff; 2 Chron i 8 ff.

Θεέ This late vocative is found in Deut iii 24, Ecclus xxiii 4, S Matt xxvii 46 See Const Ap viii. 37

Κύριε τοῦ ἐλέους. Comp. 2 Cor. i. 3. Πατὴρ τῶν οἰκτιρμῶν, and 1 Pet. v 10 Θεὸς πάσης χάριτος The reading ἐλέους σου seems to have been derived from the words below, ἐν λόγῳ σου; or the reading may have been σὺ ἐποίησας, which receives some support from the var κατεσκεύασας in the next verse

Ἐν λόγ. Ἐν, instrumental. Ps. xxxiii. 6. 'By the word of the Lord were the heavens made' Ἐν λόγ. is parallel with τῇ σοφίᾳ σου, ver 2, and adumbrates the Personal Word, as S. John i 3

2 Δεσπόζῃ Gen. i 26; Ps viii 7 Past Herm. Vis III c iv. 1 οἷς παρέδωκεν ὁ Κύριος πᾶσαν τὴν κτίσιν αὐτοῦ αὔξειν καὶ οἰκοδομεῖν καὶ δεσπόζειν τῆς κτίσεως πάσης.

3 Ἐν ὁσιότ. κ δικαιοσ. Comp S. Luke i. 75, Eph iv. 24 Ὁσιότ. 'piety towards God,' δικαιοσ 'conformity to law,' 'justice towards man'

Εὐθύτητι, 'rectitude,' 'straightforwardness of purpose' 1 Kings iii. 6.

4. Θρόνων, plur. of majesty. So ver. 12, and xviii. 15. Ps. cxxi. 5 ἐκεῖ ἐκάθισαν θρόνοι εἰς κρίσιν, θρόνοι ἐπὶ οἶκον Δαυίδ.

Πάρεδρον, 'assessor.' Prov viii 27 'When He prepared the heavens, I (Wisdom) was there' Ecclus i 1 'All wisdom cometh from the Lord, and is with Him for ever' Philo (Vit Mos. II. p 142) speaks of Justice as being πάρεδρος τῷ Θεῷ. Thus Pind Ol. viii. 28·

Διὸς ξενίου πάρεδρος θέμις.

Soph Oed. Col. 1382 Δίκη ξύνεδρος Ζηνός. The Vulg. gives 'assistricem,' ἅπ. λεγ See on viii 4 'Assestrix' occurs in Afran ap Non. Marcell 73, 29 The passage in the text seems to identify Wisdom with the Word of God. S John i 1 1 Cor. i. 24· Χριστὸν Θεοῦ δύναμιν καὶ Θεοῦ σοφίαν.

Ἀποδοκιμάσῃς, 'reject as unqualified.' Comp Ps cxvii. 22, S Matt xxi. 42, Hebr. xii. 17.

Ἐκ παίδων, 'from the number of Thy children' If God gave him not Wisdom, it would prove that he was not of the children of God Comp ii 13

5 Ὅτι introduces a consideration why God should hear his prayer. 'For I am Thy servant,' etc

'Son of Thy handmaid' (Ex xxiii 12), and therefore doubly Thy servant, according to the Hebrew law, which regarded slaves' children ('born in the house,' Gen xiv. 14, Eccl ii. 7) as slaves The phrase 'son of Thy handmaid' is common in O. T Comp. Ps. lxxxv 16; cxv 7.

Ὀλιγοχρόνιος, referring to the shortness of man's life, not to his own youth

Ἐλάσσων. Vulg. 'minor ad intellectum.' 'Too weak to understand' 1 Kings iii 7 'I am but a little child I know not how to go out or come in.' Comp ch viii 10.

6 Κἂν γάρ τις Orig. Contr. Cels vi 13 (I 639, Ben)

Τέλειος. 'Consummatus,' Vulg. 'Perfect in natural endowments,' 'accomplished.' With this verse comp 1 Cor. xiii. 1–3, and 2 Tim. iii. 16, 17. Orig in Matt. t. x 19 (III p 467, Ben) τὸ γεγραμμένον περὶ σοφίας ἐφαρμόσεις, καὶ τῇ πίστει καὶ ταῖς ἀρεταῖς κατ' εἶδος, ὥστε τοιοῦτον ποιῆσαι λόγον Κἂν γάρ τις ᾖ τέλειος ἐν πίστει ἐν υἱοῖς ἀνθρώπων, τῆς ἀπό σου δυνάμεως ἀπούσης, εἰς οὐδὲν λογισθήσεται. He goes on to apply the same words to Temperance and Justice, quoting Jer. ix. 23.

7, 8 Another reason for the need of Wisdom is that he was chosen to rule Israel and to build the Temple

7 Προείλω, 'Thou chosest me,' perhaps with the

additional notion of his being preferred to his elder brothers 1 Chr xxviii 4, 5; 2 Chr i. 9 Some think that there is here an allusion to Nathan's prediction, 2 Sam vii 12, some nine years before Solomon's birth

Υἱῶν σου κ. θυγατ. Isai xliii. 6, 7, compared with 2 Cor vi 18.

8 Εἶπας 2 Sam vii. 13; 1 Kings v 5, Ecclus xlvii 13

Ὄρει ἁγίῳ σου· Moriah, hallowed already by Abraham's sacrifice, and the altar reared by David in the threshing-floor of Araunah, 2 Sam xxiv. 16, 25 Comp. Ps. xcviii. 9. προσκυνεῖτε εἰς ὄρος ἅγιον αὐτοῦ.

Κατασκηνώσεως. 'Of thy dwelling' = where Thou dwellest. Comp Ps xlvi 4 (xlv 5, Tisch): 'the holy place of the tabernacles (τὸ σκήνωμα) of the most High.' 2 Macc. xiv. 35 And S John i 14· 'The Word was made flesh, and dwelt (ἐσκήνωσεν) among us'

Μίμημα, in app. to ναὸν and θυσιαστ Solomon's Temple was a reproduction of the First Tabernacle, the pattern of which was shown to Moses in the Mount. Ex xxv. 9, 40, Acts vii 44, Hebr viii 5 This was an image of the heavenly Temple Rev xv 5. Burton (Bampt. Lect.) and others see here a trace of Plato's doctrine of Ideas, but the author has the warrant of Scripture for all he says. Clem Al Strom. iv 8 (p 593): εἰκὼν τῆς οὐρανίου ἐκκλησίας ἡ ἐπίγειος.

Ἀπ' ἀρχῆς As Christ is the Lamb slain from the foundation of the world (Rev xiii 8), so the Temple and altar are ἀπ' ἀρχῆς Gutb

9. Μετὰ σοῦ 'Wisdom is (not 'was') with Thee,' an elucidation of πάρεδρος, ver. 4 Vulg: 'Sapientia tua.' S. Aug, De Mor. Eccl. i. 698, C, quotes 'tecum Sapientia' without 'tua'

Παροῦσα Comp Prov viii 22-30, S John i. 1 Hom Od xiii 393.

καὶ λίην τοι ἐγώγε παρέσσομαι, οὐδέ με λήσεις.

Εὐθὲς, from εὐθὴς = εὐθύς It occurs 2 Sam xix. 18, Ps xxxii 4, xci. 16, etc Philo, Leg All. 74 (I p 129).

Ἐν ἐντολαῖς σου 'According to Thy commandments.'

10 Ἁγίων οὐρ Ps xix 7: ἐξ οὐρανοῦ ἁγίου αὐτοῦ.

Πέμψον. Vulg and Eng omit this word, but it is found in all MSS There may be a distinction intended between ἐξαπόστ. and πεμψ, the former implying the sending forth of one to represent the sender, the latter denoting that the sender accompanies or escorts his messenger See Sewell, Microsc of the N. T pp 12-14

Κοπιάσῃ 'That she may be with me in my labours.'

11 Συνιεῖ. The form συνιέω = συνίημι is late. It occurs Jer xx 12, Tob iii 8, S Matt xiii 13, etc.

Ἐν τῇ δόξῃ αὐτῆς 'In sua potentia,' Vulg, so Eng. 'in her power.' Commentators compare Rom. vi 4 'by the glory of the Father,' where, they say, δόξης is used in the sense of 'power,' which is not necessarily the case Grimm explains it, 'in her brightness,' which keeps a man from straying out of the right path. Gutberlet translates· 'through her counsel,' making the expression parallel with σωφρόνως Δόξη seems to be used of the 'glorious attributes' of wisdom, including power, and counsel So 'by (ἐν) her glory' means 'by her operations' The expressions in Ps lxxii. 24 are somewhat similar, though the notion is different ἐν τῇ βουλῇ σου ὡδήγησάς με, καὶ μετὰ δόξης προσελάβου με.

12 Προσδεκτὸς occurs Prov xi. 20; xvi 15, Clem. Al p 849 Martyr S. Polyc. 14 ἐν θυσίᾳ πίονι καὶ προσδεκτῇ.

Διακρινῶ 'Disponam,' Vulg 'I shall judge,' merely an intensitive form of κρινῶ. See on i 1 The actual prayer seems to end here, though the rest of the Book is mostly addressed to God

Θρόνων See on ver. 4

13 Γάρ. The connection seems to be this· 'To rule aright the holy people of Israel demands more than human knowledge, and this cannot be attained without wisdom, the special gift of God,' ver. 17.

Τίς γάρ. Comp 1 Cor. ii 16 . τίς γὰρ ἔγνω νοῦν

Κυρίου, Rom. xi. 34 : τίς γὰρ ἔγνω νοῦν Κυρίου ; ἢ τίς σύμβουλος αὐτοῦ ἐγένετο, S Paul may have had this passage from Wisdom in his mind, but the words are found also in Isaiah xl 13, whence doubtless our author derived them.

Ἐνθυμηθήσ., 'shall think.'

Τί used for ὅ τι, as in the indirect question.

14. Δειλοί, 'poor,' 'weak,' or 'uncertain,' 'wavering' Comp. Homer's use of δειλοὶ βροτοί. See Ps. xciii. 11, 1 Cor. iii. 20.

Ἐπίνοιαι, 'notions,' 'devices.' Vulg 'Providentiae' The plur. of 'providentia' is of very late use. Tertull. Adv. Marc. ii. 4 : 'Agnosce bonitatem Dei ex providentiis' So S Aug De Trinit. iii. § 21 (viii 805 A, Ben.); S. Fulg De Verit. Praed. ii. 11.

Ἐπισφαλεῖς, 'insecure,' 'not safe,' iv 4 In Acts xxvii. 9, 'dangerous.'

15. The thought of this verse is common to heathen and Christian writers alike Comp Hor. Sat. II. ii. 77–79 ; Virg. Aen vi. 730–734. Cic. Somn Scip iii : 'Ii vivunt qui e corporum vinculis tanquam e carcere evolaverunt.' De Senect xxi : 'Dum sumus in his inclusi compagibus corporis, munere quodam necessitatis et gravi opere perfungimur. Est enim animus caelestis ex altissimo domicilio depressus et quasi demersus in terram, locum divinae naturae aeternitatique contrarium.' Comp for the Scriptural view Rom vii. 23 ; 2 Cor. v. 1–4 Thus Philo, de Migr. Abrah 2 (I. p 437) ἄπελθε ἐκ τοῦ περὶ σεαυτὸν γεώδους, τὸ παμμίαρον, ὦ οὗτος, ἐκφυγὼν δεσμωτήριον, τὸ σῶμα. Joseph. Cont. Ap. ii. 24 καὶ γὰρ ἐμφυομένη σώμασι κακοπαθεῖ ἡ ψυχή, καὶ τούτων αὖ πάλιν ὡς θανάτῳ διακριθεῖσα S Aug says : 'Non corpus aggravat animum (nam et tunc habebimus corpus), sed "corpus quod corrumpitur." Ergo carcerem facit non corpus, sed corruptio.' Enarr. in Ps. cxli. 19 Comp Serm clxxx 3, Ben

Τὸ γεῶδες σκῆνος, amplified by S. Paul 2 Cor. v. 1. ἡ ἐπίγειος ἡμῶν οἰκία τοῦ σκήνους, and ver. 4 . οἱ ὄντες ἐν τῷ σκήνει στενάζομεν βαρούμενοι. Comp Plat Phaedo, cap xxx. p. 81 C · ἐμβριθὲς δέ γε τοῦτο [τὸ σῶμα] οἴεσθαι χρὴ εἶναι καὶ βαρὺ καὶ γεῶδες καὶ ὁρατόν· ὃ δὴ καὶ ἔχουσα ἡ

τοιαύτη ψυχὴ βαρύνεται. Philo, De Somn. I. 20 (I. p 639). τὸν συμφυᾶ τῆς ψυχῆς οἶκον, τὸ σῶμα. De Migr Abrah 36 (I p. 467) τοῖς ἀγγείοις τῆς ψυχῆς, σώματι καὶ αἰσθήσει. Comp Ep ad Diognet 6, and 2 S Pet i. 14

Νοῦν and ψυχὴν seem here to be identical

Πολύφροντις. Usually, 'full of care,' here 'full of thought' Vulg. : 'multa cogitantem.' Eng . 'that museth upon many things.'

16 S John iii 12 : 'If I have told you earthly things (τὰ ἐπίγεια), and ye believe not, how shall ye believe, if I tell you of heavenly things (τὰ ἐπουράνια) ?'

Μόγις, so (not μόλις) Orig De. Orat (xi. 416), quoting vers 13–16

Τὰ ἐν χερσίν. Sin. gives τ. ε ποσὶν, which has much the same meaning, 'things immediately before us' Vulg. : 'quae in prospectu sunt.' Comp. 4 Esdr. iv. 21 · 'Quemadmodum terra silvae data est et mare fluctibus suis, sic et qui super terram inhabitant quae sunt super terram intellegere solummodo possunt, et qui super caelos quae super altitudinem caelorum.'

Ἐξιχνίασεν. If the Vulg. 'investigabit' is not simply an error for 'investigavit,' it conveys the reading of two cursive MSS. ἐξιχνιάσει. There is no variation to account for 'sciet' instead of 'scivit' in the following verse Hooker (Eccl Pol. I. vii 7) renders these two verses thus · 'A corruptible body is heavy unto the soul, and the earthly mansion keepeth down the mind that is full of cares And hardly can we discern the things that are upon earth, and with great labour find we out the things which are before us. Who can then seek out the things that are in heaven ?'

17. Βουλήν, what God means man to do.

Εἰ μὴ σὺ ἔδωκας 'Unless Thou gavest' as Thou hast done.

Σοφίαν. Πνεῦμα. Here is an identification of the Wisdom and the Holy Spirit of God. Comp Ecclus. xxiv. 3 . 'I [Wisdom] came out of the mouth of the Most High, and covered the earth as a cloud' 1 Cor. ii 10 'God hath revealed them unto us by His Spirit, for the Spirit searcheth all things, yea, the deep things of God.' See note on i. 5. Clem. Al,

Strom vi 11 (p 786, Pott.), quotes this and the following verse as in the text.

Ἀπὸ ὑψίστων = 'Heaven' So Job xxii. 12; S Luke ii 14

18 Καὶ οὕτως, i. e. while they had Wisdom to guide them, ver. 12

Διωρθ. 'were made straight.' Jer. vii. 5 Vulg. 'correctae sint' It should be 'sunt,' and 'didicerunt,' not 'didicerint' Reusch. The Vulg joins vers 17 and 18 together.

Τὰ ἀρεστά σου Bar iv. 4 (Vat) · τὰ ἀρεστὰ τοῦ Θεοῦ Jer xvi 12 τῶν ἀρεστῶν τῆς καρδίας ὑμῶν Τὸ ἀρεστὸν is used as a substantive

Ἐσώθησαν (Comp x. 4) This clause introduces a new idea, which is developed in the remainder of the Book The Vulgate adds a clause limiting this divine guidance to good men · 'Sanati sunt quicunque placuerunt tibi, Domine, a principio'—of which there is no trace in any extant Greek MS. S Aug, De Mor Eccl. I. § 28 (tom. I p. 698 D), quotes the passage without the addition. At the same time it must be noted, as Guth remarks (Einleit p. 51), that something very like it is found in the ancient Liturgies. Thus in the Lit. of S Clement· ὑπὲρ πάντων τῶν ἀπὸ αἰῶνος εὐαρεστησάντων σοι ἁγίων S. Chrys.: πάντων τῶν ἁγίων τῶν ἀπ' αἰῶνός σοι εὐαρεστησάντων. S James· ἵνα εὕρωμεν ἔλεον καὶ χάριν μετὰ πάντων τῶν ἁγίων τῶν ἀπ' αἰῶνός σοι εὐαρεστ. κατὰ γενεὰν καὶ γενεάν And S Basil as in S James So that it is possible that the MS. used by the Vulg. translator may have contained the passage. The reference to the righteous men of early times is confirmed by what follows.

CHAPTER X.

CHAPTERS X-XIX. WISDOM IN ITS HISTORICAL ASPECT.

CHAPTERS X-XII SHOWS ITSELF IN SAVING AND PUNISHING

X. 1-XI. 4. *Exhibited in the guidance of the Fathers from Adam to Moses.*

With this we may compare the effects of Faith in Heb xi.

1. Πρωτόπλαστον See on vii 1

Μόνον κτισθέντα. 'Cum solus esset creatus,' Vulg. See Gen ii. 18. The expression in the text may mean that Adam alone was created, all other men being begotten, as he is called in the genealogy (S Luke iii 38) 'son of God.' Gutberlet takes μόνον with πατέρα κόσμου, translating: 'who was created as only father of the world,' = father of the whole world Grimm and Wahl render μόνον, 'defenceless.' Probably the Vulg. is right, and the meaning is simply that Adam was created alone, with no other human being to diminish his supremacy or share his dignity. The Targum of Jonathan, on Gen. iii, has the gloss· 'The Lord said to the angels, Behold, Adam is sole (unicus, unigenitus) on the earth, as I am sole in the heavens' Etheridge, i. p 168. This Targum has also a curious note on the creation of man, which adumbrates the sanctity of his origin and the unity of his race The Lord is here said to have taken dust from Mount Moriah and from the four winds of heaven, mixed it with all the waters of the world, and created man red, black, and white, and breathed into his nostrils the breath of life.

Διεφύλαξεν, 'preserved him' from error and ignorance while in his original righteousness, 'and,' it goes on, 'delivered him after his fall.' The restoration of Adam was a very general opinion both among Jews and Christians, and occasioned a plentiful crop of legends. S. Aug. says 'it is rightly believed that Christ released Adam from hell ("ab inferni vinculis") when He preached to the spirits in prison.' This is stated as a past event by the author of Wisdom, as the Psalmist says, 'they pierced my hands,' referring to a future event. Op imperf Contr Jul. VI xxx fin

The Fathers assert generally that Adam was saved through repentance and faith in the Redeemer. Thus Tertull De Poenit. xii 'Adam exomologesi restitutus in Paradisum' S Irenaeus reasons from *a priori* grounds (Adv Haer. iii 23 § 2. p. 220, Ben) 'Cum autem salvetur homo, oportet salvari eum, qui prior formatus est, quoniam nimis irrationabile est, illum quidem, qui vehementer ab inimico laesus erat et prior captivitatem passus est, dicere non eripi ab eo, qui vicerit inimicum, ereptos vero filios ejus, quos in eadem captivitate generavit' And a little above 'Victus autem erat Adam, ablata ab eo omni vita · propter hoc victo rursus inimico recepit vitam Adam, "novissima autem inimica evacuatur mors," quae primum possederat hominem. Quapropter liberato homine, "fiet quod scriptum est. Absorpta est mors in victoria, ubi est mors victoria tua? Ubi est mors aculeus tuus?" Quod non poterit juste dici, si non ille liberatus fuerit, cui primum dominata est mors. Illius enim salus, evacuatio est mortis Domino igitur vivificante hominem, id est Adam, evacuata est et mors Mentiuntur ergo omnes qui contradicunt ejus saluti, semper seipsos excludentes a vita, in eo quod non credunt inventam ovem quae perierat. Si autem illa non est inventa, adhuc possidetur in perditione omnis hominis generatio' See also ib (pp 960, 961). Epiphanius mentions among the heresies of Tatian his opinion that Adam was not saved, Adv Haer xlvi (xli p. 840, Migne). πῶς οὐ σώζεται ὁ Ἀδάμ, ὁ παρά σοι ἀπελπιζόμενος, ὁπότε αὐτὸς ὁ Κύριος ἡμῶν Ἰησοῦς Χριστὸς, ἐλθὼν εἰς τὸν κόσμον, νεκροὺς μετὰ τὴν τελευτὴν ἐγείρει ἐν αὐτῷ τῷ σώματι; εἰ δὲ πάλιν αὐτός ἐστιν ὁ Κύριος Ἀδὰμ πλάσας, καὶ αὐτὸν τὸν πρωτόπλαστον ἀπολλύει, τοὺς δὲ ἄλλους σώζει, ὢ πολλή σου ματαιοφροσύνη, Τατιανέ Ἀδυναμίαν γὰρ τῷ Κυρίῳ κατὰ δύναμιν προσάπτεις, τῷ δυναμένῳ τὸν πρωτόπλαστον αὐτοῦ, διὰ μίαν παρακοὴν ἐκβεβλημένον τοῦ παραδείσου, καὶ παιδείας οὐ τῆς τυχούσης μετασχόντα, ἐν ἱδρῶτι καὶ καμάτῳ διατετελεκότα, καὶ κατέναντι τοῦ παραδείσου κατῳκηκότα, ὅπως μνημονεύοι τῆς ἀγαθῆς διὰ τῆς εἰς μνήμην μετανοίας σώζειν· ἡ δυναμένῳ μέν, μὴ ἐλεοῦντι δέ. And he goes on to relate how Adam in the course of time made his way to Jerusalem, died there, and was buried in Golgotha, which was called τόπος κρανίου, because his skull was afterwards discovered there. Our Saviour, shedding His blood upon the cross, watered with those precious drops the mortal remains of our first father, a token and sign of the purification of the whole race of man S Aug (?) Serm. vi in App (tom v. p. ii. 14) alludes to the same legend, adding. 'Et vere, fratres, non incongrue creditur, quia ibi erectus sit medicus, ubi jacebat aegrotus. Et dignum erat, ut ubi occiderat humana superbia, ibi se inclinaret divina misericordia, et sanguis ille pretiosus etiam corporaliter pulverem antiqui peccatoris dum dignatur stillando contingere, redemisse credatur' This sermon is probably spurious, but that Augustine believed in Adam's salvation is certain from passages in his genuine works, e g Ep. clxiv. (cap iii § 6): 'Et de illo quidem primo homine patre generis humani, quod eum inde (ex inferno) solverit Christus, Ecclesia fere tota consentit, quod eam non inaniter credidisse credendum est' Comp Ep xcix; Lib. de Haer 25. See Fabric. Cod. Pseud-epigr. V. T. vol i capp xii, xxv, xxviii; vol. ii. capp. x, xi, xix And an excellent note on this passage in Mr Churton's commentary

Ἐξείλατο, an Alexandrine form of 2 aor mid., by a change of termination to the 1 aor. See Buttm. Irr. Verbs, v αἱρέω.

Παραπτώματος ἰδίου 'His own fall,' this recovery of his not affecting his descendants. Παράπτωμα is used in relation to Adam's transgression by S. Paul, Rom. v 15, 17, 18 Comp Job xxxvi 9, Ezek.

xiv. 13 See on xii 2 There is a certain similarity between the effects of Wisdom mentioned in this chapter, and the effects of faith in Hebr xi, but the scope of the writers is entirely different. The supposition of Gfrorer (Urchrist ii 242), referred to by Bissell, that our author endorses the opinion of Philo, that Adam's fall consisted in his sinking from the condition of a pure spirit to a material existence, has no support whatever from this passage, and can only be read into it by blinded prejudice

2 This supremacy was given before the Fall (Gen i. 26, 28; ii. 20) and renewed after the Flood (Gen. ix 2), being indeed a natural attribute of man. Comp. Ps. viii. 1; Heb ii 6-8; Ecclus xvii 4

3. Ἄδικος Cain. Gen iv. 'When he in his wrath deserted Wisdom.' For the omission of the names of the characters referred to see on xix 13

Συναπώλετο 'Deperiit,' Vulg And so Gutberlet regards σύν as merely strengthening the verb. But this seems inadmissible, being without example. The word occurs in a similar connection in the prayer of Manasses, 13 μὴ συναπολέσῃς με ταῖς ἀνομίαις μου, where the Vulg translates· 'Ne simul perdas me cum iniquitatibus meis' Comp Gen xviii 23 The meaning here is that Cain perished in and with his fratricidal wrath. A tradition mentioned by Jerome (Ep xxxvi t. 1 p. 163) said that he was accidentally killed by Lamech, and some commentators see here an allusion to this legend But this is unnecessary. The 'perishing' is a spiritual death As Wisdom led Adam to repentance and salvation, so the rejection of Wisdom led Cain to destruction. See Fabric. Cod. Pseudepigr V. T. i. cap. 42, Rab. Maur. De Univ. ii. 1 (cxi p. 33, Migne), Pseudo-Aug Quaest ex Vet. Test. Qu. vi (iii 45, App).

4 Δι' ὅν, referring to ἄδικος, ver 3 The flood was the consequence of the sin of Cain and his descendants, who imitated his wickedness Comp Gen vi 4, 5, which passage connects the deluge with the giants, the progeny of Cain, and the 'sons of God.' Comp. Orig. in Joann tom xx 4 (iv p. 312, Ben)

Δι' εὐτελ. ξύλου, 'by means of valueless wood,' i e the ark. Gen vi, vii. 'Per contemptibile lignum,' Vulg. 'Contemptibilis' is a post-classical word found in Ulpian and late writers. Comp Is. xlix. 7; 1 Cor. i. 28, Vulg. Other uncommon words of like formation are these: 'incommunicabilis,' xiv. 21, 'ineffugibilis,' xvii 16, 'inexterminabilis,' ii 23; 'intelligibilis,' vii 23; 'odibilis,' xii 4; 'inextinguibilis,' vii 10

Τὸν δίκαιον. Noah, called 'just,' Gen. vi. 9, Ecclus xliv. 17. Comp. Ezek. xiv 14, Heb xi 7

5. Συγχυθέντων. 'In consensu nequitiae cum se nationes contulissent,' Vulg So Arn : 'When the nations around conspired or joined together in wickedness,' i e when they were all sunk in idolatry But as συγχέω is used of the 'confounding' at Babel, Gen. xi. 7, 9, and nowhere in the sense of 'conspiring,' it is better to translate 'After the nations had been confounded in their conspiracy of wickedness.' After the attempt at Babel, and the widespread corruption that succeeded, Wisdom knew the righteous man. A rabbinical tradition mentioned by S Jerome (Quaest. Hebr. in Gen), with a sacrifice of chronology not unusual, connects Abraham with Nimrod, making the latter cast the patriarch into a fiery furnace to punish him for renouncing idolatry. In the legend the furnace becomes a cool meadow, and Abraham suffers no harm, a circumstance which recalls the 'moist whistling wind' in the case of the three holy children See ver. 27 of the Addit to Daniel. The legend about Abraham can be read in Etheridge's translation of The Targums on the Pentateuch, vol. i. p. 191, note 5, and in Fabric Cod. Pseud. V T. vol. i cap. 107.

Ἔγνω. 'Scivit,' Vulg This reading has the authority of most MSS, ancient versions, and Orig in Johann. tom. xx (i 599) Comp 2 Tim ii 19: 'The Lord knoweth them that are His' Numb. xvi. 5. Eng · 'found out,' reading εὗρε.

Τὸν δίκαιον. Abraham. Gen. xii 1; Hebr xi. 17-19.

Ἄμεμπτον 'Sine querela,' Vulg. 'Querela,' in

the sense of 'blame,' occurs S. Luke i 6; Ecclus. viii. 10; Wisd. xiii 6; xviii. 21, Vulg

Ἐπὶ τέκνου σπλάγχνοις 'Kept him strong against his pity for his son.' Gen. xxii. 10. Ἐπὶ, 'against,' as S Luke xii 53 Σπλάγχνα, 'affection,' 'compassion.' Prov xii 10: τὰ δὲ σπλάγχνα τῶν ἀσεβῶν ἀνελεήμονα. Comp S Luke i. 78; Col iii 12.

6. Δίκαιον. Lot xix 17; 2 Pet ii. 7. See Gen. xix 17–22.

Πῦρ καταβάσιον Πενταπόλεως. 'The fi e which fell upon Pentapolis.' Καταιβάτης is used of Zeus as descending in lightning. Aristoph. Pax, 42; Aeschyl. Prom 359 The five cities were Sodom, Gomorrah, Admah, Zeboim, and Zoar or Bela Gen. xiv. 2. Zoar indeed was saved, but it is usual to speak of all the cities as perishing together. Comp. Joseph. Bell Jud. iv. 8. 4. Πεντάπολις is found in Herod. 1 144, etc., applied to a confederation of five cities.

7. Ἧς ἔτι. The preponderance of authority is in favour of this reading. The Vulg gives, 'Quibus in testimonium;' but many MSS have 'cujus,' and the other versions seem generally to have read ἧς ἔτι.

Καπνίζ καθέστηκε. 'Stands smoking.' Gen xix. 28, Deut. xxix. 23. Recent travellers have not observed this; but Philo says: μέχρι νῦν καίεται, De Abrah. 27 (II. p. 21) Joseph. Bell. Jud. iv. 8. 4: νῦν δὲ κεκαυμένη πᾶσα . . ἔστι γοῦν ἔτι λείψανα τοῦ θείου πυρός And so, other authors Thus Tertull Apologet. 40: 'Regiones affines ejus Sodoma et Gomorra igneus imber excussit [? exussit], olet adhuc incendio terra, et si qua illic arborum poma conantur oculis tenus, caeterum contacta cinerescunt' Comp. Ejusd De Pallio, 2. Tacit. Hist v 7 'Haud procul inde campi quos ferunt olim uberes magnisque urbibus habitatos fulminum ictu arsisse; et manere vestigia, terramque ipsam, specie torridam, vim frugiferam perdidisse. Nam cuncta sponte edita aut manu sata, sive herba tenus aut flore, seu solitam in speciem adolevere, atra et inania velut in cinerem vanescunt.' Strabo, XVI. ii. 44, calls the country γῆν τεφρώδη.

Καπνιζομένη 'Fumigabunda,' Vulg. This uncommon word is found in S Ambr. ii. 9 · 'fornax fumigabunda.' S. Aug uses 'fumabunda,' translating Gen. xv. 17, De Civ. xvi. 24. A word of similar formation is 'tremebundus,' Wisd. xvii 9; Hebr xii 21.

Χέρσος, 'waste land' So χέρσα, 'waste places.' Aesch. Frag 192 Cp χερσόομαι, iv 19.

Ἀτελέσιν. 'Incerto tempore fructus habentes arbores,' Vulg. 'Imperfectis germinibus fructificantes arbores,' Sabat. 'Plants bearing fruit at immature seasons' The fruits are forced by the climate into premature ripeness, and so are worthless The reference is probably to what are called The Apples of Sodom, of which Josephus speaks (Bell. Jud. iv. 8) ἔστι δὲ καὶ ἐν τοῖς καρποῖς σποδιὰν ἀναγεννωμένην, οἱ χρόαν μὲν ἔχουσι τοῖς ἐδωδίμοις ὁμοίαν, δρεψαμένων δὲ χερσὶν εἰς καπνὸν ἀναλύονται καὶ τέφραν The only fruit at all answering to this description (and that very imperfectly), now found in this region, is that of the *Calotropis Procera*. See Bible Educator, iv 312.

Ἀπιστούσης Vulg.: 'incredibilis' 'Unbelieving' In this sense 'incredibilis' is post-classical Cf Tit i. 16, Bar i. 19, Ecclus. i 36, Vulg

Στήλη ἁλός Lot's wife. Gen. xix. 26; Luke xvii. 32 Joseph. (Ant. i. 11. 4) says: ἱστόρηκα δ' αὐτήν, ἔτι γὰρ καὶ νῦν διαμένει The unscientific writers of subsequent times assigned the name of 'Lot's wife' to some of the fantastic figures which are often assumed by the crumbling rock at the south of the Dead Sea. According to the Targum of Jerusalem 'Because the wife of Lot was of the children of the people of Sodom, she looked behind to see what would be the end of her father's house, and behold she was made to stand a statue of salt, until the time of the resurrection shall come, when the dead shall rise.' Etheridge, i p 217 Clem Rom ad Cor I xi: συνεξελθούσης γὰρ αὐτῷ τῆς γυναικὸς ἑτερογνώμονος ὑπαρχούσης καὶ οὐκ ἐν ὁμονοίᾳ, εἰς τοῦτο σημεῖον ἐτέθη, ὥστε γενέσθαι αὐτὴν στήλην ἁλὸς ἕως τῆς ἡμέρας ταύτης, εἰς τὸ γνωστὸν εἶναι πᾶσιν, ὅτι οἱ δίψυχοι καὶ οἱ διστάζοντες περὶ τῆς τοῦ Θεοῦ δυνάμεως εἰς κρίμα καὶ εἰς σημείωσιν πάσαις ταῖς γενεαῖς γίνονται Other early writers speak of 'the Pillar' existing in their day, e g Iren. Adv. Haer. IV. xxxi 3, and xxxiii. 9 ; Justin M. Apol. i. 53 ; Prudent. Hamartig. 740 ff.

Ἑστηκυῖα and the other participles depend on καθέστηκε.

8 Γάρ This verse confirms ver 7

Ἐβλάβησαν 'They suffered loss so as not to know what was good' Lit: 'Were stopped from, deprived of, the knowing' 'Lapsi sunt,' Vulg., for which Reusch conjectures 'laesi sunt.' Aeschyl. Ag. 120

βλαβέντα λοισθίων δρόμων.

See Donalds New Cratyl iv 5 p 549, ed 1839.

Τῷ βίῳ 'Hominibus,' Vulg 'To the world,' Eng 'Life'='the living,' as xiv 21, 4 Macc xvii 14 Demosth. De Cor. p. 330. ἐπὶ τὸν παρόντα βίον, 'the present generation'

Ἵνα. For their punishment the knowledge of their sin is handed down to all time.

9 Θεραπεύσαντας. 'Delivered from distress those who honoured her,' referring to the instances given in the text Θεραπεύοντας, the other reading, involves a general statement. The word itself recalls to one's mind the Therapeutae, by whose teaching the author may have been influenced. See on xvi 28.

10 Φυγάδα. Jacob Gen. xxvii. 42 ff., xxviii 5, 10 Grimm. comp φυγὰς πονηρίας, Thuc vi. 92. So Philo's treatise about Jacob is called Περὶ φυγάδων.

Ἐν τρίβ. εὐθείαις. 'In straight paths,' without error

Βασιλ Θεοῦ. In his dream. Gen xxviii. 12, 17. He saw the spirit-world and the way in which God governs the universe. So Corn. a Lap., Tirin., etc. Comp Hos xii 4, 5: 'He found him in Bethel, and there He spake with us, even the Lord of hosts; the Lord in his memorial' In the Song of the Three Children, ver 32, we have εὐλογημένος εἶ ἐπὶ θρόνου τῆς βασιλείας σου. Comp S. Luke xiii 29.

Ἁγίων. 'Holy things,' 'mysteries,' parallel to 'the Kingdom of God'

Εὐπόρησεν. 'Enriched him amid hardships.' Vulg: 'honestavit' See on vii 11; cp Ecclus xi 23, Vulg

'In his travels.' Eng i. e. 'travails'='labours.' See Gen. xxx 30, 43; xxxi. 1, 41, 42.

Ἐπλήθυνε τ πόνους Either πόνους must mean (as Eng) 'the fruit of his labours,' as viii. 7; or ἐπλήθ. signifies, 'made to succeed,' 'prospered.' Πόνος in the above sense occurs Prov iii 9; Ecclus xiv 15 Comp. Past Herm. Simil IX c. xxiv. 3 ἐπλήθυνεν αὐτοὺς ἐν τοῖς κόποις τῶν χειρῶν αὐτῶν.

11. 'In the covetousness of his oppressors,' i e. Laban. Gen xxxi. 7.

Ἐπλούτισεν 'Honestum fecit,' Vulg See on vii 11; and comp Ecclus. xiii 2, 3 Esdr iii. 21, Vulg.

12 Ἐχθρῶν, 'open enemies;' ἐνεδρευόντων, 'secret enemies,' e g Laban, Esau, the Canaanites. Gen xxxiii. 4, xxxv. 5

Ἠσφαλίσατο. 'Tutavit,' Vulg. Act. for deponent forms are found elsewhere, e. g 'suffragare,' 3 Esdr. vi. 10, 'gratificare,' Eph i 6, 'demolire,' 3 Esdr. i. 55, 'lamentare,' Matt xi. 17, 'praedare,' Judith ii. 16; 'radicare,' Ecclus xxiv. 16 The form 'tutare' occurs in Plaut. Merc V ii. 24

'Invoco vos, Lares viales, ut me bene tuteris,'

where however some MSS. read 'juvetis.'

Ἐβράβευσεν 'Decided in his favour a strong conflict' Col iii 15 This refers to Jacob's wrestling with the angel Gen xxxii. 24 ff; Hos xii 3, 4. See Pusey in l. The acc with βραβεύω is to be compared with such phrases as νικᾶν ἀγῶνα, Ὀλύμπια.

Εὐσέβεια. Comp. 1 Tim. iv. 8, vi. 6. Philo, De Leg ad Cai 32 (II. p. 582). ἕως οὗ πεπρεσβεύμεθα, μὴ ἀποκόψῃς τὰς ἀμείνους ἐλπίδας μυριάδων τοσούτων, αἷς οὐχ ὑπὲρ κέρδους, ἀλλ' ὑπὲρ εὐσεβείας ἐστὶν ἡ σπουδή· καίτοι γε ἡμάρτομεν τοῦτο εἰπόντες. τί γὰρ ἂν εἴη κέρδος λυσιτελέστερον ὁσιότητος ἀνθρώποις;

13. Δίκαιον Joseph Gen xxxvii, -Acts vii 9.

Ἐξ ἁμαρτίας ἐρρ. refers to the matter with Potiphar's wife. Gen. xxxix The Vulg. renders: 'a peccatoribus liberavit eum,' taking it of Joseph's brethren; unless, indeed, as Reusch thinks, 'peccatoribus' is a mistake for 'peccato'

14 Λάκκον, the dungeon in which Potiphar confined Joseph. Gen. xxxix 20 It occurs in the same sense Exod. xii. 29: ἕως πρωτοτόκου τῆς αἰχμαλωτίδος τῆς ἐν τῷ λάκκῳ. Comp Gen. xl 15.

Σκῆπτρα Gen xli. 40–43, Acts vii. 10. The plural is commonly used in a metaphorical sense, thus Soph Oed. Col 449, Herod vii 52.

Τυραννούντων αὐτοῦ. 'Power over his oppressors,' viz. his brethren, Potiphar, etc. Gen xli. 43, xlii. 6. Ἐξουσία with gen S Matt x 1.

Τοὺς μωμησαμένους, 'those that blamed him,' refers not only to Potiphar's wife (Gen xxxix 17), but to his brethren also, who hated him for his dreams and his father's partiality. Gen. xxxvii. 4, 5.

Αἰώνιον 'Glory to all time,' handed down from age to age.

15. Λαὸν ὅσιον The Israelites. 'A holy people,' as being separated from all other nations and made God's peculiar inheritance See Ex xix 5, 6, 2 Cor vi 17, 18. Past. Herm. Sim. IX c. xviii. 4 . ἀπειληφὼς τὸν λαὸν αὐτοῦ καθαρόν.

Σπέρμα ἄμεμπτον. This is taken by some to refer to the blamelessness of the Jews as regards the Egyptians, but more probably it alludes to their official characteristic, as S. Paul calls all Christians holy' That they fell into idolatry and other sins while sojourning in Egypt is clear from Ezek. xx 8, xxiii. 3. For the deliverance spoken of see Ex. i. 12, 17, and xii. 41

16. Εἰσῆλθεν. See Ex. iv 12.

Θεράποντος Κυρίου. This, and the similar expression, δοῦλος Θεοῦ, are commonly applied to Moses in the Sept Ex. xiv. 31, Numb. xii 7; Ps civ. 26. Comp. Hebr. iii. 5.

Βασιλεῦσι. Pharaoh. So Ps. civ. 30 'even in their kings' [τῶν βασιλέων] chambers'

Τερ. καὶ σημ See on viii 8 Ps cxxxiv 9 ἐξαπέστειλε σημεῖα καὶ τέρατα ἐν μέσῳ σου, Αἴγυπτε, ἐν Φαραῷ καὶ ἐν πᾶσι τοῖς δούλοις αὐτοῦ

17 Ἀπέδωκεν The Israelites were 'repaid' for their hard labour in Egypt by the goods, jewels, etc. which they asked of the Egyptians. Ex xii 35, 36 This was according to God's promise to Abraham, Gen xv 14

Ὡδήγησεν refers to the pillar of cloud Ex xiii 21, 22; Deut. viii 2

Εἰς σκέπην ἡμέρας So Ps. civ. 39 διεπέτασε νεφέλην εἰς σκέπην αὐτοῖς. Ecclus xxxi. 19. σκιπη ἀπὸ καύσωνος καὶ σκέπη ἀπὸ μεσημβρίας (xxxiv 16)

Ἄστρων Gutb takes to mean the sun and moon, to which alone the flame of the pillar of fire would be compared But taking ἄστρον in its proper sense of 'constellation,' this seems hardly necessary Comp Ps. lxxvii. 14 ὡδήγησεν αὐτοὺς ἐν νεφέλῃ ἡμέρας, καὶ ὅλην τὴν νύκτα ἐν φωτισμῷ πυρός

18, 19 Ex xiv Ps lxxvii. 13 διέρρηξε θάλασσαν καὶ διήγαγεν αὐτοὺς, ἔστησεν ὕδατα ὡσεὶ ἀσκόν

19 Ἀνέβρασεν Vulg 'eduxit,' which is tame and inadequate 'Cast them up,' Eng, is better The Vulg. refers it to the Israelites as being restored to life from the grave, 'ab altitudine inferorum' But αὐτοὺς doubtless refers to τ ἐχθρούς, and ἀνέβρ., 'threw up,' 'ejected,' alludes to the tradition that the sea cast out the bodies of the drowned Egyptians Targum of Jerusalem 'The sea and the earth had controversy one with the other The sea said to the earth, Receive thy children, and the earth said to the sea, Receive thy murderers But the earth willed not to swallow them, and the sea willed not to overwhelm them' See Ginsburg, ap. Kitt. Cycopl. Art. 'Book of Wisdom,' note p 1116, vol III (ed 1866) Josephus, Ant. ii 16 6, mentions that all the arms and baggage of the Egyptians were driven ashore near the camp of the Israelites, who were thus provided with weapons. Comp Ex xiv 30 'And Israel saw the Egyptians dead upon the sea shore.' See next verse.

20 Διὰ τοῦτο. Because the Egyptians were found dead on the shore. See on ver 19 'Leviathan,' in Ps lxxiv. 14, refers to the Egyptians, whose corpses became a prey to the creatures that inhabit the desert

Ὕμνησαν Exod xv. Comp Is xii 5 ὑμνήσατε τὸ ὄνομα Κυρίου. Esth iv (15) additam: ἵνα ζῶντες ὑμνῶμέν σου τὸ ὄνομα, Κύριε.

Ὑπέρμαχον. 'Victricem,' Vulg. Rather 'defending,' 'that fought for them,' as xvi 17; 2 Macc viii. 36 Philo, De Somn II 42 (I p 696)· μεγάλη γε ἡ ὑπέρμαχος χείρ, referring to the same event

21 Κωφῶν. Moses, who was slow of speech (Ex iv. 10, vi 12, 30), and the people, who through fear had not dared to sing unto God in the house of bondage, now praised Him in a hymn of victory.

Νηπίων Ps viii 2. 'Out of the mouth of babes and sucklings hast Thou ordained strength'

Τρανάς from τρανός = τρανής, 'piercing,' 'distinct' Vulg., 'disertas,' vii. 22 The Vulg. rendering: 'os mutorum et linguas infantium,' seems to imply, in the eyes of some commentators, a special miracle; but there is no warrant for this in Scripture nor tradition, if we except the gloss in the spurious treatise among the works of S. Aug., De Mirab. S. Script. c. 21, where it is said that, though few out of the great multitude could have heard Moses leading the song, yet that all, young, and old, joined in it with one accord, and sang in perfect unison with him.

CHAPTER XI.

1. Εὐώδωσε.. διώδευσαν, v 2, a play of words. The subject is still Wisdom.

Ἐν χειρί. 'By the hand,' as Acts vii 35 Vulg, 'in manibus' Ps lxxvi. 21 ὡδήγησας ὡς πρόβατα τὸν λαόν σου ἐν χειρὶ Μωυσῆ καὶ Ἀαρών.

Προφήτου ἁγίου Moses Deut xviii 18, xxxiv 10-12. For the term 'holy' applied to Prophets comp. S. Luke i. 70, 2 S. Pet. iii. 2

2 Ἔπηξαν The classical word for 'pitching' a tent Plat. De Legg vii. 19 (p 817 C) σκηνὰς πήξαντας κατ' ἀγοράν. Heb viii 2 See Jer ii 6

3 Πολεμίοις, 'open enemies' in battle, as the Amalekites (Ex xvii. 8-16), Arad (Numb. xxi. 1-3); the Amorites (Numb. xxi. 21-25); and Og (Numb xxi. 33-35).

Ἐχθρούς, 'those who hated them,' as the Moabites and Midianites (Numb xxv 17, 18, xxxi 2)

4 The author omits the murmuring of the people, and alludes only to God's mercy in relieving their wants Ex xvii 4-6; Numb xx 8-11

Ἐκ πέτρας ἀκροτόμου 'De petra altissima,' Vulg. 'The flinty rock,' Eng Ἀκρότ. is 'abrupt,' 'precipitous.' It is used sometimes without πέτρα, as Ecclus. xlviii. 17. Comp. Deut. viii. 15: τοῦ ἐξαγαγόντος σαι ἐκ πέτρας ἀκροτόμου πηγὴν ὕδατος. The word is of late use. Thus Polyb Hist ix 27 4 κεῖται τὸ τεῖχος ἐπὶ πέτρας ἀκροτόμου καὶ περιρρῶγος. Philo, All. II 21 (I p. 82) ἡ γὰρ ἀκρότομος πέτρα ἡ σοφία τοῦ Θεοῦ ἐστιν. So Vit Mos I 38 (II. p. 114). λαβὼν Μωυσῆς τὴν ἱερὰν ἐκείνην βακτηρίαν... θεοφορηθεὶς τὴν ἀκρότομον παίει πέτραν. Ps. lxxvii. 15, 16, 20 See 1 Cor x 4 We may note that our author seems to have had the words of the Septuagint version before him

5 -XII. 1. *Wisdom exhibited in the punishment of God's enemies: the Egyptians*

5. The principle of retributive justice is seen to pervade all God's dealings with the Israelites and Egyptians and Canaanites

Ἐχθροὶ αὐτῶν After these words the Vulg. introduces a gloss, which is entirely without authority from the Greek 'A defectione potus sui, et in eis cum abundarent filii Israel lactati sunt' It seems to be an explanation of the text, contrasting the want of water suffered by the Egyptians when the Nile was turned into blood with the abundant supply bestowed on the

Israelites But it is most unnecessary, as the following verses sufficiently explain the allusion.

Διὰ τούτων, viz by miracles connected with water

Αὐτοί. The Israelites Ex. vii 19; xvii. 6, Numb. xx. 10, 11

6. 'Ἀενάου seems more correct than ἀεννάου. The MSS vary Bar. v 7, 2 Macc. vii 36

Αἵματι λυθρώδει ταραχθέντος 'Of a river troubled (or, turbid) with foul blood' The reference of course is to the first Plague Λυθρώδης is a very uncommon word. Λύθρον is found in Homer, meaning 'defilement from blood.' The reading ταραχθέντες introduces a harsh anacoluthon, not in accordance with our writer's habit The Vulg. differs widely from the text 'Humanum sanguinem dedisti injustis,' and it seems to translate ταραχθέντες by 'Qui cum minuerentur' Philo, Vit Mos. 17 (II p 96). συνεξαιματοῦνται δ' αὐτῷ λίμναι, διώρυχες, κρῆναι, φρέατα, πηγαὶ, σύμπασα ἡ κατ' Αἴγυπτον οὐσία ὕδατος, ὡς ἀπορία ποτοῦ τὰ παρὰ ταῖς ὄχθαις ἀναστέλλειν, τὰς δ' ἀνατεμνομένας φλέβας, καθάπερ ἐν ταῖς αἱμορραγίαις, κρουνηδὸν αὐλοὺς ἀκοντίζειν αἵματος, μηδεμιᾶς ἐνορωμένης διαυγοῦς λιβάδος. Joseph. Ant II. xiv 1: οὐχὶ τὴν χρόαν δὲ μόνον ἦν τοιοῦτος (sc. αἱματώδης), ἀλλὰ καὶ τοῖς πειρωμένοις πίνειν ἀλγήματα καὶ πικρὰν ὀδύνην προσέφερεν ἦν δὲ τοιοῦτος μὲν Αἰγυπτίοις, Ἑβραίοις δὲ γλυκὺς καὶ πότιμος, καὶ μηδὲν τοῦ κατὰ φύσιν παρηλλαγμένος So III. i. 4: ὁ αὐτὸς ποταμὸς ἐκείνοις μὲν αἷμα ἦν καὶ ἄποτος, αὐτοῖς δὲ πότιμος καὶ γλυκύς.

'Ἀντὶ μὲν with no δὲ, but the clause ἔδωκας κ.τ.λ, ver. 7, virtually contains the contrast For the regard paid by the Egyptians to their river-god Nilus or Hapiman see Wilkinson, Anc Egypt. iii. p 206

7. Εἰς ἔλεγχον. 'For reproof,' 'punishment,' referring to the verse preceding. See Ex. i. 16, 22 Vulg : 'Qui cum minuerentur in traductione infantium occisorum' For 'traductio' as the translation of ἔλεγχος comp ii. 14; xviii 5, Vulg, and see on iv 20 S Ephr Syr in Exod c vii (p 207): 'Et quidem verisimile est regem Aegypti patrio flumine statum et solenne sacrificium frequenter factitasse juxta decreta magorum, quibus plurimum deferebat. Hic Pharao, quum a Moyse Dei nomine interpellatus, Hebraeos se dimissurum negaret, Moyses percussit flumen, quod antiquus ille Pharao polluerat, ut aquae infantium sanguine foedatae in sanguinem verterentur, et pisces hominum mortuorum carnibus saginati, et ipsi morerentur.' 'All this was the Lord God of the Hebrews his doing, that the blood of the Hebrew infants might be required of the Egyptians, κατὰ ἀντιπεπανθὸς, according to the law of retaliation, or most exquisite rule of primitive justice' Jackson, ix pp 414, 415, ed 1844

Νηπιοκτόνου A new word, as τεκνοφόνος, xiv 23

Αὐτοῖς. The Israelites in the wilderness.

8. Τότε, when the Israelites were without water in the wilderness

Ἐκόλασας Ex vii 20 See on ver 5. Vulg. 'Quemadmodum tuos exaltares et adversarios illos necares,' where 'tuos exaltares et' seems to be an interpolation

9 'When they, the Israelites, were tried by thirst (although indeed it was in mercy that they were thus disciplined), they learned how the ungodly, the Egyptians, being judged in wrath, were tormented.' They recognised the different treatment accorded to them and to their enemies This passage is a good instance of the careful balancing of words and clauses affected by the writer. See Gutb. Cp Deut viii 2, 3 The Eng. Vers adds, 'thirsting in another manner than the just,' which words occur in the original at the end of ver. 14, and are found in this ver 9 neither in MSS., nor Compl, nor Ald, nor in other versions. Arn thinks it shows great sagacity in our translators to have discovered the right place for this clause, which he considers to be unmeaning in ver 14 Most readers will not agree with him Dean Jackson (bk. x. ch. 40) sees in this and similar passages what he calls an opinion 'so far from being canonical, scarce orthodoxal,' viz that the Jews, because they were the seed of Abraham, were the only righteous seed, and that the Lord, though He corrected and chastised them, would never plague them as He did the unrighteous heathen, or punish them with blindness of heart. 'The receipt or medicine for curing this disease we have set down Rom ix, 18 : "Therefore hath He mercy on whom He will

have mercy, and whom He will He hardeneth"' Works, ix. p 416 It is true that the author makes the most of the contrast between the treatment of the Jews and that shown to their heathen enemies, but he follows the line of Scripture in so doing Comp. Deut. xi. 2-4 with viii. 5, 15, 16; vii. 13, 14 with vers 15, 16.

10 Ὡς πατήρ Comp Deut viii 5, 2 Sam vii 14, Hebr xii 5, 6

Ἀπότομος, 'severe' Comp. Rom xi 22 ἴδε οὖν χρηστότητα καὶ ἀποτομίαν Θεοῦ.

Καταδικ ἐξῆτ Vulg 'interrogans condemnasti.' Sabat. 'condemnans interrogasti'

11. Ἀπόντες. 'Whether they were far away from the Israelites, or in their presence' While the Israelites were in Egypt, the Egyptians were vexed with the Plagues, when the Israelites were departed, the Egyptians were vexed with grief and envy

Ἐτρύχοντο Comp xiv 15

12 Διπλῆ γάρ Explained in ver. 13 First, the thought that their punishment brought deliverance to the Hebrews, secondly, the enforced recognition of the power of the Lord, and the nothingness of their gods.

Μνήμων τῶν παρελθόντων. 'Gemitus memor (cum memoria, Vulg) praeteritorum' Reusch. This reading has the greatest authority, that of Vat, μνημῶν τῶν παρελθουσῶν, must mean, 'groaning over past remembrances'

13 Διὰ τῶν ἰδ κολ. 'By that which punished them,' the Egyptians, e g water.

Εὐεργετουμένους, 'were being continually benefited' The reading εὐεργετημένους is the alteration of some scribe who did not understand the force of the present participle.

Ἤισθοντο τ Κυρίου, 'they took knowledge of the Lord,' recognised His hand in that which befel them xii 27 Vulg · 'Commemorati sunt Dominum, admirantes in finem exitus,' where we may note 'commemorari' used as a deponent verb (cp. Bar iii 23), and the added clause, which seems to be an interpolation from the next verse. Blunt observes that it is noteworthy that the Egyptians made no attack on the Israelites from the exodus till the reign of Rehoboam Cp Ps lxiv 9

14 Ὃν γάρ. The other reading, τὸν γὸρ, has more authority, but mars the sentence. 'For him whom, long before cast forth when the children were exposed.' The reference, of course, is to Moses Ex. ii 3 Vulg · 'In expositione prava projectum,' omitting πάλαι, or reading κακῇ Comp xviii 5; Acts vii 19, 21.

Ἀπεῖπον χλευάρ 'They rejected with scoffs,' i.e. when he was endeavouring to effect the deliverance of his people Ex v. 3, 4, vii 23, x. 10, 11, 28.

Ἐπὶ τέλει τ. ἐκβ. 'At the end of the events.' Grimm interprets this to mean, at the end of the Ten Plagues, but the succeeding clause confines the reference to the miraculous supply of water in the wilderness, marvellous stories of which may have reached the Egyptians For the reputation of Moses among the Egyptians before the Exodus see Ex. xi 3.

Διψήσαντες, i.e having themselves thirsted in a very different manner from the Hebrews Οὐχ ὅμοια, a litotes. Eng omits this clause See on ver. 9. They had no relief for their thirst when their river was turned into blood

15. Ἀντί 'For' = in punishment of 'the foolish thoughts of (proceeding from) their iniquity.' Comp. Rom. i 21. 'became vain in their imaginations (διαλογισμοῖς), and their foolish (ἀσύνετος) heart was darkened.'

Ἄλογα ἑρπετά. 'Mutos serpentes,' Vulg. Rather, 'irrational.' Ch. xvii 9, 2 Pet ii 12. The word ἑρπετά, 'reptiles,' may include crocodiles See next note.

Κνώδαλα εὐτελῆ. 'Vile, worthless animals.' The Egyptians worshipped animals of all kinds, from the crocodile to the mosquito Vulg, 'bestias supervacuas.' And so xii 24; xv. 10; xvi 29 'Useless beasts'

Ἐπαπέστειλας Deut. xxviii. 48, Ecclus. xxviii 23 (A C); Polyb I. liii 5

Ζώων, 'living creatures,' *e g* frogs, flies, lice, locusts Ex viii and x. Blunt thinks that the writer refers to the crocodiles which infest the Nile. But the reference seems to be to some of the Ten Plagues. Comp ch xvi. 9.

16. This retribution may be traced throughout the Ten Plagues, according to the distich · 'Per quod quis peccat, per idem punitur et idem.' Comp xii 23; xvi 1. S. Athan applies this principle to the circumstances of Herod's death. See below.

Καὶ κολάζ. The addition of καὶ is found in a Fragment attributed to S Athanasius (xxvi. p 1256, Migne; Montfauc ii 26)

17 Οὐ γὰρ ἠπέρει ἐπιπέμψαι. 'Non enim impossibilis erat immittere,' Vulg 'Impossibilis' is a late word, not found with the sense of 'unable,' as here, but with a passive sense = 'that cannot be done,' 'impossible.' It is here = 'impotens.'

Χείρ Pearson (On the Creed, Art. II. note e, pp. 131, 132, ed 1833) notes that as in Isai. xlviii 13, the 'hand of God' is by the Chaldee paraphrast translated the 'Word of God,' so here ἡ παντοδύναμός σου χεὶρ καὶ κτίσασα τὸν κόσμον becomes, xviii. 15, παντοδύναμός σου λόγος ἀπ' οὐρανῶν.

Ἐξ ἀμόρφου ὕλης 'Out of matter without form,' *i. e.* out of chaos. The term is Plato's, but the idea is not necessarily the same as his Our author says nothing about matter being eternal, and is speaking of the moulding and adaptation of the previously created material The commentators quote a passage from Timaeus Locr., the supposed teacher of Plato, p 94 A · ταύταν δὲ τὰν ὕλαν αἴδιον μὲν ἔφα, οὐ μὰν ἀκίνατον, ἄμορφον δὲ καθ' ἑαυτὰν καὶ ἀσχημάτιστον, δεχομέναν δὲ πᾶσαν μορφάν. The Vulg translates, 'ex materia invisa,' with reference probably to Gen 1 2 · ἡ δὲ γῆ ἦν ἀόρατος καὶ ἀκατασκεύαστος. S Aug. de Gen. ad Lit I. § 28 (t. iii. 126). 'Qui fecisti mundum ex materia informi.' But De Fid. et Symb. cap. ii. he writes 'Qui fecisti mundum ex materia invisa, vel etiam informi sicut nonnulla exemplaria tenent.' Just Mart. Apol. 1. 10. καὶ πάντα τὴν ἀρχὴν ἀγαθὸν ὄντα δημιουργῆσαι αὐτὸν ἐξ ἀμόρφου ὕλης δι' ἀνθρώπους δεδιδάγμεθα. Comp Philo, De Cherub. 35 (I. p 162) ἔστι μὲν τὸ ὑφ' οὗ, τὸ αἴτιον, ἐξ οὗ δέ, ἡ ὕλη See Orig. Περὶ Ἀρχ. iv. 33 (I. p. 192, Ben). S Aug. sees nothing erroneous in our author's statement. About this he writes thus : 'Primo ergo materia facta est confusa et informis, unde omnia fierent quae distincta atque formata sunt, quod credo a Graecis chaos appellari ... Et ideo Deus rectissime creditur omnia de nihilo fecisse, quia etiamsi omnia formata de ista materia facta sunt, haec ipsa materia tamen de omnino nihilo facta est.' De Gen. contr. Manich. i. §§ 9, 10. In the passage quoted above from De Fide et Symb he continues · 'Et si ipsum caelum et terram, *i. e.* mundum et omnia quae in eo sunt, ex aliqua materia fecerat, sicut scriptum est "Qui fecisti .. invisa," nullo modo credendum est illam ipsam materiam, de qua factus est mundus, quamvis informem, quamvis invisam, quocunque modo esset, per se ipsam esse potuisse, tamquam coaeternam et coaevam Deo sed quemlibet modum suum, quem habebat, ut quoquo modo esset, et distinctarum rerum formas posset accipere, non habebat nisi ab omnipotente Deo, cujus beneficio est res non solum quaecunque formata, sed etiam quaecunque formabilis .. Hoc autem diximus, ne quis existimet contrarias sibi esse divinarum Scripturarum sententias, quoniam et omnia Deum fecisse de nihilo scriptum est, et mundum esse factum de informi materia '

'A multitude of bears.' As God threatened the Israelites, Lev xxvi 22; Jer viii 17 Comp Philo, de Vit. Mos i. 19 (II p 97) Ἄρκος is the Alex form of ἄρκτος Bears were sent to punish the mocking children, 2 Kings ii 24, and lions punished the disobedient prophet, 1 Kings xiii. 24, and the strangers in Samaria, 2 Kings xvii 26 Comp 1 Kings xx. 36. See also ch. xii 9, and note there.

18. Νεοκτίστους, 'newly-formed' by Him who made (κτίσας) the world.

Θυμοῦ πλήρ. 'Ira plenas' Comp vii. 20; xvi. 5. Some unnecessarily have supposed that θυμός here means 'poison,' as perhaps in Deut. xxxii. 33; Job xx. 16.

Βρόμον λικμωμένους καπνοῦ. 'Fumi odorem proferentes,' Vulg. Βρόμος is here = βρῶμος, 'a stink.' The MSS. vary much in this passage. The reading in the text has most authority. The Eng. seems to have read βρόμους (V. al.) λικμωμένου (Comp.) καπνοῦ. Mr. Churton compares the description of the monster in Job xli. 20, 21.

19. Βλάβη. 'Laesura,' Vulg. A post-class. word; it occurs also xviii. 3. Tertull. De Patient. vii: 'laesura divitiarum.' Grut. Inscr. Rom. 567, 8: 'Quae vixit mecum Annis xvii. M. ii. D. iii. sine ulla animi laesura.'

Συνεκτρῖψαι. The σύν is intensive, like the prefix 'to' in old English. Thus Judg. ix. 53: 'And all to-brake his skull.' Chaucer, Knight's Tale, 2611:

'The helmes they to-hewen and to-shrede.'

20. Ἐνὶ πνεύματι ... ὑπὸ πνεύματος δυν. 'Blast.' See v. 23. So of Sennacherib it was said, 2 Kings xix. 7: 'Behold, I will send a blast (πνεῦμα) upon him.' Job iv. 9: ἀπὸ δὲ πνεύματος ὀργῆς αὐτοῦ ἀφανισθήσονται.

Ὑπὸ τῆς δίκης διωχθ. Vulg.: 'Persecutionem passi ab ipsis factis suis.' Many of these unauthorised variations from the Greek text are not noted by Gutb., whose Church considers the Vulg. of equal authority with the original. For the notion of vengeance dogging the sinner see Acts xxviii. 4.

Ἀλλὰ πάντα, κ.τ.λ. Comp. Job xxviii. 25; Isai. xl. 12. Thus 4 Esdr. iv. 36, 37: 'Quoniam in statera ponderavit saeculum, et mensura mensuravit tempora, et numero numeravit tempora.' The statement is true of the physical and moral world. Here it refers to the latter, and means generally that God, limiting His Omnipotence, awards His punishment by impartial rules, trying to lead men to repentance. The symmetry, harmony, and order that reign in the material universe are a figure and example of those which prevail in the moral government of the world. Comp. Ecclus. i. 9; xvi. 25. S. Bas. Magn. Hom. iii. in Hexaem. 5 (p. 27, Ben.): ὁ τοίνυν ἅπαντα σταθμῷ καὶ μέτρῳ διαταξάμενος (ἀριθμηταὶ γὰρ αὐτῷ, κατὰ τὸν Ἰώβ, καὶ σταγόνες εἰσὶν ὑετοῦ), ᾔδει πόσον τῷ κόσμῳ χρόνον ἀφώρισεν εἰς διαμονὴν, καὶ πόσην χρὴ τῷ πυρὶ προαποθέσθαι δαπάνην. S. Aug., too, has treated this passage at some length (De Gen. ad Lit. IV. v. § 12). Thus: 'Faciamus ita dictum esse " Omnia ... disposuisti," tanquam dictum esset, ita disposita ut haberent proprias mensuras suas, et proprios numeros, et proprium pondus, quae in eis pro sui cujusque generis mutabilitate mutarentur, augmentis et diminutionibus, multitudine et paucitate, levitate et gravitate, secundum dispositionem Dei.' Cf. contr. Jul. Op. Imp. ii. § 87 (t. x. 987).

21. Τὸ γὰρ μεγ. ἰσχ. gives the ground for 18–20.

Σοὶ πάρεστιν. Vulg.: 'Tibi soli supererat,' where 'soli' is an interpolation, and 'supererat' ought to be 'superat,' which is found in some MSS.

Τίς ἀντιστ. This is quoted by Clem. Rom., and it is remarkable as being the earliest citation of the Book of Wisdom exterior to the N. T., ἐν λόγῳ τῆς μεγαλωσύνης αὐτοῦ συνεστήσατο τὰ πάντα καὶ ἐν λόγῳ δύναται αὐτὰ καταστρέψαι. Τίς ἐρεῖ αὐτῷ· Τί ἐποίησας; ἢ τίς ἀντιστήσεται τῷ κράτει τῆς ἰσχύος αὐτοῦ; Ὅτε θέλει καὶ ὡς θέλει, ποιήσει πάντα καὶ οὐδὲν μὴ παρέλθῃ τῶν δεδογματισμένων ὑπ' αὐτοῦ. Ep. ad Cor. xxvii. See Prolegom. p. 36, and note on xii. 12.

22. Ῥοπὴ ἐκ πλαστίγγων. 'The turn of the scales.' 'Momentum staterae.' Eng.: 'Little grain of the balance;' taking ῥοπή for 'that which turns the scale.' So Grimm: 'an atom in the scale.' Is. xl. 15: ὡς ῥοπὴ ζυγοῦ.

Ὀρθρινή. 'A morning drop of dew.' Usually taken *per hypallagen* for 'a drop of morning dew;' as Vulg.: 'Gutta roris antelucani;' reading perhaps ὀρθρινῆς. Comp. Hos. vi. 4, and xiii. 3: ὡς δρόσος ὀρθρινὴ πορευομένη. Const. Apost. viii. 37: μετὰ τὸ ῥηθῆναι τὸν ὀρθρινὸν [ὕμνον], i.e. Matins.

23. Ὅτι. 'Because.' 'God's Almighty power is the foundation of His mercy.' Comp. Collect in P. B. for XIth Sund. after Trinity: 'O God, who declarest Thy Almighty power most chiefly in showing mercy and pity.' This is taken from the Sarum Missal, and

is also found in the Sacramentary of Gelasius. See ch. xii. 16, and Ecclus xviii 13.

Παρορᾷς ... μετάνοιαν. A remarkable anticipation of S Paul's language, Rom ii 4: 'Not knowing that the goodness of God leadeth thee to repentance.' Comp. Acts xvii. 30: 'The times of this ignorance God winked at (ὑπεριδών), but now commandeth all men everywhere to repent (μετανοεῖν)' 2 Pet. iii 9 Ecclus xxviii 7 πάριδε ἄγνοιαν 'Because they should amend,' Eng, where 'because'='in order that' Comp S. Matt. xx. 31. 'Rebuked them because they should hold their peace.' So 'quia' is used in late Latin for 'ut.'

24. Ἀγαπᾷς γάρ The reason of God's long-suffering and mercy. Euseb in Psalm xxiv 10 (p 93, Ben.): ἐλεεῖ γὰρ τὰ ὄντα καὶ οὐδὲν βδελύσσεται ὧν ἐποίησεν οὐδὲ γὰρ μισῶν τι κατεσκεύασε—quoting from memory.

Οὐδὲν βδελ. Comp. Coll. for Ash-Wednesday· 'Omnipotens aeterne Deus, Qui nihil odisti eorum quae fecisti;' which is the Vulg version of this passage, and is found in the Sarum Missal, with the addition of a clause from ver 23· 'Dissimulans peccata omnium propter poenitentiam.' Comp. Prov xvi. 4. S. Bas Lit. Copt: 'Deus magne et aeterne, qui hominem absque vitio condidisti, et mortem quae Satanae invidia in mundum intraverat, per adventum Filii Tui . de-struxisti' (XXXI. p. 1666, Migne) Clem Al Paed i. 8. 62 (p. 135): ἦν γὰρ οὐδὲν ὃ μισεῖ ὁ Κύριος.

Οὐδὲ γάρ 'Nec enim odiens aliquid constituisti aut fecisti,' Vulg. This is not accurate and contains an unauthorised addition. Eng. 'For never wouldest Thou have made anything if Thou hadst hated it.' 'Odiens' is a form unknown to classical Latin, but various parts of the verb 'odio' are used in the Vulg and by late authors. Thus, 'odirent,' Ps civ. 25; 'odiet,' Luke xvi 13, 'odibunt,' Prov. i 22 'odite,' Ps. xcvi. 10; 'oditur,' Tert. Apol. 3.

25. Κληθέν 'Called into being.' Is. xli. 41: 'Who hath wrought and done it, calling the generations from the beginning?' Ib. xlviii. 13, and Rom. iv 17: 'God, Who .. calleth those things which be not as though they were' Comp Neh ix 6

26. Σά ἐστι πάντα, φιλόψυχε, Orig. con. Cels. iv. 28 (I. 521, Ben.). Did De Trin. ii 6 (xxxix. 509, M) reads. ἢ τὸ μὴ βληθὲν ὑπὸ σοῦ ἐτηρήθη, φείδῃ δὲ πάντων, ὅτι πάντα σά ἐστιν, Δέσποτα φιλόψυχε, καὶ τὸ ἄφθαρτόν σου Πνεῦμά ἐστιν ἐν πᾶσι

Φιλόψυχος in classical Greek means, 'fond of life,' 'cowardly.' (Comp S. John xii 25 ὁ φιλῶν τὴν ψυχήν). Here it means, 'lover of souls,' 'qui amas animas,' a beautiful expression. Comp. i 13, Ezek xviii 4: 'Behold, all souls are Mine' S. Matt xviii. 14. See Prolegom p 27.

CHAPTER XII.

1. Τὸ γάρ gives the reason why God is 'a lover of souls,' xi. 26. The Vulg. here, as in iv 1, introduces an exclamatory sentence, not warranted by the Greek. 'O quam bonus et suavis est, Domine, spiritus Tuus in omnibus!' Some countenance is lent to this clause by the Ar. and Syr. versions, which give respectively, Arab.. 'Nam spiritus bonus omnibus inest' Syr: 'Amator es animarum, quia spiritus bonus habitat in omnibus' But the Greek MSS do not vary. S. Aug. Con Faust. xix 28 (VIII. 320 D) has 'Bonus enim spiritus Tuus est in omnibus'

Ἐν πᾶσι. Eng., 'in all things,' taking πᾶσι as neut., as πάντων, xi. 26. This is not Pantheism, but a truth expressed elsewhere in the Bible. Thus Ps. civ. 30: 'Thou sendest forth Thy Spirit, they are created: and Thou renewest the face of the earth.'

Job xxxiii. 4· 'The Spirit of God hath made me, and the breath of the Almighty hath given me life.' Comp. Gen ii 7; vi. 3 (Sept.), and see note on i. 7. It is easier however to take πᾶσι as masc. with reference to φιλόψυχε (κατὰ σύνεσιν) Gutb. quotes Thom. Aquin. 1 9 8 a 3 'Deus dicitur esse in re aliqua dupliciter: Uno modo per modum causae agentis et sic est iu omnibus rebus creatis ab ipso. Alio modo sicut objectum operationis est in operante, quod proprium est in operationibus animae, secundum quod cognitum est in cognoscente et desideratum in desiderante ... Est in omnibus per potentiam, inquantum omnia ejus potestate subduntur,' etc. The author does not mean to imply that the Spirit of God is in the same degree and in the same manner present in all men good or bad otherwise he would contradict himself. See i 3–5. So the charge of Platonism founded on this passage is futile. S. Athan, Ep. I. ad Serap 26 (I. pp 674, 675), quotes τὸ γὰρ ἀφθαρτόν σου Πνεῦμά ἐστιν ἐν πᾶσι, and then a little further on says τὸ μὲν Πνεῦμα Κυρίου πεπλήρωκε τὴν οἰκουμένην Οὕτω γὰρ καὶ ὁ Δαβὶδ ψάλλει Ποῦ πορευθῶ ἀπὸ τοῦ πνεύματός σου; καὶ πάλιν ἐν τῇ Σοφίᾳ γέγραπται Τὸ γὰρ, κ.τ.λ. And Ep. III ad Serap. 4 (p. 693), after citing the Psalm as above, Ποῦ . . Πνεύματός σου; he proceeds, ὡς μὴ ὄντος αὐτοῦ ἐν τόπῳ, ἀλλ' ἔξω μὲν τῶν πάντων, ἐν δὲ τῷ Υἱῷ ὄντος, ὡς ἐστι καὶ ὁ Υἱὸς ἐν τῷ Πατρί

2–27. *Wisdom exhibited in the punishment of God's enemies, especially the Canaanites. The lesson to be learned therefrom.*

2 Διό, i.e. because God is pitiful, xi 23–26

Παραπίπτοντας So sin is παράπτωμα, Rom xi. 11. See on x 1, and comp. vi 9 Vulg., 'eos qui exerrant' 'Exerro' is a very rare word, occurring 2 Macc ii. 2; S Cypr Ep 1 12. Stat Theb vi 444

'Spargitur in gyros, dexterque exerrat Orion'

Κατ' ὀλίγον, 'by little and little.' Vulg, 'partibus'='partim,' which is not found in Vulg 'Partibus' occurs again ver 10. The statement is general, but with special reference to the Canaanites, as the following verse shows. Comp. Ps. cxl. 5, Hebr. xii. 5–10; and see Amos iv. 6–11. 'It is a great gift of God, that He should care for us, so as to chasten us.' Pusey *in loc*.

Ὑπομιμνήσκων, by judgments which show the connection between sin and punishment, xi. 16

3 Παλ οἰκήτορας, governed by μισήσας. The 'old inhabitants' are the seven nations of Canaan conquered by the Israelites. Deut. vii 1 'Inhabitatores,' Vulg. Zeph. ii. 5. See on ver. 5 for words of similar formation.

Ἁγίας γῆς, so called 2 Macc 1 7

Μισήσας Ps v 6, 7 · ἐμίσησας πάντας τοὺς ἐργαζομένους τὴν ἀνομίαν ... ἄνδρα αἱμάτων καὶ δόλιον βδελύσσεται Κύριος. God hates the sinner's sin, though He is merciful to the sinner See ver. 8.

4. Ἐπὶ τῷ. The ground of God's hatred of them. 'For performing most odious works of sorcery and impious rites' Ex. xxii. 18; Lev. xviii 24–28, Deut xviii. 9–14

Ἔχθιστα 'Odibilia,' Vulg. So Ecclus. vii 28; Rom 1 30, Rev xviii. 2. This is an ante-classical word revived in later Latin. It occurs in Accius (B C. 136), in Prisc. p. 709 P. 'Gnati mater pessimi odibilis,' and in Lamprid Heliogab c. 18: 'Vita, moribus, improbitate ita odibilis ut ejus nomen senatus eraserit' Comp S Ambr Ep. 14, De Cain et Abel, i. 4 See note on x. 4

Φαρμακειῶν Rev ix. 21 'Witchcrafts' Ex. vii. 22, Is. xlvii. 9, 12.

5. Τέκνων τε φονέας. Fritzsche reads φονὰς, which he would join with ἔργα and τελετάς But the change is against the authority of all MSS., and unnecessary. The 'murderers of children' refer to the worshippers of Moloch and Baal, Lev xx. 2–5, 2 Kings iii 27; Ps. cvi 37, 38; Jer vii. 31, xix 5 The idea of these sacrifices was that the worth of such vicarious atonement was enhanced by the preciousness of the thing offered, the enormity of this violation of the holiest instincts being covered by the proof thus afforded of the superiority of religious to human obligations. See

further, on xiv 23 For the Vulg word 'necator' (Macrob Sat. i 22) see below.

Σπλαγχνοφάγων depends on θοῖναν, which is governed, as the other accusatives, by μισήσας, ver 3 Ἀνθρ. σαρκῶν depends on σπλαγχν., 'the feast of the entrail-eaters of men's flesh.' There is a reading σπλαγχνοφάγους found in Compl, but without MS. authority. The Vulg. may perhaps have so read, translating: 'Et comestores viscerum hominum et devoratores sanguinis' There seems to be no evidence that the Canaanites were guilty of cannibalism. It is probably an exaggeration of the author Comp. 2 Macc. vi 7. The Vulg. word 'comestor' is ἅπ λεγ 'Comessor' occurs in Tertull Adv. Marc. I i. Other unusual words of the same formation are these. 'adnuntiator,' Acts xvii 18; 'clusor,' 2 Kings xxiv. 14; 'ascensor,' Exod xv 1, 'conspector,' Ecclus xxxvi 19, 'exterminator,' 1 Cor. x. 10; 'malefactor,' 1 Pet. ii. 12, 'mediator,' Gal. iii. 19; 'miserator,' James v. 11, 'devorator' occurs Luke vii. 34, and in Tertull De Resurr. XXX. ii.

Καὶ αἵματος This clause is one of the most difficult passages in the whole Book, owing to the evident corruption of the text and the impossibility of restoring it satisfactorily The readings of the MSS will be seen in the critical note. The versions afford little help. Taking the Vat. reading, ἐκ μέσου μυσταθείας σου, as the starting-point, we have almost as many variations as MSS., and as many conjectures as editors. The Vat itself has been altered into μυσουμυστασθειασου. Vulg. 'a medio sacramento tuo,' perhaps having μυστηρίου σου The Syr gives 'Fecerunt in medio sacramento sine lege.' The Ar: 'Quum abstulissent e medio sui divinorum sacramentorum cognitionem' Of the editions, that of Basil, 1545, reads ἐκ μέσου μύστας τε θείας σου. Compl: ἐκ μέσου μύστας θείας σου, with the wonderful translation: 'De medio sacramenti Divini tui.' Basil, 1550. ἐκ μύσους μύστας τε θειασμοῦ. Reinecc and Aug as Vat Apel. αἵματος ἐκμύσου μύστας θιάσου. Grimm, 1837. ἐκμυσοῖς μύστας θιάσου. 1860. ἐκ μύσους μύστας θιάσου. Fritzsche: αἵματος ἐκ μέσου μύστας θιάσου Gutb retains the Vat reading If we can be satisfied with retaining words which occur nowhere else, we have three alternatives We may keep μυσταθείας, deriving it from μυστάθης, which Hesychius admits, explaining it εἶδός τι καὶ φρατριὰ μαντέων Or we may adopt the Sin word μυσταθίασος, a compound of μύστης and θίασος Or, leaving μύστας θιάσου, we may, with Grimm and Reusch, turn ἐκ μέσου into the new word ἐκμύσου, from ἐκμυσής, 'abominandus' Neither of these alternatives approves itself to me, and, failing any better suggestion, I am inclined to read, with Fritzsche, μύστας θιάσου, but taking καὶ αἵματος with the preceding clause

6. Καὶ αἵματος, with σπλαγχνοφάγων, 'eaters of men's flesh and of blood' This was expressly contrary to God's ordinance, Gen. ix 4, Lev xvii 10 Calmet 'Sunt qui ferant Epulum sanguinis ex medio choreae Menadum Satis constat, in Bacchi orgiis cruda exsta cruentasque carnes vorari consuevisse' Ap Migne, Script Sacr Curs.

Ἐκ μέσου μύστας θιάσου Μύστας is probably governed by ἀπολέσαι 'Thou wishedst to destroy the initiated (the votaries) from the midst of their company,' or, as Arnald words it 'Thou wast determined to destroy those priests particularly amidst all the crew of idolaters, ex medio tripudiantium coetu' This is very much the sense of the Eng version

Αὐθέντας, 'murderers with their own hand,' or 'murderers of their own flesh and blood,' like Aeschyl Agam 1573:

τρίβειν θανάτοις αὐθένταισι.

The Vulg 'auctores' is quite a mistake, as Gutb. allows, unless the word 'caedis' has dropped out 'Souls destitute of help,' i. e. their own children. The Jews learned these horrid rites from the Canaanites Thus Ps cvi 37, 38 'They sacrificed their sons and daughters unto devils, and shed innocent blood, even the blood of their sons and of their daughters, whom they sacrificed unto the idols of Canaan' Comp Jer vii 31; Deut xii. 31. See on ver. 5.

Ἀβοηθήτων, Ps lxxxvii. 5; 2 Macc. iii. 28 'Inauxiliatarum,' Vulg This is ἅπ λεγ

Πατέρων ἡμ. Ex. xxiii 23, 24, Num. xxxiii 52 ff., Deut vii, xx 16–18

7. Ἀποικίαν. This seems hardly the word to apply to the settlement of the Hebrews in what was virtually their own land, hence Grimm suspects that the author uses the word for ἐποικίαν, which would not denote removal from the mother-country. Vulg, 'peregrinationem' Eng Marg, 'new inhabitance'='population.' A. Lap · 'Ideo expulisti Chananaeos ut eorum terra, i e terrae et regiones, perciperent novam dignamque se peregrinationem, hoc est, peregrinorum et advenarum coloniam, coloniam, inquam, filiorum Dei, i e fidelium et piorum Israelitarum'

Δέξηται, 'perciperent,' Vulg. This plainly ought to be 'perciperet,' sc 'terra'

Τιμιωτάτη γῆ Deut xi. 12.

8. Ὡς ἀνθρώπων. God had mercy even on the Canaanites 'as being men' possessed of souls and weak and prone to sin. Comp. Ps lxxviii 38, 39 God's long-suffering waited till the fourth generation. Gen. xv 16

Σφῆκας. From the Sept Ex xxiii 28 ἀποστελῶ τὰς σφηκίας προτέρας σου Deut vii 20, and Josh. xxiv 12 ἐξαπέστειλε προτέραν ὑμῶν τὴν σφηκίαν The author seems to take this literally of hornets and wasps, according to the rabbinical legend; and instances are given in profane history where these insects have depopulated whole districts, as the venomous fly in Africa does now (See Smith's Dict of Bible, s v Hornets) Philo, De Praem. et Poen. § 16 (II p. 423), says the same thing. Commentators generally consider 'hornets' are to be taken metaphorically for panic. Comp. Deut. i 44. Thus S. Aug says, we do not read that the hornets were sent, so, he proceeds 'Per hoc' vespae istae" aculei timoris intelligendi sunt fortasse, quibus agitabantur memoratae gentes, ut cederent filiis Israel.' Quaest in Exod ii 93 (t iii 452).

Καταβραχὺ, 'little by little.' Thuc. 1. 64. Ex. xxiii 30. κατὰ μικρὸν μικρὸν ἐκβαλῶ αὐτοὺς ἀπὸ σοῦ. Comp Deut vii 22

Ἐξολεθρ Exod xxii 20, Acts iii 23.

9. Ἐν παρατάξει, 'in regular battle.' Judith i 6; 1 Macc iii 26

Θηρίοις Comp 2 Kings xvii 25, 26, Lev. xxvi 22, Deut xxxii. 24. See on xi 17.

Ὑφ' ἕν. Vulg : 'simul' 'Together' 'Uno eodemque momento'= πρὸς μίαν ῥοπὴν, xviii 12. Wahl.

10 Καταβραχὺ, ver 8. Vulg., 'partibus.' See on ver 2. Comp Judg ii. 21–23

Τόπον μετανοίας occurs Heb xii. 17. Comp Clem Rom Ep ad Cor vii 5 ἐν γενεᾷ καὶ γενεᾷ μετανοίας τόπον ἔδωκεν ὁ Δεσπότης τοῖς βουλομένοις ἐπιστραφῆναι ἐπ' αὐτόν Const. Ap ii 38

Οὐκ ἀγνοῶν 'Though Thou knewest well.' God's foreknowledge leaves man's free will unfettered.

Γένεσις, 'birth,' 'origin.' Vulg., 'natio'

Ἔμφυτος, 'innate,' 'planted in their very nature;' an adumbration of the doctrine of original sin, and (together with the following verse) quoted by S Aug. Contr. Julian Op. imperf iii 11(X p. 1056). 'Puto quod natura, non imitatio redarguitur, et quomodo natura nisi vitiata peccato, non in primo homine sic creata?'

Οὐ μὴ ἀλλαγῇ. 'Non poterat mutari,' Vulg. The Latin is too strong for the Greek expression, which merely implies God's absolute knowledge of their perverse abuse of free-will.

Λογισμὸς, 'way of reasoning,' as 2 Macc. vii. 21. τὸν θῆλυν λογισμὸν ἄρσενι θυμῷ διεγείρασα.

11 Κατηραμένον. Referring to the curse pronounced on Canaan by Noah, Gen ix 24–27, which had not only political but moral consequences. Joseph. Ant I vi 3 Νῶεος αἰσθόμενος τοῖς μὲν ἄλλοις παισὶν εὐδαιμονίαν εὔχεται, τῷ δὲ Χαμᾷ διὰ τὴν συγγενείαν αὐτῷ μὲν οὐ κατηράσατο, τοῖς δ' ἐκγόνοις αὐτοῦ καὶ τῶν ἄλλων διαπεφευγότων τὴν ἀρὰν, τοὺς Χαναάνου παῖδας μέτεισιν ὁ Θεός.

Εὐλαβούμενός τινα 'From fear of anyone' Ecclus xxiii 18; 2 Macc viii. 16; Job xiii 25 So εὐλάβεια, xvii 8.

Ἄδειαν. 'Indulgence,' 'impunity in those things in which they sinned'

12 Τίς γὰρ ἐρεῖ, see on xi. 21. Τίς . τί ἐποίησας; these words are found in Job ix 12

Ἃ σὺ ἐποίησας Arn takes these words thus. 'Who shall call Thee to account for the things which Thou hast done against the nations?' But the Greek rather favours the Eng version and the Vulg., 'Nationes quas tu fecisti.' The Vulg transposes the two last clauses

Εἰς κατάστασίν σοι = ἵνα καταστῇ σοι, 'In order to stand forth against Thee,' Grimm 'In conspectu tuo,' Vulg 'In Thy presence,' Eng. Marg Κατάστασιν and ἔκδικος seem rather to be used here in a forensic sense· 'Who will come to set forth the cause against Thee, as an advocate in respect of unrighteous men?'

13 Ὧι. It seems best to refer this to σοῦ 'Thou who carest for all, in order to show Thy impartiality' Ch. vi 7; 1 Pet. v 7 Whence the Eng gets 'to whom Thou mightest show' is doubtful. 'Unright' is = 'unrighteous.' The distinguishing mark of heathendom is that its gods presided only over particular provinces, not 'caring for all' See 1 Kings xx. 23.

14. Ἀντοφθαλμῆσαι, 'to look in the face,' 'to defy' Ecclus xix. 5 (Compl. and Field): ὁ δὲ ἀντοφθαλμῶν ἡδοναῖς Acts xxvii. 15. The Vulg. is very tame 'In conspectu tuo inquirent' The word occurs in Clem. Rom. Ep. ad Cor. xxxiv. 1: ὁ νωθρὸς καὶ παρειμένος οὐκ ἀντοφθαλμεῖ τῷ ἐργοπαρέκτῃ αὐτοῦ. S. Barn. Ep. v 10 ἐμβλέποντες οὐκ ἰσχύουσιν εἰς τὰς ἀκτῖνας αὐτοῦ [ἡλίου] ἀντοφθαλμῆσαι. Polyb. I xvii. 3; lxviii 7

Ἐκόλασας has more authority than ἀπώλεσας. Vulg : 'perdidisti,' proves nothing, as it translates κολάζειν, ver. 27, by 'exterminare,' Reusch.

Περὶ ὧν = περὶ ἐκείνων οὕς.

15. Αὐτόν. It is inconsistent with God's power that, as mortal judges often do, He should punish 'even' (αὐτόν) the innocent.

Δυνάμεως. 'Multi homines, ut videantur potentes, innoxios vexant, sed haec potentia est tyrannis magnaque animi impotentia Dei autem potentia vera est potentia, quia vera est aequitas veraque justitia.' Corn. a Lap.

16. Ἀρχή, 'foundation' God's almighty power is not, as man's often is, a cause of injustice and wrong, but is the basis of, and inseparably joined with, just dealing. Grimm quotes Joseph. Ant. iv 8 14. τοῦ Θεοῦ ἰσχύς ἐστι τὸ δίκαιον.

Τὸ π. σ. δεσπόζειν, 'Thy lordship over all.' Comp. xi. 23, 26; and Rom. xi. 32.

17 Ἀπιστούμενος 'When Thou art doubted, discredited, as regards the fulness, perfection of Thy power' It is then that God displays His might; e.g. in the case of Pharaoh, Ex. v. 2; and Rabshakeh, 2 Kings xviii. 32. Comp. 2 Macc. ix. 4.

Ἐν τοῖς εἰδόσι. The addition of οὐκ in A. seems to be a scribe's correction. The Vulg. (text rec.) indeed gives: 'Horum qui te nesciunt,' but many Lat MSS have 'qui sciunt,' and it is so quoted by S Aug Quaest in Hept. vi. 23. 'In the case of those who know (intellectually and theoretically) Thee, or Thy power, and acknowledge it not practically by life and action.' Comp. Rom i. 21.

Ἐξελέγχεις. 'Thou puttest their audacity to shame.' 'Audaciam traducis,' Vulg, as iv 20.

18 Δεσπόζων ἰσχύος 'Mastering, controlling Thy strength.' Vulg takes these words as a title of God. 'Dominator virtutis.' So S Aug (l. sup. cit.). 'Dominus virtutum.' But it is best rendered as above. Comp Ps lxxviii 38, 39.

Ἐν ἐπιεικείᾳ Vulg.: 'cum tranquillitate.' 'With mildness, lenity' Cant. Tr. Puer. 18; Bar. ii. 27: 'Thou hast dealt with us after all Thy goodness,' ἐπιείκειαν Comp ch ii. 19

Φειδοῦς, 'forbearance.' 'Reverentia,' Vulg. So ἐπιείκεια is translated, ii 19, q. v. It is the rendering of εὐλάβεια, Heb. v. 7 'exauditus pro sua reverentia.' Comp Esth. iii. (21), additam ἄνευ παντὸς οἴκτου καὶ φειδοῦς.

Πάρεστι.. δύνασθαι The passage is found in Const Apost vii 35. Vulg. renders well: 'Subest enim tibi, cum volueris, posse.' Cp Rom. iv. 21.

19 From this verse to the end of the chapter the author enforces the lesson of mercy and judgment to be learned from God's dealings

Φιλάνθρωπον. This is a great advance on the

Jewish principle, 'Thou shalt love thy neighbour, and hate thine enemy' (S Matt v. 43 comp Deut. vii. 2, xxiii. 6, and Tacit. Hist. V. v. 2), and an approach to the Gospel law, S. Matt. v. 44, xviii. 32, 33.

Ἐπὶ ἁμαρτ. 'On the occasion of' = 'when we sin.' Vulg· 'Judicans das locum in peccatis poenitentiae' Many MSS. omit 'judicans,' which is not in the Greek.

20 Ἐτιμώρησας A and some cursives have ἐτιμωρήσω But the act voice is used in the sense of 'taking vengeance on' Comp. Soph. Oed. Tyr. 107. Ἐτιμωρήσω occurs, without any various reading, xviii 8

Προσοχῆς, 'attention,' 'caution' Ecclus. Prol · παρακέκλησθε μετ' εὐνοίας καὶ προσοχῆς τὴν ἀνάγνωσιν ποιεῖσθαι. Comp Rom. ix. 22.

Καὶ διέσεως. 'And indulgence.' Δίεσις, 'discharge,' 'letting through.' These two words are omitted by A, some cursives, and Vulg. Διέσεως is owed to S The usual reading is καὶ δεήσεως, which is supposed to be explained by such passages as Is. lxv. 2 'I have spread out My hands all the day unto a rebellious people' Rom x 21; Prov i 24 But it seems unsuitable to God's dealings with the abominable Canaanites. The other reading, καὶ διέσωσας, probably is owed to the Sin διέσως: it certainly cannot have been the original expression, as it is quite foreign to the intention of the passage The Eng version leaves the word untranslated. It is omitted in Compl.

21. Ἀκριβείας, 'carefulness,' 'circumspection,' opp. to the rashness and partiality of men's judgments.

Ὅρκους καὶ συνθήκας. Comp. xviii 22 Deut. vii. 8; Gal. iii 16 'Juramenta et conventiones,' Vulg 'Juramentum' is a post-classical word = 'jusjurandum,' found xviii. 6, 22; Hab iii 9.

Ἀγαθ ὑποσχέσεων. Comp. Eph ii 12 τῶν διαθηκῶν τῆς ἐπαγγελίας, and 2 Pet i. 4. Wahl renders 'Foedera cum promissionibus eximiis juncta.'

22 Παιδεύων ... μαστιγοῖς. 'Chastening,' as children.. 'Thou scourgest,' as slaves. The two words occur Prov iii. 12 · ὃν γὰρ ἀγαπᾷ Κύριος παιδεύει [ἐλέγχει V], μαστιγοῖ δὲ πάντα υἱὸν ὃν παραδέχεται, quoted Heb. xii. 6. Comp. ch. xvi. 16; Ps xxxi 10: πολλαὶ αἱ μάστιγες τοῦ ἁμαρτωλοῦ, τὸν δὲ ἐλπίζοντα ἐπὶ Κύριον ἔλεος κυκλώσει

Μεριμν. κρίνοντες. 'When judging others we should think earnestly on Thy goodness.' Comp S Matt. xviii· 33

Κρινόμενοι, sc. ὑπὸ σοῦ.

23. Ὅθεν (Acts xxvi. 19; Heb iii 1), i.e. because God punished His enemies with more rigour than the Israelites. The author here and in the following verses speaks of the Egyptians. This is plain from his allusions to their being punished by the objects of their worship, which is not recorded of the Canaanites Ch xi 15, 16, xvi 1.

Τοὺς ἐν ἀφρ. ζ. β ἀδίκους. 'Whereas men have lived dissolutely and unrighteously' (ἀδίκως), Eng This is very inadequate. 'The unrighteous who persisted in folly of life,' or, 'a foolish life,' folly being sin, as i 3 Comp. Rom i 21

Βδελυγμάτων, 'abominations,' i e objects of idolatrous worship So continually in Sept. Ecclus xlix 2, 1 Kings xi. 6, Is ii 8, 20. All the Plagues were directed against the idols of Egypt 'Against all the gods (θεοῖς) of Egypt I will execute judgment,' Ex. xii 12 Thus the Nile, the sacred river, was turned to blood, the murrain on cattle discredited the worship of Apis; frogs, flies, etc., which they adored, became means of punishment; the sun-god himself had no power to shield them from the darkness

24 Τῶν πλάνης ὁδ. μακρ. ἐπλ. 'In erroris via diutius erraverunt,' Vulg. Better, as Grimm and Gutb.: 'They wandered further than the ways of error,' hyperbolically = 'they went beyond the usual limits,' 'were sunk in the grossest depths of error.'

Θεοὺς ὑπολ 'In that they held as gods even creatures which their enemies despised as being worthless,' e.g frogs, crocodiles, serpents, xi.·15; Lev. xi. 41–43; Rom i 23.

Ἄτιμα, 'supervacua,' Vulg, as xi. 16.

Δίκην, 'after the manner of,' ἅπ λεγ in Greek Scriptures, Grimm

ψευσθέντες. Vulg: 'viventes' There is no variation in the Greek MSS. Rensch suggests 'errantes.'

25. Παισὶν... ἐμπαιγμὸν.. παιγνίοις, ver. 26, a play of words. 'Cum pueris pueriliter lusisti,' Gr. The mocking judgments were the earlier and lighter Plagues.

26. Παιγνίοις ἐπιτιμήσεως. 'Play-games of punishment.' Eng. 'Correction wherein He dallied with them' Churton · 'Sportive likenesses of rebuke' So Philo, Vit. Mos. i 38 (II p 114)· τὰ παράδοξα ταῦτα καὶ παράλογα Θεοῦ παιγνιά εἰσιν Vulg · 'Ludibriis et increpationibus' Or, as some MSS. have, 'increpationis.' The word 'increpatio' is ἅπ. λεγ. in Vulg. See on vi. 18

Πειράσουσιν. The author makes a general statement, or else speaks as though he were waiting with his forefathers for the final exhibition of the 'judgment worthy of God,' i.e. the death of the firstborn, and the destruction of the host in the Red Sea.

27 The Eng. version is very confused. The Vulg. is not much better. The passage may be thus translated · 'For in the things, at suffering from which they were distressed, yea, in these same things, which they deemed to be gods, they saw, when they were punished thereby, Him whom before they had refused to know, and acknowledged Him as the true God' They saw God's hand in what happened to them through the creatures which they worshipped, xi. 13. Churton paraphrases · 'For the vexation which they felt at these petty chastisements which befel them through their gods, constrained them to acknowledge the true God whom they once denied.'

Ἡρνοῦντο. See Ex. v. 2. See on xvi. 16.

Θεὸν ἀληθῆ Ex viii. 8 ; ix 27, x. 16

Διό, because, though they were forced to recognise the Lord, yet they did not let the knowledge influence their actions Ex xiv. 5–9.

Τέρμα τῆς καταδίκης 'The extreme point of, the severest, condemnation.' Eurip Suppl. 369 .

ἐπὶ τέρμα καὶ τὸ πλέον ἐμῶν κακῶν.

Comp 1 Thess. ii 16 'The wrath is come upon them to the uttermost (εἰς τέλος)'

CHAPTER XIII.

CHAPTERS XIII, XIV THE ORIGIN, GROWTH, AND EFFECTS OF IDOLATRY, THE OPPOSITE OF WISDOM

XIII. 1–9 *Idolatry begins with the worship of nature*

1. Here commences a digression on the folly of idolatry in general, the subject springing naturally from the remarks at the end of ch xii Comp. Philo, De Monarch 1 1–3 (II pp. 213, 217).

Μάταιοι μέν, answered by ταλαίπωροι δὲ, ver. 10. Understand ἦσαν. For μάταιος and ματαιότης, applied to idolaters, see 2 Kings xvii. 15 ; Rom i 21, Eph. iv. 17. So the heathen are called, 3 Macc. vi. 11, ματαιόφρονες

Φύσει (om. by Vulg. and some other versions), here, 'the intellectual nature'

Καὶ ἐκ τ. ὁρωμ. ἀγ., sc οἱ, 'and who from the,' etc. For the sentiment comp S. Paul's speech to the people of Lystra, Acts xiv. 15–17, and Rom i 20. S Clem. ad Cor. lx. 1 σὺ τὴν ἀέναον τοῦ κόσμου σύστασιν διὰ τῶν ἐνεργουμένων ἐφανεροποίησας.. ὁ ἀγαθὸς ἐν τοῖς ὁρωμένοις καὶ πιστὸς ἐν τοῖς πεποιθόσιν ἐπὶ σέ 'De his quae videntur,' Vulg. For 'de'='ex' comp 1 Macc. xiii. 47 , S. Matt. iii 9 ; S. Luke i. 71, Vulg.

Τὸν ὄντα 'The incommunicable name of God.' Ex. iii. 14 'Ἐγώ εἰμι ὁ ὤν . Ὁ Ὢν ἀπέσταλκέ με πρὸς ὑμᾶς Comp. Rev i 4, 8. Among the Egyptians the worship of the tutelary deity of the Nile was conspicuous The annual festival called Niloa was celebrated with the utmost solemnity about the time of the summer solstice, when the river began to rise. See Wilkinson, Anc. Egyptians, iii. 369 ff. (ed. 1878).

Εἰδέναι Θεόν, 2 Thess. i. 8.

Προσσχόντες, 'by heeding,' 'attending to'

Τεχνίτην Hebr. xi. 10.

2 The objects of worship here mentioned are what S. Paul calls, Gal iv 3, 9 τὰ στοιχεῖα τοῦ κόσμου. Comp. Philo, De Decalog. 12 (II p. 189). πλάνος τὶς οὐ μικρὸς τὸ πλεῖστον τῶν ἀνθρώπων γένος κατέσχηκε, περὶ πράγματος ὅπερ ἢ μόνον ἢ μάλιστα ἦν εἰκὸς ἀπλανέστατον ταῖς ἑκάστων διανοίαις ἐνιδρύσθαι. Ἐκτεθειώκασι γὰρ οἱ μὲν τὰς τέσσαρας ἀρχάς, γῆν καὶ ὕδωρ καὶ ἀέρα καὶ πῦρ· οἱ δὲ ἥλιον καὶ σελήνην, καὶ τοὺς ἄλλους πλανήτας καὶ ἀπλανεῖς ἀστέρας· οἱ δὲ τὸν σύμπαντα κόσμον. Plat Cratyl xvi. p. 397: φαίνονταί μοι οἱ πρῶτοι τῶν ἀνθρώπων τῶν περὶ τὴν Ἑλλάδα τούτους μόνους τοὺς θεοὺς ἡγεῖσθαι, οὕσπερ νῦν πολλοὶ τῶν βαρβάρων, ἥλιον καὶ σελήνην καὶ γῆν καὶ ἄστρα καὶ οὐρανόν. Herod. (I 131) says of the Persians· θύουσι ἡλίῳ τε καὶ σελήνῃ καὶ γῇ καὶ πυρὶ καὶ ὕδατι καὶ ἀνέμοισι. τούτοισι μὲν δὴ μούνοισι θύουσι ἀρχῆθεν. Cp. 1 Cor viii. 5

Πῦρ The worship of fire prevailed among the Persians and Chaldeans. The Greek god Hephaestus was adored chiefly as the patron of arts and manufactures. The earliest form of idolatry seems to have been the worship of Nature.

Πνεῦμα. 'Wind,' as Aeolus. The Egyptians too worshipped the winds as connected with the annual overflow of the Nile, so did the Persians, Her i 131; vii. 191. See above.

Ταχινὸν ἀέρα, 'the rapid air,' like Spenser's, 'The flitting skies,' referring probably to the atmosphere, personified in Zeus and Hera.

Κύκλ ἄστρων. See Deut. iv 19; xvii. 3

Βίαιον ὕδωρ. 'Forceful water,' worshipped by the Persians, as by the Greeks under the names of Poseidon (ἐνοσίχθων), Oceanus, etc. So the Egyptians worshipped the Nile

Φωστῆρας οὐρ. The sun and moon, as Gen. i 16: τοὺς δύο φωστῆρας τοὺς μεγάλους Comp. Job xxxi. 26–28, Ecclus xliii 7 The Egyptians worshipped the sun at Heliopolis (Beth-shemesh, Jer. xliii 13) under the name of Osiris, and the moon under that of Isis. Comp. Warburton, Div. Legat. bk. iv. § 5. The Egyptian word for sun is Ra, and the royal name which we call Pharaoh is really Phrah, that is, Ra with the definite article Pi prefixed. Wilkinson, Anc. Egypt. III. 44 (ed. 1878)

Πρυτάνεις, in app. with θεοὺς, as in Eng and Vulg. So Pindar, Pyth vi 24, speaks of Κρονίδης as

βαρυόπαν στεροπᾶν κεραυνῶν τε πρύτανιν.

3 Τῇ καλλονῇ. It is rather the grandeur of the powers of nature than their beauty which influenced the Hebrew mind. But see Ecclus. xliii 9, 11. So τοῦ κάλλους γενεσιάρχης below seems to be a notion more consonant with Greek feeling than Hebrew.

Ταῦτα Reusch thinks is an interpolation, but there is sufficient authority for it S. Cypr. has: 'Quorum si propter speciem hoc aestimaverunt,' Ep. ad Fortun 1.

Τούτων is best taken with δεσπότης, as in ver. 9. Comp ὁ κατασκευάσας αὐτά, ver 4. The Vulg translates it twice. 'Quanto his dominator eorum speciosior est.' S Proclus. ὃν γὰρ ὁ νόμος κηρύττει δημιουργόν, τοῦτον ἡ ὄψις διὰ τῶν κτισμάτων πιστοῦται, Orat. II. de Incarn. (Gall. IX p. 623).

Γενεσιάρχης, ἅπ. λεγ in Sept. and unknown in older writings. Euseb. De Laud Const (p 640, Migne)· Θεὸς δὲ ὁ ἐπέκεινα Λόγου γενεσιάρχης. Epiph Adv. Haer. II ii 52 (II p. 273, Migne) The word γενάρχης is used in classical Greek for 'the founder of a family.' Comp γενεσιουργός, ver. 5.

4. Εἰ δὲ .. ἐκπλαγέντες, sc. θεοὺς ὑπελάμβανον αὐτά.

For the sentiment in vers 3, 4, Grimm· compares Lactant. Instit. II. 3, 5· 'Qui quum Dei opera mirarentur . . earum rerum obstupefacti et ipsius Artificis obliti, quem videre non poterant, ejus opera venerari et colere coeperunt, nec unquam intelligere quiverunt, quanto major quantoque mirabilior, qui illa fecit ex nihilo.' See a fine passage in S Aug, Serm lxviii, on this subject, partly quoted below on ver. 9.

5 Μεγέθ. καὶ καλλονῆς seems the best reading, the

καὶ having dropped out in some MSS. owing to the commencement of the next word Thus μέγεθος refers to δύναμιν and ἐνέργειαν, ver. 4, καλλονῇ to ver. 3. Euseb in Ps xviii. 2 (p. 71, Ben.) has ἐκ γὰρ μεγέθους καὶ καλλονῆς. So in Ps lxv 2 (p. 326, Ben), and in Ps xci 5 (p. 610, Ben). S Athan.: ἐκ μεγέθους καὶ καλλονῆς κτισμάτων ἀναλόγως ὁ γενεσιουργὸς θεωρεῖται. Contr. Gent. 44 (I. p 43, Ben.) Thus in Or ii cont Arian 32 (I. p 500, Ben) Comp Paeud-Athan contr. Ar 13 (II. p. 210, Ben.)· ἔδει οὖν καὶ σὲ ἐκ τῆς τῶν στοιχείων ἐναρέτου συμπήξεως ἀναλογίσασθαι τὸν δημιουργὸν ἀναλόγως, καὶ σαυτοῦ ἐπιγνώμονα γενέσθαι, ὅτι ἀϊδίου Θεοῦ τυγχάνει ἔργον ὁ κόσμος, οὐ κτιστὴς δὲ φύσεως, μὴ δυναμένης ἐπαρκέσαι τοσαῦτα δρᾶν.

Κτισμάτων. The Vulg reads καὶ κτισμ., as Ald. and Compl, 'A magnitudine enim speciei et creaturae.' But most of the Fathers who cite the passage omit καί. Thus S. Greg. M. 1 817· 'Per magnitudinem enim creaturae et speciem potest intelligibiliter creator videri. Τοῦ μεγέθους τῆς καλλονῆς τῶν κτισμάτων, Pseudo-Bas Comm. in Is. 161. cap. v. (I. p. 695, Ben). See Reusch.

Ἀναλόγως, 'proportionably,' Eng 'Cognoscibiliter,' Vulg 'Consequenter,' Hil. de Trin. i. p 770 'By comparing the creature with the Creator, as far as the ratio between finite and infinite will allow,' Arn Comp Rom. i 20; Acts xiv 17 The Vulg word 'cognoscibiliter' is unknown. Comp. the adverbs, 'duriter,' v 23; 'infirmiter,' iv. 4; 'sinceriter,' Tob iii. 5, 'ignoranter,' Ecclus xiv 7; 'sufficienter,' Nah. ii 12

6 'But yet,' i. e. 'though they might have known God by His works'

Ἐπὶ τούτοις, masc. 'In the case of these,' the worshippers of the heavenly bodies; the same as αὐτοὶ just after.

Ὀλίγη, 'minor,' Vulg. 'Little blame,' in comparison with the fault of those who worship idols

Καὶ γὰρ, 'etenim,' 'for truly they perhaps (τάχα) err while they seek after God and have the will to find Him.' Acts xvii. 27: 'That they should seek (ζητεῖν) the Lord, if haply they might feel after Him, and find Him (εὕροιεν).'

7. Ἀναστρεφόμενοι, like Lat. 'versari;' 'being occupied, conversant with,' referring rather to practical affairs of life than to philosophical speculations

Τῇ ὄψει, omitted by Vulg., 'persuasum habent' Sabat.: 'persuadentur aspectu' 'Let themselves be influenced by, or trust to, the appearance.'

Τὰ βλεπόμενα. Comp Heb. xi 3

8 Πάλιν δέ. 'On the other hand,' xvi. 23, 1 Cor xii. 21.

Αὐτοί, the same persons as those before spoken of. Οὐ συγγνωστοί = ἀναπολόγητοι. Rom i. 20, 21, q v

9 Ἵνα δύν., after τοσοῦτον 'Knew so much as to be able to.' For ἵνα = ὅτι cp. S. Matt. xx 33

Στοχάσασθαι τὸν αἰῶνα. 'To make guesses about,' 'to criticize' Always with gen. in classical Greek, but with acc. Deut xix. 3, Ecclus ix 14, Vat. It is here parallel with διερευνῶσι, ver 7 See 1 Cor. 1 19-21.

S Aug has a beautiful comment on this passage (Serm. lxviii ed. Ben), which ends thus 'Optime itaque et rectissime accusati sunt, qui potuerunt investigare numeros siderum, intervalla temporum, defectum luminum cognoscere et praedicere: recte accusati sunt, quoniam a quo ista facta et ordinata sunt, non invenerunt, quia quaerere neglexerunt. Tu autem non valde cura, si gyros siderum et caelestium terrenorumve corporum numeros ignores Vide pulchritudinem mundi et lauda concilium Creatoris. Vide quod fecit, ama qui fecit. tene hoc maxime Ama qui fecit. quia et te ipsum amatorem suum ad imaginem suam fecit'

Αἰών represents 'the world,' properly in its time-not its space-aspect. It is so used xiv 6, and in N T., Matt. xiii. 39; xxviii 20, Heb. i. 2; xi. 3; 1 Cor ii 7 Comp Eccl iii 11. So Lat. 'saeculum,' e. g. 4 Esdr. vi. 55. 'Propter nos creasti saeculum,' and ver. 59 'Si propter nos creatum est saeculum, quare non haereditatem possidemus cum saeculo?' Grimm See notes on chs iv 2, and xviii. 4, and compare Dr T. Lewis, Six Days of Creation, ch. xxvii, also Burton, Bampt Lect iv p 111, and note 49 (ed. 1829).

10–XIV. 13 *The worship of idols or images*

10 Ταλαίπ. δὲ, sc. οὗτοι ἦσαν

Ἐν νεκροῖς 'Inter mortuos,' Vulg. 'In dead things,' Eng The latter seems preferable Comp. ver. 18, and xv. 17: 'He worketh a dead thing (νεκρὸν) with wicked hands.' There are many similar passages in O T. *e g.* Deut iv 28; Is. xl. 18–20; xliv. 9–20, etc., Ep of Jeremy, 4 ff

Οἴτινες, 'in that they'

Ἐμμελέτημα, 'an exercise' of art The word occurs in Anth Pal. vi. 83 It is in apposition with χρυσὸν καὶ ἄργυρον. Comp Acts xvii. 29 'We ought not to think that the Godhead is like unto gold, or silver, or stone, graven by art (χαράγματι τέχνης) and man's device.'

Λίθ. ἄχρηστ, like the shapeless block of stone worshipped in Diana's Temple at Ephesus (Acts xix. 35), or the ἀρχαῖον βρέτας of Athena at Athens (Eurip. Iph Taur 977), both of which are said to have fallen from Zeus, their antiquity and unknown origin investing them with mystery.

11. Εἰ δέ The apodosis is in ver 13, ἀπείκασεν αὐτό. The whole description is similar to, and in parts identical with, Is. xl 20; xliv. 13–20, Jer x; and Bar vi. Ep. Jer. The comm compare Hor. Sat. I viii 1:

'Olim truncus eram ficulnus, inutile lignum,
Quum faber incertus scamnum faceretne Priapum,
Maluit esse deum'

Εὐκίνητον 'Meet for the purpose,' Eng. 'Rectum,' Vulg. 'Easy to handle.'

Ἐκπρίσας, 'having sawed out' from the rest of the trees

Εἰς ὑπηρ ζωῆς. Comp. πρὸς ὑπηρ. ἡμῶν, xv. 7.

12 Ἐνεπλήσθη, 'fills himself' Vulg. omits the word Is xliv 16. It is implied that the idol-maker first satisfies his own hunger before thinking of turning the refuse to account.

13. Ἐξ αὐτῶν, sc ἀποβλημάτων. 'The refuse of the refuse.'

Ὄζοις συμπεφ 'Grown thick with knots.'

Ἐν ἐπιμελείᾳ ἀργίας. 'In the industry of idleness,' such industry as a man uses when he is enjoying his leisure, a sarcastic expression, which is lost in the reading ἐργασίας, found in A and some Paris MSS Vulg, 'per vacuitatem suam' 'Vacuitas,' in the sense of 'idleness,' 'leisure,' is very uncommon.

Ἐμπειρίᾳ ἀνέσεως. 'With the skill of negligence,' 'such skill as carelessness gives.' The common reading is συνέσεως. 'Skill of his understanding,' Eng 'Per scientiam suae artis,' Vulg. But A. S., Ven., and V. prim. man, read ἀνέσεως, which I have adopted as the harder reading, and more likely to have been changed by scribes, and also as making a parallel with ἐπιμελ. ἀργίας. Thus Polyb. i. 66: διὰ πολλοῦ χρόνου τετευχότες ἀνέσεως καὶ σχολῆς.

Ἀπείκασεν Here begins the apodosis to εἰ δέ, ver. 11 So Grimm.

14. Εὐτελεῖ, 'cheap,' 'vile,' ch. x. 4; xi. 15. Vulg omits it.

Μίλτῳ, 'ochre,' or 'red lead,' 'minium.' Comp. Jer. xxii. 14; Ezek. xxiii. 14. Pliny, Hist. Nat. xxxv. 45 (see also H. N. xxxiii. 36), speaks of the statue of Jupiter being coloured red on festal days Other gods were thus adorned. Virgil, Ecl x 26 (where see Conington) ·

'Pan deus Arcadiae venit, quem vidimus ipsi
Sanguineis ebuli bacis minioque rubentem'

15 Οἴκημα, 'a shrine,' probably a niche in the wall Ἀσφαλισάμενος. (S. Matt xxvii. 65). Comp. Isai xli 7 · 'He fastened it with nails, that it should not be moved;' xl 19; Jer. x 4; Ep of Jer 27.

16. Ἵνα μέν, answered by περὶ δέ, ver 17. The helplessness of the image being contrasted with the demands made upon it.

17. Γάμων. Γάμοι, like Lat. 'nuptiae,' is used for 'marriage,' but nowhere for 'a wife.' The Vulg alters the order of the words and inserts 'inquirit,' making a new sentence at οὐκ αἰσχύνεται This has no support from MSS The well-balanced parallelism of vers 17–19 is very remarkable. Arn. compares it to the passage of S. Paul, 2 Cor. vi. 8–10. See also Jer. ii. 26–28. These private household gods, like the Roman Lares and Penates, seem to have been used among the

Hebrews in lax times. See the case of Laban's images, Gen. xxxi. 30, 34, and the Teraphim, Judg xvii. 3–5; xviii 17–20; 1 Sam. xix. 13, 16

18. Τὸ νεκρ and τὸ ἄπειρ best coincide with τὸ ἀσθενὲς and τὸ δυνάμ. The Vulg. seems to use the masc. throughout.

Ἀπειρότατον, 'inutilem,' Vulg 'That which hath least means to help,' Eng. The marg rendering is better, 'That hath no experience at all,' *i. e.* 'ignorant of the means of helping'

Βάσει, 'foot' So ποδῶν βάσις, Eur. Hec 837 See Ps. cxv 7 'Feet have they, but they walk not.'

19. Πορισμοῦ, xiv. 2; 1 Tim. vi 6, Diod. iii. 4.

Ἐργασίας, 'de operando,' Vulg 'Getting,' Eng The word may mean either 'daily labour,' or 'trade,' what we call 'business.'

Χειρῶν ἐπιτυχίας, 'good success of hands.' Polyb. L vi. 4. Vulg.. 'De omnium rerum eventu,' where the translator must either have read περὶ πάντων ἐπιτ, or written 'de manuum eventu.' Reusch.

Τὸ ἀδρανέστατον. 'Petit ab eo qui in omnibus est inutilis,' Vulg, followed by Eng, 'Asketh ability to do of him that is most unable to do anything.' It is 'that which is most feeble with its hands.'

Εὐδράνεια, ἅπ λεγ, derived from δραίνω, a desiderative verb=δρασείω. Vulg omits the word altogether Reusch suggests that 'in omnibus' is a clerical error for 'in manibus,' ταῖς χερσίν. Hooker, Eccl Pol I. viii 11, thus expresses these verses: 'He is not ashamed to speak unto that which hath no life, he calleth on him that is weak for health, he prayeth for life unto him which is dead, of him which hath no experience he requireth help, for his journey he sueth to him which is not able to go, for gains and work and success in his affairs he seeketh furtherance of him that hath no manner of power.'

CHAPTER XIV.

1 Στέλλεσθαι πλοῦν, 'to prepare for, undertake a voyage' 2 Macc. v 1 τὴν δευτέραν ἔφοδον ὁ Ἀντίοχος ἐστείλατο. Sophocles uses the active, Phil. 911 τὸν πλοῦν στελεῖν

Πλοίου. The other reading, ξύλου, is perhaps owed to a scribe who wished to make the antithesis neater

Ἐπιβοᾶται. Comp Jonah i. 5 καὶ ἐφοβήθησαν οἱ ναυτικοὶ, καὶ ἀνεβόησαν ἕκαστος πρὸς τὸν θεὸν αὐτοῦ. Probably the Pataeci, the tutelary deities of the Phoenicians, are referred to See Herod. iii. 37, and Bahr's note Comp Acts xxviii. 11. Ἔθος γάρ πως ἀεὶ ἐν ταῖς Ἀλεξανδρέων μάλιστα ναυσὶ, πρός γε τῆς πρώρης δεξιά τε καὶ εὐώνυμα, γραφὰς εἶναι τοιαύτας (sc. Διοσκούρους), S. Cyr. Al. in Cat. Act. *l. c.* These insignia were sometimes of costly material, as gold and ivory, they were at the prow of the ship; the tutelary deity ('tutela' among the Romans) was usually at the stern, though sometimes one image served both purposes. See Kuinoel in Act *l. c*, Wilkinson, Anc Egyptians, vol. i. ch. iii p. 276, ed 1878, and the woodcut, vol. ii p. 209.

2 Ἐκεῖνο, *i. e.* 'the ship.' This is made of better materials, and with greater skill than the idols.

Σοφίᾳ, 'man's natural sagacity.' The reading τεχνῖτις σοφία is not so probable; but ι and η are often interchanged in MSS. Clem Al, Strom vi 11 (p 786, Pott.), quotes formally as τὸ πρὸς τοῦ Σολομῶντος εἰρημένον τεχνῖτις δὲ σοφία.

3 Διακυβερνᾷ, 'directeth it,' the ship. Many Lat. MSS insert 'omnia,' but there is no authority for this in the original. Κυβερνήτης ('gubernator') is a 'steersman.' Comp. ver. 6. S. Chrys Hom. in Gen xi. (t. iv. p 83, Ben) οἶδε γὰρ ὁ κυβερνήτης, πότε δεῖ καθελκῦσαι τὸ πλοῖον, καὶ ἐκ τοῦ λιμένος ἐκβαλεῖν, καὶ τὰ πελάγη περαιώσασθαι καὶ πολλὴν μάλιστα παρὰ τούτοις ἔστιν ἰδεῖν τὴν σύνεσιν, ἣν ἡ τοῦ Θεοῦ σοφία ἐναπέθετο τῇ ἀνθρωπίνῃ φύσει. οὐδὲ γὰρ οὕτως οἱ τὰς λεωφόρους διατρέχοντες ἴσασι

μετὰ ἀκριβείας τὰς ἀτραποὺς, ὡς οὗτοι οἱ ἐν τοῖς ὕδασι μετὰ ἀσφαλείας τὴν πορείαν ποιοῦνται διὸ καὶ ἡ Γραφὴ ἐκπλησσομένη τὴν ὑπερβάλλουσαν τοῦ Θεοῦ σοφίαν ἔλεγεν· ὁ δοὺς ἐν θαλάσσῃ ὁδὸν κ τ λ.

Πρόνοια (xvii 2) God's providential care watches over those engaged in their lawful calling, so that they can cross the sea in ships, but idolaters have no such assurance. Πρόνοια is used by Herod., Plat., and others for 'Divine Providence.' Thus Her. iii. 108 καί κως τοῦ θείου ἡ προνοίη, ὥσπερ καὶ οἰκὸς, ἔστι ἐοῦσα σοφή. Plato speaks frequently of θεοῦ or θεῶν πρόνοια, e. g. Timae pp. 30, 44, and De Leg x. Xenophon uses the word absolutely for Divine Providence (Mem. I. iv. 6), where he introduces Socrates asserting that the eyelid in its wonderful contrivance is plainly προνοίας ἔργον It does not occur in this sense in the canonical Scriptures We have, however, in 3 Macc iv. 21 τοῦτο δὲ ἦν ἐνέργεια τῆς τοῦ βοηθοῦντος τοῖς Ἰουδαίοις ἐξ οὐρανοῦ προνοίας ἀνικήτου and 4 Macc ix 24 ἡ δικαία καὶ πάτριος ἡμῶν πρόνοια. Philo, de Mund. Op 2 (I. p 2) ὃν (τὸν κόσμον) οἱ φάσκοντες ὡς ἐστὶν ἀγένητος λελήθασι τὸ ὠφελιμώτατον καὶ ἀναγκαιότατον τῶν εἰς εὐσέβειαν ἡκόντων ὑποτεμνόμενοι, τὴν πρόνοιαν Philo wrote three treatises on Providence, which are mentioned by Euseb. Hist Eccl ii. 18, but are extant only in an Armenian version, rendered into Latin by Aucher (Opp. vol viii Richter). Comp. Jos. Bell Jud. III. viii 7; Clem Rom. Ep. I. ad Cor. xxiv. 5: ἡ μεγαλειότης τῆς προνοίας τοῦ δεσπότου. To found a charge of Platonism against the author of Wisdom from the use of the term Providence, as some have done, is quite unwarranted In all such cases we should rather admire the skill with which the writer employs the terms of heathen philosophy to convey scriptural ideas. In the present instance, the expression is parallel with that in the Collect for the Eighth Sund. after Trin 'O God, whose never-failing Providence ordereth all things both in heaven and earth.'

Ὅτι The special Providence of God was shown in the passage of the Red Sea by the Israelites Ex xiv. 22. Comp Ps. lxxvi. 20, and cvi. 23-30, Sept.

4 Ἵνα κἂν The construction is elliptical, = ἵνα τις ἐπιβῇ, κἂν ἄνευ τέχνης τις ᾖ or ἐπιβῇ. The various readings have sprung from the construction not being understood. The Vulg, as some Gr MSS, omits ἵνα; so Eng The idea is that a man may trust in God's protection even though, like Noah (ver. 6), he put to sea knowing nothing of navigation.

Τέχνης, 'the art of managing a ship.' Some Lat. MSS, by a clerical error, give 'sine rate' instead of 'sine arte;' and the commentators thereupon expound τέχνης as 'a work of art,'='a ship' Thus Houbig, and Strigel

Ἐπιβῇ, 'went on board.' Acts xxi. 2. Vulg. . 'adeat mare'

5. Ἀργὰ . . . ἔργα, a play on the words God wills that men should employ the faculties which He gives them, and use the products of sea and land which He has provided for them.

Σχεδία, 'a raft, or light boat' Prop. something hastily put together. Eng. 'weak vessel.'

Διεσώθησαν. The aorist seems to be used with some reference to the example given in the next verse, ='are saved,' generally, and 'were saved' on the particular occasion alluded to

6. Ἀρχῆς, gen. of time. 'In the beginning.' Used with a preposition in Attic

Γιγάντων, the ringleaders of the sinful race. Gen. vi. 4, 17. Comp. 3 Macc. ii. 4: σὺ τοὺς ἔμπροσθεν ἀδικίαν ποιήσαντας, ἐν οἷς καὶ Γίγαντες ἦσαν ῥώμῃ καὶ θράσει πεποιθότες, διέφθειρας, ἐπαγαγὼν αὐτοῖς ἀμέτρητον ὕδωρ. Ecclus. xvi 7; Bar. iii. 26-28.

'The hope of the world,' Noah and his family, and the creatures with him. So Virg. Aen. xii. 168 : 'Ascanius, magnae spes altera Romae.' Guth. Comp 2 Pet. ii. 5.

Αἰῶνι. The article is added in S, as xviii 4. But it is used without the art, as κόσμος, vi. 24, x 1. 'The world.' See on xiii. 9.

Σπέρμα γεν 'The seed of a new generation.' Gen ix 1, 7.

7. Some (*e.g.* Gratz, Gesch. der Jud. iii. 495)

have supposed this verse to be an interpolation by a Christian hand; but there is no reason for this notion. The Fathers have, as was natural, accommodated this passage to the idea of the cross of Christ, but the author manifestly is referring only to the material of which the ark was made, and this leads him back to his subject, viz idols of wood, ver. 8. For the application of the term 'blessed' to material things comp. 1 Tim iv. 4. As examples of the way in which the Fathers have treated this passage, take the following: S. Ambr., Serm. viii. in Ps. cxviii (p. 455), renders the words thus. 'Benedictum lignum quod fit per justitiam, maledictum autem lignum quod fit per manus hominum,' and then proceeds. 'superius ad crucem Domini retulit, posterius ad errorem gentilium qui ligna venerantur. Justitia autem quae est crucis, nisi quod adscendens illud patibulum Dominus Jesus Christus, peccatorum nostrorum chirographum crucifixit, et totius orbis peccatum suo errore mundavit?' S German Orat. i (XCVIII p 237, Migne). εὐλογίας γὰρ, ἀλλ' οὐ κατάρας ὄργανον ὁ σταυρός· ἐπειδὴ εὐλογεῖται ξύλον, κατὰ τὸν εἰπόντα, δι' οὗ γίνεται σωτηρία. Pseudo-Chrys De Ador. Cruc. (II p 823, Ben). ὅτι δὲ σεβάσμιος καὶ προσκυνητὸς ὁ τοῦ Χριστοῦ σταυρὸς καὶ ὁ τύπος αὐτοῦ, καὶ τοῦτο οἱ προφῆται διδάσκουσι . . . καὶ ὁ Σολομῶν λέγει, Εὐλογεῖτε ξύλον δι' οὗ γίνεται δικαιοσύνη. The Homilies say quaintly 'He praiseth the tree whereof the gibbet is made, as happy in comparison to the tree that an image or idol is made of, even by these very words, "Happy is the tree wherethrough righteousness cometh" (meaning the gibbet).' Against Peril of Idol pt i. p. 162 (Oxf. 1844). S. Aug. De Civit. xv. 26. 'Quod Noë homini justo . . . imperat Deus, ut arcam faciat, in qua cum suis . . . liberaretur a diluvii vastitate, proculdubio figura est peregrinantis in hoc saeculo Civitatis Dei, hoc est, Ecclesiae, quae fit salva per lignum, in quo pependit Mediator Dei et hominum homo Christus Jesus.'

Δικαιοσύνη, the carrying out of God's will, whereby the righteous was saved. Noah is called 'a preacher of righteousness,' 2 Pet. ii. 5 Comp Heb. xi 7 · 'heir of the righteousness which is by faith.' Some have thought that the reference in this verse is to Moses' rod, but the context seems to direct us to the ark.

8. Τὸ χειροπ., sc. εἴδωλον. It is a common name for idols. Comp Lev xxvi 1, Is. ii. 18, xxi. 9. θεοῖς χειροποιήτοις, Judith viii 18.

Ἐπικατάρατον, sc ἐστι, iii 13. Comp. Deut vii. 25, 26; xxvii. 15

'He is cursed because he made it, and it (is cursed) because, though it is corruptible, it is named God.' Rom. i. 23. ἤλλαξαν τὴν δόξαν τοῦ ἀφθάρτου Θεοῦ ἐν ὁμοιώματι εἰκόνος φθαρτοῦ ἀνθρώπου κ τ.λ.

9 Ἀσέβεια = 'his ungodly work.' God's hatred is known by His punishments, ver. 11. He loves His creatures (xi 24, 25), but hates the sin in them. It is shallow criticism that considers the sentiment in this verse unscriptural (See Bissell) 'Cursed be the man,' says God, Deut. xxvii. 15, 'that maketh any graven or molten image;' and He proclaims, 'I will not justify the wicked (τὸν ἀσεβῆ),' 'and by no means clear the guilty,' Exod xxiii 7; xxxiv 7 There are many passages in the Psalms to the same effect. Thus Ps. v. 5: 'Thou hatest all workers of iniquity.' Comp Ecclus. xv. 20

10 Τὸ πραχθὲν . . τῷ δράσαντι 'The work . . . the culprit.' Is. ii. 18–21.

11. Ἐν εἰδώλοις. Idols are punished by being destroyed, as symbols of devils (1 Cor x. 20, Ps xcvi. 5) and leading men astray. Ex. xii 12: 'Against all the gods of Egypt I will execute judgment.' Comp. Numb xxxiii 4; 1 Sam. v 3, 4; Is xix. 1; xlvi. 1; Jer. x. 11.

Ἐπισκοπή, 'visitation,' 'judgment,' 'punishment,' xix 15 See on iii. 7. The author probably had in mind Jer. x. 15 ἐν καιρῷ ἐπισκοπῆς αὐτῶν ἀπολοῦνται. Vulg. renders 'In idolis nationum non erit respectus.' There is no authority in Gr MSS for the insertion of the negative, which seems to have been the act of some scribe ignorant of the double use of 'respectus,' 'a visitation,' whether for reward or punishment.

Ἐν κτίσματι Θεοῦ, in the sphere of the creature of

God which is meant for His glory, idols, misusing and perverting things otherwise harmless, became an abomination. The Vulg. translates· 'Creaturae Dei in odium factae sunt,' which Gutb explains, 'creatures of God, *i e* idols, are become abominable'

Βδέλυγμα, see on xii 23

Σκάνδαλα .. παγίδα So Josh xxiii. 13; Ps. lxviii 23, Rom xi. 9 See the warnings, Deut vii. 25, 26; Exod xxxiv 12-14, S. Matt. xiii. 41.

12. Πορνείας, 'spiritual fornication,' Eng, which seems correct. Idolatry is often so called, *e g*. Lev xvii. 7, Hos. ix. 1; Rev xiv 8, xvii 2 So Philo, De Migr. Abrah. 12 (I p. 447)· ἀμφοτέρας ὁ νόμος ἐκκλησίας ἱερᾶς ἀπελήλακε, τὴν μὲν ἄθεον, τῷ θλαδίαν καὶ ἀποκεκομμένων εἴρξας ἐκκλησιάζειν· τὴν δὲ πολύθεον, τῷ τὸν ἐκ πόρνης ὁμοίως κωλύσας ἀκούειν ἢ λέγειν. ἄθεος μὲν γὰρ ὁ ἄγονος, πολύθεος δὲ ὁ ἐκ πόρνης, τυφλώττων περὶ τὸν ἀληθῆ πατέρα, καὶ διὰ τοῦτο πολλοὺς ἀνθ' ἑνὸς γονεῖς αἰνιττόμενος. As regards the reading in the text there is no variation in the MSS., but while Euseb (Praep Ev i 9) retains the text, Didym reads πρώτη πορνεία, ἐπίνοια εἰδώλων. De Trin iii 16 (XXXIX p. 865, Migne).

Ἐπίνοια, 'exquisitio' (not elsewhere in Vulg), 'the imagining,' parallel with εὕρεσις.

Εὕρεσις, 'adinventio,' Vulg. A late word occurring Ecclus xxxv 12 and elsewhere See on vi. 18.

Φθορά, 'moral corruption' (2 Pet i. 4; ii. 19), or 'seduction.'

13 Ἀπ' ἀρχῆς It was not in the first age that primitive man worshipped the creature, and even the first false worshippers probably adored the heavenly bodies without making images of them.

Εἰς τὸν αἰῶνα, 'for ever,' found in Plato, Axioch. x p. 370 C· τὰ τοῦ κόσμου παθήματα παραπήξασθαι εἰς τὸν αἰῶνα, where however Stalb. reads πρὸς τὸν αἰ. So 'in aevum,' Horat Od IV. xiv 3 For the destruction of idols comp. Isai ii. 18, Zech. xiii. 2.

14-21 *The worship of deified man*

14. Κενοδοξία, 'conceit,' 'vanity,' 'empty fancy.' Vulg (taking it as nom) translates, 'supervacuitas,' ἅπ λεγ See on vii. 5. Κενοδοξία, translated, here and Phil. ii. 3, 'vain-glory,' occurs 4 Macc. ii. 15; viii 19; Polyb. iii 81 9; Philo, De Jos 7 (I. p. 47). Ptolemy Philometer is called god on his coins; and Diod Sic i 90 says· 'The Egyptians seem to worship and honour their kings as if they were really gods.' Blunt. See note on ver 17

Εἰσῆλθεν, sc τὰ εἴδωλα A. and S insert θάνατος before εἰσῆλθε from 11 24 Αὐτῶν in the next clause shows that the subject is idols.

Εἰς τὸν κόσμον is given by S. Athan., who quotes vers. 12-21, Contr. Gent. xi. (I. p 11, Ben)

Διὰ τοῦτο, because they were originated by the vanity of men.

Ἐπενοήθη, 'is destined, intended by God,' with an allusion to ἐπίνοια, ver 12 The Eng version, 'Shall they come shortly to an end,' is no translation of the Greek.

15 Ἀώρῳ, 'untimely,'· because his son was cut off prematurely. Vulg 'acerbo,' 'unlovely.' Eurip Alc. 168: θανεῖν ἀώρους παῖδας The author gives here (vers 15, 16) one cause of the rise of idolatry, viz inordinate grief for a lost friend An instance of this tendency is seen in Cicero, who designed to raise a magnificent temple in honour of his lost daughter Tullia. See Epp ad Att xii. 35 ff The insane love of Hadrian for Antinous, which led the emperor to deify his lost favourite, and erect temples in his honour, is well known Euseb. Hist iv 8.

Ὡς θεόν, S Athan has ὡς ζῶντα, Con. Gent xi.

Τοῖς ὑποχειρίοις, 'those under his control.'

Τελετάς, 'sacrificia,' Vulg., so Eng. Rather, 'rites,' 'ceremonies.' Comp ver. 23. Μυστήρια and τελετάς would comprise all the services and initiations practised in the Mysteries so celebrated both in Egypt and Greece. S Chrys. accounts for the origin of idolatry thus, Hom de Stat. i 7 πολλοὶ καὶ πολέμους κατορθώσαντες, καὶ τρόπαια στήσαντες, καὶ πόλεις οἰκοδομήσαντες, καὶ ἕτερά τινα τοιαῦτα τοῖς τότε εὐεργετήσαντες, θεοὶ παρὰ τοῖς πολλοῖς ἐνομίσθησαν, καὶ ναοῖς ἐτιμήθησαν καὶ βωμοῖς For sons to deify their fathers was more natural and agreeable to human feeling. Thus Antiochus writes to Lysias,

2 Macc. xi. 23 · 'Since our father is translated unto the gods'

16. Ἐφυλάχθη The Vulg inserts 'hic error,' for which there is no authority in the Greek MSS. The aor. merely states the fact, the imperfect, ἐθρησκεύετο, expresses the continuance of the custom, which, from being a family institution, became a public and political one

Ἐπιταγαῖς. The word occurs xviii. 16, xix. 6; 1 Esdr. i 16, 3 Macc vii. 20, Polyb. xiii 4 3, Diod. 1. 70

Γλυπτά See on xv 13.

17. Another cause of idolatry was the erection of the statues of dreaded monarchs, such as the image on the plain of Dura, probably a statue of Nebuchadnezzar himself, Dan. iii. Some, who date this Book of Wisdom very late, see here a reference to the deification of Caligula and the attempted introduction of his statue into the temple at Jerusalem, Joseph. Ant. xviii. 8. But the statement is plainly general. See Prolegom p 33 'Mauri,' says S Cypr, 'manifeste reges colunt, nec ullo velamento hoc nomen obtexunt,' De Idol Vanit. The invocation of deified kings had early become in Egypt an addition to the worship of the traditional deities Instances of apotheosis occur in the times of the ancient Pharaohs, and the Lagidae regularly provided for the payment of divine honours to their predecessors. See Döllinger, The Gentile and Jew, I. p 486 ff., Eng. transl ; Pusey, Daniel the Prophet, p 440 and notes; Warburt. Div. Legat. ii. § 4. Hooker quotes vers 15, 16, Eccl. Pol. I viii 11

Ἐν ὄψει. 'In palam,' Vulg For examples of prepositions before adverbs see note xvii. 13.

Τὴν πόρρω ὄψιν ἀνατυπωσάμενοι, 'representing the distant face.' 'E longinquo figura eorum allata,' Vulg This translation seems to mean that they copied a picture of the king brought from far; but this is unnecessary, πόρρωθεν being used, like τὸν ἐκεῖθεν πόλεμον δεῦρο ἥξοντα, Demosth Ol. i. p 13 17, ubi vide Schaef. Syr.. 'effigiem fecerunt eorum qui procul habitabant.' For ἀνατυπόω cp. xix. 6 (Compl.), Philo, De Plant. 6 (I p. 333), Plut. ii. 329 B (Paris, 1624).

Ἐμφανῆ with εἰκόνα, 'an express, manifest image.' On the art of painting in Egypt see Wilkinson's Anc Egyptians, vol ii pp 262–267, and pp 287, 288 (new ed 1878).

Κολακεύωσι, pres. subj, implies continuance. The aor κολακεύσωσι, which some MSS read, is not so suitable.

18 A third cause of idolatry was the beauty of the image

Εἰς ἐπίτασιν, 'unto increase, intensity'

Θρησκείας. Acts xxvi. 5. Vulg., 'ad horum culturam.' Comp. Horat Ep. I. xviii. 86: 'cultura potentis amici.'

Καὶ τοὺς ἀγν, even those that knew not who was represented by the image

Προετρέψατο Cp Acts xviii 27, Xen Mem I. iv. 1

Φιλοτιμία, 'eximia diligentia,' Vulg. 'Singular diligence,' Eng. 'The artist's ambition to excel,' explained in the next verse.

19. Ὁ μὲν, the artist.

Τάχα Grimm takes to mean 'quickly,' not 'perhaps' The artist made all speed to execute the work. The Vulg omits the word. S. Athan, Contr Gent II (p 9), has ἴσως instead of τάχα. Arab. 'fortassis'

Τῷ κρατοῦντι, 'the potentate' Vulg., 'illi qui se assumpsit.' 'Him that employed him,' Douai This seems to be erroneous

Ἐξεβιάσατο, used all the efforts of his art to make the likeness assume greater beauty The verb is used by Plutarch to express the elaboration of art, τὰ Διονυσίου ζωγραφήματα τῶν Κολοφωνίων, ἰσχὺν ἔχοντα καὶ τόνον, ἐκβεβιασμένοις καὶ καταπόνοις ἔοικε, Timol 36.

20. Εὔχαρι = 'the grace' The reading εὐχαρὶς (A C) is doubtful, as the adj. εὐχαρής is not found, except perhaps in Menander, ap Walz. Rhett. Gr. vol ix p 274, 5 Steph. Thesaur sub voc. S Athan cont. Gent. II has εὔχαρι

Ἐφελκόμενον, 'abducta,' Vulg. MSS. ap. Sab.. 'adducta'

Πρὸ ὀλίγου. Comp. πρὸ μικροῦ, xv 8.

Σέβασμα, 'an object of worship' 'Deum,' Vulg Eng Comp ch xv 17, Bel and Drag. 27, 2 Thess. ii. 4; Acts xvii. 23. So Philo, De Monarch. 1 3 (II. 216), speaks of the employment of the arts of music, statuary, and painting to win men to idolatry οὐ μὴν ἀλλὰ καὶ πλαστικὴν καὶ ζωγραφίαν συνεργοὺς τῆς ἀπάτης προσέλαβον, ἵνα χρωμάτων καὶ σχημάτων καὶ ποιοτήτων εὖ δεδημιουργημέναις ἰδέαις ὑπάγοντες τοὺς ὁρῶντας καὶ τὰς ἡγεμονίδας αἰσθήσεις ὄψιν καὶ ἀκοὴν δελεάσαντες, τὴν μὲν ἀψύχοις εὐμορφίαις τὴν δὲ εὐφωνίᾳ ποιητικῇ, συναρπάσωσι τὴν ψυχὴν ἀβέβαιον καὶ ἀνίδρυτον ταύτην ἀπεργαζόμενοι

21. Τοῦτο explained by ὅτι following

Τῷ βίῳ εἰς ἔνεδρ. 'A snare to the living,' as x 8 Here again the Eng translates, 'the world.' 'Vitae humanae deceptio,' Vulg 'Fuit id mundo invidiosum,' Arab. For ἔνεδρον cp. Numb. xxv. 20, Ecclus. viii. 11, Acts xxiii 16.

Δουλεύσαντες belongs properly to τυραννίδι, but is used by zeugma with συμφορᾷ also; 'induced by calamity or humouring a tyrant.' The 'calamity' is the death of a beloved child, ver. 15; the 'tyranny' is that mentioned vers. 16–19 Vulg, 'aut affectui aut regibus deservientes'

Τὸ ἀκοινώνητον ὄνομα 'The incommunicable name.' Jehovah (as we read it) is meant by this term among the Jews. Being used here in reference to heathens it signifies merely God (In later ecclesiastical language ἀκοινώνητ came to mean 'excommunicated') See Deut. vi. 4, 14, 15, Isai xlii. 8, which passages show that the form of error intended is the distributing of the attributes of God among a host of idol deities. Thus S Athan. Cont. Gent. 17. ἐπειδὴ γὰρ τὴν τοῦ Θεοῦ ἀκοινώνητον, ὡς εἶπεν ἡ Γραφή, προσηγορίαν καὶ τιμὴν τοῖς οὐκ οὖσι θεοῖς ἐσπούδαζον ἀναθεῖναι. Comp S. Aug. De Civit vii 29, 30, of which two chapters the headings are 'Quod omnia quae physiologi ad mundum partesque ipsius retulerunt, ad unum vere Deum referre debuerint Qua pietate discernatur a creaturis Creator, ne pro uno tot dii colantur, quot sunt opera unius auctoris.'

Ἀκοινών Vulg, 'incommunicabile' See note on

Περιέθεσαν, 'conferred,' 'bestowed' Comp. 1 Cor. xi. 23· τούτοις τιμὴν περισσοτέραν περιτίθεμεν. Some MSS. and S. Athan. l. sup. cit., read περιέθηκαν, Alexandrian Greek affecting rather the 1 aor. in preference to the second.

22–31 · *Effects of idolatry on morals and life.*

22 Ἀγνοίας πολέμῳ 'War arising from ignorance,' i e the strife with all goodness and virtue occasioned by the heathens' ignorance of God. This is called τοσαῦτα κακὰ directly afterwards, and further explained in the following verses

Εἰρήνην. This war and strife and deep unrest they call peace, 'saying, Peace, peace; when there is no peace,' Jer vi. 14 Comp Tacit Agric. xxx: 'ubi solitudinem faciunt, pacem appellant'

23 Τεκνοφόνους τελ. 'rites in which children were offered in sacrifice.'

Τεκνοφ. is ἅπ. λεγ. See on xi. 7. For such sacrifices see on xii. 5, and Warburt. Div Leg. book ii § 4, notes CC, and DD; and book viii ch. 2, note G, where the whole subjects of infanticide and child-sacrifice are fully discussed They were not confined to the Canaanites. Classical readers will remember Iphigenia and Polyxena, and the circumstances mentioned in Her vii. 114. By using the pres ἄγοντες and φυλάσσουσι the author does not necessarily imply (as Grimm. supposes) that this practice obtained in his own time; but indeed it seems that in Carthage it existed till the second century A D See Guth and the article on 'Moloch' in Smith's Dict. of Bible.

Ἐμμανεῖς ἐξάλλ. θεσμ. κ., 'frantic revels of strange customs' Eng gives, 'or made revellings of strange rites,' where Arn thinks 'made' a misprint for *mad* Vulg. translates strangely, 'aut insaniae plenas vigilias habentes.' The allusion is to the orgies of Bacchus Comp 2 Macc vi. 4; Rom xiii 13 I have printed ἐξάλλων, instead of ἐξ ἄλλων, as giving a better sense So Field, Tischend., Apel, and Guth. Ἔξαλλος occurs 3 Macc iv 4; 2 Sam vi. 14, Esth iii. 8, and elsewhere For the shameful customs practised in the name of religion among the Babylonians see Herod.

i. 199. Comp also 1 Pet. iv. 3, Bar. vi. 43; Strabo, xvi. p. 1058.

24. Comp. the description of heathenism Rom i. 24-32; Gal. v. 19-21, 1 Tim. i. 9, 10; S. Barn. Ep. xx, Pseudo-Clem. Ep ii ad Cor 1. 6

Λοχῶν, 'per invidiam,' Vulg., probably a mistake for 'insidiam' or 'insidias' The correct word, λοχῶν, has been altered in S by a later hand to λοχεύων, which is quite a different word. Later Latin uses the singular form of some words instead of the classical plural. Thus S. Aug, Locut. 59 de Num, comments on the use of 'primitia' Lamprid, Commod. 16, has 'tenebra.' Plautus too writes 'delicia,' Truc. v 29 So the original word in the Vulg above is probably 'insidiam'

Νοθεύων = 'by adultery;' lit. 'making spurious, foisting a spurious offspring' Philo, De Jos 9 (II. p. 48) νοθεύων αὐτοῦ γάμον; and Quod Deus imm. 22 (I. p. 288).

25. Πάντα, 'has the great weight of authority.' 'Omnia commista sunt,' Vulg

Ἐπιμίξ, 'sine discrimine.'

Δόλος. 'Fictio,' Vulg. = 'fraus.' Comp. iv. 11; vii. 13

Θόρυβ ἀγαθ., 'persecution of good men.' 2 Tim. iii 3: ἀφιλάγαθοι.

26. Ἀμηστία. This form is more usual than ἀμνηστία, and occurs without variation, xix. 4 Vulg 'Dei immemoratio' Probably written 'Doñ' or 'Di immemoratio,' i.e 'Doni,' χάριτος, and mistaken for 'Doṁ' = 'Domini,' or 'Dei.' 'Immemoratio' occurs nowhere else.

Μιασμός = μίανσις, 1 Macc. iv. 43; 2 Pet ii. 10; Herm. Past. Sim. v. 7.

Γενέσεως ἐναλλαγή. 'Abuse of sex,' or 'sodomy.' Rom i. 26, 27. The Vulg rendering, 'nativitatis immutatio,' seems to refer to supposititious children. See Arn.

Ἀταξία. 'Nuptiarum inconstantia,' Vulg, 'unsettlement in marriages,' the marriage tie not being considered binding, and being easily dissolved. The word 'inordinatio' in Vulg seems to have been another rendering of ἀταξία, and so slipped into the text, and was then made to govern the following words It is a very unusual word, but found in S. Aug De Civit. Dei, xiv 26. 'perversa inordinatio.'

27. Ἀνωνύμων, 'having no real existence,' as ver. 29, and 1 Cor. viii 4; Gal iv. 3, or, 'mean and pitiful' Vulg, 'infandorum,' which points, as Eng., 'not to be named,' to the command in Ex xxiii 13; Josh xxiii. 7 Comp Ps. xvi. 4. Tertull De Idolatr xv · 'Daemonia nullum habent nomen singulatim, sed ibi nomen inveniunt, ubi et pignus' (p. 169).

Ἀρχὴ .. πέρας. Greg Naz., Orat. xxxviii. De Idol, calls idolatry ἔσχατον καὶ πρῶτον τῶν κακῶν. For the connection of idolatry and immorality see Jowett on Ep. to Rom pp 70 ff

28 This verse combines the chief features of vers. 23-27

Εὐφραινόμενοι Ecclus. xxx. 5; 1 Sam. xvi 5; Luke xvi. 19

29. 'Look not to be hurt,' not really believing in these deities, though they used their names in confirmation of oaths. Bar vi 35 (Ep Jer.) Vulg · 'noceri se non sperant' 'Noceo' is used with acc. Ecclus xxviii. 2; Luke iv. 35; Acts vii. 26. So Plaut. Mil Glor v. 18

'Jura te non nociturum esse hominem'

30 Ἀμφότερα, explained by ὅτι κ.τ.λ. Μετελεύσεται takes a double acc in the sense of 'prosecute.' 'Justice shall pursue them on account of both crimes.' The feeling that perjury always meets with punishment was universal. Thus Hesiod writes, Ἔργ. καὶ Ἡμ. 801:

ἐν πέμπτῃ γάρ φασιν Ἐρινύας ἀμφιπολεύειν,
Ὅρκον τινυμένας, τὸν Ἔρις τέκε πῆμ' ἐπιόρκοις.

Thus Eurip. Med 754 ·

Med. ἀρκεῖ τί δ' ὅρκῳ τῷδε μὴ 'μμένων πάθοις;
Aeg. ἃ τοῖσι δυσσεβοῦσι γίγνεται βροτῶν.

Thucydides mentions (vii. 18) that on one occasion the Lacedaemonians attributed their former failures to their breach of treaties, and were quite confident of success on another occasion because the Athenians had been the offenders The vulgar name for erysipelas, St.

Anthony's fire, is derived from the notion that the disease is sent as a punishment on those who have sworn falsely by St. Anthony's name. Superstition often stands in the place of moral principle.

Τὰ δίκαια, 'just punishment.'

Ὁσιότητος. 'Justitiam,' Vulg. 'Truth and honour.' See the case of Zedekiah in Ezek. xvii. 18, 19.

31 Τῶν ὀμνυμένων, 'the things by which one swears.' 'Numina jurata,' Ov. Her. ii 23. Grimm.

Ἡ τ ἁμαρτ δίκη, 'the punishment which God inflicts on sinners.' 'The vengeance due to perjury,' Hooker explains it, Eccl Pol. V. i 3.

Παράβασιν. 'Praevaricationem,' Vulg = 'delictum,' losing the sense of 'collusion.' Rom. ii 23, etc.

CHAPTER XV.

CHAPTERS XV-XIX CONTRAST BETWEEN THE WORSHIPPERS OF THE TRUE GOD AND IDOLATERS.

1–5. The relation of the Israelites to the true God preserved them from idolatry.

1 Σὺ δέ. In contrast to the false gods of heathendom.

Ἡμῶν, 'of us Israelites.' This is omitted by Eng version. Is lxiii. 8.

Χρηστὸς κ.τ.λ. Cp. Ex. xxxiv. 6; Numb xiv. 18.

2. Καὶ γάρ. The goodness and long-suffering of God are our hope and shield even when we fall into sin, so that we do not despair, but are rather moved to repentance. Rom ii. 4. S Aug, De Fid et Operr. xxii § 41, gives the passage thus : 'Et si peccaverimus, tui sumus, scientes potentiam tuam: non peccabimus autem, scientes quoniam tui sumus deputati.' And then he quotes 1 John ii 1, 2.

Κράτος, 'lordship,' 'supremacy.'

Οὐχ ἁμαρτησόμεθα δέ. 'Et si non peccaverimus,' Vulg., against all authority of Greek MSS., also rendering εἰδότες, 'scimus.' The Arab. gives 'si minime peccemus.' 'We will not sin' is correct, the motive following.

Λελογίσμεθα, 'we have been reckoned as the sheep of Thy pasture.' S Aug comments thus 'Quis digne cogitans habitationem apud Deum, in qua omnes praedestinatione sunt deputati, qui secundum propositum vocati sunt, non enitatur ita vivere, ut tali habitatione congruat?' De Fid et Opp xxii 41. Cp Lev xi. 44.

3 Τὸ γὰρ ἐπιστ. Comp viii 13, 17. S John xvii. 3 : 'This is life eternal, that they might know Thee the only true God and Jesus Christ whom Thou hast sent' Jer ix 23, 24. This verse is quoted by S. Method. De Sim et An. vi (XVIII p 361, Migne).

Ὁλόκληρος, 'complete,' 'omnibus numeris absolutus' S James i 4; 1 Thess v 23, 1 Macc iv. 47; 4 Macc. xv. 17. 'To know Thy power' leads to wholesome fear and awe, and so is the ground of a blessed immortality. The Vulg gives, with some confusion : 'et scire justitiam et virtutem tuam.' Comp. Ecclus i 13; and ch viii. 13.

Ῥίζα, iii 15 ; Ecclus. i 20 : 'The root of Wisdom is to fear the Lord, and the branches thereof are long life.' Comp 1 Tim. vi. 10. 'The love of money is the root of all evil.'

4 Κακότεχνος, i. 4.

Ἐπίνοια, xiv 12. 'Device' Acts xvii 29: χαράγματι τέχνης καὶ ἐνθυμήσεως ἀνθρώπου.

Οὔτε followed by οὐδὲ = 'neither .. nor yet,' is not unusual, but copyists often, as here, have altered the words for uniformity's sake.

Σκιαγράφων, 'of perspective painters.' The Vulg. renders 'umbra picturae,' reading as Compl , σκιὰ γραφῶν. Coloured statues seem to be referred to. Comp. xiii 14.

Εἶδος σπιλ in app to πόνος, 'A figure stained.' Vulg. 'effigies sculpta,' which Gutb thinks is not a mistake for 'picta,' but that σπιλωθὲν is taken as derived from σπιλάς, 'a rock,' and not from σπίλος, 'a stain.' But this is equally an error. For σπιλόω, comp. S James iii. 6; S. Jude 23; Dion. Hal vi. 93.

5. Ὧν, 'of which objects'

Ἄφρονι seems more probable than ἄφροσιν, on account of the sing. ποθεῖ Vulg. 'insensato.'

Ὄρεξιν ('concupiscentiam,' Vulg) has the highest authority. 'Enticeth fools to lust after it,' Eng. 'Turneth a reproach to the foolish,' Eng. Marg., rendering the alternative reading εἰς ὄνειδος. 'Becomes a passion in the case of a fool' The commentators quote the case of Pygmalion who fell in love with the statue of Venus, and others who have fallen victims to the same folly. S Agobardus (A. D. 779) wrote a treatise most strongly condemning image-worship, denying such representations of God and the saints the appellation of 'sacred,' and recommending that they should be utterly destroyed Galland Bibl vet Patr. ix; Migne, Patr. Lat. civ The iambic rhythm in some of the stiches, vers. 4, 5 ff., should be remarked.

6–17. *The folly of idolaters in worshipping idols of clay.*

6. Κακ ἐρασταὶ ἄξιοί τε τ ἐ. are predicates 'And worthy of such hopes,' *i e.* objects to trust in Vulg: 'Digni sunt qui spem habeant in talibus.' Comp Col i. 27. 1 Tim. i 1. 'Christ, who is our hope'

Οἱ δρῶντες, 'fabricatores,' Wahl. 'Qui faciunt illos,' Vulg Heysch, quoted by Schleusn.. δρῶντες, ποιοῦντες, ἐργαζόμενοι

7. Καὶ γὰρ gives the reason for the expressions in ver 6, κακῶν ἐρασταὶ κ.τ λ.

Θλίβων, 'kneading,' 'rubbing'

Ἐπίμοχθον, used adverbially 'Laboriose,' Vulg Or agreeing with γῆν, 'soft earth that causes trouble' in working. Gutb. takes ἁπαλὴν as predicative, 'working troublesome earth (so as to be) soft,' which is possibly right. ἐπίμοχθος is a very uncommon word It is found in Schol. Ap Aristoph Pac. 384: ὦ πόνηροι, ὦ ἐπίμοχθοι

Πρὸς ὑπηρ. ἡμῶν, like εἰς ὑπηρεσίαν ζωῆς, xiii. 11 Cp the very similar passage Rom ix. 21, and see Ecclus xxxviii. 30–34; Is. xlv. 9; lxiv. 8, Jer. xviii. 2–10.

Ἓν ἕκαστον. The ἐν seems to have fallen out of some MSS owing to the preceding word ἡμῶν. 'Unumquodque vas,' Vulg.

Ἀνεπλάσατο, 'he moulds, shapes,' in each separate case, the aorist not predicating special time, so it is used in similes.

Δοῦλα, adj. with gen. = δουλεύοντα, 'that serve clean uses,' with dat Rom. vi. 19

Πάνθ᾽ ὁμ., 'with equal toil or skill'

Πηλουργὸς occurs Lucian. Prometh. 2 (I. p. 26, Reitz)

8 Κακόμοχθος, 'labouring ill' Churton: 'with a misdirected industry.' The word is ἅπ. λεγ.

Ὃς πρὸ μικροῦ, 'he who a little while before.' Comp. πρὸ ὀλίγου, xiv. 20. See Gen. ii. 7; iii. 19.

Πορεύεται, sc εἰς γῆν ἐξ ἧς ἐλήφθη. Gen iii 19, Sept.

Ἀπαιτηθεὶς, 'when the debt of life is demanded from him' S Luke xii. 20. 'This night thy soul shall be required (ἀπαιτοῦσι) of thee' See on xv 16.

9. Κάμνειν, 'to be weak and sick,' as is shown by the contrasted phrase that follows. The Vulg., 'laboraturus est,' may have this meaning. The notion of 'labour' is foreign to the passage, and if we take it as 'die,' there is tautology

Βραχυτελῆ. The word is unknown to classical Greek, and ἅπ. λεγ. in the Greek Script, but occurs Dion. Alex 1256 A, Isid 201 B. It is explained by Suidas and Hesychius σύντομος and μικρός

Ἀλλ᾽ ἀντερείδεται The construction is slightly changed 'But he sets himself against, vies with.' The μὲν seems to be answered by χαλκοπλάστας τε See Jelf, Gr. Gram. § 765 7 a The idea is that the potter, instead of learning a lesson of his own frailty from the frailty of the materials on which he works, strives to make these assume a show of strength and solidity by giving them a metallic appearance

Χρυσουργοῖς The word is found in Pollux, vii 97 (Bekker). Χαλκοπλάστης is ἅπ λεγ

Κίβδηλα, 'counterfeits,' earthen figures coloured and glazed, or varnished to look like metal. 'Res supervacuas,' Vulg, which is wrong. Wilkinson.

'Many [counterfeit gems], in the form of beads, have been met with in different parts of Egypt, particularly at Thebes; and so far did the Egyptians carry this spirit of imitation, that even small figures, scarabaei, and objects made of ordinary porcelain, were counterfeited, being composed of still cheaper materials. A figure which was entirely of earthenware, with a glazed exterior, underwent a somewhat more complicated process than when cut out of stone, and simply covered with a vitrified coating; this last could therefore be sold at a low price, it offered all the brilliancy of the former, and its weight alone betrayed its inferiority,' Anc Egyptians, ii p 148 ed. 1878.

10 Σποδὸς ἡ καρδ αὐτ, a quotation from the Sept, Isai xliv. 20, where it differs from the Hebrew The heart of the idol-maker is dead to all noble aims, and wholly set on his worthless work. Orig., Exh. ad Mart. 32 (I. p. 294, Ben.), quotes from memory: σποδὸς ἡ καρδία τῶν εἰδώλοις λατρευόντων, καὶ πολὺ (ἰ πηλοῦ) ἀτιμότερος ὁ βίος αὐτῶν

Γῆς εὐτελεστέρα, 'cheaper, more vile than earth.' Such men have no hope of a future. Ch. iii. 18; Eph ii. 12 'having no hope, and without God in the world.' The Vulg. translates: 'terra supervacua spes illius,' reading prob. γῆ, though Jansen suggests that 'terra' is abl, 'supervacua' being = the comparative, which is more ingenious than demonstrable. These verses (10, 11) are cited by Method. Conv. dec. Virg vii (XVIII. p. 57, Migne)

11. Ἠγνόησε implies here wilful ignorance. 1 Cor 1 21

Πλάσαντα . . ἐμφυσήσαντα. Gen. ii. 7 · ἔπλασεν ὁ Θεὸς τὸν ἄνθρωπον, χοῦν ἀπὸ τῆς γῆς, καὶ ἐνεφύσησεν εἰς τὸ πρόσωπον αὐτοῦ πνοὴν ζωῆς· καὶ ἐγένετο ὁ ἄνθρωπος εἰς ψυχὴν ζῶσαν The author seems to make no very marked distinction between 'soul' and 'spirit,' only he calls the one 'active,' the other 'living.' Comp. i. 4, viii. 19; ix. 15; S. Luke i. 46, 47

12 Ἐλογίσαντο, the plural (which is doubtless the original reading, and not ἐλογίσατο,) includes all heathen, and not merely the potter and such like.

Παίγνιον, 'a plaything,' 'game' Aristotle knew better than this. He teaches that happiness stands not in amusement. See Eth. Nicom. x. 6.

Ζωὴν . . . βίον The former is mere animal life, the latter, life with its business and duties. Comp. Aristot Eth x. 6 8, where he denies to slaves the possession of βίος He says: ἀπολαύσειε τ' ἂν τῶν σωματικῶν ἡδονῶν ὁ τυχὼν καὶ ἀνδράποδον οὐχ ἧττον τοῦ ἀρίστου εὐδαιμονίας δ' οὐδεὶς ἀνδραπόδῳ μεταδίδωσιν, εἰ μὴ καὶ βίου.

Πανηγυρισμὸν ἐπικ. 'The holding of a market for gain' Dion. Hal. vii. 71, Plut Symp. Probl. 2. The Greek Panegureis were originally great national religious gatherings, which degenerated by degrees into mere fairs where articles of every sort were sold. Thus the Olympic games were called 'Mercatus Olympiacus.' Dict of Antiq s. v The saying in the text is similar to that which Cicero attributes to Pythagoras, Tuscul. Disp. V. iii. § 9: 'Pythagoram autem respondisse, similem sibi videri vitam hominum et mercatum eum, qui haberetur maximo ludorum apparatu totius Graeciae celebritate.' Read the description of Tyre in Ezek. xxvii, and cp S. James iv 13

Φησὶν, 'says one,' used generally.

Ὅθεν δὴ, 'whence one can.' κἂν, sc. ᾖ, ἐκ κακοῦ. This is like Horace's (Ep I i. 65)—

'Isne tibi melius suadet, qui rem facias, rem,
    Si possis, recte, si non, quocunque modo rem.'

The maxim would be specially appropriate to the unscrupulous commercial activity of Alexandria, then and for many centuries the greatest emporium in the world. Sophocles teaches better, Ant 312

οὐκ ἐξ ἅπαντος δεῖ τὸ κερδαίνειν φιλεῖν.

13. Παρὰ πάντας, 'more than all,' 'before all.' Comp. Rom xii. 3. The maker of such frail images must have known better than any one his imposture.

Εὔθραυστα. Some of the best MSS. read εὔθραστα, but the word nowhere occurs 'Brittle,' in the ed. of 1610, 'brickle,' with the same meaning.

Γλυπτά, 'graven images' So continually in the

Sept. Deut vii. 5; Judg. xviii. 24; Is xliv 10; 1 Macc v. 68.

14. Πάντες... ἀφρονέστατοι. This seems to be the original reading, πάντων ἀφρονέστεροι being probably a correction.

Τάλανες ὑπ. ψυχ. νηπ. Vulg · 'infelices supra modum animae superbi,' where Reusch supposes that 'superbi' is a mistake for 'pueri' Gutbert thinks that the original was 'supra animam pueri,' which became by accretions what it now is. But which is the word of God for Roman Catholics? The Douai version has merely. 'foolish and unhappy, and proud beyond measure' The words mean, ' more miserable than an infant's soul,' *i.e.* in respect of ignorance. Comp. xii. 24.

Οἱ ἐχθροὶ .. καταδυν These words cannot refer to Solomon's times, nor would it be true of the Assyrians, etc., that they accounted all other nations' idols to be gods (ver 15). The fact mentioned in ver. 18 and the present σέβονται point to the Egyptians, or Græco-Egyptians, as 'the enemies' meant. As to the time when the Jews were 'held in subjection,' we may reasonably refer it to the reign of Ptolemy Philopator, who, on his return from his repulse at Jerusalem, B.C. 217, treated the Jews most cruelly. See Proleg. p. 32. Those who attribute the Book of Wisdom to Philo quote this passage as suitable to the state of the Jews under Caligula.

15 Ἐλογίσαντο θεούς. The Greeks in Alexandria seem to have identified their gods with those of other nations, and to have honoured the images of foreign divinities equally with their own. Rome certainly did this in later times. And though the Egyptians were too vain of their own institutions to borrow other gods (Herod. ii. 79 and 91), yet they allowed them to be deities at any rate in their own special localities See on xix. 3

Οἷς οὔτε. Comp. Ps. cxv 5, 6, 7, cxxxv 16, 17.

Συνολκὴν, 'drawing together,' a very late word, apparently found nowhere else in the sense of 'breathing.' It occurs in Dioscor. De Venenis, 14, and Galen, ii. 266 C.

Ψηλάφησιν. Plut. Aemil i. 262 C, Clem Al. Paedag. iii. 5 33 (p 273 Pott.)

Ἀργοὶ πρὸς ἐπίβ, 'useless for walking.'

16 Ἐποίησεν Ps. cxv 4. They are the work of men's hands and therefore cannot have life and sense.

Δεδανεισμένος. 'Having had his spirit lent to him.' See on ver. 8. Man therefore cannot impart it to others, nor even retain it himself. Eccl. viii. 8.

Αὐτῷ = ἑαυτῷ is certainly the right reading.

17. Νεκρόν. Comp. xiii. 10, 18.

Σεβασμάτων, objects of worship, xiv. 20. Lact Inst II. ii. 13 'Melior est qui fecit quam illa quae facta sunt' Grimm. Comp. Bar. Ep. to Jer. 46.

Ἀνθ᾿ ὧν. The common reading is σεβασμ. αὐτοῦ, ὧν, where ὧν must be explained as a part. gen. connected with αὐτὸς and ἐκεῖνα, which is harsh. The Sin. MS relieves the difficulty by reading ἀνθ᾿ ὧν (suggested by Arn), 'in opposition to,' 'in contradistinction from which.' Vulg., 'quia,' perhaps reading ὡς; but it may well be the translation of ἀνθ᾿ ὧν, which is used to signify 'because,' e g Soph Ant 1068 Vulg. adds, 'cum esset mortalis,' a manifest interpolation from the beginning of the verse.

18, 19. *Greatest folly of all in beast-worship*

18. Σέβονται 'They,' viz the enemies of Thy people, 'worship,' ver. 14 'The beasts' are serpents, crocodiles, dogs, birds, and indeed nearly all animals. See Wilkinson, Anc. Egyptians, ch xiv. and vol. ii. pp. 468–471, ed 1878. The Greeks and Romans often ridiculed this animal worship See Athenae Deipnosoph vii. p. 299, ed Casaub., quoted by Wilkinson, and Juven. Sat. xv. 1 sqq Plutarch explains the origin of beast-worship by the idea that the animals consecrated to the gods became in the course of time confounded with the deities themselves See De Iside et Osir c. 71 Warburton deduces it from hieroglyphic writing, the characters of which being the figures of animals, and standing for gods and heroes, in time became the object of direct worship. Div. Legat. bk iii § 6; and bk iv. § 4.

Ἔχθιστα. 'Miserrima,' Vulg, reading perhaps αἴσχιστα. Reusch. Comp xii 24

Ἀνοίᾳ. 'In respect of folly in the worshippers,

they (beasts) are worse than the others (idols).' It is more foolish to worship a beast than an image, because the latter may be taken as the representative of the deity, but beasts, in the author's view, are worshipped in themselves, with blind adoration, hateful (ἔχθιστα) as they are. All MSS read ἄνοια, which some editors have thought to be = ἄνοα; others have suggested ἀνία, and others, as the Eng. translators, read ἔνια. Retaining the received reading, I think the above given interpretation is the most probable. If we refer ἀνοίᾳ to the beasts, it is not true that the creatures worshipped by the Egyptians were the most unintelligent of all animals. The Arm version refers it to the worshippers, rendering· 'haec est pessima stultitia' So Gutb. The Vulg. 'insensata,' points to ἄνοα, unless the var 'insensate' be the true reading. Mr. Churton paraphrases : 'The Egyptians also worshipped the vilest of animals, which appear worse than others even in the judgment of the ignorant and thoughtless' Dr Bissell reads ἄνοια, and translates: 'For being compared together as it respects stupidity some animals are worse than others;' but he does not explain how he obtains this rendering from the Greek text. Philo, De Vit. Contempl. 1 (II. p. 472)· τῶν μὲν γὰρ παρ' Αἰγυπτίοις οὐδὲ μεμνῆσθαι καλόν, οἳ ζῷα ἄλογα καὶ οὐχ ἥμερα μόνον, ἀλλὰ καὶ θηρίων τὰ ἀγριώτατα παραγηώχασιν εἰς θεῶν τιμὰς ἐξ ἑκάστου τῶν κάτω σελήνης, χερσαίων μὲν λέοντα, ἐνύδρων δὲ τὸν ἐγχώριον κροκόδειλον, ἀεροπόρων δὲ ἰκτῖνον, καὶ τὴν Αἰγυπτίαν ἶβιν. S Aug De Un. Bapt. iv 'Talia quippe novimus fuisse simulacra Aegyptiorum, ubi et instituta esse multiplicior multoque ignominosior idolatria perhibetur'

Συγκρινόμενα. Comp Philo, ub sup. προσκυνοῦσιν οἱ ἥμεροι τὰ ἀνήμερα καὶ ἀτίθασσα, καὶ οἱ λογικοὶ τὰ ἄλογα, καὶ οἱ συγγένειαν ἔχοντες πρὸς τὸ θεῖον, τὰ μηδ' ἂν θηρσί τισι συγκριθέντα, οἱ ἄρχοντες καὶ δεσπόται τὰ ὑπήκοα φύσει καὶ δοῦλα.

19. The construction is: οὐδὲ τυγχάνει καλὰ (ὄντα) ὅσον (=ἐπὶ τοσοῦτον ὥστε) ἐπιποθῆσαι (αὐτὰ) ἐν ζῴων ὄψει. In καλὰ there is an allusion to the original creation, when 'God saw everything that He had made, and, behold, it was very good (καλὰ λίαν),' Gen. i 31. The Eng. version is very clumsy; the Vulg. is impossible

Ὡς ἐν ζῴων ὄψει. Ὡς used in a limiting sense='if the question is about the appearance of beasts.' Or, 'in comparison,' as vii 9

Ἐκπέφευγε, 'Went without'='were deprived of,' referring partly to the curse upon the serpent, Gen. iii. 14, but more specially to the truth that all things employed in idolatry are *ipso facto* accursed (see xiv. 8), and become abominable in God's sight. So the very flocks and herds were to be involved in the punishment of Israel's disobedience Deut. xxviii. 18

Ἔπαινον. εὐλογίαν Gen i 28, 31; 1 Cor iv 5.

CHAPTER XVI

1-14 *Contrast at the Exodus as regards the action of beasts on the Israelites and Egyptians.*

1 In order to show more fully the folly of idolatry the author resumes the comparison, begun in ch. xi, between God's dealings with His own people and with the Egyptians.

Διὰ τοῦτο. Because they worshipped hateful beasts, xv. 18.

Κνωδάλων. Frogs, locusts, flies, etc.

2. Εὐεργετήσας is the part. Some who read οἷς εἰς ἐπιθυμίαν make it a verb (εὐεργέτησας). So A and the Vulg, 'bene disposuisti populum tuum quibus dedisti.' I have retained the V. reading, which is confirmed by C Ven. and other MSS.

Εἰς ἐπιθυμ. ὀρέξεως. Eng., 'to stir up their appetite.' This rendering is wrong, as the people showed no want of appetite, when they were lusting after the delicious food which they had eaten in Egypt (see Ex. xvi 12, 13, Numb xi. 4, 5, 18 foll.), and were punished at Kibroth-hattaavah The words are better translated in the Bishops' Bible, 'for the desire of their appetite,' or by Coverdale, 'the desire that they longed for.' So Ps lxxvii 29: τὴν ἐπιθυμίαν αὐτῶν ἤνεγκεν αὐτοῖς

Ξένην γεῦσιν 'Strange flavour' Γεῦσις here and ver. 3 seems = 'object of taste.'

Ὀρτυγομήτραν, 'quail as food' Τροφήν in opp. to γεῦσιν. Ὀρτυγομήτρα is used in Ex xvi, and Numb xi, and is explained by Hesych as ὄρτυξ ὑπερμεγέθης. Philo's account of the quails is as follows (Vit Mos. 37, II p 114). ἀλλὰ γὰρ καὶ τῶν εἰς ἀβροδίαιτον βίον οὐκ εἰς μακρὰν εὐπόρουν, ὅσαπερ ἐν οἰκουμένῃ χώρᾳ καὶ εὐδαίμονι, βουληθέντος τοῦ θεοῦ κατὰ πολλὴν περιουσίαν ἄφθονα χορηγεῖν ἐν ἐρημίᾳ. ταῖς γὰρ ἑσπέραις ὀρτυγομητρῶν νέφος συνεχὲς ἐκ θαλάττης ἐπιφερόμενον πᾶν τὸ στρατόπεδον ἐπεσκίαζε, τὰς πτήσεις προσγειοτάτας ποιούμενον εἰς τὸ εὔθηρον. συλλαμβάνοντες οὖν καὶ σκευάζοντες ὡς φίλον ἑκάστοις, κρεῶν ἀπέλαυνον ἡδίστων, ἅμα καὶ τὴν τροφὴν παρηγοροῦντες ἀναγκαίῳ προσοψήματι. The Vulg retains the word 'ortygometra' here and xix 12, using 'coturnix' elsewhere S Aug. Quaest. 62 in Ex. 'Aves quas coturnices multi Latine interpretati sunt, cum sit aliud genus avium ortygometra, quamvis coturnicibus non usquequaque dissimile.'

3 Ἐκεῖνοι. The Egyptians, as in ver 4.

Τροφήν. The S. and Ven. MSS give τροφῆς, but ἐπιθυμέω is constructed with the acc Ecclus. xvi. 1; Ex xx 17.

Εἰδέχθειαν. This almost unknown word occurs in Zonar. p 632: εἰδέχθεια ἡ ἀμορφία, and in S Chrys t. iv p. 788. Steph. Thes. in voc Εἰδεχθής is found in Polyb. xxvii 2. 1, Diod iii. 29; εἰδεχθῶς, Greg. Nyss i. p. 410: παρειᾶς εἰδεχθῶς ἐν αὐλῇ κοιλασθείσης · and ii p 701 εἰδεχθῶς καὶ γελοίως The word εἰδέχθειαν being so uncommon has been variously dealt with in the MSS. It is the reading of C 55 and some other cursives, and from its suitableness to the sense of the passage, and from the improbability of its being invented by scribes, it has found favour with most editors. It was so printed by Mai in his edition of V; but Vercellone's new edition gives δ'ιχθεισαν (sic), which appears to have been the reading of the Vulg. The verse seems to be nowhere quoted by the Fathers. The word means 'ugly look;' and the meaning of the passage is, that the Egyptians, owing to the sight of the loathsome creatures (frogs, etc) that covered everything, might lose even (καὶ) the natural desire for food (Ex. viii. 3–6.) Sabatier renders. 'Propter odiosam deformitatem eorum quae immissa sunt'

Ὄρεξιν. 'Concupiscentia,' Vulg, which translates ἐπιθυμία by the same word, Rom. vii. 7, 8; Gal. v. 24. It is a late word found in ecclesiastical authors and introduced from them into the terminology of the Church Tertull De Anim. xxxviii (p 295) 'Concupiscentia oculis arbitris utitur.' Comp. De Resur. xlv, Hieron. Ep 128

Ἀποστρέφωνται with acc., as 3 Macc. iii 23: ἀπεστρέψαντο τὴν ἀτίμητον πολιτείαν So S Matt. v. 42: τὸν θέλοντα ἀπὸ σοῦ δανείσασθαι μὴ ἀποστραφῇς Comp 2 Tim. i 15

Οὗτοι δέ. The Israelites. This seems preferable to αὐτοὶ the reading of V. and Ven So in ver. 4: τούτοις δέ.

Γεύσεως, as in ver. 2, 'diet.' The author omits all reference to the people's sin of gluttony in connection with the quails and their consequent punishment (Numb. xi 33; Ps. lxxviii. 30, 31), and dilates only on the miraculous supply vouchsafed to them because they were God's people

4 Ἀπαραίτητον, 'inexorable,' 'inevitable' So ver. 16. The lengthened distress of the Egyptians occasioned by the plagues which affected their supplies of food is contrasted with the temporary need of the Israelites so soon satisfied with abundance of delicacies.

5 Αὐτοῖς. The Israelites. 'Thy people,' Eng Marg, is a paraphrase not a translation. The reference is to the wild animals of the desert and especially to the fiery serpents, Numb. xxi. 6 ff. For θηρίων comp. Deut. xxxii. 24, and Acts xxviii. 4.

Θυμὸς Arn. wishes to translate 'poison,' comparing Deut. xxxii. 33 and Job xx 16; but 'fury' seems more correct, as it would apply to other animals beside serpents. This sense is found elsewhere in Wisdom, e g. vii 20; xi 18 q.v.

Σκολιῶν Isai xxvii 1 'Leviathan that crooked serpent,' ὄφιν σκολιών.

Οὐ μέχρι τέλους. Comp. xviii. 20; xix. 1, Heb. iii. 6.

6 Εἰς νουθεσίαν, as xi. 10: ὡς πατὴρ νουθετῶν. Judith viii. 27 · εἰς νουθέτησιν μαστιγοῖ Κύριος τοὺς ἐγγίζοντας αὐτῷ

Σύμβολον σωτηρίας (comp. ii 9), 'a sign, token of safety,' viz the Brazen Serpent, Numb. xxi 9 See the use made by our Lord of this symbol S. John iii. 14 and Wordsworth's note *in loc*. Σύμβουλον, the reading of A, S and Ven, would mean 'counsellor,' 'teacher of salvation,' which seems hardly likely to be used by the author as applied to an inanimate object. The Fathers do not help to determine the text here. S. Basil calls the serpent τύπος, which supports the reading of the text. ὁ ἐπὶ σημείου κείμενος ὄφις τοῦ σωτηρίου πάθους [τύπος] τοῦ διὰ τοῦ σταυροῦ τελεσθέντος. Just. Mart. speaks thus of the matter · καὶ κατ' ἐπίνοιαν καὶ ἐνέργειαν τὴν παρὰ τοῦ Θεοῦ γενομένην λαβεῖν τὸν Μωυσέα χαλκὸν καὶ ποιῆσαι τύπον σταυροῦ, καὶ τοῦτον στῆσαι ἐπὶ τῇ ἁγίᾳ σκηνῇ καὶ εἰπεῖν τῷ λαῷ· Ἐὰν προσβλέπητε τῷ τύπῳ τούτῳ καὶ πιστεύητε, ἐν αὐτῷ σωθήσεσθε, Apol. i. 60.

Εἰς ἀνάμνησιν is best taken as belonging to the whole sentence. The punishment and the remedy alike showed them the necessity of strictly complying with God's commandment. Philo allegorises the serpent as a type of temperance, Leg Alleg. ii 20 (I. p 80); De Agr. 22 (I p 315). It is a disputed point what the brazen serpent was intended to symbolise. Certainly the serpent was known among the Egyptians as the symbol of life and health (Wilkinson, Anc. Egyptians, ii 134, iv 375, etc), but it seems on this occasion rather to have represented the Old Serpent deprived of his poison, and, as it were, hung up as a trophy of victory And it becomes a type of the Passion of Christ, who by His death overcame death, and destroyed 'him that had the power of death' (Heb. ii. 14, Col. ii. 15). They who are wounded by sin, looking with faith to the Passion of Christ, are saved. See Theodor in Num. xxi 9, Quaest 38; Tertull De Idol v (p. 152); S Aug De Civit. x. 8; Maldonat. in John iii 14. Corn a Lap in Num xxi. 8· 'Allegorica et potissima causa fuit, ut serpens hic in ligno erectus, significaret Christum in cruce erectum, tamquam noxium et sceleratum, cujus intuitu per fidem et contritionem sanamur a letalibus peccatorum morsibus Sicut enim serpens hic habebat formam peccatoris sed non venenum, ita Christus assumpsit formam peccatoris sed non peccatum.'

7 Faith in the Great Healer was the necessary condition of safety. So Christ says (Mark ix. 23): 'If thou canst believe, all things are possible to him that believeth' The Targum of Jonathan on Numb. xxi. makes the divine voice accuse the people of ingratitude, comparing them with the serpent, who, though doomed to have dust for his food, murmured not. 'Now shall the serpents who have not complained of their food come and bite the people who complain.' And when the serpent of brass was made, if it was gazed at and the sufferer's 'heart was intent upon the name of the Word of the Lord, he lived' Etheridge, pp. 410, 411. 'Neither is it ordinarily His will to bestow the grace of sacraments on any, but by the sacraments; which grace also they that receive of sacraments or with sacraments, receive it from Him and not from them For of sacraments the very same is true which Solomon's Wisdom observeth in the brazen serpent, "He that turned towards it,"' etc. Hooker, Eccl. Pol. V. lvii. 4

Διὰ σὲ τὸν πάντ. σωτῆρα. Isai xlv. 21; 1 Tim. iv. 10: ὅς ἐστι σωτὴρ πάντων ἀνθρώπων. The author here repudiates the magical power afterwards attributed to the brazen serpent which occasioned its destruction by Hezekiah, 2 Kings xviii. 4. Corn. a Lap. refers to Philastrius, Lib de Haeres., as giving an account of the ceremonies used in the worship of this idol. Galland vii. 480.

'Salvatorem.' Vulg This word is unknown in classical Latin It occurs in one of Gruter's Inscriptions, p 19 5 'Jovi custodi, Quirino salvatori.' See note on ch xii 5.

8. Καὶ ἐν τούτῳ. 'Herein also,' as in the passage of the Red Sea, and in other instances.

Ὁ ῥυόμενος 2 Tim. iii. 11. ἐκ πάντων με ἐρρύσατο ὁ Κύριος. Ps vii. 2.

9, 10. The contrast in these verses is this: the Egyptians perished by creatures that do not generally kill men; the Israelites were saved even from poisonous serpents. Gutb.

9. Οὓς μὲν, answered by τοὺς δέ, ver. 10, is demonstrative So Matt. xiii. 8: ὃ μὲν ... ὃ δέ 2 Macc. xii. 24· πλείονες ... οἱ δέ. Polyb. I. viii. 3 οὓς μὲν ἐξέβαλον, οὓς δὲ ἀπέσφαξαν.

Ἀκρίδων, 'locusts.' Exod x. 4–15, Ps. lxxviii 46; Rev. ix 7.

Μυιῶν. Exod. viii. 16–24. Ps. lxxvii. 45. ἐξαπέστειλεν εἰς αὐτοὺς κυνόμυιαν καὶ κατέφαγεν αὐτοὺς, καὶ βάτραχον καὶ διέφθειρεν αὐτούς.

Ἀπέκτεινε. Pharaoh calls the plague of locusts 'this death,' Exod. x. 17, but we do not read there that either the locusts or flies destroyed men's lives. There are flies, especially in Africa, whose sting is deadly. Schleusner, in voc. κυνόμυια, quotes a writer who, commenting on Ps. lxxvii 45, says· κυνόμυιαν οἱ Ἑβραῖοι ἑρμηνεύουσι πλῆθος πάμμιγον ἀγρίων καὶ σαρκοβόρων θηρίων, οἱ δὲ Ἕλληνες λέγουσιν τὴν τοῦ κυνὸς ὑλακτοῦντος μυίαν Josephus (Ant. II. xiv 3) asserts that the lice destroyed men's lives, and then he describes the plague of flies thus: θηρίων παντοίων καὶ πολυτρόπων, ὧν εἰς ὄψιν οὐδεὶς ἀπηντήκει πρότερον, τὴν χώραν αὐτῶν ἐγέμισεν, ὑφ᾽ ὧν αὐτοί τε ἀπώλλυντο, καὶ ἡ γῆ τῆς ἐπιμελείας τῆς παρὰ τῶν γεωργῶν ἀπεστέρητο. εἰ δέ τι καὶ διέφυγε τὴν ὑπ᾽ ἐκείνοις ἀπώλειαν, νόσῳ τοῦτο, καὶ τῶν ἀνθρώπων ὑπομενόντων, ἐδαπανᾶτο. Philo's account is as follows: φορὰ σκνιπῶν ἐχύθη, καὶ ταθεῖσα καθάπερ νέφος ἅπασαν ἐπέσχεν Αἴγυπτον· τὸ δὲ ζῶον, εἰ καὶ βραχύτατον, ὅμως ἀργαλεώτατον. οὐ γὰρ μόνον τὴν ἐπιφάνειαν λυμαίνεται κνησμοὺς ἐμποιοῦν ἀηδεῖς καὶ βλαβερωτάτους, ἀλλὰ καὶ εἰς τὰ ἐντὸς βιάζεται διὰ μυκτήρων καὶ ὤτων. σίνεται δὲ καὶ κόρας ὀφθαλμῶν εἰσπετόμενον, εἰ μὴ φυλάξαιτό τις. φυλακὴ δὲ τίς ἔμελλε πρὸς τοσαύτην ἔσεσθαι φοράν, καὶ μάλιστα Θεοῦ κολάζοντος; Vit. Mos. i 19 (II. p 97)

10 Ἀντιπαρῆλθε. 'Adveniens,' Vulg. 'Ex adverso advenit,' Sabat. 'Came to meet,' 'came to their aid against the poison of the serpents.' It is the word used of the conduct of the Priest and Levite in the Parable of the Good Samaritan, S. Luke x. 31, 32, with a different shade of meaning The verb ἀντιπάρειμι is used by Xenophon of two armies marching along on opposite sides of a river, Anab. iv. 3. 17.

11. Εἰς ὑπόμνησιν τ. λογ. σου, parallel with εἰς ἀνάμν. ἐντολῆς νόμ. σου, ver 6. Λόγια, 'dicta divina,' 'commands,' 'laws,' as Ps. cxviii 158, 169 (Sept.); Acts vii 38.

Ἐνεκεντρίζοντο, 'were pricked with the goad.' Vulg: 'examinabantur.'

Ὀξέως, 'quickly,' as iii. 18. But Mr Churton: 'they escaped with sharp anguish.'

Ἵνα depends on ἐνεκεντρ and διεσώζοντο

Ἀπερίσπαστοι, prop 'not drawn hither and thither,' 'distracted' So Ecclus xli. 1. Here it means 'estranged from,' 'not participating in.' The Eng: 'continually mindful' is tautological. The Vulg is more to the purpose: 'Non possent Tuo uti adjutorio.'

12 Μάλαγμα. Comp. Is. i. 6: οὐκ ἔστι μάλαγμα ἐπιθεῖναι οὔτε ἔλαιον οὔτε καταδέσμους. On the use of the physician with his material remedies see Ecclus. xxxviii 1–8.

Λόγος, as ῥῆμα, ver. 26, 'the word' of God as the expression of His will. Comp. Ps. cvi. 20: ἀπέστειλε τὸν λόγον αὐτοῦ καὶ ἰάσατο αὐτούς. See on ver. 7.

13. Θανάτου. So Christ says, Rev. i 18: 'I have the keys of hell and of death'

Κατάγεις, κ.τ.λ. Comp. Deut. xxxii. 39; 1 Sam. ii. 6; Tob. xiii. 2.

Πύλας Ἅιδου. Job xxxviii. 17: ἀνοίγονται δέ σοι φόβῳ πύλαι θανάτου, πυλωροὶ δὲ ᾅδου ἰδόντες σε ἔπτηξαν; Ps. cvi. 18; Isai. xxxviii. 10. The expression in the text means, 'death, or the grave.' It is used in another sense, Matt xvi. 18 Vulg 'portas mortis' here, but 'portae inferi' in the Gospel.

Ἀνάγεις, as Heb. xiii. 20. ὁ ἀναγαγὼν ἐκ νεκρῶν τὸν ποιμένα τῶν προβάτων

14 Ἀποκτέννει, nearly all the MSS give this form. So Josh viii 24; Tob. i. 18 In N. T. it has been usually altered to ἀποκτείνω. S Aug, Spec 100, reads 'Homo autem se occidit per malitiam;' but this seems to be an error, as is the reading found in some MSS. of the Vulg. 'per malitiam animam suam.' The notion is parallel to that in Matt. x 28, viz that men may kill the body, but cannot touch the soul.

Ἀναστρέφει . . ἀναλύει, the subject of both is ἄνθρωπος 'Man killeth (man), but he bringeth not back the spirit when it hath gone forth, no, nor delivereth the soul taken to (or received in) the other world.' Comp Eccl viii. 8.

Παραληφθεῖσαν, sc εἰς Ἅιδου. The Eng translators seem to have read ψυχὴ παραληφθεῖσα, a variation found in no MSS The word is used by Polyb. iii 69 2 of taking prisoners τοὺς δὲ παραληφθέντας ἄνδρας ἀβλαβεῖς μεθ᾽ ἑαυτοῦ προῆγε.

15–29. *Contrast, as regards the action of the powers of nature, water and fire.*

15. Comp Tob. xiii 2; Amos ix 1–4; Ps. cxxxix 8

16 Ἀρνούμενοι ... εἰδέναι, 'asserting that they knew Thee not,' as xii 27 This refers to Pharaoh's speech, Ex v 2 · 'Who is the Lord that I should obey His voice to let Israel go? I know not the Lord'

Ἐμαστιγώθησαν, xii. 22, Tob xi. 14.

Ξένοις, 'strange,' 'novis,' not only because storms of rain and hail were almost unknown in Egypt, but because their character was abnormal, as it is said Exod ix 24 : ἦν δὲ ἡ χάλαζα καὶ τὸ πῦρ φλογίζον ἐν τῇ χαλάζῃ· ἡ δὲ χάλαζα πολλὴ σφόδρα σφόδρα, ἥτις οὐ γέγονε τοιαύτη ἐν Αἰγύπτῳ ἀφ᾽ οὗ γεγένηται ἐπ᾽ αὐτῆς ἔθνος 'And when Pharaoh saw that the rain and hail and the thunders were ceased, he sinned yet more,' Exod. ix 34 Comp. Philo, Vit. Mos., quoted on ver. 19. The absence of rain, especially in the inland parts of Egypt, is a marked feature of the climate, and as such is noticed Deut. xi. 10, 11, and Zech xiv. 18. Comp. Herod ii. 13, 14. Thus Philo, Vit Mos iii 24 (II. p 164) τῆς χώρας οὐχ ὑετῷ καθάπερ αἱ ἄλλαι νιφομένης, ἀλλὰ ταῖς τοῦ ποταμοῦ πλημμύραις εἰωθυίας ἀνὰ πᾶν ἔτος λιμνάζεσθαι, θεοπλαστοῦσι τῷ λόγῳ τὸν Νεῖλον Αἰγύπτιοι ὡς ἀντίμιμον οὐρανοῦ γεγονότα, καὶ περὶ τῆς χώρας σεμνηγοροῦσιν.

Ὑετοῖς ... ὄμβροις. The distinction between ὑετὸς and ὄμβρος seems to be that the former (Lat. 'nimbus') means 'a sudden heavy shower,' the latter (Lat. 'imber'), ' a lasting rain'

Ἀπαραιτήτοις See on ver. 4 Omitted in Vulg. Arn quotes Milton, Par. Reg iv .

' Fierce rain with lightning mixt, water with fire
   In ruin reconciled.'

17 Πλεῖον ἐνήργει, 'had more power than usual' Calmet refers to the account of Elijah's sacrifice, 1 Kings xviii. 38. The notion in the text is that the hail was not melted, nor the water quenched by the fires of heaven. S Ephr Syr. in Exod. c ix. (p 210): ' Ruit itaque praeceps grandinis nimbus, intermicantibus fulgetris mistus adeo nec grando ignem extinxit, nec ignis grandinem tabefecit, quin ea adjuncta, velut aggestis vepribus, flammam extulit luculentiorem. Simili miraculo grando, velut in fornace ferrum, sic igne torrente excandescere visa est, et quod etiam mirabile est, ignis grandinem inflammavit, ligna minime adussit.' Comp Ps xviii. 12, 13.

Ὑπέρμαχος, see on x. 20 The same idea is found ch v 17 foll

18. Ποτὲ μὲν ... ποτὲ δὲ refer to different times and plagues, as is shown also by the tenses of the verbs ἡμεροῦτο and φλέγει, ver. 19. The present represents the Plague of fire as present to the writer, the imperfect introduces the extinguishing of the fire as something more distant, imported for the sake of contrast. Guth.

Ἡμεροῦτο, 'mansuetabatur,' Vulg. This is ἅπ. λεγ. for the usual 'mansuefacio' 'The animals sent against the ungodly' must be the frogs, flies, lice, and locusts, but to what event in the history of these Plagues the author is alluding, is a matter of great doubt. Grimm thinks that he has erroneously combined the plagues of frogs, flies and lice with that of hail and lightning, so as to assert that the flames spared the beasts sent at that same time to plague the Egyptians. Gutberlet defends the author from this charge, and supports the explanation of Calmet, that the fires spoken of were not the lightnings of the Plague, but the artificial fires kindled by the Egyptians to disperse the noxious animals, and which had no effect on them. This however is a pure hypothesis. Arnald (whose view seems reasonable) says 'I must acknowledge that our author, in this particular, seems to have exceeded historical truth, and to have used a rhetorical exaggeration to make God's dealings with the Egyptians appear more terrible.' At the same time it is possible that the writer may allude to some old tradition on the matter, as in the case of the manna, vers. 20, 21. Comp xix 20. Philo, after describing the plague of hail, as quoted below, states that it was followed by a strong and pestilential wind which brought the locusts, but he nowhere says that the two plagues were simultaneous.

19 Φλέγει, sc φλόξ Vulg.: 'exardescebat undique,' where the tense is wrong, and 'undique' is an addition.

Γεννήματα, 'the fruits,' 'produce,' as is shown by ἀνθ᾽ ὧν, ver 20, and καρπούς, ver. 22. Vulg.: 'nationem.' See on 1 14. Philo, Vit. Mos. i 20 (II 98, 99): περιττὸν ἦν ἐν Αἰγύπτῳ χειμῶνα γενέσθαι ... ἐξαίφνης ὄντως ἐνεωτέρισεν ὁ ἀήρ, ὥσθ᾽ ὅσα ἐν τοῖς δυσχειμέροις ἀθρόα κατασκῆψαι, φοράς ὑετῶν χάλαζαν πολλὴν καὶ βαθεῖαν, ἀνέμων συμπιπτόντων, καὶ ἀντιπαταγούντων βίας, νεφῶν ῥήξεις, ἐπαλλήλους ἀστραπὰς καὶ βροντὰς, συνεχεῖς κεραυνούς, οἱ τερατωδεστάτην ὄψιν παρείχοντο θέοντες γὰρ διὰ τῆς χαλάζης, μαχομένης οὐσίας, οὔτε ἔτηκον αὐτὴν, οὔτε ἐσβέννυντο, μένοντες δ᾽ ἐν ὁμοίῳ καὶ δαλιχεύοντες ἄνω καὶ κάτω, διετήρουν τὴν χάλαζαν. ἀλλ᾽ οὐ μόνον ἡ ἐξαίσιος φορὰ πάντων τοὺς οἰκήτορας εἰς ὑπερβαλλούσας δυσθυμίας ἦγεν, ἀλλὰ καὶ τὸ τοῦ πράγματος ἀηθὲς ὑπέλαβον γὰρ, ὑπερ καὶ ἦν, ἐκ μηνι-

μάτων θείων κεκαινουργῆσθαι τὰ σύμπαντα, νεωτερίσαντος ὡς οὔπω πρότερον τοῦ ἀέρος ἐπὶ λύμῃ καὶ φθορᾷ δένδρων τε καὶ καρπῶν, οἷς συνεφθάρη ζῶα οὐκ ὀλίγα, τὰ μὲν περιψύξεσι, τὰ δὲ βάρει τῆς ἐπιπιπτούσης χαλάζης, ὥσπερ καταλευσθέντα, τὰ δὲ ὑπὸ τοῦ πυρὸς ἐξαναλωθέντα. ἔνια δὲ ἡμίφλεκτα διέμενε, τοὺς τύπους τῶν κεραυνίων τραυμάτων εἰς νουθεσίαν τῶν ὁρώντων ἐπιφερόμενα.

Καταφθείρῃ. The balance of authority is in favour of this reading, and not διαφθείρῃ (Vat.) Comp ver. 22.

20. Ἀνθ᾽ ὧν Instead of the fruits destroyed by the lightning, etc

Ἀγγέλων τροφήν, Ps. lxxvii. 24, 25 (Sept.): ἔβρεξεν αὐτοῖς μάννα φαγεῖν, καὶ ἄρτον οὐρανοῦ ἔδωκεν αὐτοῖς· ἄρτον ἀγγέλων ἔφαγεν ἄνθρωπος, ἐπισιτισμὸν ἀπέστειλεν αὐτοῖς εἰς πλησμονήν. Comp 2 Esdr. i. 19, S John vi. 31; Rev. ii. 17. See the account of the manna Ex. xvi. and Numb. xi, and Wisd xix. 21, 1 Cor. x 3

Ἐψώμισας, with double acc., as Numb. xi. 4 τίς ἡμᾶς ψωμιεῖ κρέα, Is lviii. 14 It is used in a different sense 1 Cor. xiii. 3: ἐὰν ψωμίσω πάντα τὰ ὑπάρχοντά μου

Ἕτοιμον ... ἀκοπιάτως, (or ἀκοπιάστως), 'paratum sine labore,' Vulg. These expressions, and the term 'angels' food,' imply merely that the manna was a supernatural substance, indebted to no labour of man for its production. Philo's account of the manna is given in Vit. Mos. 1. 36, 37. But his treatment of the subject is very different from our author's, as he uses the history merely as a vehicle for allegory. Thus: ἡ ψυχὴ γανωθεῖσα πολλάκις εἰπεῖν οὐκ ἔχει, τί τὸ γανῶσαν αὐτήν ἐστι· διδάσκεται δὲ ὑπὸ τοῦ ἱεροφάντου καὶ προφήτου Μωυσέως, ὃς ἐρεῖ, Οὗτός ἐστιν ὁ ἄρτος, ἡ τροφὴ ἣν ἔδωκεν ὁ Θεὸς τῇ ψυχῇ, προσενέγκασθαι τὸ ἑαυτοῦ ῥῆμα, καὶ τὸν ἑαυτοῦ λόγον οὗτος γὰρ ὁ ἄρτος ὃν δέδωκεν ἡμῖν φαγεῖν, τοῦτο τὸ ῥῆμα, Leg. Alleg iii. 60 (I. p. 121) Comp. De Prof 25 (I. p. 566). Of the way in which the Fathers have treated the subject of manna take the following examples (see also on ver. 22) S. Cyr Al in Joh iii (IV. p 318, Aub.) ἐπὰν μέν τοι γένηται πρωὶ, τουτέστιν ἀνίσχοντος ἤδη, καὶ τὴν οἰκουμένην ὅλην περιαστράπτοντος τοῦ Χριστοῦ, ἐπὰν καὶ ἡ δρόσος καταλήγῃ λοιπὸν, τοῦτ' ἔστιν ἡ παχεῖα, καὶ ἀχλυώδης τῶν νομικῶν ἐπιταγμάτων εἰσήγησις· τέλος γὰρ νόμου, καὶ προφητῶν ὁ Χριστός· τότε δὴ πάντως τὸ ἀληθὲς ἡμῖν, καὶ ἐξ οὐρανοῦ καταβήσεται μάννα, εὐαγγελικὴν δὲ δηλονότι διδασκαλίαν φαμὲν, οὐκ ἐπὶ τὴν Ἰσραελιτῶν συναγωγὴν, ἀλλὰ κύκλῳ τῆς παρεμβολῆς, εἰς πάντα δηλονότι τὰ ἔθνη, καὶ ἐπὶ πρόσωπον τῆς ἐρήμου, τοῦτ' ἔστι τῆς ἐξ ἐθνῶν Ἐκκλησίας, περὶ ἧς εἴρηταί που· "Ὅτι πολλὰ τὰ τέκνα τῆς ἐρήμου μᾶλλον ἢ τῆς ἐχούσης τὸν ἄνδρα. There is much more to the same purpose. Berengaud. Exp. in Apoc.. 'Per manna sapientia quae Christus est intelligi potest Ipse est enim panis vivus qui de caelo descendit Hoc pane aluntur omnes electi, in deserto atque in itinere hujus saeculi positi, usque dum veniant ad terram repromissionis,' i. e. 'ad caelestem beatitudinem quam repromisit Deus diligentibus se.' In App. ad Opp. S. Ambr (XVII p 861, Migne). S. Ambr. Exp in Ps cxviii Serm 18 (p 641, Ben). 'Non erat rerus ille panis, sed futuri umbra. Panem de caelo illum verum mihi servavit Pater Mihi ille panis Dei descendit de caelo, qui vitam dedit huic mundo' S. Greg. Magn Moral in Job lib xxi. c. 15 (p. 1010, Ben.). 'Manna est verbum Dei, et quidquid bene voluntas suscipientis appetit, hoc profecto in ore comedentis sapit' And again, Lib vi c 16 (p 191, Ben.): 'Manna quippe omne delectamentum atque omnis saporis in se suavitatem habuit, quod videlicet in ore spiritalium, juxta voluntatem edentium, saporem dedit, quia divinus sermo et omnibus congruens, et a semetipso non discrepans, qualitati audientium condescendit, quem dum electus quisque utiliter juxta modum suum intelligit, quasi acceptum manna involuntarium saporem vertit.' S. Aug. In Joann. Tract xxvi § 12· 'Hunc panem significavit manna, hunc panem significavit altare Dei Sacramenta illa fuerunt, in signis diversa sunt; in re quae significatur paria sunt ... Manna umbra erat, Iste veritas est'(T. III. 498).

Πᾶσαν ἡδονὴν ἰσχύοντα, this is the reading of nearly all MSS. One cursive and the Compl. insert πρὸς before πᾶσαν, and this Fritzsche has received. So Orig Exc. in Ps lxxvii. (vol XVII. p 144, Migne):

ἄρτον ἀπ' οὐρανοῦ ἔδωκεν ὁ Θεὸς τῷ λαῷ αὐτοῦ, ἀκοπιάστως πρὸς πᾶσαν ἡδονὴν ἰσχύοντα· πρὸς ὃ γάρ τις ἐβούλετο μετεκρίνατο. The Eng, Syr, and Ar versions translate as if πᾶσ. ἡδ. were in the genitive case: 'Suaviorem omni dulcedine' 'Able to content every man's delight.' The Vulg·seems to have read ἰσχοντα, 'omne delectamentum in se habentem' If we retain the usual reading, we must take ἰσχύω with acc of obj.= 'vim habeo ratione habita alicujus rei.' Wahl. 'Having power over, comprehending, every pleasure' Comp Ecclus. xliii. 15: ἴσχυσε νεφέλας, where however A. reads νεφέλαις. Bissell translates: 'strong in (with respect to) every kind of pleasant relish'

Ἁρμόνιον agrees with ἄρτον. 'Suiting every taste,' as ver 21, 'tempered itself to every man's liking.' Vulg. 'et omnis saporis suavitatem,' perhaps reading with S ἁρμονίαν The author seems to have followed some tradition in this statement the account in the Pentateuch would lead to a very different conclusion. See Ex. xvi. 31; Numb xi 6, 8; xxi. 5 Ginsburg, ap Kitt Cyclop, refers to Joma, 75, for the tradition See also Barclay, The Talmud, p 26, S. Ephr Syr in Exod. cap xvi. (p. 218): 'Subdit Scriptura: manna specie quidem coriandrum, mel autem gustu repraesentasse, ut inde intelligeremus, manna ad omnem saporem compositum fuisse' See also in Numer cap. xi (p 256) S Aug, speaking of the frequent reception of the Holy Communion, and illustrating his case with the difference of feeling exhibited by Zaccheus and the Centurion about receiving Christ into their houses, says, Ad Inquisit Jan. (Ep. liv. § 4, Ben) 'Valet etiam ad hanc similitudinem quod in primo populo unicuique manna secundum propriam voluntatem in ore sapiebat, sic uniuscujusque in corde Christiani Sacramentum illud, quo subjugatus est mundus. Nam et ille honorando non audet quotidie sumere, et ille honorando non audet ullo die praetermittere.' In his Retractations he says that if the manna had really the quality ascribed to it, the people would not have murmured as they did Thus Retract. II xx: 'Quod de manna dixi, "quia unicuique secundum propriam voluntatem in ore sapiebat," non mihi occurrit unde possit probari, nisi ex Libro Sapientiae, quem Judaei non recipiunt in auctoritatem canonicam; quod tamen fidelibus potuit provenire, non illis adversus Deum murmurantibus, qui profecto alias escas non desiderarent, si hoc eis sapeiet manna quod vellent' For ὁρμόνιος comp Clem. Al Strom ii 7· *ἁρμόνιος ἥδε ἡ δόξα.* Dion. Hal. vi. 1021, 12 (Reiske).

21. Ὑπόστασίς σου. 'Thy sustenance,' the manna sent by Thee, so called as being something firm and real, not phantom food, remaining the same in substance whatever taste it might assume subjectively. Gutb. Many commentators take the words to refer to the Person of the Logos, as Hebr i. 3 (Vulg. . 'substantia tua),' but the corresponding clause, τῇ δὲ τοῦ κ τ λ., shows that it refers to the manna. Comp Judg vi. 4 : 'And left no sustenance (ὑπόστασιν ζωῆς) for Israel.'

Γλυκύτητα The manna was sweet to the taste (Exod. xvi 31), and they who ate it tasted the sweetness and graciousness of God. Ps. xxxiv. 8, 1 Pet. ii. 3.

Τοῦ προσφερομένου, 'of the eater,' Eng προσφέρεσθαι σῖτον being a common phrase for 'taking food,' Judith xii. 9. S Aug. Ep 118 · 'In primo populo unicuique manna secundum propriam voluntatem in ore sapiebat.' Arn

Ὑπηρετῶν, sc. ἄρτος, ver. 20.

Μετεκίρνᾶτο, 'changed itself.' μετακιρνάω=μετακεράννυμι, 'to mix by pouring from one vessel into another,' here, as Vulg. translates,='converti' The Fathers continually refer to the manna as a type of the holy Eucharist S Aug. In Joh Ev Tract xxvi § 13; S Chrys. Hom xlvi in Joann (VIII p 271, Ben.). In the tract De Coena Domini, affixed to the Works of S Cyprian, we find the following apposite remarks: 'Hujus panis figura fuit manna quod in deserto pluit, sic ubi ad verum panem in terra promissionis ventum est, cibus ille defecit ... Panis iste angelorum omne delectamentum habens virtute mirifica, omnibus qui digne et devote sumunt, secundum suum desiderium sapit, et amplius quam manna illud eremi implet et satiat edentium appetitus, et omnia carnalium saporum irritamenta, et omnium exuperat dulcedinum voluptates' Ps cxv In another place (Ep 76) S Cyprian sees in the manna a figure of the grace of sacraments which is alike to all, whatever be their age, sex, or station (P 157)

22 Χιών . κρύσταλλος, *i. e.* 'the manna,' so called from its likeness to hoar-frost (Ex. xvi 14) and being an 'icy kind of heavenly meat, that was of nature apt to melt' (εὔτηκτον κρυσταλλοειδές), ch. xix 21

Ὑπέμεινε πῦρ We read that the manna was melted by the sun, Ex xvi 21; but on the sixth day that which was gathered might be seethed or baked, and kept good during the Sabbath, Ex. xvi. 23, 24. Also, though so soft by nature, it could be ground and made into cakes and baked (Numb xi 1). Both these miracles seem to be referred to in order to point the contrast with the effect of the lightning in the seventh plague on the Egyptians.

Πῦρ φλεγ. ἐν τῇ χαλάζῃ is from Ex. ix. 24, showing a knowledge of the Sept.

23 Τοῦτο, sc πῦρ

Πάλιν, see on xiii 8

Ἐπιλελῆσθαι depends on γνῶσιν, ver. 22, the construction being changed from ὅτι with indic to acc. and inf The desire of uniformity of construction has led to the change ἐπιλέλησται in many MSS., but the alternation of ὅτι with an infinitive clause is not uncommon See Jelf, Gr. Gram § 804 6 , Winer, § 64. ii 2.

24. Ἡ κτίσις, 'all created things' (Rom. viii. 22), here, specially, the element of fire. Comp ch v. 17, 20.

Ἐπιτείνεται, 'exerts, intensifies itself.' Vulg 'exardescit.' MSS Sang. et Corb 2 . 'excandescit.' S Aug. viii 871 'extenditur.'

Ἀνίεται, 'abateth (i e weakens) his strength,' Eng Exod ix 26

Εἰς σέ. The reading ἐπὶ σοί is given by Method De Resurr. xiv. (XVIII. p. 288, Migne). ἡ κτίσις σοι . . ὑπὲρ τῶν ἐπὶ σοὶ πεποιθότων.

25. Διὰ τοῦτο, because nature works out God's will.

D d

Μεταλλευομένη, sc. ἡ κτίσις, i.e. 'fire,' as ver. 24, and the manna 'Changing itself into all fashions.' See on iv. 12. The manna changed its taste according to the desire of the eater (vers. 20, 21), and fire modified its usual effects in obedience to its Maker's will

Τῇ παντ. σ. δωρεᾷ, 'Omnium nutrici gratiae Tuae,' Vulg. 'Thy mercy that provides for all' So δωρεά in the sense of 'bounty,' Eph. iv 7. Grimm and others take δωρεά to be 'the gift' of manna, which makes this verse a mere repetition of the preceding statements.

Πρὸς τ. τ. δεομέν. θέλησιν. 'In accordance with the will of those who desired it,' as ver. 21, or more generally, 'that He might give them that which they desired in their need.' Churton For θέλησις comp Tob. xii. 18; Heb. ii 4, Just. Tryph. 61.

26. Ὅτι οὐχ . ἀλλά, 'not so much .. as.' This verse is quoted by Clem Al Paedag i (p. 167, Pott).

Γενέσεις τ καρπῶν, 'races, sorts of fruits' See on i 14 'Nativitatis fructus,' Vulg; 'Nativitates fructuum,' Sabat The Vulg uses 'nativitas' in the sense of 'natural production.' See on vii 5

Τὸ ῥῆμά σου Deut. viii 3 (Sept), where 'word' (ῥῆμα) does not occur in the Hebrew See Matt. iv. 4 It stands for 'will' here, as λόγος, ver. 12 Philo, Leg. All. iii 56 (I p 119) ὁρᾷς ὅτι οὐ γηΐνοις καὶ φθαρτοῖς τρέφεται ἡ ψυχή, ἀλλ' οἷς ἂν ὁ Θεὸς ὀμβρήσῃ λόγοις, ἐκ τῆς μεταρσίου καὶ καθαρᾶς φύσεως, ἣν οὐρανὸν κέκληκεν;

27 Τὸ γάρ The proof that it is God's will alone that gives natural food its power of supporting life is seen in the facts connected with the manna, e g. it melted away in the sun and yet could be cooked and baked, Ex. xvi. 21; Numb. xi 8. We read in the Targum of Jonathan: 'They gathered from the time of the dawn until the fourth hour of the day, but at the fourth hour, when the sun had waxed hot upon it, it liquefied, and made streams of water which flowed away into the great sea, and wild animals that were clean, and cattle came to drink of it, and the sons of Israel hunted and ate them.' Etheridge, p. 500.

Ἁπλῶς, 'simply ... melted away.' Vulg.: 'statim' Thus the Israelites were taught the lesson of daily dependence upon God, in agreement with the Christian prayer, 'Give us this day our daily bread.'

28 This is one of the many beautiful passages in this Book: The lesson about early prayer is of course founded on the fact that the Israelites were obliged to gather the manna before the sun grew hot and melted it. Some commentators have inferred from this passage that the author was an Essene or Therapeut. But see Ps. v. 3; lxiii. 1. lxxxvii 14 τὸ πρωὶ ἡ προσευχή μου προφθάσει σε. Ecclus. xxxv. 14 (xxxii Eng.). Ginsburg, ap Kitto, Cyclop., refers to Mishna Berachoth, i. 2, for a tradition that prayer must be offered to God before sunrise. In his account of the Essenes Philo writes (De Vit. Cont. ii. vol. ii. p. 485). τάς τε ὄψεις καὶ ὅλον τὸ σῶμα πρὸς τὴν ἕω στάντες, ἐπὰν θεάσωνται τὸν ἥλιον ἀνίσχοντα, τὰς χεῖρας ἀνατείναντες εἰς οὐρανὸν εὐημερίαν καὶ ἀλήθειαν ἐπεύχονται καὶ ὀξυωπίαν λογισμοῦ. See also Joseph Bell. Jud. II. viii. 5 For the Essenes see Prolegom. pp 19, 20

Εὐχαριστίαν σου (like προσευχὴ τοῦ Θεοῦ, S Luke vi 12), thanksgiving of which God is the object

Πρὸς ἀνατ. φωτ, 'at sunrise,' as πρὸς ἑσπέραν, S. Luke xxiv 29. Origen reads πρὸ ἀνατολῆς φωτός, De Orat. 31 (I. p. 267, Ben)

Ἐντυγχάνειν. See on viii 21.

29. The connection is this man should be grateful for God's blessings; for without thankfulness he can have no hope of future favour.

Ἀχαρίστου looks back to εὐχαριστίαν in the preceding verse.

Χειμέριος here, as generally in Attic, a word of two terminations. Vulg 'hibernalis,' here only. Comp 'aeternalis,' Ps xxiii 7; 'originalis,' 2 Pet. ii. 5; 'annualis,' Ecclus. xxxvii. 14.

Ῥυήσεται, 'disperiet,' Vulg See on i 8 So, 'exies,' Matt. v. 26; 'exiet,' Matt ii 6, 'peries,' Ecclus. viii. 18, 'redict,' Lev. xxv. 10, 'transient,' 2 Pet. iii. 10.

CHAPTER XVII

XVII. 1–XVIII. 4. *Contrast as regards the Plague of Darkness.*

1 Γάρ This verse confirms and elucidates xvi 29, with special reference to the hardening of the heart of Pharaoh and his servants. Their sin was ingratitude for the removal of the plagues, and the author seems to view their obstinacy as a judicial punishment. See Rom. ix. 18; xi. 33.

Σου αἱ κρίσεις. 'Judgments and counsels.' The Vulg inserts 'Domine,' and 'verba Tua'

Δυσδιήγητοι. Comp. Ps xl 5; xcii 5, 6. The word δυσδιήγ is ἅπ. λεγ in Sept, and not used in classical Greek. It means, 'hard to narrate,' or 'to set forth in detail.' Comp. ἀνεκδιήγητος Pallad Hist. Laus. 33 (xxxiv. p. 1092 B, Migne).

Διὰ τοῦτο, because God's dealings with men are unsearchable

'Ἀπαίδευτοι, 'uninstructed' in matters of true religion The Egyptians made the great mistake of fighting against God in their dealings with the Israelites Vulg 'indisciplinatae' This word is found frequently in Ecclus. (e.g. v. 14, vii. 17; xxii. 3, and 4 Esdr. i 8), but not elsewhere in Vulg. It occurs in S Aug De Civ. x 29 'verbis indisciplinatis utimini.' Cypr. De Idol. Van 6 Comp. 'insensatus,' iii 12; 'discalceatus,' Deut. xxv. 10; 'pudoratus,' Ecclus. xxvi 19

2 Ὑπείληφ γάρ This paragraph confirms ἐπλανήθησαν, ver. 1. See Jer. Taylor, Duct. dub. I 1 14

Δέσμιοι σκότους. The plague of darkness (see Exod x 21–23) here referred to, miraculous in its circumstances, but proceeding from natural causes, may have been produced by a terrible and abnormal sand-storm. The Sept. calls it σκότος γνόφος θύελλα

Μακρᾶς ... νυκτός. See quotations from Philo and Josephus on ver. 5.

Πεδῆται, 'compediti,' Vulg. This is a post-classical word, occurring elsewhere in Vulg., e.g Ps. lxxviii. 11; Dan. iii. 91; and in Lactant. Inst. VII. 1. 19 Plaut. Capt V. i. 23.

'In lapicidinas compeditum condidi.'

Φυγάδες, excluded by their own act, like runaway slaves. 'Outlaws from the divine Providence' Jer. Taylor, Cases of Conscience, i. 1.

Ἔκειντο Ex x. 23. οὐκ ἐξανέστη οὐδεὶς ἐκ τῆς κοίτης αὐτοῦ τρεῖς ἡμέρας

3. They had sought darkness to hide their sins (Ps x 11), and now they were punished with darkness Eng 'While they supposed to lie hid,' a rather uncommon use of the verb 'suppose'

Ἐσκορπίσθησαν, they were dispersed, separated from one another by the solid darkness, 'the dark veil of oblivion' This, which is the usual reading, is confirmed by the S MS, which gives διεσκορπίσθησαν Fritzsche has received ἐσκοτίσθησαν, which is easier, but of inferior authority (all the ancient versions having the reading in the text), and was probably introduced by some scribe who found a difficulty in explaining ἐσκορπ Guth sees in it a reference to the mysteries (xiv 23) and orgies celebrated at night, which drew the heathen together to their 'secret sins.' This miraculous darkness drave them asunder, so that none helped or comforted other, in agreement with the view maintained xi. 15, 16, that men's own sins make the whips to scourge them withal.

Ἰνδάλμασιν, 'appearances' Sabat: 'spectris.' Lucian. Somn 5 (II p 711, Reitz). Εἴδωλον is used of the ghosts of the dead, and ἴνδαλμα is very much the same in etymology and in meaning. The author adds many circumstances in this plague which are not found in Moses' narrative. The spectres may have been the product of the Egyptians' own terrified imaginations, though there seems to be an intimation of something real in Ps lxxviii. 49: 'He cast upon them the fierceness of His anger, wrath, and indignation, by sending evil angels among them' Arn. refers to Ecclus. xxxix 28 The Vulg rendering, 'cum admiratione nimia perturbati,' is curious S Agobardus refers to this passage· 'Terrores etiam tribulationum per daemones fieri in Libr Sap legimus' Ap Galland xiii p 453

4. Μυχὸς, 'the inmost recesses of the houses,' to which they retreated.

Ἀφόβους, I have received this instead of ἀφόβως, as the author seems to use the pred adj in such cases. Comp x 5, xiv. 24

Καταράσσοντες, 'sounds rushing down' Vulg 'sonitus descendens.' The Eng addition, 'as of waters falling,' is unnecessary, as is the change from the received text to ἐκταράσσοντες (Fr.), though this may have been the original reading of V Καταράσσειν is used intr as well as trans, as our 'dashing down' The notion is amplified in ver 18

Περιεκόμπουν. 'Sounded around' This word is found in no good MS. of any classical author (the reading in Thuc. vi. 17 is spurious), it occurs in Joseph. Bell. Jud i 25 2 τούτοις περικομπήσας, καίπερ παρατεταγμένον, Ἡρώδην ὑπάγεται.

Ἀμειδ. προσώποις dep on κατηφῆ The Vulg does not keep to the Greek Jer Taylor quotes much of this chap in his treatise on Cases of Conscience, I 1

5 Comp. Philo, Vit Mos i § 21 (II. p 100) λαμπρᾶς ἡμέρας οὔσης ἐξαπιναίως ἀναχεῖται σκότος, ἴσως μὲν καὶ ἡλίου γενομένης ἐκλείψεως τῶν ἐν ἔθει τελειοτέρας ἴσως δὲ καὶ συνεχείαις νεφῶν καὶ πυκνότησιν ἀδιαστάτοις, καὶ πιλήσει βιαιοτάτῃ τῆς τῶν ἀκτίνων φορᾶς ἀνακοπείσης, ὡς ἀδιαφορεῖν ἡμέραν νυκτός καὶ τί γὰρ, ἀλλ' ἢ μίαν νύκτα νομίζεσθαι μακροτάτην, τρισὶν ἡμέραις ἴσην καὶ ταῖς ἰσαρίθμοις νυξί, τότε δὲ φασι τοὺς μὲν ἐρριμμένους ἐν ταῖς εὐναῖς μὴ τολμᾶν ἐξανίστασθαι, τοὺς δ' ὁπότε κατεπείγοι τι τῶν τῆς φύσεως ἀναγκαίων, ἐπαφωμένους τοίχων ἤ τινος ἑτέρου καθάπερ τυφλοὺς, μόλις προέρχεσθαι καὶ γὰρ τοῦ χρειώδους πυρὸς τὸ φέγγος, τὸ μὲν ὑπὸ τῆς κατεχούσης ζάλης ἐσβέννυτο, τὸ δὲ τῷ βυθεῖ τοῦ σκότους ἀμαυρούμενον ἐνηφανίζετο, ὡς τὴν ἀναγκαιοτάτην ὄψιν τῶν αἰσθήσεων ὑγιαίνουσαν, πηρὸν εἶναι, μηδὲν ὁρᾶν δυναμένην, τετράφθαι δὲ καὶ τὰς ἄλλας οἷα ὑπηκόους, πεσούσης τῆς ἡγεμονίδος. Joseph. Ant. II. xiv. 5: σκότος βαθὺ καὶ φέγγους ἄμοιρον περιχεῖται τοῖς Αἰγυπτίοις, ὑφ' οὗ τάς τε ὄψεις ἀποκλειομένοις καὶ τὰς ἀναπνοὰς ἐμφραττομένοις ὑπὸ παχύτητος οἰκτρῶς τε ἀποθνῄσκειν συνέβαινε, καὶ δεδιέναι μὴ καταποθῶσιν ὑπὸ τοῦ νέφους

The author adds some rhetorical touches to Moses' account, Ex. x. 23.

Ὑπέμενον, 'ventured,' as if the very stars feared this darkness

Στυγνήν S Matt xvi 3· πυρράζει στυγνάζων ὁ οὐρανός.

6 Διεφαίνετο, 'kept shining through' the darkness, in flashes. Arn takes μόνον with διεφ, implying that the fire was in appearance only, but the collocation of the words is against this. The Vulg. omits it. The flashes were probably electrical

Αὐτομάτη πυρά, 'a self-produced mass of fire,' in opposition to the lamps and torches used in vain by the Egyptians to dispel the darkness The Vulg gives 'subitaneus,' which occurs in this chapter, ver. 14, and xix. 16, but nowhere else in Vulg

Τῆς ... ὄψεως Eng takes as gen. of comparison after χείρω, which makes the sentence somewhat problematical, it is better taken (as Vulg) for gen of the cause after ἔκδειμα· 'Affrighted by that sight, if so be (μή) it was not beheld.' The 'sight' is the flashes of fire.

Τὰ βλεπόμενα, 'the objects seen' in the momentary flashes.

Χείρω, 'worse' than they really were The above interpretation seems to be the best which is allowed by the text as it stands There is, unfortunately, very scanty, and that inferior, authority for that which would seem to be the natural statement· 'They thought the things which they did not see to be worse than what they saw.' Calmet, Gutb., and Arn. interpret the present text nearly as I have done Thus Arn. 'Being frightened at what they had only an accidental glimpse of (for the flashes were not strong enough, nor of a continuance sufficient to view and discern things distinctly), they were more afraid of the objects that passed before them, and thought them worse than they wore.' Mr Churton paraphrases thus: 'There gleamed upon them at intervals a massive flame, burning of itself without fuel, and full of terror; and in their dread of that appearance which they durst not gaze upon, they imagined that the common objects which met their sight were changed for the worse, assuming ghastly forms from the lurid aspect which was cast upon them' (see Ezek xxxiii 7, 8) Dr Bissell 'They saw a fire, without anything to cause it, and their fear because of that which was hidden made this fire and light worse than the darkness.' This is not satisfactory, and the explanation given above is more in accordance with the received text.

7. Μαγικῆς τέχνης. 'Art magic,' Eng. From the Lat 'ars magica,' as 'arsmetrike,' in Chauc. Knight's Tale, 1900 Bible Word Book, *s v.* For μαγικὸς comp Philo, De Spec Leg 18 (II p 316), Just Apol i 14, ii. 15

Ἐμπαίγματα, 'tricks,' or 'scoffs' (Ps xxxvii 8, Isai. lxvi. 4) The latter seems preferable in connection with the succeeding parallelism So Vulg, 'derisus' See Exod. ix 11, 2 Tim iii 8, 9

Κατέκειτο, 'jacebant,' 'nihil valebant' Ex vii 22; viii. 7, 18; ix. 11. The Vulg rendering, 'appositi erant,' is unsatisfactory, unless, as Reusch suggests, 'arti,' be read, and 'apposita est' be understood with 'correptio.'

Τῆς ἐπὶ φρ 'There was ignominious reproof of their false pretensions to wisdom'

Ἐφύβριστος is a very late word, occurring in Herodian, ii. 1, vi. 7, and Clem 1 448 A (Migne), but nowhere else in Sept

8. Οἱ γάρ The wise men and magicians, as Gen xli. 8; 2 Tim. iii. 8. We may compare the proverb, 'Physician, heal thyself,' S. Luke iv 23.

Νοσούσης 1 Tim vi 4 νοσῶν περὶ ζητήσεις

Εὐλάβειαν, acc cogn, 'were sick with a laughable timidity.' See on xii. 11. The comma after 'fear' in the Eng version ought to be removed, so 'pleni' in Vulg is unnecessary Sabat 'In ridiculo timore languebant.' Ex. ix. 11

9. Ταραχῶδες, 'troubling, perplexing, object' The Vulg rendering, 'nihil ex monstris,' points to the reading τερατῶδες, which is found only in Ven, and as a correction in S.

Ἐφόβει, 'did fear them,' Eng., where 'fear' = 'frighten,' as often in Shakes, *e g* Ant and Cleop. II. vi 'Thou canst not fear us, Pompey, with thy sails'

Συρισμοῖς. The earlier form, συριγμοῖς, is given by some MSS It is probably an alteration of the original reading 'Sibilatione,' Vulg. ἅπ λεγ See on ch v. 2

Ἐκσεσοβημένοι, 'scared forth,' *i. e* from their hiding-places Ἐκπεφησθομένοι is plainly an alteration to a more usual word.

10. Διώλλυντο. Comp S Luke xxi 26. ἀποψυχόντων ἀνθρώπων ἀπὸ φόβου S Matt xxviii 4.

Ἔντρομοι 'Tremebundi,' Vulg. Comp Lucret i 96; Ovid Met iv. 133 See on x 7 For ἔντρομος comp. Ps. lxxvi. 19; Acts vii 32, Plut Fab 3 (I p 175 B).

Ἀρνούμενοι, 'refusing,' as Hebr xi. 24. They dared not look around them for fear of seeing horrible objects Some take ἀέρα for 'mist,' 'darkness,' but it is hardly likely that, after the harrowing description of the darkness given above, the author should apply to it the mild term ἀὴρ in a sense almost unknown to later writers

11. Γάρ, the reason of the magicians' fear. This verse has greatly exercised commentators The Eng. gives good sense: 'Wickedness condemned by her own witness is very timorous,' reading ἰδίῳ μάρτυρι with Compl This is also adopted by Fritzsche But then all original MSS give ἰδίως, and μάρτυρι is found only in A and some cursives. It is true that S also reads μάρτυρι, but ι is so constantly written for ει therein, that no certainty can be attributed to this (In ver. 10 S reads προσιδὶν for προσιδεῖν) I have therefore left the text as it stands in V., and we can either put a colon at μαρτυρεῖ, as Gutbl proposes, and make two coordinate clauses, thus: 'Wickedness is naturally a timid thing, it gives evidence thereof when it meets with punishment;' or keep it as one sentence, trans-

lating 'Wickedness being naturally timorous testifies the same when condemned to punishment,' or, 'Wickedness when condemned to punishment testifies that it is naturally timorous.' The Vulg, omitting ἰδίως, translates 'Cum sit enim timida nequitia dat testimonium condemnationis,' making κατοδικαζομένη depend on μαρτυρεῖ, 'testifies that it is condemned.' This is quite possible, but the sense given above seems preferable, i.e. evil men under some circumstances may hide their coward nature, but when put to the test of suffering they exhibit their base fear. As Hooker says, Eccl Pol V. i 2, referring to this passage 'Evils great and unexpected (the true touchstone of constant minds) do cause oftentimes even them to think upon divine power with fearfullest suspicions, which have been otherwise the most secure despisers thereof.' For instances of the effects of an evil conscience see Gen iii. 8; xliii 18; 1 Kings xxi 20, Job xv 20, Prov. xxviii 1, Jer ii 19

Ἀεὶ δέ, even without open punishment

Προσείληφε Eng 'forecasteth.' Vulg. 'praesumit,' reading probably προείληφε, into which the reading has been altered in S. But the received reading gives good sense 'takes in addition, aggravates evils' Comp Prov. xxviii 1, Job xv 20–22.

Συνεχομένη, 'pressed,' 'constrained.' See on ver. 20

Συνειδήσει, 'conscience,' here first occurring in this sense in the Greek version. The word indeed is found in Eccles. x. 20, but with a different meaning. It is common in N T., e g Acts xxiii. 1, Heb. xiii. 18

12 Προδοσία Vulg 'proditio cogitationis auxiliorum,' i e 'betrayal of the aids of thought.' There is a play on the word in the next verse by the introduction of προσδοκία Hooker (Eccl Pol V iii 1) renders 'Fear is a betrayer of the forces of reasonable understanding' Clemens Alex. defines fear ἔστι μὲν οὖν ἡ μὲν ἔκπληξις φόβος ἐκ φαντασίας ἀσυνήθους, ἢ ἐπ' ἀπροσδοκήτῳ φαντασίᾳ, ὅτε καὶ ἀγγελίας, φόβος δὲ ὡς γεγονότι ἢ ὄντι, ἡ θαυμασιότης ὑπερβάλλουσα The last definition of ἔκπληξις occurs Arist Top iv 5 Clemens also calls φόβος, ἄλογος ἔκκλισις, Strom. ii. 8 (p. 448, Pott).

13. The meaning seems to be. 'The expectation (of help) from within being weaker, makes the ignorance of the cause of torment greater,' i e when the succours of reason fail, the ignorance of the cause which has occasioned the terror aggravates the fear in the mind of the wicked man. Churton: 'Where there is less self-reliance or expectation of succour from within, the mind is more bewildered through its supposed ignorance of the cause whence the calamity proceeds.

Ἔνδοθεν. 'Ab intus,' Vulg. So Mark vii 21, 23. Similarly, 'ab invicem,' Acts xv 39, 'a foris,' Matt xxiii. 27, 28; 'a longe,' Matt. xxvi. 58; 'a modo,' Matt. xxiii 39, 'de foris,' Matt. xxiii. 25, 26, 'de intus,' Luke xi. 7, 'de longe,' Ps. xxxvii. 12; 'de retro,' Bar vi 5, 'de sursum,' John iii. 31, 'ex tunc,' Is. xlviii. 3; 'in palam,' Mark iv 22, 'in peregre,' Ecclus. xxix. 29

Προσδοκία, sc βοηθημάτων, ver 12.

Αἰτίας depends on ἄγνοιαν. Sabat 'Majorem computat inscientiam praebentis tormentum causae'

14. Οἱ δέ, the magicians, as in ver. 8, the passage about the terrors of a guilty conscience, vers. 11–13, being parenthetical

Τὴν ἀδύν νύκτα, acc of duration of time What the epithet ἀδύνατος, applied to νύξ and ἄδης, means is a question of some difficulty The Vulg renders 'impotentem' in the first place, and in the second leaves it untranslated: at least the words 'ab infimis et ab altissimis inferis' can hardly be meant as a translation, and are probably a corruption of the original text. The Eng gives 'intolerable,' and 'inevitable,' though the word must plainly have the same meaning in both places, the margin suggests 'wherein they could do nothing' Commentators vary between 'intolerable' (ἀδ., sc. τλῆναι), 'making men powerless,' 'incurable,' and the contradictory, 'mighty,' 'powerful' Schmid and Grimm take the epithet as applied to the darkness because it was nothing terrible or dangerous in itself, but became so only owing to the conscience-stricken terror of the Egyptians; and as appropriate to Hades as having no power upon earth, according to 1 14. Gutberlet sees in the expression a covert irony—that night which the magicians called impotent, that hell which they scoffed at as feeble. These wise men, who had disparaged the plagues, and had pretended to be superior to them, were involved in the same deadly night as the rest of the people, and like them were terrified within and without. There is much to admire in this interpretation of Gutberlet, and it is helpful in determining the sense; but ὄντως is against the epithet being merely ironical, and there is nothing to show that any irony is intended. It seems better to understand the expression thus: 'The night which was really powerless to harm and which sprung from a Hades which had no power on earth.' This is the meaning to which Grimm's interpretation points, though he errs in considering the darkness as in itself, in the author's view, nothing terrible. A glance at the previous verses refutes this at once.

Ἅιδου, as being the abode of darkness. Job x 21, 22.

Τὸν αὐτὸν ὕπνον, 'the same sleep' as the other Egyptians. This was truly ὕπνος ἄυπνος (Soph Phil. 848), troubled by the terrors of an evil conscience within and horrible sights without, ver 15. With ὕπνον κοιμώμενοι comp. τῆς κοιμήσεως τοῦ ὕπνου, S. John xi 13.

15 Ἠλαύνοντο, 'were vexed with prodigies of apparitions.' See on ver 3. S Mark vi 49.

Παρελύοντο, see on ver 19. 'Their spirit failing, they were paralysed'

Ἐπεχύθη. This seems to have been the original reading altered by copyists to ἐπῆλθεν. Comp 1 Thess v 3· αἰφνίδιος αὐτοῖς ἐφίσταται ὄλεθρος.

16 Εἶθ' οὕτως marks the transition to a different subject, all the Egyptians being here meant, and not only the magicians.

Ὅς δήποτ' οὖν ἦν, 'whosoever it was.' The punctuation of this clause has been varied by different editors. The Vulg and Eng. versions join ἦν ἐκεῖ καταπίπτων with the preceding words, 'whosoever there fell down;' and thus Holmes, Field, Tischend., and Reusch place a comma at καταπίπτων. Apel, Grimm, and Fritzsche put the stop at ἐκεῖ. But it seems very jejune to say 'whoever was there,' when they were all in the same circumstances, and the resolved form ἦν καταπίπτων would imply continuance, while here a momentary action is contemplated. It is better therefore to place the comma at ἦν, and to connect the following word with ἐφρουρεῖτο.

Ἐκεῖ καταπίπτων, 'sinking down there,' failing in limbs or spirits, or in both. Comp. ver. 2.

Ἐφρουρεῖτο Ex. x 23: 'They saw not one another, neither rose any from his place for three days.' Comp. Gal iii. 23· ὑπὸ νόμον ἐφρουρούμεθα συγκεκλεισμένοι εἰς τὴν μέλλουσαν πίστιν ἀποκαλυφθῆναι.

Ἀσίδηρον. Eurip Bacch. 1104:

ῥίζας ἀνεσπάρασσον ἀσιδήροις μοχλοῖς.

17 Ἐρημίαν, 'country away from human habitation,' 'waste.'

Προληφθεὶς, 'anticipated,' 'suddenly overtaken.' The addition of 'esset' to 'praeoccupatus' in Vulg. makes the sentence ungrammatical.

Δυσάλυκτον, a very late word. Vulg. 'ineffugibilem.' This word is found in Appuleius, Mund 280, but nowhere else in Vulg. See on x 4.

Ἔμενεν, 'sustinebat,' a use of the word not found elsewhere in Greek Test.

Ἁλύσει (2 Tim i 16) σκότους. Comp. 2 Pet ii 4: σειραῖς ζόφου ταρταρώσας παρέδωκεν

18 Ἀμφιλαφεῖς, 'far spreading,' 'thickly grown.'

Ὀρνέων. Ps liii 5: 'There were they in great fear, where no fear was.' Lev xxvi 36. 'I will send a faintness into their hearts. and the sound of a shaken leaf shall chase them, and they shall flee, as fleeing from a sword, and they shall fall when none pursueth.' As to the birds which sang in the darkness this may be only a rhetorical exaggeration; but Gutberlet affirms that in Egypt not only are there nightingales that sing at night, but other birds also, viz. a kind of lark (*Alauda arborea*), and a reed-warbler

(*Calamoherpe palustris*), and some others. The author may mean merely that the noises heard seemed to them like these sounds.

19 Explanatory of ἦχοι καταρόσσοντες, ver. 4.

Ἀπηνής, 'harsh,' 'terrible.' Instead of ἀπηνεστάτων (θηρίων) the Vulg. seems to have read ἀπηνεστάτη, 'valida bestiarum vox.'

Ἀντανακλωμένη This verb, meaning 'to reflect light or sound,' occurs in late authors, and Plut. De Placit Phil iv 20.

Κοιλότητος is certainly the right reading, κοιλοτάτων (printed erroneously by Tisch and Reusch as found in V.), having doubtless arisen from the copyist's eye catching the many genitives preceding.

Παρέλυσεν, 'disabled,' 'paralysed them.' Comp ver 15.

20 Γὰρ introduces the consideration how it was that the Egyptians' terrors were chiefly subjective.

Συνείχετο, 'was closely engaged in' Comp S Luke xii 50, Acts xviii 5 συνείχετο τῷ λόγῳ So συνέχεσθαι ὀδυρμῷ, 'lamentationibus indulgere,' Ael H. V. xiv. 22.

21 'That darkness which should afterward receive them' Comp. S Matt iii 7; viii 12; xxii 13; 2 Pet ii 4, 17; Jude 6, 13. So Tobit xiv. 10. αὐτὸς κατέβη εἰς τὸ σκότος.

Βαρύτεροι, owing to the torments of conscience.

CHAPTER XVIII.

1 Ὁσίοις The Israelites See on x 15. 'But all the children of Israel had light in their dwellings.' Ex. x 23.

Ὧν, i.e. of the Israelites The subject of ἀκούοντες, ὁρῶντες, ἐμακάριζον, is the Egyptians. Commentators have missed the sense of the passage from not seeing this The Vulgate has fallen into the same error, and then has remedied the blunder by translating ἐμακάρ., 'magnificabant Te.'

Ὅ τι μὲν οὖν, 'Whatsoever they also (the Israelites) had suffered (by reason of their bondage, etc.), they (the Egyptians) thought them happy,' compared with their own evil case. I have here adopted Gutberlet's suggestion to take ὅτι as the relative with οὖν, not that it completely satisfies me, but because I have nothing better to offer One would expect ὅτι to have the same meaning in both clauses, but then it is difficult to know in what sense to take οὖν To alter it to οἱ, on the authority of A, does not mend matters, for then the tense of ἐπεπόνθεισαν is wrong, the imperfect being required. But the preponderance of authority is largely in favour of οὖν, and we must make the best of it, as above; or else, taking ὅτι as the conj., translate: 'They (the Egyptians) deemed it a happy thing that they (the Israelites) too had suffered,' i.e. 'found comfort in thinking of the Israelites' former sufferings.' But the unusual sense thus given to μακαρίζω makes the rendering first offered most probable. Mr Churton, neglecting the force of the plup ἐπεπόνθεισαν, paraphrases: 'So they deemed them happy because of the things that happened to them.'

2 The Egyptians were grateful to the Israelites for not revenging themselves on their taskmasters. The Vulg again mistakes the sense.

Βλάπτουσι .. εὐχαριστοῦσι, hist. pres The latter verb has been changed into ηὐχαρίστουν for the sake of concinnity with ἐμακ and ἐδέοντο.

Καὶ τοῦ δ. 'Et ut esset differentia donum petebant,' Vulg. This seems to mean that the Israelites asked of God the boon that there might always be a difference in the measure dealt to them and their enemies. But the subject is still the Egyptians, and the meaning plainly is 'They begged pardon that they had been at variance' 'Inimicitiarum gratiam et veniam petebant,' Gr. Just as later they besought the Israelites to depart and pressed presents upon them Ex xii 33, 36.

3. 'Ανθ' ὧν. In contrast with the plague of darkness and its accompanying horrors. The 'propter quod' of the Vulg. does not represent this

Πυριφλεγῆ στῦλον. Ex. xiii 21· ἐν στύλῳ πυρός So Ex. xiv 24. Comp. Ps. lxxvii. 14; civ 39. Sept.

'Οδηγὸν μὲν ... ἥλιον δέ, 'a guide by day, and a sun by night.'

'Αβλαβῆ. Ps cxxi. 6. 'The sun shall not smite thee by day, nor the moon by night.'

Φιλοτίμου ξενιτείας. 'Of their glorious pilgrimage.' Ξενιτεία is properly 'service,' or, 'life, in a foreign country.' The Eng. 'to entertain them honourably,' and the Vulg.: 'solem sine laesura boni hospitii,' are equally beside the mark. Grimm makes φιλ. ξενιτείας depend on ἀβλαβῆ, but this seems unnecessary. Vatabl. renders 'Ad magnificam peregrinationem solem innocuum his exhibuisti.'

4 Ἄξιοι μὲν γάρ This verse shows the special suitableness of the punishment

Φυλακισθῆναι. Φυλακίζω is a late form for φυλάσσω. It occurs Acts xxii. 19, Clem. Rom ad Cor. xlv. 4

Ἄφθαρτον, not like the sun's light, but 'imperishable' So Christ came not to destroy the law but to fulfill. S. Matt. v 17. Εἰς κληρονομίαν ἄφθαρτον, 1 Pet i. 4

Τῷ αἰῶνι, 'the present age,' the world regarded in its temporal aspect. See on iv 2 and xiii. 9 Valck ad 1 Cor. i. 20: 'Quod Graeci Scriptores κόσμον, illud Judaei Graecienses etiam αἰῶνα dixerunt. Hinc nonnunquam κόσμος et αἰών in libb. ss. permutantur Quem Paulus vocat τὸν θεὸν τοῦ αἰῶνος τούτου (2 Cor. iv. 4), illum Joannes dixerat τὸν τοῦ κόσμου τούτου ἄρχοντα (xiv. 30).' So S Ignat. seems to use the two words interchangeably, ad Rom. vi: οὐδέν μοι ὠφελήσει τὰ τερπνὰ τοῦ κόσμου οὐδὲ αἱ βασιλείαι τοῦ αἰῶνος τούτου. The statement in the text that the light of the law was to be given to the world is noteworthy It shows that the Jews had begun to realise that the revelation made to them was not to be confined to their own nation exclusively—a truth expressed dimly in the prophets (Ps. xxii. 27, Isai. ii. 1 ff., Mic. iv. 1 ff.), but emphatically in later books, e.g Tob. xiii. 11, xiv. 6. The injunctions about the treatment of strangers in the Law (Exod xx. 10; Lev xix. 33, 34) showed that the light which they possessed was to be imparted to others. Thus Philo speaks of the Jews as possessing τὴν ὑπὲρ ἅπαντος ἀνθρώπων γένους ἱερωσύνην καὶ προφητείαν, De Abrah. 19 (II. p. 15). In another place he makes the Jewish nation the intercessor for the rest of the world, τὰς ὑπὲρ τοῦ γένους τῶν ἀνθρώπων ἁπάντων ἀει ποιησόμενον εὐχὰς, Vit. Mos. i. 27 (II. p 104) Comp. De Vict. 3 (II. p. 238).

5–25 *Contrast as regards the action of Death.*

5 A fresh contrast is here begun, the various portions being, (1) The Egyptians had sinned by the slaughter of the Israelites' children they were punished by the death of their own firstborn. (2) They drowned the children in the Nile: they were themselves drowned in the Red Sea (3) The rescue of one child was the cause of their wholesale destruction. Gutb The author still illustrates his principle (xi. 16), that a man's own sins make his punishment. For the facts alluded to see Ex. i 15, 16; ii. 3, xii. 29, xiv. 27. Philo, Vit. Mos 24 (II. p. 102). Josephus (Ant. II. ix) relates that the king of Egypt was induced to murder the male children at this time by the prevalence of a notion that a Hebrew was now to be born who would humble the power of the Egyptians and exalt the Israelites to the highest pitch of glory.

Ὁσίων. See on ver. 1.

Ἑνός. Moses, Ex ii 3, 9

Ἐκτεθέντος, the usual word for exposing children with the intention of destroying them. Herod. i 112; Aristoph Nub 531.

Εἰς ἔλεγχον, 'for their reproof,' is best taken with σωθέντος, referring to Moses' actions in after time. Vulg.. 'in traductionem illorum,' where Reusch thinks that 'illorum' ought to belong to the next clause 'illorum multitudinem filiorum abstulisti.'

Ὁμοθυμαδόν, 'conjunctim,' 'in common,' as ver. 12 Job xvi. 10 xxi 26.

6. Ἐκείνη ἡ νύξ, the night of the Exodus.

Πατράσιν Most commentators take the 'fathers' to mean the Israelites in Egypt who were made acquainted with the details of the tenth plague beforehand, Ex. xi. 4 ff., xii. 21 ff. But the Israelites are called 'God's people,' 'sons,' 'saints,' etc, but never 'fathers,' in this Book, and the opposition in the next verse introduced by δέ would be lost if πατράσιν and λαοῦ were identical. It is better therefore, with Gutb, to refer πατράσιν to the patriarchs, and the 'oath' to the promise made to Abraham (Gen xv 13 ff), and likewise to such passages as Gen. xxii. 16 ff., xxvi. 3 ff, xxviii. 13 ff

Ἀσφαλῶς εἰδότες Comp. Acts ii 36 ἀσφαλῶς οὖν γινωσκέτω πᾶς οἶκος Ἰσραήλ. See also xxii 30

Ἐπευθυμήσωσι, a word almost unknown Vulg. 'animaequiores essent' The word 'animaequus' seems almost peculiar to the Vulgate and other Latin translations of the Bible. It occurs in a Latin version of Herm Past I. i 3; Rönsch, Itala und Vulg. p 223.

7. 'So of Thy people was accepted,' Eng The translators evidently took 'the fathers' and the 'people' to be the same persons, hence they render δέ, 'so' For the same cause the Sin. MS expunges the particle, the scribe not understanding the opposition intended.

Προσεδέχθη, 'was expected' 2 Macc. viii. 11 The 'suscepta est' of the Vulg is only admissible with a very harsh zeugma

Ἀπώλεια, 'exterminatio,' Vulg. See on vi 18

8 Ὡς γάρ This, the original reading, has been altered into ᾧ to make it suit the τούτῳ, which answers to it But the combination of ὡς and the demonstrative pronoun is not unexampled, and the Vulg gives 'sicut sic' Thus Plat Rep ii 8 (p 365, D) ταύτῃ ἰτέον, ὡς τὰ ἴχνη τῶν λόγων φέρει The meaning is, that the death of the firstborn, by which the Egyptians were punished, was the means by which the Israelites were glorified.

Προσκαλεσάμενος, 'calling us to Thee,' by the institution of the Passover and the Exodus. Vulg: 'nos provocans,' reading προκαλεσάμενος

9. Κρυφῇ. The Passover, here referred to, was to be eaten in each house, Ex xii 13, 46, and so as not to offend the susceptibilities of the Egyptians, Ex viii 26 Vulg 'absconse,' 4 Esdr xiv. 26 So 'insensate,' ch. xii. 23, 'pompatice,' Amos vi. 1. 'Absconsus' = 'absconditus,' occurs vii. 21, Ecclus. i. 39; iv. 21, etc

Ἐθυσίαζον The Passover was a real sacrifice, and sacrificial terms are applied to it both in the Old and New Testaments. Ex. xii 27 θυσία τὸ πάσχα τοῦτο Κυρίῳ Deut xvi 5, 6, Ex xxiii 18; Heb xi. 28 Philo, 'In praesenti vero paschate nominato universus populus sacerdotio honoratus est; omnes enim per se peragunt sacrificium.' Quaest in Exod i. 10 (p. 455, Auch).

Παῖδες ἀγαθῶν, 'sons of good fathers' (Comp xiv 26) 'Pueri bonorum,' Vulg The children of the patriarchs, and therefore inheritors of the blessings. 'The good men' are the 'Fathers' whose praises the Israelites are said to have sung on the night of the Exodus in contrast with the Egyptians' lamentations over their dying children, θρηνούμ παίδων, ver. 10. Grimm takes ἀγαθῶν as neuter, and compares the expression υἱὸς ἀπωλείας, John xvii. 12, but the two phrases are far from corresponding, and there is here no special propriety in forcing so barbarous an idiom upon the writer Schleusner translates. 'Filii quibus destinata sunt bona paterna a Deo' It is true that the writer does not elsewhere apply the term ἀγαθοί to the Patriarchs, but that is no reason why he should not do so here We may compare Plato's expression, δεσπόταις ἀγαθοῖς τε καὶ ἐξ ἀγαθῶν, Phaedr. lviii. (p. 274, A)

Τὸν τ. θειότ νόμον. 'Established, or, came to agreement with, the divine law,' explained, as to the chief terms, in what follows Instead of θειότητος (Rom. i 20) some MSS. read ὁσιότητος, which seems to be a gloss. The Vulg. indeed gives 'justitiae legem,' but one MS. at least has 'divinitatis.' But in either case the meaning is much the same; as they celebrated the Passover, they agreed with one consent to observe the worship of God, and to share equally the dangers and the blessings consequent upon their release from Egypt. This unanimity was signified by their all eating of the lamb, and all taking of the bitter herbs and sauce that accompanied the feast

τοὺς ἁγίους is best taken with αἴνους, as Apel and Fritzsche edit. So Grimm and Gutb.

Προαναμέλποντες I have with Fr. adopted this reading from A, many cursives, the Compl., the Vulg., and the correction in S, as it seems unlikely that the author would use πατράσιν for the Patriarchs, ver 6, and πατέρων for the Israelites in this place 'While they first sang the holy praises of the Forefathers,' to whom were made the promises now about to be fulfilled The introduction of the Hallel at the Passover seems to have been of later date. But see 2 Chr xxx. 21, Sept, and 2 Chr xxxv 15 Προαναμέλπω is ἅπ λεγ

10 Διεφέρετο φωνή I have admitted φωνή in agreement with the chief authorities, Reusch's suggestion of οἰκτρά as = οἶκτος being quite inadmissible. The word has slipped out of V. and a few cursives For the 'piteous cry' over the firstborn, see Ex xi 6, xii 30. And for the contrast between the Israelites' hymns of joy and the Egyptians' mourning comp. Eurip Alc 760 ff., Med 1173 ff, Aesch. Agam 321 ff.

11. Ἦν must be supplied to the participles. For the universality of the destruction see Ex. xi. 5; xii. 29, 30. Targum of Jonathan. 'And it was in the dividing of the night of the fifteenth, that the Word of the Lord slew all the firstborn in the land of Mizraim, from the firstborn son of Pharoh, who would have sat upon the throne of his kingdom, unto the firstborn sons of the kings who were captives in the dungeon as hostages under Pharoh's hand; and who, for having rejoiced at the servitude of Israel, were punished as the Mizraee and all the firstborn of the cattle that did the work of the Mizraee died also And Pharoh rose up in that night, and all the rest of his servants, and all the rest of the Mizraee, and there was a great cry, because there was no house of the Mizraee where the firstborn was not dead. And the border of the land of Mizraim extended four hundred pharsee, but the land of Goshen was in the midst of the land of Mizraim, and the royal palace of Pharoh was at the entrance of the land of Mizraim. But when he cried to Mosheh and Aharon, in the night of the Pascha, his voice was heard unto the land of Goshen; Pharoh crying with a voice of woe, and saying thus Arise, go forth from among my people, both you and the sons of Israel . .' Etheridge, pp. 477, 478 The following is Philo's graphic account:

περὶ γὰρ μέσας νύκτας οἱ πρῶτοι πατέρας καὶ μητέρας προσειπόντες, καὶ ὑπ' ἐκείνων υἱοὶ πάλιν πρῶτον ὀνομασθέντες, ὑγιαίνοντες, καὶ τὰ σώματα ἐρρωμένοι, πάντες ἀπ' οὐδεμιᾶς προφάσεως ἡβηδὸν ἐξαπιναίως ἀνῄρηντο, καὶ οὐδεμίαν οἰκίαν ἀμοιρῆσαί φασι τότε τῆς συμφορᾶς ἅμα δὲ τῇ ἕῳ, κατὰ τὸ εἰκός, ἕκαστοι θεασάμενοι τοὺς φιλτάτους ἀπροσδοκήτως τετελευτηκότας, οἷς ὁμοδίαιτοι καὶ ὁμοτράπεζοι μέχρι τῆς ἑσπέρας ἐγεγένηντο, βαρυτάτῳ πένθει κατασχεθέντες, οἰμωγῆς πάντα ἐνέπλησαν ὥστε συνέβη καὶ διὰ τὴν κοινοπραγίαν τοῦ πάθους ἁπάντων ἀθρόως ὁμοθυμαδὸν ἐκβοησάντων, ἕνα θρῆνον ἀπὸ περάτων ἐπὶ πέρατα συνηχῆσαι κατὰ πάσης τῆς χώρας . . . ὅπερ δὲ ἐν τοῖς τοιούτοις φιλεῖ, τὰ παρόντα νομίσαντες ἀρχὴν εἶναι μειζόνων, καὶ περὶ τῆς τῶν ἔτι ζώντων ἀπωλείας καταδείσαντες, συνέδραμον εἰς τὰ βασίλεια δεδακρυμένοι, καὶ τὰς ἐσθῆτας περιερρηγμένοι κατεβόων τοῦ βασιλέως, ὡς πάντων αἰτίου τῶν συμβεβηκότων δεινῶν Vit Mos. 1. 24 (II. p. 102).

12. Ἱκανοί This is a rhetorical inference from Numb xxxiii 4, and the funeral ceremonies of the Egyptians were costly and long See on xix 3

Πρὸς μίαν ῥοπήν, 'Uno momento,' Vulg.

Ἡ ἔντιμ γένεσις αὐτ Ps cv. 36 'He smote all the firstborn in their land, the chief of all their strength.' See on iii. 13.

Διέφθαρτο, the plup seems better suited to the passage, and has higher MS. authority, than διεφθάρη, the reading of V.

13 Γάρ, further proof of the greatness of the Egyptians' calamity, seen by its effect on their minds.

Φαρμακίας, the sorceries and enchantments of the magicians. See Ex vii. 11-13, 22; viii. 7. Comp. Rev. ix 21.

Θεοῦ υἱόν, so God speaks of Israel, Ex. iv. 22, 23: 'Israel is my son, even my firstborn (υἱὸς πρωτότοκός μου); and I say unto thee (Pharaoh) let my son (τὸν λαόν μου) go that he may serve Me, and if thou refuse to let him go, behold, I will slay thy son, even thy firstborn' (τὸν υἱόν σου τὸν πρωτότοκον). Comp. Jer. xxxi 9, 20, Hos xi 1; and Matt ii. 15

14 This and part of the following verse are given in the Roman Missal as the Introit for the Sunday within the octave of Christmas, being applied to the Advent of Christ, 'the Word' of God. S. Eustath. Antioch. quotes vers 14-16, introducing them thus, De Engastrym. xix (XVIII. p. 652, Migne). εἰ δέ τις Ἰουδαϊκὴν ἀρρωστῶν ἀβλεψίαν τὰς εὐαγγελικὰς οὐ προσίεται φωνάς, ἐπακτέον αὐτῷ τὰ τοῦ Σολομῶντος ἀποφθέγματα, καὶ ῥητέον ὡδέ πως ἡσύχου γὰρ .. ἐκ θρόνων βασιλικῶν ξίφος ὀξὺ τὴν ἀνυπόκριτον ἐπιταγήν σου φέρων, στὰς ἐπλήρωσε θανάτου τὰ πάντα . ἐπὶ γῆς.

Μεσαζούσης Ex. xii 29 'At midnight the Lord smote all the firstborn in the land of Egypt' The verb μεσάζω is of late use. Comp Diod 1. 32; Herodian. Gram. Schem. p. 586, 1 (Rhet Gr viii), S Cyr. Al x 1097 B

15. Ὁ παντ. σου λόγος. The expressions in this passage are certainly applicable to the Word of God in the language of S. John. That the author had in view the passage about the destroying angel, 1 Chr. xxi 16, is very probable, and he here personifies the Almighty will of God, as Ps. cxlvii 15. 'He sendeth forth His commandment upon earth, His word runneth very swiftly.' But the personal Logos seems plainly distinguished from the spoken 'commandment' in the following verse. See Pearson, on the Creed, Art. II. note e, vol i p. 215 (ed 1833). Comp Ezek. i 24: φωνὴ τοῦ λόγου, and the description in Rev. xix. 13-16. Past Herm Vis III iii. 5: τεθεμελίωται ὁ πύργος τῷ ῥήματι τοῦ παντοκράτορος καὶ ἐνδόξου ὀνόματος. It is a most gratuitous assumption of Burton (Bampt. Lect

III. p. 75, ed. 1829), that the author in this passage speaks of the Word of God exactly in the same sense which the Platonists attached to the term 'logos' Bp Bull takes a far juster view in his Def Fid. Nic. I. i 18: 'It is clear,' he says, 'that the author is speaking of a personally-subsisting Word (λόγος ἐνυπόστατος). And it is no less evident that it is not some ministering angel, as Grotius would have it, but a divine Person, that is designated in this place; for the author calls this Word "Almighty," and also assigns Him a "royal throne in heaven."' Works, Anglo-Cath. Lib. i. p. 33 See Prolegom. p 26.

Ἀπότ. πολεμιστής. 'The Lord is a man of war,' Ex. xv. 3. Comp. Josh. v. 13, 14. For ἀπότ. see on ch. v. 20.

Τῆς ὀλεθρίας γῆς, 'the land devoted to destruction.' So (1 Kings xx. 42) Benhadad is called ἄνδρα ὀλέθριον, 'a man whom I appointed to utter destruction,' Eng

16 Ξίφος ὀξύ, 'gladius acutus,' Vulg., in app. with 'sermo;' but it is best taken in app. with ἐπιταγήν. Comp. Rev i 16 In Hebr iv. 12 the Word of God is said to be τομώτερος ὑπὲρ πᾶσαν μάχαιραν δίστομον. Comp. 1 Chr. xxi 15, 16

Ἀνυπόκριτον, (Rom. xii 9), 'insimulatum,' Vulg This Lat. word, in the sense of 'unfeigned,' occurs nowhere else. Comp. 'incoinquinatus,' iii 13, 'inauxiliatus,' xii. 6, 'inconsummatus,' iv. 5. The idea in the text is that God's decree was irreversible, and carried out its threats. Comp Numb xxiii. 19.

Ἐπιταγήν This late word often occurs in the N. T., e g Rom xvi 26; 1 Cor vii. 6, Tit. i. 3. See on xiv 16.

Καὶ οὐραν. Comp. the description of Discord in Hom Il. iv. 443, and of Fame in Virg Aen. iv. 177. As used here, the expression must mean that the command passed from heaven to earth immediately. With our later knowledge of the Personality of the Word of God it is easy to see here an adumbration of the doctrine of the Second Person of the Holy Trinity, who is God in heaven even while He walks on earth as man.

Βεβήκει, plup without augment, as commonly in N. T. 'It stood,' 'stans,' Vulg, like εὖ, ἀσφαλέως βεβηκὼς, in class Greek.

17. Δεινῶν has higher authority than δεινῶς. These dreams gave the firstborn an intimation of their fate, as explained in the two following verses Comp xvii 4

18. Ἐνεφάνιζεν, 'made clear' by words, or more probably 'proved,' that their death was a punishment from God, and no mere accident. The addition of 'mortis' in the Vulg. at the end of the verse is tautological, and is not sanctioned by some MSS.

19. Κακῶς πάσχουσιν S Matt. xvii 15

20. The author contrasts the mildness of the punishment inflicted on the Israelites, in many particulars, with the stern penalty exacted from the Egyptians

'Tetigit autem tunc,' Vulg. The unauthorised insertion of 'tunc' introduces confusion into the passage. The event alluded to is the rebellion of Korah, which happened long after the Exodus, indeed at the close of the journeyings See Numb. xvi

Πεῖρα θανάτου, 'trial,' 'experience,' as πεῖρα ὀργῆς, ver. 25

Θραῦσις, 'destruction,' the word used Numb xxi 49. 'They that died in the plague (ἐν τῇ θραύσει) were 14,700.' So Ps cv 30, and elsewhere

21. Ἀνὴρ ἄμεμπτος. Aaron, 'blameless' officially, and in this case not involved in Korah's sin

Προεμάχησε 'Stood forth as champion.' Comp Ps xcviii 6, cv. 30; Job xlii 8.

Λειτουργίας This word is used throughout the Sept. to express the ministrations of the Levitical priesthood. Exod. xxxvii. 19 (xxxviii. 21), Numb. iv 24, etc Comp Rom xv 16, Heb viii 6 For the fact referred to see Numb xvi. 46–48 In 4 Macc. vii 11 we have ὁ πατὴρ Ἀαρὼν τῷ θυμιατηρίῳ καθοπλισμένος διὰ τοῦ ἐθνοπλήκτου πυρὸς ἐπιτρέχων τὸν ἐμπυριστὴν ἐνίκησεν ἄγγελον (Joseph Opp. ii 507, Hav)

Ἐξιλασμόν. Ex. xxx. 10, Lev. xxiii. 27, Ecclus. v. 5, etc

Θυμῷ In ver. 20 it is called ὀργή The distinction between the two words, the former regarding rather the feeling, the latter its exhibition, is not maintained in late authors

Θεράπων This term is applied to Moses, Hebr iii 5

22. Ὄχλον is the reading of all MSS. except two cursives, which, as well as Compl., have ὀλοθρεύοντα. The Eng version has adopted this reading, and translates, 'the destroyer.' The old versions read ὄχλον, Fritzsche receives χόλον from a conjecture of Bauermeister. But it seems expedient to make no change in the face of this weight of authority, and to translate, 'He overcame the commotion, the trouble,' i e. the plague, and the sinfulness that caused it Mr Churton translates: 'the opposition of the multitude,' but it was not till after the awful punishment of the guilty that Aaron made the atonement Num. xvi 47.

Λόγῳ, by prayer and the remembrance of God's promises and covenant. Comp. Exod. xxxii. 13. 2 Cor. x. 4 τὰ γὰρ ὅπλα τῆς στρατείας ἡμῶν οὐ σαρκικά

Τὸν κολάζ, the plague personified.

Διαθήκας, 'covenants,' as Ex ii 24; Lev xxvi. 42, Ecclus. xliv. 11, 20 The meaning 'testament' is not found in the O T

23. Σωρηδόν. 'In heaps.' Polyb. I. xxxiv. 5, Lucian. Tim 3 (I. 105), Philo, Vit. Mos 1 17 (II. p. 96)

Μεταξύ. 'He stood between the dead and the living, and the plague was stayed' Numb' xvi. 48

Διέσχισε, 'shut off the way (of the destroyer) to the living.' Targum of Jonathan· 'Behold, the destructive burning had begun to destroy the people : but he put on incense, and made atonement for the people And Aharon stood in the midst, between the dead and the living, with the censer, and interceded in prayer; and the plague was stayed' Etheridge, p 397

24. Ἐπὶ γάρ 'For upon the garment down to the feet was the whole world ' a further illustration of the efficacy of Aaron's intercession, which had this acceptableness because it was offered by the appointed High Priest wearing his typical robes of office. For ποδήρης see Exod. xxviii 4, 31 ; Ecclus xlv. 8, and Rev i. 13 (ἅπ. λεγ. in N T) 'Poderes' occurs in Vulg, Ecclus.

xxvii 9; Rev. i 13. In the latter passage the word is used to describe the priestly garment of Christ. This robe, called the robe of the ephod, is described by Josephus, Bell Jud. V v. 7, as ποδῆρες καθύπερθεν ὑακίνθινον ἔνδυμα στρογγύλον θυσανωτὸν ἔργον τῶν δὲ θυσάνων ἀπήρτηντο κώδωνες χρύσεοι, καὶ ῥοαὶ παράλληλοι, βροντῆς μὲν οἱ κώδωνες, ἀστραπῆς δὲ αἱ ῥοαὶ σημεῖον. The High Priest's dress consisted of eight parts, viz. the breastplate, the ephod, the blue robe, the girdle, the drawers, the tunic, the turban, the mitre Lev viii 7–8; Ecclus xlv 6–12

Κόσμος. Some commentators take this word here in the sense of 'ornament,' but the allegorical interpretation, which saw a representation of the world in the form or colour of the High Priest's robes, is supported by the testimony of rabbinical and patristic tradition Thus Philo, De Monarch. ii. 5 (II. p 225) προστέτακται καὶ ἑτέρα κεχρῆσθαι πάνυ ποικίλην ἐχούσῃ κατασκευήν, ὡς ἀπεικόνισμα καὶ μίμημά τι τοῦ κόσμου δοκεῖν εἶναι So also De Profug 20 (I. p. 562): De Somn 1 37 (I p 653), Vit. Mos iii 13 (II p 154). Comp. Joseph Ant III vii. 4, 7 Clem. Alex. Strom v. 6 (p 668 Pott) τοῦ δὲ ἀρχιερέως ὁ ποδήρης κόσμου ἐστὶν αἰσθητοῦ σύμβολον See A. Lap in loc.

Πατέρων δόξαι, referring to the High Priest's breastplate, on which were engraven the names of the twelve Patriarchs. Exod xxviii 15–21, 29 'Magnalia,' Vulg, a word found often in that version (Ecclus. i. 15, Acts ii 11, etc), and in ecclesiastical writers Thus S Aug Conf xiii 27 'magnalia miraculorum' S. Cypr. Ep. lviii 'magnalia divinae protectionis' (p 96).

Ἐπὶ τετρ λίθου γλυφ, 'on the four-rowed graven stone,' 'stone of graving' being = 'graven stone,' and the whole work, which really consisted of four rows of three jewels each, being regarded as one precious stone. The variant λίθων is probably an alteration, and has the further difficulty of making τετραστίχου into a substantive, unless it be taken with γλυφῆς, which is harsh (See Ex xxviii. 17) This priestly breastplate is called λογεῖον or λόγιον by the Sept. (Ex xxviii 15), as being that by which the oracle was given. It is so named by Josephus in his description of it (Ant. III vii 5), and by Philo, De Monarch. ii 5 (II p. 226), who however considers it as a symbol of the heaven, and to be so named ἐπειδὴ τὰ ἐν οὐρανῷ πάντα λόγοις καὶ ἀναλογίαις δεδημιούργηται καὶ συντέτακται Τῶν γὰρ ἐκεῖ τοπαράπαν ἄλογον οὐδέν. The twelve precious stones in the breastplate correspond to the twelve stones in the foundations of the New Jerusalem in the Apocalypse. (Rev xxi 19, 20)

Διαδήμ Aaron's mitre had inscribed upon it, 'Holiness to the Lord' Ex xxviii. 36, xxxix. 30

25 As though the very garments of the High Priest repulsed the destroyer and were a plea for restraining God's wrath Thus Ex. xxviii. 38 : 'It shall be always upon his forehead, that they may be accepted before the Lord.'

Ὀλοθρεύων is written in some MSS ὀλεθρεύων, both here and 1 Cor x 10, and Hebr xi 28.

Ἐφοβήθη. I have taken this into the text instead of ἐφοβήθησαν (S., V and a few cursives), as possessing the higher authority and alone suiting the sense of the clause. The subject of the plural must be the Israelites, but the allusion is not to them, but to the agent of the plague The Sin MS gives indeed ἐφοβήθησαν, but the last three letters are marked as corrected, thus, ἐφοβήθησαν. Vulg 'et haec extimuit'

Πεῖρα, see on ver. 20.

CHAPTER XIX.

1–21. *Contrast as regards the powers of nature in their action on the Israelites and Egyptians.*

1. Μέχρι τέλους In contrast to the wrath against the Israelites which 'endured not long' (xviii. 20), the anger which punished the Egyptians was lasting, μέχρι τέλους, to their destruction Comp xvi. 5, and ver 4

of this chapter, where τοῦτο τὸ μέρος expresses the same view. Comp. also 1 Thess. ii. 16. Reusch notes that he has not found this nineteenth chapter quoted by any Greek or Latin writer

Προῄδει, sc. ὁ Θεός. God's foreknowledge of the Egyptians' obduracy is alleged as the ground of their final punishment (comp Exod. iii 19; vii. 4); i.e. their subsequent conduct showed that their previous chastisement had worked in them no moral change, and so God's wrath pursued them unrelentingly. The author does not mean that God punishes for sins foreseen, but not actually committed: his doctrine would be, that men not using grace given, God, foreseeing that they would make no use of further supplies, punishes accordingly. See note on i. 13

Αὐτῶν τὰ μέλλοντα, like αὐτῶν ἡ τεκοῦσα, Eurip Alc. 167, and ὁ κείνου τεκών, Id. Electr 333, the participles with the article being = substantives.

2. Ὅτι, κ.τ.λ. explanatory of τὰ μέλλοντα, ver. 1

Ἐπιστρέψαντες seems to have been the original reading, which has been altered into the easier ἐπιτρέψαντες, though the construction of this latter verb with the genitive is unusual. Ἐπιστρέφεσθαι is used with a genitive in the sense of 'to regard,' 'pay attention to,' as Soph Phil 598, 599 —

τίνος δ' Ἀτρεῖδαι τοῦδ' ἄγαν οὕτω χρόνῳ
τοσῷδ' ἐπεστρέφοντο πράγματος χάριν;

Reusch: 'Cum Aegyptii in eo elaborassent, ut Israelitae abessent.' The author uses the active in the place of the customary middle voice. 'Cum ipsi permisissent ut se educerent,' the authorised edition of the Vulg gives, but many important MSS have 'quoniam ipsi cum reversi essent,' some have both readings 'cum ipsi reversi essent et permisissent.' The reflexive form, 'se educere,' for the passive (as in French), is found iv. 2.

Ἀπεῖναι, some cursives give ἀπιέναι, but there is no necessity for the change. 'When they had provided for their absence'

Μετὰ σπ προπέμψ Ex. xii. 31–33, 39 For προπέμπω comp Acts xv 3; Tit iii 13 Philo, Vit Mos

i. 24 (II p 102) εἶτ' ἄλλος ἄλλον παρεκάλει τὸν λεὼν μετὰ πάσης σπουδῆς ἐξ ἁπάσης τῆς χώρας ἐξελαύνειν, καὶ τὸ μίαν ἡμέραν μᾶλλον δὲ ὥραν αὐτὸ μόνον κατασχεῖν πρὸς ἀνήκεστον τιμωρίαν τιθέμενοι

Διώξουσι Ex xiv. 5 ff Philo: οἱ δὲ ἐλαυνόμενοι καὶ διωκόμενοι. Ib 25.

3 Ἐν χερσὶν ἔχοντες τὰ πένθη, 'having their funeral ceremonies in hand.' These, as we learn from Herod. ii. 85–88, took a long time to complete, but before these were finished the Egyptians repented of their repentance. The Eng version is very inadequate: 'While they were yet mourning' Numb. xxxiii. 4 For the funeral rites of the Egyptians see Wilkinson, Anc Egypt. ch. xvi. vol. iii pp 427 ff, ed 1878.

Προσοδυρόμ This word is ἅπ λεγ

Ἐπεσπάσαντο, 'they seized, called in, another counsel of folly.' Josephus says that Pharaoh was influenced by the idea that all the previous sufferings were the effect of Moses' enchantments, and that now having obtained their desire and escaped from the land, the Hebrews would make no more supplication to God, and would therefore fall an easy prey to them (Antiq II. xv) He may have thought too, like the Syrians (1 Kings xx. 23), that the God of Israel was merely a local god, whose power did not extend beyond the limits of the country (comp 1 Sam. iv 8), or that Moses' commission was confined to a narrow sphere. 'Of all the infatuated resolutions which either king or people had adventured upon, the pursuing of the Israelites with such a mighty army or strong hand, after they had fairly entreated them to depart out of their coasts, may well, to every indifferent reader, seem the most stupid' Jackson, Works, vol ix p 412; Paraphr on Exod. ch 11. The Targum of Jonathan says that Pharaoh, hearing that the Israelites were bewildered near Migdol, attributed their mishap to the power of the idol Zephon, which had not been smitten with the other idols, and therefore he was the more encouraged to pursue them. Etheridge, p. 485.

Ἀνοίας S Luke vi 11 · αὐτοὶ δὲ ἐπλήσθησαν ἀνοίας.
Ἐξέβαλον Ex xi. 1 : ὅταν δὲ ἐξαποστέλλῃ ὑμᾶς σὺν

παντί, ἐκβαλεῖ ὑμᾶς ἐκβολῇ. So xii. 33 'and the Egyptians were urgent upon the people, that they might send them out of the land in haste,' σπουδῇ ἐκβαλεῖν αὐτοὺς ἀπὸ τῆς γῆς.

4 Γάρ. The Egyptians' ἄνοια, ver 3, was the consequence of the hardening of their heart Ex ix 16, xiv 17.

Ἀνάγκη. 'Destiny,' 'inevitabile fatum' This is that judicial blindness and hardness of heart which God inflicts on the wilfully disobedient. See Exod. viii. 15, 32, Rom. ix. 17, 22. On this S Aug. says, Ep. xciv. § 14, ad Sixt : 'Nec obdurat (Deus) impertiendo malitiam, sed non impertiendo misericordiam.' See Wordsw. in Rom *l. c.*

Τῶν συμβεβηκ., viz 'the plague' Ex. xiv 4. Vulg. 'Horam quae acciderant commemorationem amittebant' Reusch suggests that the right reading is, 'immemorationem immittebat,' ἀμνηστία being thus translated, xiv. 26. But 'commemoratio' is used for 'remembrance,' 'memory,' S Luke xxii 19, 1 Cor. xi. 24.

Προσαναπληρώσωσι This, the reading of A C., is far preferable to προαναπλ. of V, and is now preferred by Tischendorf in his Proleg. p xlv It occurs 2 Cor ix 12; xi 9. The Vulg. is very inexact. 'Ut quae deerant tormentis repleret punitio' Better MS Sang. 'Ut eam quae deerat tormentis replerent punitionem.' Comp Gen xv. 16 : οὔπω γὰρ ἀναπεπλήρωνται αἱ ἁμαρτίαι τῶν Ἀμορραίων ἕως τοῦ νῦν Dan viii 23, 1 Thess ii 16 See also Isai. li. 17, and 2 Macc vi. 14. ἀναμένει μακρόθυμων ὁ Δεσπότης μέχρι τοῦ καταντήσαντας αὐτοὺς πρὸς ἐκπλήρωσιν ἁμαρτιῶν κολάσαι.

5 Περάσῃ. 'Might accomplish a wonderful passage' Ex xiv. 28, 29 So in classical Greek περάω πλοῦν. Xen Oecon xxi 3. περᾶν ἡμερίους πλοῦς. The obstinate unbelief of the Egyptians became the occasion of the display of God's power and mercy towards the Israelites.

Ξένον θάν. In the sea, which obeyed the word of Moses and overwhelmed them at his command

6 The general meaning of the verse is that the elements were so changed in their operations and effects on the Israelites and Egyptians that they might seem to be a new creation.

Ἐν ἰδίῳ γένει, 'its own, proper, kind,' as ἰδίαις in the next clause.

Ἄνωθεν, 'afresh,' S. John iii. 3. With πάλιν it is tautological

Διετυποῦτο, 'refigurabatur,' Vulg. With this unusual word we may compare 'reaedificare,' Am ix. 11, 'remandare,' 'reexpectare,' Isai. xxviii. 10, 13, 'repropitiare,' Heb ii 17; 'repedare,' 2 Macc. iii. 35.

Ταῖς ἰδίαις ἐπιταγαῖς, 'the peculiar commandments given unto them,' Eng Grimm This would be equivalent to the variant ταῖς σαῖς ἐπιτ., which seems to be an alteration of the original The words mean simply 'their own commandments,' *i.e.* the commandments which they have to obey, the orders of their Creator. The facts referred to are given in the next verse.

'Serving,' Eng = 'observing,' 'keeping.'

7 'As, namely, a cloud,' Eng, 'Nubes castra eorum obumbrabat,' Vulg Both equally mistake the construction, νεφέλη and the three other subjects being constructed with ἐθεωρήθη.

Νεφέλη. The cloud which overshadowed the camp of the Israelites and gave light to them by night, while it brought darkness to the pursuing Egyptians and kept them from approaching their enemies' quarters. Ex xiii 21, 22; xiv. 19, 20. Comp Numb. ix. 18. 'As long as the cloud abode (σκιάζει) upon the tabernacle they rested in their tents' (παρεμβολοῦσιν).

Προϋφεστῶτος 'Before existing.' The verb occurs in Dion. Hal. vi 93 (II p. 1256), Plut ii 570 F.

Ἀνεμπόδιστος Isai lxiii. 13 'That led them through the deep, as an horse in the wilderness, that they should not stumble'

Χλοηφ. πεδίον, 'a plain of green grass' (Ps cv 9. ὡς ἐν ἐρήμῳ.) Gutb. justifies the epithet by a reference to the flora of the Red Sea. Most commentators take it as a poetical amplification Philo's account (Vit Mos. iii. 34) is this ῥῆξις θαλάσσης, ἀναχώρησις ἑκατέρου τμήματος, πῆξις τῶν κατὰ τὸ ῥαγὲν μέρος διὰ παντὸς τοῦ βάθους κυμάτων ἵν' ἀντὶ τειχῶν ἢ κραταιοτάτων, εὐθυτενὴς ἀνατομὴ τῆς μεγαλουργηθείσης ὁδοῦ, ἢ τῶν κρυσταλλωθέντων μεθόριος ἦν ὁδοιπορία, τοῦ ἔθνους ἀκινδύνως πεζεύοντος διὰ θαλάσσης ὡς ἐπὶ ξηραῖς ἀτραποῦ καὶ λιθώδους ἐδάφους. Ἐκραυρώθη γὰρ ἡ ψάμμος, καὶ ἡ σπορὰς αὐτῆς οὐσία συμφυεῖσα ἡνώθη (II p 174) The narrative of Josephus will be found Ant. ii 16 See note on ver. 13.

8. Πᾶν ἔθνος in apposition to the subject of διῆλθον, 'they, a whole nation.' The V reading, πανεθνί, has been altered in the MSS (see critical note), and all the best MSS give the reading of the text, though S is corrected by a later hand to πανεθνί Comp Ex x. 9.

9. Ἐνεμήθησαν, 'they pastured,' 'grazed,' here 'ranged,' as Eurip El. 1162:

ὀρεία τις ὡς λέαιν' ὀργάδων
δρύοχα νεμομένα

'Depaverunt escam,' Vulg.; ('escam' is absent from many MSS). Comp χλοηφόρον πεδίον, ver 7; Is lxii. 11–14. A Lap notes that some MSS. have ἐχρεμέτισαν, but it is not mentioned by H. and P

Διεσκίρτησαν. Ps cxiii. 4: 'The mountains skipped (ἐσκίρτησαν) like rams, and the little hills like young sheep.' Mal. iv. 2 σκιρτήσετε ὡς μοσχάρια ἐκ δεσμῶν ἀνειμένα Cp. S. Luke vi 23 The word διασκιρτάω occurs in Plut. Anim. an Corp. ii. 501 C.

Αἰνοῦντες. Ex xv 1–19

Ῥυόμενον = 'their Deliverer' The var ῥυσάμενον would refer to the particular occasioned mentioned.

10. Ἐμέμνηντο γάρ. This reflection added to their exultation at the passage of the Red Sea.

Τῶν ἐν τ παρ. αὐτῶν 'What had happened in their sojourning' in the land of Egypt. 1 Esdr. v 7: ἀναβάντες ἐκ τῆς αἰχμαλωσίας τῆς παροικίας, 'their captivity in a strange land' Acts xiii 17 τὸν λαὸν ὕψωσεν ἐν τῇ παροικίᾳ ἐν γῇ Αἰγύπτῳ. Vulg.: 'incolatu' This word 'incolatus' (from the post-class. form 'incolare') is found also Ps. cxix 5; Ezek xx. 38; 1 Pet i. 17 'The things which befell them' are explained in what follows, πῶς, κτλ.

'How the land brought forth flies instead of cattle,' Eng This version gives a wrong impression, and omits γενέσεως. The contrast is between the natural procreation of animals and their supernatural production 'How, instead of their being produced (γενέσεως, see on ver. 11) in the usual way, it was the earth that brought them forth,' Ex viii. 17. This is the view also of Gutberlet, and it certainly seems to elicit the contrast better than the Eng and other versions.

Ἐξήγαγεν Ps ciii 14: τοῦ ἐξαγαγεῖν ἄρτον ἐκ τῆς γῆς. Comp Gen i 24: ἐξαγαγέτω ἡ γῆ, κ.τ.λ.

Σκνῖπα, used collectively as in Ex. viii. 18, and as ὀρτυγομήτρα, ver. 12 The MSS vary between σκνῖπα and σκνίφα. The reading σκνίφας is probably a correction. What creature is meant by the word σκνίψ is very doubtful. Any small biting insect is called by this name, and probably 'lice' is the best translation See Exod viii 16, 17, Ps. civ 31; and the quotation from Philo, ch. xvi 9 The question is fully discussed in Smith's Dict of Bibl, s v 'lice'

Ἀντὶ δὲ ἐνύδρων, sc γενέσεως, instead of aquatic animals producing the frogs it was the water that vomited them out Ex viii 1–6.

11. Γένεσιν, 'production,' as ver 10 See ch. xvi. 2, Ex xvi. 13; Numb xi. 13; Ps. lxxviii 26–29.

Ἐπιθυμίᾳ προαχθ Ex. xvi 3; Numb xi 4, 34 'Led with (i e by) their appetite,' Eng.

12 Εἰς γὰρ παραμυθίαν. 'For their relief' 'In allocutione desiderii,' Vulg See on iii 18.

Ὀρτυγομήτρα, collectively, as σκνῖπα, ver. 10. Comp. ὁ βάτραχος, Ex viii 6, ἀκρίς, Ex. x. 12, 14. The arrival of quails from 'the sea' is in accordance with Numb xi 31. Their annual migration is a well-known fact

13. 'And punishments,' etc A new paragraph begins here. The mention of 'the sea' leads the author to think of the punishment which it inflicted on the Egyptians. Apel, Reusch, and Tisch. have only a comma at ὀρτυγομήτρα. Field has a full stop Fritzsche, Grimm, and Gutberl commence a new paragraph. So Eng begins ver. 13 here.

Ἁμαρτ, the Egyptians, the reference is to the overthrow in the Red Sea.

Προγεγονότων. V. and Ven give γεγονότων, doubtless by a clerical error Josephus, Ant. ii 16. 3, says that the judgment on the Egyptians was preceded by violent storms of rain and hail, and terrible lightning and thunder; and the Psalmist alludes to the same fact, Ps. lxxvii 16–18, 'The voice of Thy thunder was in the heaven· the lightnings lightened the world,' etc. In Ex. xiv. 24, 25 it is said that 'the Lord troubled the host of the Egyptians ... so that they said, Let us flee from the face of Israel, for the Lord fighteth for them against the Egyptians.' The Egyptians might have repented of their purpose at the first 'signs,' if they had willed to do so; their destruction was 'owing to their own wilful wickedness.'

The justice of the punishment inflicted on the Egyptians is proved by contrasting their conduct with that of the Sodomites, the mention of the storm perhaps leading to the thought of the dwellers in the Plain who were overwhelmed with a tempest of fire

Καὶ γάρ 'For they also perpetrated a harsher violation of hospitality'

Χαλεπωτέραν, i e. in comparison of others, even of the Sodomites, whose sin was punished with fire See S. Jude 7.

Μισοξενία is ἅπ. λεγ. though μισόξενος is found in Diod Excerpt. 525. 61.

14 Οἱ μὲν.. οὗτοι δέ, the Sodomites . the Egyptians The author here as elsewhere (comp ch. x.) presupposes in his readers a knowledge of the history of Bible characters sufficient to enable them to identify the persons alluded to Some suppose that the reference is to the Jewish settlers in Alexandria under the first Ptolemies, but ver 17 plainly points to the Sodomites

Τοὺς ἀγνοοῦντας. This expression has occasioned great difficulty to translators and commentators, some of whom have solved the matter by making it = ἀγνοουμένους Vulg.. 'ignotos.' Eng.: 'those whom they knew not,' a simple, but inadmissible explication. The MSS do not vary, but editors have suggested ἀγνώστους, ἀγνωμονοῦντας, ἀγνῶτας No change is necessary. As Gutb. observes, the term is contrasted with εὐεργέτας. The Egyptians illtreated those who had been their benefactors, to whom they were bound by benefits received, the Sodomites wronged persons who (speaking from the standpoint of the Sodomites) knew nothing of them See Gen. xix. Churton. 'The men of Sodom refused hospitality to strangers to whom they were unknown, and in no way indebted'

Παρόντας, 'advenas,' Vulg Mere visitors, in contrast to the Israelites, who were ξένους, 'guest friends'

Εὐεργέτας, referring to Joseph's policy, Gen. xli. 55–57; xlv 8, and to the improvements effected by the Israelites' occupation of uncultivated land. See Ex. i. 7

Ἐδουλοῦντο Recent discoveries place the expulsion of the shepherd dynasty, and the re-establishment of the native kings, in the interval between the death of Joseph and the birth of Moses. See a popular account of these discoveries in The Bible Educator, i. pp 122–124

15. This verse has exercised the wits of commentators to little purpose There is no variation in the MSS, and editors have resorted to conjecture in order to amend what they consider a corrupt text Thus some read· οὐ μόνον· ἄλλη τις. Others οὐ μόνον αὕτη, ἀλλ' ἄλλη τις ἔσται. Others· οὐ μόνον, ἀλλ' εἴ τις ἐπισκοπὴ ἔσται αὐτοῖς Gutb suggests ἀλλ' ἤ τις ἐπισκοπὴ ἔσται Apel prints καὶ οὐ μόνον, ἀλλ', ἥτις ἐπισκοπὴ ἔσται αὐτῶν This, or Gutberlet's suggestion, points the way to the right interpretation, which I conceive to be this: 'And not only so (not only is the contrast in ver. 14 true), but whatever allowance is made shall belong to them (the Sodomites), inasmuch as they received with enmity those who were strangers' This is the view taken by the English translators 'And not only so, but peradventure some respect shall be had of those, because they used strangers not friendly.' Mr. Churton, overlooking the tense of ἔσται, paraphrases. 'Besides this, it is evident that whatever visitation of judgment came upon the people of Sodom for their cruel reception of foreigners, the Egyptians merited a heavier one' Dr Bissell, with small regard

for the Greek, and in very peculiar English, translates. 'And not only so, but—for which they shall be punished—because they received strangers hostilely.'

Ἐπισκοπὴ, 'regard,' 'respect,' as ii. 20.

16 Οἱ δέ, the Egyptians, at whose invitation the Israelites had come to Egypt. See Gen. xlv. 17–20; xlvii. 6, 11.

Ἑορτασμάτων. This uncommon word occurs in S Method. Serm de Sim. 12 (p 376 B, Migne).

Δικαίων, 'rights,' 'civil privileges.' This is not expressly stated in Genesis, but may be inferred from the accounts of their reception.

Ἐκάκωσαν Ex. i. 10–14.

17 Ἐπλήγησαν. The Egyptians were effectively struck with blindness in the plague of darkness, as the Sodomites (ἐκεῖνοι) were actually at Lot's door.

Ἀορασίᾳ, a word peculiar to the Sept (Gen. xix. 11; Deut. xxviii 28, 2 Kings vi 18), is used here in the double sense of inability to see, and deprivation of sight, the darkness making the eyes of the Egyptians useless, and the Sodomites losing the power of sight.

Τοῦ δικαίου, Lot, as x 6. See Gen. xix. 11.

Ἀχανεῖ σκότει, 'yawning darkness,' or it may be 'vast,' the word ἀχανής, with ἀ intensive, being applied to the sea, an army, etc. The Vulg translates : 'subitaneis tenebris,' taking the word in the sense of 'not gaping,' 'not lethargic,' the ἀ in the compound being then negative. Mr Churton takes it in the sense of 'mute with astonishment,' 'a gloom that deprived them of speech,' the epithet appropriate to the persons being applied to the darkness This seems to be an unnecessary refinement The Vulg. word 'subitaneus' may be compared with 'temporaneus,' S. James v. 7; 'coaetaneus,' Gal. i. 14 : 'collactaneus,' Acts xiii 1. See note on xvii 6.

Τῶν αὐτοῦ θ, 'his, Lot's, door.' Gen. xix. 11. Some editors, who adopt the variant τ. ἑαυτοῦ θ., make the clause refer to the Egyptians, which seems less appropriate, as we are expressly told that under the plague of darkness none of them left their place. See xvii. 2, 17; Ex x 23

18. The general meaning of this difficult verse is this the interchange of operations in nature (in the case of the miracle mentioned) occasioned no disorder, nor marred the harmony of the Cosmos any more than the transposing of a melody to a different pitch occasions any real change in the tune. Or, if this idea is in advance of the musical practice of the age, we may take it thus the elements were no more changed in their nature than are the notes of a psaltery by their pitch and measure, which indeed give the character to the tune, but remain notes still. The author, carried away by his grand conception, has regarded meaning rather than language, and hence has made the sentence somewhat grammatically unintelligible Διαλλάσσουσι is predicated of στοιχεῖα and φθόγγοι (Gutb.), and the two members of the comparison are so mingled together, that the terms properly applicable to one only are also assigned to the other The literal rendering therefore is this : 'For the elements being differently disposed among themselves change, as in a psaltery tones do, the name of the measure, remaining always sounds.' That is, the elements retain their nature though their operations are changed.

Ψαλτήριον, a stringed instrument, Ecclus. xl 21. In the Sept the word is applied to instruments having different names in Hebrew Thus Dan iii 7, etc, it represents *pesanterin*, in Ps xxxii. 2, etc., it translates *nebel*, elsewhere rendered νάβλα. 1 Sam x. 5, etc Comp. S Athan. Ep. Encycl. 4 (p 91)

Μένοντα ἤχῳ, 'remaining (the same) in sound,' i.e in their nature, the word which applies properly to the musical instrument being applied also to στοιχεῖα.

19. The author sums up the chief instances of God's Providence in the case of the miracles that concerned land, water, and fire It seems best to confine the allusions to events connected with the Exodus

Χερσαῖα, ἔνυδρα, νηκτά, sc ζῶα 'Land animals were (for the time) turned into aquatic.' Alluding doubtless to the passage of the Israelites and their cattle through the Red Sea. Ex xii 38, xiv 29,

Ps. lxv. 6: ὁ μεταστρέφων τὴν θάλασσαν εἰς ξηρὰν, ἐν ποταμῷ διελεύσονται ποδί.

Νηκτά, the frogs that came up from the river, and covered the land, and filled the houses. Exod. viii. 3, 4 Ps civ. 30. S. Ephr in Exod. c viii (p 208): 'Perierant pisces, subsiliere ranae, alterum natantium genus, ut scilicet de vivis ranis gravissime laborarent, qui de piscibus mortuis nihil laboraverant.'

20. Ἴσχυεν accords with the tense of the other verbs It is used with a genitive in the sense of 'to be stronger than,' to 'exceed,' so that there is no need to add, as some MSS. do, ἐπιλελησμένον to govern δυνάμεως. For the allusion see on xvi 16, 17

Φύσεως. The reading δυνάμεως, found in V. and a few cursives, seems to have been introduced accidentally from the preceding clause

21. Εὐφθάρτων ζώων, 'corruptibilium animalium,' Vulg This seems to refer to the locusts. But see on xvi. 18 The author poetically regards some of the animals sent in judgment as still existing at the time of the Plague of hail and lightning Mr. Churton. 'Though they had bodies of flesh which were in no way proof against the devouring element' The unusual word 'corruptibilis' occurs Rom i. 23; 1 Cor ix 25; 1 Pet. i. 18, 23, and elsewhere; S. Aug. de Civit xiii 16 See note on x 4

Ἐμπεριπατούντων. (Lev. xxvi. 12; Job i. 7.) 'Coambulantium,' Vulg. Post-classical. Cp. 'coangustare,' Luke xix. 43, 'commanducare,' Rev xvi. 10, 'collaborare,' 2 Tim i. 8.

Οὐδὲ τηκτόν, sc. ἦν. The conjecture of Nannius, received by Grabe and Field, οὐδ᾽ ἔτηκαν, suits the Vulg. 'nec dissolvebant,' but has no MS. authority For the allusion see on xvi. 22.

Ἀμβροσίας, a classical word for οὐράνιος, and so equivalent to the 'bread from heaven,' or 'angels' food,' of xvi 20, Ps lxxvii. 24, 25. Vulg. 'bonam escam,' which is feeble.

22 Κατὰ πάντα, 'in respect of all things,' or, in every way Comp Deut. iv 6–8.

Ἐμεγάλυνας 'Magnificasti,' Vulg. This is an ante-classical word, common in the Vulg, e.g Ecclus xxxiii 10; Luke i. 46, Acts x 46; Plautus, Stich I. ii. 43 · -

'Pudicitia est, pater, eos nos magnificare, qui nos socias sumserunt sibi'

Philo deems that the Mosaic Law and the Temple and its worship are to last for ever De Vit. Mos ii 3: τὰ δὲ τούτου μόνου βέβαια, ἀσάλευτα, ἀκράδαντα, καθάπερ σφραγῖσι φύσεως αὐτῆς σεσημασμένα, μένει παγίως ἀφ᾽ ἧς ἡμέρας ἐγράφη μέχρι νῦν, καὶ πρὸς τὸν ἔπειτα πάντα διαμενεῖν ἐλπὶς αὐτὰ αἰῶνα ὥσπερ ἀθάνατα, ἕως ἂν ἥλιος καὶ σελήνη καὶ ὁ σύμπας οὐρανός τε καὶ κόσμος ᾖ (Π. p 136). De Monarch. ii. 3 ἐφ᾽ ὅσον γὰρ τὸ ἀνθρώπων γένος διαμενεῖ, ἀεὶ καὶ αἱ πρόσοδοι τοῦ ἱεροῦ φυλαχθήσονται συνδιαιωνίζουσαι παντὶ τῷ κόσμῳ (Π p. 224)

Some have thought that the Book in its present shape is incomplete, and that the author ought to have carried his history of God's dealings with the Israelites down to later times, but the present view is abundantly sufficient for the scope of the writer; and the last verse puts the finishing touch to the picture, by asserting that what God's dealings were in the period, and under the circumstances previously indicated, so they have ever been in every time and place. Εὐλογητὸς ὁ ῥύστης Ἰσραὴλ εἰς τοὺς ἀεὶ χρόνους Ἀμήν (3 Macc vii 23). On the other hand, Dean Jackson observes truly: 'The calendar made by the learned author of the Book of Wisdom, for the opposite fates or destinies of the Egyptians and of the Jews, began in his own time, and shortly after our Saviour's resurrection, to be out of date, and more than so quite inverted, "Versa tabula currebant qui modo stabant;" the lot or destiny which this good author assigned unto the ungodly Egyptians did fall upon his presumed holy ones the Jews, his countrymen' Bk x ch. xl. 26.

INDEXES

TO THE MATTER CONTAINED IN THE COMMENTARY.

I GREEK.   II. LATIN.   III. ENGLISH.

The references denote the Page and Column.

INDEX I. GREEK.

ἀβοήθητος, 175 b
ἀγαθότης, 111 a
ἀγγελία, 136 a.
ἀγερωχία, 119 b
ἄγομαι, 153 b.
ᾅδης, 197 b, 207 a.
ἀδόλως, 147 a.
ἀδύνατος, 206 b.
ἀθανασία, 156 a.
ἀθῷον, 113 b
αἴνιγμα, 155 a.
αἱρετὶς, 154 a
αἰών, αἰώνιος, 128 b, 137 a, 167 a, 181 b, 184 b, 186 a, 209 a
ἀκηλίδωτος, 151 b.
ἀκοινώνητος, 188 a.
ἀκρότομος, 168 a.
ἀμάραντος, 141 b.
ἀμβρόσιος, 220 a.
ἀμνηστία, 189 a.
ἀμόλυντος, 150 b.
ἀνάγκη, 216 a.
ἀναλύω, 117 b.
ἀνεκλιπὴς, 147 a, 156 b
ἀνεξικακία, 121 b
ἀντανακλάω, 208 a
ἀντιπαρέρχομαι, 197 b.
ἀντισχύω, 153 a.
ἀντοφθαλμέω, 177 a.
ἀνυπόκριτος, 212 b.
ἄνωθεν, 216 b.

ἄξιος, 124 b
ἀορασία, 219 a
ἀπαύγασμα, 151 b.
ἀπερίσπαστος, 197 b.
ἁπλότης, 111 b
ἀποδοκιμάζω, 159 b
ἀποικία, 176 a.
ἀπότομος, 138 a, 170 a.
ἀρετὴ, 128 a.
ἁρμόνιος, 201 a.
ἀτέλεστος, 127 b.
ἀτίμητος, 146 a
αὐθέντης, 175 b.
αὐτοσχεδίως, 118 a
ἀφθαρσία, 122 a, 143 a.
ἄφρων, 126 a.
ἀχανὴς, 219 a.
βάσανος, 123 b
βασιλεία θεοῦ, 166 a
βασίλειαν, 116 a, 137 b.
βασκανία, 131 a.
βδέλυγμα, 178 b
βίος, 166 a, 188 a, 192 b.
βλάσφημος, 113 b.
βραχυτελὴς, 191 b.
βρόμος, 172 a
γενεσιάρχης, 180 b
γένεσις, 116 a, 126 a, 217 b.
γενέτις, 147 a.
γεώδης, 161 a.
γηγενὴς, 144 b
γλυπτὰ, 187 a, 192 b

διάβολος, 123 a.
διαβούλιον, 114 b
διάγνωσις, 127 b.
διαθήκη, 213 b
διασκιρτάω, 217 a.
διατείνω, 153 a.
δίεσις, 178 a
δίκαιον, τὸ, 126 a
δικαιοσύνη, 111 a, 138 a, 154 b, 159 a, 185 a
δίκη, 172 a
δίκην, 178 b.
δοκιμάζω, 112 a, 124 b.
δόξα, 160 b
δυσάλυκτος, 207 b
δυσδιήγητος, 203 a.
ἐγκρατὴς, 158 b.
ἔθνη, 156 b.
εἰδέχθεια, 195 a.
εἰκὼν, 152 a.
ἔκβασις, 121 b.
ἐκβιάζομαι, 187 b
ἐκλεκτοὶ, 125 b, 132 b
ἐκλικμάω, 139 b.
ἐκτίθημι, 209 b.
ἔλεγχος, 114 b, 169 a, 209 b.
ἐλέγχω, 112 a, 113 a, 114 b, 119 b, 133 b.
ἐμμελέτημα, 182 a.
ἐμπεριπατέω, 220 a.
ἔνεδρον, 188 a.
ἔντρομος, 205 b

ἐντυγχάνω, 158 b.
ἐνωτίζομαι, 140 a.
ἔξαλλος, 188 b
ἐξιλασμὸς, 213 a.
ἐξιχνιάζω, 143 b, 161 b.
ἔξοδος, 124 a, 146 a
ἐπαγγέλλομαι, 120 b.
ἐπαποστέλλω, 170 b
ἐπευθυμέω, 210 a.
ἐπιείκεια, 121 b, 177 b
ἐπιλανθάνομαι, 118 b.
ἐπίμοχθος, 191 a
ἐπισκοπὴ, 122 a, 125 a, b, 127 a, 185 b
ἐπίσκοπος, 113 b, 219 a.
ἐπιστρέφω, 215 a
ἐπισφαλὴς, 129 b, 161 a.
ἐπιταγὴ, 187 a, 212 b.
ἐπιτιμία, 126 a
ἔσχατα, τὰ, 121 a.
ἐτάζω, 121 b, 140 b.
εὐδράνεια, 183 b.
εὐθὴς, 160 a.
εὐλάβεια, 176 b.
εὐστάθεια, 144 b.
εὐφυής, εὐφυΐα, 157 a.
ἐφίσταμαι, 140 b.
ἐφύβριστος, 205 a.
ζάω, 137 a
ζηλόω, 115 a.
ζητεῖν τ. Κύριον, 111 b.
ζωὴ, 192 b.

θειότης, 210 b.
θέλησις, 202 a
θραῦσις, 213 a
θυμὸς, 196 a, 213 a
ἰδιότης, 122 b
ἴνδαλμα, 203 b.
ἴσα, 145 b.
καιρὸς, 155 b
κακόμοχθος, 191 b
κακότεχνος, 112 b
καμὼν, 132 b
καταλαλιὰ, 115 b
κατάστασις, 177 a.
κατάχρεος, 112 b.
κενοδοξία, 186 a.
κίβδηλος, 121 a, 191 b.
κλῆρος, 127 a
κόσμος, 123 b
κράτησις, 140 a.
κρίνω, κριτὴς, 111 a.
κτίσις, 119 a.
λάκκος, 167 a
λαὸς, 156 a, 167 a.
λειτουργία, 213 a
Λόγος, ὁ, 151 a, 171 a, 201 a, 212.
λυθρώδης, 169 a
μαγικὸς, 205 a.
μεσάζω, 212 a
μετακιρνάω, 201 a.
μεταλλεύω, 131 b, 202 a
μετάνοια, 173 a, 176 b
μιασμὸς, 189 a
μισοξενία, 218 a.
μνημονεύω, 118 b.

μονογενὴς, 150 a.
μυστάθεια, 175
μυστήριον, 122 a, 143 b, 186 b.
μύστις, 154 a
νηπιοκτόνος, 169 a.
νοθεύω, 189 a
νόμος, 120 b
νοῦς, 161 b
ξενιτεία, 209 a
ὁλοκάρπωμα, 124 b
ὁλόκληρος, 190 b.
ὁμοθυμαδὸν, 210 a.
ὁμοιοπαθὴς, 145 a
ὁπλοποιέω, 138 a
ὀρθρίζω, 141 b
ὀρθρινὸς, 172 b
ὀρτυγομήτρα, 195 a, 217 b
ὅσια, τὰ, 141 a.
ὁσιότης, 138 a, 159 a.
ὄψει, ἐν, 146 a
παίγνιον, 179 a.
παῖς Κυρίου, 120 b
πανηγυρισμὸς, 192 b
παντοδύναμος, 150 b.
παραβολὴ, 135 a.
παραίνεσις, 155 b.
παραπίπτειν, παράπτωμα, 126 b, 141 a, 163 b, 174 a
πάρεδρος, 159 a
πειράζω, 124 b
περικομπέω, 204 a.
πετροβόλος, 139 a
πηλουργὸς, 191 b.
πλῆθος, 156 b

πληρόω, 113 b
Πνεῦμα, τὸ ἅγιον, 112 a, 113 b.
ποδήρης, 213 b.
πολυπειρία, 155 a.
πολύφροντις, 161 b.
πόνος, 154 b, 166 b
πορισμὸς, 183 a
πορνεία, 186 a
προαναμέλπω, 211 a.
πρόνοια, 184 a.
προπέμπω, 215 a.
προσαναπαύομαι, 156 b.
προσαναπληρόω, 216 a.
προσδεκτὸς, 160 b
προσέχω, 156 a.
προσοδύρομαι, 215 b
προϋφίστημι, 216 b.
προφήτης, 152 b
πρωτόπλαστος, 144 b.
ῥεμβασμὸς, 131 a
ῥοῖζος, 136 b
ῥοπὴ, 172 b
σέβασμα, 188 a, 193 b
σημεῖα καὶ τέρατα, 155 b, 167 a.
σκνὶψ, 217 b.
σκολιός, 112 a
σοφία, 112 b, 146 a, 161 b.
σπλαγχνοφάγος, 175 a
συγκλύζω, 139 b.
συγκρίνω, σύγκρισις, 146 a.
συμβίωσις, 154 a.
σύμβολον, 196 a.
συναναστροφὴ, 156 b.

συνείδησις, 206 a.
συνέχω, 113 b, 208 b
συνιέω, 160 b.
συνολκὴ, 193 a.
σύστασις, 148 a.
σωρηδὸν, 213 b.
τεκνοφόνος, 188 b.
τέλειος, τελειόω, 132 a, 159 b.
τελετὴ, 186 b.
τρανὸς, 150 a, 168 a
τρίβος, 121 a
υἱὸς Θεοῦ, 135 a
ὕλη, 171 a.
ὑπέρμαχος, 168 a.
ὑποστέλλομαι, 140 b
φθορὰ, 186 a.
φιλάγαθος, 150 b.
φιλόψυχος, 173 b.
φρόνησις, 142 a, 146 a, 154 b.
φυλακίζω, 209 a
χαλκοπλάστης, 191 b.
χάρις καὶ ἔλεος, 125 b, 132 b.
χέρσος, 165 b
χνοῦς, 137 a.
χράομαι with acc., 147 a
χρησιμεύω, 129 a.
χρόνος, 155 b.
χρυσουργὸς, 191 b
χωνευτήριον, 124 b.
ψαλτήριον, 219 b.
ψηλάφησις, 193 a
ψυχὴ, 157, 161 b.
ὥστε, 'and so,' 144 b.

INDEX II. LATIN.

Ab intus, 206 b.
Absconsus, absconse, 149 a, 210 b

Accersio, 116 b
Adinventio, 186 a.
Allocutio, 128 a, 155 b.

Anima mundi, 114 a
Assistrix, 159 a.
Boethius, 153 a.

Cogitatio, 155 b.
Cognoscibiliter, 181 a
Comessor, 175 a.

INDEX. 223

Commemoror, 170 a.
Compeditus, 203 a.
Concupiscentia, 195 b.
Correptio, 114 b
Creatura, 126 a.
Cruciatio, 141 a
Custoditio, 142 b
Detractio, 115 a.
Dignus with gen, 147 b
Doctrix, 154 a.
Duriter, 181 a.
Electrix, 154 a.
Eo, inflection of, 202 b.
Excandesco, 139 b.
Exerro, 174 a.
Exquisitio, 142 b, 186 a.
Exterminium, extermino, exterminatio, 124 a, 139 a, 142 b.
Fascino, fascinatio, 131 a.
Fictio, 189 a
Fictum, 113 a
Fumigabundus, 165 a, b

Hibernalis, 202 b.
Honestas, honestus, 146 b, 147 a
Immaculatus, 130 b.
Immemoratio, 189 a
Impossibilis, 171 a
Improperium, impropero, 120 b, 135 a.
Inauxiliatus, 175 b.
Incoinquinatus, 126 b.
Incolatus, 217 a.
Inconsummatio, inconsummatus, 127 b, 129 b.
Incredibilis, 165 b
Increpatio, 142 b, 179 a.
Indisciplinatus, 203 a
Inexterminabilis, 122 a
Inextinguibilis, 146 b.
Infirmiter, 129 b, 181 a.
Inhabitator, 174 b
Inordinatio, 189 a.
In palam, 187 a.
Insensatus, 126 a.

Insidia, 189 a
Insimulatus, 212 b.
Intelligibilis, 150 b.
Juramentum, 178 a.
Justifico, 141 a.
Laesura, 172 a.
Magnifico, 220 b.
Mansueto, 198 b
Medietas, 148 b.
Natio, 116 a
Nativitas, 143 b, 145 b, 202 a
Nimietas, 129 b, 145 b.
Noceo, with acc., 189 b
Nugacitas, 131 a, 145 b
Odibilis, 174 b.
Ortygometra, 195 a.
O sapientia, 153 a.
Partibus, 174 a, 176 b.
Poderes, 213 b, 214 a
Praeclaritas, 145 b, 157 a
Praesumo, 147 b
Praetereo, 114 b.

Praevaricatio, 190 b
Protoplastus, 144 b
Providentia, 142 a, 161 a.
Querela, 164 b.
Refiguro, 216 b.
Refrigerium, 117 b, 130 a.
Respectio, 127 a, 142 b.
Reverentia, 177 b
Sacramentum, 122 a, 143 b
Saeculum, 181 b.
Salvator, 197 a.
Sibilatio, 134 b, 142 b.
Subitaneus, 204 b.
Subitatio, 134 b, 142 b.
Supervacuus, supervacuitas, 170 b, 178 b, 186 a, 192 a.
Sustinco, 156 a.
Traductio, 121 a, 169 a.
Tuto, 166 b
Vacuitas, 182 b.
Vitulamen, 129 a.
Zelo, 115 a.

INDEX III. ENGLISH.

Aaron, 213.
Abraham, 152 a, b, 164 b, 210 a.
Adam, 144 b, 162 f
Adventure, 118 a.
Alexandria, 192 b, 193 a
Angels, 150 a.
Animal worship, 193 b, 194.
Apotheosis, 187 a
Apples of Sodom, 165 b.
Ark, the, 164 b
Art magic, 205 a.
Astronomy, 148 b
Baal, 174 b
Babel, 164 b

Bacchus, orgies of, 188 b.
Barrenness, 126 a.
Bears, 171 b.
Because, 173 a.
Bezaleel, 148 a.
Birds, Egyptian, 207 b
Blood, plague of, 168 b, 169 a.
Body and soul, 157 f., 161.
Botany, 149 a.
Breastplate of High Priest, 214.
Cain, 164 a, b -
Caligula, 187 a, 193 a.
Canaanites, 166 b, 174 a,

175 b, 176.
Chastity, 128, a, b.
Child-sacrifice, 188 b.
Christ, references to, 120, 121 b, 135 a, 149 b, 151 a, b, 152 a, 157 a, 196, 212 a.
Chronology, 148 b
Cloud, pillar of, 167 b, 216 b.
Conceit, 156 a.
Conscience, 133 b, 206 a
Continency, 158 b
Counterfeits, Egyptian, 192 a

Creationism, 157 a.
Cross of Christ, The, 185 a
Crown, crowning, 119 a, 129 a, 137 b.
Darkness, plague of, 203, 204, 219 a
Death, physical and eternal, 115, 122 a, 123 b
Devil, the, 122 b, 123 a
Egyptians, Egypt, 167 b, 168 b, 169, 170, 178 b, 193 a, 198 a, 211 b, 218 a.
Elements, the, worshipped, 180 a

INDEX.

Enoch, 130 b, 132 a.
Esau, 166 b.
Eschatology, 117, 122 a, 133 b, 134 a
Essenes, 152 b, 202 b
Eucharist, the holy, 200 b.
Eunuch, 126 b, 127 a.
Exodus, the, 210, 219 b.
Fear, to,=frighten, 205 b.
Fire, pillar of, 167 b, 209 a
Firstborn, death of the, 210 a, 211, 213 a
Flies, plague of, 197 a, 217 a
Flood, the, 164 a.
Fools, folly, 112 a.
Foreknowledge, God's, 215 a
Freewill, 176 b.
Frogs, plague of, 195 b, 198 b, 217 b, 219 b
Funeral rites, 211 b, 215 b.
Future state, 117, 118 b
Gestation, period of, 145 a.
Giants, the, 184 b.
God, son of, 120 b, 135 a.
Greeks, the, 193 a
Hades, 116 a, b.
Hail, plague of, 198 a, 218 a
Heaven, 127 a.
Hornets, 176 a
Idolatry, idols, 179 a, 180 a, 181 b, 185 b, 186, 187, 188
Image-worship, 191 a
Inhabitance, 176 a.
Jacob, 166 a, b.
Jews, renegade, 120 a, 132 a.

Joseph, 166 b, 167, 218 a.
Know God, to, 170 a.
Korah, 213 a.
Laban, 166 b
Law, Mosaic, 120 a, 209, 220 b
Lice, plague of, 197 a, 217 b
Life, eternal, 122 a, 124 a.
Lightning, plague of, 198 b, 201 b
Liturgies, ancient, 162 b.
Locusts, plague of, 197 a, 220 a.
Lot, 165 a, 219 a.
Lot's wife, 165 b
Magicians, 205 a, 212 a.
Manna, 199 b, 200, 201, 202.
Materialism, matter, 112 b, 171.
Moloch, 174 b
Moriah, 160 a
Moses, 167 a, 168 a, 170 b, 209 b, 213 b.
Nebuchadnezzar, 187 a
Neo-Platonism, 158 a
Nile, the, 169 a, 178 b, 179 b.
Nimrod, 164 b
Noah, 164 b, 176 b, 184 b.
Panoply, 137 b
Pantheism, 173 b
Passover, the, 210 b, 211.
Pataeci, the, 183 a
Patriarchs, the, 210.
Pentapolis, 165 a.
Perjury, 189 b
Pharaoh, 167 a, 169 a, 177 b, 180 b, 211, 215 b.
Physician, 197 b.

Plagues of Egypt, 139 a, 168 b, 169, 171 a, 178 b, 197 a, 199 a, 209.
Platonism, 114 a, 150 a, 151 a, 155 a, 157 b, 160 a, 171 a, 174 a, 184 a, 212 b.
Potiphar, 167 a
Predestination, 131 a.
Priest, dress of High, 213 b, 214
Prophecy, 152 b.
Providence, 184 a.
Psaltery, 219 b
Ptolemy Philopator, 193 a.
Punishment of mighty men, 140 b
Pythagoras, 157 b
Quails, 194 a, 217 b.
Rabshakeh, 177 b
Red Sea, the, 184 a, 216 b, 217 b.
Repentance, 173 a.
Riches, 136 a.
Righteousness, 111 a, 185 a.
Sacraments, the, 201 b.
Seal, 118 b.
Serpent, the brazen, 196
Serpent, the Old, 122 b, 196 a
Serpents, fiery, 196.
Serve, to, 216 b
Sin, original, 158 b, 176 b.
Sodom, Sodomites, 165, 218.
Solomon, 140 a, 141 a, 144 a, 148 b, 149 a, 155 b, 156 a, 159 a
Solstices, the, 148 b
Son of God, 120 b, 212 a.
Sorites, 142 a

Soul, the, 112 b, 123 a, 125 a, 157 a, b, 192 a.
Spirit, the Holy, 112 b, 114 a, 161 b.
Spirits, 150 b, 151 a.
Spirits, Solomon's supremacy over, 149 a.
Stoics, the, 150 a, 151 a.
Stone-bow, 139 a.
Sun, worship of the, 180 b.
Suppose, 203 b
Temple, the, 160 a
Tempt God, to, 111 b, 112 a.
Teraphim, 183 a.
Therapeutae, 126 b, 166 a.
To, the prefix, 172 a.
Traducianism, 157 a.
Travel, 166 b.
Turn, for our, 120 a.
Unright, 177 a
Virtues, the Cardinal, 154 b.
Vulgate, additions in, 119 a, 128 a, 137 a, 139 a, 143 b, 156 a, 162, 168 b, 169 b, 170 a, 172 a, b, 173 a, b, 180 b, 182 a, 187 a, 193 b
Wasps, 176 a.
Water, miracle of, 169 b, 170 b.
Wisdom, 112 b, 141 b, 142 a, 143 b, 146 a, 147 b, 149 b, 151 a, 152 b, 153 a, 155 a, 159 b.
Word, the, 159 a, 171 a, 197 b, 212.
Works, good, 147 b
Years, cycles of, 148 b.
Zoology, 148 b.

THE END.